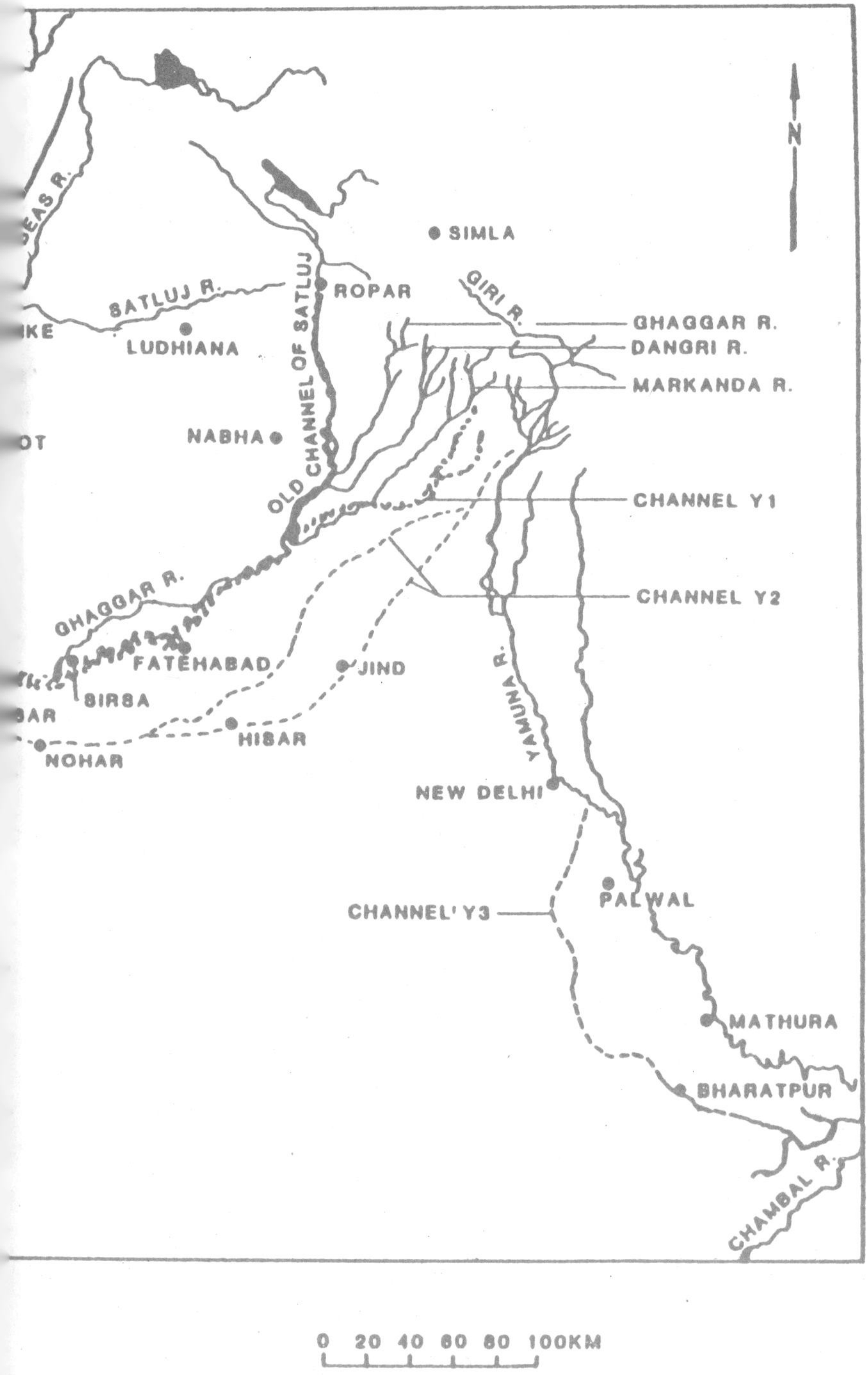
N
SIMLA
ROPAR
SATLUJ R.
LUDHIANA
GIRI R.
GHAGGAR R.
DANGRI R.
MARKANDA R.
OLD CHANNEL OF SATLUJ
NABHA
CHANNEL Y1
CHANNEL Y2
GHAGGAR R.
FATEHABAD
SIRSA
JIND
HISAR
NOHAR
YAMUNA R.
NEW DELHI
PALWAL
CHANNEL' Y3
MATHURA
BHARATPUR
CHAMBAL R.
0 20 40 60 80 100KM

Revisiting Indus-Sarasvati Age and Ancient India

Editors:

BHU DEV SHARMA
Professor of Mathematics
Xavier University of Louisiana, New Orleans, USA

and

NABARUN GHOSE
Department of Business Administration and Economics
Xavier University of Louisiana, New Orleans, USA

World Association for Vedic Studies, USA

ISBN 0-9666386-1-1

This book will be sent free of cost to
1997 members of the WAVES and also
to those who have already paid for it.

Price (including postage):
$25.00 for members
$40.00 for non-members
$99.00 for libraries

Place your order, with cheque of appropriate amount in the name of World Association for Vedic Studies (payable on a bank in USA) to
Dr. Deen B. Chandora (Treasurer),
4117 Menloway, Atlanta, GA 30340, USA
Phone (770)939-5172; Fax (770) 414-5341

Published by World Association for Vedic Studies
and typeset and printed at Urvashi Press,
49/3 Vaidwara, Meerut-250 002, India
Phone (0121)-522458; Fax (0121)-521761

PREFACE

A major conference, *International Conference on Revisiting Indus-Sarasvati Age & Ancient India*, was held in Atlanta, Georgia, USA, October 4–6, 1996. The Conference attracted a good number of scholars and participants from Austria, Belgium, Canada, India, Italy, Mauritius, Mexico, Nepal, Netherlands, Surinam, Trinidad & Tobago, UK, and USA. It was inaugurated by the Prime Minister of Trinidad & Tobago, Shri Basdeo Panday. Professor Jim Shaffer (Professor of Anthropology at Case Western Reserve University, Cleveland, OH, USA) and Professor B.B. Lal (Former Director General of the Archaeological Survey of India, and an Indian archaeologist with many excavations to his credit) were the keynote speakers.

Conference presentations were well received and hailed to be, in general, of very good quality. The participants of the Conference were so inspired that in the concluding session, they voted for founding a *multidisciplinary* academic organization ,*World Association for Vedic Studies (WAVES),* to work in the area of ancient Indian studies.

As is generally true, a paper presented in a conference has much more than what a speaker is able to present in a limited period of time during the conference. Also these papers are meant for a much bigger audience than those who attend a conference. So it was decided to bring out the Proceedings of the Atlanta Conference. A couple of papers included here are by those authors who submitted them but could not come to present at the conference, and a couple of others were submitted later after the conference.

The papers cover a variety of topics, that would fall under the disciplines of archaeology, anthropology, history, history of science and technology, social organization, culture, position of women, philosophy, scriptures, linguistics, etc. as related to ancient India.

Editors have classified them as follows:

- Papers on Indus-Sarasvati Civilization
- Papers on Vedas
- Papers on Women in Ancient India
- Papers on Ancient Indian Science
- Papers on Historical Perspectives
- Papers on Miscellaneous topics

Some papers present in-depth analysis of the topics they study and report new findings. These papers, in this volume, will serve as a source of good reference. Some other papers review the status of things, raise important issues and suggest the need and areas for further significant research. These will be found useful by enthusiastic scholars.

A few papers, that were presented in the conference, are not in this volumes for a variety of reasons. Two papers did not fit well because of their length or organization, a few others could not be got from their authors for inclusion. Notable amongst those that were not available for inclusion are papers by Shri Basdeo Panday, Professor Jim Shaffer, Professor Shiva G. Bajpai, and Dr. Edwin Bryant. However, we have included abstracts of some of these and other papers. It may be admitted here that, under the given circumstances, the editors were not able to bring further desired uniformity.

In bringing out this volume, I have received help from several persons. Firstly, individuals who greatly helped in organizing the conference were Dr. Deen B. Chandora, MD (Atlanta) and Dr. Subhash Kak (Baton Rouge). Professor Amaresh Das helped in collecting and organizing the material for the Proceedings, also in proof reading. Dr. Nabarun Ghose shared in editing responsibilities and in proof reading. I also thank Shri Dharm Prakash Gupta of Urvashi Press (Meerut, India) for his enthusiasm and care in the production of this volume.

BHU DEV SHARMA
President
World Association for Vedic Studies, Inc.
(WAVES)

CONTENTS

Page

Preface

Papers on Indus-Sarasvati Civilization

1. B.B. Lal (New Delhi, India)
India Adds New Dimensions to the Indus Civilization 1

2. Vedagya Arya (Roorkee, India)
The Vedic Sarasvati River: A Source of Indian Culture 22

3. Keonraad Elst (Belgium)
Linguistic Aspects of the Indo-European Urheimat Question 32

4. Keonraad Elst (Belgium)
Political Aspects of the Aryan Invasion Debate 48

5. S. Kalyanaraman (Chennai, India)
Sarasvati River Civilization 71

6. Avanindra Kumar (Delhi, India)
Indus Valley Civilization vis-a-vis Vedic Civilization: A Chronological Exploration 89

7. Shrikant G. Talageri (Mumbai, India)
The Indus-Sarasvati Civilization: Significance of This Name 103

8. Ram Swarup Sharma (New Delhi, India)
Aryavarta: The Original Homeland of the Aryans (Linguistic Evidence) 109

9. V. Prabhu Kumari (Chennai, India)
Antiquity of the Vedic River Sarasvati 117

10. Mahatam Singh (Surinam)
Immigration of 'Aryans' to India: A Fact or a Fiction! 130

11. Dharam Jit Jigyasu (New York, USA)
Indus-Sarasvati Age's Ṗlace in Indian History 134

Papers on Vedas

12. David Frawley (Vamadeva Shastri) (New Mexico, USA)
Vedic Literature and the New View of Ancient India 137

13. Ravi Prakash Arya (Rohtak, India)
Agniṣomīya Paśuyāga (An Operation for Rainmaking) 144

Page

14. O.P. Dwivedi (Guelph, Canada)
The Vedic Heritage for Environmental Stewardship 152

15. Rangasami L. Kashyap (Purdue University, USA)
Rigvedic Semantics: Study of All the Verses with the Word Gau 164

16. V. Krishnamurthy (New Delhi, India)
Solar Energy—Comments on a Chapter of the Yajurveda 190

17. Shyam Narayan Shukla (California, USA)
Upanishads: The Pinnacle of the Religion of Man 199

18. Rayalu Vishwanadha (Los Angeles, USA)
Vedic Language 207

19. Deborah A. Davis (Michigan, USA)
The Presence of Rta 214

Papers on Women in Ancient India

20. Shashi Tiwari (Delhi, India)
The Status of Women in the Ṛgveda 233

21. Reshmi Ramdhony (Mauritius)
Our Vedic Origin: Women Speaking for Themselves 242

22. Pandita Satwantee Pelladoah (Mauritius)
Women in Ancient India 253

23. Ramanath Sharma (Hawaii, USA)
Women in Vedic Rituals 259

24. Sudharani Shrivastava (Jabalpur, India)
The Legal Status of Women in Ancient India 269

Papers on Ancient Indian Science

25. Subhash C. Kak (Baton Rouge, USA)
Science in the Vedic Age 277

26. Narayan R. Joshi (Beaumont, TX, USA)
Tough Steel of Ancient India 288

27. S.K. Dey (Charleston, IL, USA)
A Mathematical Study of Vedanta Philosophy 295

28. P. Venugopala Rao (Atlanta, USA)
Astronomy in Ancient India: Observations and Speculations 305

29. Khila Nath Bastakoty (Kathmandu, Nepal)
Ancient Nepalese Astro-Science 311

Page

30. Richard Thompson (Florida, USA)
Anomalous Textual Artifacts in Archeo-Astronomy 317

31. Kevin H. Lee (East Lansing, MI, USA)
Illuminating the Limitations of Western/Allopathic Medicine in Light of the Wisdom of Sanatana Dharma of Ancient India 335

Papers on Historical Perspectives

32. Harry H. Hicks and Robert N. Anderson (California, USA)
Ancient India and the Vedic Aryans: New Discoveries, Scientific Procedures and Implications for History 344

33. Swami Maheshwaranand (Austria)
The Original Inhabitants of India 356

34. Jagat K. Motwani (New York, USA)
Ancient History of Bharat and Hindu Identity 361

35. Deen B. Chandora (Atlanta, GA, USA)
Distorted Historical Events and Discredited Hindu Chronology 382

36. Michael Parker (Hawaii, USA)
A Post-Modern Demand for Historic Accuracy 388

Papers on Miscellaneous Topics:

37. Joyotpaul Chaudhuri (Tempe, AR, USA)
Community and Power in Kautilya's Arthasastra 392

38. Rasik Vihari Joshi (Mexico)
The Evolution of Sanskrit Language and Literature and its Impact on Modern Languages 404

39. Klaus K. Klostermaier (Manitoba, Canada)
Jñāna: Hindu India's Greatest Gift to the World 411

40. Kamlesh Kapur (New York, USA)
The Scientific Aspects of Vedic Dharma 422

41. Gobardhan Bahadur Karki (Nepal)
Ancient Indian Culture and the Concept of Ashram 433

42. Nikoloz Kenchoshvili (Tibilisi, Georgia)
At the Source of Indo-Georgian Historical Ties (A Short Review) 437

43. Vidya Sagar Anand (England)
The Relevance of Ramayana to Mankind as it Enters the 21st Century 442

Page

44. Jerome Teelucksingh (Trinidad, West Indies)
The Caste Consciousness in Ancient India and the Distortion of Hindu History 458

45. Joseph A. Warren and Deborah Davis (East Lansing, MI, USA)
Limitations of Modern Thought with the Ancient Light of India: Freeing the Modern Mind to see the Truth in a New Dimension 465

46. K.N. Shrestha (Nepal)
The Lord Buddha and His Great Thoughts 471

47. *Abstracts of Papers not included in the Proceedings* 483

India Adds New Dimensions to the Indus Civilization

B.B. LAL
Former Director General, Archaeological Survey of India
F-7, Hauz Khas Enclave, New Delhi-110 016, India

Sometimes facts are stranger than fiction. The very river, viz., the Indus, which gave India its name, is no longer within its bounds. With the partition of the country in 1947 not only did the Indus pass on to Pakistan but, along with it, also the sites of the civilization that acquired its name from that river, viz., the Indus Civilization. Only two very insignificant sites, viz., Kotla Nihang in Panjab and Rangpur in Gujerat, remained within the Indian border, and even their identity was debated.

Such was the state of affairs in 1947. However, Indian archaeologists accepted the challenge and by 1984 (Joshi *et al.*, 1984) placed on the map of present-day India as many as 800 sites associated with various stages of that civilization. (The search is still on and the number may be much more now.) This number, incidentally, is greater than that of such sites discovered so far in Pakistan. It must also be stressed that this civilization extended far beyond the Indus valley—right into the upper Gaṅgā-Yamunā Doāb in the northeast and to as far southeast as the upper reaches of the Godavari in Maharashtra (Fig. 1). Indeed, some scholars have argued that, on the basis of such a far-flung distribution of its remains, it is no longer justified to call it the "Indus" Civilization. They have suggested a new name—the Indus-Sarasvati Civilization. But this one also suffers from the same defect, since the civilization extended far south as well. To strike a compromise, it would be better to stick to another name given to this civilization, viz., Harappan Civilization, based on the name of the site where it was first discovered.

However, let it be stressed that it is neither the number nor extent that matters. What does matter is that the Indian discoveries have added altogether new dimensions to our knowledge of this great civilization of the 3rd millenium BC. Thus, for example, Kalibangan in Rajasthan has brought to light the earliest agricultural field, dating back to *circa* 2800 BC and associated with a cultural *milieu* that preceded and contributed to the make-up of the mature stage of the Indus Civilization itself. The same site has given evidence of the earliest earthquake ever revealed through an excavation, dating back to *circa* 2600 BC. Lothal, in Gujarat, has given to the Indus Civilization the earliest dockyard. Located in the same state, Dholavira has shown that the settlement was divided into three parts—a Citadel, a Middle Town and a Lower Town. Excavations have

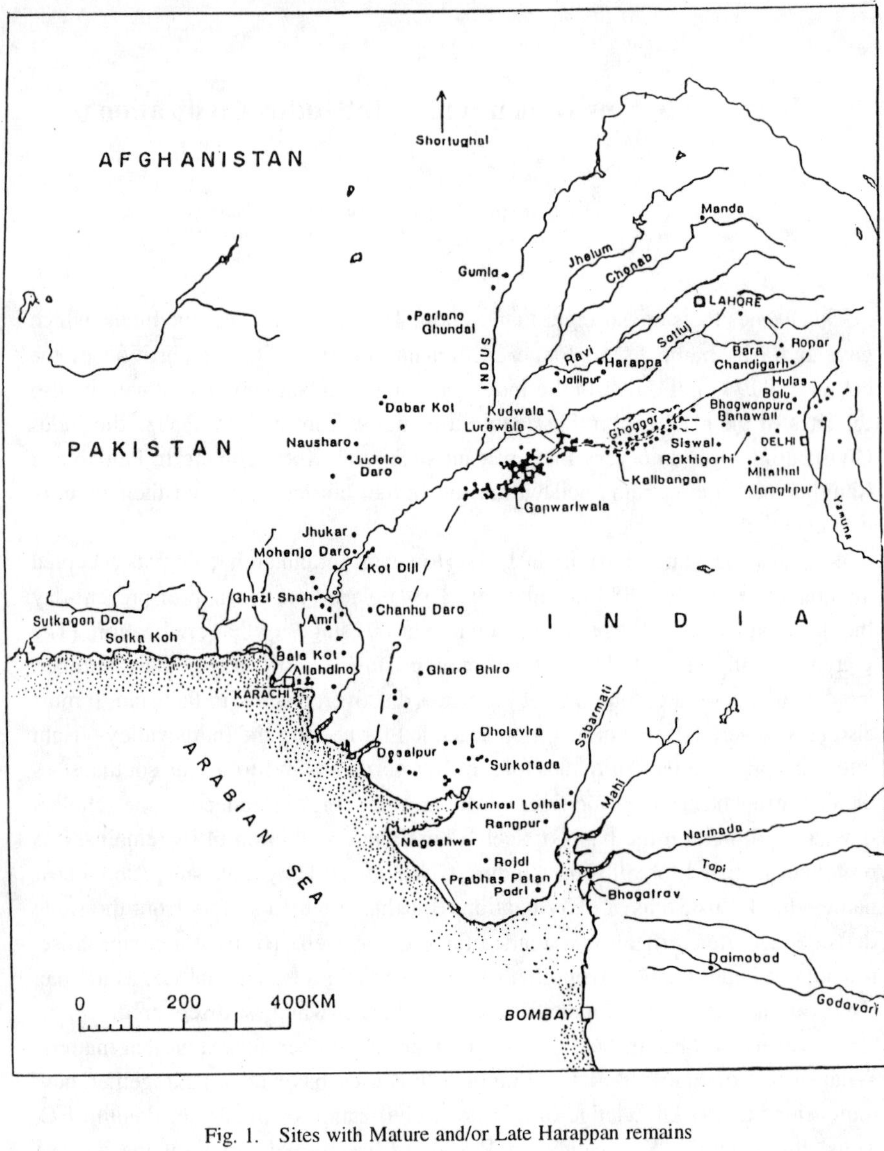

Fig. 1. Sites with Mature and/or Late Harappan remains

also thrown new light on the religion of the Indus people, as well as on their burial practices. Contrary to the general belief that thic civilization was destroyed by invading Aryans, it is now clear that there was no such destruction, much less by Aryans. Instead, there was a decline of the civilization due to several factors. The cities gave way to villages, and the latter carried down with them a good deal of Harappan legacy.

Situated on the left bank of the Ghaggar in District Hanumangarh, Rajasthan, the ancient mounds at Kalibangan lie within a perimeter of about 2 kilometres and rise to a height of about 10 metres. The river is now dry but there is ample evidence that in antiquity it was a mighty river, fed by a number of tributaries, one of which, the Sarasvati, can still be identified upstream. Scholars are of the view that in ancient times the Ghaggar itself was called the Sarasvati, identifiable with the river of the same name in the Vedic literature.

The excavations at Kalibangan have brought to light two periods of occupation, named I and II, from bottom upwards (Lal 1979; Thapar 1975). While II represented the Harappan Civilization at its maturity, I preceded it, with a break in between. Even this earlier occupation, designated variously as Pre-Harappan, Formative Harappan or Early Harappan, was characterized by a town-planning in which the streets were oriented along the cardinal directions. Further, the settlement was enclosed by a fortification wall. Five structural subperiods were noted within Period I. The houses usually comprised a courtyard around which the living rooms were located. Cooking was done in the courtyard and it is interesting to note that *tandūrs* were in vogue even then.

A noteworthy discovery relating to Period I was that of an agricultural field. It was characterized by criss-cross furrow marks, one set running north-south and the other east-west (pl. I). The intermediary distance between the furrows of the former set was 1.9 metres, whereas that in the latter only 30 centimetres. It is interesting that this kind of arrangement of the furrows is in vogue even today in parts of Rajasthan, Haryana and Panjab. These days mustard is grown in the widely distanced furrows and horse gram in the other ones and it is not unlikely that the same crop-pattern was followed in ancient days.

Dislodged walls and ruptured occupational layers mark the end of this earlier settlement and it appears that it was an earthquake that was responsible for its abandonment. However, the people returned to the site within a century or so, their material signifying, besides the earlier *milieu*, elements which mark out the Harappan Culture at its maturity. This means that within this century, viz., between *circa* 2700 and 2600 BC, a transition took place from the Formative to the Mature Stage. In fact, the evidence of such a transition is available at another site upstream in the Ghaggar-Sarasvati valley, viz., at Banawali in District Hissar, Haryana. Over there has been met with in these transitional levels a town-plan in which the typical components of the Mature Harappan times, viz., a Citadel and a Lower Town, had come into being. In this context one may well refer to yet another site, Kunal, in the same geographic area. There, in a purely Early Harappan setting, have been found steatite seals with typical Harappan perforated knob on one side and some designs (though without any inscription) on the other. Kunal is very rich in silver and gold jewellery some of which, particularly

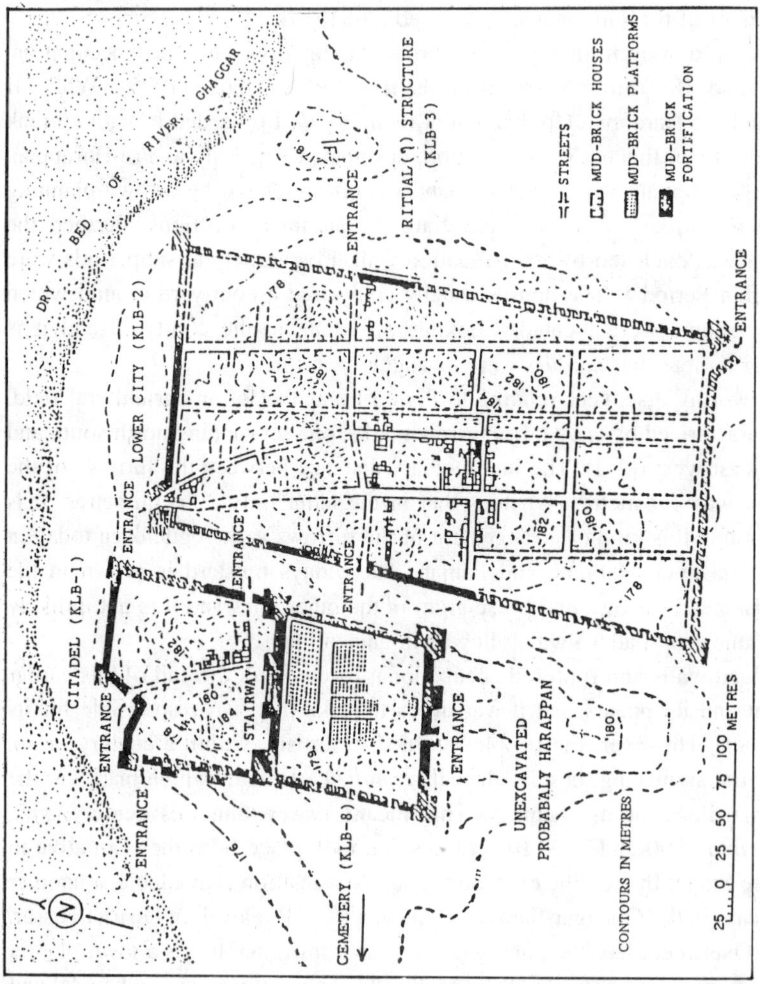

Fig. 2 Kalibangan: Harappan settlement, Period II

Plate 1. Kalibangan: Furrows of an agricultural field, Period I, *circa* 2800 BC. (*Copyright:* Archeological Survey of India)

Plate 2. Kalibangan: 'Fire-altars' in the southern half of the 'Citadel' (*Copyright*: Archeological Survey of India)

spiralled bangles and axially perforated circular beads, remind us of similar ornaments of the mature times. Period II settlement at Kalibangan was distinguished by a Citadel on the west and a Lower Town on the east, with a gap in between (Fig. 2). Both were duly fortified with separate enclosure walls. The Lower Town was divided into blocks by means of criss-cross streets, running north-south and east-west (pl. 1). It speaks volumes for the Kalibangan town-planners that even the widths of the streets were in set ratios. Thus, while the narrowest lane measured 1.8 metres in width, the next wider ones were twice, thrice and four times, measuring respectively 3.6, 5.4 and 7.2 metres.

An average house consisted of a courtyard with a series of rooms on three sides, the fourth being left out for an entrance which was usually very wide so as to allow bullock-carts and cattle to enter freely. In the courtyard troughs were provided for placing fodder and lower halves of large jars for keeping water for the cattle. Some of the rooms were paved with mud bricks. In one case a flooring of baked tiles, bearing a pleasing design of incised intersecting circles, was also observed. However, most noteworthy was the fact that one of the rooms was specially marked out for religious purposes. In it were met with what have been called 'fire altars' in the absence of a better term. An oblong shallow pit was dug into the floor. In it were placed a central cylindrical stele of clay and circular biconvex 'cakes', again of clay, around the stele. There were ash and charcoal, signifying the association of fire. It was also observed that these altars were located close to an eastern wall with the result that whosoever used them had to face the east.

The Citadel was divided into two halves by a partition wall running east-west. In the northern half there was a single street running southeast-northwest., on both sides of which there were houses. In marked contrast to the foregoing, there were no residential buildings in the southern half of the Citadel. Instead, there were several high platforms, with passages in between. Millenia of weathering and spoilation by man have robbed the platforms of the buildings they carried. However, in two cases these could be identified. Atop one of the platforms was found a row of seven contiguous 'fire altars', on the eastern side of which there was a wall, indicating once again that their user had to face the east while performing the ritual (pl. 2). Close by, there lay embedded into the ground the lower half of a jar with ashes and charcoal in it. Most likely fire was kept alive in it, to be used as and when the ritual was performed. Not far from these altars there were a well and a bathing platform, indicating that, in all likelihood, a bath constituted a part of the ritual.

On another platform there was a fairly large pit, lined with kiln-fired bricks. In it were found bovine bones and antlers. This one seems to be associated with animal sacrifice. That animal sacrifice was a part of the Harappan religion is also indicated by the prtrayals on a terracotta cake. On one side of it is engraved an animal with a noose around its neck, the rope being pulled by a human figure. On the other is shown a figure which, on the basis of its horned and feathered headgear, seems to be a deity.

Immediately to the south of the Citadel there lay the remains of houses which do not seem to have been as big as those in the Lower Town or the Citadel. Nearby were found lots of discarded pots suggesting a potter's establishment. Further, in contrast to the Citadel and the Lower Town, this area was not fortified. All this suggests that those who lived here did not belong to an economically and socially high stratum of the society. Thus, taking an overall view of the settlement-pattern at Kalibangan it would appear that the inhabitants were divided into at least three classes—an agricultural-*cum*-merchant class inhabiting the Lower Town, a priestly class occupying the Citadel and a labour class living outside these fortified areas. That there did exist such a class differentiation in the Harappan society is also suggested by similar evidence from other sites. For example, how else can one interpret the workmen's colony at Harappa in the shadow of the Citadel?

That the Harappans buried their dead in graves was already known from the evidence at Harappa itself. Besides repeating the same, Kalibangan has thrown up another kind of evidence. In the same general area within which the inhumation burials were located there also lay circular pits which contained pottery and grave furniture similar to those in the inhumation burials. But there was no skeleton. Amongst the pots there was a large jar and it was suspected that it might contain charred bones or ashes, indicative of post-cremation burial. However, in the few examples that were unearthed no such evidence was found. There is, therefore, need for further investigation.

Kalibangan has been very rich in Harappan antiquities. However, without going into the details of these, reference may here be made to an inscribed potsherd the overlap of letters on which has established once and for all that the direction of writing in the Harappan language was from right to left (pl. 3).

Further upstream in the same Ghaggar-Sarasvati system, Banawali, as stated earlier, has yielded evidence of transition from an earlier occupation (Period I) to the Mature Harappan (Period II; Bisht 1982). Towards the end of the former, viz., in Subperiod IC, there came into existence a Citadel and a Lower Town, a settlement-pattern which became diagnostic of the Mature Harappan times. Even the typical Mature Harappan ratio within the length, breadth and thickness of the bricks, viz., 4 : 2 : 1, became manifest during Subperiod IC.

Coming to the Mature Harappan times (Period II), Banawali has shown that whereas at Kalibangan the two parts of the settlement, viz., the Citadel and the Lower Town, were separate, over here the former lay within the overall area of the latter, though both were duly fortified, there being a common wall on the

Plate 3. Kalibangan: An inscribed potsherd. The overlap of letters clearly shows that the direction of writing in the Harappan script was from the right to the left. (*Copyright*: Archeological Survey of India)

southern side (Fig. 3). However, more noteworthy was the discovery of a moat outside the fortification-wall of the Lower Town. Today the dry bed of the Sarasvati is a little away from the site. However, it is not unlikely that in ancient times it may have been nearer. Even if it was not, its water from upstream could have easily been brought through a canal to feed the moat, the excess water finally discharging back into the river.

The Mature Harappan levels have revealed a well laid-out township with streets and adjacent houses. However, of unusual significance was a complex wherein were noted fire-altars enclosed within an apsidal structure, though the remains were very much disturbed. One wonders if it was an apsidal 'temple'.

There was some time-interval between the end of the Mature Harappan and the subsequent occupation at Banawali. And although many new elements made

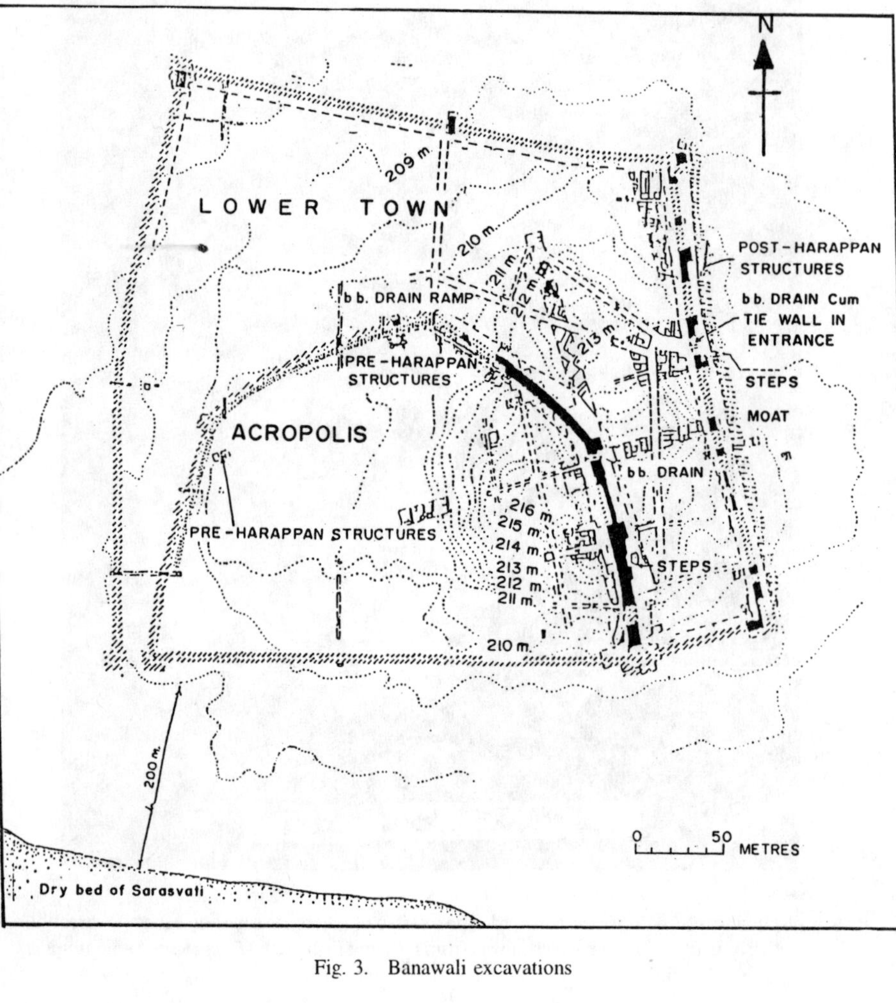

Fig. 3. Banawali excavations

their appearance in this later occupation, there is little reason to suppose that the occupants were aliens. A change and devolution had set in, the evidence of which was manifest all over the Harappan domain around the beginning oı the second millenium BC.

Amongst the other noteworthy sites in the northeastern region mention may be made of Ropar, Hulas, Alamgirpur and Bhagwanpura. While Ropar represents the Harappan Culture at its maturity, Hulas and Alamgirpur represent its late stage. Bhagwanpura, however, presents a scenario when the Harappan Civilization was getting almost diluted. Its upper levels show an interlocking with the Painted Gray Ware Culture, sometime towards the end of the second millenium BC (Joshi 1993). The combined picture presented by these sites clearly shows that the Harappan Civilization did not come to a sudden end, but gradually declined from the urban stage back to its moorings in rural life.

To come to the southern domain of the Harappan Civilization. Here at least five sites deserve mention: Surkotada, Dholavira, Daimabad, Rojdi and Lothal. Situated in the rocky terrain of Kutch in Gujarat, Surkotada offers a plan different from that of Kalibangan or Banawali. Here the two componrnts of the settlement, viz., the Citadel and the Lower Town, were juxtaposed (Joshi 1990). Both were duly fortified, there being a common wall in between, through which a gate interconnected them (Fig. 4). While the typical Mature Harappan artefacts were duly present at the site, there were some local elements as well, signifying that it was not a tightly tailored Harappan Civilization that spread all over. For example, Surkotada has yielded evidence of a different kind of burial. In the grave-pit there wasn't the usually extended body. Instead, there were fragments of human bones. Further, the pit was sometimes sealed with a large stone overlain with stone rubble. These latter features remind one of the capstone and cairn, so typical of South Indian megaliths. Although the upper occupational levels at the site have yielded white-painted black-and-red ware, from which the megalithic black-and-red ware seems to have been derived, no such pottery was found in the burial-pits. Anyway, the evidence opens up a new vista of investigation.

It has long been a matter of debate whether the Harappans were familiar with the horse. Although a terracotta figure from Mohenjo-daro had been identified as that of a horse, many scholars did not agree with that identification. Against this background, one must view the new evidence from Surkatoda. Amongst the faunal remains from this site there are definite examples of the horse (*Equus caballus* Linn.). In this evidence Kalibangan and Lothal have also joined hands (Sharma 1993). At the same time, one has yet to hear of faunal remains of the horse from the ongoing excavations at Harappa. The horse-evidence is of importance since no culture that claims to be associated with the Aryans can do so without the horse.

Dholavira offers the most elaborate town-planning amongst all the Harappan

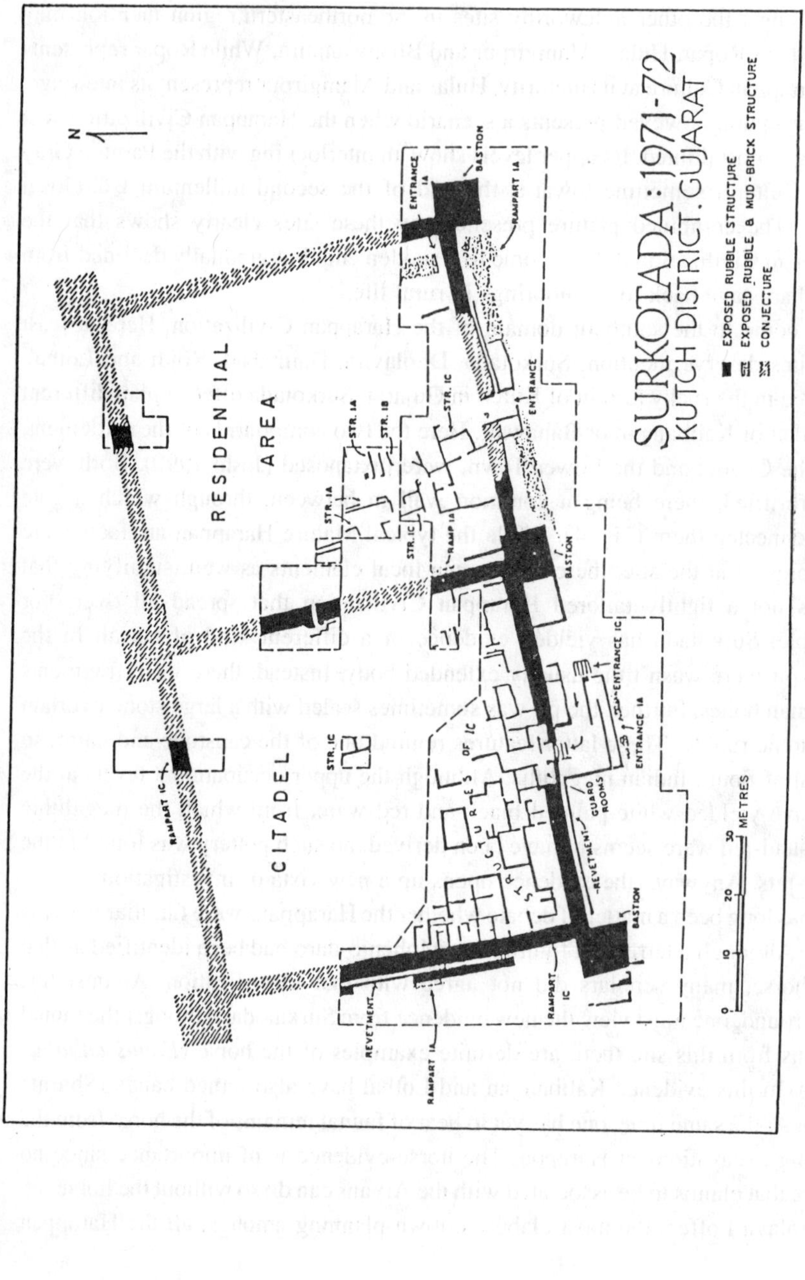

Fig. 4. Surkotada: 1971–72, Kutch District (Gujarat)

Plate 4. Dholavira: Open terrace in front of the northern gateway of the castle (*Copyright*: Archeological Survey of India)

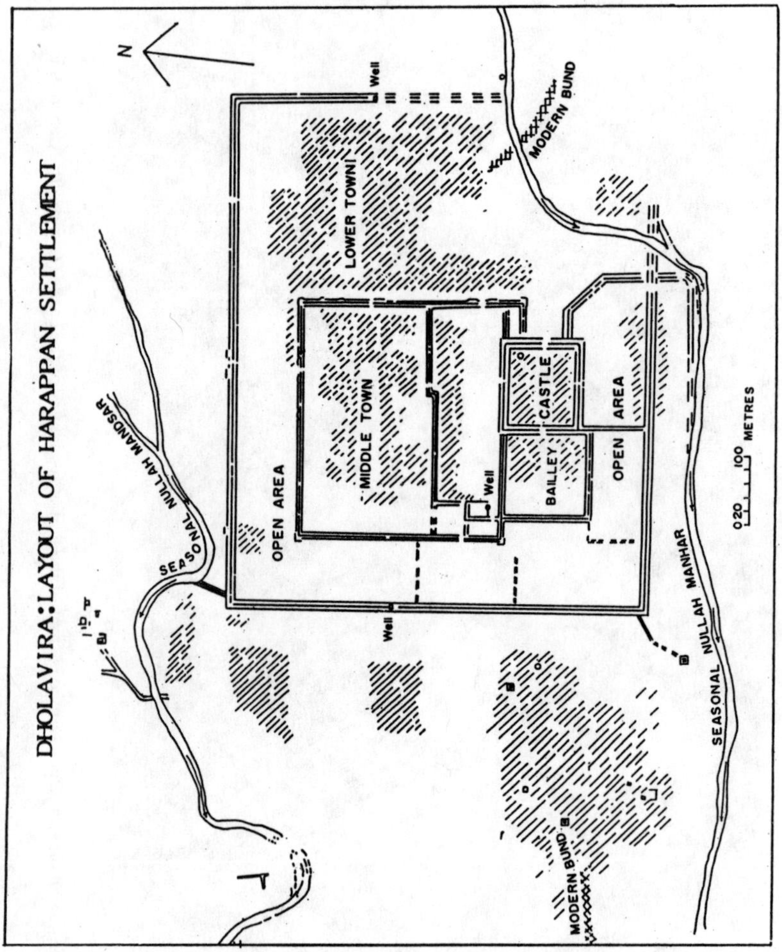

Fig. 5. Dholavira: Layout of Harappan settlement

sites (Bisht 1991). Here instead of the usual two components there were three, named respectively the Citadel, Middle Town and Lower Town (Fig. 5). Rising highest amongst the three, the Citadel was divided into two parts, which the excavator calls the Castle and Bailey. All these parts had their own enclosure walls, the Citadel and the Middle Town being also juxtaposed to each other. The overall fortification wall which enclosed the Lower Town, also enclosed the other two. Although the fortified area of the settlement measures internally 770×625 metres, ancient remains have been noted even outside it, reminding one of a similar situation at Kalibangan, Harappa, etc.

There are two seasonal streamlets, passing respectively along the northern and southern sides of the settlement. It appears that in ancient times these were bunded so as to store water carried down by them during the rainy season. This would indicate not only the concern of the Dholavira people for adequate water supply, but also their technical capabilities.

Since stone is locally available in plenty, the fortifications were built of that material, although occasionally mud bricks were also used. Of the Castle, two gateways, one on the northern side and another on the eastern, have been excavated. These are indeed very elaborate, with long staircases, side-chambers and a terrace in front (pl. 4). Structurally what is unique at Dholavira is the use of stone pillars for carrying the roof. These are not monolithic, but consist of several parts, usually with a square base and circular upper parts. Often these bear polish. Indeed, had not some parts been found *in situ*, people would have hesitated in accepting them as belonging to the Harappan Civilization since no such structural elements have been recorded earlier from any of the Harappan sites.

The site has yielded all the characteristic artefacts of the Mature Harappan Civilization: pottery, weights, metallic objects, seals with animal figurines and the monumental script. However, special mention needs to be made of an inscription, now lying on the floor of one of the gate-chambers. It consists of ten letters, each measuring 37 centimetres in height. Indeed, the inscription is a unique example of its kind.

The southernmost site associated with the Harappan Culture is Daimabad, situated in the upper reaches of the Godavari in Maharashtra. It has yielded a culture-sequence in which a late Harappan occupation is sandwiched between an earlier culture called Sawalda and a later one known by the name of the site itself (Sali 1986). Much before regular excavations were undertaken at the site, a hoard of four massive figures of copper was found by some villagers in a clandestine dig. In fact, the subsequent archaeological operations were directed to ascertain the cultural horizon of these objects. Unfortunately, nothing could be established beyond doubt. Hence there is still a debate whether or not these objects are the creation of the Harappans.

Plate 5. Lothal: Dockyard (*Copyright:* Archeological Survey of India)

The figures are solid cast, put together weigh 60 kilogrammes and comprise a chariot, a water buffalo, a rhinoceros and an elephant. While all these are unique in their own way, the chariot calls for special attention. It is 45 cm in length, is drawn by a pair of bullocks and a human figure stands on it, holding a stick in the right hand as if to make the bullocks move. Further, a dog stands on the long pole the other end of which joins the yoke placed across the necks of the bullocks. The wheels are solid and in one built with the axle, implying that these moved along with the axle. Although Harappa has yielded a metal chariot, it pales into insignificance when compared with this Daimabad example.

Located in the Saurashtra part of Gujarat, Rojdi had a peripheral wall like so many other Harappan settlements (Possehl and Raval 1989). But the dichotomy of a Citadel and a Lower Town was not there. However, more noteworthy about Rojdi is the fact that it presents a cultural *milieu* which, while having many an element of the classical Harappan Culture, has certain features of its own, which are shared by quite a few sites in the region. Indeed, the excavators are inclined to call this facet as "Sorath Harappan". All this shows that the Harappan Civilization was not monolithic as has been generally assumed.

Lothal, not far from the Gulf of Cambay in Gujarat, has given to the Indus Civilization something which no other site has—a dockyard (Rao 1979 and 1985). Juxtaposed to the eastern peripheral wall of the town, the dockyard measures around 215 metres north-south and 35 metres east-west (pl. 5). It is lined with walls of kiln-fired bricks, which are extant to a height of over 3 metres. Evidence suggests that in ancient times a river flowed past the site. Through a channel it was connected with the dockyard. This river joined the Bhogavo which in turn joined the Sabarmati, the latter falling in the Gulf of Cambay, an inlet of the Arabian Sea. The ferrying arrangement seems to have been like this. With each high tide, when the sea-water was pushing up, incoming boats were brought upstream and parked in the dockyard. Goods were unloaded and kept in a warehouse close by. Outgoing cargo was loaded on the boats. When another high tide came and was receding, along with it sailed the boats down to the sea.

The warehouse was sited on a 4-metre high mud-brick podium, covering an area about 48 × 40 metres. On it had been built a series of 3.6-metre square and 1-metre high blocks of mud bricks, of which only twelve have survived. Arranged in a grid pattern, these blocks are separated by intermediary north-south and east-west passages about 1.2 metres in width. It is surmised that the floor and superstructure of the warehouse were made of wood and the passages underneath were provided for an easy flow of air so that the material stored may be protected from moisture to which it would have been an easy prey because of the damp climate of the area. That sealed packages were kept in the warehouse is clearly indicated by the discovery in it of 65 terracotta sealings which bear on one side the impressions of the Indus seals and on the other those of the packing material and cord. The warehouse had caught fire and these sealings and a lot of burnt wood, reeds, etc. were amongst the remnants.

The general layout of the settlement at Lothal was again different from that of other sites referred to earlier. Though, as usual, there were the two components, viz., the Citadel (called Acropolis by the excavator) and the Lower Town, both lay within an overall peripheral wall and the Acropolis did not have its own fortifications. (Fig. 6). At the same time, its distinctive character was maintained by locating it on a 3.5-metre high platform, in a somewhat exclusive area.

Like other Harappans the Lothalians also buried their dead. However, it is interesting that in three graves two skeletons were found, instead of the usual one. Unfortunately, the identification of the sexes of these six skeletons has been a matter of debate amongst specialists and it is difficult to be certain that in each case a male and a female lie buried. In this context, however, it may be mentioned that the practice of burying a male and a female together in the same grave was in vogue in India in the Mesolithic times, as indicated by the evidence from D...dama in District Pratapgarh, Uttar Pradesh.

Lothal, like many other sites, has given the evidence of the gradual decline of the Harappan Civilization. Over here the occupational strata are divisible into five phases, I–V. While I belongs to an early stage, II and III present the Harappan Civilization at its full bloom. However, in Phase IV degeneration set in. There were encroachments on the streets. The dockyard began to silt up and the warehouse was scarcely used. This devolution became more apparent in Phase V, wherein all the three, viz., the dockyard, warehouse and acropolis became things of the past. Even the fortifications became non-functional. The houses were now made of brick-bats collected from the earlier walls. In terms of the artefacts, cubical weights of chert disappeared and long blades of the same material gave way to short ones of agate and chalcedony. The pottery types also underwent a change. However, in spite of these conspicuous differences between the material equipment of Phase III on the one hand and V on the other, it has to be noted that no newcomers are at all involved. It is the same Harappans who keep on getting down the hill. The story of this devolution continues at Rangpur, a site about 30 kilometres west-southwest of Lothal (Rao 1963). Here by Period III, the degeneration was complete. There weren't any longer the Harappan houses made of kiln-fired bricks. Town-planning, fortifications and monumental buildings were never heard of. Weights and measures completely disappeared, and although some of the signs of the Harappan script struggled on, it was but a poor shadow of the original.

As already stated earlier, this kind of degeneration had set in also in the northeastern domain of the Harappan Civilization. (Indeed, similar evidence is

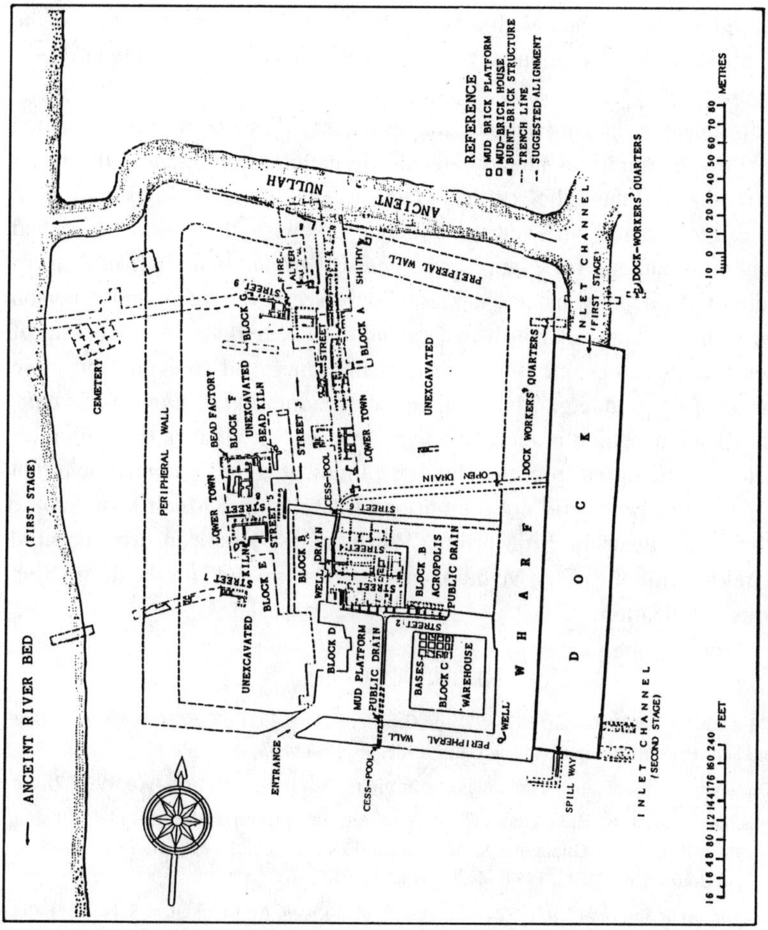

Fig. 6. Lothal: 1955–62 Plan—Period A (with alignment restored)

now available from the Indus Valley itself.) An overview of the entire panorama indicates that the gradual disappearance of weights, measures and script in the post-mature Harappan times was associated with a fall in trade, both internal as well as external. Etched carnelian beads, shell inlays, cubical chert weights, seals etc. no longer found their way into Western and Central Asia. These were also not seen circulating within the subcontinent itself. Further, climatic changes and the wearing out of the landscape may have contributed to a dwindling of agricultural production. Thus, with a fall in productivity and trade gone was the economic affluence which, about seven–eight centuries earlier, had given rise to the large centres.

Cities disappeared, leaving behind villages to carry on such traditions as suited their ethos. For example, as already stated, the pattern of ploughing the fields continued, and so did the bullock cart. In fact, strange though it may sound, even the gauge of the cart has survived the millenia. Likewise, the *tandur* has defied time. Many an ornament, for example, the *chauk*, *karadhanī* and *pāyala*, worn respectively on the head, waist and ankles, may be seen even today on the person of women in the villages of Northwestern India. Folk religion, like worship of the mother goddess, trees, etc. has withstood the time. And so even a bit more formal forms of religion, e.g., Śiva-worship or the adoration of *liṅga*s and *yoni*s. Social stratification, which is more deeply entrenched in villages than in cities, seems to have come down from the Harappan times. It is thus patently clear that the Harappan Civilization did not die out one fine morning. Much less can one agree with the late illustrious Sir Mortimer Wheeler (1947) that "on circumstantial evidence Indra [symbolic of the Vedic Aryans] stands accused" for the destruction of the Indus Civilization.

REFERENCES

R.S. Bisht, "Excavations at Banawali: 1974–77", in: Gregory L. Possehl (Ed.), *Harappan Civilization*, Oxford and IBH Publishing Co., New Delhi, 1982, pp. 113–24.

______, "Dholavira: New horizons of the Indus Civilization", *Puratattva*, **20** (1989–90), 1991, 71–82.

J.P. Joshi, Madhubala and Jassu Ram, "Indus Civilization: A reconstruction on the basis of distribution maps", in: B.B. Lal, S.P. Gupta and Shasi Asthana (Eds.), *Frontiers of the Indus Civilization*, Books and Books, New Delhi, 1984, pp. 511–30.

______, *Excavations at Surkotda, 1971–72 and Exploration in Kutch*, Archaeological Survey of India, New Delhi, 1990.

______, *Excavations at Bhagwanpura, 1975–76*, Archaeological Survey of India, New Delhi, 1993.

B.B. Lal, "The direction of writing in the Harappan script", *Antiquity*, **XL**(157), 1966, 52–55.

______, "Kalibangan and the Indus Civilization", in D.P. Agrawal and Dilip K. Chakrabarti (Eds.), *Essays in Indian Protohistory*, B.R. Publishing Corporation, Delhi, 1979, pp. 65–97.

______, "A glimpse of social stratification and political set-up of the Indus Civilization", *Harappan Studies*, Vol. I, Oxford and IBH Publishing Co., New Delhi, 1993, pp. 63–71.

______, "Chronological horizon of the mature Indus Civilization", in: Jonathan Mark Kenoyer (Ed.), *From Sumer to Meluhha*, Wisconsin Archaeological Reports, Vol. 3, 1994, pp. 15–25.

Gregory L. Possehl andcM.H, Rawal, Harappan Civilization and Rojdi, Oxford and IBH Publishing Co., New Delhi, 1989.

S.R. Rao, "Excavations at Rangpur and other explorations in Gujarat", *Ancient India*, **18 and 19** (1962 and 1963), 1963, 5–207.

______, Lothal: A Harappan Port Town (1955–62), Vol. I, Archaeological Survey of India, New Delhi, 1979.

______, *Lothal: A Harappan Port Town (1955–62),* Vol. II, Archaeological Survey of India, New Delhi, 1985.

S.A. Sali, *Daimabad 1976–77,* Archaeological Survey of India, New Delhi, 1986.

A.K. Sharma, "The Harappan horse was buried under the dune of ....", *Puratattva,* **23** (1992–93), 1993, 30–34.

B.K. Thapar, "Kalibangan: A Harappan metropolis beyond the Indus Valley", *Expedition*, Winter 1975, 19–32.

R.E.M. Wheeler, "Harappa 1946: The defences and cemetery R-37", *Ancient India*, **3**, 1947, 58–130.

The Vedic Sarasvati River: A Source of Indian Culture

VEDAGYA ARYA
40, Civil Lines, Roorkee - 247 667, India

This paper is based on various references of river Sarasvatī as these occur in the Ṛgveda, Yajurveda, and Atharvaveda. There are also some views expressed based on findings of an expedition in which the author participated in 1985. The members of the expedition traveled from Adibadri in Sivalika mountains to Prabhas Kshetra (Somanath Temple), covering about 3500 km. spread over Punjab, Haryana, Rajasthan and Gujarat.

The Sarasvtī River and the Sārasvata People

The living continuity of Indian culture was rooted on the banks of the Sarasvatī river. This river was held in the highest veneration by the Vedic people. It was a living reality flowing from the Himalayas to the Arabian Sea. It was in the river valley of the Sarasvatī that highly cultured and civilized habitation was first found on the Indian soil several thousand years ago. The soil of India also responded deeply to the Sarasvatī River where the Vedic seers built up the eternal culture and the magnificent civilization.

The Sārasvat people and the Vedic Aryans are almost synonymous and they resided on the banks of the Sarasvatī. But the nineteenth century scholars tutored in the western school of Indological studies and some of our modern pseudo-scholars term Aryans for Vedic people. They tried to establish that the Aryan people were nomadic invaders and barbarians who destroyed the Indus Valley civilization. They considered the Aryans as racial type people who migrated from Central Asia around 2000 SC. According to their opinion there was no Sarasvatī River in India, but a small stream named Haraquiti (Persian name for Sarasvatī) flowed in Western Afghanistan where the Aryan civilization originated. They are not prepared to admit that India had a long-established culture and civilization before the period of the so-called Aryan invasion.

The Harappan Culture, Indus Valley Civilization and Dravidian Culture

The Harappan culture existed much prior to the Indus civilization. The word Harappan is derived from 'Hariyupiya' and it is mentioned in the Ṛgveda. It was a city built by the Salvas who are described to be a sub-clan of Bharatas in the Vedic age. A number of sites of the Harappan culture have been discovered and all of them are found well connected with the ancient Indian culture. The Harappan culture and the Indus civilization are closely related to the Vedic culture. The Dravidians are also considered to be descendants of Vedic people. It is frequently mentioned that the great Ṛgvedic sage Agastya migrated from the north to the south. It was only due to his teachings that the south Indian Brahmins have better preserved the Vedic culture, rituals and the traditional style of chanting mantras than the north Indians. In fact all Indian culture are very much interwoven and they originate from the same Vedic culture which evolved in the Sarasvatī Valley. Thus the Sarasvatī played a dominant role in developing and shaping the Vedic culture.

The Myth of the Sarasvatī

The Sarasvatī has been described as the most important and highly sacred river in the Ṛgveda. Usually a river is considered feminine by nature and worshipped as the mother goddess in the Indian culture. She represents the dynamic force of lire, fertility and irrigation of the soil. All these significances are attributed to the Sarasvatī and she is regarded the greatest river in the Ṛgveda. The whole region of the Sarasvatī has been regarded the homeland of Vedic people. This river was so fascinating to the Ṛgvedic seers that they intimately lauded and glorified her in at least ninety hymns. They have also symbolized the Sarasvatī as the goddess of knowledge in several hymns. Three Ṛgvedic seers, namely Gṛtsamada, Bhārgava and Saunaka, together praised the Sarasvatī as the supreme mother, the greatest river and an excellent goddess among the deities.

Ambitame nadītame devitame Sarasvatī.

Ṛgveda 2:41.16[1]

This glorification of the Sarasvatī indicates three important points. Firstly she is the myth of a mother who brings up her children with milk and food. She has been compared to a cow in one of the hymns by describing that she yields milk, ghee and abundant food to the descendants of king Nahusa who resided on her banks as a mighty ruler of the region.

Rāyaścetantī bhuvanasya bhūre ghṛtam
Payo duduhe Nāhuṣāya.

Ṛgveda 7.95.2[2]

---

1 अम्बितमे नदीतमे देवितमे सरस्वति। ऋग्वेद २.४१.१६

2 रायश्चेतन्ती भुवनस्य भूरे घृतं पयो दुदुहे नाहुषाय। ऋग्वेद ७.९५.२

Secondly the Sarasvatī has been a terrestrial river not a mythical stream. She used to flow on the earth to irrigate the lands of Vedic people. Therefore she is neither a celestial river nor a spiritual one. Thirdly the Sarasvatī has been described as a divinity. It is a well known fact that a divine force has been envisioned in all natural phenomenon by Vedic Ṛṣis. This is the root cause that Indian people traditionally worship oceans, mountains, rivers and trees. Therefore the Sarasvatī has been worshipped as the goddess of learning, knowledge and wisdom. Thus she may be proved as mythical too. In fact myth and reality are so much interwoven in the old scriptures that it is difficult to draw a line of demarcation between them.

The Sarasvatī among the Seven Rivers

India is a land of many rivers. They generally flow from the Himalayas, the mount Kailash or Vindhyachala towards the west or the east and merge either into the sea or in the desert. The Punjab, before the partition, was the land of seven rivers and it was also called 'Sapta Sindhu Pradesh' in ancient times. This was the earliest name of the Punjab and it literally means a place of seven rivers (Sapta Sindhu). One of the seven rivers, named Śutudri (Sutlej), has been found to have emptied into the Sarasvatī during the Vedic period. Another river. named Vipāśā (Beas), once ran into the Indus river. Before these two rivers started merging and flowing into other currents there were seven rivers flowing independently in their courses. The Sarasvatī has been stated the most prominent and the mother of six rivers. This fact has been manifested by the Ṛgvedic sage Vaśiṣṭha in the following hymn:

Āyatsākam yaśaso vāvaśānāḥ Sarasvatī saptathtī sindhumātā
Yāḥ suṣvayanta sudughāḥ sudhārā abhiswena payasā pīpyānāḥ.

Ṛgveda 7.36.6[3]

[The Sarasvatī is flowing for an age-old time. Her flowing waters look like the white fabric woven with yarns of her reputation. She is the river and mother of all six streams. Her currents are said to be full of milk for the sons of the soil. She is very much prosperous with her own flow of waters.]

There are four points which evolve out of this hymn:

1. The glory of the Sarasvatī was well established even before the above Vedic recitation was made in her praise.
2. She is the seventh stream and the mother of six rivers. Most of the Vedic

---

[3] आयत्साकं यशसो वावशानाः सरस्वती सप्तथी सिन्धुमाता ।
याः सुष्वयन्त सुदुघाः सुधारा अभिस्वेन पयसा पीप्याना ॥ ऋग्वेद ७.३६.६

scholars agree on the following six rivers—Sutlej, Rāvi, Chināb, Jhelum, Vẏās and Sindhu (Indus) on whose banks the ancient Indus civilization flourished. 'Saptathī' means seventh one which is Sarasvatī itself.

3. The Sarasvatī used to have enough water to feed other rivers like a mother to her children.
4. 'Sindhumātā' means mother of rivers. Here Sindhu does not have the meaning of Indus river. The Sarasvatī and the Sindhu are two different river-entities and they were in existence much before the Ṛgvedic hymns were compiled.

Thus the region from the Sindhu (Indus) river to the Sarasvatī had been identified as Sapta Sindhu. Sapta-Sindhu was the earliest name of the Punjab.

The Origin and the Course of the Sarasvatī

Regarding the origin of the Sarasvatī there are four different opinions to be discussed. The scholars of Indology indicate the following origins:

1. The Mansarovar Lake at the base of Mount Kailas in Tibet. But in fact this lake is said to be the origin of the Sutlej (Śutudri). Mount Kailas is said to be the origin of the Indus river and the Brahmaputra too.
2. Devatāl (Lake of Divine People) situated in Tibet from where the Sarasvatī is said to flow near Mana village. Mana village is the last settlement of India before crossing the Tibetan border. This village is situated at a distance of 5 km. from Badrinath Temple. The river which was called Sarasvati like a tributary surprisingly runs into Alaknanda at a short distance from Mana village. Thereafter her name is not associated with Alaknandā, Bhāgirathī, Mandākinī and the Gangā. There are two very small rock-caves a little ahead of Mana village which are said to be 'Vyāsa Guphā' and 'Gaṇeśa Guphā' respectively. These caves are too small for a person to stretch his legs and to sit down comfortably. But it is said that Vedavyasā wrote Mahābhārata and eighteen Purāṇas there. It is difficult to believe this because there is no vegetation and no food is available and the whole area is snow-bound for almost six months in a year.

   According to our observation and findings there is a place called Vyāspura. At present it is named Vilāspura in Ambāla district where it is said Maharshi Vedavyāsa settled down in quest of peace after the tremendous bloodshed of Mahābhārata war. There is a Vyāsapīṭha in Vilāspura where it is believed the great seer dictated the whole story of Mahābhārata to Lord Gaṇeśa. Vilāspura is situated at a distance of 20 km down from Ādibadri where the Vedic people resided on the banks of the Sarasvatī

3. Plakṣa Prasravaṇa is the most complicated term applied for the origin of the Sarasvatī. This term is not used anywhere in the Vedas, but at the beginning of the Brahmanic scriptures it was applied to denote the origin of the 'Vedic Sarasvatī River'. Later in Mahābhārata and Purāṇas Plakṣa was applied to the holy fig tree or an ant-hill and it has been said that the Sarasvatī flowed forth from Plakṣa or the holy fig tree. The holy fig tree and an ant-hill cannot stand long if a mighty current like the Sarasvatī emerges to flow from underneath. According to Monier Williams Plakṣa Praśravaṇa is meant to be a small side door of the mountain where the Sarasvatī took her rise. It seems to be credible.
4. On the basis of the Ṛgvedic hymns the real origin of the Sarasvatī can be stated as the mountains only. A clear description is found in the following mantras:

Ekācetat Sarasvatī nadīnām suciryatī giribhya ā samudrāt.

Ṛgveda, 7.95.2[4]

[The Sarasvatī alone possesses full vitality among the rivers and being the most sacred flows from the mountains to the ocean.]

The Sarasvatī was such a turbulent and devastating river that the Ṛsi Bhāradwaj has described her as the mountain destroyer in the following hymn:

Iyam śuṣ mebhirvisakhā ivārujat sānu girīṇām tavaṣebhirūrmibhiḥ
Parātvataghnīmavase suvṛktibhiḥ Saraswatīmā vivāsema dhītibhiḥ

Ṛgveda 6.61.2[5]

[The Sarasvatī river erodes the mountain-peaks with her powerful waves as easily as breaking of the flower-petals. We designate her as the destroyer of mountains and pray to her with great devotion for our protection.]

The above quoted Ṛgvedic hymns very well prove that the mountains are the origin of the Sarasvstī where she took her rise. The Sarasvatī attributed with such eloquent descriptions and solicitations flowed for thousands of years on the Indian soil and gradually disappeared along with the glorious Vedic age. Before disappearing from the surface of the earth she left her immemorial entities in the form of several sacred places of pilgrimage from Adibadri to Prabhsas Kshetra in Gujarat.

---

[4] एकाचेतत् सरस्वती नदीनां सुचिर्यती गिरिभ्य आ समुद्रात्। ऋग्वेद ७.७५.२

[5] इयं शुष्मेभिर्विसखा इवारुजत् सानु गिरीणां तवषेभिरूर्मिभिः ।
परावतघ्नीमवसे सुवृक्तिभिः सरस्वतीमा विवासेम धीतिभिः ॥ ऋग्वेद ६.६१.२

The course of the Sarasvatī has been a subject of great controversy in the past and the present. It has drawn the attention of many scholars such as historians, indologists, archaeologists, geographers, geologists and scientists of different branches to investigate and identify its original course. A majority of them think that the Sarasvatī started flowing from the Himalayan mountains and entered the plains at Adibadri which is linked *with* Sivalik hills in the Sirmur region. Beyond Adibadri a thick forest and a long range of the mountains continue to an inaccessible place, therefore the exact original spot of the Sarasvatī can be located only in the Himalayan glaciers.

The Vedic people might have preferred the plains of low hills of the Sivalik ranges for better habitation than the flood-bound upper reaches of the Himalayas. It can be argued that due to some tectonic movements and changes in climatic conditions in the Himalayan region a smaller stream might have flowed in the region of Adibadri. Perhaps this was the time when the Sarasvatī started to disappear and reappear at several places. She is still visible on the right side of Adibadri in the form of a small stream. This flows about two km. and empties into a river called Sobha (derived from Suwarna Bhadra) which flows on the left side of Adibadri. The Sarasvatī reappears in Bhagawanpura and Mustaphabad before being joined by river Markanda, local name for Markandeya. On entering Kurukshetra her existence has been regarded in the lakes and places of pilgrimage such as Sannihitasara, Brahmasara, Prācisara, Dakṣiṇasara, Jyotiḥsara, Sthāneśwara and Prithūdakam. Evidently the Sarasvatī became very much significant by filling up the lakes with her waters. The word itself means a river of lakes and ponds. In fact she was symbolized in the living spots of the Vedic culture in the whole of Haryana and also a large portion of Punjab. There are evidences in the R̥gveda that sacrifices used to be performed on the sacred banks of the Sarasvatī, Dr̥ṣadvatī and Āpayā. Dr̥ṣadvatī is known as the river of stones. Presently this is known as Ghagger which flows making rumbling sounds. At the confluence of three rivers a famous place of pilgrimage (Mānuṣa Tīrtha) is also mentioned in the following R̥gvedic hymn

Nitwā Dadhe vara ā prithivya iḷāyāspade sudinatve ahnām
Dr̥ṣadvatyām mānuṣa āpayāyām Saraswatyām devadagne didīhi.

R̥gveda 3.23.4[6]

[O Sacrificial Fire! we (performers of sacrifice) put you in a good auspicious

[6] नित्वा दधे वर आ पृथिव्या इळायास्पदे सुदिनत्वे अह्नाम् ।
दृषद्वत्यां मानुष आपयायां सरस्वत्यां देवदग्ने दिदीहि ॥ ऋग्वेद ३.२३.४

day on the ploughed land at Mānuṣa Tīrtha situated on the banks of Dṛṣadvatī, Āpayā and Sarasvatī. We pray to you to illuminate the whole atmosphere.]

It is said that the Sarasvatī and the Dṛṣadvatī were flowing at a distance of 4 km. from each other in Kurukshetra. In fact Kurukshetra had the rare distinction of having three pious rivers. One of them named Āpayā has been mentioned as Apagi in Mahābhārata. The Sarasvatī flowing through Arunaya, Pehoa (Prithoodaka), Fatihabad, Agroha and Sirasa in Haryana entered Rajasthan.

The Saravatī flowed down in the Rajasthan desert through Nohar tehsil of Ganganagar. About 20 km. away from Nohar two famous spots of excavation, namely Soti and Karoti, were visited by the members of the expedition and some of the sacrificial items such as broken Śatachidrakumbha, earthen-wares and scales of the old culture were found. The downward course of the Sarasvatī pausing through Pallu, Rewatasara, Hanumangarh, Kalibangan, Suratgarh, Rangamahal, Anupgarh, Kolayat tehsil of Bikaner, Pokaran, Phalodi tehsil of Jodhpur, Vinjadasara near Jaisalmer, Pacbhadra. Balotra tehsil of Barmer reached Jalore before entering the Rann of Kutch. It is said that one of the currents of the Sarasvatī passed through Bahawalpur in Pakistan and joined the Indus river.

Some of the fresh evidences round from the archaeological excavations and landsat imagery indicate that the dry bed of the Sarasvatī varies in width from 3 to 10 km. in different parts of its course. This ancient course again indicates that the Sarasvatī had been once a mighty river. But when this reduced to a narrow stream, she was named Hākadā or Hākarā. The word Hākarā is derived from 'sankara' and 'sankara' also is derived from the Sanskrit word 'sankīrṇa'. It means narrow. It is evident that the broad river had shrunk and had relatively narrowed down near Bikaner and flowed onward to Jodhpur and Jaisalmer. There is Pacbhadra region beyond Barmer. Pacbhadra means a place of five rivers. There are four small streams and one is large, namely Guhya, Jojari, Leek, Dabariya and Looni. The Looni is the main river of Rajasthan. Guhya means secret or mysterious. Perhaps this indicates the Sarasvatī. The word Jojari comes from the root word Yojayati and it stands as a link stream which joins with others as the Sarasvatī joined with Sutlej and Yamuna. The word Leek means a line or tradition. This too indicates the Sarasvatī. Though the Sarasvatī disappeared long ago, she still stands alive in the minds of Indians. The word Dabariya points out a river which fills pits and ponds with water. The Sarasvatī also means one who makes lakes and fills them with water. Looni has been described as the major river or salty water of Rajasthan. When this river passes through an area which was initially a sea-bed then her water gets salty, otherwise this would be carrying sweet water. Here it is worth mentioning that an interesting observation was made by the members of the expedition. While the salt gathering process on the banks of the Looni river continues, very close by in the river bed some women of native place dig up small pits and collect sweet drinking water. They firmly believe that the sweet water comes out from the water-base of river Hakara. Thus even the Looṇi is connected with the Sarasvatī. The description of Pacbhadra or five rivers helps us to understand the visualization of the Yajurvedic seer who symbolized the Sarasvatī in five rivers and their merger again in one. The following mantra is worth-pondering

Pancanadyaḥ Sarasvatīmapi yānti sasrotasaḥ
Sarasvatī tu pancadhā so Deśe'bhavat sarit.
Yajurveda 34.11[7]

[Five rivers merge into the Sarasvatī and the Sarasvatī subsequently puts herself in five-folded diverse form existing in solidarity.]

It was quite surprising to witness gypsum and 'Multani Mitti' (yellow-clay) in abundance in some places of Rajasthan. Several truck-loads of these materials were being carried away in a routine from the spots to different parts of the country. According to the opinions of the archaeologists and the geographers the materials might have been deposited by rivers at least twenty or thirty thousand years ago, in this connection only two rivers, the Sarasvatī and the Dṛṣadvatī, having been named.

The Sarasvatī and Indra

In the Vedic literature Indra has been described as the God of rain and cultivation. Indra is very much connected with rivers. Indra is considered a mythical god in the Vedas. According to some Ṛgvedic hymns it is only Indra who destroys the dragon (Vṛtra, a term for a dragon-like glacier) to release the seven rivers to flow into the sea. In the Atharvaveda Indra has been described as the foremost god to cultivate the land and sow barley on the banks of the Sarasvatī river along with the Devas and the Marutgaṇa. Actually the Vedic age represents the agrarian civilization in which every effort had been made to highlight agriculture as the first vocation. Joint efforts of Samrāṭ Indra, Devatā and Maruts could be seen in the following Mantra

---

7 पञ्चनद्यः सरस्वतीमपि यान्ति सस्रोतसः ।
सरस्वती तु पञ्चधा सो देशेऽभवत् सरित् ॥ यजुर्वेद ३४.११

Devā imaṁ madhunā saṁyutaṁ yavaṁ Sarasvatyāmadhi maṇāvacakṛṣuḥ
Indra āsīt saripatiḥ śatakratuḥ kīnāśā āsan Marutaḥ sudānavaḥ.

Atharva 6.30.1[8]

[The gods sowed this sweet barley in the gem-like land of the Sarasvatī river. Śatakratu Indra was the lord of the plough to till the soil and the generous Maruts played a role of farmers to protect the harvest.]

Thus the foremost Vedic Sarasvatī river and the foremost Vedic god Indra, both played a significant role in developing the agrarian-culture in the Indian soil.

Sarasvatī and Vināśanam

The Sarasvatī originated from the Himalayan glacier and merges into Vināśanam. It is a Sanskrit term for the great Thar desert of Rajasthan where the Sarasvatī disappeared. This place is not yet located. Some of the scholars said that Vināśana was the gate of Niṣāda Kingdom, so that the people of the region could not see her. This is a totally mythical concept which is found in some of the descriptions of Mahābhārata and Purāṇas. The Sarasvatī has been described as generous and kind to everyone, even a low caste person. Once there was a big Satra (a term for *sacrifice*) to be performed by the sages on the banks of the Sarasvatī. A person named Kavasa wanted to attend it, but he was prevented by the performers on the ground of low caste. He started praying to the Sarasvatī at a distance and she being pleased with his sincere recitations came near him. Later on, Kavasa was included and honoured as a sage in4 the performance of sacrifice by them. This authentic event has been mentioned in Aitreyabrāhmaṇa

According to some scholars Sirsa and Kalibangan have been identified as Vināśana, but there is no vast marshy land. Both the places were examined by the members of the expedition but they found them unconvincing. It is believed that the Rann of Kutch might have been Vināśana. It can be argued on two grounds. Firstly the Sarasvatī before its final disappearance might have flowed to the Rann of Kutch in the Brahmanic age.

Secondly when the members of the expedition entered the Rann of Kutch the local people pointed out and counted seven small streams of the Sarasvatī entering the Kutch. The local people are not much educated, but they have been carrying the old tradition of the Vedic culture in which the Sarasvatī has been described as the river par excellence. One thing more. The local people call the seven streams as Sat Sarana. This word means seven currents as well as the

---

[8] देवा इमं मधुना संयुतं यवं सरस्वत्यामधि मणावचकृर्षुः ।
इन्द्र आसीत् सरिपतिः शतक्रतुः कीनाशा आसन् मरुतः सुदानवः ॥ आथर्वेद ६. ३०. १

seven sisters It is most astonishing that this fact also has been mentioned in the following Ṛgvedic hymn:

Uta naḥ priyā priyāsu sapta swasā Sujuṣṭā.
Sarasvatī stomyā bhūtaḥ

Ṛgveda 6.61.10[9]

[And all seven sisters in the form of rivers are most beloved among the dear ones. They are worthy to be served and they are highly admirable.]

It has been mentioned earlier that in the Sapta Sindhu region the Sarasvatī was the seventh river. When the same region was named as Punjab then there were five rivers namely the Sarasvatī, Sindhu, Rāvī, Vitastā and Vipāśā minus the Sutlej and the Chināb. In the Pacabhḁdra region the Sarasvatī transformed herself into five streams and in the Rann of Kutch the Sarasvatī has been described one of the seven sisters.

One should make an humble obeisance to the Vedic Ṛsis who visualized the mysterious character of the Sarasvatī River of several forms in several places.

In the end it can be stated that though the mightiest river Sarasvatī vanished but her everlasting glory is still alive in the Indian mind. When an orthodox Hindu takes bath in the morning he chants a prayer in the following śloka:

Gange ca Yamune caiva Godāvari Sarasvatī
Narmade Sindhu Kāverī jalesmin sannidhim kuru.[10]

[Oh ye Ganga and Yamuna, Godavari and Sarasvatī, oh Narmada, Sindhu, and Kaveri, reside in this water (in which I am taking my bath).]

---

[9] उत नः प्रिया प्रियासु सप्त स्वसा सुजुष्टा ।
सरस्वती स्तोम्या भूतः ॥ ऋग्वेद ६.६१.१०

[10] गङ्गे च यमुने चैव गोदावरि सरस्वती ।
नर्मदे सिन्धुकावेरी जलेऽस्मिन् सन्निधं कुरु ॥

Linguistic Aspects of the Indo-European Urheimat Question

KOENRAAD ELST
Catholic University Leuven, Belgium

1. Introduction

When evidence from archaeology and Sanskrit text studies seems to contradict the theory of the entry of the Indo-Aryan branch of the Indo-European (IE) language family in India through the so-called "Aryan Invasion" (Aryan Invasion Theory, AIT), we are usually reassured that "there is of course the linguistic evidence" for this invasion, or at least for the non-Indian origin of the IE family. Thus, when P.L. Bhargava had demonstrated all along five hundred pages that Sanskrit literature has no reference at all to such an Aryan invasion, and that on the contrary it has references to pre-Vedic and Vedic *emigrations*, he did not simply infer that the Aryan migration had been in the opposite direction; that, he opined, would be in conflict with the "well-known" (but unnamed) linguistic evidence.

A common reaction among Indians against this state of affairs is to dismiss linguistics altogether, calling it a "pseudo-science". This creates the impression that their pet theory, which makes the Aryans into natives of India rather than invaders, is not resistant to the test of linguistics. However, the fact that people fail to challenge the linguistic evidence, preferring simply to excommunicate it from the debate, does not by itself validate this body of evidence. In fact, when quizzing linguists about it, I came away with the impression that they too are not very sure of their case. By now, most of them have been trained entirely within the AIT framework, which was taken for granted and consequently not sought to be proven any more. One of them told me that he had never bothered about a linguistic justification for the AIT framework, because there was, after all, "the well-known archaeological evidence"![1]

So, let us take a look for ourselves at this fabled linguistic evidence.

2. Linguistic Ur-form and geographical Urheimat

In the 18th century, when comparative IE linguistics started, the majority opinion was that the original homeland (or *Urheimat*) of the IE language family had to be India. This had an ideological reason, viz. that Enlightenment philosophers such as Voltaire were eager to replace Biblical tradition with a more

[1]P.L. Bhargava, *India in the Vedic Age*, revised ed., Lucknow, 1971.

distant Oriental source of inspiration for European culture. China was a popular candidate, but India had the advantage of being linguistically and even racially more akin to Europe; making it the homeland of the European languages or even of the European peoples, would be helpful in the dethronement of Biblical authority, but by no means far-fetched.

But there was also a seemingly good linguistic reason for choosing India as the Urheimat: the ancient Indian language, Sanskrit, was apparently the closest to the hypothetical Proto-Indo-European (PIE) language from which all existing members of the language family descended. It had all the grammatical categories of Latin and Greek in the most complete form, plus a few more, e.g. three numbers including a dualis in declension and conjugation, and all eight declension cases. Apparently, Sanskrit was very close to if not identical with PIE, and this was taken to support the case for India as the Urheimat.

In reality, there is no necessary relation between the linguistic antiquity of a language and its proximity to the Urheimat. Thus, among the North-Germanic languages, the one closest to Proto-North-Germanic is Icelandic, yet Iceland was most definitely not its Urheimat. The relative antiquity of Sanskrit vis-a-vis PIE does not determine its proximity to the Urheimat. Conversely, the subsequent dethronement of Sanskrit, and the progressive desanskritization of reconstructed PIE does not imply a geographical remoteness of India from the Urheimat. Yet, this mistaken inference has been quite common, though more often silent and implicit than explicit.

The first major element creating a distance between PIE and Sanskrit was the *kentum/satem* divide. It was assumed, in my view (but not that of Indian scholars)[1] correctly, that palatalization is a one-way process transforming velars (k, g) into palatals (c, j) but never the reverse; so that the velar or "kentum" (Latin for "hundred", from PIE **kmtom*) forms had to be the original and the palatal or "satem" (Avestan for "hundred") forms the evolved variants.

However, it would be erroneous to infer from this that the kentum area, i.e. Western and Southern Europe, was the homeland. On the contrary, it is altogether more likely that the Urheimat was in satem territory. The alternative from the angle of an Indian Urheimat theory (IUT) would be that India had originally had the kentum form, that the dialects which first emigrated (Hittite, Italo-Celtic, Germanic, Tokharic) retained the kentum form and took it to the geographical borderlands of the IE expanse (Europe, Anatolia, China), while the dialects which emigrated later (Baltic, Thraco-Phrygian) were at a halfway stage and the

[1] E.g., Satya Swarup Mishra, The Aryan Problem, Delhi, 1992. This palatalization is known in numerous languages, e.g. Chinese (*Yangzi-kiang* > *Yangzi-jiang*), the Bantu language Chiluba (cfr. *Ki-konko, Ki-swahili*, but *Chi-luba*), Arabic (*Gabriel* > *Jibrnl*), English (*kirk* > *church*), the Romance languages, Swedish etc.

last-emigrated dialects (Slavic, Armenian, Iranian) plus the staybehind Indo-Aryan languages had adopted the satem form. This would satisfy the claim of the so-called Lateral Theory that the most conservative forms are to be found at the outskirts rather than in the metropolis. Moreover, the discovery of a small and extinct kentum language inside India (Proto-Bangani, with *koto* as its word for "hundred") tends to support the hypothesis that the older kentum form was originally present in India as well.

The second element in the progressive separation of Sanskrit from PIE was the impression that the [a/e/o] differentiation in Latin and Greek was original, and that their reduction to [a] in Sanskrit was a subsequent development (as in Greek *genos* corresponding to Sanskrit *jana*). Satya Swarup Mishra argues that it may just as well have been the other way around, and unlike the palatalization process, this vowel shift is indeed possible in either direction. Mishra cites examples from the Gypsy language, but we need look no farther than English, where [a] has practically become [e] in "back" and "bake", and [o] in "ball".

There are, however, excellent reasons to stick to the conventional view that the [a/e/o] distinctness is original and their coalescence into [a] a later development. Firstly, the reduction to [a] is typical of just one branch, viz. Indo-lranian, whereas a differentiation starting from [a] would have been a change uniformly affecting all the branches except one, which is less probable. Secondly, the different treatment of the velar consonants in reduplicated Sanskrit verb forms like *jagāma* or *cakāra* suggests a difference in subsequent vowel, with only the first vowel having a palatalizing impact on the preceding velar: *jegāma* < *gegāma* < *cekāra* < *kekāra.*

So, we see no reason to reject the conventional view that Greek vowels are closer to the PIE original than the Sanskrit vowels are. But here again, we see no reason to make geographical deductions from this. India may as well have been the homeland of Proto-Greek, which left before the shift from [a/e/o] to [a] took place.

A third element which increased the distance between reconstructed PIE and Sanskrit dramatically was the discovery of Hittite. Though Hittite displayed a very large intake of lexical and other elements from non-lE languages, some of its features were deemed to be older than their Sanskrit counterparts, e.g. the Hittite genus *commune* as opposed to Sanskrit's contrast between masculine and feminine genders, or the much-discussed laryngeal consonants, absent in Sanskrit as in all other IE languages.

It is by no means universally accepted that these features of Hittite are indeed PIE. Thus, the erosion of grammatical gender is a common phemomenon in IE languages suddenly exposed to an overdose of foreign influence, notably Persian when it was overwhelmed by Arabic, and English when it was overwhelmed by

French influence (and this in spite of the fact that both French and Arabic have grammatical gender themselves); so, it is arguable that Hittite underwent the same development when it had to absorb large doses of Hattic and other pre-IE influence. The laryngeals have been explained by competent scholars as a South-Caucasian or Semitic influence.

But for our purposes there is no need to align ourselves with these dissident opinions. Even if we go with the dominant opinion and accept these elements as PIE, that is still no reason why the Urheimat should be in the historical location of Hittite or at least outside India. As the first emigrant dialect, Hittite could have taken from India some linguistic features (genus commune, laryngeals) which were about to disappear in the dialects emigrating only later or staying behind.

3. Geographical distribution

As India went out of favour, a number of European countries started competing for the honour of being the Urheimat. Ukraine and Russia gained the upper hand with the archaeological discovery of the so-called Kurgan culture, dated to the 5th to 3rd millennium, and apparently the source of migrations into Europe. This area also fell neatly in the middle of the expansion area of IE, a fact which some took as an element in support of the Kurgan culture's Urheimat claim. However, unless IE differs in this respect from other languages and language families, this central location argues more against than in favour of the Kurgan culture's Urheimat claim. Indeed, we find very few examples of languages expanding symmetrically: Chinese spread from the Yellow River basin southward, Russian from Ukraine eastward, Arabic from Arabia westward. There is consequently nothing against an IE migration starting from India and continuing almost exclusively in a westward direction.

The reason for this observed tendency to asymmetry is that the two opposite directions from a given region are only symmetrical in a geometrical sense: climatologically, economically and demographically, the two are usually very different, e.g. the region north of the Yellow River is much less fertile and hospitable than the regions to its south. From the viewpoint of Kurgan culture emigrants, there was hardly a symmetry between the European West and the Indian Southeast: India was densely inhabited, technologically advanced and politically organized, Europe much less so. Europe could be overrun and culturally revolutionised by immigrants, while in India even large groups of immigrants were bound to be assimilated by the established civilization.

India satisfied the conditions for making the spectacular expansion of IE possible: like Europe in the colonial period, it had a demographic surplus and a technological edge over its neighbours. Food crises and political conflicts must have led to emigrations which were small by Indian standards but sizeable for the less populated countries to India's northwest. Since these emigrants, increasingly mingled with the populations they encountered along the way, retained their technological edge vis-a-vis every next population to its west (esp. in the use of horse and chariot), the expansion in western direction continued until the Atlantic Ocean stopped it. Processes of elite dominance led to the linguistic assimilation of ever more westerly populations.

It is easy to see how and why the tendency to asymmetric expansion in the case of other languages also applies to India as the Urheimat of IE. On the road to the northwest, every next region was useful for the Indo-Europeans in terms of their established lifestyle and ways of food production. The mountainous regions to the north and west of India were much less interesting, as were the mountainous areas in the Indian interior. In India, Aryan expansion was long confined to the riverine plains with economic conditions similar to those in the middle basin of the Indus, Saraswati and Ganga rivers; the Vindhya and Himalaya mountains formed a natural limit (the Vindhya mountains were first bypassed by sea, with landings on the Malabar coast). To the northwest, by contrast, after crossing the mountains of Afghanistan, emigrants could move from one riverine plain into the next: Oxus and Jaxartes, Wolga, Dniepr, Dniestr, Don, Danube, and into the European plain stretching from Poland to Holland. Only in the southwest of Europe, a more complex geography and a denser and more advanced native population slowed IE expansion down, and a number of pre-IE languages survived there into the Roman period, Basque even till today.

Another aspect of geographical distribution is the allocation of larger and smaller stretches of territory to the different branches of the IE family. We find the Iranian (covering the whole of Central Asia before 1000 AD) and Indo-Aryan branches each covering a territory as large as all the European branches (at least in the pre-colonial era) combined. We also find the Indo-Aryan branch by itself having, from antiquity till today, more speakers on the Eurasian continent (now nearing 900 million) than all other branches combined. This state of affairs could help us to see the Indo-Aryan branch as the centre and the other branches as wayward satellites; but so far, philologists have made exactly the opposite inference. It is said that this is the typical contrast between a homeland and its colony: a fragmented homeland where languages have small territories, and a large but linguistically more homogeneous colony (cfr. English, which shares its little home island with some Celtic languages, but has much larger stretches of land in North America and Australia all to itself, and with less dialect variation than in Britain; or cfr. Spanish, likewise).

It is also argued that Indo-Aryan must be a late-comer to India, for otherwise it would have been divided by now in several subfamilies as distinct from each other as, say, Celtic from Slavic. To this, we must remark first of all that the linguistic unity of Indo-Aryan should not be exaggerated. Native speakers of Indo-Aryan languages tell me that the difference between Bengali and Sindhi is bigger than that between, say, any two of the Romance languages. Further, to the extent that Indo-Aryan has preserved its unity, this may be attributed to the following factors, which have played in India to a larger extent and for longer periods than in Europe: a geographical unity from Sindh to Bengal (a continuous riverine plain) facilitating interaction between the regions, unlike the much more fragmented geography of Europe; long-time inclusion in common political units (e.g. Maurya, Gupta and Moghul empires); and continuous inclusion in a common cultural space with the common stabilizing influence of Sanskrit.

From the viewpoint of an Indian Urheimat hypothesis, the most important factor explaining the high fragmentation of IE in Europe as compared to its relative homogeneity in North India is the way in which an emigration from India to Europe must have developed. Tribes left India and mixed with the non-IE-speaking tribes of their respective corners of Central Asia and Europe. This happens to be the fastest way of making two dialects of a single language grow apart and develop distinctive new characteristics: make them mingle with different foreign languages. Thus, in the Romance family, we find little difference between Catalan, Occitan and Italian, three languages which have organically grown without much outside influence except for a short period of Germanic influence which was common to them; by contrast, Spanish and Rumanian have grown far apart (lexically, phonetically and grammatically), and this is largely due to the fact that the former has been influenced by Germanic and Arabic, while the latter was influenced by Slavic.

Similarly, under the impact of languages they encountered (now mostly extinct and beyond the reach of our searchlight), and whose speakers they took over, the dialects of the IE emigrants from India differentiated much faster from each other than the dialects of Indo-Aryan.

4. Linguistic paleontology

One of the main reasons for 19th-century philologists to exclude India as a candidate for Urheimat status was the findings of a fledgling new method called *linguistic paleontology*. The idea was that from the reconstructed vocabulary, one could deduce which flora, fauna and artefacts were familiar to the speakers of the proto-language, hence also their geographical area of habitation. The presence in the common vocabulary of words denoting northern animals like the bear, wolf, elk, otter and beaver seemed to indicate a northern Urheimat; likewise, the absence of terms for the lion or elephant seemed to exclude tropical countries like India.

It should be realized that virtually all IE-speaking areas are familiar with the cold climate and its concomitant flora and fauna. Even in hot countries, the mountainous areas provide islands of cold climate, e.g. the foothills of the Himalaya have pine trees rather than palm trees, apples rather than mangoes. Indians are therefore quite familiar with a range of flora and fauna usually associated with the north, including bears (Sanskrit *rksha*, cfr. Greek *arktos*), otters *(udra*, Hindi *ūd/ūdbilāw*) and wolves (*vṛka)*. Elks and beavers do not live in India, yet the words exist, albeit with a different but related meaning: rsha means a male antelope, *babhru* a mongoose. The shift of meaning may have taken place in either direction: it is perfectly possible that emigrants from India transferred their term for "mongoose" to the first beavers which they encountered in Russia or other mongoose-free territory.

So, the fauna terms provide no proof for a northern Urheimat. Thomas Gamkrelidze and Vyaceslav Ivanov (*IE and the Indo-Europeans*, Berlin 1995), in their bid to prove their Anatolian Urheimat theory, have gone a step further and tried to find terms for hot-climate fauna in the common IE vocabulary.[1] Thus, they relate Sanskrit *pṛdaku* with Greek *pardos* and Hittite *parsana,* all meaning "leopard", an IE term lost in some northern regions devoid of leopards. The word "lion" is found as a native word, in regular phonetic correspondence, in Greek, Italic, Germanic and Hittite, and with a vaguer meaning "beast", in Slavic and Tokharic. Moreover, it is not unreasonable to give it deeper roots in IE by linking it with a verb, Sanskrit *rav-*, "howl, roar" (alternation *r/l* is common in Sanskrit, e.g. the double form *plavaga/pravaga*, "monkey", or the noun *plava*, "frog" related to the verb *pravate*, "jump").

A word for "monkey" is common to Greek (*kepos*) and Sanskrit (*kapi*), and Gamkrelidze and Ivanov argue for its connection with the Germanic and Celtic word "ape", which does not have the initial [k], for such *k*/mute alternation (which they derive from a pre-existing laryngeal) is also found in other IE words, e.g. Greek *kapros* next to Latin *aper*, Dutch *ever*, "boar". For "elephant", they even found two distinct IE words: Sanskrit *ibha*, "male elephant", corresponds to Latin *ebur*, "ivory, elephant"; and Greek *elephant-* corresponds to Gothic *ulbandus,* Tokharic **alpi*, "camel". In the second case, the "camel" meaning may be the original one, if we assume a migration through camel-rich Central Asia to Greece, where trade contacts with Egypt made the elephant known; the word may be a derivative from a word meaning "deer", e.g. Greek *elaphos.* In the case of *ibha/ebur*, however, we have a linguistic-paleontological argument for an Urheimat with elephants.

While the commonly-assumed northern location of PIE is at least disputable even on linguistic-paleontological grounds, as just shown, the derivation of its

[1] T. Gamkrelidze and V. Ivanov: *IE and the Indo-Europeans*, Walter De Gruyter, Berlin 1995.

western location on the basis of the famous "beech" argument is indisputably flawed. The tree name *beech/fagus/bhegos* exists only in the Italic, Celtic and Germanic languages with that meaning, while in Greek (spoken in a beechless country) its meaning has shifted to "a type of oak". More easterly languages do not have this word, and their speakers are not naturally familiar with this tree, which only exists in western and central Europe. Somehow, our 19th-century predecessors deduced from this that PIE was spoken in the beech-growing part of Europe.

But in that case, one might have expected that at least some of the easterly languages had taken the word with them on their eastward exodus, applying it to other but somewhat similar trees (as Greek effectively did on its journey from central to southern Europe, a journey which it made in both the European and the Indian Urheimat scenarios). The distribution of the "beech" term is much better explained by assuming that it was an Old-European term adopted by the IE newcomers, and never known to those IE-speakers who stayed to the east of Central Europe. I do not think that anyone takes the once-decisive "beech" argument seriously anymore.

With this, we have briefly entered the game of linguistic paleontology, but not without retaining a measure of skepticism before the whole idea of reconstructing an environment of a proto-language from the vocabulary of its much younger daughter-languages. As Stefan Zimmer has written: "The long dispute about the reliability of this 'linguistic paleontology' is not yet finished, but approaching its inevitable end—with a negative result, of course."[1] This cornerstone of the European Urheimat theory is now largely discredited. Moreover, we believe we have shown that even if valid, the findings of linguistic paleontology would be compatible with an Indian Urheimat as well.

5. *Exchanges with other language families*

One of the best keys to the geographical itinerary of a language is the exchange of lexical and other elements with other languages. Two types of language contact should be distinguished. The first type of language contact is the exchange of vocabulary and other linguistic traits, whether by long-distance trade contact, by contiguity or by substratum influence, between languages which are not necessarily otherwise related. A well-known example is the transmission of terms in the sphere of cattle-breeding from IE (mostly Tokharic) to Chinese: terms for dog, horse, cow, milk, honey. This doesn't add new information but neatly confirms the long-suspected presence of Tokharic in Western China since at least the 2nd millennium BC.

[1] S. Zimmer: "On Indo-Europeanization", *JIES*. Spring 1990.

A more surprising example is the apparent influence of Hamitic on Irish: it would seem that after the Ice Age, the European west coast was repopulated from the southwest, by Basque and even Hamitic-speaking peoples, who from ca. 2000 BC were assimilated into the IE and esp. the Celtic speech community, but smuggled some of their language traits into their newly adopted language. The example is interesting but does not provide information on the Urheimat, except to confirm that it was not in Celtic Western Europe.

A few terms exchanged with Sumerian, esp. *karpasa/kapazum*, "cotton", and possibly *ager/agar*, "field", and *go/gu*, "cow" (to cite some suggestions from Gamkrelidze and Ivanov, op.cit.), would confirm the presence of IE (though not necessarily PIE if Sumerian was the borrowing language) in an area conducting trade with Sumerian in the 3rd millennium, the main candidates being Anatolia (Gamkrelidze and Ivanov's Urheimat choice) and the Indus basin.

A case of contact on a rather large scale which is taken as providing crucial information on the Urheimat question is between early IE and Uralic. It was a one-way traffic, imparting some Tokharic, dozens of Iranian and also a few seemingly Indo-Aryan terms (*sapta*, "seven, week", *asura*, "lord", *sasar*, "sister", *shata*, "hundred) to either Proto-Uralic or Proto-Finno-Ugric (i.e. mainstream Uralic after Samoyedic split off). At first sight, this would seem to confirm the European Urheimat theory: on their way from Europe, the Indo-Iranian and Tokharic tribes encountered the Uralic people in the Ural region and imparted some vocabulary to them. This would even remain possible if, as leading scholars of Uralic suggest, the Uralic languages themselves came from farther east, from the Irtysh river and Balkhash lake area.

However, two alternative explanations are equally sustainable. Imagine the first waves of emigrants from India, taking most of the ancestor-dialects of the various branches of the IE family with them, through the Oxus valley to the Wolga plain and beyond. With the exception of Tokharic which remained in the area, they did not come in contact with Uralic, and when they did, they swallowed the Uralic-speaking population without allowing it much linguistic influence. Only the Slavic branch of IE shows some substratal influence from Uralic, a fact which is neatly compatible with an India-to-Europe migration: an Uralic-speaking tribe in the peri-Caspian region got assimilated in the westwardly expanding IE-speaking population. It was the Iranians who came in contact with Uralic on a large scale, partly because they filled up the whole of Central Asia and (in the Scythian expansion) even Eastern Europe as far as Western Ukraine and Belarus, where an older Slavic population subsisted and adopted a lot of Iranian vocabulary;[1]

[1]E.g. Slavic *Bog*, "God", cfr. Sanskrit *Bhaga, Bhagwbn; mir*, "friendship, peace, society", from Persian *Mihr*, Iranian Mithra, cfr. Sanskrit *mitra*, "friend", and *Mitra*, the god of agreements.

and partly because the Uralic-speaking people were moving westward through the Urals region in a movement parallel to the Iranian westward expansion.

Now, how do the seemingly Indo-Aryan words fit in? One possibility is that these words were imparted to Uralic by non-Iranian, Indo-Aryan-speaking emigrants from India at the time of the great catastrophe in about 2000 BC, when the Saraswati river dried up and many of the Harappan cities were abandoned. This catastrophe triggered migrations in all directions: to the Malabar coast, to India's interior and east, to West Asia by sea (the Kassite dynasty in Babylon in ca. 1600 BC venerated some of the Vedic gods), and to Central Asia. The Sanskrit terms in the Mitannic language attested in West Asia in the 15th century BC seem to be a leftover of an Indo-Aryan presence in West-Asia, which presupposes an earlier Indo-Aryan migration through (an already predominantly Iranian-speaking) Central Asia. Some such emigrant group may have ended up in an Uralic-speaking environment, imparting some of its own terminology but getting assimilated over time, just like their Mitannic cousins. The Uralic term *orya*, "slave", from either Iranian *airya* or Sanskrit *arya*, may indicate that their position was not as dignified as that of the Mitannic kings and horse-trainers.

An alternative possibility is that the linguistic exchange between Proto-Uralic and Iranian took place at a much earlier stage, before Iranian had grown distinct from Indo-Aryan. It is by no means a new suggestion that these seemingly Indo-Aryan words are in fact Indo-Iranian, i.e. dating back to before the separation of Iranian from Indo-Aryan, or in effect, before the development of typical iranianisms such as the softening of initial [s] to [h]. This would mean that the vanguard of the Iranian emigration from India had not yet changed *asura* and *sapta* into *ahura* and *hafta*, and that Iranian developed its typical features (some of which it shares with Armenian and Greek, most notably the [s][h] shift) outside India. This tallies with the fact (admittedly only an argument *e silentio*) that the Vedic reports on struggles with Iranian tribes such as the Dasas and the Panis (attested in Greco-Roman sources as the East-Iranian tribes *Dahae* and *Parnoi*), the Pakthas (Pathans), Parsuas (Persians), Prthus (Parthians) and Bhalanas (Baluchis) never mention any term or phrase or name with typically Iranian features.

Even the stage before Indo-Iranian unity, viz. when Indo-Iranian had not yet replaced the PIE *kentum* forms with its own *satem* forms, may already have witnessed some lexical exchanges with Uralic: as Asko Parpola has pointed out, among the IE loans in Uralic, we find a few terms in *kentum* form which are exclusively attested in the Indo-Iranian branch of IE, e.g. Finnish *kehrd*, "spindle", from PIE **kettra*, attested in Sanskrit as *cattra*.[1] It is of course also possible that words like **kettra* once did exist in branches other than Indo-Iranian but

---

[1] A. Parpola in G. Erdosy: *The Indo-Aryans of Ancient South Asia* (Berlin 1995), p. 355.

disappeared in the intervening period along with so many other original PIE words which were replaced by non-IE loans or new IE formations. If *kettra* was indeed transmitted to Uralic by early Indo-Iranian, it may have been as a result of trade, for the Indus basin was an advanced manufacturing centre which exported gods deep into Central Asia.

This leads us to a third possibility, viz. that the seemingly Indo-Aryan words in Uralic were transmitted by long-distance traders, regardless of migrations, possibly even at a fairly date date. They may have been pure Indo-Aryan, as distinct from Iranian, normally spoken only in India itself, but brought to the Uralic people by means of long-distance trade, regardless of which languages were spoken in the territory in between, somewhat like the entry of Arabic words in European languages during the Middle Ages (e.g. *tariff, cheque, bazar, douane*). If we see India in the 3rd millennium BC as the mighty metropolis whose influence radiated deep into Central Asia (as archaeology suggests), this cannot be ruled out. At any rate, we believe we have shown enough possible ways to reasonably reconcile the lexical exchange between the eastern IE languages and Uralic with an Indian Urheimat scenario.

Another language group showing signs of early contact if not kinship with early IE or PIE is Austronesian. Remarkable lexical similarities had been reported since at least the 1930s, and they have been presented by Isidore Dyen in 1966.[1] They include pronouns (e.g. Proto-Austronesian **aku*, cfr. PIE **ego*), the four first numerals (e.g. Malay *dva*, "two"), and elementary nouns including terms for land, water, and body parts (e.g. Malay *sikel*, "leg", cfr. Greek *skelos*, "bone"). Most scholars of IE including myself know too little of Austronesian to verify this claim, and all of us tend to remind ourselves of the existence of pure coincidence when confronted with these data. Dyen's comparisons are sometimes not too obvious but satisfy the linguistic requirement of regularity.

At the same time, this lexical influence or exchange is not backed up by grammatical similarities: in contrast with the elaborate categories of IE grammar, Austronesian grammar looks very primitive, the textbook example being the Malay plural by reduplication, as in *orang*, "man", *orang-orang*, "men". The explanation could be that Austronesian came into being in India (or at least near the IE Urheimat, wherever it was) as a kind of pidgin language incorporating parts of the PIE vocabulary along with other elements, and making up its own grammar along the way. The presence in Indo-Aryan and Dravidian languages of some terms also common in Austronesian suggests a one-time presence of Proto-Austronesian in India, e.g. the twin terms *ayi/bayi*, "mother, lady", known for example in the Marathi girl's names *Tara-bai, Lakshmi-bai* etc.

[1] I. Dyen in G. Cardona: *Indo-European and Indo-Europeans*, Philadelphia, 1970.

The remarkable expansion by sea of the Austronesians, the mirror-image of the horseborne expansion of the Indo-Europeans, also suggests that they started out from a civilized country, advanced in technology as well as astronomy; this is evident when you compare the Austronesian saga with the situation of the Papuas and Australian aborigines, who never developed ocean navigation eventhough surrounded by the ocean. Even great seafarers of later centuries, like the Arabs and the Chinese, essentially stuck to coastal navigation, so the Austronesians' endeavour to cross the ocean to Madagascar and Polynesia was extremely daring and indicative of a great confidence in their tried and tested navigation skills. The Harappan or post-Harappan seafarers who colonized the Maledives and Sri Lanka may well have been in contact with the Austronesians starting on their journey. In this light, even indications longtime dismissed as flaky, such as the Easter Island inscriptions vaguely resembling the Harappan script, may assume a new significance.

Conversely, there is also a theoretical possibility that PIE was itself an offshoot of early Austronesian, which many scholars think originated in southeastern China (hence its substratum presence in Japanese, a rather hard nut to crack for an Indian Urheimat theory of Austronesian). Just imagine, a wayward Austronesian tribe sailed up the Ganga led by one Manu who, as related in the Puranas, started Aryan history in the mid-Ganga basin (Ayodhya, Prayag, Kashi), and whose progeny subsequently conquered the Indus basin. In that case, the elaborate structure of PIE would be an artificial construction due to a peculiar intellectual culture (let's call it proto-brahminism) and to the influence of local languages, including perhaps a lost branch of Semitic spoken by colonists who had brought agriculture from West Asia to the Indus settlement of Mehrgarh.

We have just presented the pro and con of some *prima facie* indications for language contacts which would imply an ancient IE and even PIE presence in Harappan and pre-Harappan India. In our opinion, none of these can presently be considered decisive evidence for an Indian Urheimat theory.

However, in the heat of this discussion, we might forget to evaluate the evidence from language contacts for the rivalling European Urheimat theory, which should be put to the same tests as the Indian Urheimat theory. The fact is that such evidence is very scarce, if not non-existent. The Old-European Basque language has no ancient links with IE. For the rest, all Old-European languages have disappeared and have not even survived as dead inscriptional languages providing us with material for linguistic comparison. Evidence of the type tentatively provided by isoglosses between IE and Semitic, between IE and Austronesian or between Indo-Iranian and Uralic, is simply not available for the westerly branches of IE or for a hypothetical Europe-based PIE. On balance, the evidence from contact with once-neighbouring languages does not provide compelling evidence for an Indian Urheimat (unless the Austronesian connection is valid), but even less evidence for a European Urheimat.

6. Deep kinship with other language families

The second type of language contact is not actual contact but a common origin: just as Portuguese and Italian have both developed out of Latin (partly by absorbing each its own dose of foreign elements), and just as both Latin and Tokharic have evolved out of a common ancestor-language provisionally called PIE, so PIE must have evolved from an even earlier language, which may at the same time have been the ancestor of other language families as well.

The most important theory in this line of research is the Nostratic superfamily theory, postulating a common origin for Eskimo-Aleut, Altaic, Uralic, IE, Afro-Asiatic, Dravidian and possibly South-Caucasian. Some people make fun of this theory, and refer it jokingly to the "nostratosphere", yet its basic postulate makes perfect sense: differentiation of ancestor-languages, as attested in detail in the case of Latin and the Romance language family, must have happened at earlier stages of history as well. Whether the present superfamily theory and the methods actually used for reconstructing the supposed Nostratic vocabulary are at all acceptable, is beyond the subject-matter of this paper.

There are a few language families which have certainly been in contact with early IE sometime in the historical period, and which have at the same time been argued to have a hoary common origin with IE. Because of the commonality of some elementary lexical items (including the first seven numerals) and of some grammatical traits, Semitic (and by implication the Chadic, Kushitic and Hamitic branches of the Afro-Asiatic family, assumed to be the result of a pre-4th-millennium immigration of early agriculturists from West Asia into North Africa) is suspected to spring from a common ancestor with IE, even by scholars skeptical of Nostratic adventures. The argument is compelling, for Semitic, like IE, has grammatically functional vowel changes, grammatical gender, conjugational categories including participles and medial and passive modes, and a range of phonemes which in Proto-Semitic was almost entirely in common with IE, and entirely so if we assume PIE laryngeals to match Semitic *aleph*, he and *'ayn.*[1]

Those who interpret the archaeological data concerning the genesis of agriculture in the Indus site of Mehrgarh as being the effect of a diffusion from West Asia may well interpret the profound kinship with Semitic as proving their point: like its material culture, Mehrgarh's language was an offshoot of a metropolitan model, viz. a Proto-Semitic-speaking culture in West Asia. This

[1]See e.g. Bernard Sergent: *Les Indo-Européens,* Payot, Paris 1995, p. 398, who believes the Kurgan people in South Russia had come from the Aral Lake area and then not from the southeast (India) but the southwest (Mesopotamia), where he assumes a common origin with Semitic.

would mean that the Indus area was indeed the homeland of the original PIE, but that in the preceding millennia, PIE had been created by the interaction of Proto-Semitic-speaking colonists from West Asia with locals.

Now that the case for an independent genesis of the Neolithic revolution (i.e. the development of agriculture) in Mehrgarh is getting stronger, we may have to reconsider the direction of such a process.

The state of the art is that we just don't know very much yet about the ancestry of PIE, especially when even the location of PIE in its heyday is still the object of debate. But just to be on the safe side in case of a breakthrough of the Nostratic theory, we do want to remark that the distribution of the alleged Nostratic language families at their earliest date of appearance, with most of them within travelling distance from the Indus-Saraswati basin (Uralic in the Ob-Irtysh basin, Altaic in Mongolia, Semitic in Mesopotamia, Elamo-Dravidian in Iran-Sindh), is certainly compatible with an Northwest-Indian Urheimat of IE, much more than with a European Urheimat. For the rest, it is best to leave these proto-proto-languages alone and concentrate on real language families.

7. Substratum elements

Apart from contact between different languages which have continued to exist, there is also influence from a disappearing language on a surviving language, often in the form of a substratum: people take to speaking a new (mostly the elite's) language, and drop their old language all while preserving some lexical items, some phonetic propensities, some grammatical ways of organizing information. The alleged presence of a large dose of "pre-Aryan" substratum features in Sanskrit and the other Indo-Aryan languages, notably from Dravidian, was historically one of the important reason for deciding against India as the Urheimat. This substratum factor is the object of an excellent paper elsewhere in this volume (Edwin Bryant: "Linguistic Substrata and the Indo-Aryan Migration Debate"), so I will treat it only very briefly.

In the 19th century, it was not yet realized how the European branches of IE are all full of substratum elements, mostly from extinct Old European languages. For Latin, this includes such elementary terms as *altus* and *urbs*, borrowed from a substratum language tentatively described as "Urbian". For Germanic, it includes some 30% of the acknowledged "Germanic" vocabulary, including such core lexical items as *sheep* and *drink*. For Greek, it amounts to some 40% of the vocabulary, both from extinct branches of the Anatolian (Hittite-related) family and from non-IE languages. The branch least affected by foreign elements is Slavic, but this need not be taken as proof of a South-Russian homeland: in an Indian Urheimat scenario, the way for Slavic would be cleared by forerunners, chiefly Germanic and Baltic, and though these languages would absorb many

Old-European elements as substratum features, they also eliminated the Old-European languages as such and prevented them from further influencing Slavic.

Even if we accept as non-IE all the elements in Sanskrit described as such by various scholars, the non-IE contribution is still not greater than in some of the European branches of IE. And, as Shrikant Talageri has shown, a large part of this so-called Dravidian contribution is highly questionable: many words routinely described as Dravidian-originated have been analyzed as pure IE.[1] At any rate, there has been so much interaction with Dravidian, including exchange of people and goods, that a Dravidian contribution (as an neighbourly or adstratum influence) is perfectly normal; it is also much smaller than the Indo-Aryan influence on the Dravidian languages, which no one tries to explain as a substratum effect.

In this respect, the testimony of the place-names may be useful. In the Hindi belt and most of Panjab, there is no evidence of a Dravidian substratum in the toponyms. By contrast, in Sindh and Gujarat, Dravidian toponyms are fairly common, e.g. names ending in *valli/palli*, "village". In Sindhi, and more so in Gujarati and Marathi, Dravidian influence is quite strong. By contrast, Hindi has much fewer Dravidian elements, even losing loanwords which had been adopted in Sanskrit. There is no reason to assume a Dravidian presence in North India, but it seems to have been there in the coastal area.

This would fit in with David McAlpin's Elamo-Dravidian theory, which puts Proto-Elamo-Dravidian on the coast of Iran, spreading westwards to Mesopatamia (Elam) and eastwards to Sindh and along the Indian coast southward.[2] This theory is supported by the similarities between the undeciphered early Elamite script and the Harappan script, and by the survival of the Brahui Dravidian speech pocket in Baluchistan. It would make the Harappan culture bi- and possibly multi-lingual: a perfectly normal situation, comparable with multi-lingual Mesopotamia or with Latin-Greek bilinguism in the Roman Empire.

But in that case, Indo-Aryan influence on Dravidian is much older than usually assumed, and dates back well into the heyday of Harappan culture. And indeed, apart from the *tatsama* (literally adopted) Sanskrit words which make up more than half of Telugu or Kannada vocabulary, and which are attributed to the influence of Brahmin families settling in South India since the turn of the Christian era, many apparent members of the Dravidian core vocabulary as attested in Sangam Tamil are actually very ancient *tadbhava* (evolved and sometimes unrecognizably changed) loans from Sanskrit or Prakrit, e.g. *ākāyam*, "sky" (*ākāsha*); *āyutham*, "weapon" (*āyudha*); *tavam*, "penance" (*tapas*); *tīvu*, "island" (*dwīpa*); *chetti*, "foreman,

[1] Shrikant Talageri: *Aryan Invasion Theory*, a Reappraisal, Aditya Prakashan, Delhi 1993.

[2] See e.g. D. McAlpin: "Linguistic Prehistory: the Dravidian Situation", in M.M. Deshpande and P.E. Hook (eds.), *Aryan and Non-Aryan in India*, Ann Arbor 1979.

merchant" (*shreshthi*).[1] It is doubtful that there ever was a pure Dravidian language in South India, Dravidian having been influenced by Sanskrit in Sindh and Gujarat before spreading south, probably as part of the great post-Harappan exodus after the ecological catastrophe in ca. 2000 BC.

Many scholars now assume that there was a third language in northwestern India, which acted as a buffer between Dravidian and Indo-Aryan before being eliminated by the latter. Many words looking like Dravidian loans in Indo-Aryan would then, in fact, have been borrowed from this third language into both. To Indian critics of linguistics ("a pseudoscience"), such a ghost language is a perfect proof of the purely speculative nature of our science. Yet, it is an entirely reasonable proposition: even Sumerian, one of the great vehicles of civilization, died out, and we have reason to assume that the Bhil tribals originally spoke a different language, possibly related to the tribal Nahali language still spoken in a few villages in Madhya Pradesh.

Such a buffer language would at any rate explain, in an Indian Urheimat theory, why there is no Dravidian influence on IE as a whole, merely on Indo-Aryan and to a very small extent, on Iranian (though it is remarkable that some of the words transmitted from Indo-Iranian to Uralic are usually credited with a Dravidian origin, e.g. *shishu,* "child", and *kota,* "house"; if correct, this would be a strong argument for an Indian Urheimat). By the time the buffer language had been swallowed and Dravidian-IE interaction began, most of the IE proto-languages had already left India.

Conclusion

It is too early to say that linguistics has proven an Indian origin for the IE family. But we can assert with confidence that the oft-invoked linguistic evidence for a European Urheimat and for an Aryan invasion of India is completely wanting. One after another, the classical proofs of the European Urheimat theory have been discredited, usually by scholars who had no knowledge of or interest in an alternative Indian Urheimat theory. In the absence of a final judgment by linguistics, other approaches deserve to be taken seriously, unhindered and uninhibited by fear of that large-looming but in fact elusive "linguistic evidence".

---

[1] R. Swaminatha Aiyar, *Dravidian Theories*, Motilal Banarsidass, Delhi 1987 (but written in 1923)..

Political Aspects of the Aryan Invasion Debate

KOENRAAD ELST
Catholic University, Leuven, Belgium

The debate on the Aryan Invasion Theory is not logically affected by the political motives of some of its participants, though these motives are sometimes palpable through the rhetoric used. Mapping these motives as a matter of history of ideas (and not as a way to decide the AIT question itself by means of political association) allows us to point out the following: on the pro-AIT side, justification of European colonialism, delegitimation of Hinduism as India's native religion by missionaries of foreign religions, Indian Marxist attempts to delegitimize Indian nationalism, and several separatisms in India seeking to bolster the case against Indian unity; and on the anti-AIT side, Indian nationalism seeking to make India's civilizational unity more robust, and to score a point against the aforementioned "anti-national forces".

Aryavarta for the Aryans

Until the mid-19th century, no Indian had ever heard of the notion that his ancestors could be Aryan invaders from Central Asia who had destroyed the native civilization and enslaved the native population. Neither had South-Indians ever dreamt that they were the rightful owners of the whole subcontinent, dispossessed by the Aryan invaders who had chased them from North India, turning it into *Aryavarta*, the land of the Aryans. Nor had the low-caste people heard that they were the original inhabitants of India, subdued by the Aryans and forced into the prisonhouse of caste which the conquerors imposed upon them as an early form of Apartheid. All these ideas had to be imported by European scholars and missionaries.

One of the first natives to interiorize these ideas was Jotirao Phule, India's first modern Mahatma, a convent-educated low-caste leader from Maharashtra. He set the tone for the political appropriation of the Aryan Invasion Theory (AIT): "Recent researches have shown beyond a shadow of doubt that the Brahmins were not the Aborigines of India (. . .) Aryans came to India not as simple emigrants with peaceful intentions of colonization, but as conquerors. They appear to have been a race imbued with very high notions of self, extremely cunning, arrogant and bigoted."[1] Ever since, the political reading of the AIT has become all-pervasive in

[1] J. Phule: *Slavery* (1873), republished by the Government of Maharashtra, Mumbai 1991, as vol.1 of *Collected Works of Mahatma Jotirao Phule*, p. xxix–xxx.

Indian textbooks as well as in all kinds of divisive propaganda pitting high and low castes, North and South Indians, speakers of Indo-Aryan and of Dravidian languages, and tribals and non-tribals, against each other.

Today, out of indignation with the socially destructive implications of the politically appropriated AIT, many Indian scholars get excited about supposed imperialist motives distorting the views of the Western scholars who first introduced the AIT. They point to the Christian missionary commitment of early sankritists like Friedrich Max MIller, John Muir and Sir M. Monier-Williams and of dravidologists like Bishop Robert Caldwell and Reverend G.U. Pope, alleging that the missionaries justify their presence in India by claiming that Aryan Hinduism is as much a foreign import as Christianity. They quote Lord Curzon as saying that the AIT is "the furniture of Empire", and explain how the British colonizers justified their conquest by claiming that India had never been anything but booty for foreign invaders, and that the Indians (or at least the upper-caste Hindus who led the Freedom Movement) were as much foreigners as their fellow-Aryans from Britain.

About the use of the AIT in the service of colonialism, there can be no doubt. Thus, during the 1935 Parliament debates on the Government of India Act, Sir Winston Churchill opposed any policy tending towards decolonization on the following ground: "We have as much right to be in India as anyone there, except perhaps for the Depressed Classes [= *the Scheduled Castes and Tribes*], who are the native stock."[1] So, the British Aryans had as much right to Aryavarta as their Vedic fellow-Aryans. Conversely, Indian loyalists justified the British presence on the same grounds, e.g. Brahmo Samaj leader Keshab Chandra Sen (mid-19th century) welcomed the British advent as a "reunion" with his Aryan "cousins".

However, it does not follow that the AIT was coined simply as a political weapon. Both in Europe and in India, many scholars have believed and still believe that the AIT is simply the most convincing hypothesis to account for a number of actual data in linguistics and other disciplines. The tendency in some Indian circles to denounce linguistics as a "pseudo-science" for having generated the AIT, or to allege that the AIT was "concocted" by political schemers, must be rejected. On the whole, the scholars concerned genuinely believed in their own hypotheses, and were sincerely trying to make sense of newly-discovered facts such as the linguistic kinship between the languages of Europe and northern India.

Paradigm inertia

If historians and linguists sometimes displayed great ingenuity in explaining away facts inconvenient to their pet theory, this should be seen as merely a case of the universal tendency to stick to established beliefs until the evidence to the

[1] Reproduced in C.H. Philips ed.: *Select Documents on the History of India and Pakistan*, part IV, p. 315.

contrary becomes really overwhelming. Scientists—in any field—abhor the disorder created by information which is incompatible with the established theory, and therefore rightfully continue to assume that a second look will smoothen this initial incompatibility and "domesticate" the new information; they have a very functional kind of immunity to facts disturbing the paradigm which underlies their research.

Even a first-rate and patriotic Indian historian like R.C. Majumdar had the same capacity to keep on ignoring facts disobeying the theory to which his mind had become accustomed, viz. the AIT. After describing how many cultural elements of the "pre-Aryan" Indus civilization have survived till today, Majumdar displays that typical academic skill of not taking even registered facts into account once they come in conflict with the paradigm: "How such a great culture and civilization could vanish without leaving any trace or even memory behind it, is a problem that cannot be solved at the present state of our knowledge."[1] Such a huge anomaly should call the theory itself into question, especially when an alternative is ready at hand, and is even suggested by facts mentioned by Majumdar himself, viz. that there is a straight continuity between the Indus civilization and the later stages of "Aryan" culture.

For another example, the allusions to armed conflict in the Rg Veda have always been taken to refer to the confrontation between the Aryan invaders and the defenders of the indigenous culture. Madhav M. Deshpande remarks about these references: "It is extremely important to recognize that all of these references to *dasyu-hattya* [= killing of the Dasyu enemies] are found in those parts of the RV which are traditionally regarded to be late parts of the text."[2] This should imply that the invaders were at first on good terms with the natives (like the *Mayflower* pioneers with the native Americans) but became hostile later.; or that the Vedic people were stable inhabitants of the region which forms the permanent background of the Vedic hymns, and were confronted with these Dasyus at a later stage, viz., when the Dasyus invaded the Vedic-Aryan territory; or that this hostility has nothing to do with a confrontation between invaders and natives.

But Deshpande doesn't even consider any of these possibilities: "This would most probably mean that even by the time of the late parts of the RV, the attitudes of the Vedic Aryans had not significantly changed, and that they still regarded the dasyus as those who deserve to be killed by Indra."[3] After saying in so many words that the earlier layers of the RV do not contain this hostility, he claims that the late parts "still" have it, and that the Aryans' attitude "had not significantly

[1]R.C. Majumdar, *Ancient India*, Motilal Banarsidass, Delhi 1991 (1952), p. 19; emphasis added.

[2]M.M. Deshpande, "Genesis of Rgvedic retroflexion" in: M.M. Deshpande and P.E. Hook, *Aryan and Non-Aryan in India*, Ann Arbor, 1079, p. 300.

[3]Ibid.

changed", when it had actually changed from neutral to hostile, as per his own summary of the Vedic data. When facts challenging the AIT stare him in the face, the scholar tends to prefer the familiar theory to the unwilling facts.

Hitler's Aryans

Even the 19th-century race theories which would feature so dramatically in crimes against humanity were not originally conceived as political ploys; in the prevailing *Zeitgeist*, most of their theorists genuinely thought that the race concept provided the best explanation for the incoming data of nascent sciences like sociology and anthropology. Nonetheless, the disruptive effects of their work have reached beyond Europe as far as India.

In the proliferating race theories of the late 19th and early 20th century, "Aryan", an early synonym of "Indo-European" (IE), became a racial term designating the purest segment of the White race. Of course, the identification of "white" with "Aryan" was an innovation made by armchair theorizers in Europe, far from and in stark disregard for the self-described Aryas in India. Better-informed India-based Britons like Rudyard Kipling summed up the Indian type as "Aryan brown".

Incorporated in the theme of Aryan whiteness, the AIT became a crown piece in Adolf Hitler's vision of white supremacy: here was the proof of both white superiority and of the need to preserve the race from admixture with inferior darker races. Had not the white invaders subdued the brown-skinned natives, and had they not lost their superior white quality by mixing with the natives and becoming more brown themselves? In the Nazi view, the Aryan invaders had retained a relative superiority vis-a-vis the pure black natives by means of the caste system, but had been too slow in instituting this early form of Apartheid, so that their type was fatally contaminated with inferior blood. The "Aryan" theme failed to kindle any sympathy in Hitler.for the brown Aryans of India: he spurned the collaboration offer by Subhash Chandra Bose because he preferred India to be under white British domination, and he ordered the extermination of the Gypsies, Indian immigrants into Europe.

Nonetheless, anti-Hindu polemicists cleverly exploit the ambiguity of the term "Aryan" to associate Hindus with Hitler. Consider this crassly false statement by a leading Marxist historian about the reform movement Arya Samaj, founded in 1875 and well-known for its anti-untouchability campaigns: "The Arya Samaj was described by its followers as 'the society of the Aryan race'. The Aryas were the upper castes and the untouchables were excluded."[1] The second sentence is precisely the Western indologist reading of the term *Arya* which the Arya Samaj sought to *counter*: the Samaj restored the original meaning of the term, viz.

[1]Romila Thapar: "The Theory of Aryan Race and India: History and Politics", *Social Scientist*, Delhi, January-March 1996, p. 8.

"civilized", in particular "belonging to or expressive of the Vedic civilization".[1] While the Samaj was not slow in acknowledging that in its own day, the untouchables were being excluded from learning the Vedic rituals and philosophies, it worked hard to *undo* this exclusion.

As for the first sentence quoted, it is not known to me where a Samaj spokesman called his own organization "the society of the Aryan race". However, it is not altogether impossible that the expression was used, because the word "race" in English (as opposed to German and post-1945 English) then had a more general, non-biological and non-racist meaning, viz. "nation, people". Sri Aurobindo, for one, has definitely used the term "Aryan race", thereby not meaning what Hitler and post-Hitlerian readers will understand by that term, but "Hindu nation".[2] To quote Hindus as speaking of the "Aryan race" without explaining the semantic itinerary of the term is tantamount to manipulating the readership into reading something into the phrase which Arya Samaj spokesmen and Aurobindo never intended.

The association of the term "Aryan" with racist doctrines had as one of its side-effects that after the collapse of Nazi Germany, the entire field of IE studies came under a shadow. Specialists of IE culture like Georges Dumizil were ipso facto (and in his case definitily wrongly) suspected of Nazi sympathies.[3] As late as 1982, a survey of Swedish national history had its chapters on the settlement of the Indo-Europeans in Scandinavia cut out; not rewritten but cut out, for the very mention of the Indo-Europeans (not even "Aryans") was considered irredeemably tainted.[4] The hysterical nature of this act of censorship comes out more clearly when you realize that the settlement of IE immigrants coming to Scandinavia from the southeast goes *against* the Nazi predilection for a North-European Urheimat of the "Aryans". Only in the last few years has normalcy in this department of historical research been restored.

This taboo on IE studies emanates from lazy or superstitious minds: rather

[1]The term is still used in that sense in the Constitution of the Hindu Kingdom of Nepal, which enjoins the King to "uphold Aryan culture".

[2]For all his "Aryan race" talk, Aurobindo was among the most clear-sighted analysts of the problem which Nazism posed. In 1939, Aurobindo advocated India's total support to the Allied cause as a matter of principle, because he saw in Hitler a force of evil; this at a time when many Indians, both Hindu and Muslim, were very fond of Hitler, and when others advocated entry into the war on purely opportunistic grounds.

[3]A list and rebuttal of the allegations against Dumézil is given in Didier Eribon: *Faut-il brûler Dumézil?* ("Should Dumézil be burned at the stake?"), Flammarion, Paris 1992. Of course, malafide authors keep on repeating the refuted allegations.

[4]The work affected is R. & G. Haland: *Bra Böckers Världhistoria*, vol.1, Höganäs 1982, as reported in Christopher Prescott & Eva Walderhaug: "The Last Frontier? Processes of Indo-Europeanization in Northern Europe: the Norwegian Case", *Journal of Indo-European Studies*, autumn/winter 1995, pp. 257–278.

than identifying exactly what was wrong with Nazism, they simply label everything which was ever associated with the Nazi regime, albeit accidentally or even illegitimately (as with the swastika, borrowed without permission from Hindu-Jain-Buddhist tradition), as being somehow the root cause of the Holocaust. In some cases, this tendency to cast the net of Nazi guilt as widely as possible is deliberate, e.g. by members of the post-war generation who enjoy putting the entire generation of their parents in the dock, or by Western secularists who like to use the Church's role in the preparation of the Nazi mind-set (authoritarianism, anti-Semitism) as arguments in their crusade against Christianity, or in this case by Christians and secularists who try to make the (largely mythical) association of ancient IE Paganism with Nazism stick to the old enemy: Paganism, including the neo-Paganism now emerging in many European countries[1]

In reality, the positive association of the IE theme with racist or Nazi ideas is quite dead except in a few extremely marginal groups. It is not really present in the main focus of contemporary ideological interest in the IE past, the French intellectual current known as the *Nouvelle Droite* ("New Right").[2] This movement, ultra-rightist in the 1960s, had shifted from "race" to "culture", from authoritarianism to participatory democracy, from crude nationalism to the celebration of multicultural difference, by the 1980s. In its search for allies against liberal-egalitarian, utilitarian, hedonistic modernity, the *Nouvelle Droite* shows a sincere interest in and respect for traditional cultures, sometimes forcing them conceptually into the mould of its own pet concerns. In contrast with the mushrooming xenophobic parties, it believes in European integration and seeks to underpin it with an awareness of pan-European cultural identity, hence its interest in the IE cultural heritage.[3]

Some of the *Nouvelle Droite* authors are very attached to the idea of the Aryan Invasion as a necessary implication of the presumed European character and origin of the IE family. As a corollary, they also accept the view of the caste

---

[1]A Christian attempt to associate Paganism with Nazism is Robert A. Pois: *National Socialism and the Religion of Nature*, Croom Helm, Beckenham GB 1986; the swastika is used to prove the essentially evil character of Hinduism in Evangelical propaganda, e.g. the 1980s' movie Gods of the New Age by Jeremiah Films, discussed with indignation by a more fair-minded missionary, Richard Young, in *Areopagus* (Hong Kong), Christmas 1990. A secularist attempt to impute a Nazi mind-set to Paganism is found in numerous passages in Bernard-Henry Livy's books *Le Testament de Dieu* (Grasset, Paris 1979) and *L'Idéologie Française* (idem 1981).

[2]Not to be confused with the Anglo-Saxon Reaganite-Thatcherite *New Right* tendency of the 1980s: the *Nouvelle Droite* is, among other things, anti-American, anti-capitalist, and pro-multiculturalist. By far the best introduction to the *Nouvelle Droite* is the winter 1993-94 issue of the American periodical Telos.

[3]The very idea that IE heritage could include other cultural items beside language is argued and pleasantly illustrated in Shan M.M. Winn: *Heaven, Heroes and Happiness. The Indo-European Roots of Western Ideology*, University Press of America, Lanham MD 1995.

system as an apartheid system between IE immigrants and Indian natives, so that in spite of their declared anti-racism, they end up reconnecting with 19th-century racist assumptions.[1] The chief sources for *Nouvelle Droite* musings about India are the late Jean Varenne, indologist; Jean Haudry, IE linguist; and most of all the late Alain Daniilou, musicologist and India-lover of socialist but pro-caste persuasion, esp. his books *Histoire de l'Inde*, which includes an imaginative processing of the AIT in all its implications, and *Les quatre sens de la vie* ("The Four Meanings of Life"), a passionate plea for the caste system conceived as a way to preserve the racial and cultural identities of different ethnic groups.[2]

The same unquestioning faith in the AIT, this time not in some sanitized modern form but in its unadulterated Nazi version, is still in evidence in ultra-Rightist fringe groups. Consider the following lament of a Belgian critic about Peter Brooke's theatre version of the Mahabharata: "Incomprehensible and shocking is that some major roles have been played by actors of African origin. It is certainly commendable to include Italians, Englishmen etc., but *Africans*? Nothing in the epic permits such a deviation. Let there be no mistake about it: the Mahabharata is not an epic written for some entity called humanity. It is a narrative by and for the Aryas as an Indo-European caste which had imposed its authority in India".[3] The poor man seems unaware that "Aryan" Mahabharata protagonists like Krishna ("the black one") and Draupadi, as well as some of the Vedic rishis, are explicitly described as dark-skinned and/or black-haired, a far cry from the *Blond Beast* (to borrow Friedrich Nietzsche's sarcastic term) which was the white racists' idea of the Superman.

So, the political reading of the AIT is not entirely dead yet in Europe, but it has been definitively marginalized. Though noteworthy as a tenacious relic of the world-view of a bygone age, it is now without political importance. The only consequential political motive to uphold the AIT is the solidarity of Western academics with their Indian counterparts who have their own reasons for defending the AIT against its challengers. By contrast, Indian political readings of the AIT still weigh heavily on India's present-day political climate.

The AIT and the "anti-national forces"

There are quite a few cases worldwide of late-medieval and modern history

---

[1]A defence of the European Urheimat hypothesis is given by Jean Haudry and Alain de Benoist in the Nouvelle Droite periodical *Nouvelle Ecole,* 1997 (issue title *Les Indo-Européens),* along with an exhaustive survey of the development of the field of IE studies, which was praised sky-high for its completeness by Edgar Polomé (who is a member of the periodical's patronage committee) in the review section of the *Journal of Indo-European Studies,* spring-summer 1997.

[2]A. Daniélou: *Histoire de l'Inde, Fayard,* Paris 1983 (1971); *Les Quatre Sens de la Vie: La Structure Sociale de l'Inde Traditionnelle,* Buchet-Chastel, Paris 1984 (1975).

[3]Ralf van den Haute: "Le Mahâbhârata ou la mémoire la plus longue", *L'Anneau* (Brussels), #22-23 (1993).

having repercussions on contemporary politics, witness the role of bad memories in ex-Yugoslavia; but I do not know of any question of ancient history which is as loaded with actual political significance as is the AIT in India. The AIT was turned into a political tool in order to question the Indian identity of the Indians, and thereby weaken the claims of Indians to their own country. This political use of the AIT continues till today. Christian "liberation theologians", Islamic missionaries, assorted separatists and like-minded anti-Hindu or anti-India activists are still highlighting the AIT in order to:

(1) Mobilize lower-caste people, supposedly the "subdued natives" forced into the Apartheid prisonhouse of caste by the invaders, against the upper-caste people, supposedly the progeny of the "invading Aryans". All this propaganda is carried out in the name of the low-caste leader Dr. B.R. Ambedkar, eventhough Ambedkar himself had strongly rejected the AIT and the notion that caste status has a racial origin: "European students of caste (. . .), themselves impregnated by colour prejudices, very readily imagined it to be the chief factor in the Caste problem. But nothing can be farther from the truth, and Dr. Ketkar is right when he insists that 'all the princes whether they belonged to the so-called Aryan race or to the so-called Dravidian race, were Aryas. Whether a tribe or a family was racially Aryan or Dravidian was a question which never troubled the people of India until foreign scholars came in and began to draw the line."[1]

(2) Mobilize Dravidian-speakers against speakers of IE languages, esp. through the Dravidian separatist movement which was started under British patronage in 1916 as the Justice Party, later refounded as the Dravida Kazhagam, and which reached its peak in the 1950s. One of its gimmicks was the glorification of the "black Dravidian" hero Ravana against the "white Aryan" hero Rama, disregarding the Ramayana information that Ravana was actually an Aryan colonizer of Sri Lanka and a performer of Vedic rituals.[2] Its most consequential success was the sabotage (masterminded by the English-speaking elite in Delhi, not in the Dravidians' but in its own interest) of the implementation of the Constitutional provision that Hindi, a North-Indian IE language, replace English as official language by 1965.

(3) Mobilize the tribals, who have been given the new name "aboriginals"

---

[1]Thus spoke Dr. B.R. Ambedkar in his paper "Castes in India", reproduced in his *Writings and Speeches* (Govt. of Maharashtra, 1986), vol.1, p. 21, with reference to S.V. Ketkar: *History of Caste in India*, Low Price Publ., Delhi 1990 (1909), p. 82; also discussed in K. Elst: *Dr. Ambedkar, a True Aryan*, Voice of India, Delhi 1993, Ch. 3.

[2]Note the agreement between the Indian Left and the European racists. In his *L'arc de Civa. poèmes antiques*, the 19th-century French poet Leconte de Lisle wrote: "*Rama, toi dont le sang est pur, toi dont le corps est blanc, (. . .) dompteur itincelant de toutes les races profanes*" ("Rama, you whose blood is pure, you whose body is white, bright subduer of all the profane races"). In fact, the Ramayana is about a struggle between two heroes who were both Aryan and both dark-skinned.

(*adivasi*) as part of this strategy, against the non-tribals, who are to be treated on a par with the European invaders of America and Australia.

(4) Mobilize Indian politicians towards delegitimizing Sanskrit, that "foreign language brought by the Aryan invaders", as India's culture language and as a school subject, in order to further dehinduize India and weaken her cultural unity: "Sanskrit should be deleted from the Eighth schedule of the Constitution because it is a foreign language brought to the country by foreign invaders—the Aryans.".[1]

(5) Mobilize world opinion against the "racist Aryans", meaning the Hindus, since they are the "Aryan invaders who imposed the caste system as a kind of Apartheid to preserve their racial purity and dominance", never mind the fact that the association of "Aryan" with "race" is a strictly European invention unknown to Hindu tradition. Now that "idolater" and "heathen" have lost their force as swearwords, "racist" is a brilliant new way of demonizing Hinduism.

The use of the AIT for political purposes is most obvious in the militant anti-Brahmin movement spearheaded by the Bangalore fortnightly *Dalit Voice*, edited by V.T. Rajshekar, a former *Indian Express* journalist fired because of his links with Khalistani terrorism. This extremist wing of the broader *Dalit movement* (*Dalit* meaning "oppressed", ex-Untouchable, a term introduced by the Hindu reform movement Arya Samaj)[2] has formulated an Indian variant of Afrocentric history, copied from the Black Muslims in the USA, with whom it co-operates closely.[3]

Thus, the theory of *continental drift*, first suggested by Abraham Ortelius in the 16th century, formulated scientifically by Alfred Wegener in 1915, is harnessed to the cart of Dalit Afrocentrism: "The Dalits were the original inhabitants of India and resemble the African in physical features. It is said that India and Africa were one land-mass until separated by the ocean. So both the Africans and the Indian Untouchables had common ancestors."[4] Of course, the break-up of the *Urkontinent* Gondwanaland took place millions of years before mankind spread across the face of the earth.

More importantly, physical anthropology does not bear out the African connec-

---

[1]A Muslim protester against the Sanskrit news service on All-India Radio, Razia Ashraf, quoting with strong approval Frank Anthony, a Christian former Member of Parliament, in *Indian Express*, 9 February 1991.

[2]We must emphasize that *Dalit Voice* is not representative (and often diametrically opposed to the goals) of the *Dalit movement*, a most necessary movement (given the slackness of the other castes in implementing social reform) as envisaged by Dr. B.R. Ambedkar. Thus, while Ambedkar became a Buddhist, *Dalit Voice* downplays the liberating message of Buddhism in favour of Christianity and Islam, religions criticized and rejected by Dr. Ambedkar.

[3]E.g., a few years ago, Black Muslims prevented the renaming of a street in Atlanta, Georgia, as *Mahatma Gandhi Square*, in deference to the hatred of the Mahatma's integrationist views by the polarizationist *Dalit Voice* group.

[4]V.T. Rajshekar: *Dalit—the Black Untouchables of India*, p. 43.

tion of India's lowest castes: they are racially far closer to the Indian upper castes than to the Africans. It does not even bear out the racial dividing-line between upper and lower castes: lower castes are genetically closer to the upper castes of their own region than to people of the same caste rank in other parts of India.[1] A recent survey has yielded this conclusion: "Detailed anthropomorphic surveys carried out among the people of Uttar Pradesh, Gujarat, Maharashtra, Bengal and Tamil Nadu revealed significant regional differences within a caste and a closer resemblance between castes of different varnas within a region than between sub-populations of the caste from different regions."[2] Yet, cranky as it is, *Dalit Voice* is strongly supported by militant Islamic centres, by Christian Liberation Theology circles and by many Western academics because they share its anti-Brahminism.[3]

Describing the Brahmins as the "Jews of India", V.T. Rajshekar combines anti-Brahminism with anti-Semitism: "Since the Brahminical Social Order is much more ancient it is quite likely that the Zionist founding fathers got their inspiration from the BSO (. . .) *Dalit Voice* has thus proved right in predicting that the Jews and the 'Jews of India' will join hands to crush Muslims, Blacks and India's Dalits."[4] He publishes calls to "get a copy of the *Protocols of the Elders of Zion* from the Iranian embassy in Delhi to understand the Zionist hatred against Blacks and Muslims".[5] Rajshekar also copies some of the classics of anti-Semitism: "The First World War, the Second World War, the establishment of Communism, the rise of Hitler, were also systematically planned and executed by Zionists."[6] His constant railing against the *CIA-Zionist-Brahminical world conspiracy* has earned him a mention in a recent authoritative survey of contemporary anti-Semitism.[7]

Even apart from this confabulated conspiracy, an analysis of anti-Brahmin rhetoric shows that it is really, down to the detail, the Indian equivalent of

---

[1]This was already argued by Dr. Ambedkar, e.g. in *Writings and Speeches*, vol. 7, p. 301, with reference to G.S. Ghurye: *Caste and Race in India*, Popular Prakashan, Mumbai 1969 (1932). It is highly significant that the vast majority of the numerous publications on caste fail to mention Ghurye's important work even in their biblography; as for Ambedkar, his rejection of the AIT explanation of caste goes equally unmentioned in the copious Ambedkarist literature.

[2]Kailash C. Malhotra interviewed by N.V. Subramaniam: "The way we are. An ASI project shatters some entrenched myths", *Sunday*, 10 April 1994.

[3]See e.g. the Flemish missionary monthly *Wereldwijd*, March 1986 and February 1991; some of Rajshekhar's separately published brochures (from Dalit Sahitya Akademi, Bangalore) are transcripts of speeches given at Christian conferences.

[4]*Dalit Voice*, 16 January 1993.

[5]*Dalit Voice*, 1 December 1991

[6]*Dalit Voice*, 16 January 1993.

[7]Lion Poliakov, ed.: *Histoire de l'antisémitisme* 1945-93 (Paris 1994), p. 395. The phenomenon of anti-Semitism in a vocal though marginal and unrepresentative section of the Dalit movement is attributed somewhat patronizingly to the "mental confusion among India's poor Dalits".

anti-Semitism. Thus, Brahmins think they are the chosen ones; they distinguish themselves by funny dress and hairstyle; they are cowards but past masters at manipulation and pitting outsiders against one another; they are pale bookworms with a transregional language of their own; they always help their own kind and deceive the others; and they monopolize wealth.[1] And worst of all, as per the AIT they are *foreigners*, usurping the rightful inheritance of the sons of the soil.

This line of anti-Brahmin rhetoric on the model of anti-Semitism comes full circle with the following allegation, originally in 1971 by K.K. Gangadharan, a Leftist sociologist from Maharashtra working in Christ College in Kanpur, since then adopted by the likes of V.T. Rajshekar: the Chitpavan Brahmins, a caste in Maharashtra which immigrated from Afghanistan when that region was islamized in the 10th century (hence their taller build and lighter colour), and which took a leadership role in the struggle against the Moghuls, the British Raj and Congress secularism, are so "arrogant" and "fanatical" because, unbeknownst to other Indians, they actually have Jewish ancestors![2]

That Brahmins monopolize wealth has even less basis in fact than the same stereotype of Jews. Brahmins always had an ideal of "simple living and high thinking", and observed a prohibition of "selling" their Vedic knowledge and ritual status; Brahmins with lucrative posts counted *ipso facto* as lower in rank. Moreover, the traditional sources of wealth for certain Brahmin families have dried up (abolition of maharaja courts, nationalization or expropriation of temples) and today poverty is rampant among all non-westernized Brahmins. But it is easy to sell the notion that the ritually highest caste must also be the richest, esp. to Western audiences brought up on one-dimensional materialism.

However, the wealth aspect of anti-Semitism does find a counterpart in the *Bania* merchant caste, which in the past few centuries and particularly in the most islamized parts of the Subcontinent occupied exactly the same niche in society as the Jews in medieval Europe: often they were the only Hindus who could buy themselves the safety which allowed them to preserve their Hindu identity, and as non-Muslim money-lenders they were allowed to practise "usury", which is prohibited to Muslims. As a fairly devout and vegetarian class, they are stereotypical Hindus, and at the same time they are a natural object of envy (as are successful Indian communities in Britain and Africa); this makes them another

---

[1]For an early example, Jotirao Phule wrote: "The Brahmin's natural (instinctive) temperament is mischievous and cantankerous, and it is so inveterate that it can never be eradicated." See *Collected Works of Mahatma Jotirao Phule*, vol.2, Government of Maharashtra, Mumbai 1992, p.73, quoted with approval in *Dalit Voice*, 16 December 1992.

[2]K.K. Gangadharan is quoted to this effect in Gérard Heuzé: *Où va l'Inde moderne?*, Paris 1994, p. 87. As for V.T. Rajshekar, see *Dalit Voice*, 1 February and 1 March 1995; and V.T. Rajshekhar: *Brahminism*, Dalit Sahitya Akademy, Bangalore n.d., p. 28.

excellent scapegoat for anti-"Aryan" crank racism in India, as exemplified by *Dalit Voice*'s regular tirades against India's most famous Bania, Mahatma Gandhi.

Political excuse for non-argumentation

One consequence of the political connotations of the rivalling theories is that people feel justified in dismissing the theory they don't like as "politically motivated" and *therefore* obviously wrong and not worth refuting. This phenomenon is in evidence in both wings of the political pro-AIT coalition, a certain European Right and a certain Indian Left. Thus, the much-applauded survey of IE studies in the French periodical *Nouvelle Ecole* devotes exactly one footnote to the entire argumentation for an Indian Urheimat, which it dismisses as "in self-evident contradiction with all the data of linguistics and comparative mythology" and as the symptom of "an exacerbated Indian nationalism".[1] This is, of course, a case of the "genetic fallacy": to assume that a position must be wrong because of the motive in which it allegedly originates. Quite apart from the fact that this motive is merely imputed, and often falsely so, no good or evil motive can make a proposition right or wrong; it is quite possible to speak the truth for the wrong reasons.

There are cases where the impression of political usefulness of a theory has stimulated research without really obstructing the researchers' objectivity and sincerity. Thus, in the 19th century, French scholars eagerly explored the possibility that the Italic and Celtic branches of the IE language family had, after separating from PIE, continued for long as a single language group: such a scenario would have helped in strengthening the French nation's historical identity, otherwise split between a biological Celtic ancestry and linguistic Latin roots. This research ultimately led to the non-desired conclusion that Celtic and Italic were, after all, not much closer to each other than either is to Germanic or Greek. Ironically, recent research has revived and given new support to the idea that Italic and Celtic did share a common itinerary for some centuries after the break-up of IE unity, and this is not any less true just because it has been a pet theory of French chauvinists.

The derivation of a judgment on the Urheimat question from the alleged motives of the proponents of the contending theories is all-pervading and vitiates the whole debate. An extreme example is the treatment given to Shrikant Talageri in a prestigious book specifically setting itself the task of countering the rising tide of doubts voiced by archaeologists and philologists about the AIT. One may or may not agree with Talageri's anti-AIT position, but he has undoubtedly built up a painstaking argumentation with ample reference to state-of-the-art scholarship, and he deserves better than this comment by George Erdosy, who locates him in the "lunatic fringe" and judges: "Unfortunately, political motivation

[1] Alain de Benoist in *Nouvelle Ecole* 49, Paris 1997, p. 44.

(usually associated with Hindu revivalism) renders this opposition devoid of scholarly value".[1] In the same volume, Michael Witzel dismisses his work as "modern Hindu exegetical or apologetic religious writing".[2]

So far, so good; Erdosy and Witzel are entitled to their opinions, even to calling a fellow scholar a "lunatic" (though I doubt that they could get their articles past the editor of an academic journal if they applied this term to a Western scholar).[3] But the point is: they don't show even the least acquaintance with the actual arguments offered by Talageri. Both Erdosy and Witzel refer to: "S.K. Telagiri: Aryan Invasion Theory and Indian Nationalism, Aditya Prakashan 1993". That is how the book's data were given in a (laudatory) review by Girilal Jain in the *Times of India* of 17 June 1993. Unfortunately, the author's real name is *Talageri*, and the book's publisher is not Aditya Prakashan (though there is another edition of the same book under a different title by Aditya Prakashan, hence the reviewer's confusion), but Voice of India.[4] This means that the book which Erdosy and Witzel dismiss in such strong terms has not even been *seen* by them.

In India too, proponents of the AIT use the alleged political connotations of the rival theory as a handy pretext for avoiding discussion of the actual evidence. Thus, historian Romila Thapar devotes a 27-page lead article in a social science periodical (which admits in an editorial note that the article's publication is a political move to counter "the Hindutva forces", falsely narrowing the non-AIT school down to "the RSS") to "The Theory of Aryan Race and India" practically without mentioning the evidence presented by the non-AIT school.[5] She invokes "the linguistic evidence" twice as proof of a late chronology for the Vedas (1500 BC), without telling us how the linguistic data prove her point. Off-hand, she brings in "the Indo-Iranian links" as proof of the same "since the earliest

---

[1]G. Erdosy, ed.: *Indo-Aryans of Ancient South Asia*, Walter De Gruyter, Berlin 1995, p.x. Incidentally, this reasoning is invalid: people with political motivations may still marshall real facts and formulate correct deductions.

[2]M. Witzel in Erdosy: *Indo-Aryans*, p.116-117. Referring to a like-minded piece by A.K. Biswas (whom he mistakenly associates with Talageri), he ridicules "the ulterior political motive of this 'scientific' piece"; op.cit., p. 111.

[3]In spite of all the "multiculturalism" and "globalization" buzz-words, numerous Westerners still treat Indians as a lesser breed which is not to be taken seriously. Prof. Ulrich Libbrecht, the Flemish pioneer of Comparative Philosophy, told me how at an international conference in Honolulu on that subject, multicultural par excellence, the average American participant treated the lectures by Indians as coffee breaks. I too have noticed many times that proposals for talks or publications by Indians are dismissed without a proper hearing on the assumption that Indians are cranks unless they have an introduction from a Western institution.

[4]Shrikant Talageri: *Aryan Invasion Theory, a Reappraisal*, Aditya Prakashan, Delhi 1993, with a foreword by Prof. S.R. Rao and minus the introductory political chapters of the Voice of India edition.

[5]R. Thapar: "The Theory of Aryan Race and India: History and Politics", *Social Scientist*, Delhi, January-March 1996, pp. 3–29.

suggested date now for Zoroaster is circa 1200 BC", ignoring the fact that the dating of Zoroaster's Avesta is itself based on the late chronology of the Vedas (the Avestan language being a slightly younger offshoot of Indo-Iranian than Vedic Sanskrit). This cavalier way of dealing with evidence apparently stems from the feeling that the anti-AIT case need not be taken seriously.

Most importantly, Romila Thapar's entire article could easily have been written several decades ago, for she totally disregards all the evidence from archaeology and archaeo-astronomy presented by her opponents in recent years, though she does mention the existence of a non-AIT school, which she explains as a symptom of an identity crisis in Non-Resident Indians (meaning US-based scientists N.S. Rajaram and Subhash Kak and historian Sushil Mittal of the *International Institute for Indian Studies* in Quibec). The same disregard for recent evidence is noticeable in R.S. Sharma's book *Looking for the Aryans*, which went to the press in November 1994 but fails to mention the pre-1994 argumentations against the AIT by K.D. Sethna, S.P. Gupta (the only RSS man in the non-AIT school), David Frawley, Shrikant Talageri and others, even in the bibliography.[1]

One case of disregarding the evidence was witnessed by the present author at the 1996 Annual South Asia Conference in Madison, Wisconsin, in a panel purportedly dealing with on the AIT debate. I knew that excellent and innovative papers by N.S. Rajaram and Shrikant Talageri had been rejected by the organizers, so I felt entitled to expect presentations of top-notch scholarship dwarfing even that of Rajaram and Talageri. Instead, what the audience got, was a canvassing session for the "Forum of Indian Leftists" without any scholarly papers. The speakers disdained to even mention any of the argumentative contents of the AIT debate, except "David Frawley's paradox" (the AIT's implication that the Harappan civilization had numerous cities but no literature, while Vedic civilization had a vast literature but no cities), which they simply laughed off without discussion *ad rem.*

Indian Marxist Biju Matthew insisted on the Stalinist position that in the social sciences, no theory ever comes without a political agenda. So, he reduced the whole AIT debate to a question of cultural policy of the Indian bourgeoisie, which was badly trying to be European. This was indeed part of the motive for the 19th-century *acceptance* of the AIT by the likes of Keshab Chandra Sen, but not of the present-day *rejection* of the AIT; but Matthew had not cared to notice the diametrical opposition between the former, colonial, and the latter, anti-colonial positions, perhaps because he counted on a knee-jerk reaction of hostility to anyone who merely utters the word "Aryan". He was all the more serious about deciding the burning question whether Non-Resident Indians should call them-

[1]R.S. Sharma: *Looking for the Aryans*, Orient Longman, Delhi 1995.

selves "Indian" or "South-Asian"; he himself opted for the latter "because it has the advantage of being anti-national". He wanted South-Asians in North America to shake off their religious and national identities and develop an "identity project" on the model of the African-Americans, which would only leave race as the distinctive trait of South-Asians in the US, a self-identification which approximates racism in its original meaning.[1]

Vijay Prashad had one interesting thing to say about the impact of the Aryan race theory on the position of Indians in the USA in the past century. It turns out that for much of the time, they were counted as "white" thanks to their IE connection, and that they strongly held on to this classification rather than to show solidarity with other, non-white minorities; but when the policy of positive discrimination for ethnic minorities started, Indians were not slow to parade their skin colour as entitling them to minority privileges. I don't know if all this is true, but it is certainly a valid topic for further research and discussion. However, Vijay Prashad revealed his destructive intentions when he called *Dalit Voice* "a wonderful paper" and praised its potentially disruptive positions, esp. its division of Indians in aboriginals and invaders. Mercifully, he did not go as far as to explicate his support for *Dalit Voice*'s motto: "What Hindus hate, we must love, and what Hindus love, we must hate."[2]

The problem with Indian Marxism

Like many academic opponents of any reopening of the AIT debate, both R.S. Sharma and Romila Thapar, mentioned above, are well-known Indian Marxists.[3] Their animosity against the native culture of India and against a theory which would strengthen its prestige is somewhat surprising, for in most Third World countries, Marxists have also been ardent nationalists in the struggle for cultural as well as political and economic decolonization. One Indian Marxist at least, historian Bhagwan Singh, has indeed contributed to the critique of the AIT, focusing specifically on the material culture and the economic data available in Vedic literature and the archaeological record of the Harappan cities.[4] Western

---

[1]I am in no position to berate African-Americans for defining their own identity in racial terms, for the total identification with their race was forced on them for centuries by Arab and later also by European slave-traders; but to drop existing non-racial identities for a racial one, that is definitely racism.

[2]*Dalit Voice*, 16 Feb. 1992.

[3]Romila Thapar insinuates ("The Theory of Aryan Race and India", p.17) that the non-AIT school merely uses the label "Marxist" as a cheap way to dismiss the Indian pro-AIT scholars like Sharma and herself without proper refutation. However, in Tom Bottomore's *Dictionary of Marxist Thought* (Blackwell, Oxford 1988), entry "Hinduism", both R.S. Sharma and Romila Thapar are mentioned and quoted as representatives of Indian Marxism.

[4]Bhagwan Singh: *The Vedic Harappans*, Aditya Prakashan, Delhi 1995.

Marxists have protested against the imperialist projection of colonial racism onto the colonized native society: "The early Indo-Aryans could no more have thought in modern terms of race prejudice than they could have invented the airplane."[1]

The mainstream of Indian Marxism, however, is true to Karl Marx's own view that Hinduism "was the ideology of an oppressive and outworn society"; Marx "shared the distaste of most Europeans for its more lurid features. (. . .) he was as sceptical as his Hindu followers were to be of any notion of a Hindu 'golden age' of the past."[2] Marx acknowledged the colonialists' historical mission of eliminating the "Asiatic mode of production", and claimed that colonial rule could only be compared (to its obvious advantage) to the memory of Turkish or the threat of Czarist rule, but not to native rule, for which India was historically unfit because it had never been a nation. In an 1853 letter, Marx wrote that "Indian society has no history at all, at least no known history. What we call its history, is but the history of the successive intruders who founded their empires on the passive basis of that unresisting and unchanging society."[3]

Marx's Indian followers, who control much of the media and of the humanities faculties, have adapted this idea to the present circumstances, e.g. to the question of India's legitimacy as a united republic.[4] They are willing to accept the unified Indian state as long as it is useful to their own ends (as in 1959–62, after their election victory in Kerala gave them hope of taking over India, a hope crushed by the embarrassing Chinese invasion of 1962), but they are just as ready to discard it, because they do not believe in it and have no loyalty towards it. They

---

[1]Quoted from Marxist theorist Oliver Gomwell Cox: *Caste, Class and Race* (1948), p.91, in Ivan Hannaford: *Race, the History of an Idea in the West*, John Hopkins University Press, Baltimore 1996, p.383. Hannaford summarizes: "The relationship between Brahmans (white), Kshatriyas (red), Vaishyas (yellow) and Shudras (black) was not a color ["*varna*"] relationship in the 'racial' sense but a metaphor identified with dharma—'a way of life virtue complex (p. 95)—that was acquired by 'the mode of livelihood' or 'the inherent qualities of nature'. His fundamental argument was that the case for color as a dominant factor in the development of caste was not supported by the evidence of historical literature, and that it was foreign scholars who had made it so."

[2]Tom Bottomore: Dictionary of Marxist Thought, p.203, paraphrasing K. Marx: *The First Indian War of Independence*, Moscow 1959 (a compilation of Marx columns on the 1857 Mutiny in the *New York Daily Tribune*), p. 156.

[3]Quoted with approval by S.K. Biswas: *Autochthon of India and the Aryan Invasions*, Genuine Publ., Delhi 1995, p. 10.

[4]The Marxist dominance of India's cultural sphere is not a convenient rumour, it can easily be documented and its genesis traced and explained. Nehru was fond of Communism though temperamentally too bourgeois to fully join it, and he promoted Marxists to important posts; but it was chiefly his daughter Indira Gandhi who (guided by her secretary P.N. Haksar), when she was critically dependent on Communist support during her intra-Congress power struggle, promoted Communists and created many new institutes for them, including Jawaharlal Nehru University.

never tire of denouncing anything that bolsters India's unity as a "myth". For them, India is an artificial unit, a prisonhouse of nations, bound to fall apart.[1]

According to a Western Marxist observer: "Uncompromising opposition to Gandhi and his cherished Hindu convictions meant that communists were cut off in a considerable measure from the mainstream of the patriotic struggle"[2] Ever since, they have supported every anti-national cause: the crushing of the *Quit India* movement (1942), Partition (1947), the Razakar terror campaign te prevent the merger of Hyderabad with India (1948), the Chinese claims to Indian territory (up to 1962: "China's chairman is also India's chairman"). In the 1990s, they have threatened secession of the states they control in the event of a Hindu-nationalist election victory.[3]

To complete the picture, it should be realized that as born upper-caste Hindus alienated by westernization, Indian Marxists are animated by a seething hatred of their ancestral culture. Unlike the British who felt some patronizing sympathy for the heathens whom God had entrusted to their civilizing care, anglicized Hindus feel a need to exorcize the remainders of Hindu heritage from themselves and their surroundings. The idea of a continuous and glorious civilization in North India dating back more than 5,000 years does not fit in well with their vision; that of the barbaric Aryans imposing foreign rule on the hapless natives is much more useful, esp. for characterizing Indian society as "oppressive". This way, lingering colonial prejudices of Western scholars and the class interests of India's anglicized elite reinforce each other to create the strange spectacle of Indians and indologists virulently opposing any rethinking of India's past which might increase the weight of India's own contribution to her own history.

A case study in contemporary AIT polemic

For a case study in anti-AIT polemic, I have chosen the article "An obscurantist argument" by the Dutch-Canadian scholar Robert J. Zydenbos.[4] His *bona fides* is unquestionable, and he represents the majority of AIT-believing scholars in that he merely accepts the predominant opinion without having a political axe to grind, though this makes him susceptible to being influenced by AIT defenders who do

[1]This assessement-cum-prediction is made quite cheerfully by Romila Thapar in her 1993 interview in the French daily *Le Monde*.

[2]Tom Bottomore: *Dictionary of Marxist Thought*, p. 205.

[3]According to Ashok Mitra, a leader of the Communist Party of India (Marxist) in West Bengal, in an interview in the Rotterdam daily *NRC Handelsblad*, 20 March 1993, "India was never the solution". He announced that in the event of a Hindu nationalist majority in parliament, the CPI(M)-controlled states will declare independence.

[4]*Indian Express*, 12 December 1993, in reply to a piece on a lecture by Prof. N.S. Rajaram, *Indian Express*, 14 November 1993, of which an expanded version constitutes the first chapter of Rajaram's book: *Aryan Invasion of India, the Myth and the Truth*, Voice of India, Delhi 1994.

have political motives. Some of the rhetoric in this article typifies the way in which certain AIT defenders in positions of authority tend to over-awe the public with references to overrated evidence, and to vilify spokesmen of the dissident non-AIT school.

The piece is an attack on N.S. Rajaram, a scientist from Karnataka (in AIT parlance: a Dravidian, not an Aryan) working in the USA, who has contributed decisive insights to the AIT debate.[1] I disagree on some important points with Prof. Rajaram, most of all with his rejection of the linguistic reconstruction of an IE protolanguage; but that is no reason to dismiss his work as "a textbook example of the quasi-religious-cum-political obscurantism that is so popúlar among alienated Non-Resident Indians", which is moreover "out of touch with what serious scholars both in India and abroad hold at present", as Zydenbos alleges. "The linguistic evidence for the Indo-European origin of Sanskrit outside India is overwhelming", he claims, in almost verbatim agreement with Prof. Romila Thapar, whom he defends against Rajaram's critique of her article "The Perennial Aryans".[2] Neither in his nor in Prof. Thapar's much lengthier article is even one item of this "overwhelming evidence" mentioned.

Zydenbos starts his crescendo of allegations by stating something Rajaram never disputed: "No scholar seriously believes that there are any 'ethnically pure' Aryans in India today (and perhaps anywhere else, either). And why should anyone care?" Actually, Rajaram himself is among those who reject the notion of 'ethnically pure Aryans', not because of the obvious fact that countless inter-ethnic marriages have taken place, but because he rejects the use of "Aryan" as an ethnic term in the first place. As he and many others have argued time and again, the Sanskrit word arya was not an ethnic term, it is Western scholars who have turned it into one.

And it is the Western participant in this duel, Dr. Zydenbos, who, even after reading Prof. Rajaram, just continues to use "Aryan" as an ethnic term: "Those who called themselves 'Aryan' 1000 years ago were already very different from the various Aryan tribes that came over 3500 years ago (. . .) This too is historical fact. One only needs to learn Sanskrit to find this out." I fear that there is something very wrong with Sanskrit courses if accomplished indologists can read arya in a racial sense unattested in the whole of Sanskrit literature.

Next, Zydenbos attacks Rajaram's reading of Romila Thapar's article, especially

---

[1]Notably *N.S. Rajaram: The Politics of History: Aryan Invasion Theory and the Subversion of Scholarship*, Voice of India, Delhi 1994; *From Saraswati River to Indus Script*, Diganta Sahitya, Mangalore 1998 (an elaboration on the Sanskrit-based decipherment of the Indus script by N. Jha: *Vedic Glossary on Indus Seals*, Ganga Kaveri Publ., Varanasi 1996); and with David Frawley: *Vedic Aryans and the Origins of Civilization*, idem 1997.

[2]Romila Thapar: "The Perennial Aryans", *Seminar* # 400 (1992).t

her insinuation (uttered much more explicitly elsewhere by other Marxist authors in India) that the anti-AIT case is motivated by some kind of Hitlerian vision of Aryanism: "Romila Thapar does not 'obviously refer to Nazi Germany' when she speaks of the fantasy of an 'Aryan nation', but to the new Indian tendency among obscurantists towards creating something parallel." If alleging that someone wants to "create something parallel to Nazi Germany" does not imply a reference to Nazi Germany, well, we might perhaps focus on the implied allegation that those Indians who question the AIT are entertaining a fantasy of creating an "Aryan nation". I challenge Prof. Thapar and Dr. Zydenbos to produce any publication of any Indian scholar presently questioning the AIT which contains even a hint of this "fantasy". I don't think that in an academic forum, one can simply get away with such extremely serious allegations; one has to offer evidence,—or apologies.

Apart from reading the works of the Indian scholars concerned, I have also privately talked with most of them, and I feel certain that no such "fantasy" is at the back of the anti-AIT polemic. In fact, what they reject in Western scholarship is precisely the creation of the conceptual framework which has made the racialist misuse of the term "Aryan" possible.

Zydenbos continues: "This includes the endorsement of blatant racism by certain Indian scholarly personalities. Thus, the archaeologist S.R. Rao, who also figures in Rajaram's article, said at a recent seminar in Mysore in response to a student's question about the Aryans that we should not listen to what 'white people' say." I don't know how Hitler would have felt about this slur on white people, but Zydenbos is quite mistaken when he infers that there is any "racism" behind Prof. Rao's remark. Rao obviously did not mean that whiteness makes one unfit for researching the question of the "Aryans". What he meant was, of course, that at present, Westerners in general are still basing their opinions about this question on theories rendered outdated by the recent findings of Indian scholars like himself, and of some paleface scholars as well,—but the latter have so far not carried Western or "white" opinion in general with them.

Dr. Zydenbos, who is described editorially as a European indological scholar living in Mysore, must have found out for himself that being "white" still connotes authority and reliability for most Indians.[1] In heated debates like the one on the Aryan question, reference to Western opinion is still treated as a trump card. If a student has been over-awed by the apparent Western consensus in favour of the AIT, Prof. Rao was right to break the spell and to put the student with his feet

[1]It is one of Mahatma Gandhi's achievements that "he made India safe for the white man", as the Indian Communists used to say around the time of Independence. The fact is that he must take credit for the friendly character of the decolonization of India, which led to the situation that Westerners who feel a strong disrespect or hostility in countries like China and Malaysia, feel like honoured guests in India.

back on the solid ground of self-reliance, esp. in a field where Western indological opinion happens to be demonstrably out of touch with the latest research.

Indeed, in his article, Dr. Zydenbos himself unwittingly plays the same game of over-awing the Indians with references to Western indologists, viz. to K.V. Zvelebil, H. Kulke and D. Rothermund, as sheer arguments of authority.[1] Zydenbos refers to Zvelebil to support this statement: "That the Indus Valley people were Dravidians is an unproven hypothesis; but the real, as yet undeciphered writings of that civilization give more support to this hypothesis than to any other." In fact, the scholars working from the Dravidian hypothesis have, after decades of intensive labour, not conclusively deciphered a single line of the Indus writings, and Zvelebil admits as much: "[The Soviet scholars] have not convincingly deciphered even one single short Harappan description, and they have not been able to offer a verifiable reading of any Harappan text."[2] Of the other teams working on the decipherment, Zvelebil has no hard results to quote either, though he praises their (and the Soviet scholars') merits in structural analysis, preparing concordances etc. He does not mention a single definite and positive (non-circular) indication that the language on the Harappan seals is Dravidian.

In Kulke and Rothermund's book *A History of India* "can be found in detail the up-to-date view concerning the Aryan migration, and confirming it", according to Zydenbos. In fact, their book does not *confirm* (with independent research findings) but merely *restate* the AIT, without refuting or even taking into account the research findings on which Prof. Rajaram and Prof. Rao base their case.

Dr. Zydenbos sums up "a few interesting questions", starting with: "Why should leading, respected Indian scholars (and even Nehru, who can hardly be accused of being politically naive or a colonial collaborator) accept the idea of the migration, if it is as patently false as our author claims it is?" We forego the occasion of preparing a list of factual reasons why "leading, respected scholars" have been found to defend the wrong position on numerous occasions in history. The interesting term in the question is "colonial collaborator", which Nehru is claimed not to have been. In fact, while politically an anti-colonial campaigner, Nehru was culturally the archetypal "collaborator" with colonialism and with the colonial view of India.

Free India's first Prime Minister never properly mastered his native Hindustani language and demanded from his relatives that they speak only English at the dinner table. He was in most cultural respects a typical colonial Englishman ("India's last Viceroy"), fully equipped with the concomitant disdain for Indian and particularly Hindu culture, of which he was 100% ignorant. About the Sanskrit traditions which

---

[1]K.V. Zvelebil: *Dravidian Linguistics: An Introduction*, Pondicherry Institute of Linguistics and Culture, 1990; and H. Kulke and D. Rothermund: A History of India, Rupa, Delhi 1991.

[2]Zvelebil: *Dravidian Linguistics*, p.90.

provide the information relevant to the Aryan question, he knew strictly nothing (in spite of his hereditary caste title *Pandit*), and he could not possibly have written anything about it except what he had read in the standard English textbooks. This can easily be verified in his book *The Discovery of India*, which reads like a chapter of a tourist guidebook, but which according to Dr. Zydenbos "in essence still holds good" in its picturesque description of the Aryan invasion.

Nehru shared with many contemporary establishment academics an ideological reason to welcome the AIT. Just as the British liked to flatter themselves with the idea that they had "created" India as a political unit, so Congress politicians liked to see Nehru as the "maker of India".[1] In this view, prior to Queen Victoria and Jawaharlal Nehru, no such cultural entity as "India" ever existed, merely a hunting-ground for ever new waves of invaders, starting with the Aryans. Zydenbos continues: "Why should it be so important that the Aryans, or the extremely remote ancestors of anyone in India for that matter, have been in the subcontinent since all eternity? That would come close to the *Blut und Boden* [blood and soil] ideology of Nazism, with its Aryan rhetoric. Why the xenophobia? Does he really not see the parallel between between Nazi attacks on synagogues in the 1930s and what happened in Ayodhya on December 6th?"

To start with the last point, we would not have believed it, but it is really printed there, black on white: an academic tries to score against a fellow academic by arbitrarily linking him with an event which had not yet taken place when the latter's paper was published, and with which he had strictly nothing to do, viz. the demolition of the Babri Masjid in Ayodhya. Add to this that he accuses Prof. Rajaram of something "close to" Nazi ideology (an old trick to associate someone with Nazism without taking the responsibility for calling him a Nazi outright and risking a court case), and I wonder: how would he fare if he accused a Western colleague in the same vein in a Western paper, considering the extreme importance which academics attach to reputation? At any rate, AIT defenders display a tendency to exceed the topic of debate and launch unwarranted attacks *ad hominem*.

Favouring the idea that the "Aryan" ancestors of the contemporary Indians have lived in the subcontinent "since all eternity" is what Zydenbos dubs "xenophobic" and "close to the *Blut und Boden* ideology of Nazism with its Aryan rhetoric". But it is not Rajaram's school of thought which has given political implications to the question of the geographical provenance of India's population; as we have seen, it is precisely the AIT which has been used systematically as a political argument against those groups considered as the progeny of the "Aryan invaders". Even most AIT opponents subscribe to the prevalent theory that mankind probably originated in Africa, so that all Indians, like all Europeans, are

[1]See e.g. M.J. Akbar: *Nehru, the Making of India* (Penguin 1992).

ultimately immigrants; the ridiculous argument of doubting the legitimacy of a community's presence in India on the basis of an ancestral immigration of 3500 years ago has been launched in all seriousness by interest groups wielding the AIT as their major intellectual weapon, not by the critics of the AIT.

As for the Nazi connection, let us first of all be clear about an easily verifiable fact: in so far as the Nazis cared about Indian history, they favoured the AIT. Establishment historians in Nazi Germany, such as Hermann Lommel, were quite explicit about their doctrine that "by invading India, the Aryans, powerful conquerors, have violated the culture which had been established there".[1] The subjugation of the black natives of India by the white Aryan invaders was, in the *Rassenkunde* ("racial science") courses in Nazi schools, the clearest illustration of the superiority of the white and especially the Aryan race. On the AIT, not Rajaram but Zydenbos is in the same camp with Hitler.

The closing paragraph of "An obscurantist argument" definitely reiterates the outdated notion that India's upper castes are the progeny of the "Aryan invaders" and pride themselves on it: "We can briefly sum up the 'Aryan problem' and the interest it creates among certain people as follows. Whatever problem is there, will not be solved by constructing a new bit of mythology on the theme of the evil foreign hand and the Indian academic community that is supposed to have no mind of its own. This has no basis in fact. Only certain people in certain castes who identify themselves strongly with the Aryans and pride themselves on being 'Aryan' rather than Indian, and thereby stress their difference from (and assume superiority to) other Indians, have a problem. As soon as the author [= N.S. Rajaram], and people of his ilk, make up their minds as to whether they are Indian or not, and whether they want to identify themselves with India and other Indians or not, the problem is solved."

That the Indian academic community "has no mind of its own" has the following basis in fact: India has not even begun to decolonize at the cultural level, and the view of Indian history instilled in the pupils of India's elite schools is still strictly the view inherited from colonial historiography. In another sense, however, the anglicized academic establishment certainly has a mind of its own: while the colonial British still had a condescending sympathy for native culture, the new elite is waging a war against it as a matter of cultural self-exorcism and of political class interest. It knows its own mind very well and has concluded that the AIT serves its interests better than a version of history which would boost native Indian self-respect. Of course, India is not the Soviet Union of Stalin's and Lysenko's days, so when the international academic opinion shifts away from the

[1]Quoted by A. van Lysebeth (*Tantra*, Flammarion, Fribourg 1988, p.24) from H. Lommel: *Les anciens Aryens*, Gallimard, Paris 1943.

AIT, the Indian establishment will have to follow suit; but as long as the matter is in the balance, it throws its entire weight on the side of the AIT.

If certain people in certain castes "pride themselves on being 'Aryan' rather than Indian", it means they have accepted the AIT, which posits the initial non-Indianness of the "Aryans" and identifies them with the upper castes. Of course, this view has no takers among traditionalist upper-caste Hindus, who pride themselves on being the progeny of the Vedic poets and epic heroes revered as the sources of *Indian* civilization. For them, it is not "Aryan rather than Indian", but "*arya*, or Indian par excellence".

Prof. Rajaram "and people of his ilk" have long made up their minds about whether they are Indian or not. That is why they feel strongly about the divisive effect to which the AIT has been used, first by interested outside forces (Zydenbos's sarcastic "evil foreign hand") who have tried to stress the difference of the "Aryans" from other Indians as a weapon against native self-reassertion, and subsequently by Indian interest groups. Their first motive for arguing against the AIT is the sound academic consideration that it seems to be contradicted by the evidence. And this evidence is not nullified at all by their secondary, political motive: the desire to stop the pernicious influence of the AIT on India's unity and integrity.

Sarasvati River Civilization

S. KALYANARAMAN[1]

Sarasvati Sindhu Research Centre
19 Temple Avenue, Chennai 600015, India

India's Sacred Sarasvati River

The mighty, sacred, Vedic Sarasvati river nourished, on her banks, an ancient, the most expansive, remarkably homogeneous, civilization of the times,

Over 1200 of the 1600 ancient settlements of the civilization circa 3000 to 1500 B.C. are on the Sarasvati river; Ganweriwala and Rakhiharhi are as large in area as Mohenjodaro. Thus, settlements on the Sarasvati River were the sustaining economic base of the civilization with Harappa and Mohenjodaro being trading outposts of the ancient civilization.

Rigveda is ecstatic about only one river—the Sarasvati—and adores Sarasvati as a river, as a mother, as a goddess; the adoration is expressed with such emotion and compassion, that this rik may be prescribed as the daily invocation song in every classroom, in every school in India:

> *ambitame nadītame devitame sarasvatī*
> *apraśastā ivāsmāsi praśastiṃ amba nas kṛdhi.* (*RV*, 2.41.16)

[O best of mothers, O best of rivers, O best of goddesses, Sarasvati, (we feel) as if given no consideration, please favour us with renown, O mother.]

Niruktam gives two meanings: *sara* as a river and as a goddess: *sarasvatī iti etasya nadi bad devatabehha nigama bhavanti.* (*Niruktam*, 2.29); *sarasvatī sarah ityudaka nāma sartes tadvati* (*Niruktam*, 9.26). In the *Ṛgbhāṣya,* Sāyaṇa says: *dvividhā hi sarasvatī vigrahavat devatā nadi rūpā ca* (*Ṛgbhāṣya* 1.3.12). The etymon, *sarasvati* means 'abundance of lakes (*saras*)'.

Mahābhārata: Balarama's pilgrimage along Sarasvatī from Dwaraka to Mathura

The great epic, *Mahābhārata*, continues the Vedic tradition of extolling the Sarasvati river and provides vivid geographical accounts of the pilgrimage sites along the river, where Balarama makes offerings to the ancestors (*pitṛs*). The pilgrimage starts from the place where Sarasvati joins the ocean.

> *tasmims tīrthe mahābhāga padma lakṣaṇa lakṣitāḥ*
> *adyāpi mudrā dṛśyante tad adbhutam arimdama*

[1]Former Sr. Exec., Asian Development Bank.

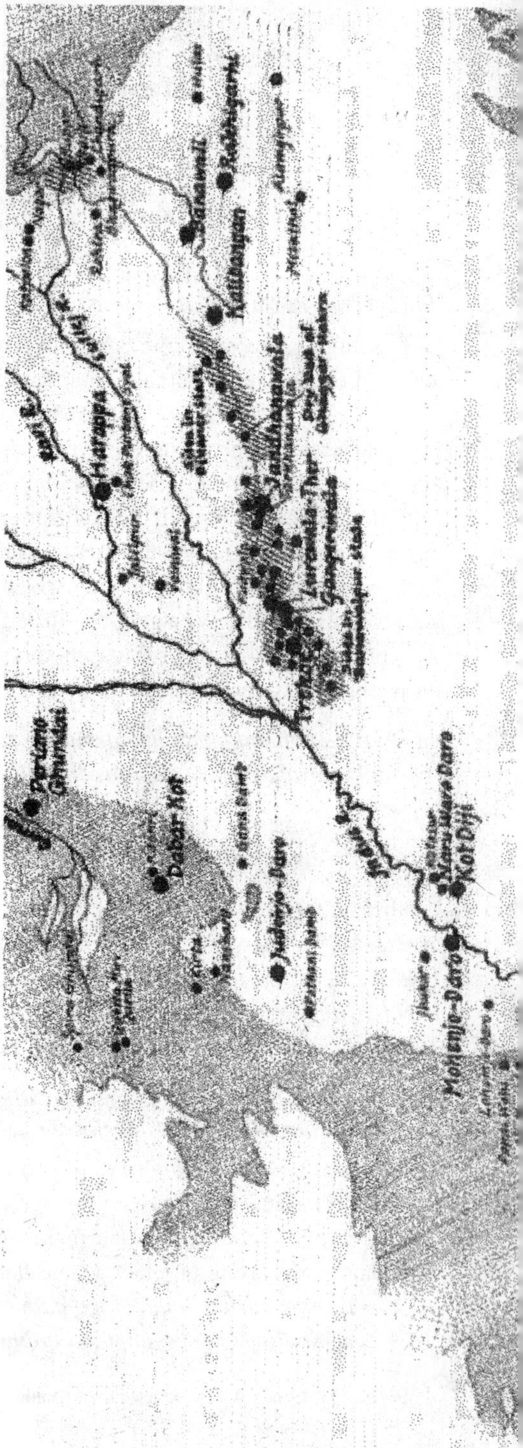
Harappa
Kalibangan
Banawali
Rakhigarhi
Dabar Kot
Periano Ghundai
Judeirjo-Daro
Mohenjo-Daro
Kot Diji

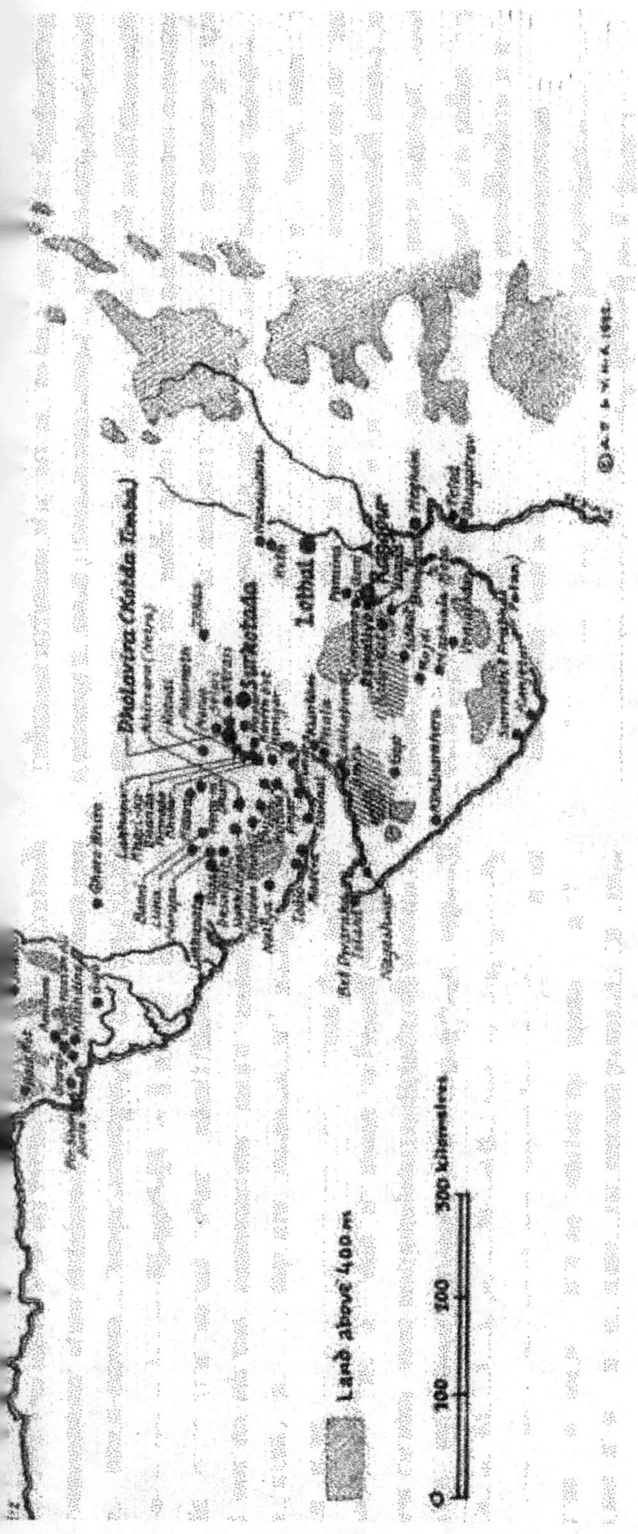

Map 1: Course of the Vedic Sarasvati River

triśūlākṣāṇi padmāni dṛśyante kurunandana
mahādevasya sāmnidhyam tatraiva bharatarṣabha (*MBh,* 3.80.84)

[In this pilgrimage site signs with lotuses are seen; even nowadays seals are seen; this is a marvelous home of faithfulness. Lotuses marked with tridents are seen there, in the presence of the great god (i.e. where Kṛṣṇa lives).]

sarasvatī puṇya vahā . . . samudragā mahā vegā (*MBh*, 3.88.2)

[(In the north) there is Sarasvatī . . . she goes to the ocean, the greatly impetuous one.]

ānayadhvam dvārakāyā agnīn vai yājakāms tathā
suvarṇam rajatam caiva dhenur vāsāmsi vājinaḥ
kuñjarāmś ca rathāmś caiva khara uṣṭram vāhanāni ca
kṣipram ānīyatām sarvam tīrtha hetoh paricchadam
pratisrotah sarasvatyā gachadhvam śīghragāminaḥ
ṛtvijaśca ānayadhvam vai śataśaś ca dvija-ṛṣabhān
tīrtha yātrām yayau rājan kurūṇām vaiśase tadā
sarasvatīm pratisrotah samudrād abhijagmivān (*MBh*, 9.34.15–8)

[(Balarāma is about to set out on a pilgrimage along the Sarasvatī ; he orders his servants:) Bring the fire from Dvārakā and the sacrificers. Bring gold, silver, cows, clothes, horses, elephants, chariots, donkeys, camels (or buffaloes), and other conveyances. Bring everything quickly, all the necessaries for traveling to the pilgrimage sites. Up the stream of Sarasvatī , set out swiftly and move on; bring also priests and hundreds of twice-born (Brahmin) sages. The procession moved swiftly to the pilgrimage sites at the time of the war of the Kurus; going upstream along the Sarasvatī , from the ocean onwards.]

Mahābhārata extols Sarasvatī as *vedānām mātaram paṣya*: the mother of the vedas (*MBh., Śāntiparvan, 12920).*

sarasvatīm īraya Veda juṣṭām eka akṣarām bahu rūpām virājam
aṅga ātmānam sama vekṣasva bālam kim ślāghase durlabhā vāda siddhiḥ
(*MBh*, 3.133.8)

[(Speak of) Sarasvatī, she who is liked for having brought to life the Vedas, she who has one syllable and many forms, she who is brilliant.]

The great epic also attests to the geophysical reality of the Sarasvatī river flowing by Kurukṣetra and Pṛthudaka (Pehoa).

puṇyam āhuḥ kurukṣetram kurukṣetrāt sarasvatīm
sarasvatyāś ca tīrthāni tīrthebhyaś ca pṛthūdakam (*MBh*, 3.81.125)

They call Kurukṣetra holy, but holier than Kurukṣetra is the Sarasvatī, holier than the Sarasvatī are the pilgrimage sites, and holier than the pilgrimage sites is Pṛthūdaka.

Vyāsa the author of the classic, *Mahābhārata*, seeks the blessings of two divinities: god *Nārāyaṇa* and goddess *Sarasvatī* before embarking upon the *magnum opus*:

> *nārāyaam namaskṛtya naram caiva narottamam*
> *devīm sarasvatīm vyāsam tato jayam udīrayet* (*MBh,* 1.1.1)

The people of this maritime, riverine civilization (with a marked preference for alluvial plains) traversed the Himalayan rivers and the oceans across the gulf of Bahrain and the gulf of Khambat. This is evident from the over 1200 settlements located along the banks of the dried-up river bed of this great river (approx. 1600 km. long) and also trade with Mesopotamia and South India (e.g. use of alloy electrum for gold ornaments in Lothal, imported from the gold mines of Hatti or Kolar in Karnataka). The Sarasvati river joined the *sāgara* (also called Hakra or Nara or Wahind or Mihran), and flowed through the Rann of Kutch into the Indian ocean at the Gulf of Khambat. Some centuries before the river dried up (circa 1500 B.C.), it should have been possible to navigate from the Indian ocean right up to Ganga-Yamuna doab, from Dwaraka to Mathura, or from Lothal to Ganweriwala or Kalibangan, on the river Sarasvati. The rise of the ocean-bed which explains the submergence of Dwaraka also explains the rise of the Aravalli ranges which was one of the principal causes for river migrations in Northern and North-West India, the river piracy, the capture of the river source of Sarasvati by the Yamuna (Chambal), a tributary of the Ganga. The eggression and recession of the sea right up to the quaternary period, right up to Kurukṣetra, explains the Luni river system, the ocean fossils near Jaisalmer and the salt marshes of the Rann of Kutch.

The river dried up in long stretches due to sand deposition (*āndhi*) and due to river piracy (Yamuna captured Sarasvati at Paonta Saheb and carried her to Prayag, Allahabad to join the Ganga; hence the myth of the sangamam of the three rivers, Sarasvati, Yamuna and Ganga). When the river was in full flow, it had borne the Himalayan glacier waters emanating from Har-ki-dun glacier (Bandarpunch massif) and of the waters of the Sutlej emanating from Mt. Kailas; thus the river had carried the present-day waters of the Sutlej, the Tons and the Yamuna.

Secular Sequence of Desiccation of the River

The Sarasvati river is not a myth; the river's ancient courses have been found from Naitwar in the Himalayas (Bandarpunch, Har-ki-dun glacier, including the earlier tributaries of Sutlej, Tons, Giri and Yamuna), through Markanda River, through Driṣadvati River, to the Indian Ocean in the Gulf of Khambat (Cambay).

About 5,000 years ago, a momentous geophysical event occurred. The Chambal (now called Yamuna) which was a tributary of the Ganga captured the Sarasvati River at Paonta Saheb and took the Sarasvati River to meet the Ganga River at Prayag, near Allahabad. Hence, the physical basis for sangamam. About 4,000 years ago another momentous geophysical event occurred. The Sutlej (Satadru) which was a tributary of the Sarasvati river (meeting at Shatrana, Punjab) migrated westwards and joined the Indus river.

These two major events in a span of a millennium, led to the drying up the mighty, sacred Sarasvati river and the migrations of people away from the banks of the Sarasvati river eastwards and southwards.

Three points have been established by the studies made by Dr. S. Kalyanaraman and published since March 1996.

First, the Sarasvati was a mighty and perennial river circa 3000 B.C. when the so-called Harappan civilization flourished, flowing from the Har-ki-dun glacier of the Himalayas in W. Garhwal into the Gulf of Khambat near Lothal, via the Little Rann and the Nall Lake (near Ahmedabad). (Thus, Gujarat was an island in the second millennium and it was possible to travel on the Sarasvati River from the Gulf of Khambat to Mathura.)

Second, as shown by the geo-physical evidence provided by hymns of the *Rigveda*, and archaeological evidence, the river sustained a maritime civilization and a metal-based economy which lasted for a millennium. Ganweriwala (Bahawalpur province) and Rakhigarhi were sites as large as Mohenjodaro. Soma, the celebrated process of the *Rigveda* has been interpreted as the processing of electrum (gold-silver quartz). The civilization was a remarkably homogeneous maritime civilization as evidenced by the artefacts unearthed from Tigris-Euphrates to the Ganga-Yamuna Doab, and showed a marked preference for establishing settlements on alluvial plains [marutam (Tamil)].

Third, at about 1500 B.C., the Sutlej river (originating from Mt. Kailas) which was also flowing into the Sarasvati river at Shatrana took a U-turn at Ropar and migrated westwards. Yamuna had drained the waters flowing into the Sarasvati (at Paonta Saheb or near ancient Plaksha Prashravana), due perhaps to the continuing rise of the Aravalli ranges and deepening of the erstwhile Chambal (now called Yamuna) tributary of the Ganga. The phenomenon of *aandhi* (sandstorms) also submerged parts of the riverbed near Jaisalmer-Pokaran in the *Marusthali*. The settlement pattern extending over approx. 1500 years indicates an eastern movement of people into the Ganga-Yamuna doab and southward along the coastline. The confluence of the Sarasvati at Sangam in Prayag is, therefore, not mythology, but based on ground truth. Similarly, the popular belief that the Sarasvati disappeared in the sands and went underground is also based on ground truth.

When Satadru river was joining Sarasvati river at Shatrana, Kalibangan, on the banks of Sarasvati river, a supply node from the Khetri copper mines (through Kanthali river, a tributary of Sarasvati) was accessible over land to Harappa on the banks of Beas (Vitasta) river. Mohenjodaro was an island caught between Sindhu and Hakra and, hence, was on the Right Bank of Sarasvati; so were Chanhudaro and Kotdiji settlements in Sind.

Due to the desiccation of the mighty river which was the life-sustenance for the civilization, there was a migratory movement of people, from circa 1500 B.C., westwards towards the Haraquaiti (Kubha, Afghanistan), towards the Ganga-Yamuna doab (Rakhigarhi), and south through the Gulf of Khambat (cf. the ancient site of Daimabad, on the banks of Pravara, a tributary of the Godavari river).

Historical Perspective: River and Settlements

Map 1 (pp. 72–73) depicts the flow of Sarasvati circa 1500 B.C. when part of the river dried up [Map based on K.S. Valdiya, 1996].

Map 2 depicts the remarkable clustering of ancient archaeological settlements

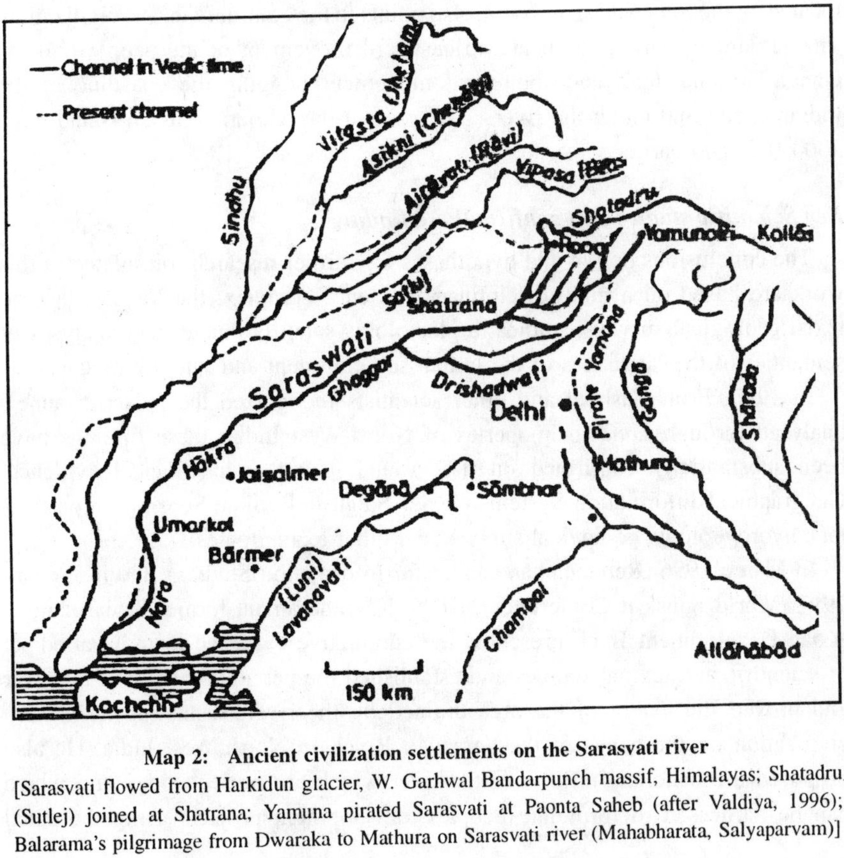

Map 2: Ancient civilization settlements on the Sarasvati river

[Sarasvati flowed from Harkidun glacier, W. Garhwal Bandarpunch massif, Himalayas; Shatadru (Sutlej) joined at Shatrana; Yamuna pirated Sarasvati at Paonta Saheb (after Valdiya, 1996); Balarama's pilgrimage from Dwaraka to Mathura on Sarasvati river (Mahabharata, Salyaparvam)]

on the banks of the Sarasvati River establishing that the settlements formed the substratum of the civilization; Harappa and Mohenjodaro were only trading outposts. [Map based on Parpola, 1994].

RADIOCARBON DATES (B.C.) OF SELECTED ANCIENT SITES ON THE SARASVATI-SINDHU RIVERS

Balakot	4150–3800	Mohenjodaro	2545–2315
Harappa	3338–3208	Lothal	2655–2185
Kunal	3016	Surkotada	2940–2540
Ganeshwar (Jodhpura)	3018–2926	Daimabad	1961–1420
Kalibangan	2950–2650	Rojdi	1947
Somnath	3055–2800	Prabhas Patan	1406
Banawali	2560–1965	Shortugai	1445
Mitathal	2435–2095		

The cumulative archaeological evidence with over 1,200 ancient settlements located on the Sarasvati river basin, also points to the continuity of the civilization. The settlement patterns indicate an eastward movement of the people into the Ganga-Yamuna doab and southward movement hugging the coastline of the Indian ocean and along the rivers. The present-day Gujarat was an island circa 3000 B.C. and earlier.

Key Scientific studies that confirm these findings

The conclusions drawn and hypotheses for further research formulated in this work are based on a multi-disciplinary evidence-complex: the Vedas, classical texts, geological surveys, studies in glaciology, satellite images and analyses of semantics of the languages of the Indian sub-continent and satellite images.

In 1980, Prof. Yashpal and other scientists recognized the palaeo-channels analysed through *Landsat* imageries of North-West India; these findings have been substantially confirmed on the ground, using archaeological evidence, Geographical Information Systems (IRS-1 Satellite Remote Sensing, in particular), hydrogeology, geological surveys and other technologies.

In March 1996 (Renganathan Centre for Information Studies), and in January 1997 (World Sanskrit Conference), Dr. S. Kalyanaraman, former Sr. Executive, Asian Development Bank presented the cumulative evidence from a varied set of scientific and textual sources and established the perennial nature of the river and proved the extent of the area drained by the river, sustaining an ancient civilization on the banks of the Sarasvati River, in North West India. He also proposed the beneficial effects of the river which are present today and which can be harnessed to formulate peoples' development projects using the canal systems network, building a NW India Drainage System and using the groundwater sanctuaries and aquifers of the Sarasvati River Basin to create micro-watershed-based agro-industrial activities, supported by solar- and wind power-based electricity generation.

In May 1996, Prof. Valdiya has traced, based on hydrogeological studies, the course of the Sarasvati River from Tons River in W. Garhwal, U.P. up to the Rann of Kutch and reiterated that river piracy by Yamuna was the principal cause for the desiccation of the Sarasvati River.

In January 1997, BARC scientists (S.M.Rao and Kulkarni) have re-confirmed the existence of the Sarasvati River and of groundwater sanctuaries and aquifers, using water samples collected from deep wells in Jaisalmer region and North-eastern Rajasthan to conduct tritium (hydrogen isotope) analysis to establish the quality of water, flow and age of the water [ranging from 4,000 to 8,000 years Before Present (B.P.)]

In October 1997, Puri and Verma have established, through glaciological and geological studies, that the Vedic Sarasvati originated in Bandarpunch (Sarasvati-Rupin glaciers confluence at Naitwar) in the Himalayas and that there was a secular sequence of desiccation of the river: (i) course through Markanda river; (ii) course through Drishadvati river; (iii) eastward migration of the river Drishadvati, linking up with Chambal and the resultant capture of the Tons (Sarasvati) River at Paonta Saheb; and (iv) signatures of palaeochannels of Satadru (which had, from Ropar, drained into Sarasvati at Shatrana) establishing the westward migration of the river with a U-turn at Ropar, ultimately joining the Sindhu river. The studies have also produced evidence of quartzite and metamorphic rocks in Paonta Doon valley and near Adh Badri in Siwalik ranges attesting to the existence of the mighty river which had brought in these rocks. In mid-eocene period (circa 35 million years ago), before the rise of the Himalayas, only three rivers originated from Mansasrovar lake (Tibet): Sindhu, Satadru and Brahmaputra. After the rise of the Himalayas, Satadru became the anchorage river of Sarasvati, joining the latter at Shatrana. Yamuna joined Tons at Paonta Saheb and flowed into Sarasvati. Ganga emerged from Gangotri with Chambal (now Yamuna) as a tributary.

Thanks to the magnificent advances being made in maritime archaeology, it should soon be possible to establish the Himalayan fingerprints of snails and shells specific to Himalayan rivers along the ancient courses of the river Sarasvati close to the Indian Ocean.

Mohenjo-daro was on the banks of the Sarasvati river

Marshall's report (1931, pp.1–6) which includes a superb map, reads thus:

> "(Mohenjo-daro) stands on what is known locally as 'The Island'—a long, narrow strip of land between the main river bed and the Western

> Nara loop, its precise position being 27.19N by 68.8E, some 7 miles by road from Dokri on NW Railway, and 25 from Larkana town . . . Twelve centuries ago, when the Ārabs first came to Sind, there were two great rivers flowing through the land: to the west, the Indus; to the east, the Great Mihran, also known as the Hakra or Wahindah. Of these two rivers the eastern one seems to have been the more important . . . Major Raverty . . . According to him, the terminal course of the Indus, which flows by Mohenjo-daro, was then a subsidiary branch of the Mihran, but its course was not the same as at present . . . the existence of two important Chalcolithic sites of Mohenjo-daro and Jhukar, the one in the near vicinity of the Indus, the other of the Western Nara loop . . ."

Griffin Vyse recalls observations that Alexander the Great had also sailed to the great lake and to the sea by this 'eastern branch of the Indus':

> . . . "the eastern or greater arm of the Mikran described by Rashid-ud-deen as branching off from above Mansura to the east, to the borders of Kutch, and known by the name of Sindh Sagara (Elliot, vol. i, p. 49). This ancient river is also identical with the Sankra Nala which was constituted by Nadir Shah the boundary between his dominions and those of the Emperor of Delhi."

Now it can be seen that Mohenjo-daro was also on the banks of one of the channels of Sarasvati, what is now called the Western Nara loop.

Sarasvati flowed into the Sāgara in the Gulf of Khambat

The Rann of Kutch was navigable in the third and second millennia B.C.

> "It is suggested by some scholars that Lothal was reached through the Little Rann and the Nal Lake which were then easily navigable. . . . Around the head of the Gulf of Cambay the ancient channels of the rivers, which are now silted up, act as drains for springtides, but otherwise remain a salt marsh." (S.R. Rao, 1979)

> "During the monsoon, the lower part of the Rann of Cambay joins the Nal Lake forming a connected sheet of water which spreads over the neighbouring tracts of Bhāl and the Nalkāntha, turning the villages into islands and cutting off communication with Ahmedabad." (*Imperial Gazetteer of India*, Bombay Presidency, Calcutta, 1901, II, p. 348)

Alex Rogers was perhaps among the earliest observers of the geology of the Gulf of Khambat (earlier called Cambay, close to Lothal). He pointed out, in

1870, that from the geological formation of the country bordering on the Rann, it appeared that the drainage of the Panjab once flowed into it. He also observed that a great river should have flowed into the Gulf of Khambat.

From Har-ki-Dun (Tons river) to the Gulf of Khambat

It would be reasonable to conclude that the ancient, perennial, Sarasvati river, originating from Har-ki-Dun (Tons river) in the Himalayas, after traversing the edges of the Great Indian desert, had flowed through the Rann of Kutch, into the Little Rann and flowed into the Gulf of Khambat by linking up with the Nall Lake. This geological reconstruction of ancient times is reinforced by the preponderance of the ancient, homogeneous, riverine/maritime settlements of the civilization, exemplified by sites such as Lothal, Rangpur, Dholavira, Kotda, Bet Dwaraka, all of which have yielded authentic material artefacts, in general, and seals with inscriptions in particular.

Metals-Lapidary-Weaver Craft-Merchant Economy

The Sarasvatī-Sindhu river valleys supported an agrarian as well as a metals-lapidary-weaver-craft economy which generated surplus commodities of trade which were transported inland and also up to the Tigris-Euphrates river valley and the Caucus-Bactria (Turkmenistan) region.

> "(Trade) routes move up the Ravi from Multan to Harappa, and thence some 60 kms. southeast to Pakpattan. This has been the traditional ferry point on the Sutlej for centuries, and is an important stage on routes connecting the Punjab with the Sarasvati Valley . . . ." (Ratnagar, Shereen, The location of Harappa, in: Possehl, Gregory L., *Harappan Civilization*, Oxford and IBH, Delhi, 1982, pp. 261–264)

The people living in the Khetri copper belt supplied the copper, lead and electrum ores. Vedic people produced *soma*, after smelting and purifying the electrum ore. The metalsmiths, weavers and lapidaries living in the river valleys and mineral-belts used the metallic ores and electrum to create (and trade in, using seals and sealings) artifacts such as clothing, ropes, agricultural implements, vessels, tools, artistic mouldings, bangles, necklaces and other ornaments using gem-stones and metal.

Most of the archaeological sites of the civilization (e.g. Kalibangan, Kotda (Dholavira), Banawali, Kunal, Rakhigarhi) are located on the Sarasvati river basin. Some sites in Gujarat are located on rocky surfaces and on the banks of seasonal rivers, for e.g. Surkotada and Dholavira in Kutch, Lothal which is located on the banks of Bhogao river. Some sites in Sindh are found on the shores of lakes, e.g. Ghazi Shah near Manchhar lake. The sites of the Arabian coast are: Balakot, Sotka Khoh in Pakistan and Kuntasi and Nageshwar in India.

Hundreds of hymns of the *Rigveda* and later-day texts attest to the importance of the Sarasvati river to Vedic people (Only a few samples will be presented in this monograph). The civilization was a maritime civilization, a metals economy with settlements on river banks and along the sea-coasts.

Rigveda attests to the Sarasvati:

"associated with the Maruts" (vii.3.8)

"associated with a desert" (vii.71.1)

"associated with the ocean" (vii.36.6)

"associated with dadvati and apay rivers" (iii.23.4)

Only one river matches these geophysical references: the Markanda-Ghaggar-Hakra-Nara (Mihran) river system in North West India.

The reference is apparently not to any of the other three Sarasvati rivers drawn on the National Atlas maps: (i) Haraquaiti (Zend Avestan version of Sarasvati) river which joins the river Kubha, a tributary of the Sindhu in Afghanistan; (ii) River Sarasvati joining the Little Rann of Kutch; and (iii) River Sarasvati originating from Pushkar, near Ajmer and joining the Luni River. These three rivers do not match the descriptions provided in the Rigveda and no major archaeological sites have been discovered on these three rivers. Naming of many rivers as Sarasvati may be a recollection of the memories of the lives of ancestors, as people migrated westward, eastward and southward.

It will be erroneous to interpret the *Rigveda* as a gazetteer of the civilization. However, the texts of the ancient texts contained in the *Rigveda* provide glimpses of the activities of the civilization. For example, there are references to traders, the paṇis [maṇika, mānya, -mān (Ta.), -vān (Skt.)] engaged in sea-borne trade, to samudra (sea), to vessels on the sea (nāvah samudriyah). The lexemes of the languages of the region contain terms such as vaṇika, vaiśya, vina-sanni.

The Vedic people had used ships to cross oceans:

anārambhaṇe tadavīrayethā manāsthāne agrabhaṇe samudre ya-daśvinā ūhathurbhujyumastam śatāritrām nāvamātasthivāmsam.

(RV. I.116.5; cf. VS. 21.7)

[referring to aśvins who rescued Bhujyu, sinking in mid-ocean using a ship with a hundred oars (*nāvam-aritraparaṇīm*).

Ye wrought that hero exploit in the ocean which giveth no support or hold or station. What time ye carried Bhujyu to his dwelling, borne in a ship with hundred oars, O Aśvins.]

Vedic culture was composed of a cooperating society among the yajñikas and others, both endeavouring to generate wealth:

samāne ūrve adhi saṅgatsaḥ saṁ jānate na yatante mitha-s-te
te devānām na minanti vratānyamardhanto vasubhir-yādamānāḥ
(*RV.*, vii.76.5)

[Being united with common people they become of one mind; they strive together as it were, nor do they injure the rituals of the gods, non-injuring each other they move with wealth. (Śāyaṇa explains *samāne ūrve* as cattle—common property of all: *sarveṣām sādhāraṇe go-samūhe*).]

The civilization worked with metals. Sarasvati was a bestower of wealth. A number of professions are indicated, particularly those of smithy:

vedā yo vīnām padamantarikṣeṇa patatām
veda nāvah samudriyah (*RV.* I.25.7)

[He knows the path of birds that fly through heaven, and Sovran of the sea (Varuṇa), He knows the ships that are thereon.]

nānānam vā u no dhiyo vivratāni janānām
takṣā riṣṭam rutam bhiṣagbrahmā
sunvantamicchatīndrāyendo risrava (*RV.* IX.112.1)

[We all have various thoughts and plans, and diverse are the ways (professions) of men. The Brahman seeks the worshipper (a professional), wright seeks the cracked, and doctor the maimed. Flow, Indu, flow for Indra's sake.]

brahmaṇaspatiretā sam karmārivādhamat
devānām pūrvye yugesatah sadajāyata (*RV.*X.72.2)

[These Brahmanaspati produced with blast and smelting, like a smith, Existence, in an earlier age of Gods, from Non-existence sprang.]

tigmam cidema mahi vapro asya bhasadaśvo na yamasāna āsā
vijehamānaḥ paraśurna jihvām dravirna drāvayati dāru dhakṣat
(*RV.* VI.3.4)

[Fierce is his gai and vast his wondrous body: he champeth like a horse with bi and bridle, And, darting forth his tongue, as 'twere a hachet, burning the woods, smelteth them like a smelter.]

taraṇiri simṣāsati vājam purandhyā yujā
ā va indram puruhūtam name girā nemi taṣṭeva sudvam
(*RV.* VII.32.20)

[With plenty for his true ally the active man will gain the spoil, Your Indra, Much-invoked, I bend with song, as bends a wright his wheel of solid wood.]

Five Peoples of the Sarasvati river

A vedic hymn refers to the endowment of metallic ores proximate to the river.

trisadhasthā saptadhātuḥ pañca jātā vardhayantī
vāji-vāje havyā bhūr (*RV.* 6.61.12)

[She who has a triple seat (being endowed with) sevenfold ores, she is the promoter of the five peoples (i.e. she makes them prosper; in every battle she is invoked).]

One of the five peoples referred to included the Pūrus. The word is as an epithet of a folk in *RV.* vii.18.13:

jeṣma pūrum vidathe mṛdhra vācam; (vi.46.8)
yad vā tṛkṣau druhyau yat pūrau; (i.108.3)
yadushu turvaśeṣu druhyuṣu pūruṣu.

The people associated are Yadus, Turvaśas and Druhyus.

ubhe yat te mahinā śubhre andhasī adhikṣiyanti pūrvaḥ
sā no bodhy avitrī marutsakhā coda rādho maghonām (*RV.* 7.96.2)

[Beautiful one, by your power the Pūrus are settled (near) both juices (*Soma* and milk); she the protector attend to us, she the friend of the Maruts incite the kindness of the munificent ones.]

citra id rājā id anyake yake sarasvatīm anu
parjanya iva tatanad dhi vṛṣṭyā sahasram ayutā dadat
(*RV.* 8.21.18)

[Citra is indeed a king, petty princes are indeed others who live along the Sarasvati; like Parjanya with the rain, so gave he one hundred, ten thousand.]

This historical reference is reminisced in the great epic, referring to the peoples living by the Sarasvati:

Śūdra ābhīra gaṇāś caiva ye ca āśritya sarasvatīm
vartayanti ca ye matsyair ye ca parvata vāsinah
(*MBh.* 2.29.9)

[(Nakula conquered) all the hosts of *Śūdras*[1] and *Ābhīras* who dwell by the Sarasvati, and those who live on fish, and those who dwell in the mountains.]

In the historical periods, *Śūdras* and *Ābhīras* (cowherds) are located as belonging to the downstream settlements of the Sarasvati river.

---

[1] '*Sudra*' is a term derived from '*ksudraka*'; in Kautilya's *Arthasastra* (1.13.13, 26; 2.13.37, 40); the term connotes a commoner engaged in minor work (in gold, such as bead-making). *Abhiras* are concordant with *aayar* in Tamil, herdsmen or cowherds. Thus the *pancajaata* cited in the *Rgveda* should connote people engaged in five trades or professions.

The Vedic period was a nascent material culture: the period had weavers; the words *sirī* and *vayitrī* denote a female weaver (*RV.* x.71.9; *PB*, I.8.9); *tasara* is referred to which is a shuttle (*RV.* xiv.2.51). Reference to women weaving is provided: *tantum tatam saṁvayanti* (*RV.* ii.3.6). Gold (*hiraṇyapiṇḍān, hiraṇyayuḥ)* was highly valued (cf. *RV*. vi.47.23, vii.78.9).

Divodāsa gave golden treasures to the Ṛṣi Gārga. Rigveda refers to niṣkagrīva (*RV* v.19.3) which is a golden ornament on the neck and necklaces of gold reaching down to the chest. *Hiraṇya* (pl.) means gold ornaments (*RV.* 1.122.2). Gold was smelted from the ores (*PB*, xviii.6.4; *JB* I,10) which evoke the Indian alchemical tradition enshrined in the *Soma rasa*, later elaborated as the science of alchemy: *rasa-vāda*. In Tamil *Soma-maṇal* means 'sand containing silver ore'. In Veda *iyal* refers to alchemy. *Ācāri* (Skt. *ācārya*) is a goldsmith. In Egyptian, *assem* means electrum; in Gypsy, *soṁnakay* means gold. Gold was won from the river-beds: Sindhu is called the *hiraṇmayī* (*RV.* x.75.8); Sarasvatī is called *hiraṇyavartanī* (*AV.* vi.61.7). [cf. the reference to *vasatīvari* waters in Vedic hymns related to *Soma*, an apparent reference to panned-gold from the Sarasvatī river-bed.] It is notable that in 1992, Rafiq Mughal (Pakistan archaeological department) has discovered a site, Ganweriwala, an industrial site on the dried-up river bed of the Sarasvati across the Rajasthan border). This site is reportedly as large as Mohenjo-daro. The Vedic people had used ships to cross oceans: *anarambhaṇe . . . agrabhaṇe samudre . . . śatāritram nāvam . . .* (*RV*. I.116.5; cf. *VS*. 21.7) referring to Aśvins who rescued Bhujyu, sinking in mid-ocean using a ship with a hundred oars (*nāvam-aritraparanīm*). There is overwhelming evidence of maritime trade by the archaeological discoveries of the so-called Harappan civilization, which can now be re-christened Sarasvati-Sindhu civilization. Some beads were reported to have been exported to Egypt from this valley (*Early Indus Civilization*, p. 149); Sumerians had acted as intermediaries for this trade (L. Wooley, *The Sumerians*, pp. 46-47; cf. *Ur Excavations*, vol. II, pp. 390–396).which extended to Anatolia and the Mediterranean.

Development Projects in the Sarasvati River Basin

The Website, *Sarasvati River* (http://www.probys.com/sarasvati), delineates a Sarasvati River Basin (NW India) Watershed Development Project proposal to use the alluvium and groundwater sanctuaries built over millennia by the Sarasvati river and to provide new livelihood opportunities to the people of Northwestern India.

A research proposal has been submitted to the Ministry of Water Resources, Govt. of India by the Sarasvati Sindhu Research Centre. The proposal is simple. The groundwater resources of the desert close to the palaeo-channels of the sacred Sarasvati river will be conserved and augmented. Thanks to the undulating terrain of the dunes, the Sarasvati lakes will naturally emerge with such replenishment of groundwater. As the irrigation and drainage systems get streamlined, further improving the drainage systems of the command areas of Rajasthan canal and other canal systems, the waters will start flowing again in the ancient, now-dried, beds of the river. There are, of course, technical problems to be carefully studied through simulation and other exercises such as the problem posed by the hard pans, underground, of calcium carbonate and calcium sulphate (lime and gypsum) deposits, the problems of waterlogging and salination on the dry-beds of the river, the problems of cultivating halophytes [such as *Salicornia brachiata*: *bholad* (Gujarati), *machula* (Hindi), *koyyalu* (Telugu), *umari* (Tamil/Malayalam)] to stem, or at least slow down, the northward march of the desert.

The revival or reclamation of the Sarasvati calls for a multi-disciplinary team of dedicated workers. The work has to be carried out, in a participatory approach, by the beneficiaries, i.e. people of the region themselves and has to be done in such a way as to ensure the preservation of the ancient archaeological and pilgrimage sites as national monuments and to make them accessible as permanent exhibitions of the cherished heritage of the sub-continent.

The salient features of the proposal are:

- The groundwater resources of the Marusthali desert can be sustained (with one million tube-wells) and augmented, conjuctively with the development of a North India Drainage System and desilting works to keep the Sarasvati River flowing almost perennially between Adhi Badri to Anupgarh;
- the northward march of the desert can be slowed down;
- the heritage sites can be preserved as national monuments;
- with the augmentation of groundwater storage using the desert as a natural underground reservoir, the Sarasvati lakes will naturally emerge; and
- the Marusthali desert can be made fertile; and the sacred Sarasvati river will come alive and start flowing again.

BIBLIOGRAPHY

D.P. Agrawal, "Metal technology of the Harappans", in: B.B. Lal and S.P. Gupta, Frontiers of the Indus Civilization, Indian Archaeological Society, Delhi, 1984, pp. 163–167.

________, "Aravali, the source of Indus Copper", in: ibid., 1984, pp. 157–162.

R.C. Agrawala and Vijay Kumar, 1982, "Ganeshwar-Jodhpura Culture", in: Gregory L. Possehl, *Harappan Civilization*, Delhi, Oxford and IBH, 1982, pp. 125-134.

Raghunath Airi, *Concept of Sarasvati in Vedic Literature*, Munshiram Manoharlal Publishers, Delhi, 1977.

P.C. Bakliwal, S.M. Ramasamy and A.K. Grover, "Use of remote sensing in identification of possible areas for groundwater, hydrocarbons and minerals in the Thar desert, Western India", *Proceeding*

Volume of the International Conference on Prospecting in Areas of Desert Terrain, The Institute of Mining and Metallurgy Publications, 14-17 April 1983, Rabat, Morocco, 121–129.

Suraj Bhan, 1972a, "Changes in the course of Yamuna and their bearing on the protohistoric cultures of Haryana", in: S.B. Deo ed., *Archaeological Congress and Seminar Papers, Nagpur University,* pp. 125–128. .

O.P. Bharadwaj, *Ancient Kurukshetra,* Harman Publishing House, Delhi, 1991, p. 69.

R.S. Bisht, "Dholavira: A new horizon of the Indus Civilization", *Puratattva,* **20**, 1991, 71–82; article in Hindi in *Aajkal,* 1994; also in: J.P. Joshi and R.S. Bisht, *India and the Indus Civilization,* National Museum Institute, Delhi, 1995.

R.S. Bisht and S. Asthana, "Banawali and some other recently excavated Harappan sites in India", in M.Taddei (Ed.), *South Asian Archaeology*, Naples, 1977, pp. 223–240.

M.N. Godbole, *Rigvedic Sarasvati*, Govt. of Rajasthan, Jaipur, 1963.

S.P. Gupta, *Indus-Sarasvati Civilization: Origins, Problems and Issues,* Pratibha Prakashan, Delhi, 1996.

G.L. Hart, The Relation Between Tamil and Classical Sanskrit Literature, Wiesbaden, 1976.

S. Kalyanaraman, *An Etymological Dictionary of South Asian Languages,* 3 vols. (CD-ROM in press, Scanrom Publications, New York); typescript 2801 pp. In C.P. Ramaswami Indological Research Institute, Madras, Asian Development Bank, Manila, 1982

______, *Indus Script—a bibliography*, Manila, 1988.

______, "Information Systems and Technologies used in the researches on Sarasvati-Sindhu Civilization circa 3000 B.C.", *Information Studies*, Bangalore, **2**(3), 1996, 176–185.

______, *Sarasvati Sindhu Civilization: Evidence from the Veda, Archaeology, Geology and Satellite,* X World Sanskrit Conference, Bangalore, January 1997.

______ (ed.), Website: http://www.investindia.com, 1997.

______, Sarasvati-Sindhu Civilization circa 3000 B.C., 1997.

Webpages: http://asnic.utexas.edu/asnic/subject/saraswatisindhucivization.html
http://www.ucl.ac.uk/ucgadkw/indus.html (indology)
http://www.investindia.com/webzine4/Discov1.html

______, *Indian Alchemy: Soma in the Veda*, 1997 (in press).

______, "A project to revive the Sarasvati river: Role of GIS", *National Seminar on Geographic Information Systems for Development Planning*, Renganathan Centre for Information Studies, Chennai, 10–12 January, 1997.

______, Website: http://www.probys.com/sarasvati (*Sarasvati River*), 1997.

N.G. Majumdar, "Explorations in Sind", *Memoirs of the Archaeological Survey of India*, No. 48, Manager of Publications, Delhi, 1934.

Sir John Marshall (Ed.), *Mohenjodaro and the Indus Civilization*, 3 vols., Arthur Probsthain, London, 1931.

Mohammad Rafique Mughal, *Ancient Cholistan: Archaeology and Architecture,* Ferozsons Pvt. Ltd., Lahore, 1997.

V.N. Misra, "Geoarchaeology of Thar Desert, Northwest India", in: S Wadia et al. (eds.), *Quaternary Environments and Geoarchaeology of India*, Geological Society of India, Bangalore, 1995, pp. 210–230.

C.F. Oldham, 1893, "The Sarasvati and the Lost River of the Indian Desert", *Journal of the Royal Asiatic Society*, 1893, 49–76.

R.D. Oldham, "On probable changes in the geography of the Punjab and its rivers: a historico-geographical study", *J. Asiatic Soc. Bengal*, **55**, 1886, 322–343.

Asko Parpola, *Deciphering the Indus Script*, Cambridge University Press, 1994.

V.M. Puri and S.P. Verma, *Glaciological and Geological Evolution of Vedic Sarasvati in the Himalayas*, Paper presented in Itihasa Sankalana Samiti meet in Delhi on 5 October 1997

K.R.Srinivasan, Monograph titled "Paleogeography, Framework of Sedimentation and Groundwater Potential of Rajasthan, IndiaùCentral Part of Erstwhile Sarasvati Basin", for presentation in Group Discussion Meeting organized by Geological Society of India on "Drainage Evolution of North-western India with particular reference to the Lost Sarasvati", December 1997 at Baroda; Two Project Reports: "Sarasvati River Basin: Development and Management of Grounwater Resources: Project Reports: (i) Kolayat Block (Bikaner District) and (ii) Osian Block (Jodhpur District)", September 1997, submitted to the Min. of Water Resources by Sarasvati Sindhu Research Centre, Chennai on 17 September 1997.

Aurel Stein, "An archaeological tour in Gedrosia", *Memoirs of the Archaeological Survey of India*, Govt. of India, Calcutta, 1931, p. 43.

Sir Aurel Stein, "A survey of ancient sites along the 'lost' Sarasvati River", *Geographical Journal*, **99**, 1942, 173–182

KS, Valdiya, "Neotectonic implication of collision of Indian and Asian plates", *Ind. J. Geology*, **61**, 1989, 1–13.

______ , "River Piracy, Sarasvati that disappeared", *Resonance*, Indian Academy of Sciences, Bangalore, **1**(5), 1996, 19–28.

L.S. Wakankar and C.N. Parchure, A Quest after the Lost Vedic Sarasvati River—An Expedition Report (tr. from Marathi), Bharatiya Itihasa Sankalana Samithi, Mysore, 1994.

Herbert Wilhemly, "Das Urstromtal am Ostrand der Indusebene und der Sarasvati-Problem", *Zeitschrift fur Geomorphologie*, Supplementband, **8**, 1969, 76–93.

Michael Witzel, "On the localisation of Vedic texts and schools", in: Gilber Pollet (Ed.), *India and the Ancient World*, Orientalia Lovanensia Analecta, Leuven, **25**, 1987, 173–213, .

Yash Pal, Baldev Sahai, R.K.Sood and D.P. Agrawal, Space Applications Centre, and PRL, Ahmedabad, "Remote sensing of the 'lost' Sarasvati river", *Proc. Indan Acad. Sci. (Earth and Planetary Sci.)*, **89**(3), Nov. 1980, 317–331.

______, "Remote sensing of the lost Sarasvati river", *Proc. Indian Acad. Sci. Earth Planet. Sci.*, **89**, 1980, 317-331; also in: B.B. Lal and S.P. Gupta, *Frontiers of the Indus Civilization*, Indian Archaeological Society, Delhi, 1980, pp. 217–226.

Indus Valley Civilization vis-a-vis Vedic Civilization: A Chronological Exploration

AVANINDRA KUMAR
Deptartment of Sanskrit, University of Delhi
Delhi-110 007, India

As a preamble to any discussion or discourse it is essential to underline the fact that intellectual integrity is the sine qua non of every academic pursuit and explorative venture. Truth, after all, is the ultimate goal of all human endeavour. Chauvinism whether individual, national or racial, is an anathema to intellectual pursuits. It is disinterested endeavour that should act as a guiding principle in the voyage of discovery. In my paper, I have been guided solely by disinterestedness, brushing aside all considerations that are not germane to the central concern.

There is not the slightest tinge of exaggeration in the assertion that Indian civilization is one of the oldest, if not the oldest~ civilizations of the world. It is not out of national jingoism or xenophobia that one should accept a fact of history to be true even if it is not and seek to reject it as untrue even when it is true. There is an enormous divergence of opinion among historians, anthropologists, archaeologists, geomorphologists, geologists, litterateurs, linguists and the like in regard to the origin and evolution of a civilization in any part of the world let alone India. The crux of the problem is whether or not India is, in verity, the cradle of the most primeval civilization in the world. There is no gainsaying the fact that Western scholars have, by and large, given a biased view of the early beginnings of Indian civilization. Their interpretations savour of academic and no less unacademic considerations. There is no denying that their approach is vitiated by national chauvinism, in that they strive to muddle up the genuineness of the antiquity of Indian civilization in comparison to other civilizations. Their vision is blurred by national pride and racial superiority. They also strive to seek and fabricate justification for the invasion, conquest and governance of India. The thrust of their argument pertains to frequent invasions of India through the ages. All invaders, including the Aryans, came from outside and drove out the natives. The Aryans, too, invaded India, drove out the natives, settled there and dominated over the weak and the servile. This is how a host of Western scholars have endeavoured to prove that people coming from outside imported with them their civilization and spread it here. Thus, indian civilization is a composite civilization consisting of native and foreign civilizations. The impact of foreign civilization has been sought to have its bearings on Indian civilization.

In this paper a candid attempt has been made to remove the cobweb of confusion, ambiguity and distortion that has shrouded the true spirit of the history of Indian civilization. For quite some time the views and interpretations of Western scholars have been in focus. However, profound studies have been made by Indian scholars as well as some Western scholars, which go to show that Indian civilization is the oldest civilization in the world. It is necessary, therefore, to put the problem in the right perspective so that distortions and the misinterptetations are repudiated and an unbiased view of history as history is allowed to emerge. There is no room for partisanship in academic matters. This paper is untinged and untainted by pride and prejudice.

Perhaps the most controversal issue in Indian history is the Aryan problem. Most of the Western scholars hold that Vedic Aryans came to India from outside. On the contrary, eminent scholars both foreign and Indian are of the view that the Aryans were Indigenous io India. They were original inhabitants of India. There are, thus, two groups of scholars holding diametrically opposed views. I do not deem it necessary to dwell on the various theories advanced by scholars, arguing in favour or against the Aryan homeland being in India or outside of it as they are all too well known.

It is pointed out that the Vedic Aryans have been rather elusive. The search for Aryans has aptly been described as looking in a dark room for a black cat, which is not there. But Vedic literature is a reality and the Aryans too have been no less a reality. This fact cannot be brushed aside just like that. It is, therefore, necessary to define the areas of their habitation, movement and activity. Vedic literature clearly records that the Aryans lived in the land of Sapta-sindhu, which can be identified as the former Punjab province of undivided India and Rajasthan, the Sarasvatī-Dṛṣadvatī basin being the main area of their activity. There is evidence to show that the Sarasvatī which was a very mighty river then was flowing through this vast region. The Sarasvatī has been identified with the Ghaggar, presently an insignificant stream that flows through the state of Haryana and dries up in the desert of Rajasthan, which is an extension of Thar-Parker desert. It should be borne in mind that the five rivers of Punjab are very important. This vast area hummed with Aryan activity. It is no exaggeration that it is one of the most fertile regions in the world easily comparable with the Nile valley of Egypt and the Tigris-Euphrates valley of Mesopotamia.

Even a cursory glance at the distribution of Vedic people is a good enough proof that they were mostly located in between the Kabul (Kubha) in the west and the Yamuna in the east in general. However, there was a heavy concentration between the tributaries of the Indus—the five rivers, viz. Śutudrī (Sutlej), Vipāśā (Beas), Paruṣṇī (Rāvī), Asiknī (Chenab) and Vitastā (Jhelum). Punjab is named after these five rivers. In the upper basin the Sarasvatī had her major tributaries Dṛṣadvatī (Chittang) and the Yamunā. Among these rivers, the most important was the Sarasvatī (Ghaggar in India and Hākrā in Pakistan). These areas were the cradle of Vedic culture nourished and nurtured by the Saravatī. In verity, the Sarasvatī was the river par excellence and been justly described as *nadītamā* (*Ṛv. II.41.16). The reference to it occurs very frequently in the Ṛgveda. It has also been described as joining the sea (Ṛv*. VI.12.8; VII.95.2). The satellite photographs of this vast region go to show that it was definitely a very large river, some 8 to 10 kms. wide and joined the Gulf of Kutch. Above all, it was not a tributary of the Indus. It was a great river in its own right. The most illustrious of the Bharatas, who have given their name to India as Bhārata had settled in the region between the Sarasvatī and the Yamunā.

Now let us have a look at the Indus Valley civilization. This civilization intruded into the Gangetic valley in the East (upto Varanasi and Ghazipur) coursed along the Ghaggar, Wahindat through Bikaner and Bahavalpur in the south-east extended over Saurashtra and Surat in the South, the Makran coast in Baluchistan in the West and stretched upto the lower limits of the present Russia including the whole of Afghanistan in the North. The Indus Civilization covered enormous area and exhibited numerous phases, contours and complexions of growth and development. Naturally, it represented the most complex culture of ancient times.

The excavations carried out on different sites have brought out a number of things which bear testimony to the existence of a developed urban culture in this vast region. The use of burnt bricks for building residential houses on an ostentatious as well as utilitarion and regulated pattern, passion for sanitation and ablution reflected in private wells, baths, privies, pipes, soak pits, sullage jars, covered drains with man-holes and elaborate provisions for public bath. Temples were marked by the absence of an imposing structure; the sanctity of bull and Pipal was the hall mark of religious creed and artistic orientation. The system of peculiar figures appearing on scales and scripts and the like distinguishes it from its Sumerian and Egyptian counterparts and proves its own individual and integrated evolution. Archaeologists maintain that the pattern of life in all townships discovered so far is more or less the same, with variations, largely insignificant, conditioned by the local climate, topography and other natural phenomenon and factors.

So far as the nomenclature of this civilization is concerned, one group of scholars calls it the Indus Valley civilization for the simple reason that the first site of the existence of this civilization was discovered around the Sindhu and its tributaries. Another group of scholars and archaeologists calls it Harappan culture. This view is based on the ground that similarities in the pattern of life in Mohenjo-daro and Harappa have also been found at such places as Ropar, Kalibangan and Lothal which do not lie in the Indus basin. Since Harappa was the first site from where a city buried under earth was discovered, it was thought proper to designate that culture as Harappan culture

The origin and authenticity of authorship of Harappan culture or Indus Valley civilization is a question that has given rise to much controversy. Sir Mortimar Wheeler is of the opinion that it was an 'explosive phenomenon.' Robert Heine Geldern holds that it was 'a sudden emergence without any trace of prior development.' W.A. Fairservis maintains that 'though the Indus Valley Civilization is the most Indianized, its essential roots are unquestionably Iranian.' Subscribing to the view of Fairservis, Dr. Buddha Prakash pleads that the Indus Valley Civilization is the culmination of a long process of social evolution originating from the rural habitations of the Indo-Iranian regions. It emerged from the same rural complex, which is common to the Indus-Valley and Iranian plateau embracing adjacent regions.

On the basis of the examination of the skulls of the people massacred in the streets of the city, it has been inferred by some scholars that it had a mixed population. Of those skulls three are defined as proto-Austroloid, six as Mediterranean, one as of the Mongolian Stock and four perhaps as Alpine. The features of the remains from cemetery H at Harappa are comparable to those of the proto-Austroloids of Mohenjo-daro. According to Dr. Guha, the Harappa remains demonstrate the presence of a non-Armenoid and Armenoid-Alpine race. The discovery of a single skull of a child at Mohenjo-daro led scholars to draw different conclusions. According to Piggott the Alpine type on this site is the same as represented at Sialk in Iran. Hrozny holds that the population of the Indus Valley represented a mixutre of Semetic and Indo-European peoples.

Other group of scholars identifies the people of Indus-Valley with the Dravidians. Dr. S.K. Chatterjee is of the opinion that the Indus-Valley Civilization is Dravidian in character. According to him, there is a pocket of Dravidian speaking people in Baluchistan in the Brahui. It is a surviving fragment of a very widespread Dravidian tract which extends from Baluchistan and Sind through Rajputana and Malwa into the present-day Maratha country and the Dravidian lands of the South. It extended north and north east in the Punjab and the Ganges Valley and probably also North-West through Afghanistan into Iran.

However, Dr. Chatterji's view has been rejected by most of the scholars on the following grounds:

(i) The Brahuis, though speaking a Dravidian language are of Turko-Iranian origin and are ethnically distinct from the people of Central and Southern India.

(ii) There is no evidence in support of the view that these people lived there in the 3rd or the 2nd millennium B.C. On the other hand, there is evidence of posting of South Indian regiments in the northern parts of the empire during the Kuṣāṇa period. A burial of the warriors of this regiment has been found at Kalalgyr I.

(iii) There is no evidence of any civilization analogous to that of the Indus Valley in the South among the Dravidians.

Some of their customs, as those of burial, differ from those of the Indus Valley people. In the Indus Valley only the poorer sections of the society buried their dead and others cremated them. Among the Dravidians burial was the prevalent form of disposing of the dead. In the Indus Valley ashes of the cremated used to be kept in large-wide-mouthed urns, containing a number of smaller vessels, bones of animals and of birds, fish and a variety of small objects such as beads, bangles and figurines and so on and sometime mixed with charcoal ashes (Sir John Marshall, *Mohenjo-daro and the Indus Valley Civilization*, Vol. 1. p. 86). A.L. Basham has also repudiated the Dravidian theory. According to him, historians have regarded the civilization of Mohenjo-daro and Harappa as Dravidian. He argues that rituals like bathing, phallic worship, the mother Goddess and the sacred bull are not essentially Dravidian. The cranial evidence from the Harappan sites is not in line with that of modern South India. In fact, there is now no Dravidian or Aryan race. The two terms are used only in linguistic and cultural contexts. (A.L. Basham, "Some Reflections on Dravidians and Aryans", *Bulletin of Instt. of the Historical Research*, Madras, Part II, 1963).

The above views regarding the identification of the authors of the Indus Valley civilization or Harappan culture are not tenable. They cannot be taken as authentic as they are based on mere hypotheses unsupported by any literary evidence. On the other hand literary evidence amply demonstrates that the Sapta-Sindhu region was the cradle of Aryan culture from the very beginning.

Until 1922, Archaeologists thought that before the rise of the Maurya Empire, a well developed and flourishing civilization had existed in India for at least one thousand years. It may be noted that of the structural monuments erected during those ages not one structure has survived save the cyclopean walls of Rajgriha (Marshall and Wheeler, *The Indus Civilization*, p. 1). This was before the Indus sites were excavated. Since the discovery of the Indus remains, a small portion of the missing chapter was found out. But even then the idea that the "Indo-Aryans" invaded the Punjab in the middle of the second millennium B.C. could not be changed. Sir John Marshall informed the scientific world about the existence of a civilization which he termed as "Pre-Aryan". According to him, the Vedic Indians were late comers in the region and "the Indus peoples of the fourth and third millennium B.C. were in possession of a highly developed culture in which no vestige of the 'Indo-Aryan' influence is to be found" (Marshall, *Mohenjo-daro and Indus Valley Civilization*, Vol. I). Sir John held that this civilization was long anterior to the Vedas and has put the anterior date of the Indus civilization to the later first quarter of the III millennium B.C. In contrasting the Indus civilization with the Vedic he found the divergences between the two, and held that so far as Sind is concerned "there is ample and convincing proof that the whole country from North to South was permeated in Chalcholithic age by a long protrected civilization which we have uncovered at Mohenjo-daro and Harappa" (Ibid). He further stated: "In my own view nothing has yet been found either at Mohenjo-daro or Harappa that conflicts with the orthodox theory that the "Indo-Aryans" entered Punjab about the middle of the second millenium B.C. But from the picture we get in the Vedas of the pre-Aryan population, I decline to think that the Indus civilization could have been but a mere shadow of its former self" (Ibid). Thus, he held the orthodox viewpoint and affirmed 1500 B.C. as the date of the arrival of the "Indo-Aryan" races in India. This view has been accepted by many occidental scholars including Sir Mortimar Wheeler and Stuart Piggot and with great zeal they support Sir John's view.

The conclusions arrived at by Sir John Marshall may be summed up as follows:

1. The Indus Valley civilization was formed and controlled by pre-Aryan people mentioned in the Ṛgveda, in which no vestige of 'Indo-European' influence is to be found. Their civilization was long anterior in date to the Vedic civilization.
2. He found nothing to change his viewpoint that the 'Indo-Aryan' invasion occurred in about the middle of the second millenium B.C. (in fact he fixed the date precisely to 1500 B.C.) from the relics dug out at the Indus sites.
3. The Indus Valley civilization was in the chalcolithic stage of culture.
4. He found dissimilarities in contrast between the Vedic and the Indus civilizations.

Now, there are some questions, which strike us in view of the conclusions arrived at by Sir John Marshall. They are: Who were the "pre-Aryan" people mentioned in the Ṛgveda? Did they form the Indus civilization? Further, the question of pre-Aryan people can only arise on the assumption that there was an 'Aryan' invasion around 1500 B.C. Still further, was Vedic culture noticeable in the Indus civilization and was it anterior in date to the Vedic or the 'Aryan' civilization?

It is hardly controvertible that the Vedic people had been living in and around the region where the Indus civilization was unveiled. Prior to the great Deluge and even before that (up to the last glaciation or pluvid), Indian dynasties had been reigning there. Thus there can be no question of 'Pre-Aryan' people in that particular region at least since Vedic Sudāsa to the time of Bhārata battle. Evidence shows that diverse tribes of people were living in and around the region during the Vedic period and they might have had linguistic-cultural differences with the Vedic Indians. The Brahuis, the prot-Austroloids and some Mongoloid groups of people also lived nearby. Vedic Indians had differences with them and the proto-Austroloids had altogether different cultures. May be that these differences led to fierce fights, referred to in the Vedas. The time when the proto-Austroloids entered India cannot be and has not been precisely determined. They might have entered from the north-African coast in days long gone by. The racial movement from African coast to the east towards Melanesia has also been verified by anthropologists. Some anthropologists hold that this movement started after the legendary Atlantis and Lemuria went under the sea at some remote past. Irrespective of the happenings, the ethnic similarity of these dark people with the Australian aborigines is a proven fact. The migratory movements of these people have also received scientific support. However, this possibility cannot be ruled out that some of them stayed in India. While in transit and during their stay they had to fight the Vedic Indians for their very existence. The question is: Were they the "Pre-Aryans", who built the Indus cities? If not, who were the people then?

From Vedic evidence, it is apparent that the Vedic Indians looked down upon the 'Dāsas', 'Dasyus', 'Rākṣasas' and 'Asuras'. A section of them were phallus-worshippers, some worshipped mad Gods, some smeared their bodies with the blood of sacrificed animals, others shouted loudly and could see better in the darkness of night but none performed the sacrificial rites according to the Vedic code. There is nothing new about Phallus worship. Phallus worshippers there have been in the hoary past and they still exist in many parts of the world. Satanic orgies have not been an isolated phenomenon in the Greco-Roman civilization and even in modern times observance of Satanic mass and also such orgies and cults are often discovered in the West including UK, USA and France. Are they, then, to be branded as 'non-Europeans'? Should they be considered as belonging to different racial types? In fact, these people are renegades and deserters from the established religious traditions. Similarly, during Vedic times also, some people indulged in such practices for various reasons; some performed such rites to acquire super-natural powers, some tried to ward off dangers and scare away enemies and still some resorted to wayward ways for reasons not known even now. It was natural that some of the Vedic Indians also indulged in such practices for reasons of their own. Such people have been referred to in the Ṛgveda derisively. It is significant to note that whenever they were spotted and identified, they were turned out and exiled from the country. Thus the words 'Dāsas', 'Dasyus' and 'Rākṣasas' have no ethnic or anthropological significance to indicate people belonging to different races. They were deviants and represented all those who acted outside the Vedic social and religious code.

A number of examples can be given to show deviation from the Vedic code of conduct. Rāvaṇa, the son of a Vedic Ṛṣi, was a Rākṣasa, his step brother Kubera was a Yakṣa. Vena, one of the early Vedic Kings and father of the great Pṛthu was called a Dānava. Kalmaśpāda, another Aryan king and the son of a king, was a Rākṣasa and Bali, who was to become the king of gods in the next Manvantara was called a Daitya. Rāvaṇa married the daugbter of Maya, the Dānava. Kṛṣṇa himself married the daughter of Jambuvān, the bear king and the sister of Vāsuki, the Nāga king married a Brāhmaṇa. Lakṣmaṇa, the brother of Rāma, fought with Lavaṇa, the Rākṣasa king of Mathurā and had relationship with most of the royal families of India. Kṛṣṇa killed Kaṁsa, the king of Mathurā, his own maternal uncle, who was a Daitya. Obviously, such epithets were used to denote people, who did not follow the traditional and orthodox religious and social code. However, the existence of the Mongoloids in nearby areas cannot be ruled out. They belonged to Nepal, Turkistan and China and they were also termed as Disas, noseless people and the like. Since their culture was different from that of Vedic Indians, they were also looked upon as inferior. Even the children of disciples of Viśvāmitra, the great sage, were described as 'Dasyus'. On the other hand, there is an example of the son of a woman of easy virtue, who received the status of a Vedic ṛṣi and was allowed to compose hymns because she followed the orthodox code. The Vedic Indians had been living in the land since the last glaciation or pluvid of 10,000 B.C. Hence there could not have been any pre-Aryan civilization existent in this area, conquered by the invading Aryans around 1500 B.C. The meagre skeletal remains found at Mohenjo-daro and Harappa are not enough to prove that this civilization was founded by proto-Austroloids. A very interesting factor known as the 'freak of Nature' has not been taken into account. Genetically speaking, Nature shows grostesque, wayward and wanton ways. The skeletal remains under reference might have been a freak or vagary of Nature. Further, the majority of the skeletal remains belong to the eastern Mediterranean group of people. They belonged to the same ethnic type as the Vedic Indians. As such, the conclusion arrived at by Sir John Marshall that the civilization was 'pre-Aryan' is farfetched and untenable. As to the point that no vestige of 'Aryan' influence is found and that the civilization was long anterior in date to the Vedic one is being taken up in the pages that follow.

Sir John's second conclusion that he found no evidence to change his view that 'Indo-Aryan' invasion occurred at about the middle of the 2nd millennium B.C. does not stand the test of evidence. From the evidence of the Greek historians including Megasthenes it is clear that (i) they found no evidence of a tradition (either from the Persian or from the Indian source.) that India was ever invaded from outside and (ii) that since Dionysus Indians reckoned 153 kings and 6453 Sandrokottas (Chandra Gupta Maurya) a contemporary of Alexander. Thus, from independent sources, it is noticed (i) that there was no invasion in India and (ii) that India had an uninterrripted history from about the middle of 8th millennium B.C. i.e. from about the last post-glaciation period. Thus, the much propagated and touted theory of 'Indo-European' invasion of India by about 1500

B.C. falls short of factual evidence and as such is no more than a speculation, a wild guess or a superimposition. Although Max Müller revised his ideas about 'Aryan' racial theory later, his followers stick to the earlier view. They argue that the 'Aryan' race invaded India by the middle of the second millennium B.C. to fit in with their pre-conceived view.

It is a well-known truism that if one goes on repeating a falsehood over and over again, it would, in the end pass for truth. Ironically enough, this is exactly what happened with several historians or Indologists with regard to the so-called Aryan invasion. They drew facile conclusions that these migratory called Aryans came to India and settled near the Indus, without examining the fact that there existed no such race as 'Indo-Europeans' in the Middle East at the time. The only race that existed in this area was the 'Mediterranean' or the 'Proto-Mediterranean' types, who spread out over a wide area from England to India and some had become fatnous in history by that time. They tailored a theory that these races migrated form the West. In order to show the validity of their theory they sought to make the migratory 'Aryans' invade the Punjab, where they met with some noseless uncultured non-Aryan people. This theory is contrived rather than evolved in the light of facts.

The startling discovery of the Indus civilization at a place where, according to the pet theory, the 'white' or 'blonde' 'Indo-Europeans' or 'Aryans' found a dark complexioned noseless uncultured people on their arrival surprised the 'Indo-European' theorists, specially those who advocated that the 'Aryans' migrated into India sometime in the middle of the second millennium B.C. Human thought, as it is, cannot easily deviate from a set line which it adopts or considers correct. This has caused much damage to scientific investigations and has stood in the way of arriving at correct conclusions. The pre-conceived idea that the 'white', 'Indo-European' race entered India by 1500 B.C. has also led scholars and investigators like Sir John Marshall, Sir Mortimar Wheeler and Stuart Piggott to find 'non-Aryan' or 'pre-Aryan' orientation in the Indus civilization. The meagre evidence of partial destruction of some of the sites to the West including the Indus ones by burning is by no means conclusive evidence that the 'Indo-Europeans' or the 'Indo-Aryans' were responsible for the same. The Ṛgvedic evidence has been twisted to fit in with their pre-conceived view and this has rendered the conclusion unscientific. The Indus civilization was dug out in an area where the Vedic Indians had settled. The township of Mohenjo-daro was situated on the west side of Sindhu, the Indus and 400 miles to the northwest was the township of Harappa on the eastern side of Paruṣṇi, now known as Rāvi. The battle of ten kings (Dāśarājña), in which many tribes of those days were involved was fought near this place. Assuming for a moment that the Indo-Europeans migrated into India about 1500 B.C. and destroyed various 'Puras' or 'Forts', built of stone belonging to the Dāsa king Śambara, it appears strange that the invaders instead of permanently occupying the townships deserted these and allowed them to be ruined. It is also strange that none of the Indus sites so far excavated was occupied for a considerable period of time after the initial destruction supposed to have been caused by Indra. This is quite unnatural and illogical. It has been pointed out that the Vedic clans had settled in the vicinity of these sites and had built hutments instead of occupying the old deserted towns. Nowhere in the history of the world has such a thing ever happened. It sounds fantastic. Nowhere has an invading army, after destroying the population of a town as stated by the excavators of the Indus sites, allowed such beautiful townships to be ruined. It is unbelievable that a migrating population, who had left their own hearth and home and occupied townships such as Mohenjo-daro and Harappa and also others between Sutkagendor and Ruper by sheer force would, instead of permanently occupying it, leave them after a little while and allow it to be ruined and build hutments nearby and reside there. The clans of Jadu, Anu, Turvasu, Druhyu and others lived in and around the area either as contemporaries or as settlers at some later date. How is it that they were not aware of these two big townships in spite of their being within a range of a few miles and on the bank of the same river? It is simply incredible that they would not speak about these towns and fortresses. Hence the inescapable conclusion is that the townships belonged to one or another of these clans and could not be of an anterior date.

It is well-known that time is the most powerful wrecker of things. In course of time these townships came to a natural end. It is also true that rivers change their courses, mountains and deserts undergo changes in their shapes and dimensions. This at one time a very great culture came to a sad end when the mighty river Sarasvatī (as described in the Ṛgveda) went dry due to metamorphic changes in the earth. There is one more logical inference explaining the end of this culture. There was a time when none cared for others. This can conceivably be no other time than the time of Bhārata war of 3137 B.C., when the whole nation was in turmoil and most of the young generation was annihilated in the great war. This is the only time that can be fixed reasonably for the beginning of the gradual decline of the city sites when during the turbulent tumultuous political upheavals and events coming as an aftermath of the war. The gradual destruction of vast townships went unnoticed. There is also a possibility that it was the Purāṇic township of 'Sauva', which Kṛṣṇa and Arjuna had destroyed. The excavators have commented that at the later stage of city's life the authorities of the municipal administration got slack and they did not observe strictness to check the deterioration of the drainage system and unauthorized constructions including factories sprang up within city limits. This is a clear indication of political turbulence in and around the country. The question is: When could there have been such a time in proto-historic India except after the battle of the ten kings that Dāśarājña war and after the Bhārata war?

Thus making an allowance for some five to six hundred years for the anticipated period of natural decay of such big townships the limit of their existence comes to about 2500 B.C. This is clear from the evidence that extensive trade which existed with Sumeria stopped almost altogether after the Sargonid period around 2350 B.C. The upper limit of the civilization should, therefore, be raised at least beyond the period of Sudāsa of the battle of the 10 kings fame till further excavations, by at least 500 years. This would bring the upper limit to about 4500–5000 B.C. and from the present state of our knowledge the existence of Indus civilization should cover the period from 5000 B.C. to 2500 B.C.

The views of the Western scholars regarding the identification of the authors of the Indus-Valley civilization or Harappan culture fail to stand to reason. They cannot be accepted as authentic since they are based on mere hypotheses unsupported by any literary evidence. On the other hand, literary evidences demonstrably show that the Sapta-Sindhu area was the heart of Aryan culture from the very beginning. In course of time, one stream of Aryans got separated from the main stream and settled in the land called Iran, a corrupt form of Aryan. So long as this group remained in touch with the Indo-Aryans it pursued the same culture and spoke the same language. But when it was cut off from the main group its culture witnessed some deviation from that of the main group. The language of this group, too, underwent a change. Dr. Narayana Bhavam Rao Paogi on the basis of literary, philological mythological, geological and archaeological evidences has attempted to prove that the centre of Aryan culture had been in the basin of the Sarasvatī in Saptasindhu region.

Here the attention of scholars is drawn towards the following facts. It is far from truth to hold that the Indus Valley civilization was a pre-Aryan civilization and the collapse of that civilization was caused by militant marauding Aryans:

(i) Eminent scholars like Bal Gangadhar Tilak and Jacobi on the basis of astronomical evidences have endeavoured to establish the fact that the upper limit of the composition of Vedic hymns goes back to 6000 B.C. Before the composition of Vedic mantras the Aryans had already developed a culture conspicuous by its advanced thinking about the life, life after death, the cosmos and its regulated functioning. Astronomical investigations and explorations are more authentic evidences than other tools regarding the determination of dates of any culture or civilization.

(ii) Great scholers like Narayana Bhavam Rao Paogi, Abinash Chandra Das, Dr. Sampurnanand etc. on the basis of literary and geological evidences have sought to establish that the Saptasindhu region was the cradle of Aryan culture. Avesta makes frequent references to *Hapahindavah*, which proves the anteriority of Saptasindhu region and its culture to the other civilizations of the period.

(iii) Prior to the advent of Vikram era, Kali era (Samvatsara) was more popular in India. Even after the Vikrama samvatsara started coming into use, the Kali era continued to be used by many to indicate the date of their writings. In a manuscript of the commentary on the Śatapatha Brāhmaṇa by Harisvāmī, the date of its composition is written as 3740 Kali varṣa. At the present time 5098 Kali varṣa is going on. It means Harisvāmī wrote his commentary on the Śatapatha Brāhmaṇa 1358 years ago in 638 A.D. From this it is evident that we have an unbroken record of events and the year calculation from 3102 B.C., the commencement of the Kali varṣa. As per Indian tradition preserved in the purāṇas and other commentaries on the Vedas, Kṛṣṇa Dvaipāyaṇa Vyāsa was the first person, who collected the Vedic Mantras composed by Vedic seers long before him and compiled them in four Saṁhitās. For determining the date of Vedas, this should be taken as an authentic line of demarcation between Mantra period and the Saṁhitā period. Kṛṣṇa Dvaipāyana Vyāsa stands on a line where the mantra period came to a close and the era of compiling mantras of the predecessor seers commenced. Since Vyāsa flourished before 3102 B.C. from where Kali era started, it follows that the Indus Valley Civilization is contemporary to the Saṁhitā and Brāhmaṇa period. This period encompasses approximately 1500 years between 3102 B.C. and 1500 B.C. The entire mantra period during which several generations of the seers like Viśvāmitra, Vaśiṣṭha, Vāmadeva, Bhāradvāja, Atri and Kaṇva etc. had contributed a large number of Mantras, had come to an end long before the so-called Indus Valley civilization came into being or Harappan culture flourished. As a matter of fact, the Indus Valley civilization was nothing but the Aryan or Vedic culture in the Brāhmaṇa and the post-Brāhmaṇa period.

(iv) Dr. Ram Bilas Sharma, an authority on West Asia and the Ṛgveda, puts forth his views thus: (a) the Sarasvatī had been a huge river in those days. The primary cause of the fall of the Indus civilization is its getting dried up. In the Ṛgveda the river has been described as full of water. As such, the Ṛgveda is prior to this civilization. (b) Voiced aspirates sounds like घ, ध, भ are still in currency in India and they are nowhere to be found in the Indo-European family. The sounds of the original language are still alive in India only. भ is the original sound not प or त, (c) When all the elements of a language undergo a change, the minimum affected element is the sound. The original Sanskrit sounds are still prevalent in colloquial slangs. In India there are 3 linguistic zones—East, West and Central. The sound of अ is spoken as ओ in the East (कोऽस्ति in Sanskrit). अ remains अ in the centre and changes to ए in the west, like सौ for शत

and सैंकड़ा, भगिनी, बहिनी, बोन and बेन are the changed forms of one single word. (d) T. Burrow, the famous linguist, supports this view. Dr Sharma opines that the origin of Sanskrit is Punjab or the North Haryana. Later on they shifted to Pañcāl (West Uttar Pradesh near Bareilly) and its main reason is the deluge and this was somewhere in the 4th millennium B.C. (e) The excavations of the Sarasvatī basin have not been completely carried out and more evidences of Vedic culture could be discovered. (f) The maps of Vedic India and the places attributed to the Indus Valley Civilization are very similar. (g) The two cultures coincide greatly and it is not possible without their similarity. (h) Some of the words of Sanskrit (from the Ṛgveda) are quite similar (in Babylonian and Sumerian languages. A terminated form *Apsu* (water) is used for water in Babylonian whereas it becomes *Abju* in Sumerian. When clothes made of cotton could be exported, then why not language? This element of language reached Sumeria from India. *Pura* is a word used for a place in Sanskrit, in Sumerian the word *ura* conveys the same meaning. These are Vedic words and that they went outside through Harappa is beyond doubt.

These evidences prove that Aryans were original inhabitants of the Saptasindhu region, not the wreckers of the land. Is it not an irony that the original inhabitants of a place have been sought to be presented and paraded as outsiders and invaders of their homeland? If it can be taken as true that the Aryans played havoc with their homeland, it follows that they were not civilized. And indeed civilized enough the Aryans were not to wreck their own homeland. The land was pillaged by marauders and invaders. It is obvious that distortion of facts, misinterpretation of evidences and misrepresentation of historical events and anthropological phenomena have cast a pall of ambiguity and confusion over the Indus Valley civilization with a view to prove that the other civilizations of the world are anterior to this civilization and that the Aryans like other invaders, were also invaders. Is not it fantastic to say that the Aryans have been branded as marauders and wreckers of their own homeland? Let alone civilized people even birds and beasts do not damage or destroy their nests, shelters and lairs. Vandals do it and India has been a victim of regular vandalism through the ages. Aryan culture remains unravished and untarnished till today despite vicissitudes it has passed through. To try to prove that the Aryans were invaders is the travesty of truth and betrays lack of intellectual integrity and intrusion of partisanship in interpretation. It is nothing short of a divine dispensation that the vital elements of Indian culture are existent in their pristine purity and splendour.

Bibliography

[1] Buddha Prakash, *Ṛgveda and the Indus Valley Civilization*, VVRI, Hoshiarpur, 1966

[2] T. Burrow, "Dravidian and the decipherment of the Indus script", *Antiquity*, **43**, 1969.

[3] W.A. Fairservis (Jr.), *The Roots of Ancient India*, 2nd Edn., Chicago, 1975

[4] John Marshal, *Mohanjo-Daro and the Indus Civilization*, 3 Vols., A. Probsthain, London, 1931.

[5] Stuart Piggot, Notes on Certain Pins and Maceheads from Harappa, *Ancient India*, **4**, 1948, 26–40.; *Prehistoric India*, Penguin, Baltimore, 1950; (Ed.) *The Down of Civilization*, London and New York, 1961.

[6] R.E.M. Wheeler, *Civilization of Indus Valley and Beyond*, McGraw-Hill, London, 1966.

[7] Ernest Mackay, Early Indus Civilization, Indological Book Corporation, N. Delhi, 1976.

[8] A.N. Chandra, *The Rigvedic Culture and the Indus Civilization*, Ratna Prakashan, Calcutta, 1980.

[9] Bhagwan Singh, *The Vedic Harappans*, Aditya Prakashan, N. Delhi, 1995.

[10] Ramvilas Sharma, *Bhāṣā aur Samāj*, N. Delhi, 1961.

The Indus-Sarasvati Civilization: Significance of This Name

SHRIKANT G. TALAGERI
C/5 Saraswat Cooperative Bldgs., Gamdevi, Mumbai-400 007, India

The Vedic culture and the Indus-Sarasvati culture, though they, singly and jointly, represent extremely significant high points in Indian history and civilization, do not represent the earliest foundations or wellsprings of this history and civilization, but only phases in it. The original homeland was in the interior of North India. The Vedic culture, as well as all Aryan (Indo-European) cultures outside India, were the result of a westward movement in two phases: firstly, from the interior of India to the Indus-Sarasvati area, and, secondly, from the Indus-Sarasvati area to lands beyond.

Introduction

The name 'Indus-Sarasvati Civilization' is one which is being increasingly used, albeit at present mostly by Hindu scholars, for what has hitherto been called the 'Harappan' or 'Indus Valley' civilization.

The use of this name is necessary for following reasons:

1. It is more appropriate than the earlier ones. The earlier names were used at a time when the excavated archaeological sites pertaining to this civilization were found mainly on the banks of the Indus. But the situation has changed now, with an ever increasing number of sites being found on what has been shown, by satellite photography, to be the banks of the now extinct Sarasvati river which dried up in the second millennium B.C.
2. It brings into focus the point that the Sarasvati river was the centre of this civilization. This alters the position of this civilization vis-a-vis the Vedic civilization. Hitherto it was presumed that the 'Indus' civilization represented a 'pre-Aryan' one which was invaded and destroyed by barbarian 'Aryans' pouring in from the northwest But the fact that both the 'Indus' and the Vedic civilizations flourished mainly on the banks of the Sarasvati, and that the 'Indus' civilization declined with the drying up of the Sarasvati, makes it clear that the Vedic and 'Indus' civilizations form a continuum in that order.

But the question which arises from all this, and one which we must face head-on, is: what is the exact position we are to assign to this civilization in Indian, and, more significantly, Indo-European history? Is the Vedic civilization to be considered identical with the Indus-Sarasvati civilization; and, if so, does the area of this civilization represent the original homeland of the 'Aryan' (Indo-European) family of languages?

Unfortunately, most Hindu scholars are agreed on these propositions. They take the Indus-Sarasvati area, the alleged Sapta-Sindhava of the Rigveda, to be the original homeland of the Vedic Aryans, who spread their Vedic culture, from this centre, both into the rest of India as well as far and wide outside India.

The Actual Situation

The homeland of the original Indo-European language speaking people, whatever their race or races, was in the interior of North India. Some of the different groups of these Indo-Europeans went and settled in the north western parts, the Indus-Sarasvati region and beyond. Of these emigrants to the northwest, one group (whom we may therefore call the Vedic Aryans) developed the Vedic culture; while some other groups emigrated from this area to Iran, Central Asia, west Asia and Europe, thereby spreading the Indo-European languages to these lands. *The unique urban civilization, which we refer to as the Indus-Sarasvati civilization, represents a later phase of a western branch of this Vedic civilization*

Hindu scholars must therefore recognize that the Vedic culture and the Indus-Sarasvati culture, though they, singly and jointly, represent extremely significant high points in Indian history and civilization, do *not* represent the earliest foundations or wellsprings of this history and civilization, but only phases in it.

So far as this question of the original homeland of the Aryan (Indo-European) family of languages is concerned there are three versions:

1. The official version is that the original homeland was somewhere in South Russia. One major group—the proto-Indo-Iranians—migrated to, and settled down in, Central Asia. Much later, they migrated in two directions: to Iran (the proto-Iranians) and India (the proto-Indo-Aryans). The Indus—Sarasvati area represents the first phase of Indo-European (i.e. Indo-Aryan or Vedic) civilization in India, before they migrated further eastwards.
2. The most generally accepted Hindu version is that the Indus-Sarasvati area was the original homeland, from where the Aryans (Indo-Europeans) migrated both east and west.
3. Our version is that the original homeland was in the interior of North India. The Vedic culture, as well as all Aryan (Indo-European) cultures

outside India, were the result of a westward movement in two phases: firstly, from the interior of India to the Indus-Sarasvati area, and, secondly, from the Indus-Sarasvati area to lands beyond.

There is no archaeological evidence proving any of the above versions, but there definitely is clear literary evidence proving:

(a) The emigration of the Vedic Aryans from the interior of India to the northwest;

(b) The emigration of the extra-Indian Aryans (i.e. the Iranians, and sections of Europeans) from the northwest to their historical habitats.

This literary record is preserved in both the Puranas and the Rigveda.

Evidence in the Puranas

The evidence in the Puranas is clear and unambiguous.

In the words of Pargiter[1], the preeminent western authority on the Puranic traditions, "Indian tradition knows nothing of any Aila or Aryan invasion of India from Afghanistan, nor of any gradual advance from thence eastwards.... tradition.... makes the earliest connexion of the Vedas to be with the eastern region and not with the Punjab...." (pp. 298, 302).

Pargiter's analysis of the Puranic tradition shows him that "the Ailas or Aryans began at Allahabad, conquered and spread out north-west, west and south, and had by Yayati's time occupied precisely the region famed as Madhyadesa.... They expanded afterwards into the Punjab and East Afghanistan, into West India and the northwest Dekhan, into East and South Bihar, and into Bengal" (p. 296).

The tradition "distinctly asserts that there was an Aila outflow of the Druhyus through the northwest into the countries beyond, where they founded various kingdoms" (p. 298). The Aryans found outside India are therefore the result of "an outflow of people from India before the fifteenth century B.C." (p.300).

Not only does Pargiter show the direction of movement of the Aryans in the Puranas; he even, *without realising* it, pinpoints the exact identity of the Vedic people from among the different ancient peoples named in these texts. Pargiter rather arbitrarily decides that the Ailas in the Puranas are Aryans, the Aikshvakus Dravidians and the Saudyumnas Austrics. However, in referring to the Vedas, he makes certain observations which, if carried to their logical end, would have enabled him to identify the Puranic identity of the Vedic Aryans. About the Rigveda, he observes that "the bulk of the Rigveda was composed in

---

[1] F. E. Pargiter: *Ancient Indian Historical Tradition*, reprinted by Motilal Banarsidas, New Delhi, 1962.

the great development of Brahmanism that arose under the successors of king Bharata who reigned in the upper Ganges-Jumna doab and plain'' (p. 297). Earlier, referring to the Bharata Kings of North Panchala, he observes: "They and their successors are the kings who play a prominent part in the Rigveda" (p.275).

The fact is that the Puranas name the different related peoples who inhabited ancient India. These people are classified as descendants of ten 'sons' of the ancient emperor Manu Vaivasvata. Of these ten groups of descendants, only two are of historical importance: The descendants of Ila (the Ailas or the 'lunar' race) and the descendants of Ikshvaku (the Aikshvakus or the 'solar' race)

The Ailas (the "lunar" race) are further divided into five main peoples: the Yadus, Turvasus, Anus, Druhyus and Purus.

The Purus were the Vedic Aryans, and, from among them, one group known as the Bharatas were in particular the Rigvedic Aryans.

The Yadus and Turvasus (as well as the Ikshvakus or the solar race) were the non-Vedic Aryans of the rest of nothern India in the interior.

The Anus and Druhyus were the Aryans who emigrated from India, and who became the linguistic ancestors of the Iranians and the Europeans.

The Puranas record the first major emigration of the Druhyus from India: from Afghanistan northwards "into the countries beyond, where they founded various kingdoms", as Pargiter puts it. The trail of these Druhyus, it may be noted, is from northwestern India to Central Asia and then further afield (i.e., to West Asia and Europe via South Russia). This documented emigration is in exactly the opposite direction to the purely hypothetical migration proposed by the academic scholars (of Aryans from South Russia to Central Asia to northwestern India).

Evidence in the Rigveda

The evidence in the Puranas is clear and unambiguous. But the academic scholars reject it on the ground that it is incompatible with the more reliable evidence in the Rigveda, which they claim clearly shows a movement from the northwest to the east.

Thus, Pusalkar[2], after describing these Puranic traditions, rejects their geographical details: "This traditional account of the Aryan expansion is, however, in conflict with the evidence of the Vedic texts. As has already been shown. . . there are good grounds to suppose that by the time the Rigveda was composed, the Aryans had not penetrated much further into the interior beyond

---

[2] A.D. Pusalkar: *The History and Culture of the Indian People*, Bharatiya Vidya Bhavan, Mumbai, Vol.1, The Vedic Age, 1965 print, p. 316.

the frontiers of the Punjab and Rajputana. . . (therefore) its (i.e. the Rigveda's) testimony is decidedly fatal to the geographical views assumed in the Puranas."

This is also the standard view of academic scholars in the west. Thus the commemorative volume[3], which devotes 37 pages to a study *'On The Localisation of Vedic Texts and Schools'* deals with the geography of the Rigveda in less than half a page. According to this, "the geographical area of the Rigveda is quickly characterized by mentioning some of the major rivers this text knows of: The Kubha, Krumu, Gomati, in the West (Kabul, Kurram, Gomal in E. Afghanistan and Pakistan); the seven rivers of the Punjab in the centre; the Yamuna and the Ganga in the East (only in a late passage) which excludes the areas, roughly speaking, East of Delhi: the Ganga-Yamuna Doab, and the tracts of land South of it" (pp. 175–176).

An examination of the geographical information in the Rigveda, however, shatters all these views.

We have undertaknen a thorough geographical and historical analysis of the material in the Rigveda in our book[4]. Without going into the details, the following picture clearly emerges from this analysis:

The Rigveda consists of ten Books known as Mandalas. These Mandalas were composed and compiled at different points of time. When these Mandalas are arranged chronologically, we get the following order:

The Early Family Mandalas:

1. Mandala 6 (The Bharadvaja Mandala)
2. Mandala 3 (The Vishvamitra Mandala)
3. Mandala 7 (The Vasishtha Mandala)

The Later Family Mandalas:

4. Mandala 4 (The Vamadeva Mandala)
5. Mandala 2 (The Gritsamada Mandala)
6. Mandala 5 (The Atri Mandala)

The Non-Family Mandalas:

7. Mandala 1 (The Shatarchin Mandala)
8. Mandala 8 (The Pragatha / Kanva Mandala)
9. Mandala 9 (The Pavamana Mandala)
10. Mandala 10

The Early Family Mandalas show a movement from an original homeland in

---

[3] Gilbert Pollet (Ed.): 'India and the Ancient World—History. Trade and Culture Before A.D. 650,' by the Department Orientalistiek, Leuven, 1987

[4] S.K. Talageri: *'The Rigveda—A Historical Analysis,'* Voice of India, New Delhi, 1998.

the east to the Punjab region: the Ganga is mentioned in the first two of these, and the Yamuna in the third of them. None of the three Mandalas refers to the rivers of the west (Kubha, Krumu, Gomati), or even to the Indus itself, even once. The first of them (Mandala 6), in fact, is centred wholly to the east of the Sarasvati river; the second one (Mandala 3) shows a movement across the two easternmost of the five rivers of the Punjab, Vipash (Beas) and Shutudri (Satlej); and the third of them (Mandala 7) shows a movement upto the next two rivers of the Punjab, Parushni (Ravi) and Asikni (Chenab).

The other Mandalas (the Later Family Mandalas and the non-Family Mandalas) show the Vedic Aryans settled over the whole of the Indus-Sarasvati region.

The Rigveda also records a major battle, known as the Dasharajna, in which the Vedic Aryans (Bharatas), led by their King Sudas, fight a confederation of ten tribes from among the Anus and Druhyus. These ten tribes are defeated on the banks of the Parushni and driven out from that region, whence they fan out westwards.

The names of these ten tribes clearly indicate the name of ten Aryan (Indo-European) peoples who, in later post-Rigvedic times, flourished or flourish in a continuous belt stretching westwards from the region of the Parushni (Ravi) right up to Southeastern Europe: the Vishanins (Pishachas), Pakthas (Pakhtoons), Bhalanas (Baluchis), Shivas (Khivs), Parshus (Persians), Parthavas (Parthians), Bhrigus (Phrygians), Druhyus (Druis or Celts, found in the Baltic area in ancient times), Alinas (Hellenes or ancient Greeks) and Shimyus (Sirmios or ancient Albanians). Incidentally, the name of another (eleventh) tribe from among the Anus, named in the Puranas and other ancient Sanskrit texts, clearly indicates the name of another such Aryan people: the Madras (Medes)

The evidence is clear: the movement of the Aryans was from east to west within India, and then westwards out of India.

The urban Indus-Sarasvati civilization, of which Indian archaeology is justifiably proud, represents a later post-Samhita Vedic phase, contemporaneous with the later Sutra texts: it is the land known as Mlecchadesha in these late and orthodox Sutras (Mleccha pronounced as Milakkha in the later Buddhist texts) and as Meluhha (pronounced Melukkha) in the Sumerian trade inscriptions.

Aryavarta: The Original Homeland of the Aryans (Linguistic Evidence)

RAM SWARUP SHARMA*
Reader, Deptment of Hindi
Deshbandhu College (University of Delhi), Delhi, India

The history of ancient India has been a puzzle for the Western scholars. The medieval invaders on this country have destroyed not only the ancient places of worship but also ruined the seats of learning like the old Universities of Takshshila and Nalanda and indiscriminately put to fire a number of ancient libraries. All such acts of barbarism have caused an irreparable loss of information and material to the extent that the true history before Buddha is not even traceable. The only reliable source of the history of the so called "Dark Age" is the Vedic literature and the structural forms of the language called Vedic Sanskrit. The question of Aryans' original homeland has been examined by scholars employing several yardsticks, like liguistics, archaeology, geology, geography, anthropology, mythology and flora and fauna, etc. Yet it needs an objective testing in the light of the new analytical method of linguistics, so that a colonial bias, often felt in the conclusions of most of the European scholars can be reexaminred. The present paper is an effort in this direction.

In 1786 A.D. Sir William Jones, as President of the Asiatic Society of Bengal, made his observations about the Sanskrit language in the following words:

> "The Sanskrit language, whatever be its antiquity, is of wonderful structure; more perfect than the Greek; more copious than Latin and more exquisitely refined than either; yet bearing to both of them a stronger affinity, both in the roots of verbs, and in the forms of grammar than could possibly have been produced by accident; so strong indeed, that no philologer could examine them all without believing them to have sprung from some common source, which perhaps no longer exists. There is a similar reason, though not quite so forcible, for supposing that both, the Gothic and the Celtic, though blended with a very different idiom, had the same origin with the Sanskrit; and the Old Persian might be added to the same family [1]."

The whole Jargon of Comparative Method and Reconstruction found its base in this pronouncement of Sir William Jones. No doubt his study of Sanskrit, inspired several Western scholars to peep into Indian history and literature through the classical literature available in Sanskrit, but at the same time the aforesaid observation also laid a foundation stone for future scholars to work on the

Residential Address: Ram Swarup Sharma, B22B, Kalkaji, New Delhi-110 019.

hypothesis that some proto language existed prior to Vedic Sanskrit. In Sir William Jones' statement, a few phrases are of great significance, e.g., "whatever be its antiquity", "to have sprung from some common source", "both the Gothic and Celtic . . . had the same origin with the Sanskrit; and the Old Persian might be added to the same family". No doubt, Sir William Jones had expressed his admiration of Sanskrit language and its literature in no uncertain terms, yet despite the proven antiquity of the language, he was not ready to accept its superiority to other ancient languages of the world in terms of grammaticalness, appropriateness and flexibility; otherwise he would not have placed Sanskrit on the same footing as that of Greek, Latin, Gothic, etc.

Prof. Max Muller was the first scholar to claim that the Aryans were originally the inhabitants of Central Asia region [2]. Though he has used comparative philology (now called comparative method in Historical Linguistics) as a tool for his analysis and conclusions, the reconstruction of an Indo-Aryan language as suggested by him is based on a strong conviction that the Aryans were invaders on Indian soil and had come from Central Asia.

In 1808, a German scholar Friederich Schlegel had declared in his work "user die sprache und weishiet der Inder" (On the language and philosiphy of the Indians) that Sanskrit is the mother of all languages. Even Franz Bopp (supposed to be the father of modern philology) admitted in 1820 that Sanskrit is nearer to some "original tongue" than Greek, Latin, etc. He says:

> "I do not believe that the Greek, Latin and other European languages are to be considered as derived from the Sanskrit in the state in which we find it in Indian books; I feel rather inclined to consider them altogether as subsequent variations of one original tongue, which, however, the Sanskrit has preserved more perfect than its kindred dialects [3]."

If Bopp's reference is to Panineeya Sanskrit in his statement, no one can disagree with him, because the original tongue as termed by him can by implication be nothing but Vedic Sanskrit. However, it was not the implied meaning of his statement. He, therefore, revised his opinion in 1845 which clearly shows his bias against Sanskrit vis-a-vis the European languages. He says:

> "I cannot, however, express myself with sufficient strength in guarding against the misapprehension of supposing that I wish to accord to Sanskrit universally the distinction of having preserved its original character. I have, on the contrary, often noticed in the earlier portion of this work and also in my *System of Conjugation* and in the *Annals of Oriental Literature* for the year 1820, that the Sanskrit has, in many points, experienced alterations where one or other of the European sister idioms has more truly transmitted to us the original form [4]."

It is evident that Bopp had not supported his hypothesis with reason. The matter did not end there. Gray propounded a new theory [3] that:

> "Lithuanian and Lettish alike are characterised by conservation in phonology and in the inflexion of the epithetologue, the vowel system of modern Lithuanian being, like that of Greek and Oscan, nearer to the Indo-European stage than in Vedic Sanskrit [5]."

Identical views are also expressed by Bal Krishna Ghosh [6]. The learned authors have first made a postulate that Greek and Latin are similar to IE in phonology and inflexional system and that Modern Lithuanian resembles Greek and Latin, hence Old Lithuanian must be nearest to IE. Is such a logic not fallacious and hence ridiculous? These authors are comparing two reconstructed languages, namely, IE and Old Lithuanian and are trying to deprive the real language (Vedic Sanskrit) of its due. Unfortunately, such self-contained illogical and colonial inferences have been prevailing over the last two centuries.

In Asia Minor, there is a place called Bogazkov (nearly 150 km from Angora) where a few records in Cuniform script had been excavated in 1893. This place was the capital of the Hittite kingdom (nearly 1365 B.C.) and thus the aforesaid records are supposed to have been written in Hittite language. In 1917, a Czech scholar B. Hrozny [7] proved that Hittite was contemporary to Indo-European. Hence the original language was termed Indo-Hittite, i.e., Sanskrit was dropped lower by one generation. This was all being done to prove that the Aryans were not the original inhabitants of India.

Even if the European chronology of languages be considered true (which the genuine Indian scholar will never accept) the period of Vedic Sanskrit is 1200 B.C. to 500 B.C. [8], while that of Greek cannot be stretched beyond 800 B.C. by any measure. How is it possible then that the linguistic feature of IE remained mostly unchanged in Greek, Latin, etc. and not in Sanskrit? Max Müller says:

> "No one supposes any longer that Sanskrit was the common source of Greek, Latin and Anglo-Saxon [9]."

Given below are a few words of Greek which are clearly derived from Sanskrit:

Sanskrit	*Greek*	*Sanskrit*	Greek
asthi	asteon	janit	genete
ārṣa	ārche	madhu	methos
uṣas	eos	mūṣ	mūs
ūrṇa	erion	śala	śchole

The similarity of the above Sasnskrit and Greek forms proves things contrary to the presumption of Max Muller. Logically, these Greek words should be taken as derived from a real language (Vedic Sanskrit) rather than from a Proto Indo-European. The situation regarding Lithuanian and Hittite is also not different in any way. For example:

Sanskrit	*Lithuanian*	*Sanskrit*	*Hittite*
agniḥ/agni	unnis	vasanam	vasanasa
vabhru	bebros	pada	pade
mātṛ	mote	kūp	kūpas (grave)
vṛṣabha	verszis	asthi	hastait

Not only this, the comparison of names of a number of gods is more interesting:

Sanskrit	Hittite
indra	indara
mitra	mittara
varuṇa	uruwana
marutas	maruttas
sūryas	surias

The phonetic changes like assimilation, epenthesis and ablaut which are found in these examples are present in Prakrit languages. For example, the 'ṛ' vowel of Sanskrit changes to various phones in Prakrit:

Sanskrit	*Prakrit*	*Phonetic changes*		
kṛṣi	kasi	ṛ > a	ṣ > s	
gṛddha	giddha	ṛ > i		
mṛta	mutu	ṛ > u	a > u	
dṛṣta	dekkha	ṛ > e		
vṛddhi	bradhi	ṛ > ra	v > b	d loss
vṛddha	bridha	ṛ > ri	v > b	d loss
vṛkṣa	rukkha	ṛ > ru	ṣ > kh	initial v loss
pitṛ	pitar	ṛ > ar		

In the examples of Lithuanian quoted earlier, it is clear that changes like Sans ṛ > Lith e (mātṛ > mote) and Sans ṛ > Lith ar (vṛṣabha > verszis) are present in the same pattern as they occur in the chain Sanskrit > Prakrit. It is evident that thousands of examples can be quoted where Sanskrit ṛ > Prakrit V (a, i, u) or CV (ra, ri, ru) or

VC (ar, ir, ur) but not a single example is available the other way round. In fact, the complicated pronunciation of ṛ caused its replacements by various phones. If we find the same changes of Sans ṛ to Lith e and ar, there is no reason to believe that Lithuanian is older than Vedic Sanskrit. It can at the most be contemporary to inscriptional Prakrit. Similarly, excess of assimilation and epenthesis available in Hittite shows that it is not a predecessor to Vedic Sanskrit. Other phonetic changes from Sanskrit to Lithuanian or Hittite like 'aspirate' > 'non-aspirate; aspirate' >'h', final 'a' > final 'o' and 'v' > 'b' etc. are quite frequent in Prakrit.

It is well known that Vedic Sanskrit has 8 vibhaktis (case frames), Lithuanian and Greek 7, Hittite and Slavics 6, Latin and Tutonic 5, Albanian 4 and Armenian and Old English 3. Lui H. Gray also states this fact in his book *Foundation of Language* [10]. The natural course of structural changes in a family of languages is from a complicated web to a simpler network.The gradual reduction of case frames in these languages again attests their comong late in a chronological order.

European scholars use archaeology for the support of their predecided conclusions arbitrarily. They declare that archaeological material (specially the pottery) excavated from a particular region belongs to a particular period and hence the chronology of various civilizations is arbitrarily decided. The detailed discussion on this aspect is beyond the scope of this paper. Nevertheless, it is proper to point out two facts on this count:

(1) The conclusions drawn about the periods of excavated materials are based on verbal logic and hence not reliable. Today several methods based on radioactivity are available which can determine the period of anything with a fair degree of accuracy. Until these scientific tests are used in an objective manner to find the true picture of the prehistoric events, the conclusions drawn earlier cannot be relied upon.

(2) Recent excavations at several places in India, e.g., at Mathura (U.P.) and in Orissa suggest that the Indian civilization is more than 12,000 years old. The same view was earlier expressed by Shri Sampoornanand by analysing the texts from the Rigveda. In his opinion the Rigveda may be 25,000 years old [11].

Is it not sufficient to overturn the applecart of the Western scholars who, by hook or by crook, want to deny India its due place on the map of ancient civilizations? Some of the European scholars also do not agree on the question of a proto Indo-European language. V. Vendriyos [12] and Bodmer [13] have differences with those philologists who have derived such a schematic system (reconstructing a proto language) and also have gone to the extent of preparing its dictionary. The fact is that even about the period of Vedic Sanskrit Western scholars are not in full agreement. Keith puts its time around 2000 B.C. whereas

Max Muller places it at 1200 B.C. Since the time of Hittite was assumed to be 1365 B.C., it became a religious duty of Western scholars to prove Vedic Sanskrit a later language. The sound changes (as shown above) provide a perfect evidence that Vedic Sanskrit is the oldest language in existence. Hence the hypothesis of any proto language is uncalled for.

If the Aryans had come from outside, there would have been two possibilities: (A) they brought the Vedas with them,. or (B) the Vedas are creations of a later period when the Aryans had settled in Aryavarta. If the first argument is taken to be correct, some earlier versions of the sacred texts would certainly have been available in their 'original homeland' either in a written form or in an oral tradition. Unfortunately there is no such evidence. Again, a number of invaders came from Central Asia (Shakas, Hunas, Turks, etc.) in the later periods, but none of them were civilized enough to be taken even at par with the contemporary Indians. Does it mean that civilization vanished from that area with the departure of the Aryans? Does it sound logical? Has it ever happened in some other case, where the civilization came to an end after the migration of a particular race? Certainly not. This means the Vedas did not exist in the Aryan treasures prior to their entry in India.

If the second view be taken as valid, there would have been a direct or indirect mention, in the Rigveda, of Aryans' migration from their 'homeland'. A race cannot altogether forget its native place so soon. Britishers, though exiled to America and Australia in earlier centuries, could not forget England and named several places after British place names (like New York, New Orleans, New Hamptonshire, etc.). Thus if this is true that the Vedas were composed in India, it must be a reality by corollary that the Aryans did not come from outside.

The whole thesis, that languages from Bengal (India) to the western coast of Europe constitute a large family called Indo-European, is based purely on the occurrence of similar words (with certain definable phonetic changes). The syntatic structure of Indian languages (SOV) is different from that of European languages (i.e., SVO), yet the scholars chose to group them in a family because of similar vocabulary. Why should then South Indian languages form a separate (Dravidian) family? All the four South Indian languages have SOV structure and a large section of their vocabulary has a common core with Sanskrit. Malayalam, the language of the extreme south, has some 45% words similar to those of Sanskrit. Can the language of the invaders influence the language of the defeated people to the extent of driving away almost half of its own vocabulary? Other languages of the South also have a large number of Sanskrit words. It seems thst the artificial separation of northern languages from southern languages is a game plan of some biased people who wanted to rule the country by fragmenting it in terms of religions, languages and regions, etc. These very people have interpreted 'Devasura Sangram' as a war between the Aryans and the Dravidians. If it is true that the Aryans destroyed the material and cultural belongings of Dravidians, defeated them, turned them to slaves and pushed them across the Vindhyas, why should the Dravidians like to have any affinity towards the Vedas, decisively an Aryan literature? We all know that out of the three authentic manuscripts of the Vedas available so far, one is from South India. Thus on the basis of the structural similarities in North Indian and South Indian languages, it is difficult to believe that the Indus Valley civilization was anything else than an earlier version of the Aryan civilization. There is no doubt that there might be regional variations in the life styles, social practices and the thought process of North India vis-a-vis South India, but that did not mean any enmity or rivalry between these two regions of the country. Even today, Shiva, Vishnu, Durga and Hanuman are worshipped alike in the north as well as in the south. Thus, whatever be the political overtones, culturally and linguistically India is one united linguistic area. Aryans are the original inhabitants of this wonderful land guarded by the Himalayas in the north and surrounded by deep sea waters on the three remaining sides. Dr Ram Vilas Sharma has also drawn the same conclusion through the analysis of the whole material available so far [14]. An overall review of the ancient history is needed.

APPENDIX

ROMAN SYMBOLS FOR DEVANAGARI ALPHABETS

स्वर (Vowels)		**व्यञ्जन (Consonants)**									
		स्पर्शी (Plosives)									
अ	a	क्	k	च्	c	ट्	ṭ	त्	t	प्	p
आ	ā	ख्	kh	छ्	ch	झ्	ṭh	थ्	th	फ्	ph
इ	i	ग्	g	ज्	j	ड्	ḍ	द्	d	ब्	b
ई	ī	घ्	gh	झ्	jh	ढ	ḍh	ध्	dh	भ्	bh
उ	u	ङ	ṅ	ञ्	ñ	ण्	ṇ	न्	n	म्	m
ऊ	ū	**अर्द्धस्वर/अर्द्धव्यञ्जन** (semi-vowels/ semi-consonants)				**संघर्षी** (Fricatives)				**संयुक्त** (Clusters)	
ऋ	ṛ										
ए	e										
ऐ	ai	य्	y			श्	ś			क्ष्	kṣ
ओ	o	र्	r			ष्	ṣ			त्र्	tr
औ	au	ल्	l			स्	s			ज्ञ्	jñ
:	ḥ	व्	v			ह्	h			श्र्	śr
						ज़	z				
						फ़	f				

References

[1] E.J. Rapson, *Ancient India*, p. 1.
[2] Max Muller, *A History of Ancient Sanskrit Literature*, p. 8.
[3] Franz Bopp, *Analytical Comparison of the Sanskrit, Greek, Latin and Teutonic Languages*, p. 48.
[4] Ibid., Vol. II, p. 354.
[5] Quoted from Bhagavaddatta, *Bhasha ka Itihas*, p. 199.
[6] Bal Krishna Ghosh, *Vedic Age*, p. 202.
[7] B. Hronzy, *Ancient History*, p. 112.
[8] E.J. Rapson, *Ancient India*, pp. 5–6.
[9] Max Muller, *India: What it can teach us*, p. 21.
[10] Lui H. Gray, *Foundation of Language*, p. 201.
[11] Sampoornanand, *Aryon ka Adi Desh*, p. 134.
[12] J. Vendryos, *Language*, p. 302.
[13] Friederich Bodmer, *The Loom of Language*, p. 183.
[14] Ram Vilas Sharma, *Pashchimee Asia aur Rigveda*, pp. 38–42.

Antiquity of the Vedic River Sarasvati

V. PRABHU KUMARI
Department of History, The Ethiraj College for Women
Ethiraj Salai, Egmore, Chennai - 600 005, India

An in-depth view into the emergence of the existing Indian culture and civilization actually projects a picture of its base to the Vedic river Sarasvati and its systematic standardization in continuing the cultural uninhabitance at every stage.[1]

The union of Sarasvati fed community with the Indo-Tibetan communities and their migration and merger with the South Indian Communities due to the makes and breaks in the Vedic river Sarasvati created a humanitarian culture throughout India. An integrated and independent study into the Vedic literature has a bearing on the lost Sarasvati as '*Naditama*' and Puranic writings as '*Sapta Sarasvata*' because it was the most extensive and mighty river known to the sages of antiquity.[2] Literal references of the Vedas especially Rigveda accord Sarasvati as one amongst the seven sisters, the mother of all streams, daughter of lighting and the spouse of *Sarasvant.*[3]

A cursory reading into the following observations gleaned from the ancient Indian lore about the mighty river Sarasvati which has now become a brook proves the authenticity of the Vedas as well as the *historicity of the river Sarasvati.*

1. Kuryanahad's son Prakasthama, one of the Indras, devastated the Shatadru city.
2. The war of Mahabharata and the war between Hariyupia and Purushni combatted near Sarasvati.
3. Vriddhashrava, the very old king, had a son Divodasa due to the benediction of river Sarasvati.
4. Prior to the Dasharajnya war, Tritsu conquered the land lying amidst Sarasvati and Yamuna.
5. In a hermitage situated on the shores of Sarasvati, hermit Dadhichi dwelled, and it is with his bones that Indra created weapons and destroyed Asuras.

---

[1]V. Prabhu Kumari, "The Saraswathi River Civilization—A New Perspective", Indian History Congress Seminar, Madras, 1996, p. 1.

[2]L.S. Wakankar and Parchure, *A Quest after the Lost Saraśvati River—A Report,* Vinayak Dhundiraj Bapat and K.A. Umapathy (Trans.), 1st Edn, Mysore, 1944, pp. 14–15.

[3]Arthur Berriedale Keith, *The Religion and Philosophy of the Vedas and Upanishas,* Charles Rockwell Lanman (Ed.), London, 1925, Vol. 3, p. 173.

6. King Videtha Madhava, impelled by the great famine on the banks of Sarasvati, carried the Vedic fire eastwards up to the Sadanira river.
7. Vaivasvata Yama acquired the name Manu, for being landed during Mana, the great flood.
8. Urvashi and Pururava's confluence took place at the Sarasvati shore.
9. On the banks of the Sarasvati river, a sacrifice was performed by Prithu Vainya.
10. Sage Rishagu resided in an abode situated near the Sarasvati river.
11. Pratishthana king Yayati brought under his sway the entire stretch of land lying in between Kosala and the Sarasvati river.
12. Strands of Sarasvati witnessed a 12 year sacrifice performed by Matinara.
13. From one deluge, Fish incarnate rescued Satyavrata, a descendant of Manu and was conceded as 'Dakshinesvara'.
14. Sahasrarjuna and many other Kshatriyas were destroyed by Jamadagni's son Parashurama near Narmada.
15. Devapi chanced to perform a penance in the surroundings of Sarasvati.
16. Sage Vishvamitra resided in Khagashatirtha, a holy site situated near river Sarasvati.
17. Prevalence of a drastic drought for 12 years and the occurrence of an exorbitant deluge thereafter during Shantanu's reign.
18. Vishvamitra along with his chariots, escorts and horses passed across the Sindhu (Indus) river. His trial to grab Vasishta's cow Nandini resulted in a prolonged feud, which ended in a long lasing peace.[1]

All these references besides establishing the veracity of the Vedas and river Sarasvati reveal that:

> The two epics represent the two aspects of our Aryan civilization, two aspects of our Indian culture, viz., moral and intellectual, individual and social; parents and elders have, for generations, used the themes and stories of these epics for imparting wisdom and instruction to the younger generations.[2]

Most discrepant and distinctive details appear in the Puranic lore which is a conglomeration of *sarga* (creation), *pratisarga* (dissolution and recreation), *vamsha* (divine genealogies), *manvantara* (ages of Manu) and *vamshanucharita* (genealogies of kings).[3] Due to their lucid language, they freed the complexities

---

[1]L.S. Wakankar and V. Prabhu Kumari, "Studies Relevant to the 'Lost' Vedic River Sarasvati", *Pulamai*, vol. 22, No. 2, 1996, pp. 81–82.

[2]Chalasani Subbarao, *Maharshi Vedavyasudu (Vyasa Darshanamu)*, Machilipatnam, 1992, p. 65

[3]Asoke Chatterjee Shastri, ""Introduction", *Purana* (Varanasi), vol. 30, No. 1, February 1989, p. 2.

of Vedic doctrines from the chosen few and spilled and popularised them amongst the masses regarding *the origin, date, diversified streams and the desertification of river Sarasvati.** At present several historians are of the opinion that they

> can trace a use of at least vamsavalis in the historical chapters given in some of the Puranas, which do certainly indicate a desire on the part of the ancient Hindus not to ignore general history altogether, and are clearly based upon ancient archives which had survived in a more or less complete shape.[1]

However, to the fraternity of occidentalists who may not accept these identifications (evidences from epics and Puranas are considered as too tenuous because they are regarded as mere mythological descriptions) references can be provided about Sarasvati from chronicles like Bana's *Harshacharita*. This furnishes a fair account of the then existing Sarasvati by elucidating Prabhakaravardhana's initiation into tantric rites at a deserted temple on the Sarasvati bank, his cremation at the same coast, his widowed wife Yashovati's attempt to plunge into the fire near the same river and the victorious march commenced by the forces of Harshavardhana at the same shore of Sarasvati[2]. These are some of the references that reiterate the historical importance of this celestial river.

Modern scientific researches conducted by the Physical Research Laboratory at Ahmedabad gravitate towards the analogous conclusions produced by the aerial photographs of Landsat Imagery about the width of the Sarasvati bed that originates in Simla and flows from the Shivalik mountains to the Rann of Kutch in Gujarat with sometimes to even 10 km breadth at certain places which dismisses the earlier mythical convictions about Sarasvati as a sheer moons line.[3] In a complete scanning of the Thar desert undertaken by NASA, an American satellite, in 1975 also picturized five different courses of Sarasvati. The Central Arid Zone Research Institute of Jodhpur reports too established that amongst five, two earlier courses flowed into the Rann of Kutch and directly submerged into the sea, whereas the

---

*A glimpse into the following citations of Bhagavata Purana itself appertaining to river Sarasvati reveals the rampantness of its references in the Puranas. "Sarasvati as a river: I. 3, 15; I. 7, 2; I. 16, 37; II. 9, 44; III. 1, 21; III. 4, 3, 6; III. 21, 6, 33, 39; II. 22, 27; III. 23, 25; III. 24, 9; III. 33, 13; IV. 16, 36; IV. 16, 24; Praci Sarasvati: IV. 19, 1; V. 19, 18; VI. 8, 40; VIII. 11, 23; IX. 4, 22; in Kurukshetra: IX. 14, 33; IX. 16, 23; X. 71, 22; X. 78, 18, 19; X. 89, 1." As given in J.E. Abbott, "The topographical list of Bhagavata Purana", *The Indian Antiquary, A Journal of Oriental Research*, Richard Carnac Temple, Bart (Ed., London, 1899, vol. 28, p. 5.

[1] *The Imperial Gazetteer of India:: The Indian Empire, Historical*, Oxford, 1909, vol. 2, p. 14.

[2] O.P. Bhardwaj, ""The Vedic Sarasvati", Haryana Sahitya Academi Journal of Indological Studies, Haryana, 1987, vol. 2, No. 1–2, p. 39.

[3] Itihasa Sankalana Samiti (Bharatiya), *Akhila Bharatheeya Itihasa Sankalana Yojana*, Hyderabad, n.d., p. 18.

remaining three confluenced with the Indus.[1] Sarasvati was fed by Beas and Sutlej on the right, Drishadvati on the left and also by Yamuna, a small tributary.[2]

Yamuna which entered Ghaggar changed its flowing direction three times, starting from ancient Ghaggar to Chautang and then to the present course of the Yamuna river. Besides Sutlej too, owing to tectonic movements, took a sharp westward right-angled diversion and this is evident from the sudden widening of the Ghaggar palaeochannel south to Patiala.[3] Drishadvati shifted several times to West from East owing to its inconceivability to flow in a flat area. Aerial photographs also include a number of its westward shifts from Didwana to Kheduli through the vicinity of Keral, Jayal and Lusinara, from Shekhawas to Dudwakhara through Sujangarh, Siwalik and ultimately to Sarasvati river after crossing Ratangarh, Parihara and Bidasar, due to morphological and climatic changes and blockages of sand and lack of water supply from the small Aravali streams.[4]

The present Sarasvati river is a small stream which flows down the mountain ranges of Sirmur bordering Ambala district in Punjab (Fig. 1). Brahmavaivarta Purana puts forth that at an informal discussion between Lord Vishnu and the Puranic triad Sarasvati, Ganga and Lakshmi, impetuous Ganga imprecated Sarasvati to turn into a river. Whereas according to Brahmanda Purana, Brahma's falsified statement provoked Lord Siva to maledict the 'vak' (speech) of Brahma, i.e., Sarasvati to flow as a river.[5] As such in the ancient Indian literature many references about Vedic Sarasvati as a goddess of rivers are found.[6] In fact, Puranic history acquiescing with the proven scientific researches of the Central Arid ZoneResearch Institute (Jodhpur) regarding the death or drying up of river Sarasvati imparts that

> The story of her quarrel with her co-wife Ganga in which both exchange curses leading to a pledge by the former to end her existence. Ultimately, as decreed by Narayana, Sarasvati is persuaded to stay on and only a small part of her self descends into the holy land of Bharata as Praci Sarasvati. This story would be easily seen to conceal a reference to the reduction in the flow of the holy river.[7]

---

[1]P.N. Phadke, "River Sarasvati and the date of Rigveda", National Seminar on Indian Civilization and Chronology, Madras, 1995, pp. 1, 4.

[2]Vimalsoni, D.C. Sharma, K.S. Srivastava and M.S. Sisodia, "Hydrogeological and geophysical study to trace the course of the buried Sarasvati river in Jaisalmer District, Rajasthan", Research paper, Ground Water Department, Department of Geology, Jodhpur, 1996, p. 1.

[3]Yashpal, Baldev Sahai, R.K. Sood and D.P. Agarwal, "Remote sensing of the 'lost' Sarasvati river", *Proc. Indian Acad. Sci. (Earth Planet. Sci.",* vol. 89, No. 3, 1980, pp. 318–19.

[4]Amal Kar and Bimal Ghose, "The Drishadvati river system of India: an assessment and new findings", *The Geographical Journal,* vol. 150, No. 2, London, 1984, pp. 222–26.

[5]Rentala Gopalakrishna, *Mana Nadulu,* Vijayawada, n.d., pp. 45–46.

[6]S.P. Gulati (Ed.), *Hindu Gods and Goddesses,* Delhi, 1986, p. 16.

[7]O.P. Bhardwaj, n. 6, p. 45.

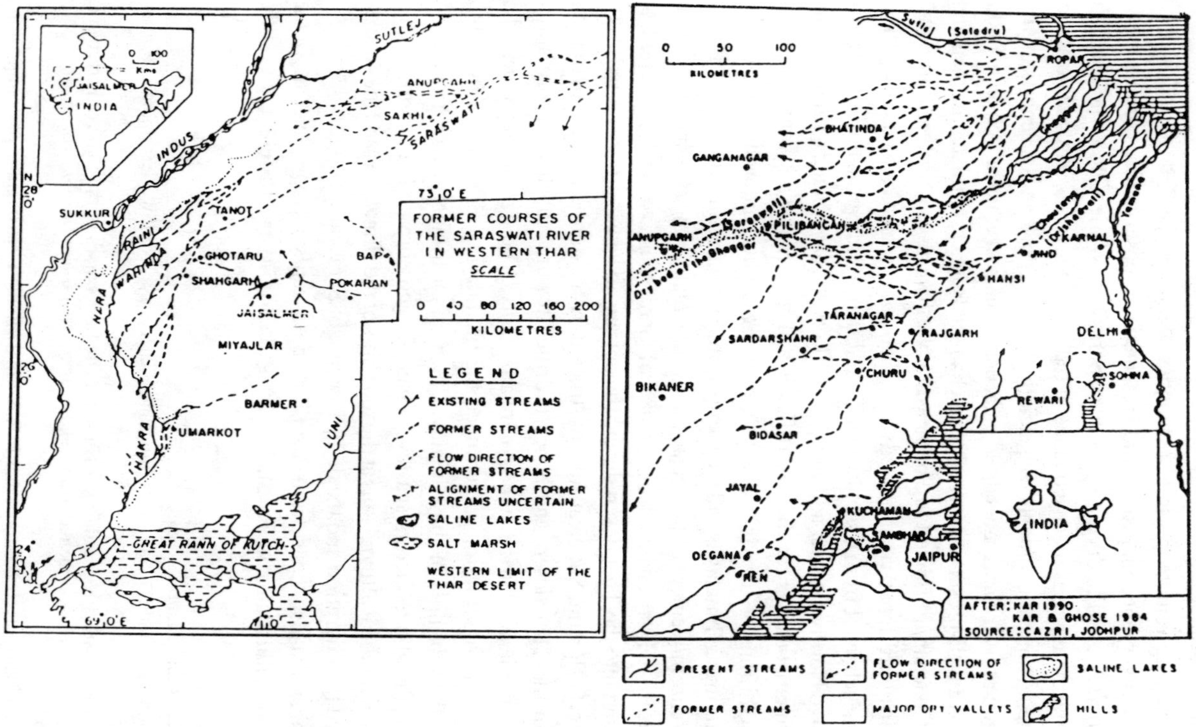

Fig. 1. (a) Former courses of Sarasvati river in Western Thar (b) Present and former stream courses in the eastern part of the Thar and its ranges (*Courtesy:* A.K. Sen and Amal Kar, ed., *Desertification in Thar, Sahara and Sahel Regions*, Jodhpur, 1993, pp. 52–53

It is still assented that amongst the two channels of Vedic Sarasvati, the river bed in Rajasthan turned into a black fertile soil and the other, i.e., subterranean Sarasvati combines with Ganga and Yamuna at Prayag which is otherwise called as 'Triveni Sangam'![1]

By employing remote sensing techniques, the scientists Ghose and Yashpal reached two divergent conclusions and presented new observations concerning the shifting courses and the drying up of river Sarasvati. While Ghose indicated the hydrographic changes as a consequence to the aeolian activity, Yashpal attributed them to the tectonic movements. Systematical analysis of Landsat reports unveils the precision of river Sarasvati's dried palaeochannel tract existing between Takhal and Sirsa as a well-preserved meandering channel. Being proximate, the meanders of this palaeochannel flowed in Southeast to Northwest, and Northeast to Southwest, i.e., in two different right-angled directions. The present Ghaggar river picking up the palaeochannel from Chandu near Takhal sharply converts its direction from Southwest to Northwest after adjoining its flanks with Johya Mala, a small stream.[2]

The principal causes for the desertification of river Sarasvati were the gradual westward shifting of the river due to advancing aridity, anthropogenic earthen movements in the Himalayas and the Rann of Kutch, contrasting climatic variations, mild tectonic movements, and palaeoenvironmental changes, especially in the Shivalik hills, which changed the course of Sarasvati river and converted the pastoral land into the Thar desert during the tertiary and post-tertiary periods.[3] The southwesterly flowing Sarasvati was obstructed by the northeasterly moving sand advance in the Thar desert and hence it drifted towards north with a rotational migration until it was buried in the Anupgarh plains.[4] The signatures picturised by the aerial photo observations determined the final drying of Sarasvati bed to the capture at the foot-hills of the Himalayas by a minor tributary river Yamuna.[5] In addition to the above factors sea level changes, geomorphic land forms such as formation of regional alluvial fans at the foot-hills of the Himalayas and the Aravalis also caused the migration and the desertification of Sarasvati in stages.

Mahabharatha also, apart from describing Sarasvati's disappearance at Vainashana, vividly illustrates in its Shalyaparva (35 to 54) the different diversified

---

[1]P.N. Phadke, n. 12, pp. 1–3.

[2]R.K. Sood and Baldev Sahai, "Hydrographic changes in Northwestern India", *Man and Environment*, vol. 7, 1983, p. 166.

[3]Bimal Ghose, Amal Kar and Zahid Husain, "The lost courses of the Sarasvati river in the great Indian desert: New evidence from Landsat imagery", *Itihas Darpan*, vol. 2, No. 1. New Delhi, 1995, p. 3.

[4]S.M. Ramasamy, P.C. Bakliwal and R.P. Verma, "Remote sensing and river migration in Western India", *International Journal of Remote Sensing*, vol. 12, No. 12, 1991, p. 2608.

[5]P.C. Bakliwal and A.K. Grover, "Signatures and migration of Sarasvati river in Thar desert, Western India", *Rec. Geological Survey of India*, vol. 116, Jaipur, 1988, p. 84.

names and streams of Sarasvati. According to Mahabharatha Baladev visited Vainashana where Sarasvati vanished and sank into the earth due to her disdain against Abhiras and Sudras. Kalidasa in his *Meghdoot* signified the intermediate beauty of Sarasvati in Brahmavarta.[1]

Multiple testimonials tested by the Central Arid Zone Research Institute, Jodhpur, based on the archaeological, geomorphological, historical and stratigraphical sources coinciding with the satellite remote sensing, in near infrared band and in FCC form, revealed Sarasvati, a once contributor for the development of a rich and thick alluvium in the desert as a river that later swang away its beds several times from its original direction and accentuated for the spread of sand-blown activity (aeolian process) in the semi-arid areas by giving way to the burial of former stream courses, disorganisation, desertification and drainage desiccation in the present Thar desert.[2]

The continuous shifting process of these rivers from one direction to another affected the natural course of the Sarasvati river and led to its desertification. Ptolemy's narration of the sacred seven rivers comprising of a dried Sarasvati bed in his account of ancient Indian geography as erratic rivers, constantly changing their course right from the Vedic age too, completely collates with the manifestations gleaned from the epics and Puranas.[3] Researches conducted by the Central Arid Zone Research Institute of Jodhpur, placed the date of the transitional and transformative history of river Sarasvati's desertification at 40,000 years.[4]

Excavations at Bheembetaka revealed to Bapu L.S. Wakankar (Lipikar) that between 40,000 to 15,000 years prevailed an age of drought. Later, the occurrence of disastrous deluges and detrimental monsoonal winds altered the geological phenomena and animated greenery in the Thar desert. The carbon-14 method advanced a steady state view about the Sarasvati's bed's sequential cultural uprise to pre-14,000 to 9,000 years. Again Sarasvati was then subjected to another destructive geological transition which created the current state of affairs. In fact,

> Elevation of the Himalayan and the Shivalik mountains continued. Feeder rivers of the Sarasvati deviated their currents. The bed of Sarasvati at Naditama, 8 km in width, began to dry up. The northern currents of the Sutlej and the Biyas deviated westward. The Choutang and the Yamuna flowed towards the Ganga. During the Rigvedic period an arm of the South Sea extended up to Bikaner. Probably this

[1]Hiralal Joshi, "Vaidik Sarasvati Nadi", Research Paper, Sarasvati Nadi Shodh Samsthan, Ujjain, 1996, p. 1.

[2]A.K. Sen and Amal Kar (Eds.), *Desertification and its Control in the Thar, Sahara and Sahel Regions*, Jodhpur, 1993, pp. 49–51.

[3]J.W. Mcrindle, *Ancient India, as described by Ptolemy*, Calcutta, 1885, p. 89.

[4]*Felicitation Address of Moropant Pingale*, World University Centre, Chennai, August 1993.

> arm and the entire South Sea receded during the period of Ram. It appears that the human habitations on the banks of Sarasvati had to transfer themselves because of a fierce drought or a deluge that occurred in the later Vedic period.[1]

The American Landsat Imagery Information about the dried up bed of Sarasvati also disclosed:

(a) The breadth of Ghaggar bed of Sarasvati from Punjab to Marot in Pakistan as huge as 6 to 8 km.
(b) Details about Markanda river and its turning flow to the northeast of Kshatrana.
(c) Width of today's Chautang river and its confluence with Ghaggar at Suratgarh through the specified dried Y-2 route.
(d) Bifurcation of the ancient Ghaggar river around Anupgarh to Marot and Baireena.[2]

The aforesaid Landsat observations support the notion of 'Naditama', a 6 to 8 km (see Fig. 2) wide river that looked like a sea and its desertification at Vainashana where Sarasvati dried (reverences offered by Balaram to his late father). If argued from archaeological premises it leads us to a path where *the expanse of the Sarasvata sites and the Sindhu-Sarasvati civilization flourished.*

The recently unearthed 5,000 year old Indus-Sarasvati script sign board at Gujarat, if deciphered, unveils the anchor that is lying around Aryan invasion and also fills up a chasm appertaining to the past secrets of India's trade apart from shedding light on the age-old Sarasvati script which was contemplated as a precedent of the Brahmi writing that influenced the Aramic and Greek scripts. While establishing the similarities of this script with Brahmi, archaeologists claimed it as a script which became extinct after the desertification of Sarasvati.[3] Moreover,

> The philosophy that the world is one family, is readily apparent from a study of the scripts of various languages.[4]

According to Manu, all the human beings acquired a knowledge of their own history from the Sarasvati basin lying in between river Sarasvati and Drishadvati. Latest archaeological excavations candidly assert the prevalence of a single culture from Uttar Pradesh to Baluchistan.[5]

---

[1]L.S. Wakankar and C.N. Parachure, n. 2, p. 19.

[2]Ibid., n. 2, pp. 14–15.

[3]*The Hindu*, Chennai, 13 August 1996.

[4]"Scientific Nagari phonography", *Organiser*, 29 January 1995.

[5]Sriram Sathe, *Maurya Chandraguptudu Kalanirnayam*, K.K. Srinivasamurthi (trans.), Hyderabad, 1984, p. 6.

Fig. 2. Synoptic view provided by the Landsat at the Northwestern Indian subcontinent showing some of the present rivers and the palaeochannels. The present Sutlej is shown taking a sharp westward turn near Ropar. The 6–8 km wide palaeochannel of the Sarasvati can be clearly seen. (Courtesy: Yashpal, Baldev Sahai, R.K. Sood and D.P. Agrawal, "Remote sensing of the 'lost' Sarasvati river", *Proc Indian Acad. Sci. (Earth Planet Sci.),* vol. 89, No. 3, p. 323)

> Archaeologists have renamed the Indus civilization as the Indus-Sarasvati civilization as now research has shown that nearly two-thirds of Indus civilization sites were on the Sarasvati river and only five per cent along the Indus. The majority of the remaining sites are in Gujarat and Uttar Pradesh, South and east of the Sarasvati.[1]

Some indigenous literary sources and foreign literary sources present an amazing overall view of the Sarasvati civilization and consider it as a cradle of the entire human civilization. *Ramapithecus*, the first human being, according to them originated on the banks of Sarasvati who afterwards matured into *Sinanthropus, Australopithecus, Homo sapiens* and *Homo bhimaveitiky*. A large number of Sarasvati seals belonging to the 35,000 year old Sarasvati fed community (worshippers of Indra, Agni and Varuna) were traced in Iran, Iraq, Sumeria, Jokhada, etc. In fact, this is a circumstantial evidence to the fact that the people living in different parts of the world can draw their roots from the Sarasvati civilization.[2]

From a scientific standpoint too, the most variegated implications implied by the spade of geologists raised a promising answer much akin to the archaeological discoveries. For them,

> fossils of many of these creatures were found in climates where they could not have thrived (fish on mountain tops, polar bears in the tropics), the earth must have undergone profound and wide-reaching changes since the time when the extinct species has lived. Such major geological changes as had occurred had come about suddenly, as the result of cataclysmic supernatural upheavals that had levelled mountains, raised seabeds towards the sky, and doomed whole species to extinction almost overnight.[3]

Further, the chronicles of Mohammedan invasions exposed to the world once again the age-old existence of the Sarasvati cicilization where innumerable mounds were traced near the fortress Sarsuti or Sarasvati. It was constituted on the Ghaggar banks which was known to the ancient civilization only as Sarasvati.[4]

Ashvagosha's *Buddhacharitra* also confesses, at the height of the Sarasvati civilization, about sage Sarasvata's preservation of the Vedic culture and imparting of samskaras, shastras and Vedas to as many as 60,000 disciples.[5]

---

[1]*The Hindu*, Chennai, 13 August 1996.

[2]Vaidik Sarasvati Nadi Shodh Samsthan, Vaidik Sarasvati Nadi Shodh Adhyayan: Ek Parichay, Jodhpur, n.d., pp. 10–11.

[3]Timothy Ferris, *Coming of Age in the Milky Way*, New Delhi, p. 224.

[4]C.F. Oldham, "The Sarasvati and the Lost River of the Indian Desert", *Journal of the Royal Asiatic Society* (N.S.), 34, pp. 51–52.

[5]V.N. Kudva, *History of the Dakshinatya Sarasvats*, Madras, 1972, p. 2.

Ghosh's archaeological journey farthest along the road leading into the depths of time corroborated the chronology of Harappa, Greyware and Rangmahal, the three riverine cultures in the Sarasvati valley. His computation towards the Sarasvati civilization is that

> Harappa culture was essentially a riverine culture, which would have been impossible had the river been dead at that time. The Greyware culture which is traced to 1,000 B.C. had a somewhat shaky source of water due to the impoverishment of the land. During the Rangmahal culture which followed 1,000 B.C., the people must have been more sure of adequate water supply and there was probably a partial resuscitation of the river system during the period. This again goes to prove that even in the recent times, in the last 3,000 years, there have been alternating periods of desiccation and adequate water supply in the region.[1] (See Fig. 3.)

In addition, Kalibangan excavations identified modern Sirasa in Haryana with the ancient *Sarasvatanagar* as a city situated to the west of Kurukshetra where the rich Sarasvata culture flourished for several centuries.[2]

As it is unfeasible for anybody to alter the planetary positions, astronomical methods (a science about the universe of space that is governed by the laws of time in a mathematical precision), were adopted by innumerable Western historians in constituting the continuous chronology of China, Egypt and Babylon.[3] Similar astronomical calculations are extensively used here to establish the association between *the Vedic river Sarasvati and the chronology of ancient India.*

Proper investigation into the astronomical observations, besides providing a detailed description of two *Rishi* lineages as *Rajarsis* and *Brahmarsis* who dwelled on the banks of the Sarasvati river. *Rigveda, Atharvaveda, Kathaka Samhita, Maitrayani Samhita, Sathpatha Brahmana, Taittiriya Samhita*, etc., supply us with lucid astronomical data which exercise a crucial role in establishing the chronology of ancient India.[4] Vasishta and his followers being royal belonged to the *Rajarshi* race. On the contrary, Vishvamitra and his community was considered as the *Brahmarshi* clan, for they were contemplated as the originators of caste races or Brahmanas.[5]

---

[1]R.L. Singh, ed., India, *A Regional Geography*, Varanasi, 1989, p. 50.

[2]P.N. Phadke, n. 12, p. 4.

[3]E. Vedavyasa, *Mana Desamu—Mana Samskrithi*, United Social, Cultural and Educational Foundation of India, 2nd Edn., 1979, p. 34.

[4]G.R. Kaye, "The nakshatras and precession", *The Indian Antiquary, a Journal of Oriental Research*, Richard Carnac Temple and Bart (Ed.), vol. 50, London, 1921, p. 46.

[5]K. Narayanaswamy Aiyer, *The Puranas in the Light of Modern Science,* Madras, 1914, p. 140.

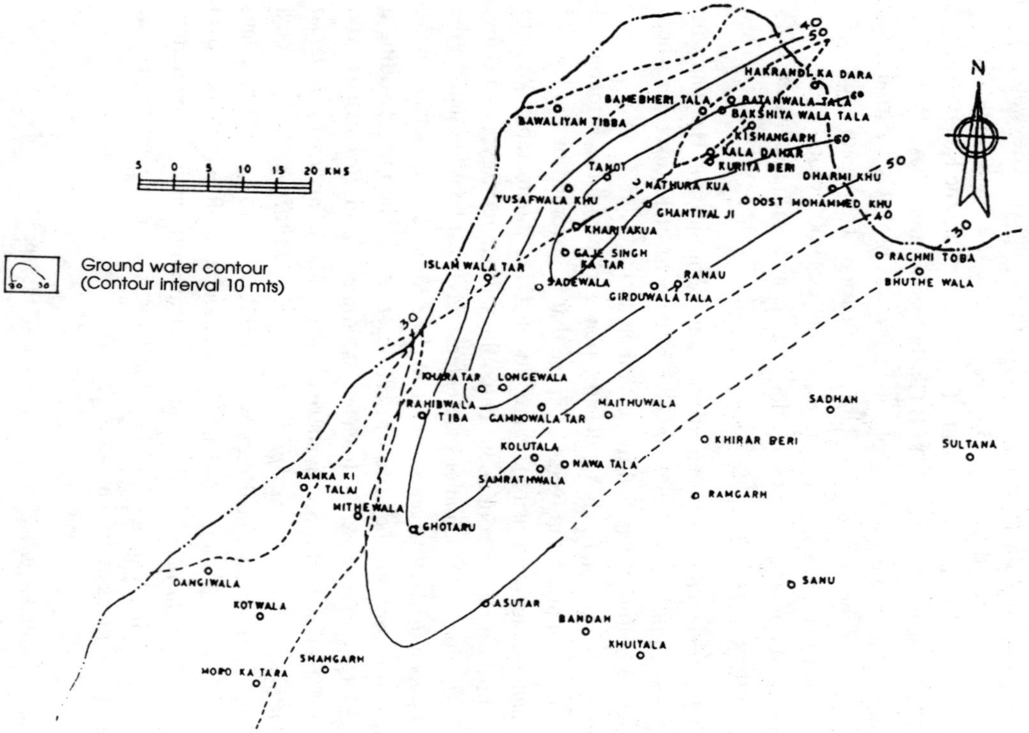

Fig. 3. Map showing ground water flow in the area of study for delineating buried Sarasvati river in Jaiselmer district (*Courtesy*: Vimal Soni, D.C. Sharma, K.S. Srivastava and M.S. Sisodia, "Hydrological and geophysical study to trace the course of buried Sarasvati river in Jaisalmer District, Rajasthan", Ground Water Department, Jodhpur, n.d., p. 10)

Besides, the tenor of abundant and oldest oriental astro-historical evidences complies with the occidental records like the ancient Jewish literature where too, like the Mahabharatha Queen Kunti, a queen disposed of her child in a basket covered by 'Naphta' into a stream that tumbled from the sky. Of course, the geological and planetological explorations applied to these astro-literary inscriptions and charts brought to limelight the collision of Venus and Earth resulting in the fall of Naphtas.

As a matter of fact, though research on Sarasvati as restricted to a chosen few, due to certain *limitations* like the inevitability to apply advanced scientific equipments, if it is subjected to further such similar inquiries, even grander estimation of the extent of Indian antiquity can be perceived.

The time has come to abandon the old paradigm of the 19th century colonial historians. The digging of the river Sarasvati promises to solve the enigmas and reveal the correct history of India. This will allow us to end the history of confusions that bedevil Indian chronology. Whatever be the argument about Sarasvati, there is no denial of the fact that in the light of available literary, archaeological and scientific evidences, the Rigvedic 'Lost River' became the cradle of the oldest living civilization.[1]

Immigration of 'Aryans' to India: A Fact or a Fiction!

MAHATAM SINGH
President Mata Gauri Foundation, Surinam

The paper presents different views on the so called Aryans and their migrations. It presents facts that are important to challenge the 'Aryan migration/invasion theory' to the Indian subcontinent. There is an independent path of historical research to study the Vedas and Puranas and the ancient annals (Itihas) of India.

Before I deal with the subject, 'immigration of Aryans to India', I like to briefly say something about the Earth, a stage on which the human drama has been played, from time immemorial to the modern time. During the last few hundred years, there has been an extraordinary enlargement of men's ideas about the visible universe in which they live. Our earth which seems vast is just a speck, in the greater vastness of space. How long the earth has endured is another question which baffles our mind. Astronomers and geologists agree that vast ages ago, the sun was a spinning, flaring mass of matter, not yet concentrated into a compact center of heat, when a series of fragments were detached from it and became planets. Astronomers and mathematicians have given us 2000 million years as the age of the earth, a body separated from the sun and about 300 million years as the length of time since life appeared upon it in abundance. There seems to be general agreement that life began in warm sunlit shallow water, in pools and lagoons along the coasts of the first formed seas.

Scientific View of Evolution and Religious Views of Man

The prevailing opinion among the men of science is that man, like all others mammals, has descended from ancestors of a lower kind, while the religious bodies were committed to the view that man was specially created. A great sensation was caused with the publication of Darwin's "Origin of Species", in which he observed how plants and animals developed in nature and how simple forms had gradually become more complex. This kind of reasoning was directly opposed to the creation of the world. As H.G. Wells in his famous treatise

'*Outline of World History*' has stated that, "no considerable Christian body indeed, now insist upon the exact and literal acceptance of the bible narrative.''

The world poet Rabindranath Tagore in his famous book, *'The Religion of Man'* has observed that "in the beginning of his career man asserted in his bodily structure, his first proclamation against the established rule of nature. At a certain bend in the path of evolution he refused to remain a four-footed creature and when his pre-occupation with the means of livelihood became less insistent, he had the leisure to create things sublime. His progress from the stage of hunting to the tillage was a great mark in the process of civilization and the saying 'culture with agriculture' had its meaning.''

As per the Indian tradition, the first king of India was Manu Svayambhu (the self-born); he was born directly from Brahma, the creator. The tenth Manu was the most famous among them and it was during his reign that the great flood occurred in which everything was submerged and only the king along with his family and seven sages survived. Lord Vishnu took the form of a large fish to which a boat was tied which took them to a mountain peak. Here the whole party stayed. It is stated that human race sprang from Manu and his family; from Manu the word '*manav*' or 'man' is derived, which mean human being.

Theory of Aryan Migration/Invasion

In the late eighteenth and early nineteenth century, another kind of evidence provided historic materials on the basis of philology, that the Indo-Europeans emerged from the region of Caspian sea and the southern Russian steppes in search of pastures and thus the 'Aryans' immigrated to India. To quote the famous scholar R. K. Mukherjee, "Sometime about the third millennium B.C. the Aryans, white-skinned, blue-eyed and sharp of nose, and riding on bright prancing horses and wheeled vehicles, appeared in the course of their immigration from central Asia in the plains of Indus and the Sarasvati." This theory stands challenged today on the ground that he historians pertaining to this view have mentioned 21 places but they have failed to pick up the definite one. Moreover none of the regions mentioned have shown evidence of such philosophical development or spiritual heritage which the 'Aryans' achieved.

Theory of Aryans migrating to West

There are Indian scholars, who regard the Aryans as indigenous inhabitants, who migrated to the different parts of Asia and Europe and were ancestors of Greeks and Romans, who spoke Aryan languages. But not much scientific base is yet available for credibly establishing this view.

Aryan Migration to India Challenged

The theory of foreign origin of Aryans stands challenged today as I have mentioned above. It is based on linguistic grounds, which have proved to be premature and superficial as many of the scholars, including Max Muller, had missionary and political axes to grind. Moreover, this has never been backed by any archaeological finds.

As stated by Shaffer, "Current archaeological data do not support the existence of Indo-Aryans or Europeans in the pre- or protohistoric periods.'' Moreover the photographs taken by the American satellites and a systematic study of recent scientific research have emphatically refuted the arguments advanced on the basis of linguistic findings. Evolution of prominent civilizations of the world has been noticed on the bank of the famous rivers. Nile, Dajlafarat, Hwang Ho and Sindhu have given birth to great civilizations. Many places of Harappa and Mohenjo Daro civilization have been found on the banks of Sindhu and its tributaries.

But to the Vedic Aryans, the holiest river was Sarasvati. In the Rigveda, Ganga is mentioned seldom, while Sarasvati is lauded on several occasions and it has been praised as '*ambitame, naditame, devitame'* etc., which means 'Sarasvati, the best of mothers, the best of rivers, the best of goddesses.' (Rigveda, ii. 41, 42)

Sarasvati, once a flourishing river along with its northern tributary, the Drishadvati, had begun to dry up as early as 3000 B.C. Here it would be wise to mention that this Sarasvati has nothing to do with the Sarasvati of Ganga, Jamuna and Sarasvati confluence in Allahabad, U.P. Recently a lot of research to ascertain its starting point and several other factors, associated through several satellite pictures, has been done. Once again we have a reference in the Rigveda, vii.95.2, regarding Sarasvati, "pure in her stream from the mountain to the sea, filled with water for the world's nourishment with her flow to the children of Nahush.''

This detailed reference to Sarasvati is actually meant to explain vividly that the Harappan civilization of the Indus valley was a continuation of the Vedic and its end coincided roughly with the final drying up of the Sarasvati about 2000 B.C. Moreover it is very clear from the recent report that Harappan civilization was part of a worldwide climatic change that affected to a greater extent all ancient civilizations and the drying up of the Sarasvati was part of the ecological calamity. This is now a scientifically established fact.

Recent research work in the field of Indology has proved that the creative Vedic age i.e. when the Vedas were still being composed and the text still fluid, had ended by 3000 B.C. when the Sarasvati had finally dried up. The closing phase of the Vedic age was the sutra period, which corresponds to Harappan archaeology of 3000–2000 B.C. This was the age when mathematical ideas flowed from India to old Babylonia and Egypt. Here we are convinced of the great Sulbha Sutra, without the mathematics of which the architectural feats of the Harappan civilization would have been impossible.

It is gradually being recognized that the Harappans of the Sarasvati-Sindhu were a literate people. The famous Harappan seals left behind are being studied by scholars to show greater affinity between the Vedic and Harappan cultures. It would be wise to mention here that all the problems relating to the script have not been fully solved. It should also be noted that Harappan seals have not as yet been fully read. But gradually it is becoming evident that the Vedic age corresponds to the Sutra period and this now rests on a solid scientific ground.

Supporting the foreign origin of Vedic Aryans, evidence of horse is also brought forward. Since the horse is a very important animal in the Vedas, this issue has been pressed into service to claim that it was brought in by outsiders—the invading Aryans, in spite of the fact that a full skeleton of horse has been found in the Harappan excavation and also in the Neolithic sites in the interior of India, going back to 6500 B.C. and evidences of both wild and domesticated varieties have been found.

We may finally conclude that the Harappan civilization of the Indus valley came at the end of the Vedic age and was part of it. It was the twilight of the Vedic age. Its end was brought about by the severe draught that began around 2200 B.C. and lasted nearly 300 years. What ended Harappan civilization ended also the Vedic civilization. And it was caused by no invasion, but by a great natural calamity. If there is one message that has come out as the result of recent scientific research, it is the following: "What ended the Harappan civilization ended also; the Vedic age; the two were one and the same."[1]

We have to adhere to the message of the great sage Swami Vivekananda that "it is for us to strike out an independent path of historical research for ourselves, to study the Vedas and Puranas and the ancient annals (Itihas) of India."

---

[1] Rajaram: *The Politics of History.*

Indus Sarasvati-Age's Place in Indian History

DHARAM JIT JIGYASU
43-49 Smart St. Flushing, NY 11355, U.S.A.

Excavations of Harappa and Mohanjo Daro were first taken up in 1921 and 1922. Only a few sites were excavated then. A number of other sites have since been excavated and it has been established that Indus-Sarasvati culture covered not only Punjab, Sind and Baluchistan, but also Gujrat, Rajasthan, Haryana and Western Uttar Pradesh. This civilization extended from Jammu in the north to Narmada in the south and from Makran see-shore in the west to Meerut in western Uttar Pradesh. Indian history in its modern form began to be written in India's British period, when India was a slave country. British coloring of Indian history still persists and a real reliable Indian history is yet to establish itself. This civilization was a part and parcel of Indian Vedic civilization and culture, and is far more older than found in the history books.

The initial excavations of Harappa and Mohanjodaro sites

In the beginning of the century people living in Harappa (District Montgomery, Punjab, India), used to find fully baked bricks when they dug the ground all around their town. They, in fact, often used them in building their own houses. This fact invoked curiosity in the mind of Shri Daya Ram Sahni, the then Director of the Indian Archaeological Department. He started excavation work there in 1921. What he found was startling. Below the ground, he found a full-fledged city, where houses built from $40 \times 20 \times 10$ or $30 \times 15 \times 75$ centimeter size baked bricks existed. Walls were sometimes as wide as 2 feet. Roads were as wide as 9 feet to 34 feet and were perpendicular to each other. The city's water and sewer system made up of baked bricks was perfect. Every house had separate kitchen and bath room. This revealed that there existed a full fledged city there about 200 to 3000 B.C.

Later in 1922 Shri Rakhal Das Benerji did some excavation work at Mohanjo Daro, locally called as '*Mouyan-da-Dara*' meaning 'the mound of the dead', in District Larkana in Sind at the place of a Buddhist Monastery. An old Harappa like city was discovered there too. In 1968–69 a pre-Harappan plough field was uncovered at Kalibagan, District Ganganagar in Rajasthan. Recently a succession of well-articulated townships of pre-Indus and Indus culture, stated to be more than 4500 years old, have been excavated at Banawali, north-west of Fatehabad in Hissar district of Haryana. The pre-Indus folks at Banawali were conversant with the technology of copper-smelting. This was proved by personal ornaments, beads of semi-precious stones, terra-cotta and bangles discovered there.

It has been established that Indus-Sarasvati culture covered not only Punjab, Sind and Baluchistan, but also Gujrat, Rajasthan, Haryana and Western Uttar Pradesh. This civilization extended from Jammu in the north to Narmada in the south and from Makran see-shore in the west to Meerut in western Uttar Pradesh.

An analysis of colored presentation by the British

Now the question is as to what are the precedents and antecedents of this civilization ? How and where did it start and how and where did it end ?

Western scholars say that this Indus-Sarasvati civilization preceded 'Aryan Vedic Civilization'. They hold that Vedas are only about 1000 B.C. to 1500 B.C. old. One difficulty in this connection is that inscriptions found in the Indus-Sarasvati civilization have not yet been properly deciphered. Secondly, whenever one begins to decipher the so-called pre-historic events, the decipherer's background and views color the whole deciphering process. Moreover, if one's background is far removed in time and space from the historical point under investigation, the coloring becomes all the more deeper. The better bet in such a situation is that one should, as far as possible, try to put oneself into the shoes of those, who were or are nearer in space and time to those whose history we are trying to decipher. Indian history in its modern form began to be written in India's British period, when India was a slave country. This is not an occasion when one can go into details as to why British coloring of Indian history still persists and real reliable Indian history has not yet fully established itself.

Two examples to refute the current theory

Let me give here only two examples amongst many, which give a very wrong perception of Indian history. I state them here because they directly affect our perception of Indus-Sarasvati civilization. The first wrong perception is that Vedas are about 1000 B.C. to 1500 B.C. old. Fortunately, Vedic mathematics and astronomy have long been established as very exact sciences. The whole world knows that Mahabharat occurred a very long time after the Vedic period. Now we are living in the year 5222 Krishna year. Then how could one say Vedic Period from 1000 B.C. to 1500 B.C.? Vedas, according to Max Muller and some other scholars, are the oldest books in the library of the world. Thus, on all counts, Vedic culture far preceded Indus-Sarasvati or any other civilization. Six angas of the Vedas make it perfectly explicit that Vedas are beyond history and have no history in them at all. The word '*arya*' in Vedas has no racial content at all. It only means 'noble', a person in complete control of his or her senses and mind. On the other hand '*dasyu*' is a person, who is slave of his or her senses and mind. It is wrong to state that 'Aryans were invaders of India'.

When we take Indus-Sarasvati civilization in its right perspective, two things clearly stand out. First, this civilization was a part and parcel of Indian Vedic civilization and culture. Secondly, it also contained some elements of the cultures of countries on the western periphery of India.

Vedic Literature and the New View of Ancient India

DAVID FRAWLEY (VAMADEVA SHASTRI)
American Institute of Vedic Studies
PO Box 8357, Santa Fe NM 87504
email vedicinst@aol.com - web www.vedanet.com

Of the ancient literature of humanity the Vedas are the largest and the best preserved, as well as probably the oldest. The Vedas are not simply one book but a compendium of many teachings, reflecting the vision of numerous sages on all levels of knowledge. The Vedas are a treasure house of the deepest wisdom in the world. Unfortunately they have not been adequately studied and appreciated, particularly in the Western world. In fact the versions of the Vedas available in English today consist of poor translations and biased interpretations designed not so much to help us perceive the deeper truths of the Vedas but designed, it appears, more to discredit the Vedas altogether.

Historical dimension of Vedas

New finds in archeology show a greater antiquity and sophistication to Vedic culture, which is once more opening the door for a new examination of this profound literature. All the available evidence today—whether that of archeological, linguistic or literary—suggests that the Vedas represent the indigenous culture of India from the beginnings of civilization now placed around 6500 BC, which is what this paper will outline.

On the other hand, to the traditional Hindu mind the Vedas are eternal and any talk of their date or historical value appears irreverent and erroneous. Yet we do live in an historical age. The modern mind has constructed a view of human history in which the Vedas are going to be placed somewhere. If those who understand the deeper import of the Vedas do not show their historical relevance, then those who are opposed to the Vedas will place Vedic culture in an historical dark age, not the age of light which the Vedas portray.

It is thus the challenge of the times to address the historical dimension of the Vedas, not as a means of denying their spiritual value, but in order to reaffirm it. As long as the Vedas are regarded as primitive documents possessing little real historical relevance few will give any attention to them. However, if we show the connection between the Vedas and the ancient civilization of India, which is now quite obvious on all fronts, then it will be hard for any student of history to ignore them. The modern materialistic view of history will have to confront the reality of the Vedic eternal view of the human soul and its journey.

The point that can be made very clearly today, even using the limited views and approaches of archaeology, is that the ancient civilization of India is Vedic. This is not to say that the ancient India invented the Vedas and their knowledge. The Vedas may indeed, at least in part, reflect a perennial tradition of wisdom which antedates even the earliest civilization of India. But ancient India does reflect the Vedas in both its land and culture. The Vedas are at least as old as the earliest civilizations of India.

The Vedas, we should note, do have an historical dimension. They were compiled at a particular point in history, just after the Mahabharata War. The Vedas do contain references to various teachers like Yajnavalkya or Vasishta, or various kings like Nahusha or Janamejaya, who existed during a particular age. The Vedas also reflect a certain type of culture via the arts, crafts, agricultural practices which they portray, albeit generally only incidentally. Hence the Vedas can be correlated with specific cultures. However in dating Vedic culture or various kings and teachers mentioned in Vedic literature, we are not dating Vedic knowledge, which as primarily knowledge of the Self (Atmavidya), indeed is eternal. We also note that most of such historical references found in the Vedas are magnified by the accounts given in the Puranas and placed in a certain chronology. We are also thereby revindicating the Puranic view.

Old model of history has changed

Today we can definitively state that the old model of ancient Indian history has collapsed. The idea that the Vedic people, the so-called Aryans, were invaders into India around 1500 BC—which has been the main view up to recently—has now been disproved and will soon be consigned to the dust bin of history. The evidence is not from one field only but from a consensus of interdisciplinary studies. Various scholars east and west are uniting in this view from various perspectives like S.R. Rao, S.P. Gupta, B.B. Lal, Subhash Kak, Navaratna Rajaram, Srikant Talageri, Jim Schaffer, Mark Kenoyer, Colin Renfrew, Georg Feuerstein, to name a few.

First let us take an overview of ancient Indian history.

Ancient India is now divided into several periods, the pre-Harappan, Harappan, and post-Harappan.

1. The pre-Harappan (6500–3000 BC) starts with early agricultural and village cultures like Mehrgarh in Pakistan which show the initial form of the type of civilization that will later dominate the subcontinent.
2. The Harappan (3000–1900 BC) is the main urban phase dominated by great cities like Mohenjodaro and Harappa located on the Indus and Sarasvati river systems.
3. The post-Harappan (1900–1000 BC) is a relocation phase that occurs after most Harappan sites are abandoned owing to ecological changes (shifting of rivers, floods, desertification, a point that we will examine in detail later.

The post-Harappan phase involves a movement eastward of the center of Indian civilization from the Sarasvati, which disappears as a perennial river, to the Ganges, the site of later classical Indian civilization. Throughout this entire period there is an organic and indigenous development of civilization in India with an unbroken continuity. Harappan civilization was not destroyed, as the Aryan invasion theory projected, but merely relocated continuing its great traditions.

Harappan India was the largest civilization of the ancient world with a number of large cities and sites found as far north as Turkestan, as far west as to the coast of Iran, as far northeast as the Ganges and as far south as Karnataka (Godavari river), with even a site on the coast of Arabia. It was larger than the entire region from Egypt to Mesopotamia, including Crete, all the other main centers of civilization of the time. Harappan cities had the most sophisticated urban planning and Harappan civilization had the greatest consistency of all the others of the time.

The main points that refute Aryan invasion theory

Below the main points refuting the Aryan invasion are summarized.

1. Geographical

India is a flood plain for several great rivers. Through time the courses of rivers and sometimes the rivers themselves change. Prior to 1900 BC Western India was watered by another perennial river other than the Indus. The Sutlej, presently of the Indus system, flowed south. The Yamuna, presently of the Ganges system, flowed west. Together along with other streams of the region, which was wetter at this time, they formed a great river, up to five miles wide, which flowed to the sea at the Rann of Kachchh, slightly to the east of the Indus. The course of the Sarasvati has been identified through satellite photography (Landsat) and through ground water studies throughout Western India.

The remains of this ancient river are today called the Ghaggar, which only has water during the monsoon season. The Ghaggar has long been identified as the Sarasvati of Vedic fame. In its upper region it flows by the Kurukshetra region of later Vedic fame. It is this same Sarasvati-Drishadvati region that is called in Manu Samhita the central land and original homeland of the Brahmins (Manu Samhita II.19). The Vedas speak of the greatest river in India not as the Indus or Ganges but as the Sarasvati, which is said to be fed by five (Shukla Yajurveda 34.11) or seven streams (Rigveda VI.61.12), and to be pure in its course from the mountains to the sea (Rigveda VII.95.2). Vedic descriptions of the Sarasvati reflect the nature of this river in Harappan and pre-Harappan times, that is as it was over four thousand years ago.

It has also now been found that the great majority of Harappan ruins lie on the dried banks of the Sarasvati, not the Indus. Therefore the so-called Indus or

Harappan culture should be renamed the "Sarasvati culture", as a number of scholars are proposing.

As the Sarasvati of Vedic fame dried up by 1900 BC, Vedic culture must be much older than this date for the Vedas to know of this river, and far older than the 1500 BC date usually ascribed for the Aryan invasion of India. Some studies suggest that the ocean going portion of the Sarasvati dried up by 3000 BC and that the Drishadvati, a Vedic confluent of the Sarasvati (RV III.23.4), also dried up around this time, which would make the Vedic age yet earlier. The dates are not specific, and further studies are needed to pinpoint them more accurately, but they are certainly much earlier than what was previously thought.

While one can interpret ruins according to one's ideas and while ancient literature, which is highly symbolic, can be given any number of interpretations, one cannot change the course of rivers to suit one's opinions. The rediscovery of the Sarasvati thus clearly vindicates the antiquity of the Vedas and dismisses the Aryan invasion as invalid.

2. Populations

Through an examination of ruins and skeletal remains in ancient India archaeologists now proclaim that there is no evidence of any significant migrations into India from the west in ancient times. Skeletal remains of four thousand or more years ago shows the same basic racial types in Punjab and Gujarat then as today. There is no evidence of any Aryan race moving into India or any Dravidian race being driven to the south, but only the continuity of the same groups of people who have considered themselves to be Hindus and Vedic in their background.

The only significant west-to-east movement of peoples in ancient India is that of the Harappan people from the Sarasvati to the Ganges after the Sarasvati went dry. This movement is mirrored in Hindu literature with the Vedas placed on the Sarasvati and the Puranas on the Ganges.

3. Astronomy

The Vedas contain various astronomical references relative to the calendar. Vedanga Jyotish, as referred to by Varaha Mihira in his Brihat Samhita (III.1), outlines a calendar wherein the summer solstice occurred in the middle of the Nakshatra Aslesha (23 20 Cancer), which yields a date of around 1400 BC. Yajurveda, Atharvaveda (XIX.7.2), and several Brahmanas place the vernal equinox in the Krittikas (Taurus), the summer solstice in Magha (Leo), and the winter solstice in Aquarius, a date of 2500–2000 BC. Such astronomical data reflect the Harappan and post-Harappan era, which one would expect to have an adequate calendar.

In this regard there is a whole reexamination of Vedic science and mathematics which is beginning. It shows that the Vedic culture had many achievements in these areas quite out of keeping with their so-called primitive nature.

4. Religion

The original excavators like Wheeler felt that the Harappan religion was a form of Shaivism, which he thought was opposed to the Vedic. Recent research shows that the predominant Harappan religion was one of fire altars. Fire altars, both private and public, have been found in most Harappan sites, with all the ritual implements and offerings as shown in the Brahmanas. Other Vedic symbols like the swastika, the Brahma bull, have been found. Figures seated in various yogic postures also appear on the seals and deities like those mentioned in the Vedic and Puranic.

5. Vedic Literature

A more critical reading of Vedic texts shows a highly advanced civilization with cities, a high development of arts and crafts, with various kingdoms spread between the two oceans (Arabian Sea and Bay of Bengal). The ocean is one of the most prominent symbols in Vedic literature, including frequent references to travel on the sea. The Vedas do not show a nomadic or tribal culture, as the Aryan invasion requires, but a maritime urban culture. Vedic culture also spread by sea and land to other regions of the world.

6. Ancient Artifacts

There is a continuity of civilization from the pre-Harappan to the Harappan and post-Harappan phases. Horses, thought to have derived from the Aryan invaders, have now been found to have existed in India in Harappan and pre-Harappan times. The Indus or Harappan script, thought to be pre-Vedic or non-Indoeuropean, has now been found to be the precursor of the Brahmi script of later India and hence probably is that of a similar Sanskritic based language.

Surprisingly, the Rigveda with its culture based on barley (yava) as a grain, cattle, and copper (ayas) as the main metal reflects the pre-Harappan era primarily (before 3000 BC), which also shows these factors. The Atharva and Yajurvedas with their references to rice and wheat and to other metals including bronze (and possibly iron) reflect the Harappan era (after 3000 BC).

Some consequences of new findings

If we recognize, as the evidence suggests, that the ancient civilization of India is Vedic to Harappan and pre-Harappan times, the following points arise:

1. The history of India, such as found in textbooks in India today, must be rewritten. The Aryan invasion theory must be set aside. The idea that Aryans and Dravidians are different races (which is also scientifically

incorrect as both the peoples of north and south India belong primarily to the same Mediterranean Branch of the Caucasian race) must be given up.

2. The history of the Indo-European peoples must be rewritten. The Harappan (Sarasvati-Vedic) culture of India shows an Indo-European group at an advanced level of civilization and urbanization in the third millennium BC or over a thousand years before the cities of the Hittites and the Greeks. This suggests Vedic India as the main center of Indo-European civilization. Hence even Europe may have a Vedic past.
3. The history of the Middle East must also be rewritten. The Sarasvati (Harappan) culture was the largest of the world during its time. Therefore it is likely that it had a great impact on and perhaps dominated, at least culturally, Mesopotamia and possibly Egypt. For example, the island of Bahrain, at the mouth of the Persian Gulf used Harappan weights and measures, not Sumerian. Hence the primacy and antiquity of Indian civilization over the Middle Eastern is a real possibility. Vedic civilization may have spread to this region as well.
4. Once these correlations have been accepted, correlations between the Vedic and other cultures in the world like those of China or America may be possible, which also exhibit similar religions of sun worship and fire sacrifices. The Vedic may come to be accepted as the original culture for humanity from which we have departed and to which we must all return.

Need for Vedic Scholarship

Once the fact that ancient Indian civilization was Vedic is recognized there must also be a new era of Vedic scholarship. Such scholarship on an outer level will look for cultural connections between Vedic literature and Harappan and pre-Harappan ruins, and to Vedic connections with various ancient cultures. The Vedas will become the most important ancient books in the world for literary research during the coming century all over the world.

This will give a need to reexamine the spiritual meaning of the Vedas. Most existent interpretations of the Vedas are based upon the Aryan invasion model of a tribal warrior culture, which is now discredited. The commentaries of Sayana deal only with the outer or ritualistic meaning of the Vedic mantras and don't go deeply into any spiritual or yogic implications. New studies and commentaries on the Vedas should be done along Adhyatmic (spiritual) lines. This approach was already outlined in the Nirukta of Yaska but not followed out by any complete commentaries that remain. Works of modern scholars of the Vedas who examined its spiritual aspect, like Swami Dayananda Sarasvati, Sri Aurobindo, and Kapali Shastri, must be given more importance.

In this regard we must reexamine Vedic language, which is not a visible or literal language, but a cryptic, symbolic mantric code in which the secrets of the universe and of cosmogenesis are hidden. Vedic language cannot be adequately understood through mere reason. It is more in such poetic-mantric works like Saundarya Lahari of Shankaracharya that we can understand what the Vedic rishis were really speaking about in their strange metaphors.

The Vedic ritual had both an inner and outer form. The outer ritual involved various priests and offerings. The inner ritual proceeded through speech (vak, hota), mind (manas, adhvaryu), breath (prana, udgata) and soul (Atma, Brahma). The inner Vedic ritual thus is a matter of yogic practice and meditation. The Vedic fire is the Kundalini, which like Agni is enkindled in the earth altar (Muladhara chakra). The Vedic Soma represents the amrit or nectar that descends from the crown chakra when the Kundalini rises up. The yogic meaning of the Vedic deities thus must be reexplored.

The Vedas have an importance relative to other Vedic sciences as well. For example, the Ayurvedic theory of Vata, Pitta and Kapha is reflected in the three main Vedic deities of Indra (Vata, Prana), Agni (Pitta), and Soma (Kapha), which represent the spiritual principles behind the three doshas. Many secrets of Ayurveda, particularly of Brahma rasayana, or the rejuvenation of the mind, are hidden in the Vedic mantras. The Soma is this power of rejuvenation hidden in the mind which can come forth through meditation.

Hence archeology, long apparently an enemy of the Vedas, has now proved to revindicate them. Through this new view of Indian history a new door on the Vedas can be opened and the Vedas can become relevant to all humanity.

In this regard India must reclaim its Vedic heritage. It must promote Vedic schools and preserve the Vedic learning which has managed to survive through this materialistic age. I think without this the nation cannot rise up because the Vedas represent the original soul of the great subcontinent. The West also needs to recognize its forgotten Vedic heritage, if not Vedic roots.

REFERENCES

David Frawley, *Myth of the Aryan Invasion* (Voice of India, 1994)

David Frawley and N.S. Rajaram, *Vedic Aryans and the Origins of Civlization,* Voice of India, 1996

David Frawley, *Gods, Sages and Kings: Vedic Secrets of Ancient Civilization*, Passage Press, 1991.

David Frawley, Feuerstein and Kak, *In Search of the Cradle of Civilization*, Quest Books, 1995

David Frawley, *Wisdom of the Ancient Seers: Selected Mantras from the Rigveda*, Passage Press, 1993.

Agniṣomīya Paśuyāga
(An Operation for Rainmaking)

RAVI PRAKASH ARYA
H.E.S., 1051, Sector 1, Rohtak,124 001, India

Vedas are the first and foremost record of great advance made first ever by humanity. Vedic *Ṛṣis* explored all the three aspects of science i.e. *ādhyātmika*[1] *(psychological), ādhidaivika* (astronomical) and *ādhibhautika*[2] (terrestrial). During their explorations they found that all the three aspects of science are interdependent. Terrestrial aspect is based on astronomical and astronomical is based on psychological aspect, psychological aspect being the primary source of evolution. Other way round, it can be maintained that from psychological evolves the astronomical and from astronomical evolves the terrestrial one. Similarly, during the time of dissolution terrestrial dissolves into astronomical and astronomical finally dissolves into psychological. Vedic scholiasts tried to define all the three inter-dependent aspects in one through equivalences. That is why the terminology and terms applied by them have the equivalences in the fields of *adhyātma*, *adhidaivata* and *adhibhūta*. The Vedic visionaries who visualized the laws of *parā* and *aparā* nature beyond time and space, applied various methods to define the laws of *parā* nature (psychology), *aparā* nature (astronomy and terrestrial sciences) such as historical, mythological and *yājñika* etc. All these methods were figurative signifying *adhyātma* (psychology), *adhidaivata* (astronomy) and *adhibhūta* (physical or terrestrial aspect). *Yajñas* were not the ends but they were means to elucidate and explain the terrestrial, astronomical and psychological intents of the Vedas. In fact, psychology was the primary intent of the Vedas, astronomy and terrestrial intents being dealt with secondarily. Similarly, Brāhmaṇic ritualism was subjected to *adhyātma* (psychology) as their primary significance and others such as *adhidaivata* (astronomy) and *adhibhūta* (terrestrial) are dealt with as the secondary significances. A close perusal of the *Brāhmaṇas* confirms this fact. The *ādhyātmika* intent of the *yajñas* has been referred to 100 times therein, while astronomical and terrestrial intents have been referred to 60 times and 9 times, respectively (for detail see RPA, 1991, 59–60).

---

[1]Ādhyātmika consists in psychological, physiological, anthropological, metaphysical and ethical aspects. All of these aspects have been indicated by the term 'psychological'.

[2]*Ādhibhautika* includes geological, geographical, social, political and economic aspects of study. All these have been referred to by the term 'terrestrial'.

In addition to this, hosts of instances may be cited where the *yajñas* can be shown to have been intended by authors of the *Brāhmaṇas* for representing the knowledge of *adhyātma.* For instance *Ś.Br.* 10.2.5.1&2 narrates the aim of *Agnicayana* ceremony as to *ātmasaṁskāra* or self-purification:

tathaivaitadyajamāna etāḥ puraḥ prapadyābhaye'nāṣṭra etam-ātmānaṁ saṁskurute.

Confer Sāyaṇa's commentary here:

tathā'yaṁ yajamāno'pi upasadormadhye agnicayanenātmānam saṁskurute.

At another place *Ś.Br.* describes all the *yajñas* aiming at *ātmasaṁpādana* or self-accomplishment, e.g.

sarvairhi yajñairātmānam sampannam vide (10.2.6.15)

At yet another place *Ś.Br.* proclaims Agnihotra as the expounder of *Ātman* or *Brahman*, i.e., supreme self, e.g.,

Śauceya ha prācinayogya uddālakamāruṇimājagāṁ brahmodyaṁ agnihotraṁ vividisisyāmi iti. (11.5.3.1)

We come across a reference in *Ś.Br.* where *Darśapūrṇamāsa* and *Cāturmāsya* sacrifices are depicted as having twofold objects of their performance, viz., *ātmayājītva* (i.e. psychological or self-realisation) and *devayājītva* (astronomical), as in

prajāpatiraha cāturmāsyairātmānam vidadhe (11.5.2.1)

Sāyaṇa's commentary is noteworthy here. According to him,

yathā darśapurṇamāsayājina ātmayājitvaṁ devayājitvaṁ ceti dvaividhyaṁ darśitaṁ evaṁ cāturmāsya yājino'pi tathātvaṁ darśayituṁ śarīrāvayavakalpanaṁ ākhyikayā racayati.

Thereupon as regards the question as to who is superior between *devayājī* and *ātmayājī*, *Ś.Br.* clarifies:

ātmayājī śreyān devayāji iti, ātmayājīti brūyāt sa ha ātmayajīyo vededaṁ me'nenāṅgam saṁskrīyate idaṁ me'nenāṅgamupadhīyata iti. (11.2.6.23)

That is '*ātmayājī* is superior between *ātmayājī* and *devayājī*. *Ātmayājī* is he who knows while performing sacrifice which of the limbs of his body is being consecrated or augmented by a particular action of *yajña* or sacrifice.'

Thus the internal evidences of the *Brāhmaṇas* give support to the view that terrestrial, astronomical and psychological meanings in order of preference were indicated by the ceremonial rituals of the *Brāhmaṇas.*

Agniṣomīya Paśuyāga (ASPY) being one in series also represents the psychological, astronomical and terresterial aspects. In psychological sense, it is the charging of an individuated consciousness with knowledge. *Paśu* here means a curious student or an individual (individuated consciousness) who is able to perceive the world around him but cannot cognize the same. *Paśu saṁjñapana* means to make the individuated consciousness surcharged with knowledge. Complete surcharging leads to the universalization of consciousness or *mokṣa* from physical body. *Agni* means a charge of knowledge and soma is a good conductor of charge or say a student worthy of charging with knowledge. A *soma* is always sacrificed to *Agn*i for the accomplishment of the process of surcharging. This subject has been handled in detail by Swami Dayananda in course of rendering his psychological translation of *Yajurveda.*[1] Here knowledge is the quality of *ātman* or consciousness and until and unless the consciousness is completely surcharged with knowledge it cannot attain universalhood or redeem itself. The seers had it as: *ṛte jñānāt na muktiḥ.*

But here it may be pointed out that the *Agniṣomīya Paśuyāga* has its equivalence at astronomical levels also which is mainly subjected to this article.

In fact, when psychological aspect is signified, the *yajñas* assume the character of *Brahmayajña;* while signifying astronomical aspect they are termed as *Devayajñas. Brahmayajña* form of *ASPY* signifies the psychological aspect and *Devayajña* form of *ASPY* signifies the astronomical sense. The purpose of *Devayajña* form of *ASPY* is narrated in the *Yājuṣa mantra* as follows:

adbhyastauṣadhibhyaḥ, (*VS.* 6.9)

i.e., 'for the sake of waters and vegetations we procure you O *havis* !'

The same *mantra* further reads:

anu tvā māta manyatāmanu pitānu bhrātā sagarbhyo'nu sakhā sayūthyaḥ. (6.9)

'Let your parent herbs, sister herbs, and simultaneously born herbs and your friendly herbs permit you to be procured for rains and growth of vegetation.'

During the course of translating this stanza Uvaṭa clarifies the same with a quotation from *Śruti.*

idaṁ hi yadāvarṣatyathauṣadhayo jāyante

'When it rains, herbs grow.'

---

[1]Dr. Veda Pal Suneeth has also made a laudable attempt in plucking out its psychological intent. See

Thus the main purpose of *Agniṣomīya* sacrifice in *adhidaivata* sense works out, as is evident from the actual verse of the *VS*, to be rainmaking. This is why the seer says that the *paśu* (vegetation) endowed with the quality of *Agni* and *Soma* is procured for sacrifice.

Agniṣomābhyām juṣṭaṁ niyunajmi (*VS*. 6.9).

And the same type of vegetation i.e. vegetations worthy of augmenting the power of *Agni* and *Soma* are consecrated. *Agniṣomābhyāṁ tvā juṣṭaṁ prokṣāmi* (6.9). In fact for making it rain, *Agni* and *Soma* are coordinated in a particular ratio.

apāṁ ca jyotiṣaśca maiśrībhāvakarmaṇo varṣa karma jāyate

(See for detail RPA 1995: 146)

These two elements *Agni* and *Soma* are defined by *Ś.Br.* as under:

dvayaṁ vā idaṁ na tṛtīyamasti. ārdaṁ caiva śuṣkaṁ ca. yac-chuṣkaṁ tadāgneyaṁ yadārdraṁ tat somyaṁ. (*Ś.Br.* 1.6.3.23)

'There are only two elements, no third is there. One is dry, another is wet. Dryness pertains to *Agni* and wetness pertains to *Soma*.'

Here the great debatable term is *Paśu*. This sacrifice has primarily taken by many ancient and modern Vedic scholiasts for animal killing. According to them, including Mahidhara, one of the commentators of *VS*, in *ASPY*, animal is sacrificed. So, the tradition of animal sacrifice is also traced back to Vedas themselves.

In fact, scholars could not make out the actual intent of *Paśu*. So they speculated *Paśu* for its literal sense, i.e., animal. Now we shall try to ascertain the actual meaning of *Paśu* intended by the seer on the basis of internal evidences of *mantras* implied in *Agniṣomīya paśuyāga* and their explanations in *Ś.Br.* in course of handling the same subject. *Ś.Br.* (3.8.4.5) defines *Paśu* broadly as life. Whatever (whether plants, animals or men) has life is called *Paśu*. *Prāṇa eva paśuḥ* (*Ś.Br.* 3.8.4.5).

In the context of *devayajña, paśu* is considered as the sacrificing material. For example, according to *Ś.Br.* (11.5.4.27), sacrificing material for all deities is known as *paśu*.

sarvāsāṁ vai devānāṁ haviḥ paśuḥ.

A.Br. also points out that *Paśu* is the sacrificing material.

havirhi paśuḥ

Now the question arises as to what was the actual nature of *Paśu* to be sacrificed as the *havi* for deities in the context of *Devayajña*. Whether it was animals or plants. To clarify it we may quote here the seer of the *Yajurveda*. According to him, *Vanaspati* or vegetation is selected for *devayajña*.

taṁ tvā juṣāmahai deva vanaspate devayajñāyai. (*VS*. 5.42).

'O vegetation, we select you as a sacrificing material for *devayajña*.'

Sacrificing material in *devayajña* is plants or foodgrains and nothing else; it is proved by the following reference of the *Ś.Br.* (1.2.1.20):

ulūkhala mūsalābhyāṁ dṛṣadupalābhyāṁ havir yajñaṁ ghnanti.

'The sacrificing material for *devayajña* is pounded with the help of *ulūkhala* and *mūsala* (i.e. mortar and wooden pestle or grinding board and muller).'

Thus the act of *paśu*'s killing with *ulūkhala* and *mūsala* is in fact the preparation of *havi* to be offered to the sacrificial fire.

ghnanti vā etat paśuṁ yadagnau juhvati. (*Ś.Br*. 3.8.1.10)

The *Śatpatha* reference further makes it clear. Accordingly by offering vegetations to *Yajñīya* fire, we are not destroying them at all.

na vā etaṁ mṛtyave nayanti yaṁ yajñāya nayanti. (*Ś.Br.* 3.8.1.10)

They cannot get eliminated by this way. In fact they become imperishable. They again grow and get back to life (flourish) on the earth.

amṛtamāyurhiraṇyaṁ. tadamṛtaṁ āyuṁṣi prātitiṣṭhati. tathāta udeti. tathā sañjīvāti. (*Ś.Br.* 3.8.1.10)

Not only the author of the *Śatapatha,* but the seer himself expresses nonetheless the similar view. He had it, as a result of the sacrifice of the plants or foodgrains to *yajña*, rainy waters flow on the Earth. These rainy waters will relieve you of the sin of cutting and destroying the vegetation, since more and more vegetations will in turn be able to grow.

idamāpaḥ pravahatāvadyaṁ ca malaṁ ca yat. yaccābhi dudrohānṛtaṁ. yacca śepe abhīruṇaṁ āpo mā tasmādenasaḥ pavamānañca muñcatu. (6.17)

Paśu was *(anna)* foodgrains. It is clearly indicated by *Ś. Br.* at one place as

na ha vā etasmā agre paśavaścakṣamire. yadannamabhaviṣyan yatheyamannaṁ bhūtā. (3.7.3.2)

'The *Paśus* were therefore not able to see' in the beginning, since foodgrains were called *Paśus*. .

Further the seer tells us as to what sort of vegetation would be worthy of use as an *Agniṣomīya Paśu* or material for sacrificing in *ASPY.*

According to the seer, the vegetation that has grown in water or has consumed lot of water is worth to be the *deva havi* in *Agniṣomīya Paśuyāga.*

apāṁ perūrasyāpo devīḥ svadantu svāttaṁ citsaddeva haviḥ. saṁ te prāno vātena gacchatāṁ samaṅgāni yajatraiḥ saṁ yajña patirāśiṣā.

(*VS.* 6.10)

So, it must be made in mind that the *havi* to be used for rainmaking or cloudseeding should be of *somīya* nature, i.e., it should have grown in the climate of high humidity and heavy rainfall.

Bṛhadāraṇyakopaniṣad also reflects an ample good light upon the rain inducing effect of *somīya āhutis, such as*

somaṁ rājānaṁ juhvati. tasyā āhūtyai vṛṣṭiḥ sambhavati.

(RPA 1995: 152)

During our experiments of rainmaking, this fact was found to be proven, since all of our experiments for cloudseeding and rainmaking were accomplished only with the help of *Somīya āhutis. This fact has been disclosed in detail by the author in his work Vedic Meteorology*, Part II, Chapter 3.

Only *somīya havi does not suffice to induce rain or seed clouds, but they should be committed to sacrificial fire in the company of Ghṛta* or fats obtained from the milk of cow. The verse had it as:

ghṛtenāktau paśūṁstrāyethā revati yajamāne priyaṁ dhā āviśa. urorantarikṣātsajurdevena vātenāsya haviṣastinanā yaja samasya tanvā bhava. varṣo yajñe yajñapatiṁ dhāḥsvāhā devebhyo devebhyaḥ svāhā. (*VS.* 6.11)

Let the *somīya āhutis* be soaked in the *Ghṛta.* Only after being soaked they should reach the *yajamāna.* They should be offered to *yajña* in the presence of air in the vast sky. This way they get expanded in volume. Since they are born in rains, they will induce rains. 'Let the *yajamāna* sacrifice them in the name of the concerned deity or to augment the power of the concerned deity.'

Not only *somīya havis* are soaked in *Ghṛta,* but the oblations of a fairly good amount of *Ghṛta* are also offered in this *yajña.*

ghṛtasya kulyā upaṛtasya pathyā anu. (*VS.* 6.12)

In our experiments of rainmaking, we discovered that *Ghee* is also one of the ingredient materials to be offered to fire of the *yajña* for rainmaking. The seer has visualized this fact thousands of years ago.

After giving a prescription of the offered material consisting of *Ghee* and other *somīya* vegetation, the seer extols the quality of celestial waters or water vapours abiding in midsphere and seeks the ability to procure them. For example, *devirāpaḥ śhuddhā voḍhvaṁ suparivistā devesu suparivistā vayaṁ parivestāro bhūyāsma.* (6.13)

'The celestial waters are pure and exist everywhere in the upper region. They have found their place among other *devas*, i.e., *Indra* etc. Let us become capable to nab them or procure them.'

In the next verse each and every part of the *havi* is purified so that it may become worthy to be offered as oblation.

vācaṁ te śundhāmi prāṇaṁ te śundhāmi, cakṣuste śundhāmi. (6.14)

Further it was prayed that each and every part of the oblatory material should be in a sound condition. For example, the seer likes it to be as:

manasta āpyāyatāṁ vākta āpyāyatāṁ prāṇasta āpyāyatāṁ cakṣusta āpyāyatāṁ śrotraṁ ta āpyāyatāṁ yatte kruraṁ yadāsthitaṁ tatta āpyāyatāṁ niṣṭyāyatāṁ tatte śudhyatu śamahobhyaḥ. (6.15)

Thus it is obvious from the foregoing that sacrificing material should be pure and in a sound condition. There should be no impurity; it should not be in a decayed position. For this purpose he asks the plant to provide the offering material intact. *Oṣadhe trāyasva* (6.15). He further suggests not to destroy the plant completely with the cutting knife or sword. *Svadhite mainaṁ hiṁsiḥ.* (6.15)

In the beginning, the seer has advised not to go for impure or mixed material, but in spite of all care duly taken in selecting the *somīya* offering, there is possibility of some material not being *somīya* and so creating anti-rain effect on sacrificing remain mixed with the original one, In such conditions, this type of material may necessarily be separated or removed. The seer explains this operation as under:

rakṣasāṁ bhāgo'si nirastaṁ rakṣa idamahaṁ rakṣa'bhitiṣṭhāmidamahaṁ rakṣo'vabādhaṁ idamahaṁ rakṣa'dhamaṁ tamo nayāmi. (6.16)

'You create anti effects. I remove you since you are anti-material. I remove this anti-material. I stop this to be used. I throw it to the heap of rubbish.'

He also discloses the process as to what happens after *somīya āhutis* are offered to fire.

According to him, on being sacrificed the *āhuti* goes to the upper layer of atmosphere along with the air drifted upward on account of the heating effect of *yajñīya* fire.

svāhākṛte ūrdhvaṁ nabhasaṁ mārutaṁ gacchataṁ. (6.16)

In fact the *āhuti* goes to the sky in the form of its essence or vapours, its carbon part scatters on the earth.

divaṁ te dhūmo gacchatu svarjyotiḥ pṛthivī bhasmanā pṛṇa svāhā. (6.21)

Thus the *āhutis* reach their concerned deities in the form of smoke.

At the end, the purpose of *Agniṣomīya paśuyāga* is further explained from the seer's prayer to *Varuṇa* to release the waters and herbs from their respective places of origin instead of destroying them. He asks for pardon because though the herbs were not worth destroying, but they had destroyed them by sacrificing into fire. He prays further, 'Let these waters and herbs be useful for us, let them be harmful for those who bear grudge against us.' The stanza reads as follows:

> *māpo mauṣadhirhiṁsī dhāmno dhāmno rājanstato varuṇa no muñca yadāhuraghnyā iti varuṇeti śapāmahe tato varuṇa no muñca. sumitriyā na āpa oṣadhayaḥ santu durmitriyastasmai santu yo asmāndveṣṭi yaṁ ca vayaṁ dviṣmaḥ.* (6.22)

'Let the waters and herbs be not destroyed. Let them flourish at the respective places of their origin. Let the *Varuṇa* release them for us from the respective places of their origin. They are said not worth destroying and we are blamed to have destroyed them. So please O *Varuṇa*, excuse us. Let both the waters and herbs be friendly (useful) with us; let them be unfriendly with those who bear grudge against us and against whom we do so.'

This stanza marks the end of *Agniṣomīya paśuyāga.* Thus it is crystal clear from the aforementioned discussion that the aim of *Agniṣomīya paśuyāga* is rainmaking or cloudseeding so far as its astronomical intent is concerned.

This *yāga* has nothing to do with animal sacrifice as proposed by ancient commentators of *Yajurveda*, viz., Uvaṭa and Mahīdhara. In fact the use of the word *paśu* creates this type of misconception in the mind of the readers. They are misled by *paśu* taking it to mean animal, but the actual intent of *paśu* here is the vegetation to be offered as an oblation to the fire.

havirhi paśuḥ

Moreover, one should not forget that the seer of *Yajurveda* himself declares that *vanaspati* or vegetation is used for *devayajña.*

> *taṁ tvā juṣāmahe deva vanaspate deva yajñayai.* (*VS.* 5.42)

So far as the various limbs to be offered to sacrificial fire are concerned, they fit suitably more in the context of *ādhyātmika* sense than in astronomical sense.

REFERENCES

Ravi Prakash Arya (RPA), *Researches into Vedic and Linguistic Studies,* Grantha Bharati Prakashan, Delhi, 1991.

__________, *Vedic Meteorology*, Parimal Publications, Delhi, 1995.

Uvaṭa and Mahīdhara, *Vājsaneyi Saṁhitā* (*VS*), Motilal Banarsidass, Varanasi.

Śatapatha Brāhmaṇa (Ś.Br.), Rashtriya Sanskrit Sansthan, Delhi, 1990.

The Vedic Heritage for Environmental Stewardship

O.P. DWIVEDI*
University of Guelph, Guelph, Canada

The concern for nature conservation and protection is ingrained in all world cultures and spiritual traditions They, each in their own way, offer a unique set of moral values and norms to guide humanity in its relationship with nature. In each culture and spiritual tradition, human beings were given a stewardship role for conservation and protection of the Creation. Nevertheless, people everywhere exploited and manipulated natural forces in the name of development with an intensity unsurpassed by any other species on earth. This manipulation, guided by the current culture of materialism and consumerism, has given rise to the view that we as human-beings have the right to use the natural environment solely for our design and purposes without consideration for the consequences of our actions on the ecosystem or on our own future generations. For our selfish ends, we the people have disregarded and to some extent mis-interpreted our spiritual heritage and values concerning nature. This presentation examines the concept of environmental stewardship and the respect for *Devi Vasundhara* as depicted in the *Prithivi-Sukta* of Atharva-Veda, as well as in other Vedic literature. The author concludes with the suggestion for building an ecological paradigm and strategy based on the concept of *Vasudhaiv Kutumbakam* and an ethic of environmental stewardship which draws on the exhortations by our Vedic seers.

1. The Background

In the past, we have witnessed the over-exploitation of nature and its resources to the point where human intervention in natural ecosystems has caused genetic mutations, the emission of heat and noxious gases into the atmosphere, destruction of forests and many other effects that are heading not only towards irreversible global damage but also to the annihilation of God's creation. These interventions are so drastic in scale and impact that our life-support systems, both locally and globally, are being threatened. Consequently, at a minimum, our activities be such that these must not endanger the natural systems that support life of all organisms on earth including the atmosphere, the waters, the soils, and the living beings. Until compatible limits on our prevailing ethic of acquisitive materialism,

*Professor O.P. Dwivedi, Ph.D., LL.D. (Hon.) teaches public administration and environmental policy and law at University of Guelph, Canada. He is past President of the Canadian Political Science Association; at present, he is Vice President of the International Association of Schools and Institutes of Administration, Brussels, Belgium.

unending growth ethic and similar demands for resource use are set, continued global ecological damage is unavoidable. It is here where the manifestation of a global community oriented towards environmental stewardship can provide the means by which local, regional and international commons/ecosystems can be maintained.

As we approach the next millennium, it is becoming increasingly clear that many of the values held by us are totally inadequate for long-term survival and sustainable development; that is why it is not surprising that we are witnessing an emergence of a wide spectrum of challenges to the traditional materialistic view. For over a millennia, guided by the Western culture, people have had blind faith in the prowess of science and technology to bring the desired material progress generally measured by economic well-being. It is only recently that we have come to understand that so-called material prosperity is not an end in itself. Slowly, a realization is emerging that spirituality and control of one's temptations/desires can bring a lasting happiness compared to materialism. However, such a realization is yet to enter in our governmental policy domain as well as in the corporate world where spiritual perspectives are generally ignored. The economic criteria which placed no value on the commons (the air, water, oceans, outer space, etc.), and which used concepts such as cost-benefit analysis, law of supply and demand, rate of return, land being a commodity and hence being a fundamental right to own property, etc. has been actually based on the delusion that has operated independently of the cultural and spiritual domain. Until now, we have taken more from our Mother Earth than ever cared to think of putting the limits on our plundering and ravaging instincts.

If environmental problems are to be solved, then a change in the way individuals think about and interact with their environment must occur. It is for this reason that the cultural and spiritual underpinnings of stewardship, which is the primary virtue in the active life of Eastern cultural and religious traditions, can be of benefit to the entire humanity. Our spiritual heritage can provide new ways of valuing, thinking, and acting that are needed if respect for nature is to be achieved and future ecological disasters are to be averted. Further, if the ecological crisis that we face today is mostly due to our attitudes towards nature, then these attitudes will have to be changed. But to change the prevailing materialistic attitudes, values and beliefs towards the environment, we shall have to draw on our spiritual and philosophical foundations and heritage—specially those foundations which enjoin us to see divinity in nature and treat it with respect. By doing this, we may evade a global ecological catastrophe.

Of course, without a change in our current value system, there will be little hope of correcting the present environmental problems we face today because "ultimately we must realize that the new images, values, and archetypes that people carry in their heads shape the institutions, technologies, and environments in their heads."[1] For this, a new consciousness will have to be developed which believes in the ethic of environmental stewardship which draws on our rich cultural and spiritual heritage. In this regard, let us examine contributions made by the Vedic heritage of India.

2. *The Vedic Heritage for Eco-care*

The relationship between human beings and nature attracted the seers of the Vedic period in a manner incomparable to any other religious and cultural traditions. The Vedic seers contemplated over the mysteries of the Creation, place of heaven and earth, and even beyond. They would not accept as final what they saw around themselves; instead they asked many penetrating questions not only about life but more about death because they were intrigued by what happens to the soul once it leaves this physical body. They were equally interested in the mystery of Creation and the establishment of the universe. Through their deep thinking, guesses, conjectures and postulations, they came to acknowledge that the material causes of this Creation happened to be the *Panch Mahabhutas* (Five Great Elements); traditionally, they are enumerated as *Prithivi* (earth), *Apah* (waters), *Tejah/Agni* (light/fire), *Akash* (space), and *Vayu* (air), although the *Taittiriya Upanishad* reverses this order (2.1). The *Aitareya Upanishad* describes them as:

Imani cha panch mahabhutani prithivi vayuh aakaash aapo jyotimshi
(*Aitareya Upanishad*, Chapter III, Verse 3)

This is the five elements: earth, air, space, water, and light.

These five Mahabhutas are cosmic elements which create, nurture, sustain all forms of life, and after death or decay, they absorb what was created earlier; and they play an important role in preserving and sustaining the environment. It should be noted that all these Mahabhutas have been deified in the Vedic and Puranic literature. Further, they, all together, have been regarded as all-pervasive and omnipresent elements; also they have the great creative potency; also together, they constitute *Brahman* who manifested the universe and whose manifestation goes on revolving forever. As mentioned in the Shvetashvatara Upanishad:

Yenavritam nityamidam hi sarvam . . .
Teneshitam karma vivartate ha prithvyaptejoanilkhani chintyam
(*Shvetashvatara Upanishad,* Chapter 6, verse 2)

---

[1] Alastair M. Taylor and Duncan Taylor, "World religions, science and technology, and the environmental crisis", in: O.P. Dwivedi (Ed.), *World Religions and the Environment*, Gitanjali Publishing, New Delhi, 1989, p. 30.

The Brahman by whom this entire universe is engulfed . . . this creation is governed by Him as well as the five great elements: earth, air, space, water and light.

Some specific description about these Mahabhutas is given below:

1. Apah (Water)

According to Shrutis, water was the first of the cosmic elements. The Rigveda says that "in the beginning, all was water, and there was darkness which engulfed it" (*Rigveda*, Book 10, Hymn 129, verse 3); as a matter of fact, in the Rigveda, four hymns have been addressed to the waters (Book 7, Hymn 47 and Hymn 49; Book 10, Hymns 9 and 30). Further, the Rigvedic Hymn 23 (Book 1, verses 16–21) considers water as the reservoir of all curative medicines and of nectar. Waters are the mothers of all beings, and they are the foundations (*pratishtha*) of all in the universe.[1] The genesis of the Universe takes place in the primeval water. The following verse from the *Atharvaveda* illustrates the place of water in our lives:

Sham ta aapo hemvatih shamu te santootsyah
Sham to sanishyadaa aapah shamu te santu varshyah
Sham ta aapo dhanvaanyah sham te santwanupyaah
Sham te khanitrima aapah sham yah kumbhebhiraabhritah
(*Atharvaveda,* Book IXX, Hymn II, verses 1 and 2)

[May the waters from the snowy mountains bring health and peace to all people; May the spring waters bring calm to you; May the swift currents be pleasing to you; and may the rains be a source of tranquillity to all. May the waters of oasis in desert be sweet to you; and so be the waters of ponds and lakes. May the waters from wells dug by humans be good to them, and may the healing powers of water be available to all beings.]

2. Tejas/Agni

Agni is considered in Vedas as the spring of our life because it creates life on the earth. Agni, in later Vedic description, is known as the sun and light. In the form of the sun, Agni is regarded as the soul, and also as the ruler and preserver of the world (Maitrayana Upanishad, 6.35). In the Rigveda, Book 10, a series of hymns (such as 1-8, 11-12, 16, 20-21, 37, 45-46, 51 etc.) have been devoted to Agni; and its almighty primordial nature is depicted as both non-existent (*asat*), and existent (*sat*); that is, the first cause and the first effect of this creation (Rigveda, Book 10, Hymns 5 and 7).

---

[1]S.K. Lal, "Pancamahabhutas: Origin and Myths in Vedic Literature", i:n Sampat Narayan (Ed.), *Prakrti: An Inte~ral Vision*, (Volume 2), Indira Gandhi National Centre for the Arts, New Delhi, 1995, p. 9.

3. Akash/Space

The word *Akash* denotes space rather than sky or ether as mentioned in some translated Shrutis. It is not a material or physical element. This word has appeared more so in Upanishads rather than in the Rigveda where its synonyms such as *nabhas, kham, antariksha* or *dyaus* have appeared. In *Chhandogya Upanishad*, a discussion takes place among three Rishis; one question is asked: where is this world *pratishthit* (that is, what is the foundation of this world); Pravaahana replies that it is in the *Akash* because it is the *Akash* (space) out of which all beings [their souls] come from, and it is where they go back after their death, because Akash is the final refuge of all beings (*Chhandogya Upanishad*, Book 1, 9th Part, verse 1).

4. Vayu/Air

In the Vedic literature, Vayu is the bond and the thread which keeps the universe together. When Uddalaka asked Yagyavalkya: what is that thread which binds this world and the other world and all beings, Rishi Yagyavalkya said: "By air indeed, O Gautama, as thread, this world, the other world, and all beings are held together" (*Brihadaranyaka Upanishad*, 7 Brahmanam, verse 2). Vayu is also liked as *Prana* (the life-sustaining breadth). Vayu is the germ of the world and a transformer of seed. Without Prana, nothing survives.

5. Prithivi/Earth

The Rigveda describes Prithivi as a divinity as well as one of the Mahabhutas. She is the mother and an upholder of all.(*Rigveda*, Book 10, Hymn 18, verse 10; and Book 1, Hymn 155, verse 2). Prithivi is also identified with goddess Aditi: a mother and protector of the holy cosmic law; she is also regarded as a divine ship, full of life-sustaining harvest. She, along with four other Mahabhutas, provide eco-care to our universe. This relationship between earth and humans is superbly depicted by Rishi Atharva in *Prithivi Sukta* (Hymn to Mother Earth) of the Atharvaveda.

3. *The Prithivi Sukta*

The Atharvaveda is perhaps the first of its kind of scripture in any spiritual tradition where the concept of respect to Earth has been propounded. An entire chapter consisting of 63 verses (Mantras) has been devoted in praise of the Mother Earth. These verses integrate much of the thoughts of Hindu seers concerning our existence on Earth. A series of verses follow, addressed to Devi Vasundhara: the Mother Earth, evoking her benevolence. Mother Earth is seen as an abode of a large and extended family (*Kutumbakam*) of all beings (humans and others alike). As the Mantra 11 tells us:

Giryaste parwata hima vantoranyam te prithvi syonamastu
Babhrum krushnam rohinim vishvarupam dhruvam bhumim prithivimin-draguptam
Ajitohato akshatoadhyatham prithivimaham.
(*Atharva Veda,* Kanda XII, Hymn I, Mantra 11)

[O Mother Earth! Sacred are thy hills, snowy mountains, and deep forests. Be kind to us and bestow upon us happiness. May you be fertile, arable, and nourisher of all. May you continue supporting people of all races and nations. May you protect us from your anger (natural disasters). And may no one exploit and subjugate your children.]

This prayer, which is based on the cosmic vision of our planet Earth, and which also relates to our consciousness towards the environment, is based on the fundamental concept of *Vasudhaiv Kutumbakam.* Every entity and organism is a part of one large extended family system which is presided by the eternal Mother Earth. It is She who supports us from her abundant endowments and riches, it is She who nourishes us, it is She who provides us with a sustainable environment, and it is She when angered by the misdeeds of her children punishes them with disasters. As one ought not to insult, unduly exploit, and violate his mother but to be kind and respectful to her, in the same way, one should behave towards the Mother Earth. Through such exhortations and various writings, Hindu religion has provided a system of moral guidelines towards environmental preservation and conservation. From the perspective of Hindu culture (as well as from the Buddhist and Jain perspectives), abuse and exploitation of nature for selfish gain is unjust and sacrilegious.

The *Prithivi Sukta* also exemplifies the relevance of environmental sustenance, agriculture, biodiversity to human beings. All the three main segments of our physical environment, that is water, air and soil, are highlighted and their usefulness is detailed. The various water resources[1] such as seas, rivers, and waterfalls flow on Earth. It consists of the three layers of brown, black and red layers of soil which is used for agricultural purposes.

The *Prithivi Sukta* maintains that attributes of earth (such as its firmness, purity and fertility) are for everyone, and that no one group or nation has special authority over it. That is why the welfare of all and hatred towards none is the core value which people on this planet ought to strive for.[2] For example, there is a prayer for the preservation of the original fragrance of earth[3] so that its natural

[1]*AtharvvVeda: Prithivi Sukta*, Chapter 12, Mantra 3, Swadhyay Mandal, Surat, India (commentary by Pandit Shripat Damodar Satvalekar).

[2]*Prithivi Sukta,* Mantra 18.

[3]*Prithivi Sukta,* Mantra 23 and 25.

legacy is sustained for the future generations. Further, there is a prayer which says that even when people dig the earth either for agricultural purposes or for extracting minerals, let it be so that her vitals are not hurt and that no serious damage is done to her body and appearance[1]; that is her natural resources and vegetation cover is conserved. Similarly, the importance of protecting medicinal herbs and other bio-diversity is mentioned in the following Mantra:

Yasyam vriksha vanaspatya dhruvastisthanti vishvaha
Prithivim vishva dhayasam dhritamacchavadamasi.
(*Atharvaveda*, Kanda XII, Hymn I, Mantra 27)

[O Mother Earth! you are the sustainer and preserver of all vegetation including medicinal plants as well as all living beings. May you the *Devi Vasundhara* nourish us as long as we live.]

The importance, as listed above, given to plants and other vegetation is further extolled by Lord Krishna in *Bhagavad Gita* where the Lord says that among all plants and trees. He is an Ashvatthah tree (a tree which grows anywhere, even on a very hard surface).[2] Further, the *Prithivi Sukta* mentions that urban centres (*Purah*) should be planned in such a way that this land remains a place worth living for all, with its natural beauty preserved.[3] The Earth is considered, after Sun, the main source of energy flowing through its vitals such as plants, minerals, and other elements; the same energy is also present in all living beings because it is that energy which drives them to work for quenching their hunger and thirst. Mantra 19 illustrates this:

Agnih bhumyam aushadhishu agnim apah vibhrati agnih ashmasu
Agnih antah purushesu goshu ashveshu agneyah.
(*Atharva Veda*, Kanda XII, Hymn I, Mantra 19)

[The Earth is full of energy, and the same energy flows through its herbs and other medicinal plants, the clouds carry energy in the form of thunder, also there is energy inside stones, and the same energy is prevalent among people and animals in the form of hunger. May that energy sustain us.]

Although man's greed and exploitative tendencies have been the main cause of environmental destruction, inter-religious and inter-cultural conflicts and wars have also contributed to the environmental problems. Therefore the *Prithivi-Sukta* enunciates the unity of all races and among all beliefs; further, the concept of secularism, multiculturalism and multilingualism, has been urged with a prayer

---

[1] *Prithivi Sukta*, Mantra 35.
[2] *Bhagavad Gita*, chapter 10, verse 26.
[3] *Prithivi Sukta*, Mantra 43.

which says that the Mother Earth bestows upon all the people living in any part of the world the same prosperity which has been pleaded by the Rishi Atharva of India.

Janam bibhrati bahudha vivacasam nandharmanam prithivi yathaukasam
Sahasram dharah dravinasya me duham dhruveva dhenurana prasphuranti.
(*Atharvaveda*, Kanda XII, Hymn I, Mantra 45)

[The Mother Earth where people belonging to different races, following separate faiths and religions, and speaking numerous languages cares for them in many ways. May that Mother Earth, like a Cosmic Cow, give us the thousand-fold prosperity without any hesitation without being outraged by our destructive actions.]

It is further mentioned that irrespective of the place of assembly of people whether in public meetings, or in woods, or even in battle ground facing each other, we should always remain respectful to our Mother Earth. Mantra 56 portrays this sentiment in the following manner:

Ye grama yadaranyam yah sabhah adhibhumyam
Ye sangramah samitayastesu charu vadem te.
(*Atharvaveda*, Kanda XII, Hymn I, Mantra 56)

[Whether we are in rural area, in woods, in battleground or in public meetings (wherever we are), we should always speak amicably about the Mother Earth and be respectful to you.]

As a matter of fact, those who defend and protect the environment are showered by blessings[1]. That is why, in the Mantra 59, the Mother Earth is implored to bless us with all kinds of nourishment and serenity so that we may live in peace and harmony.

Shantiva surahhih syona kilalodhni payasvati
Bhumiradhi bravitu me prithivi payasa saha.
(*Atharvaveda*, Kanda XII, Hymn I, Mantra 59)

[May the Mother Earth who is the provider of milk and many nourishing things, grain and other agricultural produce, fragrance and bless us with peace, tranquillity and riches.]

In summary, it can be said that the Prithivi Sukta whose entire set of 63 Mantras has been dedicated to the Mother Earth, is the foremost ancient spiritual text from India which enjoins all human beings to protect, preserve and care for the environment. This is beautifully illustrated in Mantra 16 which says that it is up to us as the progeny of Mother Earth to do to live in peace and harmony with all.

[1] *Prithivi Sukta*, Mantra 7.

Ta nah prajah sam duhatam samagra vacho madhu prithivi dhehi mahyam.
(*Atharvaveda*, Kanda XII, Hymn I, verse 16)

[O Mother Earth! you are the world for us and we are your children; let us speak in one accord, let us come together so that we live in peace and harmony, and let us be cordial and gracious in our relationship with other human beings.]

These sentiments denote the deep bond between Earth and human beings, and exemplify the true relationship between the Earth and all living beings, as well as between humans and other forms of life. Such a comprehensive exposition depicting a theory of eco-spirituality is not found in any other religious tradition and beliefs as portrayed by these 63 Mantras.. The Sukta provides us a guide to behave in an appropriate manner towards nature and our duty towards the environment.

4. The Post-Vedic Heritage

According to Hindu scriptures, people must not demand or command dominion over other creatures. They are forbidden from exploiting nature; instead they are advised to seek peace and live in harmony with nature.[1] Further, the Hindu religion demands veneration, respect and obedience to maintain and protect the natural harmonious unity of God and nature. This is further demonstrated by a series of divine incarnations, as pertinently enunciated by Dr. Karan Singh in the Assisi Declaration:

> The evolution of life on this planet is symbolized by a series of divine incarnations beginning with fish, moving through amphibious forms and mammals, and then on into human incarnations. This view clearly holds that man did not spring fully formed to dominate the lesser life forms, but rather evolved out of these forms itself, and is therefore integrally linked to the whole of creation.[2]

Hindu scriptures attest to the belief that the creation, maintenance, and annihilation of the cosmos is completely up to the Supreme Will. In the *Gita* Lord Krishna says to Arjuna: "Of all that is material and all that is spiritual in this world, know for certain that I am both its origin and dissolution and is under Me. By My will it is manifested again and again and by My will, it is annihilated at the end" (*Gita*, 9:8). Further, the Lord says: "I am the origin, the end, existence, and the maintainer (of all)" (*Gita*, 9:17–18). Thus, for Hindus, both God and

---

[1] For further discussion on the concept of divinity in Hindu religion, see O.P. Dwivedi and B.N. Tiwari, *Environmental Crisis and Hindu Religion,* Gitanjali Publishing House, New Delhi, 1987.

[2] Dr. Karan Singh, "The Hindu Declaration on Nature", the Assisi Declarations on Religion and Nature made at Assisi, Italy, WWF, Gland, Switzerland, 1986.

nature (Prakriti) are one and the same. Because the most important aspect of Hindu theology pertaining to the treatment of animal life is the belief that the Supreme Being was himself incarnated in the form of various species. The Lord says: "This form is the source and indestructible seed of multifarious incarnations within the universe, and from the particle and portion of this form, different living entities, like demi-gods, animals, human beings and others, are created" (*Srimad-Bhagavata*, Book I, Discourse III:5).[1]

The Hindu belief in the cycle of birth and rebirth wherein a person may come back as an animal or a bird gives these species not only respect, but also reverence. This provides a solid foundation for the doctrine of *ahimsa*—non-violence (or non-injury) against animals and human beings alike. Hindus have a deep faith in the doctrine of non-violence. It should be noted that the doctrine of *Ahimsa* presupposes the doctrine of *Karma* and the doctrine of rebirth (*punarjanma*). The soul continues to take birth in different life forms such as birds, fish, animals, and humans. Based on this belief, there is a profound opposition in the Hindu religion (as well as in Buddhist and Jain religions) to the institutionalized killing of animals, birds and fish for human consumption. Almost all of the Hindu scriptures place strong emphasis on the notion that God's grace can be received by not killing his creatures or harming his creation: "God, Kesava, is pleased with a person who does not harm or destroy other non-speaking creatures or animals" (*Vishnupurana*, 3.8.15). Further, the pain a human being causes other living beings to suffer will eventually be suffered by that person later, either in this life or in a later rebirth. It is through the transmigration of the soul that a link has been provided between the lowliest forms of life with the human beings.

Concerning flora in Hindu Religion: as early as in the time of the Rigveda, tree worship was quite popular and universal. The tree symbolized the various attributes of God to the Rigvedic seers. The Rigveda regarded plants as having divine powers, with one entire hymn devoted to their praise, chiefly with reference to their healing properties (*Rigveda*, 10.97). Later, during the period of the great epics and Puranas, the Hindu respect for flora expanded further. Trees were considered as being animate and feeling happiness and sorrow. Green trees were likened to a living person.

The Hindu worship of trees and plants has been based partly on utility, but mostly because of assigning divinity to them. Hindu ancestors considered it their duty to save trees; and in order to do so they attached to every tree a religious sanctity. It is still popularly believed by Hindus that every tree has a Vriksha-devata, or "tree deity", who is worshipped with prayers and offerings of water,

[1] *Srimad Bhagavata Mahapurana*, translated by C.L. Goswami and M.A. Shastri, Gita Press, Gorakhpur, India, 1982.

flowers, sweets, and encircled by sacred threads. The following deities, for example, are considered to have made their abode in these trees/plants: Goddess Lakshmi in Tulasi (*Ocimum sanctum*), Goddess Shitala in Neem, God Vishnu in Pipal/Bodhi (*Ficus religiosa*), Lord Buddha in Ashoka, Lord Shiva in Bilva/Bela (*Aegle marmelos*), Lord Brahma and Lord Vishnu in Vata (*Ficus indica*). Also, for Hindus, the planting of a tree is still a religious duty. Thus sanctity has been attached to many trees and plants.

Based on the above, one can offer a premise that every entity and living organism is a part of one large extended family system (*Kutumba*) which is presided over by the eternal Mother Earth (called by Hindus as *Devi Vasundhara*). The development of humanity from creation till now has taken place nowhere else but on the Earth. Our relationship with Earth, from birth to death, is like children and their mother. The mother—in this case Earth, has not only borne her children but also has been the main source of fulfilment of their unending desires. It is this Earth which provides energy for the sustenance of all species. And as one ought not to insult, exploit, and violate one's mother but to be kind and respectful to her, similarly, one should behave towards the Mother Earth. It enjoins us to take care of God's Creation in the form of eco-stewardship.

5. *Vedic Heritage and Global Stewardship*

Stewardship of the environment requires that one considers the entire universe as his/her extended family with all living beings in this universe as the members of the household. This concept, also known as *Vasudhaiv kutumbakam* (*Vasudha* means this earth, *Kutumba* means extended family consisting of human beings, animals, and all living beings), means that all human beings as well as other creatures living on earth are the members of the same extended family of *Devi Vasundhara*. Only by considering the entire universe as a part of our extended family, can we (individually and collectively) develop the necessary maturity and respect for all other living beings.

On this concept of *Vasudhaiv Kutumbakam*, Dr. Karan Singh has said: "that the planet we inhabit and of which we are all citizens—Planet Earth—is a single, living, pulsating entity; that the human race, in the final analysis, is an interlocking, extended family—*Vasudhaiv Kutumbakam* as the Veda has it . . ."[1] We also know that members of the extended family do not wilfully endanger the lives and livelihood of others; instead, they first think in terms of caring for others before taking an action. That is why, in order to transmit this new global consciousness, it is essential that the concept of *Vasudhaiv Kutumbakam* is encouraged. For this, the world's great religions would have to cooperate with

---

[1]Dr. Karan Singh, *Brief Sojourn*, B.R. Publishing Corporation, Delhi, 1991, p. 123.

each other. The welfare and caring of all would be realized through the golden thread of spiritual understanding and cooperation at the global level. Sustainable development, from this perspective, ought to include the upliftment (both spiritual and material) of all without exploitation and destruction of others. How to secure a development which creates conditions for *environmental Sarvodaya and Abhyudaya*, welfare of all without harming others and destroying the environment, is a challenge before India—a nation endowed with a rich Vedic heritage of eco-care.

The Vedic heritage for eco-care can lead us to master over our base characteristics such as greed, exploitation, abuse, mistreatment and defilement of nature. But before we can hope to change the exploitative tendencies, it is absolutely essential that we discipline our inner thoughts. It is here where the Vedic exhortations and Puranic injunctions may come into play for environmental stewardship. This eco-care oriented stewardship can be a mechanism which creates respect for nature by enabling people to centre their values upon the notion that there is a cosmic ordinance and a divine law which must be maintained. Further, the environmental stewardship can provide new ways of valuing and caring. It can also influence and promote sustainable development. Environmental stewardship, if globally manifested, can also provide the values necessary for an environmentally caring world and will not advance a blind belief in economic growth at all costs, creating in its wake greed, poverty, inequality and injustice as well as environmental destruction. Environmental stewardship, then, drawing upon the Vedic and Puranic precepts, may become a new focal point around which the concept of global stewardship of the environment may develop; and in this way we may usher in new values in line with an environmentally caring world.

Each spiritual tradition on earth has helped humanity. Those who see divinity in nature (or worship nature) have increased our sense of the light of beauty, the largeness and height of our life, and our aim at multi-dimensional perfection. Christianity has given us the vision of divine love and charity; Buddhism has shown us a noble way to be kinder, purer and nobler; Judaism as well as Islam has shown us how to be devoted to God and be religiously faithful in following His command. Hinduism has given us the profound spiritual possibilities beginning with the respect for nature and seeing divinity in it. Would it not be great if these God-visions could be brought together to protect and care for God's creation? All religions as well as other spiritual traditions aim to save souls, but they have yet to spiritualize the humanity. Environmental crisis facing our universe has given all of us—belonging to various religions and cultures—an opportunity to come together and work for the protection and sustenance of the entire cosmos. It is here where the Vedic heritage can help us to protect the Creation from further harm.

Rigvedic Semantics: Study of All Verses with the Word Gau

RANGASAMI L. KASHYAP
Electrical and Computer Engineering
Purdue University, West Lafayette, IN 47907
Email: kashyap@ecn.purdue.edu

Summary

Gau is a key-word in the Rigveda Samhita occurring in about 900 verses out of 10,600 in the whole text. We will study all these verses in great detail as well as those having its synonyms like *dhenu*, *usra*, etc., and arrive at a comprehensive meaning of the word based only on the Rigveda. We uncover the meanings of the recurring metaphysical phrases in the Rigveda like the loss of the *gau*, the recovery of the *gau*, smashing the hill using the *gau*, raising of the Sun, Indra's release of the Waters by killing Vrtra, etc. Figuring out the meaning of all these important words like *gau, adri*, etc., is like solving a multi-dimensional puzzle using the many hints provided by the Rigveda itself.

Even if five hundred verses out of the ten thousand in the Rigveda Samhita are read in the original Sanskrit, the impression obtained is quite different from that conveyed by the current popular essays on it by academic Western Vedicists and their Indian followers. In Indian tradition the poets of the Rigveda are sages and seers endowed with wisdom on many aspects of psychology based on spirituality and the possibility of perfection of humans. The Rigveda has a rich vocabulary of more than forty words connected with the mental operations of meditation, intellect, thought, etc. There are arresting phrases like'paths to immortality', 'mantras carved out of the heart', 'knowledge of our inner being', the collocated words 'heart, mind, intellect' etc. The Rigveda states in more than fifty verses that there is a hidden secret in the Vedas indicated by words like *ninyam, apichyam, guhyam*, etc. This secret is expressed in the form of symbolism. How can this symbolism be unveiled? Sri Aurobindo using his powerful intuition has already recovered this symbolism. This study has been augmented by the commentary of Sri Kapali Sastry and the books of Sri M.P. Pandit and Sri A. Purani. We are indicating here another approach at understanding the symbolism.

The grammar of the Rigveda follows the pattern indicated by the great grammarian Panini. The symbolism then must be in the nouns, common and proper. We do not have to worry about the verbs because once we unveil the symbolism of nouns, the symbolism behind the verbal meanings becomes obvious. We have to focus particularly on the group of common nouns associated with everyday life like *gau*, *ashva*, *adri*, *apah*, translated in everyday life as the animal cow, horse, hill, waters, etc. The second group is the meaning of the deities Agni, Indra, etc.

Every verse of the Rigveda is made of a number of distinct clauses or sentences ranging from one to four. In the group of all the verses of the Rigveda having the word *gau* or *dhenavah*, we will select a subset of sentences which have only one unknown word *gau*, all the other words having known meanings. Most members of this large subset allow for only one meaning for *gau*, namely, a Ray of Spiritual Light, or simply a ray of light.

Next we can take up the word *adri*. Again we focus on all sentences having only *gau* and *adri* as unknowns, the rest of the words having known meanings. We have many verses which state that *adri* is destroyed by means of the potent Word. Using the meaning of *gau* in such verses, we conclude that *adri* means the metaphorical hill of the forces of spiritual darkness, ignorance and inertia located in us.

Similarly *apah*, the Waters, stand for the subtle dynamic energies in a human being denoted by Kundalini and others in the later Tantrik and Yogik literature. Both the word *apah* and the water share the characteristics of flowing and nourishing, both their origins being in the higher realms.

Now we can consider the two dominant themes in the Rigveda mentioned in many verses, namely, the loss of *gau*, the Spiritual Knowledge, and its recovery, and the recovery of the Waters. The repeated loss of Spiritual Knowledge, *Veda*, and its recovery is a common theme in all later Indian scriptures like the Gita (chapter 4), the Bhagavatam and many other Puranas. Upanishads speak of the hidden knowledge in the heart. The loss of knowledge is effected by its fragmentation and the fragments devoid of their total meaning are held in the folds of the ignorance hill. The Rigveda not only celebrates the release of the hidden Spiritual Knowledge and the associated dynamical energies, the Waters, but also describes in its ten thousand verses the methods of utilizing this knowledge and the energies in our daily life.

1. Multiple Interpretation of Veda

It is not our intention to declare that the spiritual interpretation is the only correct interpretation of the Rigveda and all other interpretations are wrong and false, after the manner of certain religions which declare their own God as the "true God" and the Gods of other religions as "false Gods". In the Hindu tradition every scripture is amenable to multiple interpretations, each one reflecting the psychological viewpoints of the reader. The Rigveda, the oldest Hindu scripture, is not an exception to this rule. Also, many verses are amenable to more than one interpretation. As is the case in any high level Sanskrit poetry, Rigveda poetry is of the highest calibre according to Sanskrit and English poets who themselves have written poems of the highest calibre.

In the Indian tradition, there are three broad viewpoints of the Veda reflecting respectively their views of three different groups of persons, namely, the viewpoint of commoners, the viewpoint of the priests performing the elaborate rites and yajnas, or their sponsors, and the viewpoint of the poets of the Rigveda termed as wise sages and seers. Of course, each of these viewpoints is not monolithic.

From the perspective of the commoners (who were the spectators of the rites and rituals), the Rigveda is a record of the prayers to the higher powers, the *devas*, for preserving the health and wealth of their families, and for exposing them to some aspects of the Divine. The higher powers, the deities of the Rigveda, appeared to them not only in the form of nature powers like the sun, fire, rain, destructive storms, lightning and others, but also to their inner being in their worship and recitations.

The ritualists, known later as *mimamsakas*, believed that the correct performance of the ritual at every step will yield the material benefits associated with the ritual. Chanting of the Rigveda is only one step in this ritual. What mattered was the power associated with the chanting, not the meaning of the mantra.

The poets or the sages of the Rigveda composed these poems recording their experiences of the perennial triad of Human-World-God. They passed on their knowledge only to their students. These poets state in several verses of the Rigveda itself that there is a secret in the Veda using words like *ninyam, guhyam, apichyam*, etc. They hid the Truth in a symbolic language so that only the eager students with a high level of aspiration can have access to this secret.

The Rigveda has many commentators, but the most famous one is Sayana who lived in the fifteenth century A.D. His commentary is famous because for every word of the ten thousand verses of the Rigveda he gave a meaning and explained every verse in its entirety. No one can dispute its usefulness in the study of the many interpretations in the Rigveda. Sayana stated clearly in the commentary that his primary aim was to interpret each verse so as to throw light on the rituals that are tied to the Rigveda. Even though he had great respect for the gods of the Rigveda, he regarded them as merely nature-powers in most verses and as spiritual powers in some. The Western academic Vedicists discovered the Rigveda in the nineteenth century and gave their own interpretations. They started from Sayana's work, but stripped from it both its reverence for the gods and the poets of the Rigveda. They looked at it from an anthropological viewpoint and regarded it as the songs of the superstitious Aryan tribes. Moreover, they viewed these Aryan tribes as uncultured cattle-rearing agriculturists. These songs reflected their way of life and served as propitiation of the powers of nature such as rain, dawn, storm, etc. One of the two recurring themes of the Rigveda, the loss and recovery of *gau* translated as cows is explained by them as nothing but the theft of the cattle of the Aryan tribes by the so called cave-dwelling Dravidian tribes and the forceful release of these cattle by battle. The other recurring theme in the Rigveda is the release of waters by Indra and killing the serpent *Vrtra*, also called *Ahi*, by the use of the *Vajra*. The snake *Ahi* is identified with the cloud, *Vajra* with the bolt of thunder and lightning common in the tropics; Indra is a nature god, the god of rain. Thus the event is interpreted as Indra's shattering of the clouds with the thunderbolt causing the rain (the release of waters). These Vedicists may agree that the Rigveda contains a small number of verses of spiritual import. The verses, anyway, are in the tenth book and obviously a later interpolation. This view is accepted currently by an overwhelming majority of the academic Vedicists including those of India.

If one reads any of the essays on the Veda, one notices that the academic Vedicists have ignored ninety to ninetyfive per cent of the Rigveda stating that these constitute the "meaningless" ornamental epithets given by superstitious poets of the Rigveda to the gods. The opinion on the Rigveda by these essayists is based only on isolated phrases from a small number of verses of the Rigveda. Often entire essays are based on one word of the Rigveda, a word with one occurrence. The poems of the Rigveda (in the Sanskrit form) clearly indicate the presence of metaphors or symbols repeatedly. Moreover, it is not easy to figure out the meaning of the symbolism.

We said earlier that all these different interpretations start with Sayana's commentary. The greast weakness of Sayana's work is his penchant for giving multiple meanings to the same word. Take the word *gau* translated usually as the animal cow. Sayana gives twentysix different meanings. For the popular word *rta*, having the meaning of Cosmic Law or Truth everywhere, Sayana gives twentyone different meanings such as water, action, sacrifice, hymn, etc. Even for a word like *dhiyah*, which can be translated as thought or intellect everywhere, Sayana gives many meanings including food. For many different words, food is given as one of their meanings. We can forget a consistent interpretation of Veda if we believe that multiple meanings for words on such a large scale is inevitable.

The early Vedicist Max Muller was aware of this problem, even though he was the prime mover behind the Western interpretation. If each word, especially the common noun, has a fixed meaning, how can we recover it? Muller suggested that we should consider all the verses having that word and try to figure out the meaning. Neither he nor his associates pursued this approach. The difficulties are obvious. Many verses will have not *one* common noun, but several common nouns. When we study all the verses having the noun *x*, how do we handle the meanings of the unknown nouns *y, z* which also are in those verses. Consequently, what we are dealing with is not a one-dimensional puzzle but a multi-dimensional puzzle. We indicate an approach to handle this puzzle.

2. *A Broad Outline of Our Approach*

We focus on the common nouns in the the Rigveda which could be of widespread usage in the daily life of the Vedic people such as *gau, ashva, apah, sadana, dura, vrka,* etc., translated in common parlance as cow, horse, waters, house, door, wolf, etc. We consider all the verses in the Rigveda having that word; in the beginning we consider only the first 1500 verses of the Rigveda and select all the verses (about 120) having the particular word like *gau* or its synonyms. We investigate whether each word in this family has the same generic meaning in all the verses of the Rigveda where it appears. In the current interpretation, where *gau* is translated as cow, most verses do not have any consistent meaning, the different phrases in each verse being unrelated.

We assume the standard or primary dictionary meanings for all other nouns are correct, especially those words associated with thought, intellect, mind, ignorance, light, consciousness, etc. The Rigveda has over forty different words dealing with the mental and psychological realm, each word having a precise meaning.

For the verbs we use the standard dictionary meaning. Later we see that the Rigveda utilizes the metaphorical meaning behind the verbs. For instance, the verb *indhate* means to kindle a fire. If we read the verses carefully, we see that the kindling is done by the gods *Mitra*, *Varuna*, etc. Obviously kindling is used as a metaphor for generating the power named *Agni*.

Also we have to regard the nature and names of gods like *Agni*, *Indra*, etc., as unknowns whose meanings have to be deciphered after understanding all the verses which describe the characteristics of these gods. The precise nature of these gods is not needed for the initial decoding of the meanings of nouns like *gau*. It is enough to regard these gods as supraphysical powers endowed with consciousness. Human beings can enter into relationship with these gods by prayers, recitations, worship, etc. One of the key ideas is the manifestation of each god or the power of each god in a human being. We can decipher the precise psychological power associated with each god only after we understand the symbolic meanings of all the common nouns.

Most of the translations of the verses given here are adapted from the work of Sri Kapali Sastry and Sri M.P. Pandit. We have utilized occasionally the translations of Sri A.C. Bose.

3. *The Details of Our Procedure*

We consider the 120 verses which contain either *gau* or its synonyms *dhenavah, usriyah,* etc. Each verse breaks normally to several, two or more, relatively independent clauses each having one verb. The collection of all such clauses or sentences is our starting point. Of course, these sentences involve many unknowns like *gau, adri, apah,* etc.

Step 1: Focus on the sentences which contain only one unknown word *gau* in them excluding sentences which involve other unknowns like *adri, apah,* etc. We avoid the sentences in which the verb "giving" because of the phrase "giving *x*", where *x* is unknown, does not fix the meaning of *x*. We give a small list of such verses below containing only one unknown *gau.* In the verses below, we quote the Sanskrit word *gau* or *gava* without translating it.

1.33.1 Come here, aspirants for *gau* (*gavanta*);
Let us reach Indra who increases our needed thought (*pramatya*).
Invincible, he bestows on us the supreme (*param*) knowledge (*ketam*) of *gavam.*

1.53.2 Indra, dispel our ignorance (*amatim*) with *gobhih* and *ashvaih.*

1.53.5 O Indra, may we march together led by thy intellect fronted by *gau.*

1.62.5 You have dispelled the darkness (*andhah*) with the *gobhih* of the goddess of Dawn and Sun.

In the above quotations, we have explicitly indicated some of the Sanskrit words with their English meanings to avoid the impression that we are tailoring the English meanings of other words to fit the defined psychological meaning for *gau.*

The puzzle is to recover the meaning of *gau* in all these verses which makes each verse have a consistent meaning. Because of the presence of the words ignorance, knowledge, intelligence etc., because of the phrase "*gau* destroys ignorance", the meaning for *gau* should be something connected with the spiritual Light or Knowledge. We could consider also the meaning of a ray of ordinary light, like that of the fire or Sun. But the context of all the verses implies that the meaning of a Ray of Spiritual Light or Knowledge—*chit prakasha* in Sanskrit—is more appropriate. We use the phrase "a Ray of Light" instead of simply "Light" because the Rishis felt that the Spiritual Light also exists or operates as a bundle of Rays, each Ray standing for a particular facet or quantum of Knowledge. We capitalize Light indicating that we are not dealing with ordinary light.

Step 2: After fixing the meaning of *gau*, we should select all the verses involving only one of the other unknowns like *aditi, apah,* etc., and arrive at their meanings. The recovered psychological meanings for some of the words is given in Table 1.

TABLE 1
SYMBOLISM OF SOME COMMON NOUNS AND DEVA NAMES

Word in Sanskrit	*Common meaning*	*Psychological meaning*
gau, dhenavah, usriyah	cow	A Ray of Light A Ray of Knowledge
ashvah	horse	Life energies which give a youthful body, a happy and cheerful emotional life, mental life, and life of activity
apah	waters	The higher dynamical energies corresponding to the modern Kundalini and other subtle energies
grha, sadana	house	The subtle body of the Rishi which has a complex structure, body being viewed as a city as in the Upanishads
durah, dvarah	doors	Doors of the subtle body, openings which block the flow of the higher energies all over our bodies
adri, parvatah	hill	The forces of ignorance, inertia and the falsehood or the demons associated with those forces
prithvi	earth	The realm of cosmic matter, the realm of physical body of a human
divah, dyu	heaven	The realm of cosmic mind, realm of mind in a human
rochana	earth and heaven	Earth and Heaven
antariksha	mid-region or mid-world	The intermediate realm in a human between matter and mind, the cosmic realm of life-energies
vrka	wolf	A demonic force which cuts or divides
Agni	the deity of the physical fire	The realm of intelligent will, the force which burns dead matter or worn out emotions in human beings
Indra	god of rain	The lord of Heaven, the lord of Divine Mind and action, one who makes perfect forms
Usha	goddess of the dawn	The Dawn of Spiritual Light
Surya	physical Sun	The Supreme Light

Step 3: Now we consider all the phrases of all the 120 verses, substitute the assigned meaning for all the unknowns like *gau*, *adri*, etc. and check whether the sentence makes some sense after making sure to interpret the verb in its metaphorical manner. For example, in the phrase "Agni is kindled (*indhate*)" we have to interpret the verb *indhate* metaphorically. Another key metaphor is *vrdha* (to increase). A common prayer is: "O Agni, increase in us by our prayers" or "Indra, increase in us". Agni and Indra obviously are cosmic powers. These

prayers and chants call upon these gods to increase the effectiveness of their power in the subtle body of the singer.

Step 4: Now we consider each of the 120 verses of the Rigveda containing the word *gau*, replace all the unknown nouns by these assigned meanings, interpret the verbs by their metaphorical meanings, and check whether each verse has a consistent meaning. Strange as it may seem, all the verses make delightful sense with the indicated substitutions.

Some Comments on the Symbolism

In many cases, the psychological meaning associated with a word in the above table is suggested by its ordinary meaning. For instance, both water and its psychological meaning of higher dynamic energies share the characteristics of flow, the quality of nourishment of the human beings, etc. Both the hill and the forces of ignorance and inertia share the quality of hardness, the quality of being difficult to access, etc.

However, there is one exception of *gau*. The assignment of the psychological meaning of Light for *gau* has many reasons derived from the importance of the animal cow in the Indian culture from times immemorial. In all Indian languages, including the so-called Dravidian language, there are popular verses which describe the cow as indispensable to humans. Recall the Sanskrit *gau* stands both for the cow and the bull. The ox is the chief mode of tilling the soil and transportation needed for the grain. The key ingredients of Indian food, namely, milk, buttermilk, butter and ghee are derived from the cow. Even the urine and the stools of the cow serve as fertilizers of soil, as a disinfectant, for the preservation of the floor in the houses and other uses. After its death, its leather is used for making shoes. Hence the animal cow is considered as containing in itself all the gods, the helpful powers of the cosmos. Hence the infinite being in the Rigveda, *aditi*, whose qualities are described in many verses of of the Rigveda, such as Rigveda 1.89.8, is also hymned as a cow in Rigveda 8.101.15, and others. So much so, all the gods are hymned as *Adityas*, the children of Aditi. Even today in all temples dedicated to the deity *Vishnu*, when the doors of the inner temple or the sanctum of the deity are opened every morning, the deity is shown a cow symbolising the fact that all the gods in the Cow want to have a vision (*darshan*) of the lord. We may imagine that the Cow being so popular is a popular adjective to a hero or a noble man. (A king is assigned the epithet of *Vrishabha*, a bull, not that of *gau*, which can be a cow or a bull.)

In the Rigveda, there is one sukta (6.28) solely devoted to the *gau*. Reading this hymn clearly implies that the rishis were not thinking of cattle at all when they mentioned *gau*. We give below four verses from 6.28.3 through 6.28.6.

They (*gavo*) are not lost, nor do robbers injure them, nor the unfriendly frighten, nor wish to assail them. (3)

To me, the Rays (*gava*) are *Bhaga*, they are *Indra*.
They are a portion of the first-poured Soma. (4)

These Rays (*gavah*) that are *Indra*, O people,
The *Indra* I long for, with heart and mind. (5)

O Rays, you fatten the emaciated and make the unlovely look beautiful. (6)

4. *Discussion of the Verses in Groups*

We will divide the 120 verses in the first Ashtaka or the first eighth of the Rigveda into ten groups according to the subject matter. They are:

A. The *gau* as Rays of Light destroying ignorance and inconscience
B. The *gau* and *adri*, the metaphorical hill of the forces of inertia and ignorance
C. The goddess *aditi* and *gau*
D. The tracing and recovery of the *gau*
E. The donors of *gau* and the recipients
F. Agni, the Power of Divine Will and *gau*
G. Usha, the dawn of spiritual knowledge and *gau*
H. Ashvins and their symbolic deeds related to *gau*
I. Ribhus and *gau*
J. Waters (*apah*) asnd *gau*
K. The *gau* used as a part of a simile

We pay particular attention to the groups D and E. D deals with the recovery of the *gau* stolen by the demons. E deals with the act of giving a *gau*.

4-A. *The gau as Ray of Spiritual Light destroying ignorance and spiritual darkness*

Come here you aspirants for the Light (*gavyanta*).
Let us reach Indra who increases our needed thought (*pramatim*).
Invincible, he bestows on us the supreme (*param*) Ray of the Light (*gavam*). (1.33.1)

O Maghavan, you have protected the son of Shivitra
Who in conquering the earth remained serene
Amidst impelling currents, a hero (*vrishabhah*)
And a shaft of Light (*gam*). (1.33.15)

Praise the might of Maruts, sportive unslayable (*aghnyam*) amidst the Light (*goshu*). (1.37.5)

Indra, dispel our ignorance (*amatim*) using the Light (*gobhih*) and Life Energies (*ashvina*). (1.53.4)

O Indra, may we march together led by your superior intelligence (*pramatya*) fronted by Light (*goagraya*). (1.53.5)

Indra, you have dispelled the darkness (*andhah*) with the Light (*gobhih*) of Sun (*suryena*) and the Dawn (*usha*). (1.62.5)

We have earlier discussed three of the above, namely, 1.33.1, 1.53.5 and 1.62.5. In the last line of 1.33.15 *gam* cannot be a cow. The adjective hero is already in the text. In 1.53.4 *gobhih* cannot mean cattle. It could be interpreted as the ordinary physical light of the Sun. But in the Veda, Surya is not the physical object glowing in the sky but the spiritual Sun described as "the soul of all that moves and moves not" (1.115.1). Similarly Dawn is the goddess heralding the advent of spiritual Light in all the verses, as in 1.71.9.

Indra, the showerer, used his weapon Vajra,
With his light (*jyoti*) milked (*adukshat*)
The Rays (*ga*) from out of the darkness (*tamasa*). (1.33.10)

Vajra is the divine weapon of Light and is translated as a thunderbolt in common usage. This verse suggests that the forces of inconscience and darkness envelope the Light and by squeezing the darkness, Light can be recovered.

We will quote 5 verses from 1.84, all having the word *gau*:

The golden (or white) Light (*gaurya*) partake of the sweet Soma
Moving with beautiful Indra for the sake of splendour, they rejoice.
They abide awaiting upon his sovereignty. (1.84.10)

Soma is the Delight of Existence. The Rays of Light partake of the Soma and are nourished by it. They wait to see Indra's sovereignty established over the yajamana. A human being is a divided person. Indra, the god of Divine Mind, will establish his sovereignty over all the parts of the yajamana and make him a whole person. Translating *gaurya* as cattle and Soma as a herb can make sense of the first line but not of the second line.

Dear to Indra, the rays (*dhenavah*) urge the destructive weapon (*Vajra*).
They abide waiting upon his sovereignty. (1.84.11)

As mentioned earlier, Vajra is not a thunderbolt, but a weapon of heavenly Light and Sound (*mantra*). The Rays of the Knowledge urge the Vajra to vanquish the demonic forces, which are causing the division in a human. Once these forces are destroyed, Indra can establish his sovereignty. *Dhenavah* as cattle makes no sense at all.

The next verse is a continuation of 1.84.11. It does not explicitly mention the word *dhenavah* but uses the pronoun *tat.*

> The conscious (*prachetasah*) Rays, surrendered to his might, serve him (Indra).
> They follow his many laws (*vratani*) for advance knowledge (*purvachittaye*).
> They abide awaiting upon his sovereignty. (1.84.12)

Advance knowledge refers to the knowledge to be obtained by the yajamana when he follows the laws of Indra.

> True in his very place, home of Soma, the wise found the secret (*apichyam*) Name of the Ray (*goh*) of Twashtr. (1.84.15)

Twashtr is a solar deity associated with the Sun, the Supreme Light. The very place referred to as *Sharyanavat* mentioned in 1.84.15 is a receptacle of Soma, the Delight of Existence. Note the use of the phrase "secret name". Name in Veda is not a mere holder of a concept as in modern usage but a word endowed with power. The process of repetition results in the word yielding its power. Note also the word "secret". Also translating *goh* as cattle does not make sense at all.

> Who indeed can be so fortunate to utter in front of the Truth (Indra) the Ray (*gah*)
> Lustrous, heroic and of unbearable fury. (1.84.16)

Here *gah* is interpreted as the Spiritual Light in the form of Mantra, the potent Word.

> He whose intelligence (*mati*) is sharpened by the mighty ones. (1.83.16)

> He moves into the abode (*vraje*) of Light (*gomati*). (1.86.3)

> O *Pushan, Vishnu, Maruts*, make our thoughts (*dhiyah*) full of Light (*goagrah*).
> Make us happy (*swastimatah*). (1.90.5)

> O Soma, you have generated all the curative powers of
> The waters (*apah*), the Rays (*gah*).
> You have extended the vast mid region.
> With thy Light (*jyotisha*), you have dispelled the darkness. (1.91.22)

Agni and Soma, known to us is your power
By which the possession of the Rays (*gah*)
Was removed from the Pani.
The relic of Vrtra was thrust down.
Then was the One light (*jyotirekam*) obtained for the many.
(1.93.4)

Recall that the titans Pani and Vrtra are in possession of the Knowledge or Light. When the possession of Rays is removed from the Pani, the one Light in all its integrality is accessible to many.

4-B. Gau, the Destruction of Adri and the Result

Indra raised the Sun in Heaven for eternal vision. He burst the hill (*adrim*) with the Rays (*gobhih*). (1.7.3)

Adrim ordinarily means hill. It is difficult to see how one can burst a hill, a structure of hard matter by using the animal cow. Hence the translators assign arbitrary meanings to words to get the meaning they like to get. Griffith mistranslates *gobhih* which is in instrumental case with meaning of "with or by", by the phrase "for getting the cows" and states that Indra burst the hill for getting the cows. Wilson following Sayana renders *adrim* as cloud and *gobhih* as waters, yielding "Indra charged the clouds with the waters". To correct the whole verse, Sayana says "after the rain Sun became clear". In Griffith's translation there is no connection between the two lines. The pattern should be evident. It is as if these translators are intent on demonstrating that the Vedic verses have no deep meaning.

We recall that the Rigveda is poetry. It is impossible to imagine poetry without symbolism. In all cultures, *adrim* (hill) represents something having no flexibility, no subtlety and which is difficult to change. It is the natural symbol chosen for representing the result of the forces of ignorance both at the individual level as well as at the cosmic level.

The second line in 1.7.3 means: "Indra destroys the forces of ignorance using the Spiritual Knowledge of Light." This task is appropriate for Indra since all the epithets in the Veda for him imply that he is the Lord of the Divine Mind, i.e., the possessor and controller of all the mental aspects in their purity unmixed with turbidities. This destruction of ignorance is especially hinted at the individual aspect, i.e., the power of Indra, established in the subtle body of the Rishi with the aid of spiritual practices destroys the structure of ignorance and falsehood inside the subtle body of the Rishi.

Now there is a natural connection between the first and second sentences of the quotation (1.7.3). Sun, *Surya*, in the Rigveda is at the vertex of the hierarchy of Vedic devas. There is a Supreme Sun, within each one of us, in the microcosmos. When the ignorance is destroyed, the Sun inside becomes visible and illumines all the aspects of our inner life. Thus the Sun is raised so that all the aspects inside can have the vision of the Sun, can be influenced by the Sun. The phrase "raising of the Sun" occurs in many places in the Rigveda.

There is a verse 1.51.4 very similar in meaning to 1.7.3 with the word *adri* replaced by Vrtra, the demon who covers knowledge with ignorance (*adri*). This should confirm our assignment of meaning of ignorance to *adri*. In 1.7.3 there is the bursting of the hill. In 1.51.4 there is killing of Vritra.

> O Indra, only when after you slew Vrtra, the coverer, with thy luminous strength,
> You raised the Sun heaven for vision. (1.51.4)

> Darkness (*tamah*) obstructed the flow of dynamical Energies, Waters.
> The hill (*parvata*) was within the insides (*jathareshu*) of Vrtra.
> Indra precipitated all the Water concealed by Vrtra in the hollows. (1.54.10)

Note that the hill iis within the titan Vritra, indicating that it is not physical. The force of ignorance is trapping the flow of the dynamical energies in human beings, referred to here as Waters.

We give here the five verses from 1.62 involving *goh* here, even then only two of them involve the hill.

> Angirasa (seers), knowing the route, attained the rays (*ga*). (1.62.2)

> In the search by Indra and Angirasas
> Sarama (the Divine Intuition) discovered a foundation for the son,
> Brihaspati broke the hill (*adrim*) and attained the Rays (*gah*).
> The gods extolled the recovered Rays (*usriyabhih*). (1.62.3)

> O mighty Indra, adorned with well accented lauds
> By seven sages, Navagas and Dashgwas, waiting to go ahead,
> You did rend with thy cry (*vala*) the devourer (*adrim*) who conceals *phaligam*. (1.62.4)

In 1.62.4, Vala, the demon, is identified with *adrim*, the hill.

> O Indra, you have dispelled the ignorance (*andhah*)
> By the Rays (*gobhih*) of Dawn (*ushas*) and Sun (*Surya*). (1.62.5)

We have included 1.62.2 here even though it does not have the phrase of breaking the hill or dispelling ignorance. We have placed all the four mantras from the same hymn (sukta) to bring out the importance of context.

1.62.5 needs some more explanation. Sun, as mentioned earlier, is the Spiritual Sun. Similarly Usha, the goddess of Spiritual Dawn, represents the Rays of Knowledge obtained at the beginning of our spiritual life. Not all of it is mature. When these experiences mature, then these Rays are called Rays of the Sun, the Light of the Sun.

In 1.62.3 Brihaspati, the power of potent Word, one of the Angarasa seers, is referred to as the breaker of the hill of ignorance. The sage of the Rigveda indirectly points out the symbolism by assigning the same event (the breaking of the hill) to the different divine powers in different mantras, indicating that the event is not a physical event and is the result of all of the divine forces. Note the word *usriyabhih*, one of the synonyms of the *go*, has the same symbolism of Ray. Gods are supraphysical powers, who extol the recovered Light, not the release of physical cows. Sarama is the goddess of intuition, who indicates the place where the knowledge is hidden in the inner realm of each one of us. She points the way and the Divine Mind enters the place. By this action, she stabilizes the results (Son) of the intuition.

> With mantras, our fathers broke the places though hard,
> With their cry (*ravena*) Angirasas shattered the hill (*adrim*).
> For us, they made in us a path to the great Heaven (*brhato divah*).
> They found the Day, sunworld (*svar*), the radiant (*ketum*) Rays
> (*usrah*). (1.71.2)

Then mention of the path is reminiscent of 1.62.2. Note the shattering of the hill by the primal sound. Day stands for the waking consciousness as opposed to the sleep consciousness of Night. Sun-world is a plane of consciousness located in us like the Sun. All the actions take place in our subtle body.

> The cows of truth (*rtasya dhenavah*) enjoyed in heaven
> (*dyubhaktah*)
> With full udder have fed us desiring us.
> Flow wide to the hill (*adrim*)
> Questing for happy thought, the Rivers from Heaven beyond
> (*paravatah*). (1.73.6)

Again *dhenavah*, a synonym of *gau*, is not cattle, but Spiritual Light. Hence it is connected to Truth and it is enjoyed in the heaven (*dyu*). These Rays desire to help the humans and feed their Light. The use of *udders* indicates that the transfer of Light is a concrete process, not some vague abstraction.

4-C. Aditi, the Goddess of Infinity and a Gau

There are two important verses about Aditi in the first mandala which will be given here even though they have no word *gau*.

Which auspicious Name of God among the immortals shall we
call?
Who is he that will restore us to mighty Aditi
That I may behold the Father and the Mother. (1.24.1)

The reply is given in the next verse (1.24.2) stating that the power is Agni.

Aditi is Heaven. Aditi is Mid-region.
Aditi is Mother, Father and Son.
She is all the gods; she is the five peoples.
Aditi is all that is born and what is to be. (1.89.10)

1.43 is a hymn to Rudra.

May Aditi, the Infinite Being, facilitate Rudra's Grace on our
knowledge (*gave*). (1.43.2)

Here *gave* may be translated as cattle. But it is hard imagining the appeal to the infinite being to facilitate Rudra's grace on the cattle.

In 8.101.15, Aditi is identified as a *gau*.

Mother of Rudras is she, the daughter of Vasus, sister of Adityas,
periphery of the Truth.
Now do I speak to the human who has perception (*chikitushe*).
Hurt not the Light (*gam*) that has no stain of evil (*anagas*).
(8.101.5)

When the sons of the Rays (*gomatarah*)
Shine with their radiances, pure,
They are resplendent.
Light trails in their path. (1.85.3)

4-D. Tracing and the Recovering of Gau

Indra, you have traced and found the Rays (*usriyah*)
Using the divine helpers who break even strong places (*vilu*)
And who carry (thee) to secret places (*guhachit*). (1.6.5)

Recall 1.71.2 which speaks of the destruction of the strong places, the consolidation of the forces of ignorance.

O Indra, you opened the cave (*bilam*) of the titan Vala with the
Rays (*gomatah*).
Fearless the gods entered you speedily. (1.11.5)

Vala is a demon whose name means encircler. He is a kindred of Vrtra. Both are beings of the forces of ignorance and inconscience. Vala has stolen the

Spiritual Light or Knowledge and hidden it in the cave (*bilam*), a place of pitch darkness symbolising the inconscience, i.e., the state in which there is only a trace of consciousness on the surface. The cave is within our subtle body. Indra and the helpers break open the door to this cave and release the Knowledge. The opening of the door to the cave is mentioned in several hymns. The doors are same as the knots in the subtle body of human beings which stop the flow of the subtle energies, mentioned in the Rigveda (1.24.15, 1.25.21) as *paasha*, and as *granthi* in the Upanishads and Tantras.

In 1.11.4, Indra is addressed as the destroyer of the cities of the titans (*puram bhinduh*), the cities being the subtle structures within us erected by the titans. Indra destroys these structures which support the titans.

In 1.11.3, there is a reference to the luminous spiritual felicity or wealth (*gomatah*) given by Indra whose growth (*utayah*) does not decrease.

> O God absolute, you won the Rays (*gah*),
> Won the Soma and released the seven rivers (*sapta sindhun*).
> (1.32.12)

As mentioned, the Waters or rivers (*sapta sindhun*) symbolise the dynamic energies of all the seven planes of existence.

> O (Agni), may you, luminous,
> Uttering the word for the winning of the Light (*gavishtishu*)
> Vigorous in Life Force, be consecrated. (1.36.8)
> Indra opens his doors (*durah*) to Rays (*gah*), life energies (*ashva*)
> and material forces (*yava*);
> You are the master of instruction,
> Friend of the seekers of companionship with gods. (1.53.2)

> Truth knowers, far seeing,
> They knew the seven rivers (*sapta yahvi*) of heaven,
> The doors (*durah*) of the treasure (*rayah*).
> Sarama discovered the strong wide place (*urvam*) of the rays
> (*gavyam*).
> By that human beings enjoy happiness. (1.72.8)

Note the next verse (1.72.9) states that gods presided over the laying of the path to immortality (*amrtatvaya gatum*). The path to the Rays in 1.72.8 is the same as the path of immortality in 1.72.9. Earlier in 4B, we quoted 1.62.2 which spoke of our ancient fathers knowing the route (*padagna*) and attaining the Rays (*ga*).

> May Indra ascend the car that pours the bounty and leads to the
> Rays (*govidam*). (1.82.4)

The human who dwells amidst life energies (*ashvavati*) is the foremost to attain the Rays (*goshu*).
You pour into him plentiful wealth as the fully conscious (*vichetasah*) waters (*apah*) fill the rivers (*sindhuh*) (1.83.1)

Angirasa seers won the wealth of Rays (*gomantam*) and life energies (*ashvantam*) (1.83.4)

Atharvan laid the first path by yajna.
Then was born the pleasing Sun, guardian of laws.
Next Ushanas Kavya, the seer, obtained the Rays (*gah*). (1.83.5)

Here the birth of Sun is the manifestation of Sun Power in man. Only after the manifestation of the Sun Power is the manifestation of the Rays of consciousness possible in man. Here the particular example of the sage Ushanas is mentioned.

Soma, you have generated all the Medicinal Energies (*oshadhi*), Dynamic Energies (*apah*) and Rays (*ga*).
With thy Light you have dispelled ignorance (*tama*). (1.91.22)

Here the action dispelling ignorance is ascribed to Soma, the Lord of Divine Delight. *Oshadhih* is not merely a herb but represents the force which cures the diseases and restores the harmony of the human body. *Apah* is not merely water but Divine Energies as mentioned elsewhere. Similarly, *gah* are not physical cows but Rays of Light. These symbolic assignments are consistent with the second line.

O Mighty God Soma, with thy luminous thought direct us to our share in the felicity (*raya*).
Do thou will the discovery of the Light (*gavishtu*) for both gods and men. (1.91.23)

Indra, Lord of Rays (*gavam*) and Life Energies, we invoke for companionship. (1.101.4)

Indra, Lord of all that moves and moves not,
First found the Rays (*gah*) for the spiritual aspirants (*brahmana*). (1.104.5)

1.101.4 clearly indicates that *gavam* cannot be simply translated as cows. Indra is lord of everyrthing, not merely cows. He stabilizes in the aspirants the power of consciousness and knowledge.

Indra won the Rays (*gah*), Life Energies (*ashvan*), Herbs (*oshadhih*), Energies (*apah*) and Delights (*vanani*). (1.103.5)

Ashvins, you went to the cave to liberate the Rays (*go*) and the Energies (*arnasah*) (1.112.18)

Release of the *go* and release of the waters is described as one event.

Ashvins, you help the hero fighting for Light (*goshuyudhah*). (1.112.22)

Here the verse can mean "fighting for cattle" also.

Indra, the most Angiras, found the treasure of heaven hidden in the secret cavern like the young of the bird, within the infinite rock like a pen of cows. (1.130.3)

Here we have a reference to the secret treasure within the cave of the infinite rock. It is a heavenly treasure. It stays there like the young of a bird. He compares the treasure in the cave to the cows in a pen. Clearly the treasure cannot be the cattle themselves. The treasure is called divine. None of these verses imply that *gau* is cattle.

4-E. *Donors of the Light (Cows) and the Recipient*

O Indra, O Soma-Drinker, drink the Soma;
You are the donor of the Light (*godah*) increasing in the rapture. (1.4.2)

On the surface, the translation of *go* as cattle is possible. But Indra is the master of all worlds. Why would the wise person, the rishi, request cows from Indra? How does Indra give cows? As it is described, Indra gives rain, which causes grass to grow. Feeding the grass cows become plentiful. Thus Indra is supposed to be the donor of cows. Or Indra is viewed as an ordinary person who in his drunken condition gives cows. This analysis is far fetched to say the least.

Join to us the wealth, full of Rays (*gomat*), full of lustre (*hiranya*), opulent, mighty
Hearing of divine inspiration, the undecaying life of all (*visvayuh akshitau*) (1.9.7)

O Indra, give us mighty hearing, the Light (*dyumnam*) enjoyable by thousands, the fast moving impulsions. (1.9.8)

O master of the hill, open the doors of the home of Rays (*gavam*) and give us wealth (*radhas*). (1.10.7)

Indra, heaven and earth cannot encompass thee;
You win the waters of Svar when formidable.
Impel us towards the Rays (*gah*). (1.10.8)

He gives to the singers the wealth endowed with Rays (*gomatah*), its growth diminish not. (1.11.3)

O Indra, fulfil the desire of ours with Light (*gobhih*) and Life Energy (*ashvaih*).
We devoted by intense meditation (*svadhyay*) laud thee. (1.16.9)

The seers of the Rigveda were well versed with meditation. *Svadhyay* is derived from *dhyai*, to meditate.

O Indra, opulent, make us special among Rays (*goshu*), Life Energy (*ashveshu*), and thousandfold auspiciousness. (1.29.1)

The same phrase occurs in all the 7 verses (1.29.1–7). In the first verse (1.29.1) Indra is called as Truth (*Satya*). Again "Make us special among cows" does not make sense.

Indra secures the wealth of Rays (*gah*) to whom he favours.
Increased in us be not a Pani (miser) in giving thy plentiful delight (*vamam*). (1.33.3)

Note the phrase "increased in us". The Power of Indra increases in man. Note the use of a proper name of demon, Pani, as an adjective in the sense of miser.

You have brought forth the herd of Rays (*gotram*) for Angiras,
Found the way for Atri from the hundred doors,
Obtained for Vimada the wealth of utter rest (*sasane chid*);
You sport the stone for one engulfed in battle. (1.51.3)

Indra is the refuge of the good in need,
Donor of Rays (*gavyuh*), donor of Life Energies (*ashvayuh*).
Donor of Cars (*rathayuh*), donor of Wealth (*vasuyuh*). (1.51.14)

All wealth exceedingly luminous is known to be yours.
Gather from it and bring what is fit for us. (1.53.3)

In rapture and rapture straight dealing, he is the donor of Rays (*gavam*).
Gather in both thy hands plentiful riches,
Sharpen us, bring us wealth (*raya*). (1.81.7)

"Sharpen us" means prepare our subtle bodies to bear the spiritual felicities.

To the offerer, Soma gives cow (*dhenum*), swift life energies, hero son skilled in works. (1.91.20)
Agni and Soma, bestow the nourishment (*posham*) of the Ray (*gavam*) with heroic strength and Life Energies on the worshipper (1.93.2)

Possession of Rays (*gah*) was removed from Pani.

Then the one Light was acquired for the many. (1.93.4)

The last line of 1.93.4 clearly shows that *gava*in the first line cannot be the animal. Pani, the demon, symbolises the forces of ignorance who veil the rays of consciousness and prevent them from reaching the humans.

He (Rudra) makes for the well being of our steeds, rams, ewes,
men, women and cows (*gave*). (1.43.6)

Here *gave* can be interpreted both as cows and as Rays of Consciousness. Two possible renderings are:

"Rudra, harm not our progeny, cows (*goshu*) and steeds"

and

"Harm not our disciples, Rays of Knowledge and Life Energies."

But if we look at the context and the epithets for Rudra, the translation of *goshu* as Light or Rays and *ashveshu* as Life Energies is appropriate.

4-F. Agni, the Power of the Divine Will and Gau

O Agni, the gods made thee the first human being. (1.31.11)

O Agni, you are the protector of the Rays (*gavam*) and their offspring. (1.31.12)

Obviously the physical fire cannot protect the cows. Agni, the power of Divine Will, the will endowed with wisdom, the power of human aspiration can protect both the knowledge and its derivatives.

With the sight of Sun, the Rays (*gavah*) travel towards him (Agni). (1.66.5)

Agni, you establish your word in the Rays (*goshu*) and the Delight (*vaneshu*). (1.70.5)

With his Rays (*gobhih*) and Waters (*adbhih*)
He (Agni) assumes his excellent form in the mid region.
Seerr Agni cleanses the source.
Such thoughts extended by the gods become the function of
gods. (1.95.8)

When Agni cleanses the source of Light and Energies, the Heaven (*dyu*), the pure thought that arises, becomes the meeting ground of the divine powers, the gods.

Agni, son of strength,
You united with the Rays (*gomatah*)
Are the Lord of all plenitude. (1.79.4)

4-G. Usha and Gau

Usha is the goddess of spiritual Dawn. She represents the force behind a human being's first intimation of the divine.

> The dawns have harnessed (to their car) the radiant Rays (*gah*) easily yoked.
> As before, they have brought the knowings.
> The bright Dawns have attained the fulgent Sun (*bhanum*). (1.92.2)
>
> Usha, bring all the gods from the mid-region to drink the Soma.
> O Usha, establish within us (*asmasu*)
> The Rays of Light (*gomat*), the Life Energies,
> The plenitude of hero-might lauded in hymns. (1.48.12)

The verse makes excellent sense as is. Spiritual Light is established within us, in our subtle bodies. Persons trying to force the meaning of cattle on *gomat* in 1.48.12 claim that *asmasu* should be interpreted in the sense of "near us" or "near our home".

> O Usha, give us plenty of impulsions of the human Rays (*gomatih*) (1.48.15)
>
> Goddess Mahi, full of Rays (*gomatih*), happy Truth flowing abundantly. (1.8.8)
>
> Usha bestowing Rays (*gomatih*), heroes, the Life Energies (*ashva*) on the giver. (1.113.18)
>
> These Dawns have created Light and manifest it.
>
> These Rays (*gavah*) radiant mothers, onward come. (1.92.1)

Dawns, in the spiritual context, signify outbreaks of higher consciousness occurring repeatedly in the life of a Rishi. Consequently, the rays of consciousness which nourish the humans also come.

> O Usha, full of Rays (*gomatih*) and Life Energies, shine on us the luminous wealth. (1.92.14)

4-H. Ashvins and their Symbolic Deeds Related to Gau

Ashvins are the lords of bliss who render the human body free of disease and prepare it to receive the force of immortality. We give two translations of 1.116.22.

> Ashvins, you filled the barren cow with milk for the sake of Shayu. (1.116.22)

Or

> You filled the superficial knowledge receptacle (of knowledge) with deep knowledge. (1.116.22)

In the first translation, Ashvin's deed is a miracle with no explanation. The second indicates a spiritual experience of the divine filling the empty human body with knowledge. Just as ordinary milk is a product of cow, milk in the spiritual sense is a product of knowledge. The same symbolism is repeated in several verses given below.

> You filled the emaciated barren milkless cow with milk for Shayu. (1.117.20)
>
> O Ashvins, fill our consciousness (*gah*) with immortality. (1.118.2)
>
> O Ashvins, you generated milk (*avasam*) in Shayu's knowledge-receptacle (*gavi*). (1.119.6)
>
> O Ashvins, you filled the barren (*asvam*) cow (*dhenum*). (1.112.3)
>
> O Ashvins, never may our cows (*dhenavah*) nourishing with milk stray from our homes. (1.120.8)

1.120.8 declares "Let not knowledge depart from us".

> Prepare us for the power (*ishe*)
> United with Rays (*dhenumatyai*). (1.120.9)
>
> Direct the car of yours,
> O Ashvins, to our house (body) endowed with radiant (*gomat*) and lustrous (*hiranya*). (1.92.16)
>
> May your (Ashvins') coming be full of Rays (*gomat*) and lustrous (*hiranya*). (1.30.17)

4-I. Ribhus and Gau

Ribhus in the Rigveda are the devas who are the artisans of immortality. They build the subtle human body to receive the knowledge and power.

> Ribhus fashioned the nectar yielding cow (*subar dugham*). (1.20.3)
>
> Ribhu separated the soul (*gam*) from its physical covering (*charmanah*) and united the mother with its calf. (1.110.8)

We translate *gam* as soul, which is the concentration of the Rays of Knowledge. The soul of man is covered by the outer body. Ribhus remove the covering and restore the soul (the calf) to the infinite consciousness (the Mother), Aditi.

The usual translation of 1.110.8, given below, is only enigmatic but not enlightening.

> "Ribhus separated the cow from the hide and united the mother with the calf."

4-J. Gau and Apah, the Waters

Apah, translated as Waters, symbolises all the cosmic energies which shower all the inhabitants of the earth as well as the subtle energies found in the subtle body of the human being, later termed as Kundilini. They have the power of purifying, removing all falsehood. This idea becomes by studying the subhymn (1.23.16 through 23). We will quote only two verses to indicate the symbolism of Waters.

I call the Waters (*apah*), goddesses in whom
Our knowledge (*gavah*) nourish. (1.23.18)

Immortality (*amrtam*) is in the Waters,
The healer is in the Waters. (1.23.19)

I have now attained the Waters.
We have become one with their essence. (1.23.23)

We will quote here some verses involving both the Waters and *gau*. If we take *gau* as cattle, then the idea of cows drinking water is natural. However, the entire verse or hymn does not allow for such a simplistic explanation.

O hero, God absolute,
You won the Rays (*gah*), won the Soma,
You released the seven rivers to flow. (1.32.12)

O Soma, you have generated
All the Waters (*apah*), Rays (*gah*) and herbs.
With thy Light, you have dispelled darkness. (1.91.22)

Have faith in Indra's prowess by which
He won the Rays (*gah*), won the Life Energies,
Won the Waters (*apah*), won the herbs, and
Won the Delights (*vanani*). (1.103.5)

Both 1.32.12 and 1.103.5 refer to the cosmic battle between the forces of Light and the forces of darkness culminating in the release of the hidden lnowledge (*gah*), the delight of existence, Soma, the flowing energies or rivers and Waters (*apah*). Interpreting Soma as a herb, the rivers as the five rivers of Northern India implies that the Rishis placed all sorts of disjoint phrases in a single verse.

Again in 1.91.22, Soma with his Light, is said to dispel darkness. Clearly Soma cannot be the herb. Clearly a herb cannot generate waters. Thus the references Soma, *apah*, etc. must be symbolic.

4-K. Gau as a Simile

Gau is used as a part of simile in twelve verses (1.3.8, 1.23.15, 1.25.16,

1.32.11, 1.38.2, 1.61.10, 1.61.12, 1.71.1, 1.87.1, 1.91.3, 1.92.4, 1.95.6). *Dhenavah* is used as a simile in five verses (1.32.2, 1.32.9, 1.66..1, 1.4.1, 1.69.2). In these verses, *gau* refers to the cows. Even in such cases as in 1.87.1, the word *gau* could be interpreted as Light.

5. *Gau in Hymn 121*

We will quote here all the verses of this hymn, the last one of the first eight of the book (*ashtaka*) which contain the *gau* word. The entire quotation will give a clue to the general pattern of the hymn.

The first verse (1.121.1) does not contain *gau*. It sets the theme of the hymn: "When will Indra listen to our prayers and manifest himself with us?" The verses 2 and 4 describe some of Indra's powers. The verse 5 gives a specific procedure for feeling Indra's presence. Verse 6 declares that Indra is manifested. Verses 7 through 14 again describe some of Indra's actions. The last verse is a prayer for Indra for sharing in his knowledge.

We quote verses 1, 2, 5, 6, 7, 8, 9 and 15.

> When will Indra, the guardian of men, impeller of the seekers of
> God, listen to these prayers of Angiras?
> When he comes to the inner being (*harmasya*) of yajmana,
> He is to be worshipped and he greatly exults. (1.121.1)

> Indra upholds the heavens. He has made the Life Energy
> (*ashvasva*) the mother of Rays (*go*). (1.121.2)

The literal translation is "he has made the horse, the mother of cow". The esoteric meaning is straightforward. To manifest the knowledge a human being needs a body endowed with life energy so that it can withstand the force of knowledge. Otherwise it breaks like an unbaked jar quoted in the Rigveda. This verse states that Indra manifests the rays of knowledge in the human body through a profusion of life energies, i.e., life energies act like a mother and yield the knowledge.

> When the yajamana offered the pure and most rich milk (*payah*)
> for the nectar streaming (*sabardugah*) Light (*usriyayah*). (121.5)

> Then is Indra manifested. (121.6)

Milk is a product of the cow. Here it symbolises a product of knowledge. Only when the yajamana offers his higher thoughts and feelings to Indra which have been purified by removing all the petty human feelings, then Indra is manifested.

> The impeller Indra dispels the *coverings* over the Rays (*goh*) in
> the yajna.

When the Soma, brightly shining, seeks to flow,
When you shine forth through the days of action, the senses
(*pashveshu*) are readed
For both the motionless and the active. (121.7)

This verse refers to the removal of the coverings on the knowledge. When the covering is removed, the knowledge manifests everywhere, both in action and in making the senses keener to appreciate the presence of the Divine everywhere, both in motionless subjects as well as in moving ones

The next two verses describe the battle of Indra with the adversary forces of ignorance and the release of Soma as described earlier.

O warrior, overcome the adversary shadowing the Light
(*dyumnasham*)
When the rapturous Soma, invigorating like the ox (*gorabhasam*)
is poured out for thy increase. (1.121.8)

Note the increase refers to the increase of the power of Indra in the inner body of the poet.

For getting the Rays you did hurl the Vajra brought from Heaven
by Ribhu. (1.121.9)

This verse is reminiscent of 1.33.10, 1.7.3, etc. Vajra is not a mere thunderbolt, but a force of Divine Light and Sound. Indra uses the Vajra to break the hill of ignorance and release the captive Rays of Consciousness.

The last verse is a prayer for sharing in the knowledge of Indra.

O Indra, never may thy grace fail us.
Make us share in the rays (*goshu*).
Most eager in thy worship
May we rejoice together with you. (1.121.15)

In the Rigveda the poets do not propitiate the gods. They believe that they are collaborators with the gods in the divine action and want to rejoice along with Indra.

6. Conclusions

We have shown that in all the verses of the first ashtaka, the first eighth of the Rigveda, *gau* or *dhenavah* has the consistent meaning of Spiritual Light or Spiritual Knowledge. Even the words associated with gau (or cow), words like *payas* or *ghrta* translated as milk and ghee (melted butter) have corresponding symbolic meanings like product of knowledge and clarity. The use of the symbolic meanings for the common nouns indicated in the table yields a consistent meaning not only for each verse but also for the entire hymn. We mentioned earlier that in some of the verses, especially those involving similes, *gau* can be translated as the animal cow or even as rays of ordinary light. But such meanings cannot be sustained in all the verses.

Since *gau* is no longer cattle, the theft of cattle cannot be one of the main themes of the Rigveda. Spiritual Knowledge is lost by human beings due to the forces of others. Only the force of Divine Mind can smash the forces of ignorance and retrieve the spiritual knowledge, whose loss is mentioned in many books.

Acknowledgements

I want to thank Dr. Sadagopan of the Indian Institute of Management, Bangalore and Mr. R. Ramabhadran for help in preparing this essay.

References

[1] Sri Aurobindo, *The Secret of the Veda, Hymns to the Mystic Fire*, Sri Aurobindo Ashram, Pondicherry, 1956.

[2] Sri Kapil Sastry, *Light on the Veda*, Vol. I of Collected Works; *Translation of Hymns 1 through 121 of First Mandala*, Vols. IV, VI and X of Collected Works, Dipti Publications, Aurobindo Ashram (Lotus Light Publications, P.O. Box 2, Wilmot, WI 53192).

[3] Sri M.P. Pandit, *Wisdom of the Veda* (translation of some selected verses of Rigveda), Lotus Light Publications, P.O. Box 2, Wilmot, WI 53192.

[4] A.B. Purani, *Studies in Vedic Interpretation*, Chowkhambha Sanskrit Series, Varanasi-1, India.

[5] Abinash Chandra Bose, *Hymns from the Rigveda*, Asia Publishing House, Bombay, 1966.

Solar Energy—Comments on a Chapter of the Yajurveda

V. KRISHNAMURTHY

Director, K.K. Birla Academy, B4 Shivalik, New Delhi, 110017, India.

Of the 101 branches of the Yajurveda only two are extant now. Of these two, the Taittiriya sakha has a chapter which has 32 paragraphs. This chapter of the Vedas is called the Surya-Namaskara Prasna. The Mantras of this chapter have great spiritual significance. The worship of the Sun is considered to be most important and powerful. This physical sun is not what we are worshipping. Hinduism is not Nature Worship. Behind every form and object of nature there is the Ultimate Supreme which is the one reality present everywhere and at all times. The Kenopanishad makes this very clear in no uncertain terms. Whatever cannot be seen by the eyes but by which the eyes see, that is Brahman—not the one that you see physically and worship.

Surya Namaskaara Mantras

As an expression of the divine power there is nothing to beat the Sun. Ever since the Vedic times the Sun (Surya) has been worshipped, adored and revered. It is true that the invisible rays of the sun can kill bacteria and give life to the plant world. But the Sun was revered not just for these but for being the only visible symbol of the infinite power, majesty and glory of the 'Unseen Almighty'. Of the 101 branches (= Sakhas) of the Yajurveda only two are extant now. Of these two the *Taittiriya sakha* has a chapter which has 32 paragraphs (known as *Anuvakas)* divided into 130 sub-paragraphs, each called a *panchasat.* Each such *panchasat* has 10 sentences except when it occurs at the end of a paragraph. The entire matter is a compendium of information on the Sun as was 'seen' by Vedic seers. It has been the tradition among Brahmins educated in the Vedas to recite this chapter and make a full prostration to the Sun in the east at the end of each *panchasat,* particularly every Sunday morning. This ritual is called *Surya-Namaskara.* That is why this chapter of the Vedas is called the *Surya-Namaskara Prasna.* The *Mantras* of this chapter have great spiritual significance. The benefits of the physical exercise that one derives from this ritual are only incidental. Their real benefit is esoteric in terms of a spiritual evolution. There is such a firm belief in these benefits, both physical and spiritual, that performance of this ritual is recommended even by proxy, i.e., if one is either incapable of doing it either because of ill-health or because of lack of training in the scriptures—that is, one engages a professional pundit to do it for him.

Rama's Worship of the Sun-God

The worship of the Sun is considered to be most important and powerful. This worship is usually done through the supreme *mantra* named *Gayatri.* In this worship, the Sun-God is the ultimate Godhead itself. The Sun is probably the most practical example of God's immanence in everything. Recall that right in the Rigveda we are told that the Sun is the soul of the moving and the stable world[1]. There are three formal texts which are used to worship the Sun. One is the *Gayatri Mantra.* The other is through *Aditya-hridayam,* a *stotra* which occurs in the Valmiki Ramayana. The scene is the war between Rama's armies when almost every leader except Ravana has been killed and the war is reaching its final climax. The face-to-face battles between Rama and Ravana are taking place. On the very last day, in the morning, the sage Agastya appears before Rama and teaches him the *Aditya-hridayam* in eighteen verses. Rama absorbs it, recites it and meditates on it. It was on that day that he finally won the battle by vanquishing Ravana. This *Aaitya-hridaya-stotra* is a very easy and popular one. Among the many *stotras* that are systematically recited by the faithful every day, *Aditya-hridayam* would find one of the foremost places.

Not Nature Worship but Worship of the Absolute

In the matter of worshipping the Sun-god and similar other gods a standard misconception has to be cleared. What we are worshipping is not the physical sun before us, not the visible sun that scientists have charted out for us as the centre of our solar system, our nearest star, at the centre of which there is a large accumulation of nuclear matter, which supplies through its nuclear reactions a constant flow of enormous energy to our terrestrial environment, in such a way that this flow reaches us in eight minutes of its organization and all the time that sun itself is moving away from the centre of the galaxy, the Milky Way. This physical sun is not what we are worshipping. The external manifestation is only secondary; the Absolute Supreme that is behind is primary. The *Kenopanishad* makes this very clear in no uncertain terms,

"Whatever cannot be seen by the eyes but by which the eyes see, that is *Brahman*—not the one that you see physically and worship."[2]

So behind the physical sun there is the *Surya-devata,* the Sun-God. It is not

---

[1] *Surya atma jagatas-tastushascha.* Rigveda 1.115.1

[2] Kena Upanishad, 1 to 6.

visible to the physical eyes. That is what we are supposed to be worshipping. "He who inhabits the Sun but is within it, whom the Sun does not know, whose body is the Sun and who controls the Sun from within, is the Inner Controller, your own immortal Self" says the *Brihadaranyaka Upanishad.*[3] In fact if we understand this principle of Hindu worship well we will discover that no amount of scientific advance and breakthrough can ever upset the esoteric philosophical foundations of the religion called Hinduism. Whatever object we worship, whether it is the waters, or the fire, or the wind, or the Earth, or even the Sun, there is always an abstraction into a divine element behind the physical element or object and that abstraction is the object of our worship. Man may land on the moon and inhabit it. But that cannot deny the status of the Moon-God to the Moon and its status as the seat of the *pitr's*, the ancestral souls, which is part of the Hindu culture, religion and tradition. The Earth is also worshipped as *Bhuma-devi.* We stand, sit and sleep on the Earth and we do all sorts of contamination on it. This does not preclude a Hindu scientist praying to *Bhuma-devi* every morning when he gets up from bed and invoking Her pardon and forgiveness for his day's activities to start, with all the pollution of the Earth that these involve. Thus it should be clear that Hinduism is not Nature Worship. Behind every form and object of nature there is the Ultimate Supreme which is the one reality present everywhere and at all times. This statement can never be overemphasized as any careful reader of the Vedas would have observed. In fact the *Gayatri Mantra* which is explained to the uninitiated as Sun-worship is called *Savitri,* because the object of worship is *Brahman* embedded in the region of *Savita,* the Sun. This would show that *Gayatri-Upasana* is actually the *upasana,* worship, of *Brahman.*

Surya-namaskara-prasna

We shall briefly comment on the parts of the text of the *Surya-namaskara-prasna*. The very first prayer which appeals to the Divines that only good things should happen, uses, as usual with most of the prayers in Hinduism: "With our ears may we hear what is good; with our eyes may we behold thy righteousness … ." This is a characteristic of most of the Vedic prayers and, in their wake, of all of the Puranic prayers. The one who chants the mantras offers his prayer for the entire world. After this prayer the chapter starts with a prayer for the divine elements embedded in the waters. "By these *Mantras* I shall make these waters extremely powerful." Note that only by the Sun's rays the waters and the food and medicinal products that grow out of these waters become fruitful. "By my doing this may all good come to us, and may the goddess Sarasvati be

[3] III, 7–9.

beneficent to all of us." After these and such other prayers, the text gets into business.

First Anuvaka on Concept of Time

First there is a whole paragraph, *Anuvaka,* which is a treatise on the concept of Time. The visible universe of the solar system, including the Sun, is known to us by four means of knowledge: memory, direct perception, historical records and inference. Time flows like a river—endlessly, as it were. And it goes on and on. It never turns back. We measure the passage of time by calling them days, months and years. It keeps trickling by minute units as well as large chunks of such measure. But all this is only in the phenomenal world. The passage of time is only for the empirical world of the visible universe. *There is something absolute beyond all this. That is not visible to us.* There is no world there, no Sun, no animals. This is the real nature of the absolute behind the Sun. There is something absolute behind Time and the Vedas are so kind to tell us that even if we do not understand it, it does not matter. This is in concordance with the thought expressed in the Gita, in the third chapter: "Do not create a confusion of understanding in the ignorant who are attached to their works."[4] The context there is the requirement that those who are unattached to the ephemeral, would do their actions exactly as those who are attached do; the difference is only in the attitude and not in the external way of doing things.

Surya-Namaskara Prasna: On Faith

The third paragraph has beautiful pieces about Faith, *sraddha.* The context is that we should have faith in the Vedas. Faith is response in the heart, not just intellectual acceptance. Continuous intellectual study sometimes only results in vanity, false satisfaction and undigested information. It has been rightly said that the greatest weakness of man is intellectual doubt. The Vedas are our best friend. It tells us what is best for us. We should not mistrust our best friend. To bring forth this idea the text goes on thus: "Is there a friend who mistrusts a friend from whom he has derived only good? Whoever discards such a good friend in mistrust and doubt, for him there is no right to read and hear the scriptures any more; even if he hears them, he listens in vain. The Bhagavad-Gita, in its sixteenth chapter discusses *sraddha* and declares it is a condition in which the heart is pleasantly inclined towards the article of faith and so "*whatever is that will, faith or constituting belief in the person, he is that and that is he.*" "Faith does not admit of telling; it has to be lived and then it becomes self-propagating" said Mahatma Gandhi. One is reminded of the words

---

[4] Gita, III-26.

of Jesus[5]: "Have faith in God. I tell you the truth, if any one says to this mountain, 'Go throw yourself into the sea,' and does not doubt in his heart but believes that what he says will happen, it will be done for him. Therefore I tell you, whatever you ask for in prayer, believe that you have received it and it will be yours." The Gita also says: "The ignorant who has no faith, the soul of doubt, perishes; neither this world nor the supreme world nor any happiness is for the soul full of doubts. To the question: 'Without actual experience of God, what is the good of mere belief?' one has to recall the experience of the ultimate oneness with God that so many saints over the centuries have described. Their experience teaches us that one starts with faith, goes through an intellectual pursuit and then ends up, by transcending the intellect, with a feeling of oneness with God." Incidentally we note in this paragraph the use of the *Sakti Pranava 'im'* for the Vedas. The Vedas personify God and the symbol for *Saguna Brahman* is '*im'* just as '*aum'* is the symbol for *nirgun Brahman.*

Anuvaka Six: Significance of Namaskara

In paragraphs 3, 4 and 5 the seasons are described poetically. The seasons, remember, are the handiwork of the Sun's rays. We know today they are the consequence of the Earth's rotation round the Sun. But more fundamental than this is the fact that the rays fall in different angles We now go to the sixth paragraph. The essential secret of the significance of *Surya Namaskara* is hidden here. In the sixth paragraph a mention is made about how in the winter season, one cuddles up near the fire and this cuddling up with knees bent is itself an act of prostration to the divines of the seasons. "With knees bent and touching the ground, with hands folded up at the chest, as if in an act of 'anjali' (meaning, in respectful bowing to a god or elder, as it were),—this very act is taken by the gods of the seasons as a prostration and to such a person, it is said, the seasons themselves bow in respect; he who thus coordinates with the seasons in the knowledge of, and respect to, the seasons, he gets the position of leadership of men." The use of the syllable *'ni'* in two meanings in two places in this extract is real poetic smartness. *'Ni'* means 'touching the feet' (*nyag-bhuta*) — this is the use in the construction: *ni janu kame-nyanjalika*[6]. The word *janu* means 'knee'. '*ni*' also indicates the folding posture; it is so used in the compound word '*nyanjalika*'. In this context, one should recall the Vedic emphasis on *namaskara,* full prostration, in several contexts and places. The word 'namah' has a very significant connotation in the Hindu religion. It means,

---

[5] Mark 11: 22-24

[6] *Ni janu kamenyanjalika: ami vacham upasatam iti tasmai sarva ritavo namante; maryadakaratvatprapurodham; Brahmana apnoti.*

simply, prostration. But there is more to it. The two syllables '*na*' and '*ma*' are said to indicate the attitude of '*na-mama-kara*'—that is, not mine, not mine. Whatever I have, Oh Lord, is yours, not mine. So let me prostrate to you with that feeling of total detachment from what I call my possessions,—which includes everything that I call 'mine',. including my body, limbs, mind, thoughts, expressions, feelings, certainly my physical possessions, my kith and kin and, finally, my egoism, my personality, my name. This attitude of total surrender, and identification with the Absolute, is the summum bonum of all knowledge and realization because there is nothing else other than the Absolute, in the final counting. The *Surya Namaskára* itself is to inculcate in us this attitude of recognition of the One Absolute—of which the visible Power is the Sun—and the action of repeated prostrations to the Sun-God is to imprint on us this recognition for ever. The *Taittiriya Upanishad* says, at one point, that those who worship Him with the word '*namah*' on their lips are so special that all desires will fall and bow at their feet. The *Isavasyopanishad,* in its very last *Mantra,* which therefore is the last *Mantra* of the entire *Sukla-yajur-veda,* says to the Fire-God—as explained earlier, this means, to the same Ultimate Reality of which the Fire is a visible manifestation—'we will make innumerable repetitions of *namah* to You, please take us along the right path.'

Anuvaka on Seven Suns

The seventh *Anuvaka* reveals some unusually interesting insights about the Sun. In fact modern solar energy studies must include a research into this portion of the *Suryanamaskara prasna*. First it names seven Suns! Does it mean these are the seven colours in the spectrum of the Sun? It does not say so. But throughout this chapter which is itself a treatise on the Sun, and throughout the entire body of scriptures, whenever the Sun-God is mentioned, the number seven goes along with it either in the form of references to the number of horses in His chariot or to these seven Suns. The names are: *aroga, braja; patara, patanga, swarna, jyotishirnan, vibhasa.* 'These heat the entire space,' goes the text, 'in such a way that no damage is done but they enrich everything with the downpour of strength-giving rain, etc.' Then it says—here comes the surprise: 'There is an eighth Sun: *Kasyapa,* by name. He never leaves the *Maha-meru'*. The *Mantra* goes on: 'Oh *Kasyapa,* by the skill that You have in enriching the power of our senses, in the life-giving dalliant rays of Yours which bestow nutrition on us, by that skill—in which the seven Suns are linked to You—may we be blessed to be in the highest peak of our efficiency.'

Then the text goes on to talk about the various speculations about what it has itself just declared. 'Some say,' the text goes on, 'these seven suns are the vital airs that dwell in the face; others say that they are the five senses of perception, plus the mind and the intellect.' Incidentally the seven points of entry into the body which are in the face—namely, the two eyes, the two ears, the two nostrils and the mouth—are the holes which allow the seven *adhyatma-pranas,* that is the vital airs classified as pertaining to the soul within. The five elemental fundamentals—earth, water, fire, air and space—together with the two principles called *mahat* and *ahamkara,* are the seven *adhi-bhautika pranas,* that is, the vital airs belonging to the physical plane. The seven Suns, named above, are the *adhidaivata-pranas,* that is the vital airs pertaining to the celestial plane.

An Eighth Sun Beyond

Then comes the passage narrating the claims of great sages about their experience of the seven Suns and the eighth Sun. Two sages by name *Pancha-karna,* son of *Vatsa* and *Sapta-karna*, son of *Plaksha,* claim to have seen the seven Suns; but, say the two, they have not been able to go to the *Maha-Meru* and see the eighth Sun. But everybody strongly recommends, says the text, that Man should strive to go to the *Maha-Meru* and see that One-ness of Divinity, called *Kasyapa.* It becomes clear that they are referring to the Supreme Reality here which is the substratum of all the Seven Suns. '*Tasya bhasa sarvam idamm vibhati*' say the scriptures in another place. So these seven Suns themselves derive their strength and dalliance from the eighth Sun, namely *Kasyapa.* The seven Suns originated from *Kasyapa,* says the text. The very name *Kasyapa* is extolled and its meaning derived by going into its etymology. *Kasyapah pasyako bhavati*—is the statement later, in the eighth paragraph of the chapter. It means *Kasyapa* is the One that sees. Meaning, He sees rightly. The next sentence explains this. *Yat sarvam pari-pasyati-iti saukshmyat.* Because it sees everything in all its subtlety. The root word for seeing is '*dris*' which, when conjugated becomes '*pasyati*'. There is another esoteric significance here. The word '*Kasyapa*' has three syllables: *Ka, sya* and *pa* in that order. Reverse the order of these syllables. We get *pa, sya*, and *ka* and they make up, in that order, the word *Pasyaka*—which means One who Sees. That is why, *Kasyapah Pasyako bhavati! Bhavati* means, 'becomes'. *Kasyapah* happens to be the *Pasyaka.* The existence of this eighth Sun in the form of the Ultimate Supreme (Who sees, as things are to be seen) is given only in the scriptures and one wonders whether this could have implications for the understanding of what Solar Energy is, really. It is at this point there arises the need for modern research into the conceptual foundations of the Theory of Solar Energy. The Scripture says there is an eighth Sun beyond and that is the source of the strength, power and glory of the visible Sun. Can this eighth Sun be researched on? What would be our equipment? What would be our scientific conjecture on this, on which we may test with further experiments and observation? These are all unanswered questions. Only those who have some faith in the scriptures would dare research on these matters! At the end of all this adventurist description of the eight Suns, the passage ends with the same prayer with which the *Suka Yajurveda* ends

Anuvaka on Death

The eighth paragraph contains, among other things, a discussion on the concept of Death (*mrityu).* Death is a consequence of Time-flow. Nobody can escape death. So the Sun is the ultimate supreme cause of inescapable Death. But there are other minor causes of death, namely, the loss of life-giving air—which can be countered by breathing exercises like *Pranayama* and the like; the fire of consumption within the stomach, called *Jatharagni,* for which there are medicinal cures; and thirdly, the Moon, which is the deity for food and herbs and such death is due to lack of food, and wrong medication—which again can be countered. Thus it turns out to be that the Sun, by which we mean the flow of Time (kala) is the greatest and supreme Cause of Death and this we can never escape.

Anuvaka on Tapas

The eleventh *Anuvaka* has interesting things to say on *Tapas.* The great *Mantra* of the Sun is the most powerful purifier of all but it is not possible to obtain it except by intense *tapas* (askesis). *Tapas* is the process by which irrespective of what happens to the physical and mental body one concentrates on some particular goal, usually spiritual, works for it and does not stop until that is obtained. The root word '*tap*' means to torture or to heat. *Tapas* therefore indicates heat, particularly the heat energy generated by ritual activity and personal mortification of the body through fasting, sexual abstinence or any other severe self-discipline. Even voluntary poverty is a form of *tapas*. In fact, every form of pursuit of self-control is *tapas*, says the *Narayanopanishad.* By means of a body which has not gone through a torture of the necessary effort in the form of *tapas*, one is like a food which is not ripe and so would not obtain the cherished goal—says the text. Doing one's duty with a persistent religious zeal is doing tapas; others are prey to desires and their life is vain—says the ancient author of *Tirukkural* in Tamil. The thought that not doing tapas in some form or other is a life spent in vain is also echoed in the Gita: He who does not follow the Cosmic Law but is totally subservient to his senses lives in vain; his life is just a sinful life. It should be pointed out however that the concept of *tapas*, though important in the entire Hindu mythology and metaphysics, is only a means to a spiritual end, not an end in itself.

Names, Only in Name

That Ultimate Status which one looks for and works for, by *tapas,* is described eloquently in the scriptures. Here in the context of the *Surya,* the same is talked about in the language relevant to the physical Sun. The Sun hides the stars in the daytime. It is as if it is withdrawing all these rays—which are the ones which are making the stars invisible—at night time. And then the stars become visible. So also we human beings give undue importance to the names given to us, which pertain only to this body of flesh and bones. This name is so much linked to this body that it becomes meaningless when Real Enlightenment dawns. The names which are caused by association with the body become meaningless in reality and they are names only in name! *Nama namaiva nama me*—this is a famous line in this paragraph. *Nama* means name.

Death on the Wings

In the fourteenth paragraph, for example, the units of time are systematically used to impress upon us the ephemeral nature of man's life. When the Sun rises its rise symbolizes the passing away of one night in the life of human beings and in this sense the Sun's rise is like taking away a slice of life-span from everybody. When the Sun sets it has taken away one day from the lives of each one of us. When the days pass by, when the months and years pass by, this is what is happening to us. Every movement of the Sun across the sky implies this passing away of our lives. This continual reduction in the remaining part of our lives is something the scriptures never fail to point out, because even after all this, we tend to forget this, especially in crucial moments of self-consciousness, anger, jealousy or passion. The fourteenth paragraph has a number of perorations on this, starting with the rise of the sun, the setting of the sun, then the fortnights, the months, and the years.

After this, the *Surya-Namaskara Prasna* gets into technical detail. Particularly throughout the last one-third part it elaborates a ritual called *aruna-ketuka-yajna.* In sum, the *Surya-Namaskara Prasna*, in addition to being a treatise on the Sun, proves to us by its philosophical and esoteric implications that Hindu religion is not just a system of beliefs nor just a formalized effort to wheedle a little pity out of God by offering Him pleading self-condemning prayers and propitiatory rites. Instead, Hindu rituals, each one of them, is a constant reminder to us of the Oneness of God and His omnipresence. The act of reminding and remembering is itself a part of the total process of approach to that Divinity.

Upanishads: The Pinnacle of the Religion of Man

SHYAM NARAYAN SHUKLA
Project Manager, Lawrence Livermore National Laboratory
University of California, Livermore, CA
(44949 Cougar Circle, Fremont, CA-94539, USA)

All the world religions created the concept of heavens as a reward for their followers who abided by their dictates. According to these religions the ultimate goal of a human being is to acquire a place in the heaven, after this life. Hindu religion is not an exception to this philosophy either. However, the Hindu sages did not stop there. Like scientists they continued their experiments to achieve freedom from the effect of space and time. Ultimately they realized that once they caught hold of 'that', which is not relative but is full and absolute, they could live eternally in that experience. The main theme of the Upanishads deals with that state of mind in which all shackles are destroyed.

The Upanishads form the *Jnanakanda* of the Vedas. The word 'Upanishad' literally means 'to sit near'. The secret knowledge of *Brahman* taught to the disciple by sitting near the preceptor was Upanishad. The Upanishads propound the subtle truth. It is latent in the Vedas. Its knowledge is called *Rahasya* or secret. They were such confidential personalized instructions that they were taught only to those who were fit to receive them. It was Sage Veda Vyasa who made the secret knowledge of the Upanishads easily comprehensible, by putting it in the Bhagvadgita, which is considered the gist of the Upanishads. He also wrote Brahmasutra to put the knowledge in the form of aphorisms. The Upanishads give four Mahavakyas, one from each of the four Vedas. The *Mahavakyas* are very important thought provoking sentences which the sages formulated after having reached the end of their journey and realizing the ultimate objective. The Upanishadic philosophy forms the pinnacle of human religion unparalleled in world history.

Introduction

The principal objective of all the religions of the world has been to make sure that their followers have a fulfilling life on this earth. If a person abides by certain laws of nature he would enjoy his life better here. If he leads a disciplined life he would be physically and emotionally stronger. With these basic principles in mind the prophets or founders of the religions preached to their followers during their life time. Their teachings, when written in the form of books, eventually became the scriptures of the religions. All the religions have one commonality. That is the concept of the Heavens. If a person follows the dictates of religion he would be rewarded with a place in Heaven, where there is long lasting peace and happiness. The Hindu religion did not have a prophet or a founder. However, it too has heaven and hell for good and evil people, respectively.

The Hindu sages did not feel contented with the concept of Heaven as the ultimate goal. They were very innovative people like the scientists. They continued in their search for achieving freedom from the effect of time and space. They discovered that when a man identifies himself with his body, with all its limitations, then he is a tiny, weak and mortal creature in this vast universe. On the other hand, when he identifies himself with his inner self, the Atman, which is limitless, immortal and blissful, he achieves divinity in this very life. The Upanishads are collections of their teachings. They are the unique gifts from our sages of Ancient India to this world. The Upanishadic teachings are not a mere philosophical concept but are realized facts experienced by our sages. Those teachings inspired when they were composed and they inspire even today, thousands of years later. They are as inspirational in America as they are in India. The Upanishads are beyond time and space.

Veda and Vedanta

When each Veda *shakha* is taken, first comes the *Samhita*, then the *Brahmana* and lastly the *Aranyaka* [1]. The Upanishads occur in the concluding portion of the Aranyaka. Since the Upanishads occur at the end of the Vedas they are called the Vedanta, which literally means 'the end of the Vedas'. The ultimate goal of the Vedas is contained in the Upanishads. Also because they are the end products of the Vedas, they are appropriately called the Vedanta. The part of a Veda where there are methods of rituals and sacrifices, are the *Karmakanda* and the part where the supreme knowledge of the Vedanta is dealt with is the *Jnanakanda*.

The Western scholars have done more research on the Vedas than Indian scholars. They have tried to establish the time when the Vedas and the Upanishads were written. The estimate ranges from 1500 B.C. to 3000 B.C. According to Bal Gangadhar Tilak the Vedas came into existence around 6000 B.C. However, according to one school of traditional vedic scholars, the Vedas are considered *anadi* or without beginning. It is stated in the Vedas that they are vast and endless (*ananta vai Vedah*). They are also without human authorship (*apaurusheya*). What we have is a small portion of what God created as the Vedas. A portion of what was revealed to the Rishis is available to us today. Therefore, a Rishi who wrote down an Upanishad or a shakha of a Veda, is not its creator or *karta* but is its seer or *drishta*.

It was Sage Vyas who organized the Vedas and wrote *Bhagvadgita* and *Brahma-sutra*, which made it possible for the scholars to know how deep the philosophy of the Upanishads is. In the Bhagvadgita Vyas put the essence of the Upanishads in the form of a conversation between Arjuna, the disciple, and Lord Krishna, the teacher.

About 1200 years ago, when the Vedic knowledge was in danger of extinction, Adi Shankaracharya (788–820 A.D.) came as a teacher of the era (*yuga pravartaka*). He wrote commentaries to the Bhagvadgita, Brahmasutra and some principal Upanishads: Only then the mystic knowledge of the Vedanta became easier to comprehend for others.

However, mere study of the Upanishads is not enough to fathom the depth of the philosophy or to achieve the supreme knowledge which is their main theme. In the Chhandogya Upanishad there is a story of Narada who approached Sanatkumara and said that he had studied all the scriptures and all the sciences and arts. He knew only the mantras but he had no knowledge of the Atman *(Mantravideva asmi na atmavid)*. The Upanishads have to be studied at the feet of a *Brahmajnani* teacher (a teacher who has achieved the Brahman). That is why it is called the Upanishad, which literally means 'to sit near (with devotion)'. It also means [2] 'secret teachings'. When a student studies in a *Gurukul*, the mystic knowledge permeates into the student's mind by the subtle manner the teacher explains the subject, by merely observing his daily *sadhana* and his way of life. The teacher imparts the secret knowledge of Brahman only to those students who are spiritually ready for it. That is why the Katha Upanishad says, "Many, though they hear of it, do not understand it. Wonderful is he who speaks of it. Blessed is he who, taught by a good teacher, is able to comprehend it." The Upanishads mention that the meditation on 'Om' is the meditation on the Atman or the Brahman which resides within a man [3]. Chhandogya Upanishad says that all the sacrifices prescribed in the Vedas cannot bring salvation. It is meditation on *Om* that leads one, step by step, to the highest object of the Upanishads, that is, the realization of the Brahman.

Do Vedas and Vedanta Contradict Each Other?

Some people believe that the Vedas and Vedanta clash with each other. To prove their point they quote Lord Krishna. In the Gita Lord Krishna says:

Vedavadaratah Partha nanyadasteeti vadinah

(*Gita* II-42)

Kamatmanah svargapara janmakarmaphala pradam

(*Gita* II-43)

"O Partha, those who follow the words of the Vedas literally and say that there is nothing other than this, are full of desire to dwell in Heaven, which leads to new birth as a result of their actions."

Also,

Traigunya vishaya veda nistraigunyo bhavarjuna

(*Gita* II-45)

"O Arjun, the Vedas deal with the three gunas (*satva, raja* and *tama*). You should transcend these three gunas."

These verses give an impression that Lord Krishna encourages us to follow the teachings of the Upanishads directly, and ignore the rituals prescribed in the Vedas. The traditional *Vedantis* (scholars of the Vedanta) tell us that jumping to the study of the Upanishads directly, without preliminary preparation of purifying the mind and body does not help a student to realize Atman. The mind and body are disciplined by the *yajnas* and worships prescribed in the Vedas. Only after undergoing that discipline we are qualified to take up the study of the Upanishads. When the mind is purified by yajnas, then the world around us ceases to be real. Then all the actions we perform become yajnas and we are no more separate from the Brahman. Then we are ready to merge in Him. That is why Adi Shankaracharya tells us in his book, *Sopana Panchaka* that first we must study and recite the Vedas, perform the prescribed rituals, be guided by the *Mahavakyas*, meditate on them constantly and then only try to reach the Brahman. (We will discuss about the Mahavakyas in a later paragraph). The fact that the seers of the Upanishads quoted hymns from the Vedas in support of their teachings shows that they were not against the Vedas.

The reason why Lord Krishna says the above about the Vedas has to be understood in the context of the *Mahabharata* period. During those days a majority of the people performed yajnas as a means to achieve worldly and heavenly pleasures. They behaved as if that was the ultimate teaching of the Vedas. They almost ignored the teachings of the Upanishads, that realization of the Brahman is the ultimate goal in their lives. Lord Krishna has chastised those people in the Gita. He rebuked those who took the Karma path and did not go beyond it to adopt the Jnana path in their lives. He would have certainly taken to task those also who would directly go to study the Upanishads without performing the Vedic Karmas.

Even in the time of Shankaracharya many great scholars specialized only in the Karma path of the Vedas. Mandan Mishra, a famous Vedic scholar of Varanasi, was a staunch follower of *Poorva Meemansa* (scholarly analysis of the Karmakanda of the Vedas), before he became a disciple of Shankaracharya. After he entered *Samnyasa Ashrama* and became Sureshwaracharya he shifted from karma to jnana path. He wrote the *Vartika* (explanation) of the Shankara Bhashya on the Brahmasutra.

The Principal Upanishads

It is believed that there are about two hundred Upanishads [3]. However, only one hundred and eight have been preserved [2]. The principal Upanishads are those which Adi Shankaracharya selected to comment upon. They are ten in number and are traditionally studied in a certain order. The following *shloka* [1] (Sanskrit verse) enumerates the principal Upanishads in that order:

Isha Kena Katha Prashna Munda Mandukya Taittiri
Aitareyam cha Chandogyam Brhadaranyakam dasha

Isha, Kena, Katha, Prashna, Mundaka, Mandukya, Taittiriya, Aitareya, Chhandogya and Brhadaranyaka are the ten (principal) Upanishads.

Shankaracharya also commented on an eleventh Upanishad, the *Shvetasvatara.* In his commentary on the Brahmasutra he has made references to four more Upanishads. They are: *Kausheetakee, Jabala, Mahanarayana* and *Paingala.*

Ishopanishad (or Ishavasyopanishad)

Usually the Upanishads appear at the end of an Aranyaka. As an exception this Upanishad appears in the Samhita portion of Shukla Yajurveda. The very opening verse of this Upanishad contains the central theme of all the Upanishads. It says that Ishvara or God pervades the whole universe and we should realize Him by offering the fruits of all our actions to Him. Offering the fruits of action to Brahman is *Karmayoga* in a nutshell. This is the first time that the principle of Karmayoga is introduced in the Upanishads. Only in the Gita we see its more elaborate form.

Kenopanishad

It is also called 'Talvakara Upanishad' because it occurs in the Talvakara Brahmana of the Jaimini Shakha of Samaveda. This Upanishad, teaches through an allegorical story, that all our powers are derived from the *Mahashakti*, the Supreme God or the *Parmatma.* The Paramatma is without beginning or end.

Kathopanishad

The Kathopanishad occurs in the Katha Shakha of the Krishna Yajurveda. This Upanishad became very popular for its fascinating story of young Nachiketa going to Yama, the God of Death, and asking him to teach him about what happens to the soul after one's death. Yama then tells him about the true nature of the soul or the *Atman.* It defines Atman as divine, without birth and death, indestructible, etc.

Prashnopanishad

This belongs to the Atharvaveda. As the name implies (prashna means question) this answers six questions on how creation began; who are the devas; how does life get connected to the body; what is the truth about the states of awakening, sleep and dreaming; why should one worship Onkara; and what is the relationship between Purusha and Jeeva.

Mundakopanishad

This Upanishad too is from the Atharvaveda. Mundak means shaven head. Its teachings are meant for the *Samnyasis* or monks who are free from worldly attachment. It talks of *Akshar Brahman* which is free from destruction. It classifies the knowledge into *para*, higher and *apara*, lower. The knowledge of Atman is para and all other knowledge is apara.

Mandukyopanishad

This is the third Upanishad from the Atharvaveda. Manduka means a frog. This Upanishad shows the way to pass the three stages of waking, dream and dreamless sleep and reach the fourth stage of *Turiya* in one leap. Turiya is the stage of pure consciousness which reveals the Atman.

Taittiriyopanishad

This is the most widely studied Upanishad. Its first part Shikshavalli teaches self controls involved in Brahmacharya, the order in which the Vedas should be studied, the worship of Pranava, etc. The precepts such as 'speak the truth', 'follow the dharma', 'treat mother, father and teacher as divinities' appear in this. Its second part Anandvalli describes how there is an ascending order of bliss, starting from that of a human being and culminating into Brahmananda. Bhriguvalli, the third part, is what Varun taught to his son, Bhrigu.

Aitareyopanishad

This Upanishad occurs in the Rigveda. It talks about how a Jiva (soul) takes birth again and again according to sin and merit and how liberation from birth and death is possible only through the realization of the true nature of the Atman. The Upanishad proclaims that the thought (Prajna) itself is the Brahman.

Chhandogyopanishad

The last two Upanishads, namely, the Chhandogya and the Brihdaranyaka are large in size. The Chhandogya Upanishad appears in the Chhandogya Brahmana of the Samaveda. Chhandogya means one who sings the 'sama gana' (singing of the Samaveda hymns, which are the source of the Indian classical music, praising all the gods). This Upanishad introduces us to devout truth seekers like Satyakama, Shvetaketu and Narada and learned spiritual teachers like Aruni, Sanatkumara and Prajapati. The Upanishad teaches that there is no difference between the Atman within a person and the Brahman. It tells us how starting from purity of food and going up to purity of mind and soul we reach a stage when we get rid of all the bonds and achieve Atmananda (bliss).

Brhadaranyakopanishad

'Brhad' means large and 'Aranyaka' means forest. As its name suggests this is the largest of all the Upanishads and it is a forest of spiritual inspiration and thoughts. Usually the Upanishads appear at the end of an Aranyaka as mentioned earlier. The entire Aranyaka of the Shukla Yajurveda forms the Brahadaranyaka Upanishad. (The Samhita of Shukla Yajus contains the Isha Upanishad). We learn of two Kshatriya kings, namely, Ajat Shatru and Janaka who were well versed in the Vedantic philosophy. Then there is an interesting anecdote and philosophical dialogue of Sage Yagyavalkya and his learned wife Maitreyi. Yagyavalkya says that the nature of the Atman is love and happiness. The Upanishad expounds the central theme of all the Upanishad that man is divine and that this whole universe is Brahman.

The Four Mahavakyas

There are four *Mahavakyas* or 'great statements' in the Upanishads. An Upanishad from each of the four Vedas proclaims boldly the ultimate conclusion of its philosophy, in the form of a Mahavakya. The Aitareya Upanishad of the Rig Veda proclaims, *Prajnanam Brahma*—'Brahman is pure consciousness'. The Brhadaranyaka Upanishad of the Shukla Yajurveda says, *Aham Brahmasmi* —'I am Brahman'. The Mahavakya of the Chhandogya Upanishad of the Samaveda is, *Tat Tvamasi*—'You are That'. Here 'That' means Brahman, according to the language of the Upanishads. Finally, the Mandukya Upanishad of the Atharvaveda proclaims as a Mahavakya, *Ayamatma Brahma*—'This Atman is Brahman'.

This kind of bold proclamation, that a human being has Atman (soul) within him or her which is none other than the Supreme Brahman Himself, is unparalleled in the history of religions anywhere other than in the Vedas.

The Concept of Brahman in the Upanishads

It is very difficult to describe [5] the Brahman or the Supreme God in words. That is why it is said: *Ekam Sat, vipra bahudha vadanti*, or "Truth is one, the wise speak of It in different ways." The devotees usually heap many highest human qualities on the God to describe him. Even then they are unable to describe Him adequately and end up making Him human-like. The Rishis finally gave up human like description of the Brahman and described Him by saying "Not this, not this." In the Upanishads the Brahman is compared to a spider and His creation with the spider's cobweb, which comes out of it. The whole universe comes out of the Brahman who resides in the center of it. The Atman residing within the body is Brahman too. Taittiriya Upanishad says, "Brahman is That from which these beings are born, That by which they live when born, and That into which they enter on passing away." There is a subtle difference between the God (Ishvara) and the Brahman. Ishvara is God when viewed through human eyes, in relation to the universe. It is then *Saguna* Brahman. When Brahman is God as He is and viewed independently, He is Brahman, or *Nirguna* Brahman. Some sages believed that the best way of indicating Brahman is by silence.

Conclusion

The Upanishads form the Jnanakanda, or the portion dealing with the supreme knowledge, of the Vedas. They contain the ultimate messages of the Vedas. They tell us that a human being is not only made up of a body which is subject to old age, decay and death, but also of Atman within it, which is divine, eternal and blissful. A person can realize the Atman by meditating on Om, the symbol of the Supreme God, and become immortal and blissful in this very life.

REFERENCES

[1] Sri Chandrasekharendra Saraswati (Shankaracharya of Kanchi Kamakoti Peetham), *The Vedas*, Bharatiya Vidya Bhavan, Bombay, 1991.

[2] Swami Prabhavananda, *The Upanishads*, Sri Ramakrishna Math, Madras, 1979.

[3] F. Max Muller, *The Upanishads*, Part 1, Dover Publications, Inc., New York, 1884.

[4] Swami Ranganathananda, *The Message of the Upanishads*, Bharatiya Vidya Bhavan, Bombay, 1968.

[5] D.S. Sarma, *The Upanishads: an Anthology*, Bharatiya Vidya Bhavan, Bombay, 1964.

Vedic Language

RAYALU VISHWANADHA
114, S. Oxford Ave., #103
Los Angeles, CA-90004, USA

When we presume Sanskrit is the language of Veda we get into trouble in understanding the text. There is difficulty in understanding the meanings of words and sentences. Doubts arise in following the thought itself.

Words

For instance the words *svāhā, svadha,* and *vashat* are very common in Veda but their precise meaning is not known.

Svāhā stōmasya vardhanā (*Ṛgveda* 8-8-5)

Yajñō vai Svāhākaraḥ (*Śatapatha Br* 3-1-3)

Vashatkārēna juhuyāt vashatkṛtēvā (*Śatapatha Br* 7-2-3)

What these sentences mean can be fully understood only when the exact meanings of the words *svāhā* and *vashat* are known.

Sentences

Mā candaḥ (*Tai. Sam.* 4-3-7)

Annam vaĭ candramāḥ (*Tai. Br.* 3-2-3)

Sahasra sṛngō vṛṣabhō jātavēdāḥ (*Tai. Br.* 3-7-2)

Unless we know the meaning of each word in these sentences, we cannot even guess what the sentences mean. If we consider them as Sanskrit words, sentences will not convey convincing meanings. Some Vedic words like *mutram, purisham* etc. convey obscene meanings. By quoting Sanskrit meanings, some of the modern writers are even entering the area of pornography in explaining Vedic statements.

Thought

Agnimabhi pavatē
Agnimabhi sampavatē (*Tai. Br.* 2-3-9)

Is there any significant difference in the above two statements? Does the Mantra need repetition to just add an adverb *sam* (Upasarga) to the verb '*pavate*', when the latter sentence alone could have done the job, particularly when we know that the Veda uses minimum words with maximum efficiency?

Manō gāyatrī yai
Gāyatrī trishtubhē
Trishtubjagatai
Jagatyanushtubhē (*Tai. Br.* 3-7-6)

What is the underlying thought?

Vachē^nnam
Brahmana ōdanam (*Tai. Br.* 3-10)

What is Veda conveying in these two sentences?

Akshara Variation

It looks a single Akshara makes a difference in the meaning of the same word, and same Rik, in different sections of the Veda.

Iḷāmagnē	(*Ṛg* 3-1-23)	*Idāmagne*	(*Tai. Sam.* 4-2-4)
Parīnasō	(*Ṛg* 8-84-7)	*Parīnasi*	(*Sa. Sam. Purv. Arch.* 34)
Pra yam rāye	(*Ṛg* 8-103-4)	*Pra yō rāyē*	(*Sa. Sam. Purv. Arch.* 58)
Yātyagnirā	(*Ṛg* 10-8-1)	*Bhātyagnirā*	(*Ath. Veda* 18-3-65 and *Tai. Ar.* 6-3-1)

How to explain the change of Aksharas, when the texts are being carried from the very beginning to this day without any distortion by oral tradition?

Svargà is the word used in all the other three Veda Samhitas, but in the Yajussamhita alone, it is replaced bu *Suvarga*. Does a simple vowel 'u' make all the difference?

Different Language

These variations suggest that the Vedic language is different from the conventional languages which we know and use.

Veda talks about the importance of Akshara at many places. There are many Rik and Yajur mantras emphasizing the importance of Akshara. 11th Anuvaka of 7th Prasna in 1st Kanda of Taittiriya Samhita is all about Aksharas, starting with "*Agni rekaksarena vacha mudajayat*".

There are Riks with a single Akshara as a complete word:

Ūrdhva ū shu ṇō adhvarasya hōtaragnē . . . (*Rig.* 4-6-1)

How to understand the Rik without knowing the meaning of single-akshara words?

Earlier Vedic scholars (Saunaka, being one of them) wrote books on the language structure of Veda. They are called Pratisakhya Granthas. Each one of those books deals at length about Akshara.

Hence we have to look at our speech system, the source of all Aksharas to understand the Vedic language.

Vedic Alphabet

When we speak or hear, the speech sounds are Aksharas. When we put them to writing, their name is alphabet. Vedic alphabet are shown below as per their articulation points in the speaking machine (mouth).

A अ	Ka क	Ca च	Ta ट	Ta त	Pa प	Ha ह	Ya य
I ई	Ga ग	Ja ज	Da ड	Da द	Ba ब	Sha ष	Ra र
U ऊ	Jna ङ	Cna ञ	Na ण	Na न	Ma म	Sa श	La ल
						Sa स	Va व

1. The arrangement of the positions of articulation in the mouth, either from left to right or from top to bottom is shown above. Everyone can verify for himself/herself the arrangement.
2. Main vowels only are shown as the remaining vowels are just combinations of the prime vowels (a + i = e; a + u = o; a + e = ai; a + o = au; and a + a = a; i + i = i; u + u = u).
3. Only articulation points (and not all Aksharas) are shown. Akshara Kha has no separate point of touch. The articulation point is the same as Ka. Similar is the case with other aspirants: Cha, Jha, etc.
4. The vowel "a" is added to each consonant (Ka) to make it an Akshara. Combination of vowel and the consonant results in an Akshara, a separate recognizable "sound unit". This automatic combining capability of both the vowel and the consonant is innate in every man. Consonant sounds alone cannot be sustained for more than half matra duration (Matra is the time period required to utter an Akshara to be clearly audible and recognizable). Veda calls this natural union "Samhita". It is the vowel sound that gives "life" and makes the consonant stand the full matra period. The vowel-consonant combination is the basic Samhita on which the entire speech system depends.
5. The live energetic vibrant Akshara matrix, embedded in the mouth of every human being, is the basis on which the Vedic language is built.
6. When we look at the matrix, we notice an orderly system in the arrangement of the Akshara positions:
   (a) There are three main lines with eight Aksharas in each line and a fourth subsidiary one with two Aksharas.
   (b) If we look from top to bottom, they are separated into three broad

groups: vowels in the left (1 row), consonants (stops) Aksharas in the centre (5 rows), and the last two rows (7th and 8th) are different from both vowels and stops. Sanskrit linguists call the 7th row Aksharas *Ushma* type and of the 8th row, *Antastha* type. *Ushma* Aksharas require more air to utter. The nature of effort to pronounce *Antastha* Akshara is different from that for all other types. Sanskrit grammar texts refer to consonants in the middle as *Sparsha* Aksharas and the vowels as *Prana* Aksharas.

(c) Vowel speaking area is spread from the throat to the lips and indicates the boundaries of the speaking machine. Similarly, the limits of active area for each group are clear, both lengthwise and breadthwise, from the orderly arrangement of the articulation points in the mouth.

(d) *Sparsha* Aksharas are in three horizontal lines. The first line consists of Aksharas with minimum resonance, the second with those of higher resonance and the last, highest resonance (nasal sounds).

(e) The arrangement is so scientific and perfect that the tongue can jump to any point and pick up the consonant before the vowel sound comes to join.

Akshara in Vedic Language

How does Veda apportion meaning to each Akshara?

Every Akshara has a specific and significant position in the matrix. Also the nature and intensity of effort involved in uttering differ from Akshara to Akshara and also from one group to another. All the variations and characteristics of each Akshara are reflected in its meaning.

Our life is a continuum of actions and events. Area of articulation is the main area where actions and events are taking place. Every action is a Yajna. Satapatha Brahmana says: "*Vaghi yajnah*". Where our ideas, intentions and desires are converted into Aksharas is the Yajnashala. Speech action is representative of all actions in our life.

Sparsha Aksharas are in three lines. Human existence has three aspects. The first one refers to activities associated with daily routine. The second one is connected with our ideals, dreaming goals and emotional hours. The third is the world of knowledge, thinking and awareness. Aksharas in the three rows are correspondingly used in Vedic language. All *Nasikyas* (nasal sounds) are used to identify and describe the various Jnana activities. The Akshara *Ma*, last in the line, is reserved for mind (*Manas*).

Ushma Aksharas are used to identify *Prana* area (forces responsible for living).

Man has four traits. The four *Antastha* Aksharas are used for the four traits as given below:

1. Man always does one thing or the other (*Ya*).
2. He is an individual, separate Jiva (*Ra*).
3. He is not the same individual but a different one when he is dreaming to achieve higher goals, gripped by *Devo bhava* (*La*).
4. He can speak to express himself, *Vak* (*Va*).

We can see that the matrix is the miniature audio picture of man himself and Vedic language expands it into a full blown audio picture.

Examples of Actual Use

Vowels are spread over the entire Yajnashala. 'A' is located at the entrance, 'I' in the middle and 'U' at the end. They are taking part in the formation of every Akshara. They represent the time and the potential needed for the Yajna.

Broadly there are three stages of time for any incident or event (Yajna)—past, present and future. Veda attributes the three stages to the three prime vowels A, I and U respectively since their positions of articulation are in the same order. A is also used for the ever present tense since when we open our mouth to speak, the first sound coming out is that of A and is present when the other vowels are not in operation.

Agnimīlē purōhitam

is the first sentence of Rigveda and *Agni* is the first word. The word starts with A. So *Agni* is ever present. The word ends in I. *Agni* is now being used in the Yajna. Whatever be the meaning of the word, two features of the "object" meant by the word *Agni* are clear. Rigveda starts with Agni, the ever present force and constantly in use with every Yajna (action). Rigveda deals with all aspects of Yajna up to the point of start. Yajnas in Veda cover the entire spectrum of actions in life and the resulting behavior. Yajna is an attempt to improve ourselves from the existing state. When a Yajna is completed successfully, the driving force *Agni* invoked for the purpose becomes a part of us. Then it will be *Agna* and not *Agni*. So Samaveda, which deals with final stages of Yajna starts with the word *Agna*—"*Agna ayahi vitaye*" (*Sa. Veda* 1). *Agni,* the driving force of the achievement has become *Agna*, ever present in us as the new capability achieved. But for change of vowels, we will not know the two different states of *Agni*.

'I' indicates present tense (time during which Yajna is conducted), and 'U', the future. Yajurveda, describing implementing procedures in detail, starts with both vowels in the first two sentences.

"*Ishētvōrjētvā*" (*Ishētvā* + *ūrjētvā*)

All our actions (Yajnas) are only with a purpose to achieve. *Isha* is our present requirement, hence starts with the vowel 'I'. The word *Urja* is our hopefully achievable future want and has to start with 'U'. The two sentences are combined into one (*Samhita*) to indicate that human nature is to keep an eye on the future while working for the present.

Vedic Word

In Sanskrit and other languages only the word has a meaning but not its component Aksharas. Vedic word is a combination of Vedic Aksharas. The meaning of the word is summation of their individual meanings. The meaning of the word can be deduced by linking the meanings of individual Aksharas in a logical way.

Akshara is a Vedic word. Its formation is as:

All the vowels we can speak are represented by	A
All *Sparsha* Aksharas are represented by	Ka
All *Ushma* Aksharas are represented by	Sha
All *Antastha* Aksharas are represented by	Ra
All *Nasikya* Aksharas are represented by	M
Samhita capability is indicated by the compound Akshara	Ksha

The word not only indicates all the audio capsules the mouth can produce, but also its *Samhita* capability. The word 'Akshara' means what it sounds!

One more example to indicate how the Vedic words are coined. *Om* is a very common word in Veda and *Om iti ekaksharam Brahma* is an oft quoted sentence from Veda. Akshara 'O' is the result of combining the vowels 'a' and 'u'. They are located at the beginning and middle of the speech tunnel. 'M' the consonant is at the end of the tunnel. All the three combined represent all "objects" that have a beginning, existence and the end. *Om* has been made into a single Akshara with a purpose. All "objects" combine into only one "big object", the universe. Brahma, the universal creative force, is known only through its creation. *Om* represents Brahma through its manifestation, having the properties of *a*, *u* and *m*.

Different Language

Veda uses the Aksharas as they are located in the matrix to bring out the various forces working inside to change our intentions into Aksharas. In fact, Vedic language uses its words and Aksharas as windows through which we can see the working of the subtle body.

Vedic language is made to express the various forces of the microcosm, whereas all our languages are meant to express what we see and know outside of us. All our languages combined will not contain what man does not know. Vedic language talks only of what we do not know. Vedic language uses its words and Aksharas to name the forces within us. We use that Akshara to name the items we know and want to refer. So Vedic language is apart from all the languages we know and use in our daily life.

Time of Origin

Many scholars have strived to find the meanings for many Vedic words and have recorded their views. It is well known that there are more than a few meanings for some Vedic words. But all these ages no scholar has ever questioned the usefulness of the language. Probably there were no people speaking the language and owning it as a mother tongue. The fact leads us to believe that Vedic language and Vedas must be existing prior to all known languages including Sanskrit. It is fairly reasonable to say that Vedic language is the oldest of all languages.

Veda is a Single Book

The same language is found in all sections of Veda—Samhitas, Brahmanas, Aranyakas and Upanishats. The same words with the same meanings are found in all parts of Veda.

Yajna is the subject, Veda deals in all its sections and we cannot have a complete picture of Yajna unless we go through the entire book.

Evern to have a complete picture of Vedic language, we have to go through the whole book, since the Aksharas and their related forces are not listed at one place. Veda is about the Maha Yajna, our life itself, and is not a language text book. The importance of Akshara is detailed in Taittiriya Samhita. What Samhita means is explained in Taittiriya Upanishat. Source of Akshara is described in Shatapatha Brahmana. If these different volumes came out at different times, it is impossible to understand the earlier texts. In such a situation, anyone born in Rigveda times should have had to wait till the Upanishat age to know what Samhita is.

Veda is a single book with all its sections put together and Vedic language is the oldest of all languages. It is a unique language with a purpose. It is not a language for communication and was never intended to be so. Hence it had never been used and will never be used.

The Presence of *Rta*

DEBORAH A. DAVIS
College of Human Ecology, Michigan State University
(89 Moultine Creek Circle, St. Augustine, FL 32086, USA)

This paper will briefly discuss the early 19th century Western European intellectual history and the 20th century U.S. Family Systems Theory, as expressions of the Vedic Rta ("the setting in motion"), and the principle of the universe that regulates the matrix patterns and processes of all manifest things. I am identifying Hegel's dialectic and Family Systems Theory's multi-paradigmatic framework with the Vedic principle of rta, and am suggesting that rta could integrate social sciences, humanities, and sciences. In the Appendix additional examples of rta's presence in other academic disciplines are presented.

Western European Intellectual History

In *The Passion of the Western Mind* (1991), a narrative history of dominant Western thought and world-view from the ancient Greek to the postmodern, author Richard Tarnas recounts the late 18th and early 19th centuries' effort in Western Europe to synthesize the growing schism between the scientific and humanistic imperatives. The German poet and the natural scientist, Johann Wolfgang von Goethe (1749-1832) tried to unite empirical observation and spiritual intuition into a natural science that would be more revealing than Newton's and capable of grasping nature's organic archetypal forms. In Goethe's view, a scientist could not arrive at nature's deeper truths if he was out of context, not in relationship with nature, and employed only cognitive instruments to understand it—if he registered the external world only like a machine. Such a strategy guaranteed that the observed reality would be very incomplete, a grey picture whose depths had been veiled in some way. Only by bringing observation and imaginative intuition into intimate interaction could man penetrate nature's appearances and discover its essence, argued Goethe.

Then the archetypal form in each phenomenon could be elicited; then the universal could be recognized in the particular and reunited with it.

In Goethe's worldview, nature permeated everything, including the human mind and imagination; nature's truth did not exist as something independent, objective, and "out there," but was revealed in the act of human cognition itself. The human spirit did not simply impose its order on nature, as Goethe's older contemporary Immanuel Kant had argued, but rather nature's spirit brought forth its own order through man, who was an embodiment of nature's self-revelation. Nature was not distinct from spirit, but was itself spirit, inseparable from man and God. God did not exist as a remote governor over nature, but "holds her close to His breast," so that nature's processes breathe God's own spirit and power. Thus did Goethe unite the poet and the scientist in an analysis of nature that reflected his distinctly sensuous religiosity.

Similarly, the metaphysical speculations of the German Idealists after Kant culminated in the extraordinary philosophical achievement of Georg W.F. Hegel (1770–1831). Steeped in classical Greek philosophy, Christian mysticism, and German Romanticism, Hegel set forth a conception of reality that sought to relate and unify man and nature, spirit and matter, human and divine, time and eternity. At the foundation of Hegel's thought was his understanding of dialectic, according to which all things unfold in a continuing, evolving process in which every state of being inevitably brings forth its opposite. The interaction between these opposites then generates a third stage in which the opposites are integrated—they are at once overcome and fulfilled—into a richer and higher synthesis, which in turn becomes the basis for another dialectical process of opposition and synthesis. The crucial German word through which Hegel expressed his concept of dialectical integration was *aufheben*, meaning both "to cancel" and "to lift up." In the moment of synthesis, the antithetical state is both preserved and transcended, negated and fulfilled.

Hegel's overriding impulse was to comprehend all dimensions of existence as dialectically integrated in one unitary whole. In Hegel's view, all human thought and all reality was pervaded by contradiction, which alone made possible the development of higher states of consciousness and higher states of being. Each phase of being contained an "other" within itself, a self-contradiction or complement, which served as the engine for its movement to a higher and more complete phase. Through a continuing dialectical process of opposition and synthesis, the world was always in the process of completing itself. Whereas for most of the history of Western philosophy from Aristotle to the present, "separative vision" has reigned and defined opposites as logically contradictory and mutually exclusive; for Hegel all opposites were logically necessary and mutually implicated complements in a larger truth, a truth that is thus radically paradoxical.

Hegel possessed a profound faith in human reason, believing that it was ultimately grounded in divine reason. Whereas Kant had argued that human reason could not penetrate the veil of phenomena to reach ultimate reality because man's finite reason inevitably became caught in contradiction whenever it attempted to do so, Hegel saw human reason as fundamentally an expression of a universal Spirit or Mind (*Geist*), through the power of which, as in love, all opposites could be transcended in a higher synthesis. When all of Hegel's philosophy, metaphysical, and religious understanding—characterized by the same dialectical process—was set forth in the early nineteenth century, and for several decades afterward, this great structure of thought was regarded by many as the most satisfying and indeed ultimate philosophical conception in the history of the Western mind, the culmination of philosophy's long development since the Greeks. Every aspect of existence and human culture found a place in this world conception, embraced by its all-encompassing totality. Hegel's influence was considerable, first in Germany and later in English-speaking countries, encouraging a revival of classical and historical studies from an Idealist perspective and providing a metaphysical bulwark for spiritually inclined intellectuals who argued against the forces of secular materialism. Hegel's dialectic engendered an understanding of history as motivated ultimately not by material factors (political, economic, or biological), but rather by consciousness itself, by the self-unfolding of thought and the power of ideas.

Eventually, Hegel's Idealism also aroused much criticism. For some, the absolutist closures of his system appeared to limit the unpredictable possibilities of the universe and the personal autonomy of the human individual. His stress on the rational determinism of the Absolute Spirit and the ultimate overcoming of all oppositions seemed to undercut the problematic contingency and irrationality of life, and to ignore the concrete emotional and existential actuality of human experience. His abstract metaphysical certitudes seemed to avoid the grim reality of death, and to disregard the human experience of God's remoteness and inscrutability. Often Hegel's historical judgements seemed peremptory, while his political and religious implications were ambiguous, and his language confusing. And his scientific views, though informed, were unorthodox. While the modern Western mind did indeed incorporate much of Hegel, especially his dialectical logic and his recognition of the power of history, it did so in a dry, abstract manner. The grace and aesthetic beauty, which were the heart of Hegel's Idealism, lost out to a ruder materialistic "science" (actually, an arrogant and crude notion of that mode of inquiry). In fulfillment of its own theory, Hegelianism was eventually submerged by the very reactions it helped to provoke: irrationalism and existentialism (Schopenhauer and Kierkegaard), dialectical materialism (Marx and Engels), pluralistic pragmatism (James and Dewey), logical positivism (Russell and Carnap), and linguistic analysis (Moore and Wittgenstein)—all movements increasingly more reflective of "separative vision" and the loss of felt connection, the general tenor of modern experience. As an entirety, the Hegelian synthesis was not sustained by the modern Western mind.

Modern Families

Today, about 150 years later, Hegel is remembered only by philosophers and other academics, and is no longer a famous public figure. But the Hegelian synthesis has reappeared, so to speak, in research on family dynamics. Dissatisfied with all the theories about families, two social psychologist/family therapists in Boston decided to conduct a qualitative research project and actually observe what and how families do what they do. Nineteen families volunteered. Placing audio tape recorders and graduate student observers in these families, David Kantor and William Lehr's project (*Inside the Family: Toward a Theory of Family Process*, 1975) was an inductive *tour de force* for the 1960s. Their data eventually revealed to them three major types of family process, which they termed: Closed, Open, and Random. Kantor's student, Larry Constantine, elaborated this work with a fourth type, called Synchronous, and substantiated the clinical therapeutic value of Family Systems Theory (*Family Paradigms, The Practice of Theory in Family Therapy*, 1986).

Each of these four family types has its own distinct style of goal-directed behavior. In the language of Kantor, Lehr, and Constantine, the Closed type seeks stability by adhering to (local) tradition and moving directly toward its goal. The Random type is the opposite of Closed and seeks variety by means of innovation. This type follows any path that spontaneously presents itself and may lose sight of its initial goal or targets, accepting alternative targets that appear along the way. The Open type is a synthesis of Closed and Random, and seeks adaptability by using much verbal negotiation. This type will accept alternative goals/targets along the way, and does not lose sight of its initial goal. The Synchronous type seeks harmony through identification. This type aligns its strategic pathway with the seasons, the cycles of nature—this process of alignment is its goal. Whatever other targets/goals appear along the way will be accepted or rejected. These four distinct styles of movement are drawn below:

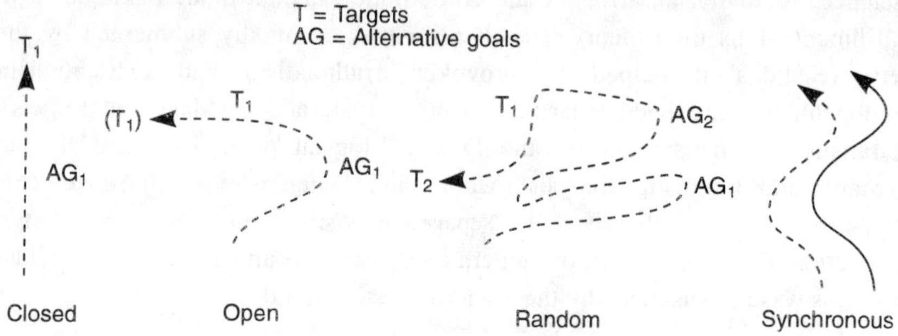

Fig. 1 Styles of movement by paradigmatic family type

Constantine has described the whole system of four family paradigms as "an extended form of a *dialectic*: one form, a *thesis*, is succeeded by its *antithesis*, then, in turn, by a *synthesis* of these forms, to be followed ultimately by an *antisynthesis*, which is antithetical to synthesis, that is, a negation of the dialectic" (1986, p. 97). And he has further stated (1992, pp. 48–9) that the quintessential characteristic of each family type corresponds mathematically to a vector, an arrow pointing in the direction of "paradigmatic purity." Because it not only defines a given type but also distinguishes it from alternative types, such a vector also incorporates and models interrelationships among types: Closed families rely on a hierarchy of authority to pattern their process, but in their purest forms, neither Random nor Open nor Synchronous families require a hierarchy. Only Random families characteristically accept everyone "doing their own thing" as a regular expression of their family style. The other three paradigms are based on some form of common group solution or activity, whether determined by tradition (Closed), arrived at by discussion (Open), or resulting from tacit agreement with unstated expectations (Synchronous). It is not that people in Closed, Open, or Synchronous families never go off on their own, but that such divergence is not characteristic of them. The distinguishing feature of Open families is their reliance on consensus built through negotiation and self-examination. Open families are reflexive. They examine and consider their own rules, structure, and process in the search for solutions. Synchronous families are distinguished by their reliance on pre-existing, tacit agreement based on the way members share in and are aligned with a common set of implicit rules, which Constantine called "consentaneity." However, the more familiar management term is "alignment." The four taxonomic vectors are thus: hierarchy, divergence, reflexivity, and alignment, and are summarized by Constantine in the following table:

TABLE 1. TAXONOMIC VECTORS OF THE PARADIGMATIC FAMILY TYPES

Taxon	Taxonomic vector	Description
closed	hierarchy	degree of reliance on a hierarchy of authority to regulate process and determine solutions [pure forms of the other paradigms are nonhierarchical]
random	divergence	degree of reliance on completely different and independent action by individuals as acceptable forms of group solution and activity [purely closed, open, and synchronous all require a common group solution]
open	reflexivity	degree of reliance on exploration and examination of family's own stucture and process for developing solutions and making decisions [closed, random, and synchronous in pure forms do not "process"]
synchronous	alignment	degree of reliance on preexisting, tacit agreement with a shared set of values, goals, and ideas to regulate process and define solutions [pure forms of closed, random, and open rely only on interaction and feedback regulation]

Today, in Family Systems Theory, we understand this multi-paradigmatic framework as a pluralism of types in which no one type is better than any other. All types are equal in their capacity to serve as effective models for successful family functioning. Thus there are several kinds, at least four, of normal, healthy families, which can differ profoundly from one another over a wide but understandable range. Curiously, while the modern Western mind could not sustain the Hegelian synthesis 190 years ago, today modern Western families are a living embodiment of this four-fold dialectical movement. Modern Western individuals are also a living embodiment of this four-fold dialectical movement, and when students in courses in Family and Child Ecology recognize in themselves the four paradigmatic types, they experience a transformation of consciousness, that which the Greeks called metanoia, and the early Christians called epiphany.

Meditations Through the Rg Veda

In an extraordinary work about the origin and originality of human language, reason, and conceptual articulation, philosopher Antonio T. de Nicolás takes his reader into the very ancient *Rg Veda*, a text at considerable distance from the 20th century that has not suffered from "separative vision" and the loss of felt connection as we have. Between the *Rg Veda* and now, human beings have systematically strived to divide and reduce everything into such manageable sizes that things, cultures, worlds, theories, gods, disciplines, images, and we ourselves, are manageable and controllable-in-use at every level. But in the *Rg Veda* we come face to face with language before it became prose and logic, poetry and imagination, or music and meter—when it was all three, combined and inseparable, in an intentional unity. The Rg Vedic Aryans realized that "the sacrifice" (the first sacrifice was the separation of heaven and earth) was the origin of the multiplicity of perspectives within their culture, and they also strived through the sacrifice for an open culture where all human flesh would feel itself at home. In this sense, Rg Vedic society was open to accept others within its fold on only one condition: that they also accept the sacrifice, not only in its ritualistic form, but as the radical activity of humans so that all people may live in innovation and continuity. The reason why Rg Vedic people do not accept any way of understanding the human role other than as an original and continuous sacrifice (an activity rather than a theory), is because any identification of people with a "theory of people" obscures the fact that any and all such theories are made of the radical dismemberment of ourselves, and distract us from engaging in our only original and primary activity: the sacrificing of all theories about ourselves so that we may recreate ourselves anew.

The Hymns and Sacrifice in the *Rg Veda* come to us in primary and discreet intentionality—structures through which and to which any statement, chant, or song in the *Rg Veda* reverts for meaning, or from which it derives its meaning. Nicolás declares that there are four intentionality-structures: the languages of Non-existence (*Asat*), Existence (*Sat),* Images and Sacrifice (*Yajña*), and Embodied Vision (*Rtadhih*). These four languages, with their multiple perspectives, function as four spaces of discourse within which human action takes place, and from which any statement in the text gains meaning. The "languages," or sub-linguistic systems, of Non-existence, Existence, and Images and Sacrifice show the human situation within disparate linguistic contexts embodying different ways of viewing the world. These may be integrated within a transcendent context, not by rejecting the reality of any of the previous frameworks, but only by changing to a transcendent "view", and looking at the world as the result of the internal dynamic activity of the languages themselves—by allowing Language to be the integrating and transcendent context. Language is, after all, anonymous as an activity, neither fully speakable, nor reducible to any theory; and because it is primarily action, it contains the totality of the possibilities of manifestation, while simultaneously orienting its movement in view of the cultural norm (*Rta*)—which is also the cultural and individual body. In this manner, Language always remains simultaneously an open possibility and a Cultural Norm, while each manifestation will always be a part of a sub-linguistic system. Thus Nicolás suggests a complementarity of languages within a transcendent and unifying Language-activity, by dropping the opposing demands of exclusivity in the original context-languages for a way of viewing and acting in the world which is eternally (*nitya*) efficient (*rtu*) and follows the Norm (*Rta*). Thus any statements in the Rg Veda can be traced to an original language source, either *Asat, Sat, Yajña,* or *Rtadhih*, where the meaning of those statements is grounded. Each one of these languages is also the ground of a particular intentional acting through a particular intentionality: *Nirrti* (non-action) is the modality of being in the world of *Asat*, either as possibilities to be discovered, or as stagnant dogmatic attitudes; *Satya* is the modality of acting in the world of *Sat*, as the truth to be built, formed, or established; *Rta* is the modality of acting in the world of *Yajña*, as the activity of regathering the dismembered sensorium and the multiplicity of the worlds of *Sat* by sacrificing their multiple and exclusive ontologies; and *Rtadhih* (embodied-vision) is the modality of *having gone through*, and being in, a world which remains continuously moving because it comprehends the totality of the cultural movement on which it is grounded. Simultaneously with the languages as origins of meaning, and of the activities through which these meanings are originated, there is also a multiplicity of images which synthesize, and embody, both the languages and the activities of a whole cultural orientation. Thus, we have *Vrtra*, the dragon, and his cohort of ophidians, as the prototypes (*pratirupa*) of the *Asat*, covering up the possibilities of cultural woman and man, either through inaction or dogmatism. Heroes like Indra and a multitude of gods are the prototype of the multiple ontologies of the *Sat*. Agni, Varuna, Prajapati, etc., are the prototypes of the *Yajña;* while *Rta* embodies the totality of languages, activities, images, and in general, the total cultural movement that needs its own continuous sacrifice of particular perspectives so that the whole cultural body may remain totally alive without partial amputations.

To understand the fabric of Rg Vedic methodology, one must bear in mind that it does not rest on a naive epistemology of "looking out" and seeing the objective world out there, or of "looking in" and seeing the contents of consciousness. Instead, the focus is on insight and embodied-viewpoint: the original generators of consciousness and its objects, which can be recreated continuously by partaking of that original viewpoint. Furthermore, while not much may be said about the origins of the world (R.V. 1.164.4 and R.V. 10.129), much can be said of the worlds which appear in the consciousness of the *kavis* (from the root *ku-* "to have the intention of") and *rsis* ("one sharing the viewpoint of the gods"). That is, originally dragons, heroes, and gods were undifferentiated (*Asat*); they became differentiated (*Sat*) with the birth of interpretation; but this differentiation has to be sacrificed (*yajña*) in the wake of insights and vision, because originally, and finally, there is no story at all for any identification whatever, for life goes on.

Recognizing Rta: Sight v. Sound

These four Rg Vedic "languages" that Nicolás defines have their counterparts in the foundation of all theories of music (McClain, 1976, p.3). The language of Non-existence (*Asat*) is exemplified by the pitch continuum within each music interval as well as by the whole undifferentiated gamut—chaos—from low to high. The language of Existence (*Sat*) is exemplified by every tone, by every distinction of pitch, thus ultimately by every number which defines an interval, a scale, a tuning system, or the associated metric schemes of the poets, which are quite elaborate in the *Rg Veda*. The language of Images and Sacrifice (*Yajña*) is exemplified by the multitude of alternate tone-sets and the conflict of alternate values which always results in some accuracy being "sacrificed" to keep the system within manageable limits. The language of Embodied (*Rta*) Vision (*Dhih*) is required to protect the validity of alternate tuning systems and alternate metric schemes by refusing to grant dominion to any one of them.

We talk about the Random (*Asat*), Closed (*Sat*), and Open (*Yajña*) types of families in much the same way in Family Systems Theory. Chaos, or Constantine's "divergence," is a characteristic feature of Random families. Explicit and extensive delineation of rules and procedures, the quintessence of "hierarchy," is a characteristic feature of Closed families. Keeping the system within manageable limits, or "sacrifice," is the result of the Open family's "reflexivity," their characteristic feature of reviewing and reconsidering their goals, structure, and processes. While we don't perceive Synchronous families in terms similar to *Rtadhih*, we do talk about the whole multi-paradigmatic family system as a plurality in which no one type is any better than another—no one type has dominion over any other.

These four Rg Vedic "languages" are the expressions of a sensorium which organizes itself primarily on a model of sound. "Sound," writes Nicolás, "is the greatest clue we have to interiority, our own and that of others" (1971, p.134). The structure of the *Rg Veda* takes sound and its criteria as the radical presupposition through which the sensorium and the cultural body orient themselves in the Rg Vedic world. In our world, sight and its criteria are organizing our sensorium and are the presupposition of our "separative vision." For most of us, sight travels on the surface, spying object after object, providing us with discontinuity. Sound, in spite of its evanescence, gave Rg Vedic people the instance of eternal presence and unity they so well used to develop their world according to *rta*, the well-formed instant. We are accustomed to an analytical (prosaic), discursive, conceptual "ground" that differentiates (divides) and expands linearly, a one-dimensional centrifugal movement. Occasionally we think about synthesis as an assemblage, some sort of patchwork, of analytically located elements. We do not perceive synthesis as a centripetal movement of "sacrificing," of letting go of all the differentiation. We assume that meaning can be reduced to explicit statements; the *Rg Veda*'s song-poems acquired their meaning from their harmonics. These song-poems were not just oral creations, they were chanted revelations. Rg Vedic people were enveloped in sound, sound as vibration, sound as the original substance of the world. They were surrounded by sound, excited by sound, made aware of presences by sound. They looked for centers of experience in the experience of sound, and they found the model of complete, absolute instantaneity and communication in sound—such was their embodied vision. They structured their sensorium in such an interiorist way so as to become, in one instant moment, the total presence and power of absolute and efficient communion.

The Source of Faith

Nicolás asserts that *Rta* is perhaps the most significant contribution both to practical reason and to social acting which Indian Tradition has to offer. The Rg Vedic seers were very profuse in making clear that the *Rta* is both a Norm established from old, *rtam purvyam* (R.V. 1.105), and also an inspired way of acting leading to the same kind of efficacy, *rtasya tantuh* or *rtasya dhara* (R.V. 9.73.9; 5.12.2), as a thread to be woven or a stream to be followed.

Rta comes from the root *r*—to move, to go, meaning that which is already in movement, going, or gone. It is the world created by *Varuna* (R.V. 7.61.4), and in general, it is the result of the sacrificers (R.V. 10.61.11). It is also a given world, already made; and in this sense, already a tradition and a gift (*radha*) resulting from the first sacrifice which separated the heavens and the earth and opened the free spaces (*varivas*) (R.V. 1.46.11), thus redeeming people from the anguish of the darkness which surrounds them from everywhere (*vidvamhas*) (R.V. 4.3.14). It is in *Rta*, as the embodied tradition of human beings, that Rg Vedic people find the source of their faith (*sraddha*), their guiding light, their guarantee that the Norm works and is effective. Examples of this insight may be seen in R.V. 9.113.3; 9.1.6; and in 10.151:

1. *By faith is Agni kindled, by Faith his oblation offered.*
   Full of happiness we rejoice in Faith.
2. *Just as the gods had faith even in the powerful*
   Asuras, make this wish of mind come true for
   Those who are generous in the Sacrifice.

3. *Faith by sacrificing.*
   Men gain Faith through the instilled desires of
   The Heart Protected by Vayu, both men and gods increase in
   and become richer through Faith.
4. *Faith in the early morning, Faith at noon we*
   Implore, Faith at the setting of the Sun.
   Faith, increase our Faith.

Rta offers Rg Vedic people two very important aspects from which to guide their lives: it is the store of all that has been rightly formed (*sukrta*) (R.V. 4.3.1), and it is the guide for action of all that can be formed and integrated within its cosmic form (R.V. 2.28.4). As the first, it becomes a common body of Law, a Norm; as the second, it is a guidance for exact action (*satya*).

Rta unifies the whole activity of all the characters of the *Rg Veda* according to its Norm: Agni extends the Earth and Heaven according to *Rta* (R.V. 5.1.7), he sacrifices according to *Rta* (R.V. 7.39.1), he guides his chariot according to *Rta* (R.V. 3.2.26); he is the guide to all those searching for *Rta* (R.V. 8.23.9); in fact, Agni is the first-born of *Rta* (R.V. 10.5.7), the creator of *Rta* (R.V. 10.61.14); for he knows *Rta*'s meaning (R.V. 5.12.2), is able to open its path to others (R.V. 5.12.2), and holds the paths of *Rta* opened through the Sacrifice (R.V. 5.12.2).

Mitra-Varuna make people aware of the *Rta* (R.V. 6.57.19) and show people how to cross over to the *Rta* from the darkness (R.V. 7.66.3).

The path of *Usa* (the Dawn) is the path of *Rta* (R.V. 1.124.3), its horses are yoked to *Rta* (R.V. 1.124.3), because the Dawn was born of *Rta* (R.V. 1.124.3) and the Dawn and Night show people the path of *Rta* (R.V. 4.51.6).

Indra's activity is to lead people to *Rta*, for only through *Rta* can they liberate what is hidden in the Cave. Even his intoxication with Soma, the increase in his own vigor, is only the sign of his approaching the path of *Rta* (R.V. 8.25.3).

Aditi holds *Rta*, and thus gives birth to all the gods. The Rivers rush to *Rta* (R.V. 1.75.8), the waters flow from *Rta*, *Vena* shines in *Rta* (R.V. 7.87.3). *Rta* flows from *Dhenu*, the milch-cows (R.V. 3.55.13), where the sacrificer finds *Rta* (R.V. 10.61.19), and so does *Ila* (light) (R.V. 2.55.13).

Brhaspati finds *Rta* by voicing *Rta* (R.V. 10.67.2). The *Angirasas* destroy the mountain (*Vrtra*) through *Rta* (R.V. 4.3.11), for they learned to voice their songs from the bow-string of *Rta* (R.V. 2.24.8), and so they destroy the Cavern through *Rta* (R.V. 10.62.2) and allow the Sun to ascend to heaven through *Rta* (R.V. 10.62.2). All the gods (*Visvadevas*) know the path of *Rta* (R.V. 10.66.8); they drink in the streams of *Rta* (R.V. 7.43.3), and in general, there is no effective thought which is not born of *Rta* (R.V. 10.67.1) as the only way for the "Cows" (light) to enter *Rta* is through *Rta* (R.V. 4.33.9).

Soma is also born from *Rta* and returns to *Rta* roaring (R.V. 9.97.32). It is in *Rta* that people may profit from Soma (R.V. 9.86.32), while Soma's use is made right through the intentionality of *Rta* (R.V. 9.113.2), and so Soma engenders *Rta* (R.V. 9.66.24) and his boat goes straight to *Rta* (R.V. 9.97.4).

Rta appears with the *Rg Veda*, and then mysteriously disappears. Though it's always presupposed in later Indian life and philosophy, between the Vedic text and the following Indian texts there are great cultural gaps. In these later texts/contexts, the word of the *Rg Veda* becomes 'holy word.' No longer dynamic, it becomes stagnant in order to achieve external ends: the *rc*, alive and dripping inspiration, changes into a mantra, but by then the integrity of the *Rgveda* is lost and we have instead and in succession; liturgy (*Brahmanas*), speculative philosophy (*Upanisads*), and even historical poetry (Epics).

Notes and Additional Remarks

In addition to the embodiment of Hegel's dialectic in this qualitative research and theory of family dynamics, Family Systems Theory, students of Professor David R. Imig have recognized the four-fold paradigmatic framework, actually the relations of complements (or "interrelationships among types" as Constantine described it), in many other academic disciplines as well. To date, the list includes:

Family Dynamics

Kantor and Lehr (1975); Constantine (1986, 1992); Imig and Phillips (1992); Imig (1994); Redfield (1994); Gottman (1994)

Other Social Sciences

Sociology—Parsons (1956), Junker (1972), Stevens (1946); Psychology—Grof (1980 etc.)

Humanities and Arts

Educational philosophies of homeschooling (Hood, 1995); Ways of knowing (Belenky, 1986), Musicology (McClain, 1976); Philosophy (Nicolás, 1976); Family housing design (Beyer, 1955 and Schousboe, 1991)

Sciences

Causal metatypes in biological and social sciences (Maruyama, 1985);New science of human systems (Allen, 1989)

Theoretical chemistry (Prigogine and Stengers, 1984); Logic of quantum mechanics (Heelan, 1972)

Topology of volcanic tremors, Belousov-Zhabotinski chemical reaction, and phase-locked feedback system of spiral nebulae (Rösseler attractor; Talcott Parsons and Neil J. Smelser, 1956: *Economy and Society, A Study in the Integration of Economic and Social Theory,* Glencoe, Illinois: The Free Press).

The four fundamental system problems under which a system of action, in particular a social system, operates are: latent pattern maintenance (including tension management) [Synchrnous], goal attainment [Closed], adaptation [Random], and integration [Open]. Their gross relations to each other are schematically represented in figure 1 (pp. 18-19).

A Adaptive Instrumental Object Manipulation	*G* Instrumental-Expressive Consummatory Performance and Gratification
L Latent-Receptive Meaning Integration and Energy Regulation Tension build-up and drain-off	*I* Integrative - Expressive Sign Manipulation

1. A Adaptation
2. G Goal Gratificatioin
3. I Integration
4. L Latent-Pattern Maintenance and Tension Management

Fig. 1. The Functional Imperatives of a System of Action*

*Adapted from Figure 2, p. 182, in *Working Papers, op. cit.* The above figure deals with the "Functional imperatives" aspect of the system of action; that in the Working Papers deals with the "phase movement" aspect. Cf. Chap. IV, pp. 242–45.

- B.H. JUNKER, 1972: *Fieldwork: An Introduction to the Social Sciences* (CHICAGO: UNIVERSITY OF CHICAGO PRESS).

  The social roles of the participant observer can be described as a continuum ranging from complete participation, through participant as observer, and observer as participant, to the complete observer:

  Complete Participants: Conceal their observational activity from those under observation, becoming *totally involved* in the group's lifestyle, behavior, and concerns. [Random]

  Participant as Observer: Does not conceal observational activity while engaging *in relative involvement* with the group. [Open]

  Observer as Participant: The observer declares the intention to observe from the outset, and this public disclosure ensures relative detachment. The observer remains peripheral to the group, *in* the world of the group, but not *of* it. [Synchronous]

Complete Observer: The observer has complete detachment, without any contact with group members. The observer sees *acts* rather than experiencing *actions*; by failing to share the experiential world of the group under observation, the full meaning of group actions is lost. [Closed]

- S. S. STEVENS, 1946: "On the theory of scales of measurement," *Science*, 103: 677–680.

The Nominal Level: Different states of a concept quantified at a nominal level can only be labeled, and no statement about differences between different states is possible, except to say that they are recognized as different.—The nominal level gives categorization without giving order, or sequence. [It is flexible and separate: Random]

The Ordinal Level: Ordinal level of quantification applies to concepts that vary in such a way that different states of the concept can be rank ordered with respect to some characteristic.—The ordinal level indicates non-equal differences that are arranged on some basis. [It is flexible and connected: Open]

The Interval Level: An interval level of quantification is one in which states of the concept are not only rank ordered, but also the difference between the states has meaning.—The interval level provides order, sequence, and equal (meaningful-in-the-same-way) units. [It is structured and separate: Synchronous]

The Ratio Level: If the location of zero on an interval scale has some meaning, either in terms of a theoretical concept or as a measurement procedure, then it is useful to compute the ratio of two numbers.—The ratio level provides order, sequence, equal units, and a true zero point. [It is structured and connected: Closed]

- STANISLAV GROF (1980).

- MARY E. HOOD, 1995: "Contemporary Philosophical Influences on the Homeschooling Movement," *Home School Reader*, Vol. 7, No. 1, pp. 1–8.

By means of content analysis, Dr. Mary E. Hood identified four educational philosophies amo0ng home educators, which she called essentialism, progressivism, perennialism, and existentialism:

Essentialism: One of the primary goals of essentialism…is the preservation of traditional values and a democratic way of life. The term itself is derived from the belief that these educators know, without question, what knowledge and skills are most essential for students to acquire in order to become adequately prepared for adult life," and authority, hard work, obedience, and an orderly environment are emphasized. [Closed]

Progressivism: The educational ideas associated with progressivism are rooted in the philosophy of pragmatism of the 1870s in America. Pragmatic philosophers…"focused their attention on the importance of change, adaptation, and growth, and on the interrelationship of individuals and their social and physical movements… . Morality was no longer based on the authority of family, customs, or religion." [Open]

Perennialism: Educators who adhere to perennialist ideals believe in the existence of absolute values, which are timeless and exist in all cultures. They therefore advocate the use of a single classical curriculum for all students, which emphasizes the presentation of these perennial values. [Synchronous]

Existentialism: Existentialists emphasize…"the individual and his or her relationship to the world and to other people." In education, "an emphasis is placed on the right of individual learners to enter into authentic relationships with their parents, teachers, and fellow students; to choose their own curricula; and to retain their individuality by avoiding exposure to measurement devices and labels.

- BELENKY, CLINCHY, GOLDBERGER, and TARULE, 1986: *Women's Ways of Knowing, The Development of Self, Voice, and Mind* (San Francisco: Harper Collins Publishers).

- GLENN H. BEYER, 1955. *Houses Are For People, A Study of Home Buyers' Motivations* (Ithaca, New York: Cornell University Housing Research Center).

  In 1952 Cornell University's Housing Research Center conducted a survey of modest-income families in Buffalo, New York, in order to see how social and psychological values might relate to housing design. The Cornell study identified nine variables, which they clustered into three groups: Economy (30.0%), Personal (13.6%), and Family (30.1%), with 26% of the data unclassified. The clustered values were then given to an architect, who was asked to design homes that would fit the preferences of the different groups.

  The Economy Group [Closed, middle class] of families wanted a house that was practical, rectangular, simple, and economical to construct that would always have a good re-sale value. A house for families in the Personal

Group [Random] had separate private areas as well as larger undifferentiated areas that could be closed off for various private uses. Family came first for the people in the Family Group [Open]. This house had an open plan so that family members could be together and share one another's activities and pleasures. A fourth design, the Prestige House, was added to this study by the researchers. The Prestige House [Closed, upper class] was an expression of social position, with a formal dining room separate from the kitchen and a fireplace that was a status symbol rather than an actual center for family gatherings.

- KAREN SCHOUSBOE, 1991: "Housing Beyond 2000 May Not Be All That Different," *Denmark Review*, no. 4.

  In 1991 Denmark's Institute for Futures Studies surveyed about 1000 Danish families, asking them what they would like for a "dream house of the future." The responses from these Danish families were easily grouped into four categories: Hansen, Frandsen, Hermansen, and Petersen.

  The "Hansens" [Closed] were families that wanted their house to be a fortress against the outside world's uncertainty; their dream was for a future of certainty, stability, and constancy. "Frandsen's" [Random] were a family on the move, viewing their house as a resting place between activities; their dream was of a creative, adventurous life full of change. "Hermansen's" [Open] used their home as a showcase, emphasizing stylishness and status; their dream was for a future of economic and social prosperity, but not of change [Closed/Open]. "Petersen's" [Synchronous] wanted a house where the kitchen was the "togetherness" room, while another room would be used solely for relaxation and meditation; their dream was for a visibly coherent life.

- MAGOROH MARUYAMA, 1985: "Four Different Causal Metatypes in Biological and Social Sciences," *Self-Organization and Dissipative Structures, Applications in the Physical and Social Sciences*, William C. Schieve and Peter M. Allen, eds. (Austin, Texas: University of Texas Press).

  Among the current theories in the biological and social sciences, it is useful to recognize at least four different types of causal models at the metalevel, keeping in mind that there are many other types and mixtures between various types:

  1. *Nonreciprocal causal models:* Causal relations may be either probabilistic or deterministic, but it is assumed that they cannot form loops. They obey the transitive law. [Closed]

2. *Independent-event models:* It is assumed that the most probable states of the universe or an isolated system are states of random distribution of independent events, each having its own probability. Non-independent relations and nonrandom structures exist, but they are considered less probable and therefore tend to decay to more random, unstructured, homogeneous states. [Random]
3. *Homeostatic causal loop models:* Causal relations may be probabilistic or deterministic and can form loops. Structures and patterns of heterogeneity can be maintained by homeostatic causal loops. [Closed]
4. *Morphogenetic causal loop models:* Probabilistic or deterministic causal loops can increase heterogeneity, generate new patterns and symbiosis, and raise the level of the sophistication of the system.

- PETER M. ALLEN, 1989: "Towards a new science of human systems." *International Social Science Journal*, v. 41, n. 1, p. 81(11), February.

Physicist Peter M. Allen mathematically modeled the Canadian fisheries industry, a complex dynamical system with many aspects: the physical behavior of the ocean or coastal waters; the complexity of the marine ecosystem with its many levels and species in constant evolution; the behavior and technology of fishermen deciding what and where to fish; the needs and directives of the fish-processing industry which buys much of what is landed; the need for employment in both the fishing and processing industries the demand from both local and foreign consumers and the competition with other foodstuffs in the international and domestic marketplace.

Allen's computer models also generated the spatial behavior of the fishing fleets and the fish stocks, and showed how extraordinarily complex behavior emerged. The models identified two extremes in the decision-making behavior of the skippers. At one limit were the "Stochasts," who paid absolutely no attention to economic rationality and diffused at random [Random]. At the other extreme were the "Cartesians," who weighed every bit of information available and moved with the first probability to the point with the greatest attractivity—even if this was only marginally better than elsewhere [Closed]. In the Canadian fleets, as elsewhere, there were "risk takers," who made the discoveries of new fish aggregates, and the others, who were content to rely on the information generated by risk takers:

Obviously, fishermen fall somewhere between these two extremes, but nevertheless, the idea of "Stochasts" and "Cartesians" seems to capture a basic truth about people… . What our model allows us to do is to explore the evolution of such a system, and we find that a population of "Cartesians" alone survives poorly on a small part of the system's potential, never exploring beyond this. However, although "Stochasts" can beat "Cartesians," they remain too dispersed to exploit their discoveries efficiently. A more efficient strategy for the fishing fleets as a whole, is to have "Cartesians" which "spy" on "Stochasts" [Open]. We can show that, providing say 10 per cent of the information about a catch gets through to them, they succeed in creaming off the good fishing areas discovered by the "Stochasts," and in making a good living. (p. 88)

Had Professor Allen also included methods of Native Fisherman, taking just exactly what is needed and no more and thanking the fish for their "offering," his model would also have had the Synchronous archetype.

- ILYA PRIGOGINE and ISABELLE STENGERS, 1984: *Order Out of Chaos, Man's Dialogue With Nature* (New York: Bantam Books).

  Although the effects of "nonlinear" reactions (the presence of the reaction product) have a feedback action on their "cause" and are comparatively rare in the inorganic world, molecular biology has discovered that they are virtually the rule as far as living systems are concerned.

  Auto-catalysis (the presence of X accelerates its own synthesis [Random]), autoinhibition (the presence of X blocks a catalysis needed to synthesize it [Closed]), and cross-catalysis (two products belonging to two different reaction chains activate each other's synthesis [Open]) provide the classical regulation mechanism guaranteeing the coherence of the metabolic function. (p. 153)

- PATRICK HEELAN, 1972: Rösseler attractor—topology of volcanic tremors, Belousov-Zhabotinskii chemical reaction, and phase-locked feedback system of spiral nebulae

REFERENCES

Constantine, Larry L.: *Family Paradigms: The Practice of Theory in Family Therapy*, Guilford Press, New York, 1986

Constantine, Larry L.: "The Structure of Family Paradigms: An Analytical Model of Family Variation," *Journal of Marital and Family Therapy*, Vol. 19 (1993.), 39-70.

Kantor, David and William Lehr: *Inside the Family: Toward a Theory of Family Process* (San Francisco: Jossey-Bass, 1975).

McClain, Ernest G.: *The Myth of Invariance: The Origin of the Gods, Mathematics and Music From the Rg Veda to Plato* (York Beach, ME: Nicolas-Hays, Inc., 1976).

Nicolás, Antonio T. de: *Four-Dimensional Man, Meditations Through the Rg Veda* (Stony Brook, NY: Nicolas Hays Ltd., 1976).

Tarnas, Richard: *The Passion of the Western Mind, Understanding the Ideas That Have Shaped Our World View* (New York: Harmony Books, 1991).

The Status of Women in the Ṛgveda

SHASHI TIWARI
Reader, Maitreyi College
University of Delhi, Delhi, India.

The condition and status of women in Indian society changed substantially from the early period to the beginning of the present century. Vedic literature depicts an ideal society, where women enjoyed an honourable and high status. Like every patriarchal society here also the father is he commanding authority, but in the household affairs the mother is considered to be supreme.Though limited in number, Vedic goddesses were as powerful as the gods.

In the Ṛgveda there is no reference to an instance where the birth of a girl was considered inauspicious. That the girl received education is evident from the composition of hymns by the female seers. The daughter of the Ṛgvedic times was bold, strong and free. The maiden seems to have been free to make her choice of husband as appears in the verse *ṚV*, X-27-12 and was supported in her choice by her parents. Probably a maiden having no brother had her legal right to inherit the paternal property. The wife was a partner in the performance of sacrifices. She was the empress in her home. In the Ṛgveda we get few references to polygamy because monogamy was the rule. On the basis of some verses it can be said that the custom of widow remarriage existed.

Other social evils relating to women, such as burning of widows, purdah system and child marriage were not found in the Ṛgvedic society. Hence, this Ṛgvedic picture of womanhood is the real heritage of India.

The condition and status of women in Indian society changed substantially from the early period to the beginning of the present century. Vedic literature depicts an ideal society, where women enjoyed an honourable and high status. The Bṛhadāraṇyaka Upaniṣad records one of the best periods of Indian history, when women were admitted into philosophical groups and were allowed to discuss the highest spiritual truths of life. In the court of the king Janaka, Gārgī questioned Yājñavalkya about the nature of Brahman [1]. In Ṛgveda, women occupy a very prestigious and remarkable place. We find certain women referred to with great admiration and respect in the context of domestic affairs, social organisation, education, warfare and spiritual debate.

Later on, in the medieval period of Indian history the position of women gradually degraded. Due to all sorts of foreign influences, women were one of the most oppressed and pitiable section of society. Eleventh century onwards, the repeated Muslim invasions and their rule led to further deterioration in the

Residential Address: Dr. Shashi Tiwari, 54, Saakshara Apartments, A-3, Paschim Vihar, New Delhi-110 063, India. Tel 0191-11-5585237

position of women. Orthodox Hindu society was constantly threatened by the fear of the invaders' attacks on their women. The birth of a daughter was unwelcome because she was considered to be a cause of expense, troubles and anxiety to her parents, since they merely had custody of her till her marriage. Woman's liberty was restricted as she had no choice in the selection of her husband. She was married at an early age when she was incapable of understanding the real significance of marriage and in exercising her own judgement and discretion. Womanhood was sacrificed at the altar of supposed social conveniences and purity. With her degeneration began the degeneration of Indian society.

In the nineteenth century the question of woman's position was initially raised by reformers through a number of organisations. The issues included sati, widow-remarriage, polygamy, child-marriage, women's property rights and female education. Raja Ramamohan Roy and Swami Dayananda Sarasvati were the foremost Indians in the modern times to challenge the accepted views on women. Certainly the true knowledge of original Indian culture based on the study of scriptures is needed to condemn the subsequent degraded position of Indian women.

The Vedas are part of the great literary heritage of India, in which our basic thoughts, aspirations, cultural and ethical values are reflected. In fact, the pulse of the real national life can be felt in the Vedic hymns. So, for knowing the ideal, and in fact the original, view-point of Indian thinkers about the status of women in ancient society, the deep study and thorough analysis of Vedic verses are required. Here in this paper only the oldest Vedic text namely 'Ṛgveda-Samhitā' is studied to draw conclusions regarding the life and status of women in the Ṛgvedic age. Obviously such a survey would be limited in scope but deep in observations.

The Ṛgvedic society is founded on the home and the family, as well established institutions, with a proper place assigned to women under an advanced system of material laws. Like every patriarchal society here also the father is the commanding authority, but in the household affairs the mother is considered to be supreme. The Ṛgvedic expression "the wife is the home" [2] shows how the woman was the central point of domestic life. The home with its focus on love between husband and wife and between father and the son is an eminent feature of the life of Ṛgvedic people. In the verses assigned to 'Dampatī' we get a glimpse of the happy and cooperative family life of the Ṛgvedic time. Here the couple lived in harmony, helping each other in their daily routine work. "May the husband and wife with one accord press out and wash the soma juice. May they come united to the sacred grass and never do they fail in strength." [3]

The concept of mother is as old as mankind. The first thought appears to have been of mother as one 'who gives birth to'. And then other ideas like the one who feeds and sustains, looks after, protects and loves, appear to have gathered, in the world of human emotions and thoughts, around the term mother. The seers of Ṛgveda are aware of these emotions about mother. The idea of the mother as a creator and protector of human life is expressed in many ways. The imagery of mother is used in the context of giving birth, protecting and looking after offsprings. Heaven and Earth are described as Father and Mother. [4] The mother in the household of Ṛgvedic Aryans set the model for the concept of Ṛgvedic goddess. The strength of the women who ruled the home of ṛṣi and yajamāna was unconsciously reflected in the pleasing counterparts whom he addressed his prayers. Though limited in number, Vedic goddesses were as powerful as the gods. The goddesses invoked in the Vedas are Uṣas, Rātri, Vāk, Purandhī, Aditi, Pṛthvī, Eṛā, Sarasvatī, etc. Aditi is the ideal mother of many gods. Many times she is spoken of as protecting men from distress and danger [5]. So in Ṛgveda the motherhood is, no doubt, the essential and the most characteristic trait of woman and she is placed on a highly respectable platform in the domestic and social context [6].

The status of the women in any society may be truly judged by the way in which the birth of the girl is celebrated. In the Ṛgveda there is no reference to an instance where the birth of a girl was considered inauspicious. Certainly we find prayers for the birth of a son [7], not for a daughter. But the prayers for the birth of a child may not always be meant for the birth of the son only. The semantic study of the various names for son or male child in the Ṛgveda shows that often it is for descendants only. In Ṛgveda a number of names are used to denote a maiden in her different stages of life. It is important to know that among them Kanya, Kanā, Kanīnaka, Kanyanā are for a maiden and Duhitā is for a daughter meaning 'Milkmaid' . The etymology of her names indicates her principal duty in the Ṛgvedic family, namely the milking of the cows. Her association with milk and its other preparations is brought out in several instances [8]. Thus it may be said that the maiden was mainly occupied with the domestic work. Affection was bestowed on the maiden by her relatives and she had a place of importance in the family.

The position of the maiden in home and society may best be measured by the freedom she enjoys for her education, for going out and for choosing her companion. In the Ṛgveda the fact that girls received education is evident from the composition of hymns by the female seers. Female seers had visualised the mantras like the male seers. The number of female seers or the speakers of the Vedic mantras comes to about thirty [9]. Ghoṣā, Lopāmudrā [9], Apālā, Romasā, Sūryā, Juhū Brahmajāyā, Śraddhā, Yamī, Indrāṇī, Mamtā, Agastyasvasā, Ātreyī, Śāśvatī, Viśvavārā etc. are few important names in this intellectual field. They performed sacrifices, offered hymns to gods and occupied glorious positions in the temple of fame. Also as a qualification for marriage education of the maiden was considered as important as that of the groom. The exact nature of the maiden's education is difficult to determine by the study of the Ṛksamhitā, but it is certain that education was imparted to her in her maidenhood and under the eye of her parents.

The daughter of the Ṛgvedic times was bold, strong and free. She, as a maiden, was quite free to move anywhere she liked. There is description of Samana in various hymns of the Ṛgveda [10], mostly with the word 'Yoṣa', the lady. Sāyaṇācārya has explained according to the context and in some cases has given a meaning to fit in with the sacrificial ceremony. Pischel thinks it to be a popular festival or social gathering in which men and women took part [11]. Griffith has rendered the word as a 'gathering' or 'festal meeting'. In some places Samana gives us the picture of a battle. So the meaning of the word is doubtful, but if taken in the sense of a festival gathering, as most of the interpretations suggest, women—young and grown up—are described as decorating themselves to participate in it.

> The dawn shines with the rays of the sun and decorates herself like a crowd of people going to a festival [12].
>
> From olden times the matron goes to feast and general sacrifice [13].
>
> They come to him as dames to an assembly [14].
>
> Like maidens going to a gathering or festivities [15].

Here the word Agruvaḥ is used for young ladies. Perhaps there is some purpose of fully decorated young ladies in going to such assemblies. They desire to secure companions. Since the twin gods, Aśvins were accepted by the daughter of the sun-god by her own choice, there must have been a custom of young girls choosing their companions freely. This is only a surmise based on the references of 'Samana' and not a statement supported by actual facts in the Ṛgveda.

The maiden seems to have been free to make her choice of husband as appears from the verse. "If the girl be both good and fair of features, she finds herself a friend among the people" [16]. In the description of Uṣas, the goddess of Dawn, certain phases of a maiden's life are revealed. She is described as marching in the Heavens, not with any hesitation but radiant in the pride of her beauty [17]. Here the word for a lover is Jāra. Sun is described as a Jāra to Uṣas who follows her when she travels alone in the sky [18]. The existence of love of an unlawful type was not permitted by the society, but women enjoyed sometimes too much freedom to be morally safe. Thus the Ṛgveda reflects a society, where there was freedom to both sexes prior to marriage [19]. Here marriage was a union of two persons who were fully developed. No reference regarding age or its limitations, as are found in the later works, can be traced in the Ṛgveda. Certainly marriage between the grown-ups was the order of the day. We read of old age marriages.

A well known example of such was Ghoṣā [20]. Child marriages did not exist in Ṛgvedic times as no reference is available. The marriage hymn (X.85) of Sūryā contains several references which show that the bride at the time of her marriage was quite grown up. In the Ṛgveda we have no conclusive evidence whether there were any definite forms of marriage which later on came into existence.

As marriage also depended on the choice of the maiden and supported by her parents, it was often very difficult to select a proper bridegroom for her, who would be worthy of her in every way. In case the girl failed to secure a worthy husband, she had to pass the rest of her life in her father's or brother's house being dependent on them. So the marriage of a girl was not always compulsory. Unmarried maidens are called 'Amājur'. This epithet used three times [21] denotes maidens who grew old at home, without finding husbands or as they are called 'Pitṛ-ṣad', who sit with their father [22]. Sometimes the unmarried daughter was given a share of paternal property along with the brothers for her independent support and maintenance [23].

For a maiden having no brother, an epithet Abhrātṛ is found in two passages of the Ṛgveda [24]. They refer to the case where a daughter is the only child. The one verse says, "She seeks men, as she who has no brother, mounting her car, as it were to gather riches" [25]. It means that a brotherless maiden used to come back to her father. The purpose is explained differently. Probably she used to come back to her father's house to look after her parents or to perform the funeral rites of her father, even after she had been given away in marriage. This shows her legal right to inherit the paternal property and also that she is considered equal to a son.

Woman as a wife is denoted by the words Jāyā, Jani, Janī, Patnī, Supatnī, Gnā, Jāni,Vadhū, Strī, Yoṣa, Yoṣaṇā, Nārī, Venā, Menā etc. in the Ṛgveda [26]. Each word indicates special aspects of wifehood. Vadhū denotes the meaning that she was respectfully brought from one home to another. The word Jāyā has a special sense of the share of the husband's affection. The words Patnī and Supatnī clearly mean that she was a partner in the performance of sacrifices. A patnī has a right to offer oblations to fire. Mithuna or Dampatī are husband and wife who performed religious functions together.

> The couples desirous of thine aid are presenting oblations together. [27].

> He, whom the two, a pair of equal age dwelling in the same place, and engaged in the same ceremony, worship night and day [28].

The words Jani, Janī and Jāni reflect that besides performing religious and domestic duties she was the mother of children. Here motherhood supersedes wifehood. She reached the zenith of her powers when she became a mother. Surely her high status may be realised by the fact that the word Mātarā alone was enough to signify both the parents. In the gambler's hymn (X.34) we see the love and fidelity of a wife, who never got vexed or angry with her husband and at last her distracted husband realised the right path. The dignity of the wife was recognised in the Ṛgvedic society. She was not only the manager of the household but was the centre of the home. She was the empress (sāmrājñī) in her home [29]. The husband identified her with his very home.

"O Maghavan! A wife is home and dwelling" [30].

She was auspicious (Kalyāṇī) [31] and the most auspicious (Śivatamā) [32]. The love of husband and wife was the base of domestic happiness [33]. Their conjugal relationship was a matter of pride to the Ṛgvedic seers as they refer to it occasionally [34]. It seems that she used to help her husband in all sorts of activities. Mudgalāṇī, wife of the sage Mudgala, helped her husband in the pursuit of robbers who had stolen their cows and drove the car for her husband when he was put in a tight corner [35]. Though the wife was obedient to her husband and subservient to his will, she was treated by him with proper respect. She dressed herself well and gracefully [36] and always put on a smiling countenance [37] to please her husband. So, on marriage, a woman was not only given a very honourable position in the household but could offer oblations to the fire in performing sacrifices. She was the mistress of all—young and old—in the home.

All this is comprehensible only on the supposition that monogamy was the rule. And this is pointed to directly by the text [38]. However, there are some traces of the existence of polygamy [39], though it was recognised that plurality of wives never contributed to domestic happiness and often made the life of a husband miserable [40]. It may be concluded that kings and nobles were mostly polygamous as Indra has been several times alluded to as having a number of wives.

In the Ṛgveda we get few indirect references to widows and their remarriage. The evidences are mostly of an inconclusive nature. On the basis of some verses we can say that in Ṛgvedic society widows had a normal place [41]. There is no evidence of widow remarriage in the proper sense of the word in the Ṛgveda. But a custom seems to have existed according to which a childless widow could live with her dead husband's brother (devṛ) in order to produce a child. The verse records [42]:

Where are ye, Aśvins, in the evening, where at morn?
Where is your halting place, where rest ye for the night?
Who brings you homeward, as the widow bedward draws her husband's brother, as the bride attracts the groom [43].

The nature of widow-remarriage is uncertain but it is obvious that the widow was comfortably adjusted in the society and her condition was not pitiable. As for the burning of the widows (Satī custom) the practice did not exist in the *Ṛgveda*, because there is not a single reference in this context. *ṚV* X.18.7 is regarded by some scholars as an evidence of widow-burning but the meaning of the verse is very doubtful. So that view cannot be truly accepted.

In the Ṛgvedic times the compulsion of veil (purdāh system) was not in vogue. Women used to take part in social and religious activity with men. They went unveiled in festive gatherings.

Regarding the legal position of the women nothing has been clearly said in the Ṛgvedic verses. The legal status of the daughter is hinted in a few passages, which are not quite conclusive. It seems that the brother was the inheritor of the ancestral property. But in the absence of her brother she inherited the property of her father in her own right before her marriage. Unmarried old maidens (Amājur) used to live in the father's home, but if the only child daughter had become mother, her son could be the heir to the property of his maternal grandfather [44]. The woman surely was dependent on man to a great extent even when she was kept comparatively in high honour. But she was not the helpless creature as in later times. She had a right to grumble and protest and she could raise her voice against her troubles. The gambler's wife suffered inwardly without a complaint but after some time she was bitter to her husband and left him [45].

Thus in household management woman was supreme and it was her voice that mostly prevailed. As a daughter and sister her role was not of much significance, but as a mother and wife she was free, decisive and lovable, enjoying her life with sons, daughters and husband [46]. Besides, it was always her absolute supremacy as housewife or mother. The Ṛgvedic women had her equality with her husband recognised by the society. In social and religious matters she was his equal partner.

In later times Indian woman became a non-individual creature. Social evils, related to women—uneducation, sati-custom, purdah system, dowry, widow's neglect, child marriage, restriction of freedom of movement, unwelcome to female birth, disrespect to women, discrimination between male and female child etc., which developed in the medieval and modern age were not found in the Ṛgvedic society. The Ṛgvedic picture of womanhood is the real heritage of India. It was an ideal state where womanhood was given maximum honour. Preservation of our best traditions is, in fact, the need of the present hour and this can be restored by hearing, contemplating and propagating the hymns of the Ṛgveda.

References and Notes

[1] *Bṛha. Upa.*, 3-6.

[2] जायेदस्तम्। *ṚV*, III-53-4.

[3] या दम्पती समनसा सुनुत आ च धावतः।
देवासो नित्ययाशिरा॥
प्रति प्राशव्या इतः सम्यञ्चा बर्हिराशते।
न ता वाजेषु वायतः॥ *ṚV*, VIII-31-5,6

[4] द्यौर्वः पिता पृथिवी माता। *ṚV*, I-191-6

[5] *ṚV*, X-100; I-94-15.

[6] "Mātā aur Pitā ke Vāchaka Śabdon kā Artha-vaijñānika Adhyayana", Shashi Tiwari, in: *Vyutpatti aur Artha Nirdhāraṇa*, M. Bharatiya, Ghaziabad, 1988, pp. 35–44.

[7] *ṚV*, I-91-20; I-92-13; III-1-23; X-85-25; X-183-1.

[8] B.S. Upadhyaya, *Woman in the Ṛgveda*, 1974, p. 44.

[9] Shashi Tiwari, *Ṛṣikas of Ṛgveda*, in: *Kalyāṇa Kalpataru*, Women number, 1995, pp. 23–28.

[10] *ṚV*, I-48-6; I-124-8; IV-58-8; VI-75-4; VII-2-5; X-86-10; X-168-2.

[11] *Vedische Studien*, II, p. 314.

[12] वपुच्छन्ती रात्रिभिः सूर्यस्याज्ज्यङ्क्ते समनगा इव व्राः। *ṚV*, I-124-8.

[13] सहोत्रं स्म पुरा नारी समनं वाव गच्छति। *ṚV*, X-86-10.

[14] ऐनं गच्छन्ति समनं न योषाः। *ṚV*, X-168-2.

[15] समग्रुवो न समनेष्वञ्जन्। *ṚV*, VII.2-5.

[16] भद्रा वधूर्भवति यत् सुपेशाः स्वयं सा मित्रं
वनुते जने चित्। *ṚV*, X-27-12.

[17] *ṚV*, VI-65-1.

[18] *ṚV*, I-115-2.

[19] *ṚV*, X-85-7.

[20] घोषायै चित् पितृषदे दुरोणे पतिं जूर्यन्त्या अश्विनावदत्तम्।*ṚV*, I-117-7.

[21] *ṚV*, II-17-7; VIII-21-15; X-39-3.

[22] *ṚV*, I-117-7.

[23] अमाजूरिव पित्रोः सचा सती समानादा
सदसस्त्वामियें भगम्। *ṚV*, II-17-7.

[24] *ṚV*, I-124-7; IV-5-5.

[25] अभ्रातेव पुंस एति प्रतीची गर्तारुगिव सनये धनानाम्।*ṚV*, I-124-7. Translation by Grffith, I, p. 172.

[26] Shashi Tiwari, "Ṛksamhitā Me Patnī Ke Vācaka Śabda", in: *Studies in Sanskrit and Musicology (Saṁskṛta-Saṅgīta Vaijayantī)*, S. Kulshreshtha (Ed.), Delhi, 1992, pp. 25–37.

[27] वि त्वा ततस्रे मिथुना अवस्यवः। *ṚV*, I-131-3.

[28] यमीं द्वा सवयसा सपर्यतः समाने सोना मिथुना समोकसा।
दिवा न नक्तं पलितो युवाजनि . . . .। *ṚV*, I-144-4.

[29] सम्राज्ञी श्वसुरे भवे। *ṚV*, X-85-46.

[30] जायेदस्तं मघवन्त्सेदु योनिः। *ṚV*, III-53-4.

[31] *ṚV*, IV-58-8; III-53-6.

[32] *ṚV*, X-85-37.

[33] *ṚV,* I-122-2; X-32-3.

[34] *ṚV,* I-66-3; I-73-3; I-82-5; VIII-31-5; X-149-4.

[35] *ṚV,* X-102-2.

[36] *ṚV,* IV-3-2; IV-58-9.

[37] *ṚV,* IV-58-8.

[38] *ṚV,* I-124-7; IV-3-2; X-71-1; X-71-4; X-104-3; X-105-8.

[39] *ṚV,* I-62-11; I-71-1; I-104-3; I-105-8; I-186-7.

[40] *ṚV,* I-105-8; X-33-2.

[41] *ṚV,* IV-18-12; X-18-7; X-40-8.

[42] कुह स्विद् दोषा कुह वस्तोरश्विना
कुहाभिपित्वं करत: कुहोषतु:।
को वां शयुत्रा विधवेव देवरं
मर्यं न योषा कृणुते सधस्थस्या।। *ṚV,* X-40-2.

[43] R.T.H. Griffith, *The Hymns of Ṛgveda*, Vol. II, p. 438.

[44] शासद् बह्निर्दुहितुर्नप्त्यं गाद्
विद्वाँ ऋतस्य दीधितिं सपर्यन्। *ṚV,* III-31-1.

[45] द्वेष्टि श्वाश्रूरप जाया रुणद्धि। *ṚV,* X-34-3.

[46] पुत्रिणा ता कुमारिणा विश्वमायुर्व्यश्नुत:।
उभा हिरण्यपेशसा।। *ṚV,* VIII-31-8.

On Our Vedic Origin: Women Speaking for Themselves

RESHMI RAMDHONY
Senior Lecturer, Head of Hindi Dept., Mahatma Gandhi Institute, Moka, Mauritius
('Rasmeita', Maurice Prudent Ave. Floreal, Mauritius)

The Rgvedic womanhood comprise symbolic figures—Sarasvati, Usha, Shakti, Apsaras, etc. Upanishadic rituals recommend for ensuring the birth of scholarly daughters to women scholars in Vedas. Matrimonial regimes, divorce, pregnancy, niyoga, widowhood and socio-religious customs are considered in Vedas. Also, the position of woman is explained concerning their duties, morals, manners, status in family. The paper also brings out interesting mentions about their looks, fashion, trends, habits, marriage, education and legal status.

Introduction

Before the Vedic period, according to different authorities, the Indian subcontinent was probably matriarchal. The elementary concept was that men were dependent upon women, because like Earth, she gave life, sustenance and strength. Siva, the oldest known deity, found in Indus Valley civilization, describes Sakti as the creating, sustaining and destroying force.

If we go to the Vedic age, we get a clear idea of the status of women. It would not be an exaggeration to say that Indians not only honored women but also kept them on a high pedestal in domestic and social life. We find reference in the Vedic literature, of a ritual recommended for ensuring the birth of a scholarly daughter. It says, "If it's a girl, let it be born with wisdom, inner joy and beauty."[1] Through the Rigveda, we perceive the actual condition of the Hindus, at a date long anterior to the dawn of Grecian civilization—prior to the oldest Hebrew writings and posterior only to the Egyptian dynasties. The community had long turned patriarchal although quite a large number of names still continue to be matronymic.

---

[1] Brihadaranyaka Upanishad.

Rgvedic Woman

The Rigvedic conception of womanhood at its best can be seen through the beautiful hymns addressed to the goddesses—the strength of a woman who ruled the household of the Rsi was unconsciously reflected in the transcendent woman whom he created and to whom he addressed his impassioned prayers. First in importance among the goddesses is Aditi, typifying motherhood. She is the ideal mother like Maat of Egypt and Themis of Greece. The Rigvedic seers used to run to her for protection. She is sometimes identified with a cow which typifies motherhood by providing milk. Aditi's name is invoked eighty times in the Rigveda.

We also have many other incarnations, like Sita, Ratri, Indrani, Surya, Bharati, etc. Sarasvati is the flowing knowledge. Significantly, learning itself was deified as a feminine symbol. She is the Indian Minerva who incites all pleasant songs and inspires all gracious speculations. The most beautiful vision of a goddess which the Rigveda presents is that of Usa—the Dawn. Macdonell, a translator of Vedic hymns, writes: "Usa is the most graceful creation of Vedic poetry and there is no more charming figure in the descriptive religious lyrics of any other literature."

She is the most tender and mighty conception of human mind, the veritable dawn of poetical genius. Clothed in light, the maiden appears in the eastern horizon and unveils her maddening charms to her beholders. Rising resplendent as from a bath, showing her charm, she approaches with light, dispelling darkness. A celestial class of celestial woman, Apsaras, have also been treated as goddesses in the Rigveda. They are endowed with seductive charms of feminine beauty, this is more so in the Puranic mythology and in the epic. A capital instance is seduction of Vishvamitra by the nymph Menaka, the result of which was the birth of Shakuntala whose story forms the subject matter of Kalidasa's immortal play. The most prominent among those are Urvashi, Rambha, Chitralekha and Tilottama.

Thus we see that prayers become the personified goddesses, and though they are addressed to gods, the sacrifice is presided over by Goddesses. Gods alone are not the guests at the sacrifice. Their wives must accompany them. Hence the sage croons the prayer, "Unite them Agni with their dames." But it be remarked that the Rigvedic goddess was never too free. Just as the wife in the earthly home of the Rsi commanded her household always under the protection of the kind loving husband, so also did her divine sister behave under her Lord of Heaven. Even the Dawn, the freest, is conceived as the mother of a mighty son, the daughter of a great father and the beloved of a brilliant Surya. Thus it is clear that in the spiritual sphere, which was more important for the devout man of the Rigveda than the secular one, the part played by the woman was deeply permeating.

Every family had an altar which was lit at the time of the wedding. Here man and wife together offered their worship. From this originated the idea that the man could not worship alone, that he was only half a being. This ritual partnership between man and woman was proof of the wife's equal status at the highest level. The Rigvedic people were devoted to home, wife and children were their anxious concern who received all their love and care. We find frequent references to daughters being fondly caressed by parents. They were lovingly treated by their mothers and shielded by the strength of their brother and father. The fate of the daughter in the medieval Rajput community was, in contrast, horrible. Many a time, the cruel hand of man snapped the thread of her life.

The maiden's principal duty in the Rigvedic family was the milking of the cow and preparing clarified butter and curds. She also wove cloth, embroidered garments, brought water in jars from wells and watched the fields, singing as she did so.

Legal Status

Concerning her legal status, it would seem that the daughter had some share in the property of her father as she was allowed to grow old in her father's family if she chose to remain unmarried. Mention is made about wealth being given away by the spouse's brother to his brother-in-law. This is a clear reference to dowry of later times. An unmarried daughter had her own jewelry which she could dispose of as she liked. It was at the time of marriage generally that she gave away riches and ornaments to Brahmins. There are allusions in which it is said that girls lacking in charms, education and culture could get good husbands if they had money. The Rigvedic system was very alive to the susceptibilities of the woman as the daughter's son could succeed to the property of the maternal grandfather.

The family itself had become an institution for imparting education. The teaching of the hymns was mainly by rote. The daughters also mingled their voices. The maiden who had to seek a husband for herself would find it easier if her intellectual attainments were added to her physical charms. The Rigveda is emphatic in its support of female education. Music and dancing also made her an accomplished woman. Singing was her favorite pastime. Women also had the knowledge of the use of the bow and arrow. Sometimes we find them going to battles along with their husbands. Vishpala, the wife of King Khela, is such an amazon. Like Kaikeyi of the Ramayana she accompanies her lord to the battle field where she loses a leg which is replaced with an iron one. The field of spiritual instruction was open as well to them. We have names of women who contributed about 200 hymns in the composition of the Vedas. We have instances of Visvavara and Apala, Atri's daughter, who as old maids living in their father's house, were able to compose hymns in praise of the Gods. The example of the philosopher Gargi, who boldly challenged her husband sage, Yajnavalkya, in abstruse philosophical argument concerning life and death, soul and God, is quite well known. In later times, we have the example of Bharati, well-versed in Hindu scriptures and metaphysics, who acted as the umpire in the debate which took place between her husband and Adi Sankaracarya and which lasted for seven days. She declared Sankaracarya the winner. In the Aitareya Upanisad, we have an instance where ladies are directed to leave the hall of learning where some principles of gynecology were explained, which are indelicate for the female ear.

Marriage and Virtues of Woman

Thus always was the woman the centre of happiness and the abode of grace; the best part of her breeding consisted in her training to be modest, to conduct herself with grace and form excellent habits. Girls for instance were to "cast their eyes downward and keep their feet close together." Their education aimed at making them good and kind rather than clever or learned. The Vedic girl was taught that marriage was not for lust, but for domestic life and progeny. The measure of her success was the extent to which she could identify herself with her husband's home. In one hymn we have a housewife reminding her husband that ancient sages did attend to the begetting of progeny and did not consider their spiritual progress hampered thereby. The chief lesson impressed on the Vedic girl was how to prove a fit mother and nurse. She was recognized as the first educator whose influence in the nine months of pregnancy could make or mar the child's welfare in after-life. The expectant mother had her surroundings solemn and silent which lay the foundation of the spiritual training of the future child. This extremely important aspect of the Vedic woman's life is taken up by Swami Vivekananda and Mahatma Gandhi who felt that all the problems of the Indian women would be solved as soon as she received education on the right lines. For a woman, the heart is the essence of the personality. Education should help to expand her heart, to strengthen her capacity to love, cherish and protect. M. Gandhi also said, "let her transfer that love to the whole humanity, let her occupy her proud position by the side of man as his mother, maker or silent leader."

Five Examples of Indian Womanhood: Panchkanya

Women were married at a mature age and had full freedom in the choice of their husbands. It is significant that there is not a single reference to child marriage in the whole of the Rg Samhita. They were treated as useful members of the society, walked around freely, involved in all activities from agriculture and crafts to scholarship and were termed "grihalakshmis." They were also prominent in the teaching profession. The Atharva Veda says, "the success of women in married life depends on the proper training given during brahmacharya." In any social milieu, the institution of marriage is crucial to the status of women. The Artha-sastra that enumerates eight types of marriages in the Vedic society, says that in addition to these, any form is approvable provided it pleases all those concerned. Though polygamy was permitted, the husband, before he married another, had to settle a certain amount on the one superseded. While monogamy was the normal custom, divorce was permissible. In his book "*Some Aspects of the Early Sociological History of India*" Professor Sarkar remarks that "the Vedic prince and his priest who could give and receive scores of slave girls as wives, were no doubt living in an age of flourishing polygamy." Indeed we read of several instances of slave girls being given away along with the princesses and when it suited the pleasure of their master, they readily became his wives. It must however be pointed out that from the solemn affirmations and promises made by the bride and the bridegroom to each other, it appears that monogamy was generally prevalent.

The ancients have not dilated much on the life of a widow because her life was not so very different from that of the other women. To keep these women in the same family, marriage of the widow with the younger brother of the deceased husband was allowed. There is a passage in the Rgveda addressed to the widow. "Rise up woman, thou art lying by one whose life is gone, come to the world of the living, away from the husband." Thus it is clear that, unlike the widow of medieval India, the most miserable creature of the Hindu society, her Rgvedic sister enjoyed more freely the air of liberty and the dictates of her conscience, and when remarried, she was a full-fledged wife meant "for love, progeny and prosperity." The chief object of her marriage being the propagation of race by procreating children, her motherhood was considered as the most distinguished trait in a woman. The begetting of children was considered so very important that the impotency, absence or death of a husband was no bar to her giving birth to children. This makeshift was termed as "Niyoga" in later literature. Although niyoga could be practiced on a woman by any kinsman of her husband, her *devar* seems to have been the favorite and the first preference. In that society sexual relationship was determined by other factors than what later came to be termed morality, One has only to look at the genealogy of several of Mahabharata's outstanding personalities who by later code would be termed illegitimate or extramarital progeny. They have sometimes been described as chivalrous but not less "virtuous" in terms of the later measuring codes.

To Kunti, the mother of the Pandava princes, this happens twice. Once while she was still a maid, when she is wooed by Surya. She hesitates as she believed that only parents can bestow her on a man. Surya firmly asserts that a young lady is free; in fact, he avows that the law of nature makes all men free in their sexual desire. So Karna is born. Later the same Kunti, after her marriage, is exhorted by her husband, King Pandu, to have relations outside their marriage, since he cannot produce children himself, and assures her that this is in keeping with Vedic customs, approved of and respected by Rsis and lay people alike. Thus the Pandava princes were born of levirate.

There are instances which show that the system of polyandry is a form of union in which a woman has more than one husband at a time, or in which brothers share a wife or wives in common. Originally, in the matriarchal system, the woman lived with her mother, the children belonged to her. In the next stage, she lived on her own, the husband or husbands only visiting and the children and property still with her. Next came the stage when the husbands were restricted to brothers and lived in the same house. So now the woman moved in with them and the domination of the male started. The children were at first jointly shared, but in course of time, the eldest brother established himself as the head. The prevalence of this system comes out clearly in the Rg and Atharvaveda and at the time when Draupadi's father declined to marry his daughter to five Pandavas and Yudhisthira, the eldest, pacified him, proving this was not strange, by relating several such examples. Actually this form of union was practiced in both northern and Southern India but when Manu came and denounced this practice this tradition had perforce to be explained away because it had become unpalatable by the time of the final redaction of the Mahabharata. Thus the story tells how Arjuna performs a feat and wins over Draupadi. Back home, the brothers asked their mother to open the door and receive them who had returned with pretty alms that day. Not knowing what they referred to, she asked them from behind the door to divide it among themselves. Thus Draupadi became their common wife.

The absence of rigidity, in fact considerable liberalism, in conjugal relationship and the woman's right to her own lifestyle is vividly reflected in the choice of the five women: Sita, Mandodari, Draupadi, Tara and Ahalya, known as the *panchakanyas.* These were ordinary housewives who were held up as an ideal, but obviously not for being worshipful wives.

Sita showed courage to give her expression to the contempt she felt for Rama when he showed flaws in his personality though presumed to be perfect. When he is banishing her, she shows not her anger or sorrow so much as utter disdain for his weak character. She had shown a similar reaction when he feared to take her with him in exile.

In Mandodari, we see the same strength which rises out of integrity. She has the courage to warn and reprimand Ravana against his pursuit of Sita, and the seizing of unwilling women for pleasure. She also agrees to marry Vibhisana after Ravana's death.

Draupadi has been considered as outstanding among the epic women, learned and described as Pandita. As a wife, she seemed a superwoman to be able to manage her marital life with ingenuity. She was anything but a submissive wife to the five highly individualistic husbands. On the contrary, she was a highly spirited woman, a fearless and determined character boldly speaking out her mind, who could even rail at the gods and upbraid her weak husbands for their many failings. She maintained her personality in the face of much dishonor, she vowed destruction to her tormentors, and saw to it that this was carried out through Krsna, inflaming his anger when he showed signs of toning down. She even dared to deny the goodness of God, "I see the noble and good in distress and the wicked enjoying the good things of life.... God does not show for all mankind the love of a parent or the concern of the wise guardian. God is partial.... caprice and blind will appear to be distinctive, not justice and mercy."

It is very significant that two others included in this galaxy of ideal women would not have been accepted as virtuous by the standards ulterior to the Vedic ones, they would even be condemned as immoral and unethical. It must be remembered that the Puranic traditions according to which this classification has been made, in most cases illustrate the condition of society prevailing prior to the Rgvedic. Tara, the chief wife of Bali, seems to have willingly given herself to Sugriva, Bali's brother. She is honored not as a devoted wife but as a forceful personality, cool-headed, calculating, one who could play important roles in her husband's affairs, especially as she is shown holding her own in argument with an opponent and resolving a difficult situation. This speaks volumes for an entirely different set of ideals and roles for women than that of the meek submissive wife.

The case of Ahalya, also included in the five ideal women, is even more puzzling. The honored wife of the famous sage Gautama is alleged to have committed adultery and was cursed to be an immobile stone until rescued by

Rama. Here, with your permission, I'll open a bracket to pass on some information The word 'Ahalya' literally means 'unploughed'. Gautama tries to keep her in this stage while Indra tries to cultivate her, transgressing his limits, and, in the process, Ahalya loses her original form and become 'halya'. It is in this context that the story of Ahalya has to be understood. She is given the first and foremost place among the five celebrated maidens of Hinduism mainly on account of all alphabets. 'A' the first of the vowels and Hal—the inert consonants and the vowels that make them alert. She is thus the embodiment of all the sounds, syllables and spells whose significance get faded by a momentary contact with Indra, the Lord of the senses, and then regain their significance by coming into contact with Rama whose name is more significant than his form. In other words, the son of Dashratha rises to the level of Rama, the mystic spell of the Vedas, only after the episode of Ahalya. I'm sorry I could not simplify this explanation any further.

Beauty and Decoration of Woman

Let us now come to more interesting and colorful themes, namely beauty and adornment. Though Rgvedic life is generally classified as plain, simple and based on very few necessities, we know that culture has a lot to do with a woman's beauty and we have seen how the Rgvedic girls were free to choose their husbands. Well, surely in that society decoration or 'sringar' counted for a great deal. Like Eve who, the day she became conscious of her nakedness, plucked the leaves of a cabbage to cover herself, thereby setting foot in the world of fashion and ornament, the Rgvedic daughter was alive to this need of hers and she took pains to adorn herself in the most attractive manner. Even in a description of Usa, it's written: "She decks her beauty shining forth with sunbeams like women trooping to the bridal feast."

Many references make it clear that these people were not merely spiritual but they also cared for mundane affairs and there were many articles of dress. It appeared that the materials were of three kinds, namely skin, wool and cotton. In classical literature, we find Shakuntala wearing skin robe which bore knots on the shoulders. Sita in the like manner dressed up in skins in the hermitage of Valmiki. The garment consisted of three items, an upper garment, an undergarment and an over-garment, occasionally there was a kind of scarf. For weddings, there was a head-dress.

Reference is also made to an outer loose-flowing garment, perhaps a shawl covering the entire person of the woman except her head. Its use was made when women went out to attend social functions. There is a passage in the Samhita that reads: "Women dressed in white garments and moving slowly like the milk that colors it." These women seem to have been well advanced in the art of weaving, dyeing and bleaching. Brocades were known and rich gold threads were interwoven with fibers of wool and cotton. The Rgveda also refers to beautiful dresses worn by dancing girls. There is no reference to the saris anywhere in the Vedas though we know that the classical Indian beauty is described in a two-dimensional visual, firstly we have the doting mother with her long, thick, plaited hair falling neatly down the back of her sari and choli and secondly the one with a hint of the voluptuous charms and mysteries of the Kama Sutra. In the whole range of the Rgveda, we nowhere come across a single reference to the footwear. Prof. Sarkar thinks that by view of both the men and women wearing anklets the use of footwear must have been limited.

Love of ornaments has been a racial trait of the Hindus. These have always had material as well as symbolical value in the life of the woman. Gold was the metal used. The frequency with which gold has been mentioned attests to the fact that it abounded in the country and ornaments made of gold and precious stones were worn in profusion. From the earlier pieces of terracottas and sculptures, from the description of chariots decked with pearls and precious stones, we cannot but naturally infer the women had access to dazzling jewelry. There is mention of anklets on feet, gold chains on breast, visors wrought of gold on head, a particular kind of gold coin, ear pendants, and ornaments for shoulders. No one has an idea how these were. As for the nose ring, Dr. Altekar has shown in his "Position of Women in Hindu Civilization" that the post-Muslim period began to show the nose-ring for the first time.

Much attention seems to have been paid to the hair. Hair war well combed, piled, parted and braided. Often, we have reference to dames with lovely hands, broad plaits and ample hips, loose tresses hanging beautifully on the back. Mention is also made of the use of ointments and perfumes. We read that wives attending the funeral were expected to embellish their bodies with odorous sweets. This finished, the women put unguent to their eyes. All these accomplishments were considered a mark of good manner in the *beau monde* of ancient Hindu India.

Mention should also be made of the 'nritya' or the professional dancer whom Vatsyayan will refer to as Devdasis in the 4th century A.D. in his Kamasutra. They enjoyed a respectable status as repositories of art. Some of these institutions like the Devdasi, in spite of their exalted origin, however got corrupted like so many other practices. Their pristine growth was clouded and they began to lose their privileged position in the medieval period.

Manusmriti and Status of Woman in Post-Vedic Period

In the post-Vedic age, with the Manusmriti we find restrictions that tended to deprive woman of her traditional status. The 'upnayan' ceremony came to be confined only to male children, girls were also prohibited from access to the Vedas. He further ordained that there should be no sacrifices or vratas for women without the husband's consent. Manu also said women should never think of independence from the father, the husband or the sons. It's all very complicated because Manu himself is known to have said beautiful words like: "Where women are honored, there the gods delight." And "The man of' faith must accept wholesome teaching even from an inferior, high principles from even the lowliest, and the gem of a lady even from an inferior family." Manu was backed by the Epic and Puranic writers, later by saint poets like Tukaram and Kabir, who called woman a hellish well. The condition of women became appalling in the later Hindu society and already during the time of Bhartrhari women had come to be spoken of "as incapable of being chaste", when the adolescent daughters came to be compared to a basket of snakes which the father has to carry.

Jawaharlal Nehru remarks in his "*Discovery of India*" as follows: "The legal position of women, according to Manu, the earliest exponent of Indian law, was definitely bad. They were treated in law almost as chattels. And yet from the numerous instances in the epics this law was not applied very rigidly and they held an honored place in the home and in society. Bad as the legal position of women was in Ancient India judged by modern standards, it was far better than in Greece, and Rome, in early Christianity, in the canon law of medieval Europe and indeed right up to comparatively modern lines at the beginning of the 19th century.

Later on, movements like Buddhism in the 6th century B.C. had the greatest impact on women's status. Buddha's compassion and respect for human beings served to raise the position of women. Ugly trends like child marriage, dowry, Sati, etc. were discarded. Women *bhikhunis* assumed equal part in religious pursuits. When Yashodhara, Buddha's wife, appeared in public without a veil, Buddha declared that modesty in women could be preserved by the women themselves through their own sense of discipline, not by an artificial veil.[2]

---

[2] There is no mention of women students at Taxashila or any of the Buddhist Universities, but some of them did function as students somewhere, for there is repeated mention of learned and scholarly women.

Hindu society, however, became somewhat rigid in its attitude towards women with the advent of Islam. Her freedom was severely curtailed and her fate became particularly miserable.

Muslim Rule and Later Period of Reforms

As a reaction to Muslim domination as well as to the unjust practices of orthodox Hindus, the Bhakti movement delivered a new message of love and hope through the saint poetesses like Andal and Mirabai. However limited, Christianity had some impact on the woman's sphere. Providing education to women also led to women taking to professions.

Then came the social reforms with stalwarts like Swami Dayananda, Swami Vivekananda, Gandhi, Tagore and Aurobindo who gave to the modern woman the sanctions of the national spiritual heritage to move in the wider world of wider opportunities.

For the liberated Indian woman, the situation is far more complex. She manifests the tradition versus modernity war in far more real terms. The old Indian woman has been nourished on the ideals of Sita, Savitri, Damayanti. In the limited world in which she functioned, these ideals sufficed to sustain her. Not that our women are insensitive to these appeals, but they find their never ending aspirations and energies unsustained by them. Hence their persisting sense of guilt, their unsteady steps, and the rest you know.

Women in Ancient India

PANDITA SATWANTEE PELLADOAH
Arya Sabha, Mauritius

1. INTRODUCTION

To grasp the history of women in India, the study of the Vedas, the most ancient scriptures since the creation of the world, becomes very important. The Vedas have always been considered as a gift of divine eloquence for the benefit of mankind. As the science of life, the Vedas clearly establish the fact of women's role and the place they occupied in ancient India. The Vedas are regarded as the source of knowledge, and the extremely important pivotal place of women in society, as expounded in the Vedas, has hardly been disputed so far. According to the early Vedic period the upbringing and education of women was extremely well established. Women were then playing prominent roles as individuals, as members of the family, in social life as well as in national affairs. Women in ancient India were endowed with exceptionally pure qualities, amongst others—motherly attitude, sympathy, patience, care, ambition, bravery and fearlessness. They were considered as the repository of faith in truth. The status, rights, qualities and struggle for identity have evolved through the ages.

In the Vedic age, known as Sat Yug, women have been acknowledged for their duty, responsibilities, education, etc. In the Treta Yug (the Ramayana being the landmark of this period, although written well afterwards), women enjoyed the same status as in the Vedic age. Dwapar Yug (the Mahabharata and the Bhagawadgita being vivid examples of this age) also depicts the emancipation of women as in the two previous periods. With the advent of Kaliyug women were still enjoying a high place in society. But with the passing of time, when the rulers of the country started mismanaging the affairs of the nation, invasion by foreigners being partly responsible, women started losing their rightful place which they had so far been enjoying. Their education started declining. They were degraded from their status, being considered as a lower human being within the family and in the society at large, with impacting consequences on the very social fabric which they were supporting.

2. STATUS OF WOMEN

Just as the ancient Rishis experienced the Vedas through the divine voice, known as Shruti, so did the Rishikas (women Rishis). This fact reveals that women during that period were highly qualified and cultured. In the Rigveda there are 24 Rishikas and in the Atharvaveda, 5 Rishikas who experienced more than 422 mantras.

For example, in the Rigveda, Mandal 10, Sukta 85, fortyseven mantras are attributed to Rishika Surya Savitri. Rishika Ghosha Kakshivati (Mandal 10, Suktas 39 and 40) dedicated 28 mantras. Rishika Siki Nivavri has contributed 20 mantras in Mandal 9, Sukta 86. Similarly, Rishika Indrani in Mandal 10, Suktas 86 and 145 received 17 mantras. Rishikas Yami Vaivasvati, Dakshina Prajapatya and Aditi have all mostly gifted us with their mantras in the tenth Mandal of the Rigveda.

Likewise, in the Atharvaveda, Rishika Surya Savitri has gifted us with 139 mantras and Rishika Matrinama with 40 mantras. In the same way, Rishikas Indrani, Devajamayia and Sarparajiyayi have bestowed upon humanity their eternal encounters with God.

This leaves no doubt as to the fact that during the Vedic age women had achieved a very high degree of cultural maturity. Women were exposed to an advanced civilization which promoted education. Only the evolution in such a cultural environment could have promoted such Rishikas. The Rishikas stand out as thinkers, philosophers, religious reformers and leading figures of their time. This leads us to think that women in general benefited from this educational and cultural atmosphere. While being part of the material world, women were in union with God. This communion was what they imparted for the benefit of humanity.

3. Qualities and Contribution of Women in Ancient India

Rishikas and other highly educated women establish one important and revealing fact. Women are the source of knowledge, which we now call university. The mother is considered as the greatest university in life. Women in ancient India were the source of all development of knowledge. The process of learning starts well before birth, right from the womb of the mother. This was what they established and practised.

The legacy of the eight mantras from the eighth Rishika, Vak Ambhrini, in Mandal 10, Vak Sukta of the Rigveda, relating to the science of speech, gives an insight into the analytical approach developed by the Rishika. She has established that speech constitutes the first pillar of education.

The 18th Rishika, caled Shraddha Kamayani, has laid down five mantras related to the study of psychology, without the application of which knowledge remains inadequate and meaningless, psychology being the life blood of pure knowledge in the same way as the soul activates the body.

Rishika Surya Savitri, in the Vivah Sukta, has expounded the merits of marriage (Vivah Sanskar). She has explained marriage as an institution which perpetuates life within the meaning of the Vivah Sanskar. Similarly, in the Indrani Sukta, she brings to light woman's dignity, honour, glory and values.

From Rishika Romasha Brahmavadini we learn that women also studied and discoursed on spiritual knowledge. In Atharvaveda, Kand 1, Sukta 27, Mantra 4 Rishika Indrani has given to the world the science of war. She teaches about the invocation of God before engaging in a battle, organising the army, leading and conducting battles and techniques about uplifting the morale of soldiers to win.

"*Indrani ye tu prathama jyetu.*"

This clearly proves that women had equal education, knowledge and rights to enable them to succeed in the daily battle of life.

In the Vedas, women have been called "Brahma". "*Stri hi Brahma babhuvita.*" Brahma is the cradle of knowledge. Women are the educators. Those who have had access to the knowledge of the Vedas have always imparted the best education to the world—education based on truth. This is the path that has been followed by Arya women so far under the spiritual revival of Maharshi Swami Dayanand.

Regarding the strength of women, the Atharvaveda strongly points out that women are not the weaker elements of society. On the contrary, they are the more powerful elements. This is underlined in the Indrani Sukta "Shastra Virya". Woman is fearless, strong and brave. The Yajurveda also supports these words and emphasises that women are a million times more powerful. They are the destroyer of all negative and harmful actions emanating from the body, mind and speech of the enemy.

The Vedas were not accessible to the common woman due to the complexity of the Vedic Sanskrit language. To remedy this lacuna, Panini, Patanjali and Parashar Rishis and Munis dedicated their Brahman Granthas, Grihyasutra, Ashtadhyayi, Upanishads and Mahabhashya to propagate the essence of Vedic knowledge.

The Brahman Granthas have thus simplified the Vedas within easy reach of women who have thus greatly benefited from them. Women have been given a high status just as Manu Maharaj has clearly underlined.

"*Yatra naryastu pujyante ramante tatra devata.*
Yatra etastu na pujyante sarvastatraphala kriyah."

(Where women are given due respect and dignity, there devatas have their abode. Where the dignity of women is trampled upon and disrespect is shown towards them, there duty and action are fruitless.)

This is the reason why during those days women participating in the yajnas were given nectar as a sign of respect.

4. Women's Rights and Responsibilities

According to the granthas mentioned above, women were enjoying proper rights in society. "*Striya striyam sama dadhat.*" Women were considered as the wealth of the household, "Grihalakshmi". They have been defined as "*Yosha*" in the Shatapath Brahman, one who is responsible for the welfare of the family. From this we can deduce that we are incomplete human beings without the support of women during the various phases of our life. Through her family and her household the ancient Indian woman asserted herself in her own right, in directing the members of the family towards a path that led to a healthy framework of life.

The education she was exposed to gave her the freedom to judge for herself the duty she had to shoulder as a daughter. She had the moral responsibility not to let down her parents' trust.

In those days unmarried women could become Rishikas. Married women, while having to look after their household, could also freely participate in constructive social work. Even two hundred years before Christ, women were enjoying a long established tradition of political and social rights.

Women enjoyed all the above rights in the Vedic age called Sat Yuga. The study of the Treta and Dwapar Yugas reveals that women had the same rightful place in society as men. We find in the Ramayana Queen Kaushalya lecturing on the techniques of governing and managing the affairs of the nation. In Ayodhya Kand mother Sumitra educates her son about the essence of the relationship amongst brothers. We also find Queen Kaushalya teaching her sons the importance of devotion to God by performing yajna and and through prayers, and by chanting the Veda mantras. In the Shanti Parva of the Mahabharata "*Naste matri samah guru*" clarifies the place women occupied as gurus. Likewise in Stree Parva mother Kuntee assumes her rights as a mother by inculcating the importance of power in Yudhisthir. Regarding the proper exercise of power she advises him that it is the king who shapes the future of a nation and not the future that makes the king. This indicates that women in ancient India were also well versed in politics and government.

During the same era a daughter was given equal rights in the succession of her father's wealth. It is known that Sita was requested to succeed Rama on the throne when he was ordered to abdicate. This proves that women were capable of governing a country or ruling a kingdom.

The cornerstones of women's rights and responsibilities are characterised by the three D's, Daya, Daman and Daan. Through Daya she is capable of moulding the individual, the family, the society and the nation. Through Daman (sacrifice) the woman participates in social activities and fights against injustice. She sacrifices her own desires for the benefit of her family and society. Through Daan (enlightened self-interest) she shares the exixtence of her womanhood and motherly love for the benefit of humanity.

5. Education of Women in Ancient India

In ancient India the education of women was well established. This explains the high place they achieved as intellectuals. The aforementioned Granthas have written about women's education in that era. Women achieved high education not only because they studied but because they grasped the essential teachings of the Vedas, Vedic grammar, Mimamsa Darshan, etc. and other serious subjects as well. They became great scholars and teachers of men as well. Female teachers were called Acharyas. Women who studied the Kath Shakha of Yajurveda were known as Kathi. The title Briha Vrichi was given to a woman who took to the study of of the Briha Vrikshaka. Those who studied Apishali grammar were known as Apishala Brahmani and those who studied Panini grammar were known as Paninya.

During that period women were given the Yajnopavita in the same manner as men before undertaking studies under the guidance of noble teachers. They were also subjected to all the samskaras in the same way.

Through Panini we come to learn that besides the mental development through education women enjoyed sports and games, that is, physical education as well. Special sports centres for women were known as "Udyan Krida Shal Bhanjika" and "Ashok Pushp Prachayika".

This was the situation of the educational background women were enjoying in the Treta and Dwapar Yugas. But because of certain difficulties starting after the Vedic Yuga the studies of the Vedas became remote. Then the importance of the various Granthas to understand and study the Vedas began to be felt.

Because of the lack of the understanding of the Vedas, the status of women started declining gradually. By the end of the Mahabharat battle these changes affected women's status considerably. The establishment of various kingdoms and governments ruling different parts of India gave birth to different institutions having little or no concern for the welfare of women. Because of these negative developments the ancient rich customs supporting the education and upliftment of women received a serious blow. Sacrifice and devotion gave way to pleasure, material gains and vices. Women started to be looked upon as the lowest members of society.

A ban on women's education gradually crept in, thus annihilating the gains during the previous yugas. Education was eventually reserved for a handful of privileged women from extremely rich background.

Between the 12th and 16th centuries during the Turkish and Persian invasions, even the defence and protection of women became very difficult. To defend their customs, rites, religion and culture child marriages started taking place. Young women preferred to die along with their husbands to protect themselves from the invaders (called Sati Pratha). This also gave rise to the wearing of veils (or Parda) to evade the vicious looks of the foreigners. Whereas they used to be brave, now a wind of cowardice and fear started blowing on women. This decline in the fate of Indian women continued, causing an erosion of their self-respect..

This state of affairs persisted until the reform movement of the Arya Samaj was started by Maharshi Dayanand. This movement amplified with the objective of redressing the balance through the education of women as during the Vedic era.

Indian women can regain their rightful place in society through the Vedic vision of Swami Dayanand Sarasvati. Gurukulas and Vidyalayas have reopened for the education of women and men based on the strictures of the Vedic era.

Women in Vedic Rituals

RAMA NATH SHARMA
Professor of Sanskrit and Chairman
Department of Hawaiian and Indo-Pacific Languages
University of Hawaii at Manoa
2540 Maile Way., Spalding 255, Honolulu, HI 96825
Email: rama@hawaii.edu

I

It is common knowledge that the Hindu society believes in performing elaborate rituals (*saṁskāras*). There are generally sixteen major rituals spread over a span of human life beginning with conception (*garbhādhāna*). Initiation (*upanayana*), marriage (*vivāha*) and death (*mṛtyu*) are three leading rituals which have attracted most attention. I have accepted a much wider usage of the word ritual for purposes of this paper. I consider rituals as religious practices which symbolize social behavioral norms, expectations and injunctions. This broader sense of ritual includes every religious activity which the Hindus not only had through millenia, but which they also nurtured and practiced with dedication. For, their performance accrued them merits (*puṇya*), responsible for bringing bliss in this life and the life beyond. More importantly, rituals serve as agents of purification: *saṁskriyate anena vā saṁskāraḥ* (that by means of which purification is accomplished). Purification from what? From agents of pollution which may come to bear upon performance of dutiful actions (*dharma*). These pollutants have generally been referred to as *guṇas* (qualities). Philosophers of the *Vaiśeṣika* school consider the totality of *guṇas* to be twentyfour. The last *guṇa* has been named *saṁskāra* and one inherits it in one's blood. The ritual *saṁskāras* which are performed at birth serve as purificatory agents. Their purpose is to boot up the inherited *saṁskāras* of the previous birth, if you may, and prepare them to form the basis for the *saṁskāras* of the present life. All the pollutant qualities introduced through seeding and pregnancy are thus removed by the *saṁskāras* performed at birth.

It is very difficult, if not impossible, to exactly define the nature of rituals in the developmental aspect of the Hindu society. The Vedas, particularly the *Ṛgveda,* are our most ancient text. It is not known precisely when the Vedic Indians learned how to write. We know for sure from Harappa that the inhabitants of the Indus Valley definitely knew how to write. The Vedic Indians must have had the Vedas before they reduced them to writing. That writing must have come very late in the transmission of the Vedic texts is also attested by internal evidence pertaining to recitation. Thus, we find that reciting from a written text was considered as one of the six most sinful ways of recitation:

gitī śighrī śiraḥkampī tathā likhitapāṭhakāḥ /
anarthajño'lpakaṇṭhaśca ṣaḍ ete pāṭhakādhamāḥ //

(Sing-song, fast speed, head-shaking and reciting from a text, not knowing the meaning and lacking enough modulation in voice, are six despicable reciters.)

The Vedic Indians reduced the Vedas into writing at a time when the society was much more developed and the text of the Vedas had become fairly standardized. This must have happened at least in the very early part of the development of the Classical Sanskrit language. It can be safely assumed that, by the time of the Buddha (6th BC), the Hindu society had fully developed and settled into structures we can easily verify through available documents. The four Vedas, the *Ṛk*, *Yajuṣ*, *Sāma* and *Atharva*, later on developed into many thousand branches and subbranches. The *saṁhitā* texts of the Vedas are most valuable sources for studying the nature and development of the Vedic society. The texts of the *brāhmaṇas* and the *gṛhyasūtras* offer rich elaborations and interpretations of rituals. The development of the *saṁhitā, brāhmaṇa* and *gṛhyasūtra* texts must have taken a minimum of one thousand years before the Buddha. Our Vedic texts thus date back to at least a minimum of 1,500 years before Christ. One can easily assume that at least a thousand years must have elapsed before this time when the Vedic texts were reduced to writing. The Vedic society which reduced the Vedas to writing must have preceded Christ by at least 2,500 years. We are thus talking about a ritualist Vedic society which existed in the Indo-Gangetic plains of North India about 5,000 years before. When did the precursor of this civilization establish itself on the east of the Euphrates and the Tigris rivers, and when did it flourish beyond the region of *Saptasindhu* (seven oceanlike rivers), over formidable odds presented by a very well developed culture of the Indus Valley, must be determined within a time-frame certainly going way beyond a few thousand years before the Buddha.

It is very difficult to know exactly what rituals this society practiced and how. We know that fires (*Agni*) of various kinds, the most important of which is called the *gārhaspatya* (belonging to the lord of the household, or simply the household), were commonplace. Heaping, maintaining and using these fires for daily rituals formed the main focus of attention in the early days of this ritualistic society. We later on find the development of elaborate ritual sacrifices (*yajña*) encompassing a wide range of them: from the *agnicayana* (heaping of (ritual) fire) to *naramedha* (human sacrifice). Most of the Vedic rituals are lost. Heaping and maintaining of ritual fires is also mostly lost. Though there are a few homes in the North, and many more in the South, where the *gārhaspatya* is still well maintained. I have just stated that most of the Vedic rituals are lost. It is for this reason that we must evaluate and rediscover our concept of rituals.

A cursory look at the developmental history of rituals suggests that Buddhism introduced major changes to the ritual scene of North India. The rituals that were performed prior to the Buddha can be safely called Vedic rituals. These rituals mostly used Vedic hymns. The post-Buddhist Hindu rituals developed clearly with a Vedic base, but under the influence of the tantra and Śaivite practices. The more elaborate rituals, such as the *rājasūya* (ritual sacrifice for king of kings) and *aśvamedha* (horse sacrifice), were reserved mostly for the kings and elites. Rituals such as the *cāndrāyaṇa* were very difficult to perform since they both entailed intense physical and mental discipline. Some rituals resorted to brevity but were generally structured to bring quick results. Another twist to the structure of rituals was added by the immeasurable impact of the Purāṇas on the Hindu society. Consequently, what we have now is the Purāṇic structure of rituals, of course with the traditional base of Vedic hymns. This paper will try to present the status of women in ancient Ṛgvedic India as reflected in rituals. These rituals are mostly Purāṇic but I have taken the liberty of calling them Vedic because of their predominant use of the Vedic hymns.

Status of women, be it inside or outside the context of rituals, cannot be determined unless one understands the role of women in society. The assertion that *vinā nārīm niṣphalā lokayātrā* (a journey through this world (of mortals) is fruitless without a woman) must be taken very seriously in the Indian ritualist context. The earliest concept of woman in the Vedic literature is more like an abstraction in the form of Aditi: the mother of gods, the woman who encompasses heaven and earth (*dyāvā-pṛthivī*); one who is the mother, tthe father and the son (*mātā sa pitā saputraḥ*). This concept of Aditi, when contrasted with its counterpart Diti, gave rise later on to the concept of Śakti. Recall in this connection that the manifestation of Pārvatī in the form of Satī, the daughter of Dakṣa, is nothing but the Purāṇic counterpart of the same Śakti. The Sanskrit word for woman is *Nārī*, a counterpart of *nara* (man). Etymologically, a man is called *nara* because he is supposed to be engrossed in action, i.e., inferred as dancing. A woman, similarly, is also thought to be engaged in action side by side her man. This is why *nara* and *nārī* are compared with two wheels of a cart. This is why a trip through this world below the heaven becomes useless in the absence of a woman.

Who is this woman? A mother, sister, wife and a daughter. These four are the most important faces of woman celebrated in the ritual literature. As a wife she is a friend, a lover, i.e., the other wheel of the cart without which going becomes impossible. Finally, the tradition has seen a wife primarily as one who serves as the field (*kṣetra*) for the seeds (*bīja*) which sprout within her and which bear him sons. A son is the most important product a woman can offer. A son is called *putra* because he protects the ancestors from the *naraka* (hell). It is ironical that a woman is born as a daughter and, in many ways, also completes her cycle of voyage to this world by giving birth to a daughter but her worth is measured by the birth of a son. Technically, *putrī* can also be accepted as a female who protects her ancestors from the *naraka*. Within this journey from being a daughter to giving birth to a daughter, a woman assumes many roles and contributes many things. But her single most important contribution must be a son. It is perhaps because this that a *putrī* cannot be accepted as one who can also protect the ancestors from the *naraka*. The *Aitareya-brāhmaṇa* perhaps best sums up the discriminatory sentiment of Hindu society concerning the importance of a son against a daughter.

ātmā hi yajñaḥ ātmanaḥ sa irāvatī atitāriṇī /
sakhā ha jāyā, kṛpaṇaṁ duhitā jyotir ha putraḥ parame vyoman /
taj jāyā jāyā bhavati yad asyāṁ jāyate punaḥ /
nā putrasya loko'sti //

(A man is born again in his son; a son is the boat which takes across the ocean of this world; a wife is a companion; the son serves as a light not only for this world but also for the world beyond; a daughter is pitiable (nothing but misery); a wife is no wife until one gets born as a son in her; this world is no world for a son-less.)

This indeed was a patriarchal society where sons were preferred over daughters. It is no wonder that Indra's blessings were invoked for planting ten sons in the womb of a woman so that she could become "a woman with eleven men". Of course, the eleventh will be her husband. The sages do not say anything about invoking the blessings of any god for the birth of a daughter.

Pumāṁsaṁ putraṁ janayatāṁ pumānaṁ anu jāyatāṁ /
bhvāsi putrāṇāṁ mātā jātānāṁ janayāṣ ca yān //

(You be the mother of sons you have given birth to, and of those who you will give birth to, hereafter.)

The *Ṛgveda* does not clearly state against the birth of a daughter. The emphasis was so much on giving birth to a son that the birth of a daughter became insignificant. A son was always conceived to be a brave slayer of enemies (*śatru hantā*) and, above all, a facilitator for the father's (and ancestors') sinless ascension to heaven, away from hell (*naraka*). A daughter, when born, was always prayed to become rich and prosperous: *mama putrāḥ śhatruhaṇo'tho me duhitā virāṭ*.. It is hard to believe that a girl who, in her youth, gives birth to brave sons and who commands respect equal to water (*āp*) and earth (*pṛthivī*), the two most important entities sustaining life, is treated as undesired by the seers of the *Atharvaveda*.

A general look at the history of civilizations attests beyond any reasonable doubt that women were generally not treated as equal to men in all societies. The Vedic societies were no exception to it. Women were generally supposed to follow men: *striyaḥ puṁso'nuvartmāno bhāvukāḥ.* Their life was limited to family, husband, offsprings, generally sons. A bride was considered as auspicious (*sumaṅgalī*). She was also desired to become the queen of her household. This household of which she was to become the queen would have a husband who will earn money with a hundred hands and spend with a thousand (*śatahasta-samāhara sahasrahasta saṁkira).* There will be no affection lost between spouses, no conflicts between the offsprings. That a woman's world was limited to family and household is further attested by a hymn of the *MaitrāyaṇOī-saṁhitā.* See what a woman says to her husband:

ahaṁ vadāmi neta tvaṁ sabhāyāṁ aha tvaṁ vada

(I alone speak here (at home), you (go ahead and) speak at gatherings.)

No wonder that the *Maitrāyaṇī-saṁhitā.* regards women as superior to men: *striyaḥ puṁso'tiricyante.* The majority of literatures respect woman as a mother and wife. But in general it also treats women as inferior to men. Except for a female with no brother, women in general were blocked from receiving inheritance (*dāya*). There is also evidence of women with immoral conduct (*duśśīla*). And then there are also extreme references to women in general characterized with contempt. There is a great deal of evidence where women were offered as gifts. *Śatapatha-brāhmaṇa* records that, at the end of an *aśvamedha*, women, including an unmarried girl and hundreds of maids, were offered as gifts.

II

I shall now return to individual rituals and see how women are treated in them. The *gṛhyasūtras* and the *smṛtis* differ on the number of *saṁskāras.* They vary between 25 to 13. The following 16, however, are the generally accepted *saṁskāras.*

A. *Three before birth*
   1. Pregnancy (*garbhādhāna*)
   2. Sprouting (*Puṁsavana)*
   3. Veil-lifting (*sīmantonnayana*)

B. *Six after birth through adolescence*
   4. Birth (*jātakarma*)
   5. Naming (*nāmakaraṇa*)
   6. Outing (*Niṣkramaṇa*)
   7. Food-tasting (*annaprāśana*)
   8. Hair-cutting (*cūḍā*)
   9. Ear-piercing (*karṇabedha*)

C. *Three concerning education*
   10. Initiation (*upanayana*)
   11. Study of the Vedas (*Vedādhyayana*)
   12. Graduation (*samāvartana*)
D. *Household rituals*
   13. Marriage (*vivāha*)
   14. Retirement (*vānaprastha*)
   15. Renunciation (*saṁnyasa*)
E. *End*
   16. Last rite (*antyeṣṭi*)

Note that the study of the Vedas, graduation, retirement and renunciation, these four are not very commonly practiced rituals. The tradition had many other rituals which focussed more on the Vedic ritual *śrāvaṇī*, *agnihotra*, *agniṣṭoma* and *atirātras*, etc., than on the purificatory *saṁskāras.* Manu claims that these *saṁskāras* were to be performed for getting rid of polluting agents received in the process of seeding and pregnancy:

baijikaṁ gārbhikaṁ caino dvijānāṁ apasṛjyate

(The sins—both seed and womb related—of those who are reborn through this *saṁskāra,* get far removed.)

Whether the word *dvija* here means *brāhmaṇa* is debatable.

It is generally believed that all *saṁskāras* were to be performed for boys and girls alike. However, there are marked differences and discriminatory practices. I shall discuss seeding, sprouting and veil-lifting in connection with my discussion of marriage. I shall presently consider birthing (*jātakarma*), naming (*nāmakaraṇa*), outing (*Niṣkramaṇa*), food-tasting (*annaprāśana*), hair-cutting, (*cūḍā*) and ear-piercing (*karṇabedha*) which are major rituals for children. The earlier *gṛhyasūtras* generally allow these rituals for boys and girls with no distinctions. However, by the time of the *Dharmasūtras* we find a clear difference in performing these rituals for boys and girls. For example, the *Viṣṇudharmasūtra* states that birth-related rituals for girls should be performed without chanting of any *mantra*:

amantrikā tu kāryeyaṁ strīṇāṁ āvṛd aśeṣataḥ /
saṁskārārthaṁ śarīrasya yathākālaṁ yathākramaṁ //

Yājñavalkya in the *ācārādhyāya* declares that *saṁskāras* for women, with the exception of marriage, must be performed quietly without uttering the *mantras*:

tūṣṇīṁ etaḥ kriyāḥ strī ṇāṁ vivāhas tu samantrakaḥ /

The reasons given for such practices is clearly chauvinistic. In a nutshell, a woman cannot be trusted. This is exactly similar to later sentiments which have been expressed rather rudely as:

nadīnāṁ nakhīnāṁ caiva śṛṅgiṇāṁ śastrapāṇināṁ /
viśsvāso naiva kartavyaḥ strīṣu rājakuleṣu ca //

(Rivers, animals with nails and horns, men with weapons in their hands: these plus women and royalty should never be trusted.)

It is perhaps for this same reason that Manu says:

pitā rakṣati kaumāre bharttā rakṣati yauvane /
putro rakṣati vārdhakye na strī svātantryaṁ arhati //

(Father protects her in adolescence, husband in youth, the son protects her in old age; a woman never deserves freedom.)

Perhaps this is not as bad as the sentiment of the ascetic school where a woman is characterized as *narakasya dvāraṁ* (gateway to *naraka* (hell)). But do not despair; the tradition also believes that:

yatra nāryas tu pūjyante ramante tatra devatāḥ

(Gods rejoice at the place where women are worshipped.)

The *gṛhyasūtras* recommend two names for each child, where the first name is private and the second for use in the public. A name should consist of two or four syllables. The first part of a name should be a *saṁjñā* (name), the second part could be a verb form. Names should generally contain one long vowel and *visarga* (*ḥ*) at the end. One should have a voiced consonant (*g, gh, j, jh, d, dh, b, bh,* etc.) at the beginning and *y*, *v*, *r* and *l* in the middle. One name is private. A girl's name should have uneven number of syllables, generally not exceeding three syllables. It is preferred to have them end in *ā* and be a derivative with a *taddhita* (patronymic) affix:

dvyakṣaraṁ chaturakṣaraṁ vā nāmapūrvaṁ ākhyātottaraṁ dīrghābhi-
niṇāṭhānāntaṁ ghoṣavad ādyantarantasthaṁ /
ayujākṣaraṁ kumāryāḥ . . . (*Āpastambagṛhyasūtra*)

Many still prefer a girl's name to end in *dā*. That is, Shubhadā, Priyamvadā, etc. It is stated that a girl's name should not have words denoting the name of a river, constellation (*nakṣatra*), moon, sun or Pūṣan. Gaṅgā, Bhāgīrathī, Yamunā, Narmadā, Kṛṣṇā, Tārā and Śaś, watch out. Female names must also not end in *dattā* (given (by or to)) and *rakṣitā* (protected). Why were women then named as Cārudattā and Tiṣyarakṣitā? Manu has a list of such words which not only should not be made part of a girl's name, but girls with such names should not be chosen as a bride. The naming ceremony is strictly private, and is performed on the tenth or twelfth day after birth: *daśamyāṁ putrasya nāma vidadhyāt* . . .

Outing and food-tasting follow naming in the series of early childhood rituals. Outing basically involves introducing the child to the outside world. The Vedic seers considered the outside world as primarily consisting of nature. Thus, sun, moon, vegetations (*oṣadhi*) or elements encompassing the realm extending from heaven to earth, were all invoked for blessing:

śivās te santv oṣadhayaḥ uttvāhārṣaṁ
adharasyā uttarāṁ pṛthivīṁ abhi /
tatra tva ādityau rakṣatāṁ
sūryyācandramasāv ubhau //

This ritual was performed generally on the twelfth day, or prior to the fourth month, after birth. Parents, or maternal uncle, were supposed to perform it. Food-tasting follows outing in the order of the childhood rituals. The tradition calls *anna* (food) as *prāṇa* (life) for the reason that it sustains life. This ritual was performed in the sixth, eighth, tenth or twelfth month after birth. For girls it was performed in the uneven seventh, ninth or the eleventh month. Normally it was timed after teething and development of the digestive system. Haircutting was normally done in the first or the third year. Girls lost out on this *saṁskāra* early on. There are references where a symbolic haircutting was performed for girls at the time of marriage. Ear-piercing for girls stayed in practice but, toward the beginning of this century, it got completely lost in case of boys. The medicinal literature indicates that ear-piercing also served purposes of warding off some afflictions (*Suśruta-saṁhitā*).

Initiation (*upanayana*), at least in case of the *brāhmaṇa* boys, is still considered as important. Boys, in ancient India, were brought close to the teacher for initiation. The initiation ritual for *brāhmaṇa, kṣatriya* and *vaiśya* boys were ideally performed in the eighth, eleventh and twelfth years after conception (*Manu*, II.36). It was perhaps by the classical period (5th BC) that initiation of girls was altogether abandoned. There are clear references in the *saṁhitās* which attest that girls not only used to be initiated but they also were allowed to wear the thread and girdle (*mekhalā*), and study the Vedas. Initiation symbolized the onset of studies, austere life and celibacy. We find references to many women in the Vedas who were accomplished scholars and seers. The classical period witnessed the codification of restrictions aimed against women.

Marriage perhaps best represents the status of women in rituals. Earlier literatures state that a boy, after completing his studies and with due permission from the teacher, should marry a girl of respectable family. The Vedic period emphasized on performance of *yajñas* (ritual sacrifices). Since a man was not allowed to perform any *yajña* without his wife, marriage became the most important ritual in life (*ayajñiyo vā eṣa yo' patnīkaḥ* (*Śatapatha-brāhmaṇa*)). Performance of *yajña* became the most important purpose of marriage. The next important purpose of marriage was progeny (*santāna*). Sex was considered as the third important purpose of marriage.

> *apatyaṁ dharmakāryāṇi suśruṣā ratir uttamā /*
> *dārādhīnas tathā svargaḥ pitṝṇāṁ ātmanaś ca ha //*

(Offsprings, religious duties, service and best of sex; these thus went under the control of a wife, (for) sure heaven for ancestors and his own self.)

Note that the preceding is the opinion of Manu who, in turn, is regarded as very harsh to women. But even he recognizes that a woman controls the fate of his man as well as of his forefathers, insofar as their residence in heaven is concerned. The *Saṁhitā* period, however, considers birth of sons as the primary purpose of marriage. Progeny, understandably through sexual union, and welfare in life as a householder, were to follow marriage as its natural results. Since the society laid considerable emphasis on control of senses and celibacy, sex was treated as an instrument needed for procreation only. This was the reason why the society considered sexual union with any woman other than one's wife as a sin. This is also the reason why, for purposes of procreation, sexual contact with another man was arranged vide the ritual practice of *niyoga*. An interesting description of types of sons, both produced through sexual union and other instrumentalities of procurement, is related by Pāṇḍu, the father of the Pāṇḍava brothers, to his wife Kuntī (the *Mahābhārata, Ādiparvan*).

I have already mentioned rituals like seeding, sprouting and veil-lifting. Seeding was performed with great austerity for the birth of brave sons. That is why, the newly-weds had to wait for three nights after their wedding for sexual union. Basically, it involved invoking blessings of gods prior to sexual union. Sprouting and veil-lifting were rituals for safe carrying and delivery of the child in the womb. Here again we find that sons were favourites. Marriage is the only ritual where a woman's position is treated as that of one equal to man. *Saptapadī* is one of the famous marriage rituals where pledges are made. The groom at the end of the seventh step calls the bride: *sakhe saptapadā bhava* (O companion, be one who has walked seven steps with me). The tradition considers a walk as little as seven steps with someone establishes friendship. The groom invites the bride to be friends with him. Thus, husband and wife do not become 'man' and 'wife'. Instead, they become friends.

Dharma, artha, kāma and *mokṣa* are considered as fourfold goals of life. A householder strives his best to attain these. *Dharma* is performance of deeds prescribed by the religious codes as duty. Bringing about the birth of offsprings and raising them in accord with the standards of the society was considered as the primary duty of a householder. Giving to the needy was also one of the prescribed duties. Enjoying the pleasures of this world within limits was yet another part of his duty. The pleasures were to be consumed by the householder only to the extent that they, in turn, did not start consuming him. *Mokṣa* was the supreme goal. Husband and wife strived for the best of *dharma, artha* and *kāma* in life. *Mokṣa* has always been more individual and hard to obtain. As a householder, women have been treated well by the Indian society. They had the rights and they asserted their rights. As daughters they did not receive equal treatment. As young girls they were also discriminated against. They did not have as much freedom as the boys had. They were always considered as protectorates and hence did not enjoy full freedom. They did not receive full education and did not have any leading roles in the society. As widows they were miserable. The Vedic society was much more liberal. Women enjoyed more freedom and opportunities in the Vedic society than they did subsequently.

The Legal Status of Women in Ancient India

SUDHA RANI SHRIVASTAVA
Advocate, M.P. High Court
208/2, Garh Phatak, Jabalpur-482 002 (M.P.), India

Introduction

In India there are different views regarding the legal status of women in ancient India. Sarasvati is the goddess of learning, Laxmi is the goddess of wealth and Durga is the goddess of power. In ancient time people believed in this saying.

"यत्र नार्यस्तु पूज्यन्ते रमन्ते तत्र देवता।

(where woman is worshipped, gods stay there.)

But there is a vast gap in theory and practice. A woman's position is not equal to man in society. Though the women of mythology are worshipped up till now, but the legal status of women was not equal to man. Manu says:

"पिता रक्षति कौमार्ये, भर्ता रक्षति यौवने।
पुत्रो रक्षति वार्धक्ये, न स्त्री स्वातन्त्र्यमर्हति।।.

(A woman is not entitled to independence. Her father protects her in her maidenhood, her husband in her youth and the son in her old age.)

Yajnyavalkya says:

रक्षेत कन्यां पिता, निन्नां पतिः, पुत्रास्तु वार्धक्ये।
अभावे ज्ञानयस्तेषां, न स्वातन्त्र्यं क्वचित् स्त्रियाः।।

(A woman is never entitled to independence. Let the father protect her in maidenhood, husband in youth and son in her old age.)

There are many other sayings on this, on the same view, that a woman should not be considered at any stage of her life independent—independent in the sense of any work, whether of household or of property matter. The argument for the view that woman is ever dependent of men in her whole life, is:

"स्त्रियो निरिन्द्रिया अदायादिः।"

(Women are considered as destitute of strength and of a share.)

On one hand people worship goddess Durga who is symbolised as the goddess of strength, and on the other hand the rule-making saint says the above sayings. So the status of woman in ancient India was in a muddled position. In theory the woman is a goddess, and in practice the woman is a dependent. She is aloof from share in property, education and in any other field. Maitreyi and Gargi are some exceptions, but the legal status of a woman was no better in ancient times. Moreover, in society a man could keep many women but a woman could not keep more than one husband. The argument for plurality of wives was that the family lineage was from male and not from female, but there is the story of Satyakama, often used at the time of argument, that why the name of father for identification and not the name of mother? In Chandogya Upanishad there is the story of Jabala the mother of Satyakama:

> Once upon a time Satyakam addressed his mother Jabala: " Mother, I desire to live as a celibate student of sacred knowledge in the teacher's house; so tell me of what lineage I am." The mother replied, "Son, I am a servant of the Ashram, and I am engaged in many works of saints, such as cleaning, washing, cooking etc., meanwhile I have to satisfy the lust of the people of the Ashram. This was the cause of your birth, and I am unable to tell your father's name. However, I am Jabala by name and you are named Satyakam. So you go to Acharya Haridrumta Gautam and say: "I desire to live under you, O revered Sir, as a Brahmacharin. May I approch your venerable self?" For the same Gautam asked him: "Dear boy, of what lineage are you?" Satyakam firmly replied: "Sir, I do not know of what lineage I am. I asked my mother for this. She replied that she was engaged in many works and in attending on others got me in her youth. Having been such, I could not know of what lineage I am. However, I am Jabala's son Satyakam. So, Sir, I am Satyakam Jabala." Gautam said, "No blood other than Brahman can speak thus, dear boy! Bring the sarcificial fuel. I shall initiate you as a Brahmacharin."

This indicates the status of woman as Paricharini (servant). Though this story is often used when there is any talk, conference or workshop on "status of women", yet the hidden manly pride is not explained anywhere that Satyakam was not educated in the Ashram because he was the son of Jabala, but because by his words Gautam could draw the inference that only Brahman blood could speak thus, or, in other words, that Satyakam was out of Brahman lineage. It may also be argued that why Jabala sent Satyakam in Gautam's Ashram. Maybe Satyakam was his son. Anyway, Jabala started a term of mother's name, which may be said to be the lineage from mother's side.

Sources of Hindu Law

According to Yajnyavalkya, Sruti, Smriti and custom are the original sources of Hindu Law:

"श्रुतिः, स्मृतिः, सदाचारः, स्वास्थ्य च प्रियमात्मनः।
सम्यक् संकल्पजः कामो, धर्ममूलम् इदं स्मृतम्।।

(The Sruti, the Smriti, the approved usage, what is agreeable to one's good conscience and desire sprung from due deliberation are the foundations of Dharma.)

The word 'Sruti' is derived from the root 'Sru' meaning 'to hear' and believed to contain the very words of the Deity, meaning what was heard by sages in a revelation by God. This is of supreme authority being given a divine source. The Sruti consists of the four Vedas and the Upanishads dealing chiefly with religion, rites and the means of attaining true knowledge.

Each of these four Vedas consists of two parts: Samhita and Brahman. Samhita is a collection of Mantras in praise of the Almighty and the Brahmans are the theological expositions of the Mantras. Both the Samhita and the Brahmans are supposed to have emanated from tho Divine. Both of them together are called Sruti. From these both the Sutras come into existence.

Smritis

The Sutras of Sruti fall into three classes known as Srut Sutra (श्रुत सूत्र), Grihya Sutra (गृह्य सूत्र) and Dharma Sutra (धर्म सूत्र). Of these the Dharma Sutras alone are to be considered the source of Hindu Law called Smritis. The meaning of 'Smritis' is 'what was remembered'. This can be said to be of human origin, and is believed to be the recollection of sages handed down to their students and thus hand to hand exists up till now. Smritis have two parts: primary Smritis and secondary Smritis. The primary Smritis are classified into two parts: Sutras (सूत्र) and Dharmashastra (धर्मशास्त्र). Manu, Gautam, Bodhayan, Apastamba, Vashishth, Vishnu, etc. are the chief Sutra writers of Dharmashastras. Of these Manu is the paramount authority on secular law and flourished about 200 B.C. It can be said that these Dharmshastra Sutras are the root of law in society. The word Dharma is generally rendered into Law and includes all kinds of rules, religious, moral, legal, physical, metaphysical or scientific, in the same way as law does in its widest sense. 'Dhri' (धृ) is the root of Dharmashastra which means 'to hold', support or maintain, and it means the law or duty which is essential to govern the society's protection to human life. But the word Dharmashastra is often used to designate the Smritis alone with a view to make their practical importance. Manu says:

ऋतुस्तु वेदो विक्षेयो धर्मशास्त्रन्तु वै स्मृतिः।

(Vedas are known by Sruti, and Dharmshastra is known by Smriti).

Custom

Customs are of very great importance, being the rules by which the people are actually guided in practice. It can be said that the customary laws even overriding the Smritis were accepted. These customs indicate rules of conduct. In other words, such customs are presumed to be based on unrecorded revelations. Manu and Yajnyavalkya declare good conduct (सदाचार) which means approved custom or usage to be evidence of Law. Some of the other sages use the word शिष्टाचार meaning the way of behaviour. Antiquity, certainty, reasoning and continuity are the essentials of custom.

The word 'family' is the outcome of the customary law.

Woman as Defined in Law

After attaining maidenhood, a girl is donated to her bridegroom. In ancient times marriage involved the idea of transfer of dominion over the damsel, from the father to the husband. Slavery, or the proprietary right of man over woman, was a recognised institution among all ancient nations, and it appears to have owed its origin to the father's dominion and unlimited power over his child. The status of a daughter in ancient India was only as an item of property, which by Kanyadan he donated to another man for his services. Kanyadan was much better, and still remains, but the ancient father had the customary right to sell, gift or otherwise alienate her like any other property.

पिता दध्यात् स्वयं कन्या। (नारद)

So, a gap between theory and practice continues up till now. On one hand woman is a goddess and on the other hand she is a sheer part of property. Woman as defined in the Dharmashastras as a mother, wife (*patni*), daughter, sister, aunt, etc. These are her family relations; but apart from these family relations woman's union with man is defined as a wanton woman (*swairini*), a prostitute (*veshya*), a deserted woman (*nishkasini*), a keep of man (*bhujishya*), a servant (*dasi* or *paricharini*) and after the death of husband, widow etc. In every way an ancient woman had to serve man, she had no separate status, she was known by the name of her father or husband only.

Status of Woman as Goddess

As it is said above there is a vast gap between theory and practice. Woman was a goddess in theory and a slave in practice. All Dharmashastras keep woman inferior to man. The contrasting views are given below:

या देवी सर्वभूतेषु शक्तिरूपेण संस्थिता।
नमस्तस्यै नमस्तस्यै नमस्तस्यै नमो नमः।।

(O goddess! You exist in every creature as a strength. So I bow to you, I bow to you, I bow to you.)

Durga is called the goddess of strength and power but the Dharmshastra says that:

"स्त्रियो निरिन्द्रिया अदायादि:।"

(Women are considered as destitute of strength and of a share.)

In theory a goddess protects creatures while a woman is protected by father in childhood, by husband in youth and by son in old age. Though Saraswati is the goddess of art and knowledge, Luxmi of wealth and Durga of strength, yet the woman as a creature has no independent status either in society or in the legal sphere.

Vedic Culture

The word Hindu is the indication of a culture which is Vedic culture which means a culture derived from the Vedas and the Upanishads. According to Indians the Vedas are not the work of any human being; they are an eternal creation. In a historical way it can be said that sages after thinking for generations wrote the Vedas and the Upanishads. They are not the work of a single person. This mass of sacred literature is divided into two parts: Karmakand and Gyanakand. Karmakand is the work portion and Gyanakand is the knowledge portion. The work portion consists of ceremonials like sacrifices. The Gyanakand or the spiritual portion comprises the Upanishads, also called the Vedantas.

The literal meaning of Vedanta is the gist, the essence of life in its social sense. That means the human life is not only for self-benefit, but sacrificiation for others forms the concept of society. In Geeta Bhagawan Krishna says:

यो मां पश्यति सर्वत्र सर्वं च मदीय पश्यति।
तस्यामहं न प्रणश्यामि स च मे न प्रणश्यति।।

This feeling of fraternity is the essence of Vedic culture.

Man and woman are the pivot of society—woman is mother, wife, sister and daughter. The mother is an ideal of Indian womanhood because she gives birth to man. This is also fascinating that nature made woman less in strength, but still she gives birth to a strong man. She keeps this strong man in her womb for nine long months. That's why the status of mother is very high not only in anciet India but today also. There is a sloka in Durga Saptapadi:

या देवी सर्वभूतेषु शक्तिरूपेण संस्थिता।
नमस्तस्यै नमस्तस्यै नमस्तस्यै नमो नम:।।

(O goddess! You exist as a mother in every creature. So I bow to you, I bow to you, I bow to you.)

Motherhood is the ideal of Indian womanhood. According to Vivekanand, "The word 'woman' calls up the idea of mother to the Indian mind. And even God is conceived of from the mother. All religions like Islam, Christianity, Yahudi etc. recognize and honour the mother."

After the mother there is the place of wife, sister and daughter. The Dharmshastras speak about the duty of a man towards the mother, towards the sister, towards the daughter, towards the wife or widow of elder or younger brother or son; yet the control over the property and the person of the woman was in man's hand. As it is said:

न स्त्री स्वातन्त्र्यमर्हति।

(A woman is not entitled to independence.)

Comparative Position of Ancient and Modern Women in India

As has been said above, Sruti, Smriti and custom play an important role in governing Indian society. It may be said that the governing agency of society were the Dharmashastras. Social good was called Punya (virtue) and wrong was called Pap (sin). These were the two wheels towards progress. There was a vast difference between what is Punya for woman and for man, or what is Pap for woman and for man. A man could marry as he liked, but the woman was not free for remarriage. If her husband died in early age, there were only two options for her: either she could adopt the path of Sati or serve her parents or in-laws all her life without enjoying the worldly charms. As far as the Hindu Law concerns, before the British empire, Hindus were governed by these Dharmshastras. Before 1774 there were Hindu and Muslim Laws in Indian courts. The British judges had to face difficulty to decide the cases of Hindus and Muslims, so by the help of Pandits and Mullas they codified the law. It was also difficult to decide who is Hindu? For that in Hindu Law, Hindus had been defined first. This legislature was based on Srutis, Smritis and custom, as explained in the above paragraphs. The situation of women was no better in this Hindu Law. There were many restrictions for woman, such as:

(a) No absolute property right to woman.
(b) She could not remarry.
(c) She could not divorce her husband.
(d) She could not get the custody of her child.
(e) She could not express her opinion as she was dependent for whole life, and so on . . .

Marriage and sonship constitute some of the unique chapters in the literature of ancient Hindu Law. As early as the time of the Rigveda marriage had assumed the sacred character of a sacrament and the sanction of religion had heightened the character and importance of the institution of marriage. The Rigveda pronounces some impressive texts, that after completing the seventh step of Saptapadi the bridegroom says: "With these seven steps we have become friends." The basic thought was that marriage was a prime necessity, for that alone could enable a person to discharge properly his religious and secular obligations. Hindu marriage is a sacred thing in religion. It is not a contract. This belief still exists in India. There are 8 forms of marriages recognized in ancient times, i.e., (1) Brahma, (2) Daiva, (3) Arsha, (4) Prajapatya, (5) Asura, (6) Gandharva, (7) Rakshasa, and (8) Paishacha. The first four are the approved forms of marriage and the last four are unapproved. The Hindu Marriage Law prior to the Hindu Code Bill 1955 gives the following reliefs:

(a) *Decree of nullity of marriage*: That means any void marriage or minor marriage is not approved in Law.

This still exists.

(b) *Decree for divorce*: In the prior Law only the husband could file a case for divorce on specific grounds but after the passing of the Hindu Code Bill in 1955 the Hindu Marriage Act 1955 came into force and the wife could also file a case for the relief of divorce on some specific grounds.

This is a major change in Hindu Law. The ancient wife had no right to seek divorce, and her whole life she had to suffer cruelty, adultery, desertion and the uncurable diseases etc. of her husband. Now she can take divorce on these grounds

(c) *Legitimacy of illegitimate child*: In the old law a child born out of void or voidable marriage was called illegitimate child, who had no right in his father's property, but according to the Hindu Code Bill a child born out of void or voidable marriage can be declared by law a legitimate one, and gets all the rights in the paternal property.

These were some of the major changes in the Hindu Marriage Act. In property also, prior to the Hindu Code Bill, the daughter and widow had no succession rights like her brothers and her own male children. Though a female has still no coparcenary rights in ancestral property, yet she now has survivorship rights in her father and husband's self-acquired property.

CONCLUSION

Change is an essential element of nature. The situation in the Vedic age was something else and now something else. Even then the position of women is not as much better as the need of the era. The Constitution of India has provided many facilities to Indian women. There is a special provision in Article 15(3) of the Constitution of India, which empowers the States to make laws for the welfare of women and children.

The root of dual policy is very deep in India. From ancient times a woman's needs have had a secondary importance. Even now the woman cannot enjoy even her own earning without the permission of her husband or father. One good thing towards progress is that now women are working in every field and they are in a much better position to snatch their rights from the dominating male. A woman knows where she needs legal protection and how she can amend the law. Thus the legal position or status of the modern Indian woman is much better than that of the ancient women.

Science in the Vedic Age

SUBHASH C. KAK
Department of Electrical and Computer Engineering
Louisiana State University
Baton Rouge, LA 70803-5901, USA

This paper reviews our current understanding of the contributions to science in the Vedic times. In particular, the physical sciences, mathematics, astronomy and the science of the mind are examined.

'Veda' means knowledge. Since we call our earliest period Vedic, this is suggestive of the importance of knowledge and science, as a means of acquiring that knowledge, to that period of Indian history. For quite some time scholars believed that this knowledge amounted to no more than speculations regarding the self; this is what we are still told in some schoolbook accounts. New insights in archaeology, astronomy, history of science and Vedic scholarship have shown that such a view is wrong. We now know that Vedic knowledge embraced physics, mathematics, astronomy, logic, cognition and other disciplines. We find that Vedic science is the earliest science that has come down to us. This has significant implications in our understanding of the history of ideas and the evolution of early civilizations.

Reconstructions of our earliest science are based not only on the Vedas but also on their appendicies called the Vedangas. The six Vedangas deal with: *kalpa*, performance of ritual with its basis of geometry, mathematics and calendrics; *shiksha*, phonetics; *chhandas*, metrical structures; *nirukta*, etymology; *vyakarana*, grammar; and *jyotisha*, astronomy and other cyclical phenomena. Then there are naturalistic descriptions in the various Vedic books that tell us a lot about scientific ideas of those times.

Vedic World View

Briefly, the Vedic texts present a tripartite and recursive world view. The universe is viewed as three regions of earth, space, and sky with the corresponding entities of Vishve Devah (all gods), Indra, and Agni. Counting separately the joining regions leads to a total of five categories where, as we see in Fig. 1, water separates earth and fire, and air separates fire and ether.

In Vedic ritual the three regions are assigned different fire altars. Furthermore, the five categories are represented in terms of altars of five layers. The great altars

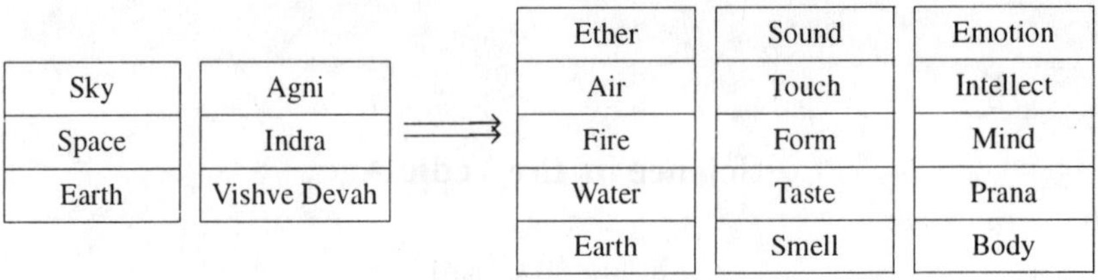

Fig. 1. From the tripartite model to five categories of analysis

were built of a thousand bricks to a variety of dimensions. The discovery that the details of the altar constructions code astronomical knowledge is a fascinating chapter in the history of astronomy (Kak 1994a; 1995a,b).

In the Vedic world view, the processes in the sky, on earth, and within the mind are taken to be connected.

The Vedic rishis were aware that all descriptions of the universe lead to logical paradox. The one category transcending all oppositions was termed brahman. Understanding the nature of consciousness was of paramount importance in this view but this did not mean that other sciences were ignored. Vedic ritual was a symbolic retelling of this world view.

Chronology

To place Vedic science in context it is necessary to have a proper understanding of the chronology of the Vedic literature. There are astronomical references in the Vedas which recall events in the third or the fourth millennium B.C. and earlier. The recent discovery (e.g. Feuerstein 1995) that Sarasvati, the preeminent river of the Rigvedic times, went dry around 1900 B.C. due to tectonic upheavels implies that the Rigveda is to be dated prior to this epoch, perhaps prior to 2000 B.C. since the literature that immediately followed the Rigveda does not speak of any geological catastrophe. But we cannot be very precise about our estimates. There exist traditional accounts in the Puranas that assign greater antiquity to the Rigveda: for example, the Kaliyuga tradition speaks of 3100 B.C. and the Varāhamihira tradition mentions 2400 B.C. According to Henri-Paul Francfort (1992) of the Indo-French team that surveyed this area, the Sarasvati river had ceased to be a perennial river by the third millennium B.C.; this supports those who argue for the older dates. But in the absence of conclusive evidence, it is prudent to take the most conservative of these dates, namely 2000 B.C. as the latest period to be associated with the Rigveda.

The textbook accounts of the past century or so were based on the now disproven supposition that the Rigveda is to be dated to about 1500–1000 B.C. and, therefore, the question of the dates assigned to the Brahmanas, Sutras and other literature remains open. The detailed chronology of the literature that followed Rigveda has not yet been worked out. A chronology of this literature was attempted based solely on the internal astronomical evidence in the important book "Ancient Indian Chronology" by the historian of science P.C. Sengupta in 1947. Although Sengupta's dates have the virtue of inner consistency, they have neither been examined carefully by other scholars nor checked against archaeological evidence.

This means that we can only speak in the most generalities regarding the chronology of the texts: assign Rigveda to the third millennium B.C. and earlier and the Brahmanas to the second millennium. This also implies that the archaeological finds of the Indus-Sarasvati period, which are coeval with Rigveda literature, can be used to cross-check textual evidence.

No comprehensive studies of ancient Indian science exist. The textbook accounts like the one to be found in Basham's "The Wonder that was India" are hopelessly out of date. But there are some excellent surveys of selected material. The task of putting it all together into a comprehensive whole will be a major task for historians of science.

This essay presents an assortment of topics from ancient Indian science. We begin with an outline of the models used in the Vedic cognitive science; these models parallel those used in ancient Indian physics. We also review mathematics, astronomy, grammar, logic and medicine.

1. Vedic cognitive science

The Rigveda speaks of cosmic order. It is assumed that there exist equivalences of various kinds between the outer and the inner worlds. It is these connections that make it possible for our minds to comprehend the universe. It is noteworthy that the analytical methods are used both in the examination of the outer world as well as the inner world. This allowed the Vedic rishis to place in sharp focus paradoxical aspects of analytical knowledge. Such paradoxes have become only too familiar to the contemporary scientist in all branches of inquiry (Kak 1986).

In the Vedic view, the complementary nature of the mind and the outer world, is of fundamental significance. Knowledge is classified in two ways: the lower or dual; and the higher or unified. What this means is that knowledge is superficially dual and paradoxical but at a deeper level it has a unity. The Vedic view claims that the material and the conscious are aspects of the same transcendental reality.

The idea of complementarity was at the basis of the systematization of Indian philosophic traditions as well, so that complementary approaches were paired together. We have the groups of: logic (*nyaya*) and physics (*vaisheshika*), cosmology (*sankhya*) and psychology (*yoga*), and language (*mimamsa*) and reality (*vedanta*). Although these philosophical schools were formalized in the post-Vedic age, we find an echo of these ideas in the Vedic texts.

In the Rigveda there is reference to the yoking of the horses to the chariot of Indra, Ashvins, or Agni; and we are told elsewhere that these gods represent the essential mind. The same metaphor of the chariot for a person is encountered in Katha Upanishad and the Bhagavad Gita; this chariot is pulled in different directions by the horses, representing senses. which are yoked to it. The mind is the driver who holds the reins to these horses; but next to the mind sits the true observer, the self, who represents a universal unity. Without this self no coherent behaviour is possible.

The Five Levels

In the Taittiriya Upanishad, the individual is represented in terms of five different sheaths or levels that enclose the individual's self. These levels, shown in an ascending order, are:

- The physical body (*annamaya kosha*)
- Energy sheath (*pranamaya kosha*)
- Mental sheath (*manomaya kosha*)
- Intellect sheath (*vijnanamaya kosha*)
- Emotion sheath (*anandamaya kosha*)

These sheaths are defined at increasingly finer levels. At the highest level, above the emotion sheath, is the self. It is significant that emotion is placed higher than the intellect. This is a recognition of the fact that eventually meaning is communicated by associations which are influenced by the emotional state.

The energy that underlies physical and mental processes is called prana. One may look at an individual in three different levels. At the lowest level is the physical body, at the next higher level is the energy systems at work, and at the next higher level are the thoughts. Since the three levels are interrelated, the energy situation may be changed by inputs either at the physical level or at the mental level. When the energy state is agitated and restless, it is characterized by *rajas*; when it is dull and lethargic, it is characterized by *tamas*; the state of equilibrium and balance is termed *sattva*.

The key notion is that each higher level represents characteristics that are emergent on the ground of the previous level. In this theory mind is an emergent entity, but this emergence requires the presence of the self.

The Structure of the Mind

The Sankhya system takes the mind as consisting of five components: *manas, ahankara, chitta, buddhi,* and *atman*. Again these categories parallel those of Fig. 1.

Manas is the lower mind which collects sense impressions. Its perceptions shift from moment to moment. This sensory-motor mind obtains its inputs from the senses of hearing, touch, sight, taste, and smell. Each of these senses may be taken to be governed by a separate agent.

Ahankara is the sense of I-ness that associates some perceptions to a subjective and personal experience. Once sensory impressions have been related to I-ness by *ahankara*, their evaluation and resulting decisions are arrived at by *buddhi*, the intellect. *Manas*, *ahankara* and *buddhi* are collectively called the internal instruments of the mind.

Next we come to *chitta*, which is the memory bank of the mind. These memories constitute the foundation on which the rest of the mind operates. But *chitta* is not merely a passive instrument. The organization of the new impressions throws up instinctual or primitive urges which creates different emotional states.

This mental complex surrounds the innermost aspect of consciousness which is called *atman*, the self, *brahman*, or *jiva*. *Atman* is considered to be beyond a finite enumeration of categories.

All this amounts to a brilliant analysis of the individual. The traditions of *yoga* and *tantra* have been based on such analysis. No wonder, this model has continued to inspire people around the world to this day.

2. *Mathematical and physical sciences*

Here we review some new findings related to the early period of Indian science which show that the outer world was not ignored at the expense of the inner.

Geometry and mathematics

Seidenberg, by examining the evidence in the *Shatapatha Brahmana*, showed that Indian geometry predates Greek geometry by centuries. Seidenberg argues that the birth of geometry and mathematics had a ritual origin. For example, the earth was represented by a circular altar and the heavens were represented by a square altar and the ritual consisted of converting the circle into a square of an identical area. There we see the beginnings of geometry! In his famous paper on the origin of mathematics, Seidenberg (1978) concluded: "Old-Babylonia [1700 BC] got the theorem of Pythagoras from India or that both Old-Babylonia and India got it from a third source. Now the Sanskrit scholars do not give me a date so far back as 1700 B.C. Therefore I *postulate* a pre-Old-Babylonian (i.e., pre-1700 B.C.) source of the kind of geometric rituals we see preserved in the Sulvasutras, or at least for the *mathematics* involved in these rituals." That was before archaeological finds disproved the earlier assumption of a break in Indian civilization in the second millennium B.C.; it was this assumption of the Sanskritists that led Seidenberg to postulate a third earlier source. Now with our new knowledge, Seidenberg's conclusion of India being the source of the geometric and mathematical knowledge of the ancient world fits in with the new chronology of the texts.

Astronomy

Using hitherto neglected texts related to ritual and the Vedic indices, an astronomy of the third millennium B.C. has been discovered (Kak 1994a; 1995a,b). Here the altars symbolized different parts of the year. In one ritual, pebbles were placed around the altars for the earth, the atmosphere, and the sky. The number of these pebbles were 21, 78, and 261, respectively. These numbers add up to the 360 days of the year. There were other features related to the design of the altars which suggested that the ritualists were aware that the length of the year was between 365 and 366 days.

The organization of the Vedic books was also according to an astronomical code. To give just one simple example, the total number of verses in all the Vedas is 20,358 which equals 261×78, a product of the sky and atmosphere numbers! The Vedic ritual followed the seasons hence the importance of astronomy.

The second millennium text *Vedanga Jyotisha* went beyond the earlier calendrical astronomy to develop a theory for the mean motions of the sun and the moon. This marked the beginnings of the application of mathematics to the motions of the heavenly bodies.

Planetary knowledge

The Vedic planetary model is given in Fig. 2. The sun was taken to be midway in the skies. A considerable amount of Vedic mythology regarding the struggle between the demons and the gods is a metaphorical retelling of the motions of Venus and Mars (Frawley 1994). The famous myth of Vishnu's three strides measuring the universe becomes intelligible when we note that early texts equate Vishnu and Mercury. The myth appears to celebrate the first measurement of the period of Mercury (Kak 1996a) since three periods equals the number assigned in altar ritual to the heavens. Other arguments suggest that the Vedic people knew the periods of the five classical planets.

Writing

Cryptological analysis has revealed that the Brahmi script of the Mauryan times evolved out of the third millennium Sarasvati (Indus) script. The Sarasvati script was perhaps the first true alphabetic script. The worship of Sarasvati as the goddess of learning remembers the development of writing on the banks of the Sarasvati river. It also appears that the symbol for zero was derived from the fish sign that stood for "ten" in Brahmi and this occurred around 50 B.C.–50 C.E. (Kak 1994b).

Binary numbers

Barend van Nooten (1993) has shown that binary numbers were known at the

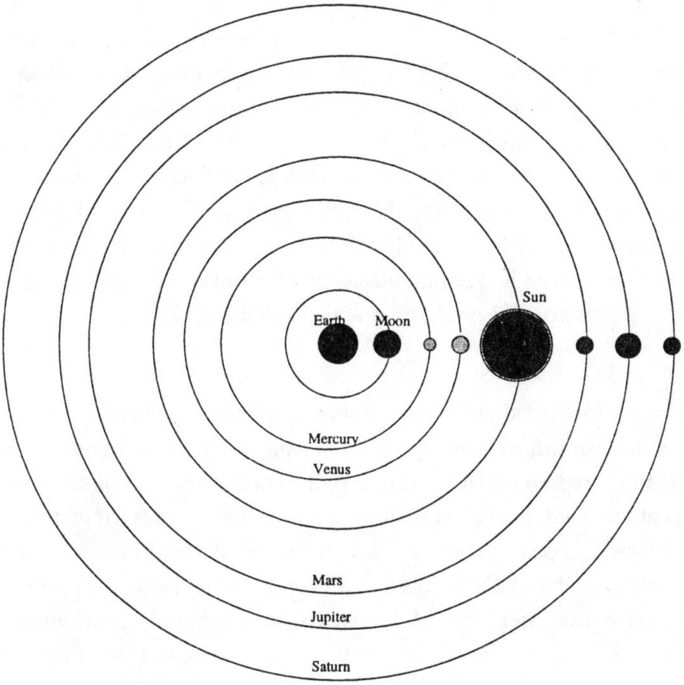

Fig. 2. The Vedic planetary model

time of Pingala's *Chhandahshastra*. Pingala, who lived around the early first century B.C., used binary numbers to classify Vedic meters. The knowledge of binary numbers indicates a deep understanding of arithmetic. A binary representation requires the use of only two symbols, rather than the ten required in the usual decimal representation, and it has now become the basis of information storage in terms of sequences of 0s and 1s in modern-day computers.

Music

Ernest McClain (1978) has described the tonal basis of early myth. McClain argues that the connections between music and myth are even deeper than astronomy and myth. The invariances at the basis of tones could very well have served as the ideal for the development of the earliest astronomy. The tonal invariances of music may have suggested the search of similar invariances in the heavenly phenomena.

The Samaveda, where the hymns were supposed to be sung, was compared to the sky. Apparently, this comparison was to emphasize the musical basis of astronomy. The Vedic hymns are according to a variety of meters; but what purpose, if any, lay behind a specific choice is unknown.

Grammar

Panini's grammar (6th century B.C. or earlier) provides 4,000 rules that describe the sanskrit of his day completely. This grammar is acknowledged to be one of the greatest intellectual achievements of all time. The great variety of language mirrors, in many ways, the complexity of nature. What is remarkable is that Panini set out to describe the entire grammar in terms of a *finite* number of rules. Frits Staal (1988) has shown that the grammar of Panini represents a universal grammatical and computing system. From this perspective it anticipates the logical framework of modern computers (Kak 1987).

Medicine

There is a close parallel between Indian and Greek medicine. For example, the idea of breath (*prana* in Sanskrit, and *pneuma* in Greek) is central to both. Jean Filliozat (1970) has argued that the idea of the correct association between the three elements of the wind, the gall, and the phlegm, which was described first by Plato in Greek medicine, appears to be derived from the earlier *tridosha* theory of Ayurveda. Filliozat suggests that the transmission occurred via the Persian empire.

These discoveries not only call for a revision of the textbook accounts of Indian science but also call for new research to assess the impact on other civilizations of these ideas.

3. *Rhythms of life*

We have spoken before of how the Vedas speak of the connections between the external and the internal worlds. The hymns speak often of the stars and the planets. These are sometimes the luminaries in the sky, or those in the firmament of our inner landscapes or both.

To the question on how can the motions of an object, millions of miles away, have any influence on the life of a human being one can only say that the universe is interconnected. In this ecological perspective the physical planets do not influence the individual directly. Rather, the intricate clockwork of the universe runs on forces that are reflected in the periodicities of the astral bodies as also the cycles of behaviors of all terrestrial beings and plants.

It is not the gravitational pull of the planet that causes a certain response, but an internal clock governed by the genes. We know this because in some mutant organisms the internal clock works according to periods that have no apparent astronomical basis. So these cycles can be considered to be a manifestation of the motions of the body's inner "planets." In the language of evolution theory one would argue that these periods get reflected in the genetic inheritance of the biological system as a result of the advantage over millions of years that they must have provided for survival.

The most fundamental rhythms are matched to the periods of the sun or the moon. It is reasonable to assume that with their emphasis on time bound rituals and the calendar, the ancients had discovered many of the biological periods. This would include the 24-hour-50-minute circadian rhythm, the connection of the menstrual cycle with the motions of the moon, the life cycles of various plants, and the semimonthly estrus cycle of sheep, the three-week cycles of cattle and pigs, and the six-month cycle of dogs.

The moon (*Soma*) is called the "lord of speech" (*Vachaspati*) in the Rigveda. It is also taken to awaken eager thoughts. Other many references suggest that in the Rigvedic times the moon was taken to be connected with the mind.

This is stated most directly in the famous *Purushasukta*, the Cosmic Man hymn, of the Rigveda where it is stated that the mind is born of the moon and in *Shatapatha Brahmana* where we have "the mind is the moon." Considering the fact that the relationships between the astronomical and the terrestrial were taken in terms of periodicities, doubtless, this slogan indicates that the mind is governed by the period of the moon.

Fire, having become speech, entered the mouth
Air, becoming scent, entered the nostrils
The sun, becoming sight, entered the eyes
The regions becoming hearing, entered the ears
The plants, becoming hairs, entered the skin
The moon, having become mind, entered the heart.
Aitareya Aranyaka, 2.4.2.4

This verse from the Upanishadic period speaks at many levels. At the literal level there is an association of the elements with various cognitive centers. At another level, the verse connects the time evolution of the external object to the cognitive center.

Fire represents consciousness and this ebbs and flows with a daily rhythm. Air represents seasons so here the rhythm is longer. The sun and sight have a 24-hour cycle. The regions denote other motions in the skies so hearing manifests cycles that are connected to the planets. The plants have daily and annual periods; the hairs of the body have an annual period. The mind has a period of 24 hours and 50 minutes like that of the moon.

What are the seats of these cycles? According to tantra the chakras of the body are the centers of the different elements as well as cognitive capacities and rhythms related to "internal planets." The knowledge of these rhythms appears to have led to astrology.

4. Cosmology

We have seen how the logical apparatus that was brought to bear on the outer world was applied to the analysis of the mind. But the question remains: How does inanimate matter come to have awareness? This metaphysical question was answered by postulating entities for smell, taste, form, touch, and sound as in Fig. 1. In the Sankhya system, a total of twenty-four such categories are assumed. These categories are supposed to emerge at the end of a long chain of evolution and they may be considered to be material. The breath of life into the instruments of sight, touch, hearing and so on is provided by the twenty-fifth category, which is *purusha*, the soul.

The recursive Vedic world-view requires that the universe itself go through cycles of creation and destruction. This view became a part of the astronomical framework and ultimately very long cycles of billions of years were assumed. The *Sankhya* evolution takes the life forms to evolve into an increasingly complex system until the end of the cycle.

The categories of *Sankhya* operate at the level of the individual as well. Life mirrors the entire creation cycle and cognition mirrors a life-history. Surprisingly similar are the modern slogan: ontogeny is phylogeny, and microgeny (the cognitive process) is a speeded-up ontogeny (Brown 1994).

5. *Concluding Remarks*

We are in the midst of a paradigm shift in our understanding of Vedic science and cosmology. We now know that measurement astronomy is to be dated to at least the third millennium B.C. which is more than a thousand years earlier than was believed only a decade ago; and mathematics and geometry date to at least the beginning of the second millennium B.C. Indian mythology is being interpreted in terms of its underlying astronomy or/and cognitive science. We find that many Indians dates are much earlier than the corresponding dates elsewhere. What does it all mean for our understanding of the Indian civilization and its interactions with Mesopotamia, Egypt, China and Greece? Was Indian knowledge carried to the other nations or do we have a case here for independent discovery in different places?

Contemporary science has begun to examine Vedic theories on the nature of the "self" and see if they might be of value in the search for a science of consciousness (e.g. Kak 1996b). Man has mastered the outer world and Vedic science formed the basis for that enterprise; it is now possible that the exploration of the inner world, which is the heart of modern science, will also be along paths long heralded by Vedic *rishis*.

References

J.W. Brown, "Morphogenesis and mental process", *Development and Psychopathology*, **6**, 1994, 551–563.

G. Feuerstein, S. Kak and D. Frawley, *In Search of the Cradle of Civilization*, Quest Books, Wheaton, 1995.

J. Filliozat, "The expansion of Indian medicine abroad", in: Lokesh Chandra (Ed.), *India's Contributions to World Thought and Culture*, Vivekananda Memorial Committee, Madras, 1970, pp. 67–70.

H.-P. Francfort, "Evidence for Harappan irrigation system in Haryana and Rajasthan", *Eastern Anthropologist*, **45,** 1992, 87–103.

D. Frawley, "Planets in the Vedic literature", *Indian Journal of History of Science*, **29**, 1994, 495–506.

S. Kak, *The Nature of Physical Reality*, Peter Lang, New York, 1986.

______, "The Paninian approach to natural language processing", *Intl. Journal of Approximate Reasoning*, **1**, 1987, 117–130.

______, *The Astronomical Code of the Rgveda*, Aditya, New Delhi,1994a.

______, "The evolution of writing in India", *Indian Journal of History of Science*, **28**, 1994b, 375–88.

______, "The astronomy of the age of geometric altars", *Quarterly Journal of the Royal Astronomical Society*, **36**,1995a, 385–396..

______, "From Vedic science to Vedānta", *The Adyar Library Bulletin*, 59, 1995b, 1–36.

______, "Knowledge of planets in the third millennium B.C.", *Quarterly Journal of the Royal Astronomical Society*, **37**, 1996a, 709–715.

______, "Reflections in clouded mirrors: selfhood in animals and machines", in: K.H. Pribram and J. King (Eds.), *Learning as Self-Organization*, Lawrence Erlbaum, NJ, Mahwah, 1996b.

E.G. McClain, *The Myth of Invariance*, Shambhala, Boulder, 1978.

A. Seidenberg, "The origin of mathematics", *Archive for History of Exact Sciences*, **18**, 1978, 301–342.

P.C. Sengupta, *Ancient Indian Chronology*, University of Calcutta Press, Calcutta, 1947.

F. Staal, *Universals*, University of Chicago Press, Chicago, 1988.

B. van Nooten, "Binary numbers in Indian antiquity", *Journal of Indian Philosophy*, **21**, 1993, 31–50.

Tough Steel of Ancient India

NARAYAN R. JOSHI
Department of Civil Engineering
Prairie View A & M University
Texas A & M University System, Prairie View , Texas 77446

The role of iron and steel in the development of human civilization from 500 BC till this day is indisputable. The applications of low carbon steels are numerous. Those of ultra-high carbon steels, however, are less common. The ultra-high carbon steels have interesting history because of their use in making the famous swords in middle ages. Although the swords were hammered in many towns of Asia, steel bars were imported from India. High carbon content makes steel brittle. The ancient Indian steel had high carbon content but it was not brittle. On the contrary it was tough. For that reason Indian swords never broke in wars while European swords used to bend and break. The secret of this special steel resided in the proper thermo-mechanical heat treatment. This research paper will present the technical details of this ancient art using the modern discipline of Materials Science.

Introduction

In the middle ages, Damascus swords were famous throughout the Islamic world. The blades of these swords were exceptionally strong in compression. They were hard yet tough enough to absorb blows in combat without breaking. They owed their superb mechanical properties as well as their wavy surface markings (the legendary Damask) to the material from which they were forged—Damascus Steel. The name Damascus Steel, however, is misleading because the steel was actually produced in India. It was traded in the form of castings or cakes from which sword blades were forged in Persia and Syria. Steel is an alloy of iron and carbon with the percentage of carbon ranging from 0.2 to 2.0. Figure 1 shows the standard Iron-Carbon thermodynamic phase equilibrium diagram. The diagram delineates various phases of steel at different carbon content and temperatures. Although the applications of the low and medium carbon steels (carbon less than 0.4 per cent) are numerous, those of ultra-high carbon steels (carbon between 1 to 2.1 per cent) are less common. This is so because the increased carbon content in the steel, though increases its strength, makes steel less ductile and more brittle. Damascus steels were actually ultra-high carbon steels. Yet they were not brittle but were the opposite of brittle. They were tough!

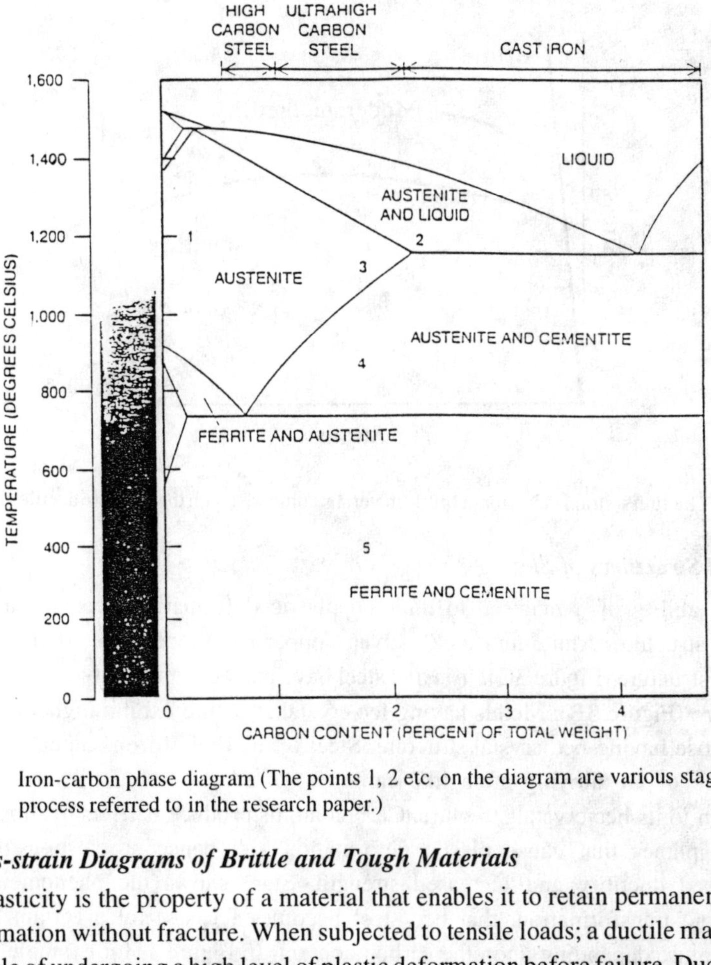

Fig. 1. Iron-carbon phase diagram (The points 1, 2 etc. on the diagram are various stages in the process referred to in the research paper.)

Stress-strain Diagrams of Brittle and Tough Materials

Plasticity is the property of a material that enables it to retain permanent set or deformation without fracture. When subjected to tensile loads; a ductile material is capable of undergoing a high level of plastic deformation before failure. Ductility is a property that allows the material to undergo change of form without breaking. Gold, silver, aluminum, copper, wrought iron are examples of materials having good ductility. These materials exhibit a large amount of plastic deformation before failure (Figure 2). Ceramic material like a brick does not undergo much plastic deformation after the elastic region (Figure 2). It is a brittle material. Toughness represents the ability of a material to support loads even after yielding or forming cracks. Toughness is also defined as the ability of the material to absorb energy without falling apart. For most materials the toughness is measured as the area under the stress-strain diagram. An increase in toughness relates to an increase in the amount of energy needed to produce a specified damage condition. Figure 2 shows three stress-strain curves of a brittle, moderately ductile and highly ductile materials.

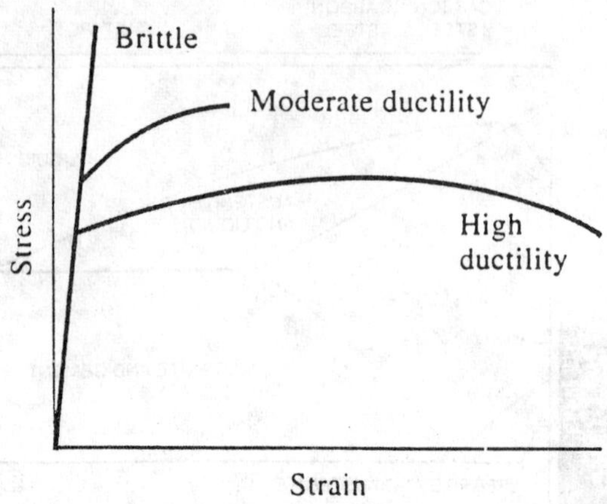

Fig. 2. The stress-strain behavior of brittle materials compared with that of more ductile materials

Crystal Structures of Steel

The ability of a material to undergo plastic deformation depends upon its crystal structure. Aluminum, gold, silver, copper have face-centered cubic (fcc) crystal structure (Figure 3C). Iron and steel have body centered cubic (bcc) crystal structure (Figure 3B). Metals having fcc crystal structure exhibit higher ductility than those having bcc crystal structure. Steel is an alloy of iron and carbon. The presence of an alloying atom like carbon also affects the ductility of iron in addition to its bcc crystal structure. Carbon atoms produce barriers to slipping of crystal planes that cause plastic deformation and hence are responsible for decreased ductility and increased strength. Steel shows the phenomenon of allotropic transformation, that bcc steel becomes fcc steel at a certain higher temperature depending upon the carbon content. In Figure 1, for example, at the carbon content of 0.77 per cent and at the temperature 727°C, the crystal structure changes from bcc to fcc with increasing temperature.

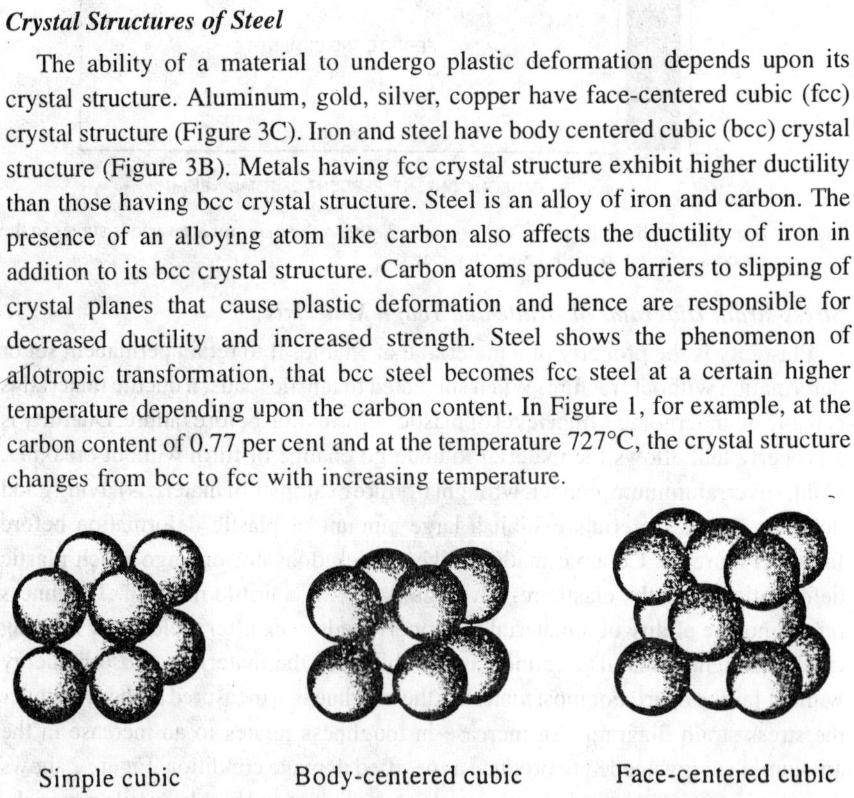

Fig. 3. The models of crystal structures: (A) Simple cubic, (B) Body-centred cubic, (C) Face-centred cubic

Secret of Damascus Steels

At Stanford University, Dr. Sherby and Dr. Wadsworth [1, 2] produced samples of the ultra-high carbon steels that, like Damascus Steels, are strong and ductile at the same time at ambient temperatures. They followed the procedure in their laboratory similar to that followed in the smithies (Houses of Ghisadi people) of India, Persia and Syria. The study of Damascus swords with surface markings called Damask indicated that the pattern became visible only after the finished blade was polished and etched with an acid that preferentially attacked the iron background. The whitish areas in the alternate layer pattern were of iron carbide or cementite and the dark background was iron containing considerably less carbon. It was found that Damascus blades were toughened by forging which dispersed the coarse cementite network around the large grains of austenite formed during slow equilibrium cooling. The spheroidal carbide particles produced as a result of breaking of the continuous cementite network still served the function of strengthening the steel, but because they no longer formed a continuous network, the metal was not brittle.

Forging and Hardening Operations

When wrought iron and charcoal were heated to 1200°C (the point I in Figure 1) in a crucible, the iron converted into fcc austenite. Carbon from the charcoal can dissolve in the iron, decreasing its melting temperature. Molten cast iron formed at the surface of the iron particles when the carbon content of the surface layer exceeded 2 per cent (the point 2 in Figure 1). Slow cooling allowed the carbon to diffuse through the metal producing a steel with an average carbon

Fig. 4. Coarse grain of austenite (dark color) surrounded by the network of cementite (white color lines)

content between 1.5 and 2 per cent (the point 3 in Figure 1). It also allowed the austenite grain to grow to a coarse size (Figure 4A). When the temperature fell below about 1000 degree C (the point 4 in Figure 1), carbon precipitated out of solution as cementite at the grain boundaries (Figure 4A). The coarse cementite network was the source of the whitish damask markings. At this point the steel cake called wootz underwent forging operations at temperatures between 850°C and 650°C. Higher temperatures would have caused the cementite to dissolve again in the austenite. Hammering the wootz cake at a temperature below 850°C, on the other hand, broke up the continuous cementite network into spheroidal particles. The carbide particles still served the function of strengthening the steel, but because they no longer formed a continuous network, the metal was not brittle.

As the temperature fell below 727°C, fcc austenite converted into alternating layers of cementite and carbon-poor, bcc ferrite (the point 5 in Figure 1). The blades were hardened by being reheated above 727°C, and then quenching it in water. When ultra-high carbon steels are allowed to cool slowly from austenite phase, as in the initial casting of wootz, the austenite is converted into pearlite. Pearlite is made up of alternate layers of soft, carbon-poor ferrite and carbon-rich cementite. If the steel is quenched, however, the transformation of austenite into pearlite is suppressed. The iron crystals become body-centered, but they are stretched from a cubic form into a tetragonal one (Figure 5). This structure, called martensite, still has room for carbon atoms, and so it is hard.

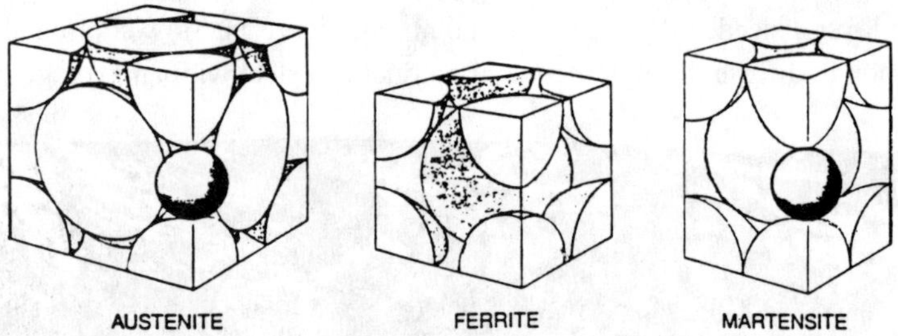

Fig. 5. Allotropic transformation of steel crystal structures

History of Indian Steel

As mentioned earlier, the steel of Damascus swords was produced in India. How far back does the art and science of steel making go in Indian history? Well, the Greek historian Herodotus wrote that the Indians in the Persian army were armed with iron. Ktesias, who was in the court of Persia in the 5th century BC, wrote that he was presented with two remarkable swords of Indian steel by the Persian emperor and his mother respectively. Quintus Curtius mentioned that around 326 BC [3, 4] Alexander Javanani, the Macedonian, received a gift of 100 talents or 30 lb of Indian steel from the Indian king Porus of Taxashila, located in the northwest region of the present day Pakistan. Pliny (first century AD) refers to fine swords made of Indian steel. The Periplus of the Erythrean Sea of the first century AD describes the occurrence of Indian iron and steel in the African ports and Ethiopia. The Romans were fascinated by the Indian steel which they imported to make fine cutlery and armors. The Indian army of Chandragupta (Maurya) who freed the land of Afghanistan from Seleucus Nikator carried weapons of the special Indian steel. Hannibal's soldiers armed with swords of Indian steel hammered at Toledo, scattered the Roman legions at the battle of Cannae in 216 BC. Damascus steels got their name not from their place of origin but from the place (Damascus) where Europeans first encountered them during the Wars of Crusades around 1192 AD. Since that time Europeans were interested in uncovering the secret of making wootz, the second name of the ultra-high carbon Indian steel.

Research on Bulat

With the rise of Islam after 600 AD when Arabs developed keen interest in Indian sciences, they realized the strength of Indian steel which they called Hinduwanig (Indian sword or iron). The word wootz may have its origin in the word Hinduwani. The swords of this special steel carried by Rajput armies did protect Indian borders and hence were known in the middle ages by the name "Jawab-i-Hind", ("the Answer of India"). Although the geographical distribution of Damascus steels generally followed the spread of the Islamic faith, they were known in medieval Russia where they were called Bulat. The British scientist Michael Faraday famous for the laws of electromagnetic induction spent many years in uncovering the secret of wootz and achieved partial success around 1819 AD. Faraday's paper inspired Jean Robert Breant who in 1821 discovered that wootz got its strength, toughness and beauty from its high carbon content. The Russian metallurgist, Anossoff, in 1841 published a monograph on Damascus steel with the title "On the Bulat." Anossoff dedicated his life to the study of Bulat. In Arabia, Persia and Syria, it was known as Pulad. In India it was called Polad, or Faulad. In this name, there exists connection of this strong steel to the tender flowers, Blue Lilies.

Blue Lotus Flower

In the Hindu religious philosophy, the human mind is thought of as the blue lotus flower of 1000 petals with the flame of consciousness rising up from the center. To Indians, and especially to Hindu Rajputs, the blue lotus flower is the symbol of truth and spiritual beauty. In the Hindi movie "Neel-Kamal" (Blue Lotus) directed by the late famous Indian director Raj Kapoor, the heroine who sacrificed her life was like a Neel Kamal, full of pure love and spiritual beauty. In ancient India, people living in the province of Gandhara (the North-West

Frontier Province of the present day Pakistan) were fond of blue lilies. The ancient capital of Gandhara was the city of Pushkaravati. Pushkara means blue lotus flower or blue lily in Sanskrit. In the city Pushkaravati, there were many beautiful lakes in which grew blue lilies. Pushkaravati was the great trading center around 1 AD and was also the center of production of the special ultra-high carbon Indian steel. Thus in the ancient world steel coming from Pushkaravati was known as Pushkaravata in Sanskrit language and Pokkhalavat in Pali language. With the course of time, the word Pokkhalavata was corrupted into Pohalavada, Polavaden and in recent times to Pulad, Faulad, Bulad, Bolod in living languages like Arabian, Turkish, Russian and Hindi. Thus the strong material steel got its name Bulat from the name of the tender flower of Pushkar or Neelotpal—the Blue Lily!

REFERENCES

[1] Oleg D. Sherby and Jeffrey Wadsworth, "Damascus steels", *Scientific American,* February 1985, 112–120.

[2] Jeffrey Wadsworth and Oleg D. Sherby, "On the Bulat-Damascus steels revisited," *Progress in Materials Science,* **25**, 1980, 35–68.

[3] D M. Bose, S. N. Sen and B.V. Subbarayappa, *A Concise History of Science in India,* Indian National Science Academy, New Delhi, 1971, p. 290

[4] N.R. Banerjee, *The Iron Age in India,* Munshiram Manoharlal, New Delhi, India, Chapter 6.

[5] Floyd L. Darrow, *Masters of Science and Invention,* Harcourt, Brace and Company, 1923, p. 173.

A Mathematical Study of Vedanta Philosophy

S.K. Dey
Professor of Mathematics
Eastern Illinois University, Charleston, IL. 61920, USA
Email: cfskd@eiu.edu

In ancient India, Aryan pundits developed Vedanta philosophy. It proclaims that every object—animate or inanimate, from the minutest atom to the prodigious universe itself—is divine. We all are essentially divine. In this article an attempt has been made to analyze this sublime philosophy mathematically. In no way one should think that Vedanta could be fully explained by mathematics which is the sole language of science. Indeed it is still far beyond the grip of modern science.

Introduction

Historians state that more than 4000 years ago, the people who lived in India were tall white people [16] highly proficient in archery, astronomy, arithmetic, art, and agriculture. Dr. Lucille Schulberg, a famous historian stated [8]; "Historically India is not a country. It is a culture, one of the oldest and most consistent on earth. That culture has been contemporary to almost all civilizations . . . The culture consists predominantly of a religion and a mode of living called Hinduism." Hinduism is based upon the dictums of a set of books, known as the Vedas. These books were composed by the Aryans and adored most highly by them. Aryans called them the books of knowledge. At the end of these books a philosophy is expounded in several books, called the Upanishads. This is Vedanta philosophy. Hindus claim that this is the pinnacle of wisdom, the highest form of knowledge that one can possess. Can such a claim carry any scientific merit? Or, is it purely emotional, fanned by religious fervor? Highest form of knowledge definitely implies the existence of a state of the Absolute. We live in a world where everything is measured relative to some given standard of measurement or a frame, which also exists relative to another frame and so on. Can there be anything which is the Absolute, beyond the world of dualism and yet be scientifically acceptable?

Before we start answering these questions let us study the fundamentals of Vedanta Philosophy [1]. The primary assumption is the existence of an apparently fictitious being who is called "Brahman". Brahman is the Absolute—the omnipotent, the omnipresent and the omniscient—beyond time, space and causation, birthless, deathless, conserved and the Eternal. Brahman is holy, divine, and God—the supreme operator of the universe. This lofty philosophy has several apparent contradictions. Chandogya Upanishad [1] states: "... as by knowing one nugget of gold, all that is made of gold is known, the difference being only in name, and the truth being that all is gold," similarly it states "... it is that knowledge, knowing which we know everything." Scientists unanimously agree that knowledge is endless. How can one accept that there exists a knowledge, knowing which one knows everything. Brihadaranyaka Upanishad [1] states: "Aham Brahmasmi" (I am Brahman). Am I birthless, deathless? Do I have any of the attributes of Brahman stated above? The answer certainly is "NO". This is another contradiction. Svetasvatara Upanishad states [1]: "It (Brahman) is not female. It is not male nor it is neuter. Whatever body it takes with that it becomes united." If this is true a piece of rock is also a manifestation of Brahman. How could a piece of rock be divine? Chandogya Upanishad states [1]: "Thou art that" or "You are Brahman." Can we say this to a rapist or a murderer, or in other words, can evil be divine? Vedanta claims that divinity, which is the essential characteristic of this universe must be realized. Once this sublime truth is experienced, a person goes beyond time, space, and causation. Such a person then realizes that this colorful phenomenal universe is unreal. In sanskrit it is called "Maya." Another most interesting property of Brahman is that—Brahman is detached although, he is the real doer—THE OPERATOR behind all operations. From the motion of the elements smaller that a quark to the motion of the vast cosmos—all are controlled by Brahman. Brihadaranyaka Upanishad states [1]: "He (Brahman) has nothing sticking to Him, for He does not stick to anything."

To understand these philosophical tents, I will apply rigorous mathematical logic—which is stringent and stern, robust and rigorous.

Mathematical Operators

In mathematics one studies functions. When a cause is changed to an effect or symbolically a quantity X is changed into a quantity Y, we say that this is done by a function F and write

$$F : X \to Y. \tag{1}$$

F is also called an operator.

Mathematically, every change—the minutest one or the massive one—is caused by an operator. F is, however, neither attached to X nor to Y. For instance when clouds are changed into rains, it is done by an operator which is neither cloud nor rain. Brahman is certainly not *just* a mathematical operator (because no mathematical operator can be omniscient), but there are some aspects of Brahman which may be simulated by a mathematical operator.

In 1905 Einstein proved [4] that everything in the universe is changing. Nothing is stationary. Long before Einstein, over 6000 years ago, Hindus used the Sanskrit word "Jagat" which means the phenomenal world. The word "Jagat" is derived from the Sanskrit words meaning "that which is continuously in motion." Thus "Jagat" literally means "the ever changing cosmos." A piece of rock may appear to be stationary, but in fact, if we see it through a powerful microscope, we will notice many tiny atoms moving all over it. The question is who causes such a motion? The mathematical answer is: An operator. In the Bhagavad Gita [2], which the synopsis of all the Upanishads, Lord Krishna (whom Hindus accept as an incarnation of Brahman) stated in Chapter 10, Bibhuti Yoga, that although He is present everywhere, still degree of manifestation of Brahman varies from one object to the other. For instance, in the animal world He is most potent in man—who has the ability to conquer instinct applying intellect. Shri Ramakrishna an Indian saint born in the nineteenth century said that the degree of manifestation of Brahman varies from one object to the other only quantitatively. Qualitatively there exists no difference. Mathematically there are weak operators and strong operators. Strong operators have much larger norms (magnitudes) than weak operators. For instance, potential energy in one object could be much greater than that in another object, and thus when it is transformed into kinetic energy, one can do more work than the other. Vedanta also states that there exists modes of transformation that makes it possible to extract an infinite amount of energy from any object which could be infinitely small (Reference: Svetāsvatara Upanishad [1] states: "Know the embodied soul (Brahman) to be a part of the hundredth part of the point of a hair divided a hundred times, yet it is infinite.") This implies that even in the sub-atomic particle, the infinite and imperishable Brahman exists and thus It has the resources to hold a vast amount of energy. This has a great deal of similarity with Einstein's equation $E = mc^2$ where E = the energy, m = mass and c = the velocity of light (186,000 miles per second). This equation reveals that a tiny mass could be the source of a vast amount of energy.

Another name of Brahman is the "Self," which exists in all objects according to Vedanta. Aitereya Upanishad states that Brahman is the inner operator "by which one sees, by which one hears, also by which one smells odor, and by which one utters speech and by which one tastes the sweet and the sour." Kena Upanishad [1] elaborates this much further stating that: "That which cannot be expressed by speech, but by which speech is expressed—that alone is known as Brahman. That which mind cannot comprehend but by which mind comprehends—that alone is known as Brahman. That which cannot be seen by eyes, but by which eyes can see—that alone is known as Brahman. That which cannot be heard by ear, but by which ears can hear—that alone is Brahman. That which cannot be breathed, but by which breathing system works—that alone is Brahman." Let us analyze the very first statement. "That which cannot be expressed by speech" definitely means, whatever "That" is, is detached from our expression or beyond expression; "but by which speech is expressed" means "That" must activate our mechanism of speech—or more precisely must operate on those constituents of our body which activate the mechanisms of speech. If D_1 = all constituents of the mechanisms of speech and R_1 = all speeches which are spoken, then "That" who is Brahman is represented mathematically by

$$\text{Brahman} : D_1 \to R_1 \tag{2}$$

This is similar to equation (1). If we combine all such statements in the Upanishads, we get

$$\text{Brahman} : \bigcup_{n=1}^{\infty} D_n \to \bigcup_{n=1}^{\infty} R_n \tag{3}$$

where $\bigcup_{n=1}^{\infty} D_n$ = union of all constituents of infinitely many mechanisms existing in the cosmos, and $\bigcup_{n=1}^{\infty} R_n$ = union of all the outcomes from all of these various mechanisms.

By virtue of this definition, we see that there exists no operator in the realm of mathematics more potent than "Brahman". We must analyze now why He is beyond time, space and causation.

The State of the Absolute

From physics we understand that for the entire universe, if at a given time t, $a(t)$ = potential energy of the universe and $b(t)$ = kinetic energy of the universe, then

$$a(t) + b(t) = K \tag{4}$$

where K is an absolute constant independent of t. The universe being always in motion, potential energy is continuously being converted into kinetic energy and work is done. If we set $t = 0$ at the time when the universe was just about to be born, then in the absence of motion

$$b(0) = 0 \tag{5}$$

Thus

$$a(0) = \mathrm{K} \tag{6}$$

Therefore K is equal to the vast amount of potential energy which must have existed before the universe was born. Since energy cannot transform itself, mathematically there must have existed an operator who must have converted the potential energy $a(0)$ into kinetic energy so that the universe may be born and motion could ensue. As motion starts, time flows and space is generated. Taittiriya Upanishad states: "... all that exists is inalienable from Brahman in time and space, Brahman being the cause of time and space." Aitareya Upanishad [1] states: "In the beginning there was but the Absolute Self alone. There was nothing else whatsoever that winked." Analyzing (5) and (6) one can comprehend the validity of the above statements.

If at least two objects exist, then the concept of dualism or relative existence can be ascertained. But if only one object exists and nothing else exists, then the concept of dualism is meaningless. Thus at $t = 0$ when the universe was non- existent, no operator of the world of science was present, then Brahman was the sole operator changing potential energy into kinetic energy so that creation may take place. Therefore, He must be beyond dualism or in other words, He must be the Absolute.

When we think of God, we visualize a person who is superior to all of us for all times to come and divinity is the attribute which is glued to Him. Thus God must be the Absolute. Since there cannot be two Absolutes, Brahman must be the same whose other name is God. Thus Brahman is divine. Brahman is not an ordinary operator of mathematics.

Origin of the Universe

First question that one should ask is "How did $a(0)$ come into existence?" Vedanta states that in us, potential energy is generated and stored by the Self. Similarly $a(0)$ was generated in the vast cosmos by the Self who is Brahman. Vedantists have gone far deeper than this to explain the origin of the universe. Īśa Upanishad states: "There exists a universe which is invisible, infinite and complete. Out of this universe, another universe has come out which is visible, infinite and complete." The former universe is Brahman Himself. The second universe is the vast cosmos—our visible universe. Let us analyze these statements. In mathematics, the word "complete" means, if X is any element of a set S and it goes through an infinite number of changes, namely, $X_1, X_2, \ldots$ and if ζ is the final point, beyond which there is no change, then S contains all the changes of X including ζ, the final point. This is precisely what Vedanta meant by the word 'complete'. As Shri Ramakrishna [14] said: "Everything is contained in Him. Nothing exists beyond Him." Also if a set A contains all numbers, positive, negative and zero, then A has an infinite number of elements. If a set B contains only the positive numbers, then B is also an infinite set. Now if B is taken out of A, then A still remains infinite. This is mathematically accurate. Thus since Brahman is infinite, when this infinite universe came out of Him, He still remained infinite. Thus all forms of matter (and, according to Prasna Upanishad [1] antimatter as well) are formed out of Brahman. Since Brahman is changeless, It must be conserved. Thus matter must be conserved. The laws of conservation in Physics states that both mass and energy of the universe are conserved. Einstein [15] stated while talking about Relativity that he simply combined the laws of conservation of energy and conservation of mass into one law: The Law of Conservation of Matter.

Rig Veda states: "Before the universe (visible universe) became manifest, there was manifest Hiranyagarbha". In Sanskrit, the word "Hiranya" means golden and "Garbha" means womb. Thus, according to Rigveda, when this universe was born, there were flashes of light. This is precisely what scientists called "The Big Bang". The other name of Hiranyagarbha is Brahma. Hindus worship Brahma and call Him the Creator. George Gamow [7] called it a "Universal cooking Era". He assumed the existence of the sub-atomic particles which formed $a(0)$ in equation (6) and wrote that these particles were "squeezed to extremely high density and subjected to high temperatures providing favorable conditions for all kinds of nuclear transformations." Who could have done this "squeezing"? Mathematically an operator must have existed then to do this operation. Vedanta states that the operator is Brahman.

The Vibrating Cosmos

Katha Upanishad [1] claims: "Whatever there is . . . the whole universe vibrates because it has gone forth from (the realization of) Brahman." Vibration is the most essential feature of every element of this visible universe. From the subatomic particle to the cosmos itself—everything is vibrating in time and space. Why? Vedanta states that the visible universe has nine fundamental characteristics: (i) three modes of existence which are projection, preservation and destruction, (ii) three factors of existence which are time, space and causation, and (iii) three Gunas (inclinations) or "Avyaktams" (the undifferentiated) which are basically three subtle, random, natural forces and are called Sattva, Rajas and Tamas. With these nine elements and Brahman which is represented by "null" because He is the starting point, Hindus in ancient India invented the decimal system [10,13]. Every element of this visible universe is being continuously bombarded at random by these three subtle forces of Nature. Vedanta states that these three forces are never balanced. Therefore everything must vibrate. This is mathematically correct and it matches perfectly with the findings of Quantum Mechanics. The Law of Entropy also states that the visible universe is being continuously bombarded by an arbitrary number of subtle, random forces in Nature and these bombardments increase with time. Vedanta claims there are only three such fundamental forces. Vedantists really called them "gunas" which mean "inclinations". The word "force" was not used in the Upanishads. In the theory of Relativity Einstein said that all objects are *inclined* towards each other causing changes of curvature of their orbits in the space-time manifold.

The three gunas, affecting the entire visible universe, have made it vibrate, according to Vedanta. In the Chapter 9, Verse 7, Raja Vidya Rajaguha Yoga of the Bhagavad Gita [2], Lord Krishna said that this universe will stay manifest for one "kalpa," unmanifest for one "kalpa" and will reappear at the beginning of the next "kalpa." This Hindu almanac when translated into the modern scientific language shows that: one kalpa equals 4.32×10^9 years [11, Vol. 11, page 509]. Thus the period of vibration of the universe is 8.64×10^9. In this regard, Dr. Carl Sagan [9] wrote: "The Hindu religion is the only one of the world's great faiths dedicated to the idea that the cosmos itself undergoes an immense, indeed an infinite number of deaths and rebirths. It is the only religion in which the time scales correspond, no doubt by accident, to those of modern scientific cosmology. Its cycles run from our ordinary day and night to a day and night of Brahma, 8.64×10^9 years long, longer than the age of the earth or the sun and about half the time since the Big Bang." Since this huge arithmetic computation (of the length of two kalpas = the period of vibration of the cosmos) was done by Lord Krishna who had a track record of such massive computations, I simply disagree with Dr. Sagan that Lord Krishna found it accidentally. Those who have studied the Bhagavad Gita have seen that in Akshara Brahma Yoga, Chapter 8, Verses 24 and 25, Lord Krishna described that the sun stays above the celestial equator for six months and below it for six months. This implies that Lord Krishna must have studied the Spherical Geometry very thoroughly, knew how to solve spherical triangles to compute the length of a day at a given time, knew about the ecliptic which is the orbit of the sun relative to the earth and conducted massive computations to find the length of a month and the length of a year. Historians stated that the prince Siddhartha (who later became Lord Buddha) and many other Hindus did many large-scale arithmetic computations in the days of antiquity in India [17]. Scientific analysis of the life history of Lord Krishna as conducted by Professor De [5] and Mr. Chatterjee [6] showed that Krishna was born around 1510 B.C. in Mathura, India and was an expert in astronomy, arithmetic, archery, biology and medicine.

Avyaktams and Human Psychology

According to Vedanta, all forces in Nature physical or metaphysical are various combinations of the Avyaktams—Sattva, Rajas and Tamas. Thus human psychology is strongly governed by them. In Gunatraya Bibhaga Yoga (Bhagavad Gita, Chapter 14) Lord Krishna described the properties of Sattva, Rajas and Tamas and explained how do these Avyaktams affect our psychology.

In verse 6 (Chapter 14, Bhagavad Gita) Lord Krishna said: " . . . Sattva, being stainless, is luminous and unobstructive. It binds (us) by creating attachment to (internal) happiness and attachment to knowledge." In verse 7, he said: "know

Rajas to be the nature of passion, the source of thirst and attachment; it binds (us) fast by attachment of action." In verse 8 he said: "But know Tamas to be born of ignorance, deluding all embodied beings; it binds (us) fast by heedlessness, indolence and sleep." Thus Sattva is an internal force that elevates moral virtues of life and generates an environment of peace and serenity. Rajas generates an external force to go into action and Tamas attempts to balance both Sattva and Rajas by generating corruption, evil ideas and wickedness. Brahman being with all of us, we all are capable to generate our free wills. But if these free wills are overpowered by the forces of Tamas, or in other words, if one decides to be more activated by the inclination of Tamas, the person becomes an evil person, although the basic element in him/her is "Brahman" or divinity.

Attainment of the State of Brahman

Since we all are essentially divine, Vedanta states it is our birthright to realize this highest state of existence or the state of divinity. How can this be achieved? Katha Upanishad states: "This knowledge cannot be attained by reasoning" or by "studying books." One can obtain only "by means of concentration on the Self". Mundaka Upanishad states: " . . . a person whose mind is completely serene and whose senses are controlled" is eligible to acquire the knowledge of Brahman. In Moksha Samnyasa Yoga (The Bhagavad Gita, Chapter 18), verse 53, Lord Krishna states: "Having abandoned egoism, violence, arrogance, desire, enmity, property, free from the notion of 'mine' (attachment) and peaceful, the person is fit to be (bestowed with the knowledge of) Brahman." This is possible if one can overcome the brutal bombardments of Sattva, Rajas, and Tamas by meditation and concentration on the "Self." Many saints and seers have proved that as meditation gets deeper and deeper, concentration gets stronger and stronger and the bombardments of the Avyaktams get weaker and weaker. Anyone who does meditation can experience this, at least partially. Meditation generates a feeling of a peaceful environment. Mind becomes calm and instincts are controlled by intellect so that they can do no harm to our mind and stress is alleviated. When mind is calm and serene, thoughts do not grow at random. They all become single-pointed and concentrated towards one *final* objective. Let us denote it by "A." Thus "A" is the object which mind *does not* and *cannot* change. If "A" is an element of the cosmos, then "A" is subjected to the bombardments by the Avyaktams or the Law of Entropy, which means "A" is subject to change, which is a contradiction. Thus "A" must be beyond the cosmos. If "A" is subject to time, space and causation, then again "A" must be an element of the cosmos and "A" must change, which again is a contradiction. Thus "A" must be beyond the cosmos. In the earlier part of this article we have studied the Vedic assumption that the cosmos originated from "Brahman" and only Brahman is beyond the cosmos and unaffected by the laws of Nature. Thus "A" must be Brahman, the Absolute. The state of attainment of "A" is called the state of "Trance" in psychology. Vedanta calls it "Samadhi". Upanishads claim that: "Brahman is Abanmanasagochor" meaning that Brahman is beyond words and beyond the reach of our mind. Why? If we describe anything say "X" then "X" must be an element of the cosmos and thus, it is subject to change. If mind can dwell upon "X", then again "X" must be changed by mind because of the fact that mind is subject to bombardment by the Avyaktams. Since "A" is changeless, "A" must be beyond words and mind. When Shri Ramakrishna attained the state of "Samadhi" and was requested by his disciples to describe this royal state to them, he said that at this state everything melts into the Absolute (Brahman) just as a doll made of a chunk of salt loses its identity in an ocean. Chandogya Upanishad [1] states that this is a state "where one sees nothing else, hears nothing else, understands nothing else." Subāla Upanishad [18] states: "In the supreme, there is neither existence nor non-existence, nor existence and non-existence." Our concepts of "existence" and "non-existence" are applicable only to this universe. Thus the Absolute is beyond all of these. Brihadāranyaka Upanishad [1] states "In this state a father is no more a father, a mother is no more a mother, the worlds are no more the worlds, the gods are no more the gods ". In the state of the Absolute dualisms do not exist. In order that a father may exist, a child has to exist. But at the state of "A" only one—the Absolute Brahman—exists and thus all others must cease to exist. No law of the universe is applicable there. Whatever exists in this world is relative. Thus nothing that exists here, exists there.

In [12] a more rigorous mathematical logic has been applied to analyze the attainment of the state of the Absolute.. But this analysis falls far short to describe this supreme state.

Conclusion

In this article, I have just made an attempt to explain certain aspects of Vedanta by applying mathematical logic. In the true sense of the term, Vedanta is beyond scientific explanation. Mathematics may be applied to explain whatever may exist and/or may cease to exist within the framework of the visible universe. But whatever exists beyond the existence of this universe is beyond the realm of science. Thus mathematicians, I believe, may be able to take steps towards the right direction, make very stringent and logical approach but at the very end all glamour and glaze of mathematical graphs are bound to graze in a domain where the very definition of mathematics loses its identity. The truth of the Absolute is governed by the law of the Omniscience [14]—which scientists have yet to know.

References

[1] Swami Nikhilananda, *The Upanishads*, Bell Publishing Company, New York, 1962.

[2] Swami Chidbhavananda, *The Bhagavad Gita*, Tamil Nadu, India, 1960.

[3] Swami Vivekananda, *Thoughts on Vedanta*, Udbodhon, Calcutta, India, 1964.

[4] James R. Newman, *The World of Mathematics*, Simon and Schuster, New York, 1956.

[5] G.D. De, *Shree Radha and Shree Krishna of Vrindavan*, University of Calcutta, 1964.

[6] B.C. Chatterjee, *Krishna Charitra*, Calcutta, 1890.

[7] G. Gamow, *The Creation of the Universe*, The New American Library, 1960.

[8] L. Schulberg, *Historic India*, Time-Life Books, 1968.

[9] Carl Sagen, *Cosmos*, Balentine Books, New York, 1980.

[10] V. Sanford, *A Short History of Mathematics*, Houghton Mifflin Co., 1930.

[11] *Encyclopedia Britannica*, 1967.

[12] S.K. Dey, "Mathematical Analysis of Consciousness in Vedanta Philosophy", *Informatica*, 1997 (accepted for publication).

[13] S.K. Dey, *Invention of Zero*, Proceedings of History of Mathematics, Professor J.D. Wine (Ed.), University of Wisconsin, La Crosse, 1997.

[14] Swami Nikhilananda, *The Gospel of Shri Ramakrishna*, Calcutta, India, 1976.

[15] .P. French, *Special Relativity*, W.W. Norton & Comp.Inc. New York, 1968.

[16] David Frawley, *Gods, Sages and Kings: Vedic Secrets of Ancient Civilization*, Passage Press, Salt Lake City, Utay, 1991.

[17] D. E. Smith, *History of Mathematics*, Ginn, Boston, 1923.

[18] S. Radhakrishnan, *The Principal Upanishads*, Harper Collins Publishers, India, 1994.

Astronomy in Ancient India: Observations and Speculations

P. VENUGOPALA RAO
Department of Physics
Emory University, Atlanta, Georgia 30322
Email: phspvr@physics-emory.edu

There is evidence that knowledge of astronomy began to accumulate as far back as Indus valley civilization times. Nakshatras or asterisms are the main divisions of the region around the ecliptic, which we now refer to as Zodiac. The movement of the equinoxes is clearly observed and probably its significance is understood. They have a well organized calendar system which is intimately connected with their sacrifice rites. And they used a luni-solar calendar. They have used a sidereal year instead of tropical year. They balanced the lunar and solar year by intercalary days or months. They are very much into astrology but it is based upon asterisms or nakshatras. These asterisms divide the Zodiac not into equal segments but segments of different lengths.

How do we define astronomy, especially in the context of a historical period usually referred to as ancient? Astronomy as we understand today refers to the large scale activity of observing the universe with the aid of not only ordinary telescopes but all the technologically sophisticated instruments of data collection including robot satellites. But observing with naked eye the sky and its contents is an age-old pastime and if we can include all such activity in the domain of astronomy, it is a discipline practiced by humans since ancient times all over the world. To know how our ancestors lived and learned from the Nature can be not only a source of pride but also a glimpse into their intellectual activities and pursuits. If we do not let ourselves arrogantly place the ancients into a class of barbarians, we may actually learn something from our past.

The main features of the apparent motions of the heavenly bodies must have been observed from the very earliest times all over the world. No one could have failed to notice the alterations of the day and night, the recurring phases of the moon, the association of summer season with the sun high in the sky, and return of the seasons at regular intervals. A casual study too would have revealed the fact that the whole sky appears to be turning round about a certain point, approximately once in a day and night, giving the appearance of the rising of the heavenly bodies in the east, their gradual upward path and then the downward path till they finally set in the west. It is not unreasonable to assume that they could notice that while certain stars remained fixed as regards their relative positions, the planets were not so fixed, sometimes in an easterly, sometimes in a westerly direction, yet being confined to a certain belt of the sky.

But a casual observation is not enough to call it astronomy. There must be careful observations that are remembered, passed on and utilized in some way to make it astronomy. You may ask what gives rise to such a need? The well known answer is "the necessity of having a measure of time" in the activities of life. In the development of civilization we associate such a need with the beginning of agricultural economy and life style. This is from the perspective of a historian, who studies the beginning, development and end of civilizations. We shall adopt this point of view. A civilization thriving on vast agricultural surplus cannot do without a developed calendar system. And the development of a calendrical system is not conceivable without astronomical knowledge.

Indus Valley Civilization

The first urbanization that took place in the Indian subcontinent was in the Indus valley, where a civilization flourished between 3000 BC and 1500 BC. Historians have enough data to say with some confidence about the dawn, evolution and devolution of the Indus civilization, now referred to as Harappa culture by scholars. This civilization is not just confined to a small area around the Indus river. The archaeological evidence suggests it is spread over a vast area on the subcontinent. Historians have identified the course of an ancient river, Saraswati that flowed through these regions. We know a lot more about this civilization now compared to say fifty years ago. And here is a little summary that appeared in a recent book by S.R. Rao on Indus civilization [1]. "The Indus Civilization made several permanent contributions to the progress of man, the greatest among them being the simplified alphabetic system of writing which facilitated quick communication and recording of thought. Without such an easy system of writing sophistication would not have been possible. The Harappan metrology laid the foundation of science and technology. The engineering skill of the Harappans, especially in building docks after a careful study of tides, waves and currents is remarkable for the age. They not only followed modern principles in building docks, warehouses, drains and baths but also achieved advanced standards of construction. For navigational purposes they observed and even fixed the position of stars with the help of an instrument similar to the sextant . . ."

The question is: Is there evidence to presume the existence of astronomy in the Indus civilization? We know that the entire civilization flowered forth as a result of surplus agriculture economy. The Harappans must have possessed the knowledge of stars for, without it, it is difficult to account for the rigid north-south and east-west orientation of the streets and lanes. In the burials the bodies of the dead were oriented, head pointing to north and feet towards south. The identification of pole star for this purpose has to be credited to the Harappans.

Thick circular ring-like objects of conch shell have been found at Lothal, Mohenjodaro, Harappa and Dhola Vira. These two shell instruments, which contain the slits in the lower half as well as the upper half, were supposedly invented for measuring the eight or twelve whole sections of the horizon and sky and not merely the lines, points and degrees on a plain surface. There is also evidence to say that Harappans were navigators. Thus almost two thousand years before the Greeks had thought of an eightfold or a twelvefold division of the sky and the horizon, the Indus people seem to have achieved it and invented an instrument to measure the angles and the position of the stars for navigational purposes.

Vedic Times

Ancient Indians of Vedic times have left us with enough evidence to let us know that they were not only skilful and discerning observers of the sky, but had used that knowledge in their lives in a very significant way.

I recently came across a study of Rigveda by Dr. Y. Venkatramiah, who identifies some hymns, in particular the 35th hymn in the first Mandala [2]. He identifies Savitar with Aurora Borealis. If we make the assumption that Vedic rishis credited the forces of nature with conscious individuality and worshipped them as gods, the obvious conclusion is that these were human beings who once inhabited a region illuminated nightly by Savitar and that, at one time in the past, Arctic regions were also probably the home of the Aryans.

One has only to scan patiently through the Vedic literature that they have handed down to us, that is, their collections of hymns, ritual descriptions and philosophical speculations in order to know about their astronomy. Vedas indeed serve as a guidepost for us to grasp their knowledge of the heavens because we are left with no other physical evidence, such as huge monuments and structures.

The first mention of this subject of astronomy is of course in the Rigveda. The Rigveda (and also Satapatha-brahmana) refers to the five planets as gods and mentions Brihaspathi (Jupiter) and Vena (Venus). At this very early period a clear conception of the ecliptic emerges. It was divided into 28 lunar mansions or nakshatras or asterisms. These nakshatras are connected with the daily motion of the Moon in the sky. The names of these asterisms appear in Taittiriya Samhita, Kathaka Samhita, Maitrayini Samhita and the 19th book of Atharvaveda. At a subsequent date the zodiac was rearranged and divided into 27 nakshatras so that they agree more nearly with the mean daily motion of the Moon.

In those days nakshatras generally meant asterisms and not zodiacal portions. The zodiac was divided not by compass but by means of the leading stars. The principal star of each nakshatra or asterism was called the Yogatara. So one who knows Yogataras by sight has 27 fixed points in the sky and uses them to describe the position of any object on the ecliptic. The ecliptic is like a great dial graduated at irregular distances by the positions of yogataras.

All the lists of the nakshatras in the Vedic sources always begin with Krittikas, because the vernal equinox coincided with them when the list was made. The convention obviously was to start counting the first Nakshatra from the vernal equinox. Sometime after the commencement of the Christian era, the vernal equinox coincided with the first point of the lunar asterism Aswini, and it is from this fixed point, the first of Aswini, we measure the longitudes now. It has been shown by scholars that the vernal equinox is at the end of Revathi at about 490 AD. Presumably around that time we started counting Nakshatras from Aswini.

By means of observations extending over a long period, the Hindus became aquainted with the precession of the equinoxes. That needs fixing the equinox point in the sky with good accuracy. This of course is done by the observations of the solistial points. The observation of solistial point is something that was practiced all over the world at various times in the ancient past. As a matter of fact, there is enough evidence in the Vedic literature to note that there were references to times when vernal equinox is not in Krittika but in other asterisms as indicated below [3]

Vernal equinox	*Summer solstice*
Aswini	Pausha
Krittika	Magha
Mrigashira	Phalguna
Punarvasu	Chitra

This is an indication that the Vedic priests have been following the motions of the heavenly bodies continuously for a long period of antiquity. They were adjusting the calendar year, the beginning and the end of it, following these observations. By the time of Varahamihira in 5th century AD, the Aswini system was introduced.

We also know that the sacrificial rites of Brahmins depended upon knowing time very carefully. There were Sattras which lasted for a year, typical of sun's yearly course. Brahmins prepared their calendar mainly for sacrificial purposes and the performances of various sacrifices facilitated in its turn, the keeping of the calendar. The sacrifice and calendar have become synonymous terms. The priests were not only the sacrificers of the community, but were also its time-keepers.

What kind of a calendar they have used with this knowledge of astronomy? The civil day (Savana) or the solar day is the natural day from sunrise to sunrise. Thirty days in a month and twelve months in a year—360 days in a year—these units formed the basis of the earliest calendar. Remember a day can be measured differently by looking at the stars, by returning to the same position of a particular star. That we call a sidereal day. But we also know the month was determined by the Moon. Names of the months are found in Taittiriya Samhita. Here again we have two ways of looking at the revolution of Moon around earth. A lunar sidereal month cannot correspond with thirty civil days. Lunar year is 354 days. To balance the lunar year with the solar year an intercalary month or days were inserted. The year is divided into twelve lunar months, a thirteenth intercalary month being added when necessary to adjust the correspondence between lunar and solar years and thus with the seasons of the year.

We also know that the solar year in the Vedic literature is most probably sidereal year and not the tropical year. The tropical year is the time of passage of the sun from one vernal equinox to the next. Sidereal year is the time between two successive arrivals of the sun at the same fixed star. Tropical year is about 20 minutes shorter than the sidereal year. For the early observers of heavens, it is easy to determine the position of the sun in the ecliptic by observing every morning the fixed stars near the sun. The year would be said to be complete when the sun returned to the same fixed star.

In the early Vedic days the year began when the sun was in the vernal equinox; as the sun passed from the south to the north of the equator it was also the commencement of the northern journey (uttarayana). The year, sattras, vasanta, uttarayana (devayana)—all commenced at vernal equinox. The equinox is known as Vishuvan, which literally means the time when day and night are equal. The middle day of the annual sattra is called the Vishuvan day, and it is expressly stated that this central day divides sattra into two equal halves, in the same way as the Vishuvan or equinoxial day divides the year.

It appears then that in the Vedic times a mixture of lunar and solar calendars is used—a luni-solar calendar, which we do even today in different parts of our country. It also appears that they possessed quite sufficient mathematics of their own for the purpose of their astronomy.

Returning to the subject of Indus civilization, a special note about Krittika is worth mentioning. "The Krittikas rise exactly in the east" asserts the Satapatha Brahmana. We know they did not rise exactly in the east during the period of Satapatha Brahmana (not earlier than 1000 BC). But they did arise exactly in the east about 2334 BC, which is the peak period of Harappan culture.

Vedanga Jyothisha talks about the longest day and shortest night and gives a number for the difference between them, which is 6 muhurtas. A relation between the longest day and shortest night does not hold good globally. It depends upon the latitude. So we can infer that the latitude where this observation is made is about 34.5 degrees north. This falls within the cultural frontier of Indus civilization.

Astrology and Astronomy

There is simultaneous cultivation of astronomy and astrology in ancient India. They have acted and reacted on one another. At least several centuries before Christ, Jyothisha attained the position of being one of the six angas of Veda. But the astrology was based on Nakshatras. There are plenty of references to the desirability of recognizing an auspicious or inauspicious Nakshatra both for natural and individual events.

But even in those days there were people who believed in Nakshtara astrology and those who did not believe. In fact some of the best minds in India did not believe in it. For example Buddha allowed the study of nakshatras but condemned forecasting. There are ancient sutras that declare that those who practice astrology are unfit in the same row with brahmins for dinner. Kautilya regarded as reprehensible the extreme reliance on astrology.

But we know that an auspicious nakshatra is a key element in all Vedic rites. On the other hand tithi was rarely mentioned. Weekday was not mentioned. Rasi was not mentioned. No planets were mentioned in connection with astrology.

REFERENCES

[1] S.R.Rao, *Dawn and Devolution of the Indus Civilization*, Aditya Prakashan, New Delhi, 1991.

[2] Y. Venkataramiah, *Savitar or Aurora Borealis: A Study in the Rigveda*, Lodhra Press, Madras, 1941.

[3] B.G.Tilak, *The Orion or Researches into the Antiquity of the Vedas*, Fourth Edition, Tilak Brothers, Poona, 1955.

Ancient Nepalese Astro-Science

KHILA NATH BASTAKOTY
G.P.O. Box 6660, Kathmandu, Nepal

Astro-science in Nepal has been of great importance because of its unique culture, tradition and beliefs. Its use has traditionally been recognized and is enhanced in recent days as the predictions of the astrologers have been found, in most cases, relevant.

Kathmandu, the capital of Nepal, contains over 25 thousand scrolls in two libraries only, dating back to some 1,500 years. Nepal, hence, is believed as a hidden treasure of the greatest palm-leaf manuscripts. It is also exemplified by the frequent visits of foreign scholars in its research. The contributions of Sidda Purush and Kaptad Baḅa have been the inspiration for working more to generate information about the creative epoch of Nepal's history.

This paper will document the present status of, and will critically examine the implications of, ancient astro-science in the Nepalese perspective, and its contribution to belief. Literature review of various documents, in particular the Sanati Shastra, Karmakanda Vidhi, Sumati Tantra, Yajnyavalkya Smriti, Bhrigu Samhita, Durga Saptashati, Kal-Chakra, Ratna Karandika, Yavana Jatakam and Hara Mekhala, will be made in this paper with support from recent research findings. The paper will highlight the elements contained in the Sumati Tantra, as it is one of the important books, written in the Kathmandu Valley, some 1,400 years ago. The paper will also include recommendations to expand the scope of astro-science in modern society.

Nepalese Astro-Science as Viewed in the Present Scenario

Nepal is a South Asian land-locked country, situated at 80.12° to 87°E longitude and 26.21° to 30.27° N latitude. China lies in the north and India in the east, west and south. This country extends 880 km. from east to west and spreads 193 km. from north to south. The size of this country is 1,47,181 square kilometres.

The population of Nepal is 2,11,26,636 as estimated from the census of 1990, in which the male population is 1,05,99,478 and the female population is 1,05,27,158. Over 98% females and 95% males believe in their respective religions. Population by religion is also diversified. The Hindus are 86.51%, the Buddhists 7.78%, the Muslims 3.53%, and the Christians are 0.17%.

Talking about the present status of Nepalese astro-science, more than 95% of the people have firm faith in astrology. After all, people in Nepal believe in astrology; even some scientists too have come to believe in astrology after due course of events or new happenings. Thus, it is obvious that majority of people believe in astrology for one reason or the other.

More than 15,000 astrologers are working in their respective areas in different parts of Nepal. Eminent astrologers are scattered in most of the village development committees.

As regards calculating of the National Almanac or Panchangas and the standard of Nepalese time, it is worth mentioning, as time is the central object of specification in this branch of study, that since 13 April 1985, Nepalese standard time has been recognized to have 5 hours and 45 minutes difference from GMT.

The position of mathematical astrology and the calculation of Panchangas have been widely spread. Seven Panchangas are in use presently by different astro-scientists. The National Panchangas Decision Committee (NPDC) has fixed strict regulations for the publication of Panchangas. Any Panchanga approved by this committee can be published and distributed here. Without prior approval of NPDC, no one has the right of Panchanga publication. This committee was formed in the year 1970 under the chairmanship of Dr. Mangal Raj Joshi, a royal astrologer. The theories of our Panchanga calculation are based on "Surya Siddhant," "Ram Vinod Chart," "Grahalaghav," and "Jyotir Ganit."

The tradition of astrological studies has been a long course of Nepalese life. There were very few astro-teaching centres and organizations 10 years ago, but now there are mushrooming astrological organizations and institutions in Kathmandu and the outlying areas of the capital city. We have taken this trend as a bright aspect of astrology.

The last quarter of this century has witnessed a great renaissance in Nepal, specially in the field of astrology. Efforts are being made by government agencies and non-government agencies equally. In this context, some of the major institutions and astrological schools in Nepal are as follows:

1. Tribhuvan University and its affiliated colleges
2. Mahendra Sanskrit University and its affiliated Mahavidyalaya
3. Some secondary schools of Sanskrit
4. Tradition of teacher-disciple education
5. Self-studied personalities and their teachings
6. Some non-government agencies, such as,
   —National Astro-Science Committee, Kathmandu, Nepal
   —Himalaya Astro-Geographical Society, Lalitpur, Nepal
   —International Astro-Research, Training and Forecasting Center, Parbat
   —Nepali Astrological Development Committee, Kathmandu, Nepal

—Asian Astrologers' Congress, Nepal Chapter

—World Federation of Astrologers, Kathmandu, Nepal

Besides these astronomical and astrological organizations, eminent writers of astro-science, such as Professor Naya Raj Panta and his disciples, Dr. K eshav Ram Joshi, Dr. Samba Raj Acharya, Dr. Mangal Raj Joshi and other contemporary scholars have made a great deal of contribution to the development and expansion of astro-science in this region. Professor Naya Raj Panta is the towering personality who has been working for the research and development of the Nepalese astro-system and history for the last 70 years. More than a dozen of his astrological and historical publications have been the everlasting pieces of astro-science.

There are several methods of forecasting in practice. Some are following the horoscope methods, a few the planetary transit systems, some others palm readings, and still others are following mundane astrology. Some are also using the horary system for astrological diagnosis. In the case of *Nakshatra Dasha*, *Vimshottari Tribhagi* (80 years of calculation instead of 120 years) and *Yogini Dasha* without calculating *Bhukti* are popular in Nepal. Research results have proved that more than 68% of the astrologers use these two systems as the main tools of forecast.

Recently the 8th Asian Astrologers' Conference was held in Dhaka, the capital city of Bangladesh, from 6th to 8th September 1996, under the auspices of Asian Astrologers' Congress and the Bangladesh National Astrologers' Federation in which five Asian countries—Nepal, India, Srilanka, Bangladesh and Malaysia—had taken part. In that conference it was decided that "Asian Institute of Astro-Science (ASIS)" and "Central Asian Library of Astro-Science (CALA)" should be established in Nepal. Similarly, the 10th Asian Astrologers' Conference is going to be held in Nepal in October 1998. The AAC has given top priority to develop Nepal as a centre of astro-science in the near future as Nepal has been the centre of astrological studies from the very beginning.

Thinking about Ancient Nepalese Astro-science

It is believed that the human beings have been in existence on this earth for about ten lakh years. For the last 6000 years they have been acqainted with the art of writing. When talking about the *Himavat Khanda* and the lap of the Himalayas, there are a number of remaining signs of the Indus Valley civilization more or less in the same manner. As legend says, *Brahma Yamal*, written around one thousand years ago in this region, was a Tantric book on a grand scale. It was penned with an eye on *Pratima Lakshana*, the concept of deities. The dialogues between *Shiva* and *Shakti* were as fresh as ever. In this fully documented work the principle of the installation of deities was expounded, as the deity rides a camel. She was also camel-faced, holding a sceptre, with dishevelled hair and outstretched hands. She had a bizarre look. It is very near to the concept of a local god in the period of the Indus Valley Civilization. Legend further says that the six hundred year old *Sumati Tantra* was a rarity and the work of a sensitive intellect.This astrological treatise was based on *Kathmandu Udayamana* instead of *Lankodaya.* The precious *Shiva Siddhanta,* lost in dim antiquity, was said to be presented in this manuscript without ever detracting from its value.

The history of ancient Nepal also shows that in those days the Kathmandu valley was the centre of Asian astrology and astronomy. We can collect evidences of this thought from different valuable Granths or manuscripts of ancient Nepalese writers of astro-science.

Similarly, *Yavana Jatakam* has a unique flavour. It was the pride of the Orient. It was said to be written by the sage *Yavaṇa Muni*, the literary lion in *Himavat Khanda.* In this greatest work on astrology, model horoscopes of emperors, kings, statesmen and dacoits are given. One can see this important manuscript in the library of Nepal.

It is clear that mathematics plays a vital role in astrology. Correct recording of the time and place of birth is very essential, otherwise every calculation goes wrong. Therefore, it would not be an exaggeration to mention here that religion and astro-science are interwoven and require a new dimension of tremendous research work on this important subject.

Moreover, let me avail the opportunity of placing my small views regarding the close link between science and astrology. If I understand the matter at all, science and astrology are two sides of a coin, one expressing the eternal order of things in terms of feeling, the other in terms of thought. When men no longer love nor hate, when suffering causes no pity and the tale of great deeds causes no thrill, when the city or the field shall seem no longer more beautifully arranged than Solomon in all his glory, and when awe has vanished from the snow-capped peaks and the deep ravine, then indeed science may have the world to itself; but it will not be because the monster has devoured astrology but because one side of human nature is dead and because men have lost one half of their ancient and present attributes.

Now let us move to the front side. One can see some of the important traditional systems of Indus Valley Civilization (IVC) which are still alive in Nepal. For example, we can mention the following systems:

- *Swastic* sign has been seen in IVC. The sign was later accepted by Vedic conquerors. This sign is used everywhere including Nepal.
- Traditional use of *Purna Ghat (Kalash)* is still alive in Nepal as it was in the first civilization (that is, IVC).
- The first planned city was seen in the Indus Valley. The same technique with the use of oil-coated bricks has been used for the first time at Bhaktapur town area of Kathmandu valley around 1100 A.D.
- "*Yajna Chiti*" construction system mentioned in the "*Sulva Sutra*" (500

B.C.) is believed to have existed in the Sarasvati age. The sample type of *"Yajna Chiti"* is still in use in Nepal for religious performances.

- The traditionsal Ananta of IVC time still exists in Nepal. Even now one can see Ananta on the Royal Nepal Academy gate.
- System of worship of "Kumari" has been seen in IVC. The same tradition is still alive in Nepal in different forms.
  - (a) *"Taleju Bhavani Puja"* (worship of the Goddess Taleju) is believed to have continued from IVC which entered into Nepal with some modification of Maharashtriyan culture.
  - (b) *"Kanya Puja"* (worship of unmarried girls before teen age), specially in Navaratra of Dashain, is popular in Nepal, which is more or less similar to the tradition of the first civilization.
  - (c) The widely popular "*Kumari Puja*" (worship of a girl as a living goddess) in Kathmandu is another example of the old tradition of the Mohanjodaro civilization or IVC. Worship of Kumari or living girl and worship of Pashupati (Lord of all living creatures) are directly connected with IVC period which are still alive in Nepalese society.

Instead of systematizing my paper, now I am a little bit diverted from the topic because I want to draw the attention of research scho;ars and institutions to open their eyes to this barren land of ancient astro-science and culture.

Conclusion

Nepal, where a number of remains of IVC are still in use, is mainly connected with the geography of ancient *Bharatvarsha* itself. But the North Indian belt and the Himalayan ranges have been the shelter of defeated crowds from the very beginning as it is today of Bhutanese refugees. So it is believed that the defeated groups from the Indus Valley moved to the secure mountainous areas with their culture, values and techniques. At the same time, conquerors of the Indus Valley also expanded their territory toward the plain areas and came up to the plain belt of Northern India. Thus the southern lap of the *Himavat Khanda* became the centre of a mixed culture, both in terms of safety and more or less a sound condition.

Yet there are sociocultural as well as astrological indications which are likely to suggest a continuity of some features of IVC, after it met its obliteration by 1750 B.C. I am tempted to think that Nepal's ancient astro-science might be connected to the post-Indus culture astro-science which definitely continued in the Himalayan sub-continent after the Vedic and post-Vedic second urbanization (700 B.C. onwards) in the sub-Himalayan North Indian plains.

Last, but not the least, it is obvious that Nepal has been rich enough in the field of astro-science from ancient times. We have many important manuscripts unpublished due to lack of funding. In fact, we have lots of expertise but we need joint ventures, mutual exchange of ideas and technology transfer on the forecasting systems, methods and techniques of one country to another for unity and development of astro-science in this universe.

Anomalous Textual Artifacts in Archeo-Astronomy

RICHARD THOMPSON
Bhaktivedanta Institute
P.O. Box 1920, Alachua, Florida 32616-1920

Ancient artifacts can survive within written texts, as well as within the strata of the earth. In this paper, two examples of anomalous textual artefacts are discussed. The first is a verse from the medieval Indian astronomy text *Sūrya-siddhānta* which seems to encode accurate values for the diameters of the planets. The second is a system of cosmic geography from the *Bhāgavata Purāṇa* which contains what seems to be a realistic map of planetary orbits in the solar system. We discuss these examples in relation to the controversial claim that there existed a premodem civilization with advanced astronomical knowledge.

Introduction

Reconstructions of ancient history are necessarily based on fragmentary artefacts and documents that have survived wars, social upheavals, and processes of gradual attrition. In some cases, extensive technological developments are completely lost to recorded history and then revealed by a chance discovery. For example, in 1900 an astronomical computerwas uncovered from a shipwreck of the 1st century B.C. near the Greek island of Antikythera (de Solla Price, 1962). This machine used an ingenious system of gears to exhibit positions of the sun, moon, and probably the planets on a series of dials. Nothing like it is described in surviving ancient literature, but a machine of such sophistication implies the existence of a well-developed technological tradition.

In India, in 1958, a realistic cast head of what looks like a Vedic warrior was rescued from being melted down (Hicks and Anderson, 1990). It has been dated to 3700 ± 800 B.C. by MASCA corrected carbon-14 dating. At present, it seems to be the only surviving sculpture of its kind. In this case, the find corroborates popular traditions about ancient Vedic civilization, but it stands out as an anomaly in established reconstructions of ancient history.

Information in old texts may also sometimes provide a unique glimpse into a forgotten past. One type of textual artefact consists of knowledge that seems too advanced for the historical period of the text. In cases where comparable knowledge was acquired in modern times through extensive scientific efforts, it can be argued that the knowledge may be a remnant from an earlier, advanced civilization that is lost to historical memory. In this paper, we will discuss two examples of textual artefacts that suggest the existence of advanced astronomical knowledge in the distant past.

Planetary Diameters

We begin with a medieval Indian astronomical text called the *Sūrya-siddhānta* (Burgess, 1989). In chapter 7 of this text, the 13th verse gives the following rule for calculating the apparent diameters of the planets Mars, Saturn, Mercury, Jupiter, and Venus: "The diameters upon the moon's orbit of Mars, Saturn, Mercury, and Jupiter, are declared to be thirty, increased successively by half the half; that of Venus is sixty."

The meaning is as follows: The diameters are measured in a unit of distance called the *yojana*, which in the *Sūrya-siddhānta* is about five miles. The phrase "upon the moon's orbit" means that the planets look from our vantage point as though they were globes of the indicated diameters situated at the distance of the moon. (Our vantage point is ideally the center of the earth.) Half the half of 30 is 7.5. Thus the verse says that the diameters "upon the moon 5 orbit" of the indicated planets are given by 30, 37.5, 45, 52.5, and 60 *yojanas*, respectively.

The next verse uses this information to compute the angular diameters of the planets. This computation takes into account the variable distance of the planets from the earth, but for the purposes of this paper it is enough to consider the angular diameters at mean planetary distances. The diameters upon the moon's orbit were given for the planets at these mean distances from the earth. The *Sūrya-siddhānta* says that there are 15 *yojanas* per minute of arc at the distance of the moon (giving 324,000 *yojanas* as the circumference of the moon's orbit). Thus the mean angular diameters of the planets can be computed by dividing the diameters upon the moon's orbit by 15. Table 1 gives the results of this computation and lists other estimates of planetary angular diameters for comparison.

TABLE 1

Planet	*Sūrya siddhānta*	Ptolemy	Tycho Brahe	Modern Minimum	Modern Maximum
Mars	2.0	1.57	1.67	.067	.450
Saturn	2.5	1.74	1.83	.250	.350
Mercury	3.0	2.09	2.17	.067	.200
Jupiter	3.5	2.61	2.75	.333	.817
Venus	4.0	3.13	3.25	.150	1.233

Angular diameters of planets in minutes of arc. The modern angular diameters are for the greatest and least distances of the planets from the earth. Those of Claudius Ptolemy are from his book *Planetary Hypotheses*.

The figures of Ptolemy and Brahe were obtained by naked-eye astronomy. They are roughly comparable with the *Sūrya-siddhānta* figures and are clearly much larger than the angular diameters measured in more recent times by means of telescopes (Burgess, 1989). It is well known that a small, distant light source looks larger to the naked eye than it really is. This phenomenon makes it likely that angular diameters of planets would inevitably have been over-estimated by astronomers before the age of the telescope. However, there is evidence indicating that the *Sūrya-siddhānta* angular diameters were not simply based on naked-eye observation. To see this, we must consider the orbits of the planets.

Orbital Dimensions in the Sūrya-siddhānta

Verses 12.85–90 of the *Sūrya-siddhānta* give the circumferences of the planetary orbits in *yojanas*, and these figures are reproduced in Table 2. The orbits are represented as simple circles centered on the earth, and their circumferences are proportional to the mean orbital periods of the planets. For Mercury and Venus, the mean planetary position is the same as the position of the sun, and thus the orbital circumferences in the table are the same for Mercury, Venus, and the Sun. For Mars, Jupiter, and Saturn, the mean position corresponds to the average motion of the planet in its heliocentric orbit.

Verse 1.59 of the *Sūrya-siddhānta* gives the diameter of the earth as 1,600 *yojanas*. Several scholars have argued that the *yojana* in the *Sūrya-siddhānta* is about 5 miles, thereby bringing the earth's diameter to the realistic value of $5 \times 1{,}600 = 8{,}000$ miles. Examples are Sarma (1956), Dikshit (1969), and Burgess (1989, p. 44). Using modern data for the mean diameter of the earth, the exact value should be 4.948 miles/*yojana*. We will see later on that it is worthwhile to consider this exact value, rather than the rough estimate of 5 miles.

Different standards were adopted for the *yojana* by different medieval Indian astronomers. This was noted by the astronomer Parameśvara (1380–1450 A.D.), who said that "What is given by Āryabhaṭa as the measure of the earth and the distances [of the planets from it], etc., is given as more than one and a half times by other [astronomers]; this is due to the difference in the measure of the *yojana* [adopted by them]" (Sarma, 1956). In fact, using Āryabhaṭa's earth diameter of 1,051 *yojanas*, we get 7.54 miles/*yojana* (Clark, 1930, p. 15).

Verse 4.1 of the *Sūrya-siddhānta* gives the diameters of the sun and moon as 6,500 and 480 *yojanas*, respectively. Given 4.948 miles per *yojana*, the resulting lunar diameter of 2,375 miles is about 10% higher than the modern value. The corresponding earth-moon distance of about 255,000 miles is high by 7%. However, the sun's diameter comes to 32,164 miles, which is far too small.

It is easy to see why the diameter of the moon should be reasonably accurate. The dimensions of the moon and its orbit were well known in ancient times. For example, the lunar diameter given by Ptolemy in his *Planetary Hypotheses* falls within about 7% of the modern value, if we convert his earth-diameters into miles using the modern diameter of the earth (Swerdlow, 1968).

TABLE 2

Planet	*Sūrya-siddhānta orbital circumference (yojanas)*	*Modern orbital period (days)*
Moon	324,000	27.32166
Mercury	4,331,500	365.256
Venus	4,331,500	365.256
Sun	4,331,500	365.256
Mars	8,146,909	686.98
Jupiter	51,375,764	4,332.587
Saturn	127,668,255	10,759.2

Geocentric orbital circumferences, as given in texts 12.85–90 of the *Sūrya-siddhānta*. The circumferences are nearly proportional to the geocentric planetary periods listed in the second column.

It is also easy to see why the diameter for the sun is too small. Ancient Greek astronomers tended to greatly underestimate the earth-sun distance, and this also happened in the *Sūrya-siddhānta*. The angular diameter of the sun is easily seen to be about the same as that of the moon—about 1/2 degree. This angular diameter, combined with a small earth-sun distance, leads inevitably to a small estimate for the diameter of the sun. Ptolemy's solar diameter figure is similar to the *Sūrya-siddhānta*'s.

Computing Planetary Diameters

What about the planets? Ptolemy listed wildly inaccurate diameters for Mercury, Venus, Mars, Jupiter, and Saturn in his *Planetary Hypotheses*. To see what the *Sūrya-siddhānta* says about the diameters of these planets, we should scale up the diameters on the moon's orbit by multiplying them by the orbital circumference of the planet, divided by the orbital circumference of the moon. This is done in Table 3. (These results were reported in Thompson (1997), assuming 5 miles per *yojana*, rather than the 4.948 used here.)

TABLE 3

Planet	*Modern diameter*	*Sūrya-siddhānta* diameter	*% Error*
Mercury	3031	2977	–2
Venus	7520	3969	–47
Mars	4217	3733	–11
Jupiter	88729	41195	–54
Saturn	74565	73120	–2

Planetary diameters in miles, computed using the *Sūrya-siddhānta* orbital radii from Table 2 and the rule of verse 7.13. The error percentages compare the *Sūrya-siddhānta* diameters with the corresponding modern planetary diameters.

Note that even though the angular diameters are too large, and the orbital radii are too small, the calculated diameters are close to modern values for Mercury, Mars, and.Saturn. For Venus and Jupiter, they are too small by about 50%, and it appears that they may represent radii. As we will see below, in this case they differ from modern values by 6% and –7%.

One might argue that this balancing is due to pure chance. However, the balancing works for five distinct cases. It is therefore worthwhile to estimate just how probable it is.

This probability can be evaluated by randomly choosing 5 pairs of numbers representing modern and ancient planetary diameters. For each pair (x, y), the number $P = 1 - \min(x/y, y/x)$ is a measure of how close x is to y. The sum of the P's for all 5 pairs is a measure of how well they agree. This sum can be computed for the 5 pairs in Table 3, and we can calculate how probable it is that randomly chosen pairs will give a lower sum and a better match. This probability comes to .0175, and therefore there is at most 1 chance in 57 that we would get the results in Table 3 by chance.

If the observed correlation did not happen by chance, then perhaps it happened by design. One hypothesis is that at some time in the past, ancient astronomers possessed realistic values for the diameters of the planets. They might have acquired this knowledge during a forgotten period in which astronomy reached a high level of sophistication. Later on, much of this knowledge was lost, but fragmentary remnants were preserved and eventually incorporated into texts such as the *Sūrya-siddhānta.* In particular, the real diameters of the planets were later combined with erroneous orbital circumferences to compute the diameters "upon the moon" given in verse 7.13. These figures were then accepted because they gave realistic values for the angular diameters of the planets as seen by the naked eye.

This hypothesis is supported by the fact that the *Sūrya-siddhānta* diameters of Jupiter and Venus in Table 2 are almost exactly half of the corresponding modern diameters. If we multiply these *Sūrya-siddhānta* diameters by 2, we get 82,390 miles for Jupiter and 7,939 miles for Venus. These figures differ from the corresponding modern values by 6% and –7%. Given this correction, the root-mean-square error for all five planets comes to 6.6%.

One can argue that the *Sūrya-siddhānta* diameters for Jupiter and Venus were actually the radii for these planets, and somehow they were accepted as diameters by mistake. Or radii might have been deliberately used instead of diameters in order to allow for the simple rule of $30 + 7.5i$ used in verse 7.13. This is consistent with the fact that such verses were intended as memory aids and brevity was considered to be a virtue.

In the probability estimate discussed above, the *Sūrya-siddhānta* diameters of

Jupiter and Venus were not interpreted as radii. Thus the probability estimate of .0175 is for the unedited *Sūrya-siddhānta* diameters. If we do double the diameters of Venus and Jupiter (taking them to be radii), then the probability estimate becomes 1.3×10^{-5}, or about 1 chance in 75,000.

Alternative Explanations

One possible explanation is that verse 7.13 may have been written recently, using modern planetary data, and falsely interpolated into the text. But this is ruled out by the fact that there is a manuscript of the *Sūrya-siddhānta* that scholars date to the year A.D. 1431 (Shukla, 1957). This manuscript includes a commentary by Parameśvara, who died in A.D. 1450, and thus it definitely dates back to the 15th century. Verse 7.13 is present in this manuscript, and it agrees with the Burgess translation quoted above. The commentary explains the verse point by point, and thus it confirms that the verse was present in the manuscript in the same form in which it appears today.

In 15th century Europe, the prevailing ideas concerning the sizes of the planets came from medieval Islamic astronomers who were following the teachings of Ptolemy. The first telescopic observations of planets were made by Galileo in 1609–10 (Drake, 1976). As late as 1631, Pierre Gassendi of Paris was shocked when his telescopic observation of a transit of Mercury across the sun revealed that its angular diameter was much smaller than he had believed possible (Van Helden, 1976). It is clear that the information on planetary diameters in the *Sūrya-siddhānta* antedates the development of modern knowledge of these diameters.

It is also clear that Hellenistic astronomers did not have accurate diameters for the planets. Ptolemy computed planetary diameters from his angular diameters and his estimates of planetary distances, and these were reproduced without significant change by European and Islamic astronomers for centuries (Swerdlow, 1968). However, his figures disagree strongly both with modern data and with the diameters computed from *Sūrya-siddhānta* in Table 3.

If we hypothesize that verse 7.13 incorporates knowledge of the actual diameters of the planets, then one natural question is this: If one started with the modern diameters of the planets and the *Sūrya-siddhānta* orbital circumferences, could one calculate backwards and arrive at the rule given in this verse? It turns out that the answer is yes. For each planet, multiply its modern diameter, converted to *yojanas*, by the ratio between the orbital circumferences of the moon and the given planet, as listed in Table 2. Here we use the radius in place of the diameter for Jupiter and Venus. The resulting values can be approximated by an arithmetic progression of the form $ai + b$ either by trial and error or by using an optimization method such as least squares. If we divide by 15 to get minutes of arc and then round off, we get the angular diameters given by *Sūrya-siddhānta.*

Planetary Orbits

The *Sūrya-siddhānta* makes the planetary orbits too small, and this was also done by ancient Greek astronomers. However, it turns out that in the *Bhāgavata Purāṇa*, the orbits of the planets are implicitly represented with good accuracy.

The *Bhāgavata Purāṇa* is a Sanskrit text sacred to the Vaiṣṇavas or worshippers of Viṣṇu. Modern scholars generally date it somewhere between the 5th and the 10th centuries A.D., but Indian tradition assigns it to about 3000 B.C.

The *Bhāgavatam* contains a section (the Fifth Skanda) which deals with cosmology. This describes the earth as a disk, called Bhūmaṇḍala or earth maṇḍala, which is 500 million *yojanas* in diameter. This disk is divided into a series of concentric ring-shaped oceans and islands. The islands, called *dvīpas*, are further subdivided by mountains, rivers, and other geographical features. The radii of the *dvīpas*, oceans, and ring mountains are given in the text in *yojanas*.

TABLE 4

No.	*Radius*	*Thickness*	*Feature*
1	50	50	Jambūdvīpa
2	100	100	Salt ocean
3	350	200	Plakṣadvīpa
4	550	200	Sugarcane ocean
5	950	400	Śālmalīdvīpa
6	1350	400	Liquor ocean
7	2150	800	Kuśadvīpa
8	2950	800	Ghee ocean
9	4550	1600	Krauñcadvīpa
10	6150	1600	Milk ocean
11	9350	3200	Śakadvīpa
12	12550	3200	Yogurt ocean
13	15750	3200	Manasottara Mt.
14	18950	3200	Puṣkaradvīpa
15	25350	6400	Sweet water ocean
16	41100	15750	Inhabited land
17	125000	83900	Golden land
18	250000	125000	Aloka varṣa

The radii in thousands of yojanas of the circular features of Bhūmaṇḍala, as given in the *Bhāgavata Purāaṇa*.

At first glance, Bhūmaṇḍala seems to be a poetic but utterly mythological description of the earth as a flat disk. However, the sizes of the *dvīpas* have a curious feature. They are far too small for the universe of stars and galaxies and far too large for the earth globe. But, given traditional values for the length of the *yojana*, they look right for the solar system.

The *Bhāgavatam* describes the path of the sun over Bhū-maṇḍala in detail, and from this one can deduce that Bhū-maṇḍala corresponds roughly with the plane of the ecliptic in modern astronomy. It is therefore natural to ask how the orbits of the planets compare with the geographical features of Bhū-maṇḍala.

Since the earth as we know it corresponds with the center of the Bhū-maṇḍala disk, we need to look at planetary orbits from a geocentric point of view. For each planet, we did this by taking the planet's heliocentric position vector and subtracting the earth's heliocentric position vector. By using an up-to-date ephemeris program, one can thus obtain the geocentric orbits of the planets as given by modern astronomy.

To compare the geocentric orbits of the planets with the *dvīpas* of Bhū-maṇḍala, we need to convert the *dvīpa* radii from *yojanas* to miles or kilometers. We have already observed that there are different standards for the length of the *yojana*, with 4.948 miles bringing the earth to its correct diameter for *Sūrya-siddhānta.*

Hiuen Thsang, a Buddhist pilgrim who visited India in the 7th century A.D., said that a *yojana* consists of 40 *li* according to tradition, but the measure in customary use was equal to 30 *li*, and the measure given in sacred texts was only 16 *li* (Burgess, 1989, p. 43). Joseph Needham (1962, p.52) pointed out that the *li* has taken many values during China's history, but in the Thang dynasty (when Hiuen Thsang lived), there was a long *li* of 532 meters and a short *li* of 442 meters. This gives about 4.4 to 5.3 miles for the 16-*li yojana* and 8.2 to 9.9 miles for the 30-*li yojana.* These figures roughly agree with the *yojana* of the *Sūrya-siddhānta* and with the popular valuation of 8 to 9 miles per *yojana* given by Cunningham (1990, p. 486). Of course, the *yojana* of 40 *li* is substantially larger than these values.

If we use a value of about 8 miles per *yojana*, we find that the geocentric orbits of Mercury, Venus, Mars, Jupiter, and Saturn, projected to the plane of the ecliptic, are in striking agreement with the features of Bhū-maṇḍala. We observe that the apogees and perigees of these orbits (their points of greatest and smallest distance from the earth) seem to line up with the boundaries of *dvīpas* and oceans, as listed in Table 4.

A geocentric orbit looks like a spirograph tracing that loops around the earth (see Figures 2–5). There are points of closest approach, were the curve swings in toward the center, levels off, and then moves out. These points of closest approach range from a minimum (the perigee) to a maximum. Likewise, the points of greatest distance, where the orbit turns in after moving away, range from a minimum to a maximum (the apogee). These four minima and maxima can be called the turning points of the orbit, and they help describe what the orbit looks like when plotted on a sheet of paper.

We can define a measure of "goodness of fit", showing how well the orbits line up with the *dvīpa* radii given in the *Bhāgavatam.* For each planet, find the shortest distance between a *dvīpa* radius and an orbital turning point. Take the root mean square of these distances for Mercury, Venus, Mars, Jupiter, and Saturn. The reciprocal of this is large if the orbits line up well with *dvīpas*, and it is small if they do not line up well.

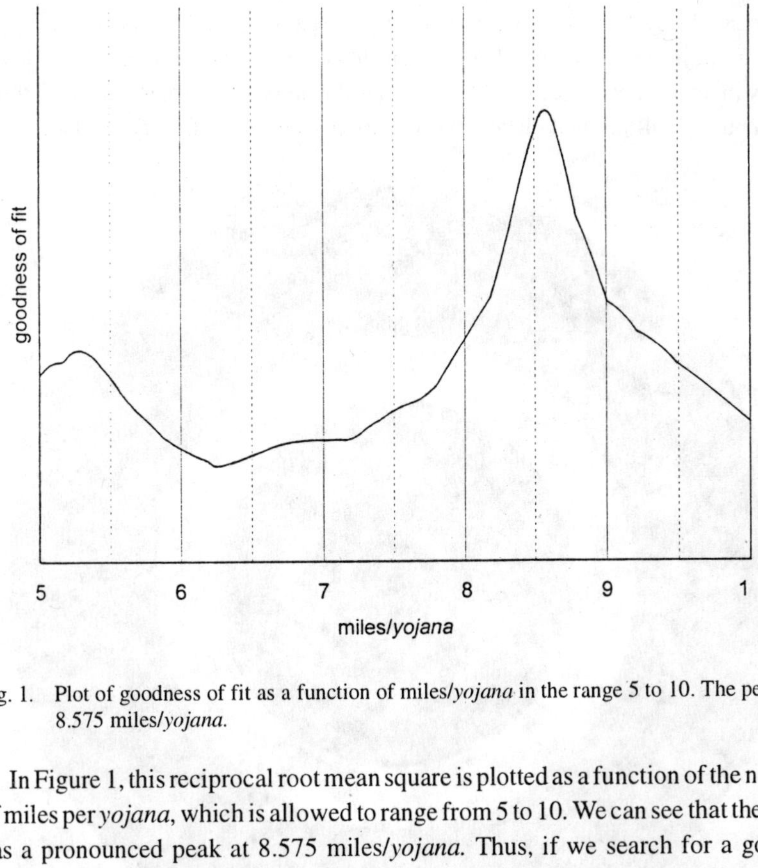

Fig. 1. Plot of goodness of fit as a function of miles/*yojana* in the range 5 to 10. The peak is at 8.575 miles/*yojana.*

In Figure 1, this reciprocal root mean square is plotted as a function of the number of miles per *yojana,* which is allowed to range from 5 to 10. We can see that the curve has a pronounced peak at 8.575 miles/*yojana.* Thus, if we search for a good fit between orbits and *dvīpas*, we automatically arrive at a value for the number of miles/*yojana* that agrees with customary usage and with the *yojana* of 30 *li.*

This calculation makes use of orbital calculations for the epoch of 3102 B.C., the traditional starting date of Kali-yuga. This date was chosen since it marks the traditional time period of the civilization described in the *Bhāgavatam.* In general, it was found that, due to gradual shifting of the planetary orbits, the optimal number of miles/*yojana* changes from about 8.52 in A.D. 2000 to 8.605

in 4000 B.C. The shift in miles per *yojana* is too gradual to determine the date of the orbit/*dvīpa* alignment, but it is consistent with the traditional date.

At 8.575 miles/*yojana,* we find the following alignments between orbital turning points and *dvīpa* radii. (These are listed in Table 5.)

We should note that calculation for the optimal miles/*yojana* took into account the radii of Table 4, except for Manasottara mountain (feature 13). This oversight was brought about by the fact that this feature is a "mountain" rather than a boundary of a ring-shaped region. It is one of two ring-shaped mountains in the Bhū-maṇḍala system (the other being Lokāloka mountain marking the outer boundary of the Golden Land, feature 17). However, it turns out that this mountain closely matches the apogee of Mercury. Thus the perigees and apogees of Mercury and Venus are all aligned closely with circular features of Bhū-maṇḍala.

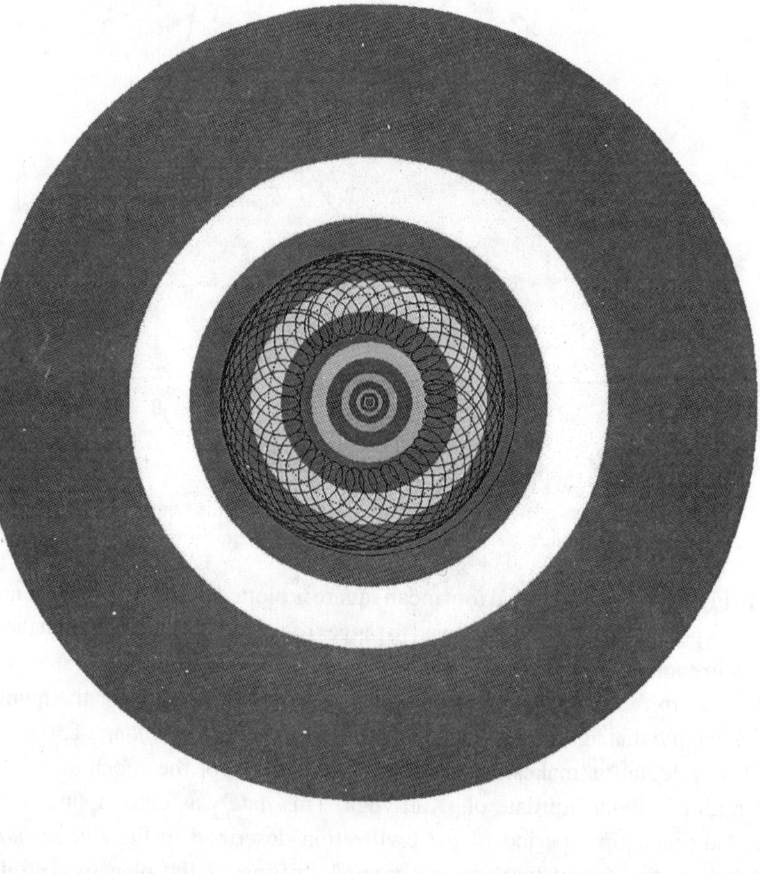

Fig. 2. Plot of the geocentric orbit of Mercury (continuous line) and the geocentric orbit of the sun (dotted line) superimposed on Bhū-maṇḍala. The epoch is 3102 B.C. and the plot assumes 8.575 miles/ *yojana.*

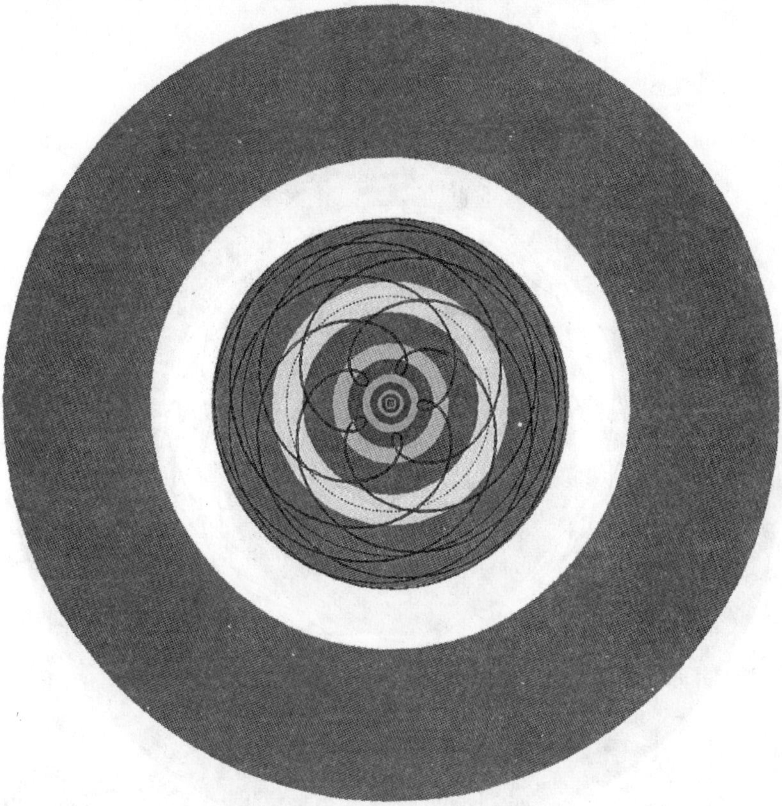

Fig. 3. Plot of the geocentric orbit of Venus (continuous line) and the geocentric orbit of the sun (dotted line) superimposed on Bhū-maṇḍala.

TABLE 5

CORRELATION BETWEEN DVIPA RADII AND ORBITAL TURNING POINTS.

No.	*Planet*	Turning point	Turning point radius	Dvīpa radius	Error percentage
1	Mercury	Perigee	5,976.0	6,150	2.9
2	Mercury	Apogee	15,701.1	15,750	0.3
3	Venus	Perigee	2,851.0	2,950	3.5
4	Venus	Apogee	18, 813.0	18,950	0.7
5	Mars	Perigee	4,090.0	4,550	11.2
6	Mars	Apogee	25,736.5	25,350	–1.5
7	Jupiter	Perigee	43,422.8	41,100	–5.3
8	Saturn	Apogee	121,599.6	125,000	2.8
9	Sun	Mean	10,840.4	10,950	1.0
10	Ceres	Perigee	16,312.8	15,750	–3.4
11	ZCeres	Apogee	42,683.2	41,100	–3.7
12	Uranus	Apogee	229,811.0	250,000	8.8

The *dvīpa* radii are from Table 4. Error percentage gives the error in the *dvīpa* radius relative to the corresponding orbital turning point. The orbital turning points are calculated for the beginning of Kali-yuga, using the ephemeris programs of Duffett-Smith (1985).

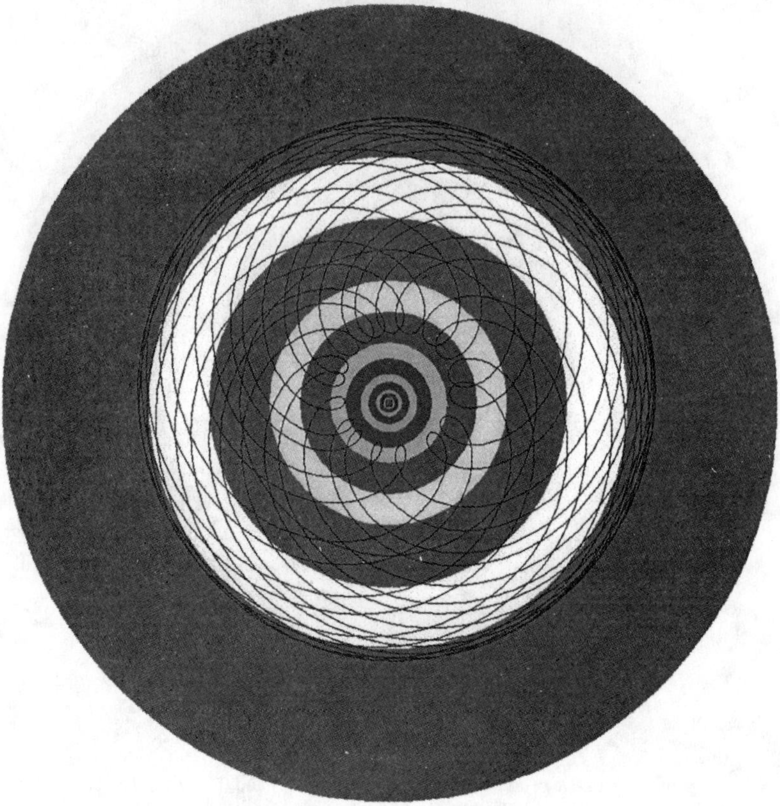

Fig. 4. Plot of the geocentric orbit of Mars superimposed on Bhū-maṇḍala.

In the case of Mars, the minimum of the envelope of outer turning points lines up with the outer boundary of the Sweet water ocean (feature 15). This is called apogee—to distinguish it from the apogee proper, which is the maximum of the outer turning points. The perigee of Mars lines up with the outer boundary of Krauñcadvīpa (feature 9), but the error is greater than that of the other correlations, and Mars partially penetrates the interior of Krauñcadvīpa. (Perhaps coincidentally, the *Bhāgavata* 5.20.19 states that Krauñcadvīpa was attacked by Kārttikeya, who is the regent of Mars.)

The perigee of Jupiter and the apogee of Saturn line up with the inner and outer boundaries of the region known as Golden land (features 16 and 17). The outer boundary—called Lokāloka mountain—is said to divide the regions lit by the sun from those not lit by the sun (*Bhāgavata,* 5.20.34). Saturn, the outermost of the five traditional planets, orbits just within this boundary.

The sun, of course, is one of the most important elements of *Bhāgavata*

Fig. 5. Plot of the geocentric orbit of Jupiter (continuous line) and Saturn (dotted line) superimposed on Bhū-maṇḍala.

cosmology. The geocentric orbit of the sun is nearly circular and falls close to the midpoint of the Yogurt ocean (feature 12). This midpoint comes to 10,950 = (9,350 + 12,550)/2 thousand *yojanas*.

When these correlations emerged, it was natural to ask about the other planets in the solar system. Neptune and Pluto lie outside the outer boundary of Bhū-maṇḍala, but the apogee of Uranus is within this boundary (feature 18) and close to it. Even the asteroid Ceres lines up with *dvīpa* boundaries in Bhū-maṇḍala. Ceres is the largest asteroid, and it marks the orbit of the famous missing planet between Mars and Jupiter. Since the orbital elements of Uranus and Ceres are not as well known as those of the other planets, the calculations for Uranus and Ceres were made for the epoch of A.D. 2000, rather than the third millennium B.C. (using, as always, 8.575 miles/*yojana*).

We made an effort to test these correlations statistically. The strategy is to focus attention on the correlations that emerged from the original optimization program used to find miles/*yojana*. For the purpose of statistical testing, other correlations that were noticed later were ignored.

The statistical test was performed by generating random sets of concentric circles and comparing them with the geocentric orbits of the planets. To keep these similar to the actual Bhū-maṇḍala system, the thicknesses from Table 4 were multiplied by pseudo-random numbers in the range of 0.25 to 1.75, and pseudo-radii were computed by adding these thicknesses. The optimal miles/*yojana* figure within the range 5 to 9 was then computed for the five planets Mercury through Saturn, and the reciprocal root mean square measure of correlation was also computed. This process was repeated 10,000 times.

It was found that in 9 cases out of 10, the level of correlation was less than that obtained for the actual Bhūmaṇḍala system. Thus the original pattern of alignments found by the optimization program is statistically significant. The additional alignments observed later can be regarded as icing on the cake.

The Length of the Yojana

The value of 8.575 miles/*yojana* was calculated by fitting orbits to *dvīpas*, but it turns out to be closely related to the dimensions of the earth. There are 68.70843 miles per degree of latitude at the equator. At 8.575 miles/*yojana*, we have 8.013 *yojanas* per degree. Since this is very close to 8, it is possible that the *yojana* was intended to be 1/8 of a degree of latitude at the equator, or 8.589 miles. This would be consistent with the fact that units of distance have often been defined in terms of latitude, both in modern and in ancient times. This is true of the meter (which is close to 1/10,000,000 of the distance from the equator to the pole on the Paris meridian) and the Greek stadium (which was 1/600 of a degree of latitude).

The *yojana* is often stated to be four *krośas* of 2,000 or 1,000 *dhanus* (bow-lengths). A *dhanu* is 4 *hastas*, where a *hasta* of 24 *aṅgulas* (fingers) corresponds to a Western cubit (Burgess, 1989, p. 43). The *yojana* thus comes to 32,000 or 16,000 *hastas*. Let us refer to these units as a long and short *yojana*, respectively.

If a long *yojana* is defined as 1/8 of a degree of latitude, then a *hasta* comes to 431.936 millimetres. I would like to suggest that the long *yojana* may correspond to the 30-*li* *yojana* mentioned by Ĥiuen Thsang, and the short *yojana* may correspond to his 16-*li* *yojana*. If so, the *hasta* of the short *yojana* must be 32/30 times the *hasta* of the long *yojana*. This comes to 460.732 millimetres.

This is within 0.2 per cent of the "geographic cubit" which was used extensively in ancient Near Eastern and Western civilizations for geographical measurements. Livio Stecchini, a scholar specializing in the history of measures, has explained in detail the use of the geographic cubit in ancient Egypt, and he defines it as 461.6935 millimeters (Stecchini, 1971, p. 351). He also points out that the Greek stadium was 400 "Greek cubits" of 462.4147 millimeters and was considered to be 1/600 of a degree of latitude.

Stecchini argues that the difference between these two cubits is due to the variation of the length of a degree of latitude at different latitudes. The Greek cubit corresponds to the latitude of Mycenae, and the latitude for the geographic cubit lies in Egypt. For comparison, we have defined the *hasta* of 460.732 millimeters in terms of the degree of latitude at the equator. This agrees well with our findings regarding planetary orbits.

The connection between the *yojana* and the Greek and geographic cubits is corroborated by Strabo, who describes the experiences of Megasthenes, a Greek ambassador to India in the period following Alexander the Great. Strabo cites Megasthenes as saying that along the royal road to the Indian capital of Palibothra (thought to be modern Patna), there were pillars set up every 10 stadia. The British scholar Alexander Cunningham argues that the pillars marked an interval of one *krośa* (Cunningham, 1990, p. 484). Since the stadium was defined as 400 Greek cubits, there must be 4,000 cubits per *krośa* and 16,000 per *yojana*. This agrees nicely with our conclusion that the short *yojana* should consist of 16,000 of the geographic or Greek cubits.

According to this interpretation, the pilgrim Hiuen Thsang learned the proportions of three sizes of *yojanas* from his Indian hosts, but he expressed their absolute lengths only approximately in his native *li.* (Of these, the first two are our short and long *yojanas*, and the third remains unidentified.) This might be expected of a pilgrim, whose concern with units of distance was simply to provide travel directions for his fellow pilgrims.

In contrast, the close agreement between 10 stadia and the *krośas* of the short *yojana* suggests a long-standing connection between India and the West. Note that since the stadium was 1/600 of a degree of latitude, the *krośa* of the short *yojana* comes to 1/60 of a degree, or 1 minute. The short *yojana* itself is 1/15 of a degree.

As we have already noted, the *hasta* of the short *yojana* is 32/30 of the 431.936 millimeter *hasta* of the long *yojana*. This number of millimeters, in turn, is very close to 4 times 108, a number that shows up repeatedly in ancient Indian literature and in the ancient world in general.

Here a key observation is that the meter is very close to 1/10,000,000 of the length of the meridian from the equator to the north pole. (It was fixed at this value after the French Revolution, but later remeasurements led to a slight revision in the length of the meridian in meters.) Thus, the *hasta* of the long *yojana* is close to 432 ten billionths of the length of this meridian, or 108 ten billionths of the circumference of the earth through the poles.

In a perfect sphere, the circumference through the poles is 360 times the degree of latitude at the equator. But in the oblate spheroid of the earth, this ratio is slightly higher. We can approximate it by taking a degree of latitude at the equator to be 8 long *yojanas* of 32,000 *hastas* of 108 ten billionths of the circumference through the poles. This gives us a value of 361.690 = 10,000,000/(256 × 108), where 256 is 2 to the 8th power. In fact, this simple estimate is low by only 0.04.%.

Another expression for the flattening of the earth at the poles can be derived by considering the *yojana* of 4.948 miles that figured in the study of planetary diameters in the *Sūrya-Siddhānta.* We pointed out above that the figure of 4.948 miles would prove to be important. Recall that this figure was obtained by dividing the exact mean diameter of the earth in miles by 1,600, the number of *yojanas* in the diameter of the earth according to the *Sūrya-Siddhānta.*

Now, 4.948 differs substantially from the short *yojana* of 4.58 miles. However, 4.948/4.58 is within 0.03% of 1.08. Whether this is a coincidence or not, it is a fact that 1,600 × 1.08 short *yojanas* is very close to the mean diameter of the earth. The short *yojana* is 8/15 of the long *yojana*, which we just expressed as a fraction of the circumference of the earth through the poles. By multiplying these numbers together, we can estimate the ratio between the polar circumference and the earth's mean diameter to be 150,000,000/(4,096 × 108 × 108), where 4,096 is 2 to the 12th power. This estimate comes to 3.13967, a number that is close to π, but slightly lower, due to the earth's equatorial bulge.

We can also compute this ratio using calculus and the flattening factor of f = 1/298.257 from a modern spherical astronomy text (Green, 1985, p.100). The result of this calculation is 3.13984, a figure that is 0.006% higher than the estimate obtained from the study of the *yojana.* It is not likely that one could come so close to this number simply by chance. It appears that the *yojana* in its different forms reflects real knowledge of the dimensions of the earth.

In view of these findings, we should briefly mention the role of 108 in India and other parts of the world. The Egyptologist Jane Sellers (1992) has documented the repeated appearance of 108, 432, 360, and related numbers in many different ancient and medieval traditions. These numbers also show up over and over again in ancient Indian texts, such as the *Ṛgveda* (Kak, 1987, 1993).

Sellers interprets these numbers as evidence for ancient knowledge of precession of the equinoxes. In Indian texts there may also be a connection with precession, but it is clear that these numbers play a variety of astronomical roles. For example, in the *Bhāgavata Purāṇa*, the period of Jupiter is given very simply as 12 × 360 = 4,320 days and the period of Saturn is given as 30 × 360 = 10,800 days (the actual figures being 4332.6 days and 10,759.2 days). The additional role played by 108 in the *yojana* and the dimensions of the earth suggests that this number may have been part of a sophisticated ancient system of mathematics and astronomy.

As a final point, recall that the mean earth-sun distance listed in Table 5 is 10,840.5 thousand *yojanas* and is close to the 10,950-thousand-*yojana* midpoint of feature 12. Here we have another possible example involving 108 and 360. Note that 10,800 = 30 × 360, and 10,950 = 30 × 365.

Conclusions

There is evidence that Bhū-maṇḍala, as described in the *Bhāgavata Purāṇa*, can be interpreted as an accurate map of the solar system showing how the planets move relative to the earth. This map is expressed in terms of distance units based on accurate knowledge of the dimensions of the earth.

There is also evidence that realistic knowledge of the diameters of the planets lies behind text 7.13 of the *Sūrya-siddhānta*. This knowledge is expressed in a unit of measurement that seems to be related to the unit used in the *Bhāgavatam*, and the relationship leads to an accurate expression for the ratio between the circumference of the earth through the poles and the earth's mean diameter.

This evidence of advanced astronomical knowledge suggests the existence of a civilization with well developed sciences of astronomy and geography. But when could such a civilization have flourished? The *Sūrya-siddhānta* and other medieval Indian astronomy texts strongly underestimate the distances of the planets, and this was also done by Greek astronomers from Aristarchus to Ptolemy.

The astronomy of Bhū-maṇḍala in the *Bhāgavatam* was not understood by medieval Indian astronomers. Thus Bhāskārācārya, the 11th-century author of *Siddhānta-Śiromaṇi*, said that he could not reconcile the relatively small diameter of the earth globe with the immense size attributed to the earth by the Purāṇas (Wilkinson, 1861, pp. 114–15). Likewise, the 15th-century astronomer Parameśvara stated that the Puāṇic account of seven *dvīpas* and oceans is something "given only for religious meditation" and is not acceptable to astronomers (Sarma, 1956, p.85). Since these astronomers severely underestimated planetary distances, they could not see the correspondence between the "earth maṇḍala" and the solar system.

The known astronomy of the first millennium B.C. and earlier is even more rudimentary than that of the Greeks or medieval Indians (Neugebauer, 1975). Thus, if accurate information about planetary distances and diameters was known in the past, this knowledge must date back well before the first millennium B.C. It must be coming down to us in fragmentary form from an earlier high civilization that was followed by a period of collapse and eventual recovery.

The connection between the *yojana* and the geographical cubit may indicate a tradition of knowledge dating back at least as far as the building of the great pyramid in about 2500 B.C. The correlation of planetary orbits with Bhū-maṇḍala gives a *yojana* that is exactly 1/8 of a degree of equatorial latitude at some time in the 4th millennium B.C. (This is due to the slow shifting of the orbits with the passage of time.) These indications of a date between 2500 and 4000 B.C. are consistent with the evidence indicating that astronomical knowledge was crude from the first millennium B.C. up to the medieval period.

In recent times, knowledge of planetary distances and diameters was obtained using the telescope, aided by Newtonian physics. It is not apparent how equivalent knowledge may have been obtained in the distant past. However, further research may yield greater insight into the advanced scientific achievements of ancient civilizations.

References

Ebenezer Burgess (trans.), *The Sūrya Siddhānta*, P. Gangooly (ed.), Motilal Banarsidass, Delhi, 1989..

Alexander Cunningham, *The Ancient Geography of India*, Low Price Publications, Delhi, 1990.

Derek de Solla Price, "Unworldly mechanics", *Natural History*, **71**, March 1962, 8–17.

S.B. Dikshit, English Translation of *Bharatiya Jyotish Sastra*, R.V. Vaidya (trans.), Manager of Publications, Civil Lines, Delhi, 1969.

Stillman Drake, "Galileo's first telescopic observations", *Journal for the History of Astronomy*, **7**, 1976, 153–168.

Peter Duffett-Smith, *Astronomy with Your Personal Computer*, Cambridge University Press, Cambridge, 1985.

Robin Green, *Spherical Astronomy*, Cambridge University Press, Cambridge, 1985.

Harry Hicks and Robert Anderson, "Analysis of an Indo-European Vedic Aryan head—4th millenium B.C.", *Jour. of Indo-European Studies*, **18**, 1990.

Subash Kak, "On astronomy in Ancient India", *Indian Jour. of the History of Science*, **22**(3), 1987, 205–221.

______, "The structure of the Ṛgveda", *Indian Jour. of the History of Science*, **28**(2), 1993, 71–79.

Joseph Needham, *Science and Civilization in China*, Vol. 4, part I, Cambridge University Press, Cambridge, 1962.

O. Neugebauer, *A History of Ancient Mathematical Astronomy*, Springer-Verlag, 1975.

K.V. Sarma (trans.) *The Goladīpikā by Parameśvara*, The Adyar Library and Research Center, Chennai.

Jane B. Sellers, *The Deaṭh of Gods in Ancient Egypt*, Penguin, London, 1992.

K.S. Shukla, *The Sūrya Siddhānta with the Commentary of Parameśvara*, Dept. of Mathematics and Astronomy, Lucknow University, 1957.

Livio Catullo Stecchini, "Notes on the relation of ancient measures to the Great Pyramid", in: Peter Tompkins, *Secrets of the Great Pyramid*, Harper & Row, New York, 1971, pp. 287–382.

Noel Mark Swerdlow, "Ptolemy's theory of the distances and sizes of the planets: A study of the scientific foundations of medieval cosmology", Ph.D. thesis, Yale Univ., 1968.

Richard Thompson, "Planetary diameters in the *Sūrya-siddhānta*", *Jour. of Scientific Exploration*, 1997 (to appear).

Albert Van Helden, 1976. "The importance of the transit of Mercury of 1631", *Jour. for the History of Astronomy*, **7**, 1976, 1–10.

L. Wilkinson (trans.), *Siddhānta-Śiromani of Bhāskarācārya*, B.D. Sastrin (Rev.), Baptist Mission Press, Calcutta; reprinted in *Bibliotheca Indica*, New Series, No. 1: Hindu Astronomy I.

Illuminating the Limitations of Western/Allopathic Medicine in Light of the Wisdom of Sanatana Dharma of Ancient India

KEVIN H. LEE
OsteopAthic Physician and Ayurvedic PracTItioner
Lansing, MI ,USA

As we rapidly approach the dawn of the third millennium of the common era we find ourselves in a fractured world—a world of burgeoning population whose resources become smaller every day, a world of cultural and religious diversity which is rushing headlong toward a kind of economic and ideological homogenization as the West is emulated by nations globally.

The Euro-American ethics of egocentrism and materialism have captured the global imagination. The sentient fruits of the industrial revolution, born of the European post-medieval "renaissance" in the material sciences, have become all too visible in a twentieth-century world polarized into "haves" and "have-nots".

Increasingly sophisticated and "intelligent" technologies make the images and icons of Western culture ubiquitously available to non-Western peoples whom the West views simply as an expanded global marketplace. These same technologies, increasingly electronic, mobile, and information-based, have during the latter half of the present century made this "dream" of the Euro-American lifestyle a tangible reality even to developing "third-world" nations.

But is this vision of reality truly a "dream" or might it be a global "nightmare?" Does this Western egocentric, cognocentric, materialistic vision of human existence represent the true nature of reality or does it more closely resemble the Vedic concept of "maya", the veil of avidya (ignorance) or unreality.

Even as this global culturo-economic homogenization proceeds at an alarming rate, the Faustian costs to our environment, our health and well-being, and to future generations, are becoming abundantly evident.

Deforestation, pollution of our waters and oceans, acid-rain, ozone depletion, birth-defects, mutating viruses and microbes, carcinogenic food additives, and nuclear wastes are but a small fraction of the all too familiar lexicon of the planetary "nightmare" in which we find ourselves enmeshed.

In addition, as the global community has become progressively smaller during this same enigmatic century, we have witnessed a prodigious explosion of violence; wars, political and ideological conflicts, racial tension, human abuses, imprisonment, and drug and alcohol abuse have become commonplace.

We must ask ourselves how we have arrived at this critical juncture. The question we must face is: if the dominant Western culturo-economic model truly offers such a unifying field-view of reality, why have we arrived at such a fractured, self-destructive world, whose very survival into the next millennium is uncertain? What ideological paths have led us here? Is there another source of wisdom which can shed light upon our limitations and offer us a path of liberation?

The first thesis of this paper is that indeed there is such a reservoir of illuminating wisdom available to us as a species. The ancient traditions of India, rooted in the knowledge of the Vedic Rishis as reflected in the Vedas, offer us a true understanding of the nature of reality.

The wisdom of the Vedas proceeds directly from the inner source of all knowledge, the True Self, the ground of being underlying all existence and all appearances. Such direct experiential knowledge is accessible only through the seat of consciousness which resides in the heart, and not by the conceptual mechanisms of the human intellect.

The Vedic and Vedantic teachings represent the oldest and most comprehensive spiritual tradition in the world. The heart of this tradition is expressed in the "eternal teaching," or "Sanatana Dharma." Known also as "Satya Dharma," the way of truth, or simply as "Dharma," this is the essence of true religion, and refers to the Universal Law or the true nature of the Self. The ancient religious traditions of India may collectively be called the "Dharmic traditions" as they share a common set of core principles.

The core principles of this Sanatana Dharma may be expressed as follows: that the one true religion is to be found in the eternal truth within the Self; that direct knowledge of this truth is available to each soul through Self-Realization; and, finally, that this Self-Realization is the very reason for our human existence.

The second thesis of this paper is that the reason why our faulty intellectually-based Western ideologies have brought the world to the brink of self-destruction is precisely because we have departed from (or have forgotten) this Dharma, and that only by embracing (or remembering) this Universal Law can we begin to bring ourselves into harmony with ourselves and others.

Since the focus of this paper is the application of these principles to the field of medicine, particularly allopathic medicine as it is practiced in the contemporary West, let us look at the origins of the present crisis in medicine and health care, and how the theses previously mentioned may play a role.

The origins of "modern" Western medical science are often traced to a number of influential practitioners throughout Western historical civilization, from the Greeks, Aristotle, Hippocrates and Galen, to the later Europeans such as William Harvey, Louis Pasteur, and others.

Yet the "biomedical model" which has come to dominate Western medicine, and which has become synonymous with our "medical model," was born in the seventeenth century under the influence of the Cartesian-Newtonian mechanistic world-view. Descartes' *Discourse on Method* in 1637 proposed his contentions that all natural objects were machines ruled by mechanistic principles, and that scientific knowledge, arrived at through the senses, is absolutely certain. Later Newton, in his *Principia Mathematica,* presented his completed mathematical formulations of this mechanistic view of nature.

This non-organic, reductionistic, mechanical view of the world gave rise to the dominant paradigm in Western medicine, indeed in Western culture, for the past three hundred years.

Medicine, as a discipline, and as a field of human service, may be seen to mirror our socioeconomic culture at large. As such we may be able to use the practice of medicine as a microcosmic "model" reflecting the qualities, problems, and perhaps opportunities for change which may exist in the Western cultural experience.

Emergency medicine, in particular, is often seen as the quintessential example of allopathic medicine. The allopathic principle is that of opposing the apparent symptoms of a disease process with an agent (medicine) which causes precisely the opposite effect in the body. In the emergency setting, this pharmacological reversal of symptomatology is accomplished very rapidly and effectively, often through invasive interventions.

The third thesis of this paper is that the system of medical care delivery within the Western model is essentially an "Adharmic" system. This can be seen in many aspects and at all levels, from the origins of Western medical sciences, to the methods with which medical research is carried out, to the ways in which health care is delivered to patients.

Let us examine some examples of the influences of this "Dharmic void" on contemporary medical practice. Where appropriate I will draw from my own experiences as an emergency room physician.

First, as the human biological organism is viewed as a machine with so many "parts," healing is reduced to fixing or replacing "broken" parts. This is in contradistinction to the holistic and ecological view held by the ancient Indian disciplines of Yoga and Ayurveda. Thus we "treat and street" patients in busy emergency departments. This means we reverse the symptoms of their disease as quickly as possible and discharge them. Now, if the patient is viewed as simply the reductionistic sum of mechanical processes, then this can be considered to be the essence of "healing." But according to Ayurveda this could not be farther from the truth. The underlying cause of the disease is essentially missed.

Second, the mechanistic medical model leaves no room for an underlying spiritual principle, the soul or "Atman," as the source of consciousness itself.

Without remembrance of spiritual knowledge, or "jnana," "consciousness" is seen simply as a by-product of neurochemistry, rather than our Atmanic union with the ground of being itself.

Thus we treat those patients who have lost demonstrable higher cortical brain activity as if they lack consciousness; i.e., "brain-dead." And we treat individuals without development as yet of somatolinguistic communicative awareness as non-persons; i.e., first trimester fetuses. Thus euthanasia and fetal abortion are commonplace in a culture where the Dharmic principle of "Ahimsa" (reverence for all sentient and non-sentient life) has been forgotten.

Recent neuroanatomical research by P. MacLean has suggested what he calls man's "triune brain," the neurophysiological result of the sequencial evolution, in man, of the "reptilian," "mammalian," and finally the "neocortical" brain.

The *Mandukya Upanishad* describes the four states of consciousness, the first three of which may correspond to the components of this "triune brain" of man. Man may be said to "sleep dreamlessly" in his "reptilian" brain, to "dream" in his "mammalian" brain, and to "think awake" in his "neocortex." The fourth state of consciousness, the pure transcendent awareness of Atman, according to many scriptures such as the *Katha Upanishad*, is "concealed in the Heart of all beings."

Further research by P. MacLean, J. C. Pearce and others has begun to reveal what Indian mystics have known for millennia. The heart is the actual source of consciousness. The intellect merely reflects this consciousness as the moon reflects the light generated by the sun. For example in the *Upadesa Saram,* Ramana Maharshi states that the heart (Hridaya) is that which is the essence of Human existence, i.e., the Atman-Brahman."

Paul Muller-Ortega, in *The Triadic Heart of Siva*, similarly quotes Abhinavagupta: "For just as in the body, which is made up of all the principles and depends on various different parts, such as the skin, etc., that heart is called the place where there is a repose in the pure light and pure consciousness . . . When the heart is free of stains and a light occurs which illuminates the supreme plane, by immersion in this shining light, one obtains identity with the Supreme Siva, that is, with consciousness."

Third, as the Cartesian model of reality holds that "all science is certain, evident knowledge," medical science rejects all knowledge unverifiable through the interaction of the intellect and the senses. Though science has developed many marvelous diagnostic imaging tools such as x-ray, CAT, MRI, PET, etc., they are simply extensions of the external senses and the intellect.

By contrast the Buddhist and Yogic "inner science" of direct, immediate awareness of reality is not subject to the perceptual distortions of the mental and sensory phenomena. Not until very recently has Western science begun to recognize the importance of intuitive nonrational perception in the healing arts.

Fourth, as nearly anyone living in the later twentieth century knows, our culture and our world are under siege by an epidemic plague of addictions and addictive behaviors. As the Buddha expounded his Four Noble Truths in his first sermon at Sarnath, he stated that the root of all suffering is craving, grasping, or attachment, i.e., "addiction." Since all attachment is rooted in self-ignorance (avidya), and by this ignorance is meant the false identification with the "ego" or false self, all addiction is ultimately rooted in addiction to ego. Here again the forgetting of Dharma is the prerequisite and *sine qua non* of the ignorance of ego-identification.

Emergency departments are literally overrun daily by legions of sufferers of the consequences of addictions. The protean manifestations of addictive behaviors are truly the "bread and butter" of ER census. The typical emergency department is little more than a "revolving door" for the recycling of victims of self-abuse or other-abuse. Discharged patients not infrequently are returned to the street only to return to the ER, sometimes multiple times in a given shift.

Drug addicts and alcoholics commonly account for repeated admissions to emergency departments. Yet such so-called "substance-addictions" represent only the more visible part of a vast and deep-rooted condition in which, according to Anne Wilson Shay, who wrote *The Addictive Society*, "98% of our society is addicted."

Other so-called "process-addictions" involve cyclical self-destructive addictive behaviors ranging from food and sexual addictions, to gambling and stealing addictions, to a myriad of victimizing and "victimless" violent behaviors. As widespread as many of these behaviors have become in our society, we often don't see the "forest for the trees." These behaviors and their images are such an integral part of our advertising, entertainment, and consumer-based industries that we have become almost insensitive to their continuous presence. In the final analysis we find ourselves addicted to addiction itself.

Even the common, "expected" diseases characteristic of our stressful, fast-paced, over-indulging society, such as obesity, cardiovascular disease, strokes, emphysema, and many forms of cancer are largely the end results of commonly accepted addictive behaviors.

Thus, in as much as Adharmic ignorance is a part of our human experience, addiction itself is not an aberration of a few of our fellow human beings, homeless drunks inhabiting the bowels of our cities; but rather addiction *is* the human condition. Such is the message of the Buddha.

Fifth, as "Dharma" is understood to mean that every element and every individual takes its proper place in the universal scheme of natural law, our ego-centered culture has created an expectation of "entitlement" among an entire generation. Many individuals believe that others, individually and collectively, "owe" them flawless services and unearned commitments, even though their own flaws are to be overlooked or denied. Hence we live and work in the paralytic crisis of an increasingly litigious society. This adharmic toxic legalism serves only the agendas of an elite noncompassionate few, and poisons the well of social interdependence from which we used to draw trust in and good-will toward others.

Certainly the time-honored relationship between the doctor and patient is being so poisoned. Indeed billions of health care dollars are consumed annually, in the United States alone, in "defensive medicine." Such "legal preventative" procedures are performed every day in every emergency department in this country. And this problem is only getting worse. As Mahatma Gandhi observed, "privilege without responsibility" is truly an anathema to civilization.

Sixth, and corollary to the above, is the widespread perception that we have "freedom" of action when we act with apparent impunity, uncensored, or if our actions go undetected by human authorities. The Dharmic principle of "Karma" having been forgotten, many people live their lives as if moral behavior conducted in unrewarded obscurity is useless, and as if amoral deeds done without getting caught may advance one further in life. That all one's thoughts, speech, and actions are causal in nature, or that this lifetime is only one pearl in an endless string of lives, are concepts lost on a "me first; me now" generation.

We have examined some of the ways in which the ancient Indian understanding of the spiritual principle of "Dharma" has been forgotten in Western society. We have looked at modern Western medicine as a mirror of the crisis brought about by this "Adharma."

We have seen that, in spite of the many so-called "miracles" offered by modern medicine, it remains bound within the realm of materialism, the intellect and the senses. Thus, limited to the relative realm of the phenomenal in nature, it is incapable of that transcendent awareness of the noumenal, that direct experiential knowledge which is the very nature, "Sat-Chit-Ananda." of consciousness itself.

Thus in Western culture's blind idolatry of corporate materialism's "goose-that-lays-the-golden-eggs." we tenaciously cling to our biomedical model of reality, failing to recognize or adequately address the underlying spiritual bankruptcy that afflicts us. As a result the "health care crisis" grows more costly, more materialistic, and spirals ever more out of control.

Perhaps the solution is to be found in a fundamental shift in our understanding of the nature of reality itself; a move away from the dominant materialistic Cartesian-Newtonian paradigm to a deeper, more comprehensive mapping of reality based on Dharma, the wisdom of the Vedas, and rooted in the non-dualism of the "inner science" of the Dharmic traditions of ancient India.

Such a paradigm-shift would entail a transformation of our understanding; from the reflected consciousness of the intellect to the source of consciousness, intelligence, and Being; from a nonorganic reductionism to a living holism that acknowledges the Atmanic divinity within man; and from an egocentric idolatry of and identification with the false Self to a Dharma-centric expression of Karma-yoga, where the true Self may be served and realized.

Significantly, the twentieth century has witnessed the emergence of examples of such a paradigm-shift in several key disciplines. Not unexpectedly the earliest and most fundamental indications of "cracks" in the Cartesian-Newtonian view of reality in nature began to become apparent in the field of particle physics early in this century.

Physicist-explorers such as Plank, Heisenberg, Einstein, Bohr, Oppenheimer, and others began to discover a subatomic universe whose properties, as revealed by ever more sophisticated technology, no longer conformed to the rules and formulas by which the "Newtonian" universe had previously been conceived to operate.

Mysteriously, this world within "atoms" unfolded to show an increasingly parallel resemblance to the mystical religious philosophies of Hinduism, Buddhism, and Taoism. Terms such as "relativity," "uncertainty," "wave-particle duality," "nonlocality," etc. were becoming the new vocabulary of quantum mechanical physics, ushering in a new view of the basic fabric of nature itself.

In the conceptual pyramid of the natural sciences, physics represents the base. Not surprisingly a profound paradigm-shift in the field of physics might be expected to precede and presage similar transformations to follow in the biological and applied sciences. This is exactly what we are beginning to witness at the close of the twentieth century.

One such emergence has been the development of the "12-step programs" of addiction-recovery which were developed in the first half of this century. Dr. Bill Wilson, the cofounder of "Alcoholics Anonymous," some say was divinely inspired to birth this program.

Driven by his own desperate struggles with addiction to alcohol, and wrestling with repeated failures to overcome its ravages, in spite of a deep and profound desire to quit drinking, he was influenced by a letter he received from Carl G. Jung, the eminent Swiss psychiatrist.

Concerning an individual these two men had each seen as a patient, C. G. Jung noted that the patient, an intransigent alcoholic, had recovered only after undergoing a consummate spiritual transformation. Jung observed that this disease of addiction to alcoholic "spirits" was indeed itself a "spiritual" disease, and in true "homeopathic" reasoning, stated, "*Spiritis contra spiritum*" ("A spiritual disease requires a spiritual cure").

Jung had borrowed these ideas from a contemporary psychologist, William James, whose own studies had been influenced by the tradition of the "Perennial

Philosophy", a term coined earlier by Liepniz and later used by Aldous Huxley in this century. Subsequently popularized through the work of Annie Besant and the Theosophical Society, the term refers to that essential spiritual core existing in all religions throughout all ages, whose origins in turn trace to the Sanatana Dharma.

That the 12-step programs of recovery from a host of addictions have been an answer to the global epidemic of addiction and a salvation to millions worldwide, is well known. What is less well appreciated is that its origins directly reflect the wisdom of the ancient Vedas.

Another example of this paradigm-shift, occurring in the area of psychology, is the growing movement of "Transpersonal Psychology," whose primary exponent is the Czechoslovakian psychiatrist, Stanley Grof. Dr. Grof's work has utilized voluntary alterations in respiratory pattern, based on Yogic *pranayama* techniques to access the therapeutic potential inherent in altered states of consciousness. Dr. Grof uses this "Holotropic Breathwork" to transport the patient's mental awareness to the subconscious origins behind the expressions of psychological disease states.

In Grof's view of the transpersonal psychological universe, the ground of being-consciousness is the substratum from which our individual experiences of personal consciousness arise. That force of desire continually urging us back toward the source of consciousness itself he calls "Holotropic" (i.e. "toward wholeness"). While that opposite tendency of consciousness to move from wholeness to separateness, from the formless to the multiplicity of forms, he calls "Heilotropic" (i.e. "away from wholeness").

Grof has compared the continual equilibrium of these two opposing psychological forces to the eternal dance of Siva-Nataraj, the creation and destruction dance of the cosmos from the formless consciousness of "Brahman" to the infinite manifestations of "Maya."

The psychological paradigm that has dominated Western medical science and psychiatry in this century has been based on the work of Sigmund Freud. Freud's model of the personality with its id, ego, and superego, conforms to basic Newtonian mechanical forces expressed in psychological terms. Grof's transpersonal psychology represents the same transformational departure from Freud's model that Quantum mechanics represents in relation to Newtonian physics.

As we approach the new millennium we stand on the threshold of cataclysmic transformation. The violent upheavals within our society and the decay and dissolution in our natural environment reflect the constrictive, materialistic, ego-centered worm's-eye-view of reality we, in the West, have chosen to cling to. Presently our very survival depends upon our detachment from the limitations of identification with the ego, intellect and the senses, and a rediscovery of the liberating reality of man's immortal soul, and an expanded awareness of the source of consciousness underlying all forms, all religions, and all natural law.

The Dharmic traditions of India and the eternal wisdom of the Vedas are an ancient repository of the deepest truths concerning man and his relationship to the universe. If we have the courage to reflect on why we are here and where we are going, this wisdom can offer us an opportunity to bring to our collective remembrance the message of "Sanatana Dharma," allowing it to transform and enlighten our sciences and our society.

Ancient India and the Vedic Aryans: New Discoveries, Scientific Procedures and Implications for History

HARRY H. HICKS,
Director, Foundation for Cultural Preservation
P.O. Box 111, Menlo Park, CA 94026, USA

ROBERT N. ANDERSON
Emeritus Professor, San Jose State University, CA, USA

Scientific tests on an ancient Vedic Aryan head that was cast nearly 6,000 years ago, research and related astronomical and scientific calculations, ongoing archaeological work, the use of recent technologies such as satellite photography, research relating to the Sulba-Sutras and discoveries such as the astronomical code in the Rigveda, strongly support ancient Indian traditions and belief and change the perception of ancient Indian science. They indicate a need to correct some misconceptions that have been held for over 100 years concerning the time and events relating to the Vedic-Aryans and the extent of their early cosmic and mathematical knowledge.

The new knowledge determines a more accurate time frame and indicates an earlier flux, merging and some reflux of proto-Indo-Europeans, Indo-Europeans, Kurganians, Indo-Aryans, and Vedic-Aryans concomitant with their movements and migrations. Hopefully this will clarify, and help to sort out some of the cross-cultural contacts, descendent sub-cultures and other inter-relationships, and the confusion arising from racial miscegenation and the many evolved names and designations.

Introduction

New discoveries support old traditions: Extensive scientific tests on an ancient Vedic Aryan head using advanced techniques and new methods, indicate it was cast nearly 6000 years ago. It was found in old Delhi where it had been brought to be melted down.

Ingenious research and related astronomical and scientific calculations, ongoing archaeological work, the use of recent technologies such as satellite photography, research relating to the Shulba-Sutras and discoveries such as the astronomical code in the Rigveda, strongly support ancient Indian traditions and belief and change the perception of ancient Indian science. They indicate the need to correct some misconceptions that have been held for well over 100 years concerning the time and events relating to the Vedic-Aryans and the extent of their early cosmic and mathematical knowledge. In general archaeology deals with physical evidence, the Vedas are unique in that they enlighten us as to abstract, creative and inspired thoughts of that ancient time. The facts and information are available and need to be properly presented and recognized. Regretfully, a lack of communication between outstanding scholars in the various disciplines involved has delayed this recognition, though, in fairness, much of the information is relatively recent. With the new technologies, scientific analysis can and should be used to greater advantage. There is a human factor as well, a reluctance to change old concepts even when proven incorrect and to adjust to new concepts in keeping with new discoveries and information which, surprising as it may be to some, lend support to traditional accounts and dates. Be that as it may, the charting of a more accurate chronological framework now appears possible and timely. Perhaps it would be best in a graphic form or overlay, a broad synthesis of ancient movements showing the flux and reflux of proto-Indo-European, Indo-European, Kurganian, Indo-Aryan, Vedic Aryan and other movements and migrations, and hopefully clarifying even cross-cultural contacts, descendant sub-cultures and other interrelationships. There is an implicit request for input, suggestions and constructive criticism from scholars of all disciplines, and those with interest and knowledge to assist in more accurately charting these migrations in correlation with the early history and movements of contemporaneous neighboring societies in the light of current knowledge.

This is a broad-brush attempt to correlate and. synthesize the interrelationships of the East and the West, Europe and Asia, and possibly even the "new world". Movements and migrations occurred from the earliest times, and while earlier on there were somewhat isolated enclaves there was, and has been, an ever increasing acceleration of miscegenation throughout the centuries. Drawing on the work of others, this is an effort toward a brief gestaltic view of some of those movements and their far reaching effects, with a focus on India and the Vedic Aryans.

In the Beginning

Various postulations, a blending of facts, sound reasoning and conjecture by respected scholars.

Luca L. Cavalli-Sforza, in his DNA studies, indicates early migrations from Africa into Europe and Asia. "The corresponding times of separation suggested by paleoanthropology are in similar ratios: 100,000 years for the separation between Africans and Asians, about 55,000 to 80,000 years for that between Asians and Australians, and 35,000 to 40,000 years for that between Asians and Europeans." It appears that there was a common trunk with one branch going to Europe and another to India. It also appears that India had early well developed agricultural communities and probably extensive astronomical and mathematical knowledge before the arrival of the Indo-European Kurganians. Cavalli-Sforza believes a symbiosis developed between pastoral nomads and farmers who originally owned the land. Furthermore, those "nomads often generated a hierarchical society in which their aristocracy formed the highest class...as was introduced in the Indian continent." Ammerman and Cavalli-Sforza in 1984 argued that the spread of farming after 7000 B.C. could be seen as a diffusionary process brought about by a combination of cultural diffusion, population growth and displacement, which they called "demic" diffusion. Linguistic scholars "are now theorizing that the proto-Indo-European language is itself a small branch of a much larger tree that stretches back to the dawn of mankind." A proto-world language ca.10,000 to 20,000 B.C. was given the name "Nostratic" (our language) during the time of hunter gatherers. This was followed by a proto-language called "Indo-European" around 8,000 years ago.

Indo-European Migrations

Colin Renfrew believes there was an agricultural expansion beginning ca. 7,000 B.C. and that the first Indo-European languages (PIE) came to Europe from Anatolia around 6000 B.C. with the first agriculturists, (Note: they had fertility goddesses, not male gods) and spread across Europe during the sixth and fifth millennia B.C. replacing or amalgamating the non-Indo-European speaking Mesolithic populations. He uses the estimated average expansion rate of ca. one km./year suggested by Ammerman and Cavalli-Sforza. Others felt it more likely that Danubian agriculturalists in a pincer movement encircled the Basques, meeting in France ca. 4000–3500 B.C., and that not enough consideration had been given by Renfrew to the results of comparative studies of Indo-European mythology, history and folklore and supported by archeology, that the Indo-European religion had sky oriented male Gods. (There are even indications that the Danes were on the North American continent in Greenland ca. 5000 B.C.) Renfrew also makes the point that the new, longer chronology de-emphasises the significance of the shared Indo-European heritage and that local conditions must be sought to explain the development of sophisticated social organizations in Asia and Europe.

Marija Gimbutas believes that there were several major "Kurganian" migratory waves. The first major thrust, ca. 4400 B.C. to 4300 B.C., consisted of a movement initiating from between the Don and Volga Rivers of Steppe pastoralists, nomadic horse riding "Kurganians" (refering to their mound graves called kurgans), moving south, east and west. She believes the importance of the horse in Indo-European society and religion cannot be over-estimated. The swift horse provided the transport and ability to strike out across great distances, instigating not only trade and the accumulation of wealth and social differentiation, but also raids and violence. It is possible but not clearly established that there was a collision of the early Kurgan culture with the Old European in E. Central Europe and the Old Indian (Indo-Aryan) culture in the Indus Valley. Cambridge's "History of India" indicates that the Indo-Europeans came "into S. Afghanistan and thence by the valleys of the Kabul river, Kurran and Gumal (all of them well known to the poets of the Rigveda) into the N.W. Frontier and the Punjab. In the age of the Rigveda they found five peoples each consisting of a number of tribes in which the women were of the same race as their husbands. This is proved conclusively by their social and religious status. We may be certain therefore that the invasions were no mere incursions of armies, but gradual progressive movements of whole tribes." (Note: Kurganians had patriarchal male gods.) These Indo-European warriors often formed a superstratum in invaded lands. There were early hill forts and probable rule from the hill forts along with the spread of the Indo-European Chiefdom system in Europe and India (Cambridge 1920). "There can be little doubt that Dravidian languages were actually flourishing in the western regions of northern India in the period when languages of the Indo-European type were introduced, possibly by the Kurganian migrations from the north-west. Dravidian characteristics have been traced alike in Vedic and classical Sanskrit and in the prakrits..."(note the island of Dravidian Brahui speech in distant Baluchistan and Elamite connection). There apparently was some friction and fighting between some of the Vedic Aryans and the Dasyus who had formerly been assumed to have been Dravidians; however, it now appears likely that much or most of the friction and fighting was between various Vedic groups.

Some of the Kurganians had moved along the Russian Steppes toward the Altai area and others along the Russian Steppes (and likely some from the Anatolia area) possibly bringing an advanced knowledge of metallurgy and other contributions into India. Some may even have come to India by sea. (Note: Vashistha's mother's name indicates association with the peoples of the sea.) Gimbutas believes there were two additional major waves of Kurganian migrations, the second ca. 3400–3200 B.C., the third ca. 3000–2000 B.C. They went across prehistoric Europe as well. Gimbutas feels "the late Kurgan migrations ended the long cycle of movements which had continued for nearly 2,500 years." I would merely emphasize the probability that there was considerable flux and reflux involved and my feeling that the late migrations were probably more from east to west.

New Discoveries—New Theories

The brilliant and comprehensive research by Subhash Kak, including his work on the Vedic codes, establishes that the Vedic-Aryans knew advanced astronomy. Navaratna S. Rajaram, a mathematician and historian, is currently studying the scientific foundation of history, primarily in India, and his work includes the Shulba-Sutras and the comparative mathematical time frames of Old Babylonia, the Egyptian Middle Kingdom and indicates the earlier knowledge of Ancient India. David Frawley's "*Gods, Sages and Kings*" refers to astronomical references in the Rig Veda preserving the memory of things going back to ca. 6500 B.C., and corroborates the work of other earlier scholars such as Tilak and Jacobi. Their work makes possible a much more accurate chronological summary for the ancient age of India. Borrowing from their creative work, as well as that of Marija Gimbutas, Colin Renfrew, Luca Cavalli-Sforza and others, and our own work with the Vedic Aryan head, with some trepidation and demonstrating some courage (since there have been prestigious and knowledgeable differences of concept), but with the benefit of new information and the recent guide posts, I suggest for critical review the following tentative hypothesis:

A. The Rig-Vedic Age

Probably beginning shortly after the major Indo-European "Kurganian" migration of ca. 4,400 to 4,300 BC. as described by Gimbutas, the Rigvedic age, apparently with its inspired concepts, conceived in India, (Cambridge: "The Hymns of the Rig Veda were composed in the N.W., the country of the 7 rivers") was still flowering at the time of King Sudas, Vasishtha, and the Battle of Ten Kings ca. 3700 B. C.. "Narayana" (Creator of Man) was apparently their original Supreme God-Head. Contemporaneous neighboring societies included the First Dynasty of Egypt, Proto-Assyrian, and an earlier agricultural Old Indian culture long before 3700 B.C. (based on considerable archaeological and literary evidence probably dating from ca. 6,500 B.C.). There appears to have been a merging of fertility symbols and concepts and a likely assimilation of

Figure 1. Newly recognized Indo-European Vedic Aryan Head. From the Collection of the Hicks Foundation for Cultural Preservation. Extensive tests and mutually corroborative and interrelated physical, stylistic and historical evidence indicate it was cast in the 4th millennium B.C. The life sized, hollow, copper-based head in a human likeness may be the first hard evidence relating to the original Vedic Aryans in India as well as the oldest discovered worshipped image of any practicing religion.

knowledge that India had already achieved combining with the knowledge the Indo-European groups may have brought with them along with their patriarchal and sky God concepts. (Cambridge: The Hymns "were collected and arranged between the Yamuna and Ganges, the 'Country of the Holy Sages', where Brahmanism assumed its final form, a form which in its religious aspect and universal principles appears to be a merging of Vedic and Old-Indian ideas and the result of the contact of different races.")

B.G. Sidharth in his "*Is the Rig Vedic Civilization the Oldest?*" based on an astronomical interpretation of some of the hymns in the Rig Veda and published findings concerning the excavations at Nevali Cori (dating ca. 7300 B.C.), led him to the conclusion that the Rig Vedic composers either belonged to an elite Anatolian clergy or at the very least had contact with it.

The human-like Vedic Aryan head with the warrior's mustache and the hair style of Vasishtha, dating at ca. 3700 B.C., is an important guide post, being hard evidence that helps establish the migrational time frame and level of technology of the period (as for instance in metallurgy) as well as a better understanding of the early layers of the Rig Veda. Tests indicate that the metal composing the head probably came from the mines in Anarak or Sialk in Mesopotamia which were heavy in sulphide ores. The Head's natural style and eye treatment also provide evidence of the continuity of Vedic Aryan art styles of the 4th/3rd millennium B.C., the Harappan and Mesopotamian art, and the evolution into later Hellenistic and classical Indian art.

Some believe the Vedic Aryan culture possibly received its spark from a powerful fusion of the knowledge of an Indo-European Kurganian superstratum, enriched by a wealth of knowledge from Indo-Aryan and/or the "Old Indian" culture. Whoever it was, whatever they were, it was an inspired "Fountain Head" which not only had some perceptions very similar to current scientific thought, but has impacted the entire world and its concepts to this day. Archaeological excavation of the Sarasvati civilization along with better interdisciplinary (and eastern and western) communication, and use of the new technologies in scientific analysis, will hopefully give further insight into who they were.

B. The Middle Sarasvati Civilization

The Middle Sarasvati civilization flourished ca. 3700 to 3000 B.C.. The Mahabharata War (based on early accounts and the time ascribed to the event) may have been fought ca. 3100 B.C. Perhaps it was the beginning of the end of the Vedic age and was also the time of the First and Second Dynasties of Egypt, the Proto-Sumerians and Proto-Assyrians.

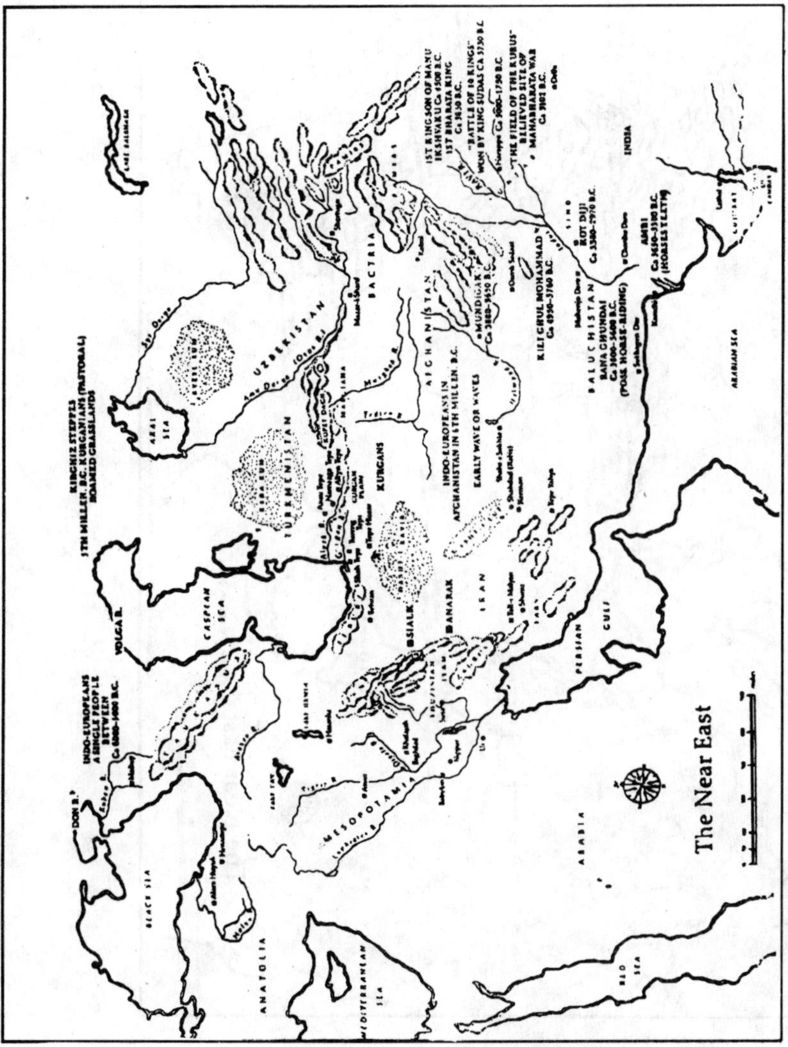

Fig. 2. Map of the Near East

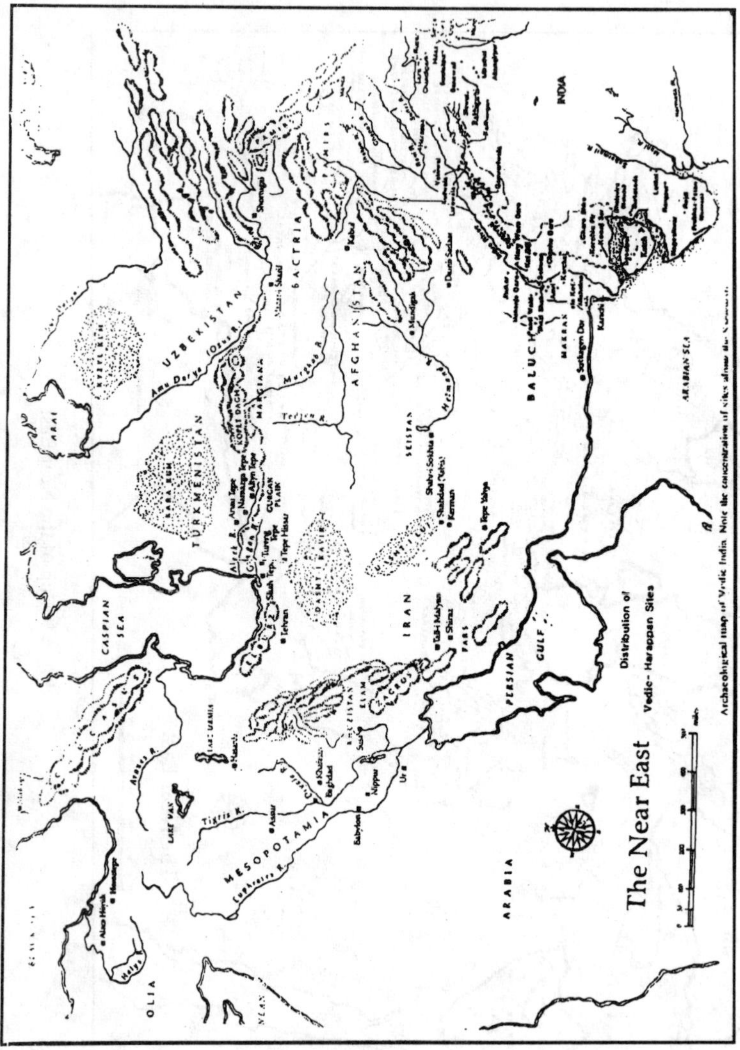
The Near East
Distribution of Vedic- Harappan Sites
Archaeological map of Vedic India. Note the concentration of sites along the
CASPIAN SEA
ARAL
TURKMENISTAN
UZBEKISTAN
KARA KUM
KYZYL KUM
Amu Darya (Oxus R.)
KOPET DAGH
MARGIANA
BACTRIA
AFGHANISTAN
Murghab R.
Tejen R.
Helmand
SEISTAN
IRAN
PARS
ELAM
ZAGROS
ELBURZ
DASHT-I KAVIR
MESOPOTAMIA
Tigris R.
Euphrates R.
LAKE VAN
ARABIA
PERSIAN GULF
ARABIAN SEA
INDIA
MAKRAN
Babylon
Nippur
Ur
Susa
Baghdad
Assur
Tehran
Shiraz
Kerman
Tal-i Malyan
Tepe Yahya
Shahr-i Sokhta
Shahdad
Tepe Hissar
Namazga Tepe
Altyn Tepe
Kabul
Mundigak
Shortugai
Karachi

Fig. 2A

C. The Late Sarasvati ca. 3000 to 1900 B.C.

Brahmavarta, "the Holy Land", probably was still principally Vedic. Archaeological excavation of the newly located cities along the old Sarasvati river will hopefully shed light on the matter. *Brahmarshidesa*, "the Country of the Holy Sages" between the Yamuna and the Ganges, apparently was where Brahmanism assumed its final form. It was the age of the Sutras and Brahmanas and the Trinity of Shiva, Vishnu and Brahma, the Sumerians, Egyptian Third and Fourth Dynasties, and the drying up of the Sarasvati River by 1900 B.C. In *the Harappan civilization* note the two art styles from the Harappan digs, i.e., the small natural and human like torso and dancer, and the stylized priest. There seems a possibility that the unpopular Elamites in Mesopotamia (who raided for women and cattle) were attacked and forced to migrate and settled in Harappa and possibly Mohanjo Daro, ca. 3000 to 2500 B.C. There were some migrations to the West. Gimbutas felt that around the 20th century B.C. the "movement of Asiatic peoples was responsible for the break-up of the Old Empire of Egypt." There were movements into Mesopotamia, and further west into Anatolia. Druids and their priests are believed to have arrived in the British Isles ca. 3000 to 2500 B.C. according to British archaeological calculations.

Talagiri identifies the Druids with the Druhyu people of north-western India. Apparently according to Indian records, the Indian emperor Mandhatr (who had marriage connections with the Purus) and possibly also Sudas, in a series of campaigns, drove a large segment of the Druhyus out of the N.W. and Afghanistan. Perhaps some went north and others became the Celtic Druids of England. The Druids in England claimed their origin to be far to the east ca. 3903 B.C.. There are indications the first Druids arrived in England in the third millennium B.C. with their trinity of God the creator, God the preserver, and God the destroyer and recreator, but called by different names than Hinduism's Brahma, Vishnu and Shiva. Possibly this gives a further clue as to where they may have come from and when. Perhaps of particular interest to the western world, the Druids also apparently had a prophecy that there would come a Messiah by the name of Jesu, which later led many of them to convert to Christianity.

D. After 1900 B.C.

After 1900 BC.was a time of turmoil and considerable migration, some to the West, i.e., West Asia and Mesopotamia and beyond; founding of the Kassite, Hittite and Mittani Empires, Celts, Scythians, etc.; centuries of raiders and plunderers. There was also some movement east to the Ganges-Yamuna area. Ultimately political supremacy passed from the Bharata King Sudas' Dynasty on the Sarasvati (later merged with the Kurus) to the Magadha Kingdom on the

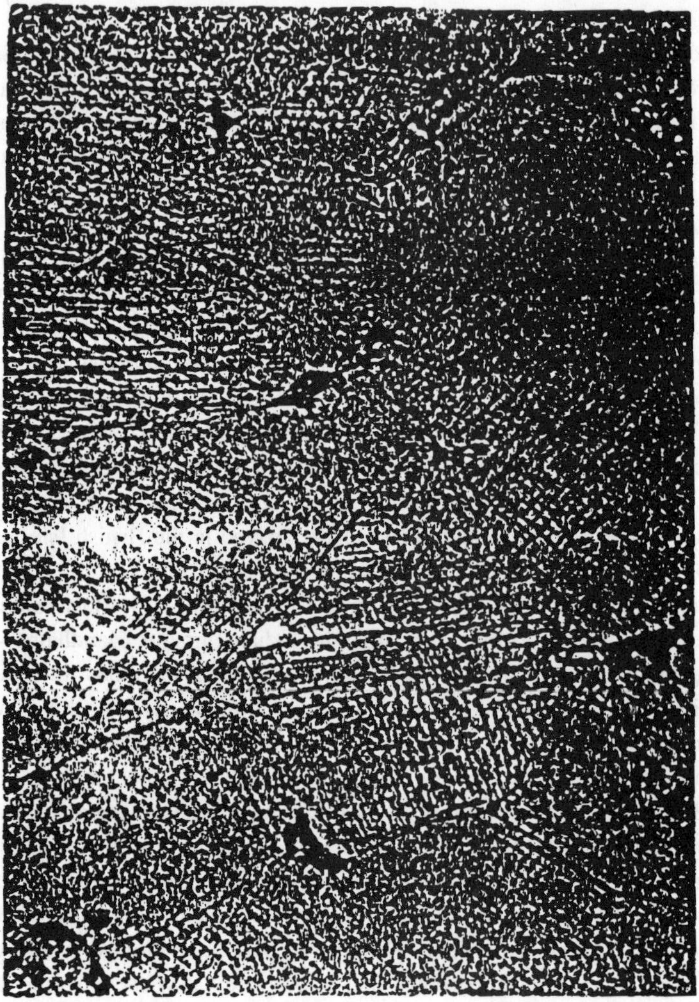

Figure 3. This metallographic picture is taken of a piece of metal removed from the neck in the area of the crack. The absence of sharp angles in the grains shows that the grains have recrystallized. The grain boundaries also show pitting and attack

Ganges. For many centuries Magadha was the dominant power in North India until the Hepthalite Huns, ca. the 5th or 6th century A.D. The life sized Vedic head with the hair style of Vasishtha, found in the Delhi area ca. 1958, was apparently damaged long ago, possibly as late as during the time of the Muslim conquests of the Delhi area in the 13th and 14th century A.D. It is worthy of note that the inscription is off centered to the face and either by accident or design is centered to avoid the damaged area. Scientific tests indicate the inscription, identifying the Head as the ancient Vedic God "Narayana" (creator of man), was inscribed a minimum of 4,500 yrs. after being cast and in a script not used after the 14th century A.D. This possibly indicates the Head may have been actively involved in over 5000 years of the history of India. If it was damaged by the Huns, it would coincide remarkably with the date of ca. 3,700 B.C. for King Sudas. There are indications of a great tectonic disturbance in India, ca. 1900 B.C., which changed the flow of the Vedic-Aryan's "Mother River", the Sarasvati, causing it to dry up and forcing the abandonment of hundreds of settlements (just recently discovered with the assistance of satellite photography) along its previous banks. It is believed some of these Indo-Aryan groups may have migrated into Mesopotamia around this time or shortly thereafter (possibly as the Kassites) and conquered the area. Others may have gone into Iran or Persia. (Zarathustra may have been a descendent.)

The Indo-European Yueh Chi: The Big Yueh Chi apparently came back from near Mongolia and went into N.W. India ca. the 2nd century B.C. and became the Kushan. The Little Yueh Chi may have gone farther west and/or south.

The North American Continent

While controversial, there is a great deal of evidence indicating there was trade going on between the Mediterranean area and the east coast of North America in the 1st millenium B.C. While fault may be found for example with some of the assumptions made by Barry Fell in his "*America B.C.*" or with Joseph B. Mahan in his book "*The Secret*" (*America in world history before Columbus*) there appears to be too much substance to dismiss lightly. There is a new publication as well which may shed some light on the subject, "*Ancient American Inscriptions: Plow Marks or History?*" by W.R. McGlone, P.M. Leonard, J.L. Guthrie, R.W. Gillespie and J.P. Whittall, Jr. from the Early Sites Research Society. Those interested in researching the matter might find the two volumes of "*Pre-Columbian Contact with the Americas across the Oceans: An Annotated Bibliography*" by John L. Sorenson and Martin H. Raish (Research Press, Provo Utah) of some assistance. Among the many artifacts indicating an Indo-European contact is a bone dating at ca. 700 B.C. taken from a tomb in the Alabama-Tennessee area with what is believed to be Proto-Ogam (Celtiberian) writing on it. A number of other artifacts have been found, along with inscriptions and writings, indicating Phoenicians, Carthagenians, Syrians, Egyptians, Celtiberians and even the Yueh Chi may have been a part of this contact. The matter appears worthy of further objective research and study.

The Original Inhabitants of India

SWAMI MAHESHWARANAND
Vienna, Austria

India is a country of manifold diversity of physical and social type, language, custom and religion. The so called Indus-Valley civilization stretched over a vast area covering a million and a half square kilometers. Thus it was the most extensive in the ancient world. It exceeded in size and sophistication ancient Egypt and Mesopotamia combined together. Max Muller and some other scholars would like us to believe that the Rigveda was composed near about 1200 B.C. It is difficult to believe this theory. The theory of the Aryan invasion into India is not a scientific reconstruction of our remote past based on archaeological finds. Max Muller was not an archaeologist. He was a linguist. The theory of Aryan invasion is based on the similarities between Sanskrit and European languages.

Introduction

I am happy to participate in this World Conference on *Revisiting Indus-Sarasvati Age, Ancient India and Vedas*. I am happy to find that a group of brilliant scholars and academicians present here are engaged in the Herculean task of gathering the new pieces of evidence that have come to light recently as a result of excavations and satellite studies and trying to understand the Vedic age in their light in an objective, dispassionate and scientific manner free from racial and national prejudices.

As you know, the geography of India, its physical features, its mountains and rivers have had a decisive influence on its history. Walled off by the impenetrable Himalayan ranges on the north and flanked on the sides by lesser ranges, India enjoys a practically isolated position in the Asian continent. With the waters of the ocean separating her from Africa on one side and Malaysia and the islands of the Indonesian Archipelago on the other, India was from the beginning of history isolated to a large extent in her evolution. The fact that the area so isolated was large and contained at all times a variety of racial elements, wide differences of climate, soil and physical characteristics, not only prevented it from becoming stagnant, but gave it a continental character, capable of generating the forces of action and reaction which lead to the development of civilization. One comes across every kind of climate in India, from the scorching heat of the deserts of

Rajasthan to the snowing cold of the Himalayan ranges, from the dry rocky tablelands of the Deccan to the moist tropical luxuriance of Bengal and Kerala.

The outstanding feature of Indian Geography are the Himalayas. The incalculable influence of the Himalayas on India can be imagined from the fact that the Indus and its great tributaries, the Ganga and its major tributaries and the Brahmaputra—the three river systems on which the life of Hindustan depends, take their rise on the Himalayas. The now nonexistent Sarasvati Drishadvati also flew from the Himalayas. It is the protective wall of the Himalayas that has given to India the continuity of its civilization and social structure from the earliest times to our own days.

No careful student of our history can help being struck by one supreme characteristic of the Indian people. It is their vitality as a distinct type, with a distinct civilization of their own and a mind as active after centuries of foreign rule as ever in the past. The Indian people today are no doubt a composite ethnic product; but whatever their different constituent elements may have been in origin, they have all acquired a common Indian stamp, and have all been contributing to a common culture and building up a common type of tradition, thought and literature. Beneath the manifold diversity of physical and social type, language, custom and religion, which strikes the observer in India, there can still be discerned a certain underlying uniformity of life from the Himalayas to Cape Comorin.

Some of the enriching and distinct characteristics of Indians

The history of India revolves around the Aryans not only because they were the first among the races whose records have been preserved, but chiefly because they have succeeded in impressing the stamp of their religion, philosophy, vocabulary, literary form and tradition, administrative system, in their ideas and culture, upon the other races of India. Tribes that cannot claim with truth to have a drop of Aryan blood in their veins have accepted the Aryan influence and tried desperately to give their ancestors an Aryan pedigree. Aryan culture with the addition of some elements borrowed from the Dravidians but transformed in its own way rules all India and gives to it an inner unity, in spite of the diversity created by our geography, ethnology and political history.

The Aryans have enriched Indian life with the following six gifts:

1. A lofty spirituality which has sublimated even the non-Aryan elements borrowed in the course of that grand synthesis which is called Hinduism.
2. The spirit of systematizing the methodical arrangement of every branch of thought by a minute analysis of its parts.
3. Ordered imagination in literary and artistic creation as distinguished from extravagances, grotesqueness, emotional abandon.

4. The grading of the people into mutually exclusive castes, based upon differences of function and of supposed ancestry.
5. Honour to women while rejecting feminist institutions like matriarchy and polyandry, which prevailed in the south and north of the then Aryan wedge driven into Aryavarta.
6. The institution of Gurukulas which were distinct alike from the city universities and the celebite monasteries of Europe.

Who are Aryans!

Who were the Aryans? Were they the sons of the soil or invaders? If they were invaders, what was their native country? When did they invade India? When did they compose the Vedas? These are the questions which the scholars have tried to answer.

Until 1921, it was commonly believed that the Aryan civilization was the oldest civilization in India. In 1922, as a result of excavations conducted in Harappa and Mohenjo Daro, it trasnspired that the cities of Harappa and Mohenjo Daro, which are the best known cities of another civilization older than the Aryan one, show extremely advanced architectural features like carefully planned buildings and public facilities, drainage and water supply. All the books on Ancient Indian History say that this Harappan civilization disappeared near about 150 B.C., most likely due to the invasion of the Aryans.

These Aryans are reported to have composed the Vedas in 1200 B.C. after destroying the civilization of the Dravidians of the Indus Valley in 1500 B.C. The destroyed civilization was named Harappan or Indus-Valley civilization but we know that the so called Indus-Valley civilization stretched over a vast area covering a million and a half square kilometres. Thus it was the most extensive in the ancient world. It exceeded in size and sophistication ancient Egypt and Mesopotamia combined together.

Max Muller and some other scholars would like us to believe that the Rigveda was composed near about 1200 B.C. It is difficult to believe this theory. The theory of the Aryan invasion into India is not a scientific reconstruction of our remote past based on archaeological finds. Max Muller was not an archaeologist, he was a linguist. The theory of Aryan invasion is based on the similarities between Sanskrit and European languages.

Some Major Modern Findings

After examining all the available archaeological evidence, Sri N.S. Rajaram, in his book *History of Politics*, states: "Archaeology therefore tells us that the whole of ancient Indian civilization, from the earliest times, was largely an indigenous evolution. The idea that the Indian civilization has always been an import—an alien imposition at every stage—is a politically motivated dogma that receives no scientific support."

Ganga is now the holiest river in the eyes of the Hindus. But to the Vedic Aryans the holiest was Sarasvati. There are not less than fifty references to Sarasvati in the Rigveda, whereas Ganga is mentioned only once.

- Vasishta in the 7th Mandala of the Rigveda describes Sarasvati as a mighty river flowing from the mountains to the sea sustaining the lives of the Vedic people.
- Visvamitra, the mantra-drashta of the 3rd Mandala of the Rigveda, sings: "I kindle you, O blessed fire at Ila, the most glorious place on earth. In the pure brilliance of the auspicious day, on the Drisadvati, the Sarasvati, the Apaya, may you enlighten all men." (Rigveda III, 23.4)
- Gritsamad; the seer of the 2nd Mandala, speaks of Sarasvati as "the best of mothers, the best of rivers, the best of goddesses." (Rigveda II, 42.16)
- At one place in the Rigveda, Indra is invoked to shower nectar on the place where Kapila, Hiranaya and Prachi Sarasvati meet. This place is Prabhas Patan famous for the temple of Lord Somnath.

The Rigveda was composed before the drying up of Sarasvati, otherwise the seers would not have sung its praises. According to the exploration of Wakankar, before 2000 B.C. a great river was to flow through Haryana, Punjab and Rajasthan mingling with the Arabian Sea at modern Bharuch. This is also confirmed by the American satellite photography. We know now that the Sarasvati gradually became weaker and began to dry up as early as 3000 B.C. It finally dried up completely around 1900 or 2000 B.C. This is confirmed by the archaeological sites of this period found on the river-bed itself indicating that the river must have been dry by the time they were established.

According to Sri Raja Ram the verdict of science is clear. The Rigveda describes the geography of North India before the Sarasvati dried up. The Harappan civilization of the Indus Valley was a continuation of the Vedic, its end coinciding roughly with the final drying up of the Sarasvati in 2000 B.C. So the theory of the Aryan invasion in 1500 B.C. and the composition of the Rigveda in 1200 B.C. is pure fiction.

Raja Ram would like to believe that the Sarasvati-Sindhu civilization spanned 5000 years. Its contribution includes the science of language, mathematics, metallurgy and in all probability alphabetical writing. Then there is the great contribution of the Vedas, the Upanishads, Yoga and other philosophical works that taken together make it the greatest civilization the world has ever known. The heartland of this civilization was not the Indus but the once mighty Sarasvati. All this makes the theory of Aryan invasion a myth, and the same is true of the Aryan-Dravidian conflicts.

I never had any formal schooling in history, but from what I have read, I find that Sri Raja Ram, Mr. David Frawley, Sri Subhas Kak, Sri S.R. Rao and Dr. S.P. Gupta have done remarkable work to present a correct and candid picture of Ancient India. Their works are based on the latest explorations in the Indus-Sarasvati area, archaeological excavations and satellite data. The picture that emerges from their studies is:

1. The Vedic age commenced near about 8000–7000 B.C. The Rigvedic age ends in 3750 B.C.
2. The Sarasvati river completely dried up near about 2200 to 2000 B.C. There was a great drought during 2200–1900 B.C. Indian Aryans migrated out of India into Iran, Mesopotamia and Asia around 2000 B.C. This was caused by the great drought.
3. The Vedic age ended in 2000 B.C. with the complete drying up of the Sarasvati. The closing phase of the Vedic age was the Sutra period which corresponds to Harappan archaeology of 3000 to 2000 B.C.
4. Aryans were not invaders into India.

Even earlier scholars like Dr. Sampurna Nand, Dr. Avinash Chandra Das, Dr. Ganga Nath Jha, Dr. L.D. Kala and Dr. Raj Bali Pande had contended that the original home of the Aryans was India, but they did not have access to the data which is available today. The result was that they could not convince others.

Now things are different and I hope that the scholars of the present generation will be successful in reconstructing India's ancient History. I wish them success in their endeavour.

Ancient History of Bharat and Hindu Identity

DR. JAGAT K. MOTWANI
2 Court, Dix Hills, Ny 11, Langhans 746

This paper is a product of a library-based research. Its main hypothesis is that much of the ancient history of Bharat is false and ill-based. It has adversely affected Indian identity in general and Hindu identity in particular.

The paper addresses itself to the following issues:

(a) The importance of ancient history and its impact on the cultural identity of its people;

(b) Wrong history is being taught in schools and colleges—meaning thereby that Hinduism/Sanatana Dharma didn't exist prior to the alleged Aryan invasion; prior to Aryan invasion of Bharat in 1500 BC, the natives of Bharat were barbarous; chronology of the important Hindu epics and Vedas has been advanced to period after 1500 BC to fit into the so called Aryan invasion theory; Indus civilization is considered different from Vedic civilization; different scholars have suggested different original homes of Aryans.

Primary approach is to expose contradictions, implicit and explicit, within the one and the same author/book. I present some interpretations that show ignorance and clear bias. Distortions and misinterpretations are scientifically exposed with the support of documented evidences.

If you want to weaken a nation, you must distort its ancient history and confuse its identity. This is what the European colonialists, especially the British did to Bharat. This paper is a product of a library-based research which is still in progress. Its first part is intended to find out about Bharat's ancient history, about who wrote it, and what, with what intentions, and why the native Aryans didn't. Were those historians competent and well qualified? Were they bias-free and men of professional integrity? It also wants to find out how they have stripped the descendants of native Aryans of their ancestral identity. What did they do to their ancient holy scriptures, Vedas, and to Sanskrit, the family language of their ancient seers. Vedas were too ancient and too distant for historians, more so for biased foreigners, to be able to meaningfully comprehend.

The second part of this paper addresses itself to refuting the theory of *'Aryan Invasion of India'*, which, in David Frawley's (1991a) words, has been "one of the main ideas used to interpret and generally devalue the ancient history of India."

My basic approach to refute the theory has been to use their own material against themselves. Let the readers and authors themselves see what they have written, implicitly and explicitly, is self-contradictory and how they have been contradicting others or writing different things. Different books and encyclopedias are contradicting one another. One page contradicts what is written on the other page of the same book. Sometimes contradictions appear in the same page, or even the same paragraph. The authors, it seems, were aware of the contradictions, and seemingly to cover up they had to make it ambiguous, foggy and vague. They have confused the readers with their illogical, ill-based, and speculative interpretations and vague representations. It is hard to understand why; rather, they have not tried to correct it in the light of the discovery of the Indus civilization. The ancient pre-histories should never be considered final, especially in the present atmosphere of increasing archaeological appetite.

In the third part, the most important one, an attempt has been made to trace the history of ancient Asia Minor region and to identify its ancient languages, social structure and religions, so as to ascertain if Asia Minor had the people with *Vedic* orientations and if they knew *Sanskrit* or any Indic language. Most historians tell that the original home *of Sanskrit* and *Vedas* is somewhere in that region. My hunch is that there were some immigrants who had Vedic religious and linguistic orientations. They must have gone there from Bharat, as has been discussed later (p. 5); and some of them might have migrated back in 1500 B.C..

History and the National Identity

The Western scholars have written Bharat's ancient history. Several historians have rightly portrayed Hindus as indifferent to their own ancient cultural history.

> "India has always been an immensely heterogeneous land of provincial fastness, linguistic and racial diversity, torn by conflict and invasions. Its people have had little opportunity until recent times to develop a pervasive sense of historical continuity or of nation awareness, and much of ancient Indian history is still shrouded in mystery. However, during the past century immense strides have taken in archaeological research" (Garraty and Gay, 1981: 95).

Perhaps, the English literate elite have not yet realized the value of the history of their heritage and its impact on identity. It is evident from the mass allergy to the traditional name *'Bharat'*. Ceylon went back to its original name 'Sri Lanka' immediately after its independence. India's long subjugation under Muslim and later European rulers had numbed their ethnic sensitivity, which seems to have started regaining gradual consciousness, this august convention is a heartening evidence of.

Wrong History is More Dangerous than Its Ignorance

The strength of a nation and the identity of its people owe a lot to its history. Herbert J. Muller in *'The Loom of the History'* (1958) emphasizes the significance of history and laments its abuse by historians. He says that from the past, as is given to us by history, come all our customs, institutions, skills, arts, rights, duties and faiths. We draw upon the history of our civilization, however unconsciously, whenever we make up our minds about any matter of importance.

Muller believes that a superficial, confused, distorted notion of history is far more dangerous than ignorance of it. Muller has expressed his pain at the intentional mutilation of the history of the ancient Eastern civilizations by Western historians. There are distortions, misrepresentations, ambiguities, incongruities and deliberate well calculated complexities and gaps.

> "In particular, it develops the historic theme of East and West. This is a much-abused theme, commonly oversimplified by the prejudices of the West; the earnest talk about *One World* is still clouded by the notion that never the two shall meet, or always the West must win." (Herbert J. Muller, 1958: xiii).

According to Muller (1958: 28), this kind of historic prejudice and conceit led Paul Valery to call history "the most dangerous product ever concocted by the chemistry of the brain." He has talked about what Herbert Butterfield, a distinguished historian, thought about history:

> "The national history taught in schools has tended to encourage the most general and terrifying of existing evils, human presumptions and particularly intellectual arrogance, or in other words self-righteousness. Wrong history is being taught in all countries, all the time, unavoidably. While we have great need of history, our first need is to unlearn most of what we have been taught."

Western Cultural Arrogance and History in Classrooms

The Western institutions of higher learning have been very cautious about what and how much should be taught about non-Western cultures. According to William H. Honan *"Curriculum and Culture: New Round is Opened in a Scholarly Fist-Fight"* (*NY Times*, August 21,1996), Allan Bloom, in his book, *"The Closing of the American Mind"* (1987), has argued that efforts to include non-Western cultures in the curriculum were displacing what he regarded as the more valuable teaching of the Western culture. Lawrence W. Levine, the author of "*The Opening of the American Mind*" (1996) has said that he was appalled by the fact that he graduated from the City College of New York in the 1950s, "knowing very little about the vast majority of the peoples in the world. We studied Northern and Western Europe, nothing on Africa, Asia and Latin America."

The Lake County (Florida) School Board voted by three votes to two in early May, 1994, that all students must be taught that the "United States' culture is superior to other foreign or historic cultures." Opponents said that the School Board was being jingoistic. The Board majority and its supporters said they won't have the children of Lake County sucked into the swamps of multi-culturalism and moral relativism. On the CNN Crossfire (May 18,1994) under the title: *"Culture Clash,"* Pat Buchaanan, former (1992 and 1996) Presidential candidate, supporting the proposition, said: "If we believe our country, its culture, and its institutions are the best *in* the world, why not instill these ideas in America's children in order to instill patriotism and love of country in them."

Some Western historians, anthropologists and archaeologists have been interpreting oriental cultures from their own biased perspectives. They need to know and be able to identify with the foreign cultures they are writing about. They should make conscious effort to be objective.

British East Indian Company and Prostitution of the Ancient History of Bharat

This was about what has been done to history in general at international level. Now, let us talk about the history of India. Dr. K. M. Munshi, the founder of the *Bharatiya Vidya Bhavan,* in his foreword to Majmudar's *"History and Culture of the Indian People"* (1988: 8–9) has indicated what harm several British scholars have intentionally done to the history of the Hindu culture:

> "The attempts of British scholars, with the exception of Tod, wherever they have taken these *'histories'* as reliable source-books, have hindered rather than helped the study of Indian history. Unfortunately for us, during the last two hundred years we have not only to study such histories but unconsciously to mould our whole outlook on life upon them."

The British East India Company employed a well planned three-pronged (missionary, history and education) assault on Hindu culture. Max Muller (Bharti, 1992: 64–71) basically missionary, was presented to India as a Sanskrit scholar. He was hired at the age of 25 years in 1847 to translate the *Vedas* into English. If they were really interested in translations, they could hire an indigenous scholar with proficiency in *Sanskrit,* authentic historic perspectives on the *Vedas* and a genuine feel of the *Vedic* religion. Max Muller had none of the three. Neither English nor was Sanskrit his mother tongue. He didn't have a genuine feel of, nor respect for, the Vedas; he was hired to translate. Only his 'plus' from point of British interest was his firm commitment to his Christian Mission. He very tactfully, with the help of a couple of hired poor (who could be easily bribed) *Sanskrit Pundits,* misinterpreted *Vedas* to humiliate Hindu religion. For example, the mantras praising Aryan (Hindu) heroes were attributed to the invading Aryans. They shortened the ages of the four *Vedas* and the two epics, *Ramayana* and *Mahabharata,* and dated them after the so-called "Aryan Invasion of India" (1500 B.C.), so as to give credit for all the good things in the *Sanskrit* literature and *Hindu* culture to the invading *Aryans,* and bad things attributed to Hindus. The exponents of the theory wrote that prior to the advent of the light-skinned *Aryans* from Asia Minor, the natives of India were dark-skinned uncivilized *Dravidians* who were pushed down to the South and sowed the seeds of difference and division between the North and the South. The world is aware of the age-old British doctrine, 'Divide and rule.'

Wolpert's (1993: 37) talk about "invading barbaric hordes" and "their more civilized pre-Aryan 'slaves' " clearly suggests that native *Aryans* were more civilized than the invading *Aryans.* He has characterized *Aryan* conquest of India as their gradual "institutional assimilation and socio-cultural integration", not as their "overwhelming linguistic, religious and cultural influence" over the native *Aryan* society.

Max Muller worked enthusiastically to project Hinduism in unfavorable colors. His vicious design is well reflected in his letter to Chevalier Bunsen (The *Life and Letters of Max Muller*, Vol. 1:17).

> "Your Excellency, I have no doubt, whatever, that something can be written about the *Veda* which would reach even the dullest ears. Nevertheless I of course shall be glad if the *Rig Veda* is dealt with in the *Edinburgh Review,* and if Wilson would write from the standpoint of a missionary, and would show how the knowledge and bringing into light of the *Veda* would upset the whole existing system of Indian theology. It might become of real interest.
>
> The Christianity of 19th century will hardly be the Christianity of India. But the ancient religion of India is doomed—and if Christianity does not step in, whose fault it would be."

Thomas Babington Macaulay, another missionary behind the mask of an educationist (Bharti 1992:66) had told his father in 1836 that if his plans of education were followed up, there will be no high caste Hindu left in Bengal after 30 years. It is hard to understand why Bengal, even now, continues to be more so under the world renowned 'Nobel' flag a target of missionary work.

Both Max Muller and Macaulay worked hard to distort and mutilate the history of the *Vedic* culture by way of shortening the age of the *Vedas* with a purpose to induce in *Hindu's* cultural inferiority complex and confuse their identity.

The British did the same thing with Zoroastrians too:

> "In the area of doctrine, problems arose in the 19th century, when European scholars began to translate and interpret Zoroastrian texts, challenging the traditional view of them. As a result, various reform movements were founded in Bombay, and still remain at variance with one another." (Peter B. Clarke, 1993: 123).

Munshi (in Majmudar, 1988: 9) has drawn our attention to the harm several European scholars have intentionally done to Hindu culture: "It (history) does not give us the real India. Unfortunately for us, during the last two hundred years we had not only to study such histories but unconsciously to mould our whole outlook on life upon them." We find consolation in Munshi's assuring note:

> "History, as I see it, is being consciously lived by Indians. History is a witness to the fact that politically motivated recorded history of India has been disappointed by the history given down to us orally by our *Vedas* and *Upainshads"* (Munshi in Majmudar, 1988: 9).

Munshi (in Majmudar, 1988: 9) laments how failures of Hindus have been highlighted and successes ignored. During our school or college career, generation after generation, we were told about the successive foreign invasions of the country, but little about how we resisted them and less about our victories. We were taught to decry the Hindu social systems; but we have never been told how this system came into existence as a synthesis of political, social, economic and cultural forces; and how it developed in the people the tenacity to survive catastrophic changes.

Pakistan—History and Indus Civilization

Changes in political situation in a country can distort its ancient history. A case in point is Pakistan which was created in 1947 as a result of the partition of Bharat. The titles of the following two books, recently published in Pakistan, would tell the story how the history can get distorted:

1. Sirmar Temarvellar, "Five Thousand Years of Pak."
2. G.M. Syed, "Sindhu Desh: A Study in its Separate Identity through the Ages"

Unfortunately, Pakistan occupies almost all the area of the Indus civilization and both of its main ancient cities, *Mohenjo Daro* and *Harappa,* are in Pakistan. With the passage of time, worldwide increasing cultural clash and depreciating professional integrity of historians, the history will one day forget that *Mohenjo Daro* and *Harappa* are reminders of the pride of the ancient Hindus. History has already forgotten *"Vishal Bharat"* (Greater India) which extended itself without defined borders in all directions, especially in the far South-East touching Bali and in the North-West *Gandhar Desh* and *Avesthan* (Iran).

Sacred Hindu Isles in the West

Let me tell you the long-forgotten 'Sacred Isles of Hindus' in Europe. This statement by Captain F. Wilford shed relevant light on what I want to tell.

> "The sacred Isles in the West, of which *Swetadweepa,* or the White Island, is the principal, and the most famous, in fact, the holy land of the *Hindus.* There the fundamental and mysterious transaction of the history of their (Hindu) religion, in its rise and progress, took place…. This I conceive to be a most favorable circumstance; in the present case, the learned have little more to do with than to ascertain whether the White Island be England, and the Sacred Isles of the Hindus, the British Isles. After having maturely considered the subject, I think they are." (8th volume of *Asiatic Researches,* Sir William Jones, Ed., 1787: 246).

On page 257, Wilford tells the story of two doves "found by Mohammed in the *Cabba* at *Mecca;* which they claim, with some reason, as a place of worship belonging originally to the *Hindus."* John Bently (*Asiatic Researches*, pp. 377–497) talks about the influence of *Vedas* in Europe and Persia.

Max Muller (1891: 298), writes that the old name of Ireland is *Eriu* and the ancient name of *Irish Celts* is *Er* or Eri, as preserved in the Anglo-Saxon name of their country *Ireland.* It is maintained by O'Reily that this *"er"* is used in Irish in the sense of noble, like the Sanskrit *Arya.*

Swastika: A Sacred Symbol of the Celts

The following quotation taken from the book, *"The Celts: Sacred Symbols*" (1995) would explain the influence of Hinduism among Celts which spread in Europe, including British Isles and Germany:

> "One of the great enduring symbols of the whole of the Ancient World, the swastika, had wide currency as a sign of good luck and of solar beneficence. The motif occurs throughout the lands occupied by the Celts, sometimes on stonework in the company of images of the spoked wheel, another powerful sun symbol."

Mandala: A Potent Sacred Symbol of Mankind

The book "*Mandala*" (Thames and Hudson Inc., New York, 1995) describes the *Mandala* as a sacred symbol of mankind:

"Although most immediately associated with the religions and cults of India and Tibet, the *mandala*, literally circle, is one of the most potent symbols of humankind. Its circular form and concentric structure reflect the shape of the universe outside and the sense of perfection within. Concentration on its form and content is an aid to prayer and meditation, leading eventually to a complete at-oneness with the world."

The book further says:

"The potency of concentric circles around a centre point, the most intense expression of the divine, pervades all cultures and religions. Among the Huichol tribes of California and Mexico, such a vision of circles, the *nierika*, is a prayer offering, a reflection of the face of the god, and a means of realizing the most concentrated experience of the sacred, symbolized by the centre point."

The book also talks about a Christian *mandala*, giving diagrams which include cross and *Swastika*.

The Madonna and Hittite kingdoms, as described earlier, vouch for *Vedic* influence in *Mesopotamia* including Asia Minor, at least over 3,500 years back from today.

Several characteristics of American Indians [Brandon (1969), Driver (1869), Parkes (1988)] similar to India's, such as *Swastika,* cremation, a priestly caste, brownish complexion, incarnated gods, sacrifice rituals, worship of nature gods (fire, rain, earth, trees, sun, etc.), worship of serpent god *(Nagdevta),* pottery, textiles, half man-half animal god, carving of wood, blowing of conch *(Shankh)* in temples, carvings of pillars and elephant on one Maya temple, oral transmission of religious poetry from generation to generation, all support my hypothesis that at least some of the migrants from Asia to Americas were Vedic Aryans from India and/or from Asia Minor, Europe etc. where they had migrated and settled in very old ancient times.

Theory of Aryan Invasion of India

The focus of the study is on the *'Theory of Aryan Invasion of India',* which has been responsible for distorting the ancient history of Bharat. Before submission of the findings of this research, let us understand what the theory is, as stated by some historians:

"About 1500 B.C. or earlier, a series of invasions of India began by light-skinned nomads who came through the Afghan passes and settled in the Ganges plains... . These nomad invaders were the Aryans; in Sanskrit the word "Arya" means gentleman or one high born. The Aryans had their own literature; their early books are called Vedas, or scriptures. Veda literally means knowledge... . The Aryans very early developed an

> exceedingly complicated form of worship, which became Hinduism" (Gunther, 1939: 373).
>
> "From 1500 to 500 B.C., the Aryans brought the Sanskrit language, the horse, and iron products… . Since its origin around 3000 B.C., Hinduism has had great influence on Indian society… . Chiefly worshipped (gods) are: Brahma, the creator; Vishnu, the preserver; and Shiva, the destroyer." (Osborne et al; 1988: 59).

If *Hinduism* originated in India around 3000 B.C., how then Osborne could say that *Sanskrit* came from outside? How could Gunther claim that *Vedas* were brought in by the invading Aryans? If Hindus worshipped *Shiva* in around 3000 B.C., how then do some historians say that *Shiva* was borrowed from the Indus civilization by the native Aryans (Hindus) living in the rest of Bharat? On page 61 Osborne et al. have mentioned that Vedas were the sacred writings of Hinduism. They have also said: "The Indus Valley (3000 B.C.) is the birthplace of India's civilization. Two early city states were Mohenjo Daro and Harappa." Contradictions are apparent.

Let us examine how Wolpert's (1993) statements are self-contradicting, confusing and vague.

> "We have no archaeological evidence for the first centuries of India's *Aryan* age (from about 1500 to 1000 B.C.), but we have been able to piece together some picture of the era from the Aryans' religious 'Books of Knowledge,' or Vedas… . It *(Rig Veda)* is the earliest surviving Indo—European literature …. the *Rig Veda* was not *written* down before about 600 B.C. The *Rig Veda,* however, is unconscious of that journey and of the Aryan 'invasion' of India, yet it does mention *Aryan* victories against 'fortified places' *(pur)* … . This was the most important invasion in all of India's history, since the *Aryans* brought with their Caucasian genes a new language—*Sanskrit—and* a new pantheon of gods." (Wolpert, 1993: 25–27).

If the *Rig Veda* was written not before 600 B.C., why then the invading *Aryans* themselves would ignore mention of the arrival of their ancestors m the *Rig Veda* they created? It is also said that the *Vedas* were created after their arrival. Wolpert says that the *Rig Veda* records *Aryan* victories over the dark-skinned *'dasas'*. Why not even one Anatolian Aryan name is mentioned in those stories of their victories in the *Rig Veda?* Wolpert has mentioned (page 10) Anatolian names—*"Subiluliuma"* and *"Mattiwaza"* of Hittite and Mittanni kingdoms respectively who invoked names of Hindu gods as divine witnesses in the treaty they concluded in about 1200 B.C. Since there is no archeological evidence and the *Rig Veda* was silent, how historians were able to piece together some picture of the era (1500 to 1000 B.C.) from the Vedas?

> "The *Aryans* ("noble ones") were part of a large Indo-European migration which left a common cultural heritage from Greece through Iran into India. The religious and social institutions of these invaders are reflected in the oldest stratum of the *Veda* (sacred "knowledge")—the most revered sector of traditional *Hindu* religious literature.... Our knowledge of *Aryan* culture is derived primarily from the *Samhita* ("Collection") of the *Rig-Veda* ("Veda of hymns"). It was put into final form at a relatively late date, but reflects the chore of a very archaic tradition. The hymns were preserved by priestly specialists, the *Brahmans*". (Garraty and Gay, 1981: 97–98).

The above quotation is a classic example of a confusing statement by confused historians seemingly with an intention to confuse the readers. Does Greece reflect even faintest glimpses of *Vedic* religious and social institutions? Any remainders of the 'traditional Hindu religious literature' in Greece and its vicinity? History has yet to see traditions don't die out in the land where its seeds were sown and flourish in a foreign land thousands miles away. How then can they be called traditions?

The source of the knowledge of the Aryan culture is based on the assumption that Rig Veda was created only after the Aryan invasion. The antiquity of the Vedas, especially the *Rig Veda* and the age of the Vedic (Hindu) religion have been distorted by the Western scholars. Frawley (1990, 1991, 1991a, 1992a, 1994) and Kak (1987, 1992, 1992a, 1994) have taken an aggressive lead to refute the distorted antiquity of *Vedas* by extending their '*Sarasvati*' and 'astronomical' evidences. Several other scholars, like Abhayankar, Gidwani, Rajaram, Rao, Sidharth, etc. have refuted the theory by giving several different evidences—astronomical, archaeological, Sarasvati, demographic, linguistic, etc., which for space reasons will not be discussed here

Nehru (1946: 76–77): Antiquity and Significance of Rig Veda

Antiquity:

"The earliest records of Hindu culture." "The (Vedic) literature is earlier than that of Greece or Israel." "Some of the earliest documents of the human mind." "The *Rig Veda,* the earliest book that humanity possesses." "Yet behind the *Rig Veda* itself lay ages of civilized existence and thought, during which the Indus Valley and the Mesopotamian and other civilizations had grown."

Significance:

"Revealed scriptures." "The unfolding of the human mind in the earliest stages of thought." "The first outpouring of the human mind." "The glow of poetry, the rapture at nature's loveliness and mystery."

Wolpert (1993: 25) has said that the *Rig Veda* is the earliest surviving Indo-European literature. Nehru quotes Max Muller: "The first word spoken by the *Aryan* man." and Prof Winternitz: "The beginnings of the *Vedic* literature go back to 2,000 B.C. or even 2,500 B.C."

No Invading Power has Overwhelmed Hinduism: History is a Witness

The long history of India is a witness to the fact that no invading race has made any significant dent in the *Hindu / Vedic / Sanatan Dharma* nor has faded its color, because of its synthesizing, absorbing and inclusive nature. Nehru (1946: 76) has talked about India's traditional "some inner urge towards synthesis, derived essentially from the Indian philosophic outlook."

> "Each incursion of foreign elements was a challenge to this culture, but it was met successfully by a new synthesis and a process of absorption. This was also a process of rejuvenation and new blooms of culture arose out of it, the background and essential basis, however, remaining much the same" (Nehru, 1946, p.76).

Aryans and Sanskrit: Two Ancient Siblings

The first word, the first *Aryan* spoke, was in *Sanskrit. Bharat* was the mother of the twins. In order to establish that none but Bharat is the original home of *Vedic Aryans,* it becomes necessary to meaningfully weave the five interrelated strings—*Aryans, Sanskrit, Vedas, Vedic religion* and *Swastika,* into a rainbow ethnic tapestry. Origins of all the five basic elements of the ancient *Bharatiya* civilization are so closely interrelated that the geography of their respective origins cannot be other than one and the same. The five, if all are not known to have born at the same time, are at least genetically connected; and were born in far ancient times, too remote for scholars to chronicle their respective origins. It doesn't become logical to say that any of them migrated into India from outside, when *Sanskrit,* one of the most ancient languages of the world, is an irrefutable common ingredient to clan all the five together. For example, since *"Arya", "Vedas"* and *"Swastika"* are *Sanskrit* words and *Vedas,* the scriptures of Aryan religion, are written in *Sanskrit,* it will be illogical for history to dictate that *Aryans, Sanskrit, Swastika* and *Vedas* were foreign to the ancient *Bharat.*

Sanskrit: Its Original Home, 'Bharat'

All dictionaries and encyclopedias have talked about 'Indo-European Family of Languages.' The Random House Webster's dictionary (1995: 685) has defined the word 'Indo' as "combining form representing India." It further indicates that the word 'India' has originated from the Latin 'Indus' and Greek 'Ind' or 'Indos'. It clearly suggests that the 'Indo-European' family can be classified into two major groups of languages, 'Indian' and 'European'. This dictionary, like many other dictionaries and encyclopedias, in order to be specific about their subgroups, talks about 'Indo-Aryan' (which includes Sanskrit, Hindi and other modern languages of India), Indo-Iranian, Indo-German, Indo-Hittite, etc.. All this proves beyond doubt that Sanskrit and its descendent regional languages originated nowhere but in *Bharat.*

> "Sanskrit language and literature (were) developed in ancient India.... The term Vedic refers to the Vedas, the oldest sacred scriptures of *Hinduism"* (W.B Ency., 1984,17: 101).
>
> "The Hindus are the only nation that cultivated the science of grammar without having received any impulse, directly or indirectly, from the Greeks. As Greek grammar owed its origin to the critical study of Homer, Sanskrit grammar arose from the study of the Vedas, the most ancient poetry of the Brahmans." (Max Muller, 1891: 124–5).

In Max Muller (1889: 225–6), it is said that the discovery of *Sanskrit* came on Lord Monboddo, like a thunderbolt just after he had finished his great work *'Of the Origins and Progress of Languages'* (2nd edition, 6 volumes, Edinburgh, 1774), in which he says all the dialects of the world were derived from a language originally framed by some Egyptian gods. Later in 1792 Monboddo writes: "There is a language (Sanskrit) still existing, and preserved among the Brahmins of India, which is richer and in every respect a finer language than even the Greek of Homer. All the other languages of India have a great resemblance to this language, which is called the Shanscrit." According to Max Muller, Monboddo once believed that "Greek is derived from the Shanscrit."

> "Of the three Oriental dramas, Sanskrit, Chinese, Japanese—the oldest is Sanskrit, although the dates of its origin are uncertain. Sanskrit drama is part of Sanskrit literature which flourished from about 1500 B.C. to A.D. 1100" (Columbia Encyclopedia, 1993: 163–4).

If Sanskrit literature flourished in India from about 1500 B.C., it means there was Sanskrit and Sanskrit literature in its rudimentary form prior to 1500 B.C., the advent of invading Aryans.

The Natives of Asia Minor and Aryan Invasion of India

In order to substantiate, refute or understand the *'Theory of Aryan Invasion of India'* it would be required to ascertain if the ancient natives of Asia Minor were Sanskrit knowing Aryans who had Vedas and Vedic religion, they allegedly took with themselves to India around 1500 B.C. Quite a few encyclopedias and books of World History have been looked into to find out who were the ancient natives of the Asia Minor region, especially around 1500 B.C. and to know their linguistic, socio-cultural and religious affinities. It is also important to know if their population had remained static or fluid; in other words, if there were any infiltration of foreign elements.

My hypotheses in this research are:

1. The invading Aryans were not the ancient natives of Asia Minor.
2. They were foreigners who had invaded the Asia Minor region long before 1500 B.C.
3. Their linguistic, socio-cultural and religious affinities were different from those of the natives.

> "In ancient times most Oriental and Occidental civilizations intersected in Asia Minor, for it was connected with Mesopotamia by the Tigris and Euphrates rivers and with Greece by the Aegean and Meditarian seas. The Rittite established the first major civilization in Asia Minor about 1800 B.C." (Columbia Encyclopedia, 1993: 163).

An inference, be it speculative if not definitive, can safely be drawn that at least some immigrants/invaders with oriental civilization orientation could be from India. The Hittite civilization, which was established in Asia Minor in 1800 B.C., was not entirely/purely its original civilization.

Langer (1975: 34) talks about the Hurrian invasions during 1700–1500 B.C. that "the Hurrians, biblical Horites, began to drift south from the Caucasus and penetrated into whole of Mesopotamia, Syria and eastern Anatolia."

> "Strange to say, that the ruling class of the Hurrians bore not Hurrian but Indo-Aryan names. Evidently the Aryans drove both the Hurrians and Kassites before them in the 17th century, overrunning the former and establishing themselves as an aristocracy. Probably they won their position as chariot warriors, since it seems likely that the horse-drawn chariot, introduced in the 18th century and widely used in the 17th century, originated among Aryan peoples. The symbiosis of Hurrian and Indo-Aryan elements is characteristic of Hurrian society wherever we come upon it" (Langer, 975: 34). Note they were Indo-Aryans, not Indo-Europeans.

Starr (199: 101) while talking about Hittite and archeological hints and linguistic distributions, has said:

> "It is generally agreed that they came into Asia Minor from the outside, either from Europe or across the Caucasus mountains. The outpouring of Indo-Europeans at the turn from the third to the second millennium B.C., though the Hittite themselves were in Asia Minor before 2000 B.C."

According to Langer (1975: 34) small Haran principalities were united toward 1500 B.C. into the Kingdom of Madonna. According to T. Burrow (1973), the Aryan Hittite and Madonna kingdoms signed a treaty in around 1400 B.C. As witnesses they put the names of Hindu gods, like *Indra, Mitra, Varuna* and *Nasalyas.* The *Aryan* Kassites of the ancient Middle East worshipped Vedic gods, like Surya, etc.

> "The culture of this state (Madonna) was a fascinating medley from many sources. The Haran speech, like several other tongues of the mountain belt in the Near East, does not fit into any major linguistic group; but the rulers of Madonna had names akin to those of the Indo-European invaders of India, as did such of their major gods as Indra and Varuna" (Chester, 1991: 86).

The ancient archaeology (BE 1968, 11: 551) has failed to provide unequivocal ethnic data on ancient Hittite. It points to "an infusion of foreign elements plausibly connected with the arrival of the Indo European Hittite." On page 554, it has talked about "Increasing seepage of pronouncedly oriental influence into Haiti." The history has not been able to determine the route of the migration, more inclined to an eastern route. The word 'Indo-European Hittite' suggests that immigrants/invaders were not the native Hittite and they had Indo-European affinities, and some of them could be Indo-Aryans. History (BE 1968, 11: 551) has talked about an eminent city state *"Burushatum"* (Hittite *Purushanda*), very close to Hindu name "Purushottam". Hittite (BE 1968,11: 555) was esse ntially a feudal society and the ruling "gentry constituted a kind of higher warrior caste and provided the armed chariotry which formed the backbone of offensive military might." On page 557, the encyclopedia talks about the burial practices of the Hittite: "Royal burial entailed cremation of the body on a pyre on the day or night of the death."

All these things mentioned above, such as migration of Indo-Europeans, their eastern route, infusion of the foreign elements, oriental influence, Sanskrit names of city states, high caste chariot warriors, worship of Hindu gods by royalty and their custom of cremation, all suggest that the warriors *(Kshyatries)* had migrated into Asia Minor long back and their descendants returned to Bharat around 1500 B.C. They had *Vedic* orientation and knowledge of horse-driven chariots. It is also quite clear that only the rulers, not commoners, had their names and gods akin to the Indo-European invaders of India who were none but Vedic Aryans, returning to the home of their ancestors. More research is needed.

Language and Religion of the Natives and Invading Aryans

The above mentioned encyclopedias, dictionaries and the world history books, included in the attached bibliography, have mentioned quite a few Indo-European Anatolian languages, such as Hittite, Hieroglyphic Hittite, Akhadian, Arzawa, Canaanite, Lydian, Lycian, Luwian, Palaic etc., almost all of them are dead. There were some non-Indo-European languages were spoken in ancient Asia Minor, such as Ligurian, Messapian, Illyrian, Thracian, Pirrygian, all of which are dead. Garraty and Gay (1981: 86) have said, "The grammatical structure of the Hittite language relates it to the Indo-European group, but the vocabulary is mainly that of the non-Indo-European indigenous peoples of Anatolia." They had adopted the cuneiform script, the use of which ceased after the fall of the Hittite Empire around 1200 B.C., no Indo-Aryan script. At present, it seems Turkish is the main language, prevalent in the region. Nowhere even a slight reference has been made to *Sanskrit* or any other Indic language as the language of Asia Minor at present or any time in the past.

How is it possible that Sanskrit, Vedas and Vedic religion originated in this or that country where they are no longer alive? It has been historically proved that a living language has very rarely become extinct in the land of its origin and that it has flourished in a foreign far-distant land where a small fraction of the people have immigrated into. Persian language of the Indian Parsees who were forced out by Muslim invaders from Persia (Iran) in early 8th century (706 A.D.) has virtually died out in India as their spoken language; although it is being taught in schools and colleges as a classical language. Persian is alive in Iran, the country of its origin.

Religion

Like Hinduism there has been reference to 'thousand gods of Haiti'. But the names of their gods, such as goddess 'Inaras', the war god 'Sulinkatte' or 'Wurunkatte', 'Tauri', etc don't show any affinity to Hindu gods. It proves that the religion of the natives of the region was completely different from Vedic/Hindu religion, the invading Aryans brought to India, as some historians claim. The mention of the Hindu gods *Indra, Mitra, Varuna* as witness in a treaty between the kingdoms of Hittite and Mitttani in 1400 B.C. should not be interpreted that Vedic religion was prevalent among the masses. As a matter of fact, only the kings, who seem to be Indo-Aryan, might be worshipping Vedic gods. This is corroborated by the fact that the kings were socio-culturally different from the commoners. As said earlier that royalty practiced cremation, different from the burial practice of the commoners.

It doesn't mean that the region, *Aryans* came from, was the land of origin of *Sanskrit, Vedas* and *Vedic* religion. Books tell that there was a heavy migration of peoples speaking several Indo-European (Aryan) languages from Asia Minor to several countries including Andante Iran. India must have received only a small portion, because India was at the end of the migration route. India's share must have been too small to overwhelm, religio-culturally and linguistically, its extremely gigantic population and that also widely dispersed in vast diverse geography of India. Some authors have rightly observed that the invaders/immigrants called themselves Aryans and got culturally assimilated and absorbed. It is hard to believe that chariots were able to negotiate and cross thorough the Khyber Pass of *Hindu Kush* mountains.

Langer and Burrow clearly suggest that the ruling class of the Hurrians, Hittite, Cassittes and Madonnas were not the native commoners of the region (Asia Minor) but they were Indo-Aryan chariot warriors and aristocrats who might have introduced horse-driven chariots. This explains that in about 1500 B.C. some of them, whatever they had reasons, returned to *Bharat.* The history says they got assimilated into the Indo-Aryan cultures. The returning Aryans naturally might have been influenced by the then native Asia Minor culture, which has been, as earlier said, the symbiotic synthesis of the Oriental and Occidental cultures. The culture of the returning Indo-Aryans might have contributed toward the Vedic religion which, we know, has been both receptive to and absorber of the foreign cultures and religions.

Survival Instincts of Hinduism and Hindustan

It is my unshakable optimism, as that of most *Hindus,* that no assault, physical or psychological, from outside or from within, can uproot the Hindu society which has its roots too deep down into the ancient sacred earth. The roots have crept into the *Patal* (below the bottom of the earth) too distant even for *Shaitan* to dare to reach. Dr. K.M. Munshi and Pt. Jawaharlal Nehru both have identified and beautifully portrayed the basic *'survival instincts'* of *Hinduism,* fortified by ancient Aryan tenacity, conservative strength, elasticity, and vitality and 'India's traditional urge towards synthesis and its process of absorption' which in Nehru's opinion is "derived essentially from the Indian philosophic outlook." Hindus don't need any formal education to incorporate and nourish all these prized characteristics. They get them by birth. The in-built Hindu oral traditions and social institutions, especially family, continue to fertilize and nurture them.

Illiteracy: A Blessing in Disguise

Paradoxically, illiteracy in the villages has been a blessing in disguise. It has insulated the *"Jahil"* villagers of India against the undesirable psychological inroads of the foreign-written ancient history. Illiteracy has provided them with the cultural immunity. They, unlike the elite, have remained correctly informed about their culture and heritage, the *Vedic* knowledge of which is being passed down to them orally from generation to generation. Good that they have been unable to read the garbage, others have written about their ancient heritage. This will be better explained by what Alan Roland, an eminent American psycho-analyst, has said in his research-based book: *"In Search of Self in India and Japan"* (1988, p.18):

> "British administrative, educational, and missionary attitudes all conveyed intense attitudes of British superiority and Indian inferiority in numerous shades and ways over the two centuries of their colonial presence. This had enormous psychological impact, particularly on the Western-educated elite who were more closely associated with the raj. Since the men were more exposed to British attitudes than women, they were much more affected by colonial denigration."

The educated elite of India, in order to become learned in a real sense, need to unlearn a lot. Nehru's *Discovery of India* is, in essence, a history book. Nehru very well knew that it is the heritage which gives the people a proud identity. We Indians have been suffering from ethno-cultural inferiority complex. I wish Prime Minister Nehru had taken an effective interest to find the truth about the theory of *"Aryan Invasion of India"* and had ordered to rewrite India's ancient history. It is never too late. I wish the free *Bharat* would wake up from her millenniums long *Kumbhakarna* slumber to reconstruct and rewrite her own ancient history to discover her true identity, her future generations would feel proud of. No nation should let others write its history. Autobiographies are much less contaminated than biographies.

> "To be a history in the true sense of the word, the work must be the story of the people inhabiting a country.... The central purpose of a history must, therefore, be to investigate and unfold the values which age after age have inspired the inhabitants of a country to develop their collective will and to express it through the manifold activities of their life. Such a history of India is still to be written" (Munshi in Majmudar, 1988: 8).

Bibliography

Abhayankar, K.D and B.G. Sidhartha (eds.): *Treasures of Ancient Indian Astronomy,* Ajanta Publications, New Delhi, 1993.

Bharti, Brahm Datt: *Max Muller: A Lifelong Masquerade,* Erabooks, New Delhi, 1992.

Brandon, William: *Indians,* Houghton Mifflin Company, Boston, 1989.

CNN Crossfire, *Culture Clash,* May 18, 1994.

Cambridge History of India, Vol l, Cambridge, 1922.

Cannon, Garland and Kevin R. Brine (ed.): *Objects of Enquiry: The Life, Contributions, and Influences of Sir William Jones,* New York University Press, New York, 1995. (DHL 954,0072, OBJ.)

Childe, V.G.: *The Aryans: A Study of Indo-European Origins,* London, 1926.

_________ : *The Aryans*, New York, London, 1926 (Majmudar, p. 545).

_________ : *New Light on the Most Ancient East,* Frederick A. Praeger, New York, 1928.

Clark, Grahame: *World Prehistory in New Perspective*, Cambridge University Press, Cambridge, 1993.

Clark, Grahame and Stuart Piggot: *Prehistoric Societies,* Alfred A. Knopf, New York, 1968.

Clarke, Peter B.: *The World's Religions, Understanding the Living Faiths,* Marshall Editions Limited, Pleasantville, 1993.

Colebrooke, H.T.: "Sanscrit and Pracrit Languages" (written in 1780's), in Sir William Jones (ed.), *Asiatic Researches* (Vol. 7, Ch. VII), Cosmo Publications, New Delhi, 1979a.

_________ : "On the Vedas, or Sacred Writings of the Hindus" (written in 1780's), in Sir William Jones (ed.), *Asiatic Researches* (Vol. 8, Ch. V, pp. 377–497), Cosmo Publications, New Delhi, 1979b.

Cream,C. W.: *The Secret of the Hittites,* Alfred A. Knopf, New York, 1956.

Driver, Harold E.: *Indians of North America,* The University of Chicago Press, Chicago, 1969.

Durant, Will: *Our Oriental Heritage,* MJF Books, New York, 1935.

Dutt, R.C.: *History of Civilization in Ancient India,* London, 1893.

Eliade, Mircea: *A History of Religious Ideas* (Vol. I, From the Stone Age to the Eleusinian Mysteries), The University of Chicago Press, Chicago, 1978.

Elst, Koenraad: "*Indigenous Indians: Agastya to Ambedkar*", Voice of India, New Delhi, 1993.

_________ : *Dr. Ambedkar: A True Arya,* Voice of India, New Delhi, 1993a.

Embree, Ainslie T. (ed.): *Sources of Indian Tradition* (Vol. I, from the beginning to 1800), Columbia University Press, New York, 1988.

Fairservis,W.A.: *The Roots of Ancient India* (2nd ed.), University of Chicago Press, Chicago, 1975.

Frawley, David: *From the River of Heaven: Hindu and Vedic Knowledge for the Modern Age,* Passage Press, Salt Lake City, 1990.

_________ : *Gods, Sages and Kings,* Passage Press, Salt Lake City, 1991.

_________ : "On the Banks of the Sarasvati: The Ancient History of India Revised," in *The Quest,* Autumn 1992a.

_________ : *The Myth of the Aryan Invasion of India*, Voice of India, New Delhi, 1994.

Garraty, John A. and Peter Gay: *The Columbia History of the World*, Harper & Row, New York, 1981.

Gaur, Albertine: *History of Writing,* Charles Scribner's Sons, 1985 (DHL: Q 411.09).

Gidwani, Bhagwan S.: *Return of the Aryans*, Penguin Books (India), New Delhi, 1994

Grun, Bernard, *The Timetables of History*, Touchstone Books, New York, 1975.

Gunther, John: *Inside Asia,* Harper & Brothers, New York, 1939.

Gurney, O.R.: *The Hittites.* (Rev ed.), Penguin, 1975.

Honan, William H.: "Curriculum and Culture: New Round in a Scholarly Fistfight", *New York Times,* August 21, 1996.

Ions, Veronica: *Indian Mythology*, Peter Bedrick Books, New York, 1983.

Jones, Sir Williams: Supplement to the Essay on Indian Chronology (written in 1780s), in Sir William Jones (Ed.), *Asiatic Researches* (Vol. 2, Ch. XXVII, pp. 303–314), Cosmo Publications, New Delhi, 1979f.

Kak, Subash C.: "On the Chronology of Ancient India", in *Indian Journal of History of Science*, 22 (1987), 222–234.

__________ : The Architecture of the Rgveda, 1992.

__________ : "The Astronomy of the Vedic Altars and Rgveda" in *The Mankind Quaterly* 32 (1992),

__________ : "The Astronomical Code of the Rgveda", Aditya Prakashan, New Delhi, 1994.

Linton, Ralph: *The Tree of Culture,* Alfred A. Knopf, New York, 1955.

Mackay, Ernest: *The Indus Civilization,* Lovat Dickson & Thompson Ltd., London, 1935.

MacQueen, J.G.: *The Hittites and Their Contemporaries in Asia Minor* (Rev. Ed.), Thames and Hudson, New York, 1986.

Majmudar, R.C. (Ed.): *History and Culture of the Indian People,* 11 Volumes, Fifth edition, Bharatiya Vidya Bhavan, Bombay, 1988.

Mansfleld, Peter: *The Middle East: A Political and Economic Survey* (5th edition), Oxford.

Marshal, Sir John: *Mohenjo-Daro and the Indus Civilization,* 3 Vols., London, 1931.

McCrindle, J.W.: *Ancient India*, Vol. IV, Bombay, 1885.

Muller, F. Max.: *History of Sanskrit Literature* (2nd edition). London, 1960.

__________: *Science of Language* (Vol. 1), Charles Scribner's Sons, New York, 1891.

Muller, Herbert J.: *The Loom of History,* Harper & Brothers, New York, 1958.

Narain, A.K.: *The Indo-Greeks,* Oxford, 1957.

__________ : "Indo-Europeans in Inner Asia" in Denis Sinor (Ed.), *The Cambridge History of Early Inner Asia,* Cambridge Uni. Press, Newcastle, pp. 151–176, 1990.

Nehru, Jawaharlal: *The Discovery of India,* The Signet Press, Calcutta, 1946.

Osborne, John et al.: *Global Studies: A Regents Review Text,* N.N Publishing Company, 1989.

Parkes, Henry Bamford: *A History of Mexico,* Houghton Mifflin Company, Boston, Middletown, New York, 1988.

Piggott, S.: *Prehistoric India to 1000 B.C.*, London, 1962.

Pradhan, S.N.: *Chronology ofAncient India,* Calcutta, 1927.

Quaritch Wales, H.G.: *The Making of Greater India,* London, 1951.

Rajaram, Navaratna S.: *Aryan Invasion of India, The Myth and the Truth,* Voice of India, New Delhi, 1993.

__________ : *The Politics of History: Aryan Invasion Theory and the Subversion of Scholarship,* Voice of India, New Delhi, 1995.

Rao, S.R.: *Dawn and Devolution of the Indus Civilization,* Aditya Prakashan, New Delhi, 1991.

__________ : *Excavation of Submerged Ports: Dwarka, a Case Study,* National Institute of Oceanography, Goa, India.

Roberts, J.M.: *History of the World,* Penguin Books Ltd., London, 1987.

Rubel, David.: *Concise Chronology of World History, 3000 BC–1993*, Thomas Nelson Publishers, Nashville, 1993.

Sarasvati, Svami Dayanand (Translated by Dr. Parmanand): *Rgvedadi-Bhasya-Bhumika,* Meharchand Lachhmandas, New Delhi.

Schmidt, Karl J.: *An Atlas and Survey of South Asian History,* New York, 1995.

Sen, S.N.: *Ancient Indian History and Civilization,* Wiley Eastern Limited, New Delhi, 1988.

Sethna, K.D.: "Karpasa in Prehistoric India", *Voice of India,* New Delhi, 1982.

__________ : "The Problem of Aryan Origins", Voice of India, New Delhi, 1992.

Sidharth, B.G.: "The Unmythical Puranas: A Study in Reverse Symbolism", in *Grifith Observer,* April 1989.

__________ : *The Antiquity of The Rig Veda,* B.M. Birla Science Centre, Hyderabad, 1991.

__________ : *Mahayuga: The Great Cosmic Cycle and the Date of the Rig Veda,* B.M. Birla Science Centre, Hyderabad, 1991a.

__________ : *The Astronomical Symbolism of Vishnu from the Vedas to the Puranas,* B.M. Birla Science Centre, Hyderabad, 1991b.

__________ : *A Lost Anatolian Civilization: Is It Vedic?,* B.M. Birla Science Centre, Hyderabad, 1992.

__________ : *Calendaric Astronomy, Astronomical Dating and Archaeology: A New View of Antiquity and its Science,* B.M. Birla Science Centre, Hyderabad, 1993a.

Sinor, Denis (Ed.): *The Cambridge History of Early Inner Asia,* Cambridge University Press, Newcastle (U.K.), 1990.

__________ : "The Hun Period", in Denis Sinor (Ed.), *The Cambridge History of Early Inner Asia,* Cambridge University Press, Newcastle (U.K.), 1990a, pp. 177–205.

__________ : *"The Establishment and Dissolution of the Turk Empire,"* in Denis Sinor *(Ed.), The Cambridge History of Early Inner Asia,* Newcastle (UK.), 1990b, pp. 285–316.

Starr, Chester G.: *A History of the Ancient World,* Oxford University Press, New York, 1991.

Stewart, Dugald: *Conjectures Concerning the Origin of the Sanskrit.*

Syed, G.M.: *Sindhu Desh: A Study in its Separate Identity through the Ages,* G.M. Syed Academy, Karachi, 1992.

Talageri, Shrikant G.: *Aryan Invasion Theory and Indian Nationalism,* Voice of India, New Delhi, 1993.

__________ : *Aryan Invasion Theory: A Reappraisal,* Voice of India, New Delhi, 1993a.

Thapar, Romila: *A History of India,* Vol. 1, Penguin Books India (P) Ltd., New Delhi, 1966.

Thieme, P.: "The `Aryan' Gods of the Mitanni Treaties," in *Journal of the American Oriental Society,* Vol. 80 (1960), pp. 301 ff.

Tilak, Lokmanya Bal Gangadhar: *The Arctic Home in the Vedas,* Messrs Tilak Bros., Poona (India), 1971.

Trager, James: *The People's Chronology,* Henry Holt and Company, New York, 1992.

Vaidya, C.V.: *History of Sanskrit, Vol. 1: Sruti (Vedic) Period,* Poona, 1930.

Vakharia, Niranjan N.: *Cosmological Truths of Ancient Indian Religion, Jainism and Hinduism,* Parichay Printers, Ahmedabad, 1978.

Wilford, Francis: "Chronology of the Hindus." in Sir William Jones, *Asiatic Researches,* Vol. 5, Cosmo Publications, New Delhi, 1979, pp. 241–295.

__________ : "An Essay on the Sacred Isles in the West" (written in 1780's), in Sir William Jones (ed.), *Asiatic Researches*, Vol. 8, Cosmo Publications, New Delhi, 1979a, pp. 245–375.

__________ : "On the Ancient Geography of India" (written in 1780's), in Sir William Jones, *Asiatic Researches,* Vol. 14, Ch.VII, Cosmo Publications, New Delhi, 1980, pp. 373–470.

Winternitz, M.: *History of Indian Literature* (English trans. by S. Ketkar), Vol.1, Calcutta, 1927.

Wolpert, Stanley: *A New History of India,* Oxford University Press, New York, 1993.

Encyclopedias

Chernow, Barbara A. and George A. Vallasi (Eds.): *The Columbia Encyclopedia,* Fifth Edition, Columbia University Press, New York, 1993.

Encyclopedia Britannica, 1968.

Hammond Standard World Atlas, Hammond Incorporated, New York, 1969.

Siepmann, Katherine Baker (ed.): *Reader's Encyclopedia,* Benet's 3rd edition, Harper Collins Publishers, New York, 1987.

The Illustrated Encyclopedia of Knowledge, Vol 19, The Educational Book Guild, Inc.,1957.

The World Book Encyclopedia, World Book, Inc., Chicago, 1984.

Distorted Historical Events and Discredited Hindu Chronology

DEEN B. CHANDORA, M.D.,
4117 Menlo Way Atlanta, GA. 30340, USA

This paper takes up for critical analysis the material written in the book "*World Literature*", taught in the tenth grade of Dekalb County's High School, Georgia, U.S.A., published by Holt, Rinehart, and Winston Inc., in respect of what is said there about Indian-Hindu history, religion and civilization. Books like "*World Literature*" are taught throughout the western world. This is not an isolated incidence, but a well-planned strategy by intellectuals to discredit and disgrace any other philosophy which is not in their favor, even though the philosophy, civilization and history are real facts which have been in existence since time immemorial.

Distortions of any kind are either due to ignorance or due to intentions. Ignorance induced distortion can be corrected by education, understanding and appropriate social interventions. On the other hand, intentionally implemented distortions continue unabated as the malevolent force perpetuates it; therefore these distortions become a part and parcel of societal life. This subtle brainwashing cannot be screened even by the best of the intellectuals who are themselves raised in that society where distortions permeate. Only rare brilliant dedicated scholars can identify these distortions and can present them to the society for correction. Therefore, it is the social responsibility of an individual to undertake this task to correct these distortions and present the facts.

Following are a few examples of many major fallacies taught in the US high schools, taken here from the source book followed in the 10th grade in Georgia as a part of 'World Literature' course:

1. Aryans are labeled as a race and they are shown as invaders to India.
2. Invasion occurred around 1500 B.C.
3. Vedic period: 1500–500 B.C.
4. Rig Veda was written: 1000 B.C.
5. Mahabharata period: 400 B.C.–400 A.D.
6. Ramayana period: 200 B.C.–200 A.D.
7. "Vyasa" meaning compiler or arranger.
8. "Krishna" is represented as a cult leader.
9. "A very human god": author's comments.

There are several other similar comments and presentations about Indian-Hindu history, tradition, religion and culture.

As would be testified by any person understanding India's heritage, these writings do not present a correct picture. These are devoid of a balanced approach and do not give factual anthropological, archaeological, sociological and scientific data of diverse Western and Indian scholars. Thus their comments and interpretations are inaccurate and discredit the history.

These matters are about Indians and their history and things mentioned in these books do not agree with any original Indian account or tradition. We enunciate below views of ancient and modern scholars of India, not unduly influenced by Western distortions.

Austria and Germany etc. Misused the Word `Arya'

The word 'Arya' (or Aryan) means noble in Sanskrit language. It does not indicate any race, religion, creed or color. It is qualitative and denotes the virtues of a person. In this regard, Yogi Aurobindo has written, *"The word Arya expresses a particular ethical and social order of well-governed life, courage, gentleness, purity, humanity, compassion, protection of the weak, liberty, observance of social duties, eagerness for knowledge, respect for the wise and the learned and the social accomplishment. There is no word in human speech that has a nobler history."*

The Theory of 'Aryans Invading India'

The theory of 'Aryans invading India' is a pure concoction. They are, in fact, the original inhabitants of Himalayan regions and later on some of their groups moved westward to Europe through Gandhar (Afghanistan) when the Sarasvati river dried up, many millennia B.C. This is now researched and confirmed by the satellite technology, cultural, anthropology and indological studies. Many indigenous modern scholars like Maharshi Dayananda Sarasvati, Swami Vivekananda, Swami Shradhananda, Ramatirtha, Yogi Aurobindo, and Nobel Laureate Rabindranath Tagore, researched and concluded that the Himalayas and its river banks were the original abode of the Aryans [1–4, 6–8, 10–12].

A Conspiracy on the Part of British Rulers

It is worthwhile to mention that the decision to distort facts about India was not a result of any misunderstood idea put forth by any genuine scholar or academic. It was a pure and simple act of conspiracy on the part of British rulers. On April 10, 1866, a secret meeting was held in the Royal Asiatic Society, in London, UK, when a conspiracy was hatched 'to induct the theory of the Aryan invasion of India, *so that no Indian may say that English are foreigners. ... India was ruled all along by outsiders and so the country must remain a slave under the benign Christian rule."* "A clever clergyman, Edward Thomas, spelled the theory with Lord Stangford in the chair."[3] This was a political move and as part of this conspiracy, Britishers made this theory a part of curriculum in schools and colleges.

Events of human and natural history are well recorded in different scriptures of India, using a very wide scale of time. According to these sources, the total period elapsed since the dawn of Vedic civilization is 1.96 billion years up to 1995 A.D. [4, 10–12]. Here it may be mentioned that Carl Sagan, professor of Astronomy and Space Sciences, Cornell University, determined the life of the earth as 4.6 billion years and that of the sun as 5 billion years. [15].

Any follower of Hindu, Jain and Sikh religions knows that Ramayana period preceded Mahabharata period and not the other way around as the authors have portrayed. Ramayana period, called Treta yuga, preceded the Mahabharata period, Dwapar yuga, by many millennia. Mahabharata was written in Dwapar yuga. The "death" of Shri Krishna marks the end of Dwapar yuga and the beginning of present yuga called Kali yuga. Since then 5,097 years have passed till 1995 AD [8, 10–13].

These authors comment about "Vyasa" meaning compiler or arranger. The fact is: Ved Vyasa is the name of the sage who wrote the historical events of the Mahabharata war. [10–13].

Incorrect Use of the Word 'Cult'

Saying that Shri Krishna started a cult is also not correct. Devotees of Shri Krishna are called as *Vaishnava. Vaishnava* is a major Hindu denomination, and not a cult [9, 14]. *Worldwide, more than five hundred million Hindus belong to Vaishnava denomination. A man of great eminence, Mahatma Gandhi, was a Vaishnava too!!* The authors' intent to disgrace Hindu history becomes clear by the use of the word "cult" for Vaishnava denomination as *Krishna cult, thereby putting it in the same category as Jim Jones and David Koresh,* just to name a few! Cult is an ugly epithet according to contemporary American society. Literally, cult is used to describe a fad.

It seems these writers are unaware of important sociological terms. They fail to differentiate between cult, denomination and religion [5]. These intellectuals were born and bought up in an American society. They ought to be cognizant of the contemptuous impact of the term cult in current American communities. Either they are ignorant or are planning a far fetched strategy to subtly brain-wash young adults to destroy the historical facts for some ulterior motives.

I may like to point out that recently, we were instrumental in getting the "cult" word corrected by the American Psychiatric Association when Hare Krishna devotees were labeled as cult followers, rather than being called as "Vaishnava" which they have been rightfully recognized for 5000 years [14].

The authors have neglected the teaching of "Gita", where Shri Krishna teaches, "action and responsibilities, dedication, devotion to duty, to achieve one's goals" [9]. Moreover, the authors have painted a bleak picture of Hindu society, by depicting Shri Krishna as a womanizer—"Krishna's charming personality and good look made him irresistible to women ... the fact that even married women left their homes to follow Krishna's flute..."—the sanctity of family life of married Hindu women is put at stake.

Ancient travelers' documents and cross-culture studies done by Megasthenes, the Greek Ambassador to Chandragupta Maurya, a 400 B.C. Indian Emperor, were not mentioned. His book, 'Indika', is a living testimony of the Indian civilization of that time [9]. It does not mention of any ongoing war, neither Rama's war (Ramayana) nor Krishna's war (Mahabharata).

The authors' comment of "A Very Human God" for Shri Krishna is undesirable as they are unaware of "Satyartha Prakash" (1884), a magnum opus of Maharshi Dayanand Sarasvati (1825-1883) containing logical analysis and systematic comparative study of world religions and translated in almost all world languages (published in English as "Light of Truth" [12]), forcefully and openly not only disputed the 'Very Human God' but also refuted the worship of 'Son of God' as other religion followers do. The father of Hindu renaissance movement, Maharshi Dayanand Sarasvati, in his superb balancing literary work of Satyartha Prakash reflected his utter desire to seek the truth. These authors in question have lacked entirely this spirit of balancing the literature factually.

Cross references from ancient texts (Purana) [13] were not even considered. Also cross-geo-anthropological studies of Thai and Bali (Indonesian) people and their history were not taken into account in determining Ramayana and Mahabharata periods.

The Indian-Hindu time-line has appeared in *Hinduism Today* (December 94 issue), a newspaper, and this [8] may serve as an initial reference for many authors writing on historical aspects of Hindu history.

Ancient history of India by R.C. Majumdar [16] refers the date of Mahabharata War as 3102 BC. This book is accepted by the Government of India and her universities as an authentic text and reference book. This very important and true historical fact is completely omitted!

One billion Hindus of the world reject the authenticity of the "chronological and historical sequences" as described in the Indian literature chapter of the book "*World Literature*". This book is taught in the tenth grade of Dekalb County's high school, Georgia, U.S.A. and is published by Holt, Rinehart, and Winston Inc. Please write to the Publishers of this book to correct the distortion. This distorted "*World Literature*" is taught throughout the western world. This is not an isolated incidence, but a well-planned strategy by these intellectuals to discredit and disgrace any other philosophy which is not in their favor, even though the philosophy, civilization and history are real facts which have been in existence since time immemorial.

Indeed, it is the need of time to correct the "*World Literature*" like any other scientific document, where facts, opposing views and theories are to be addressed equally. The authors of the "*World Literature*" have categorically avoided the scientific and archaeological discoveries and the pertinent views of Indian and other scholars. Therefore, their writings are unjust, unbalanced and devoid of authenticity.

Academically, these fallacies have serious impact on our children at schools and colleges. Our students are cognizant of correct chronology but the teachers mark them negatively since they are unaware of the facts and follow only what is given in the text. Academically, anthropologically, archaeologically, psychologically, sociologically, scientifically, etc. all concepts, controversies, conflicts and theories are to be addressed on factual grounds to disseminate knowledge in schools and colleges.

REFERENCES

1. Yogi Aurobindo: *Arya,* volume I, p. 1963.
2. David Frawley: Gods, Sages, and Kings: Ancient Secrets of Ancient and World Civilization, Passage Press, Utah, 1990.
3. Swami Jyotirmayanand: "*Vivekanand—His Gospel of Man-Making with a Garland of Tribune and a Chronicle of His Life and Times with Pictures,*" 1, M.V. Naidu St., Panchavati, Chetput, Madras-600 031, India, October 1986.
4. Deen B. Chandora, M.D.: *Hindu Dharma: Vedic Light*, Sarvdeshik Arya Pratinidhi Sabha, New Delhi, India, Nov. 1991.
5. Robertson: *Sociology*, Third Edition, New York, 1987.
6. Swami Vidhyanand Sarasvati: *Original Home of Aryans*, Sarvdeshik Arya Pratinidhi Sabha, New Delhi, India, July 1987.
7. David Frawley: *The Myth of Aryan Invasion of India*, Voice of India Publication, New Delhi, India, 1994.
8. *Time-Line, Hinduism Today,* Himalaya Academy, Hawaii, December 1994.
9. R. Charles: *The Hare Krishna's in India*, Princeton University Press, NJ, 1989.
10. K.N. Kapur: *Age of Mahabharat War*, Vedic Light, New Delhi, India, April 1981.

11. K.N. Kapur: *Dawn of Indian History*, Sarvadeshik Arya Pratinidhi Sabha, New Delhi, India, April 1990.
12. Dayanand Sarasvati: *Truth of Light*, Sarvadeshik Arya Pratinidhi Sabha, New Delhi, India 1884.
13. Paramhansa Jagdeeshwaranand Sarasvati: *Shrimad Valmiki Ramayan*, Govindram Hasanand, Publishers, Nai Sarak, Delhi, India, 1988.
14. *Western Psychiatrist*: Hinduism Today, Himalaya Academy, Hawaii, USA, September 1991.
15. Carl Sagan: *Cosmos and Pale Blue Dot: A Vision of Human Future in Space*, The Commonwealth Club of California, San Francisco, Volume 89, January 16, 1995.
16. Majumdar, R.C., *et al.*: *An Advanced History of India*, Macmillan, New York, 3rd Edition, 1967.

A Post-Modern Demand for Historic Accuracy

MICHAEL PARKER
Honolulu, Hawaii, USA

In the western world there are many misconceptions and prejudices about Vedic tradition and culture. Academicians and scholars need to review them in the light of colonial designs of the past where they originated. The honesty in scholarship demands that there be truth brought out. Also, because of its own historical turns, the West has, perhaps, a lot in its inheritance and connections with the Vedic culture that is denied.

In some Greek episodes, words like 'arya' and 'swastika' occur; also in the several countries of the Europe and other cultures, names resembling Rama are found. With correct understanding and interpretations, one is bound to discover important historical truths.

Introduction

In any investigation one must use evidence. The evidence can come from many sources, but a conscientious investigator is not swayed by the various prejudices and biases, that he or she will be confronted with. The present state of world history, as taught in a majority of schools, is fraught with theories, assumptions and outright cultural and racial prejudices. This is especially clear in the current field of Indian historical studies. Many of the current theories find their roots in the 19th century, a time of European world domination. From the genocidal doctrine of America's 'Manifest Destiny' to the British colonial and Christian missionaries' 'Theory of White Man's Burden', one can clearly see the unworthy and unstable foundations upon which Western historical research stands. The fact is that the expansionist agendas of the 19th century European/American nations were enthusiastically supported by many of the intellectual elite, who devoted volumes of the books to the scholarly rationalization of European world domination. This fact alone not only damages the validity of their opinions, but actually discredits them. If presented in a legal setting, this so-called scholarly evidence would be thrown out of court.

Western Misconception about Vedic View of Woman

Another Western misconception is the supposed anti-women bias of Vedic culture. The truth is the Vedic culture promotes the greatest potential of femininity, whereas Western culture perceives equality to mean the masculinization of woman. Another fallacy of the modern theorists is the assumption that humanity has always been driven by animalistic drives such as lust, greed, jealousy, etc. The problem is compounded by their attempts to measure past human events by comparing them with current trends in human affairs. With such an unscientific approach to historical research, the need for an accurate and objective revision is extreme.

Was not Alexander Defeated by Porus?

It is obvious that the Aryan/Indo-European theories evolved out of the colonial era's expansionist mold. With these theories now exposed false, there are many questions that remain 'officially' unanswered. Many aspects of ancient Indian history demand to be reviewed, researched and, in many cases, revised. For example, 'Alexander the Great's' ambiguous retreat from India. Why would his victorious armies mutiny on the threshold of reaching their goal of India? Mysteriously, after allegedly defeating the powerful king Puru (Poros), the Greeks decided to mutiny and march back to Persia. These inconsistencies are analyzed by H.C. Seth in his paper, 'Was Poros the victor at the battle of Jhelum?' Also the ancient Ethiopic Text (edited and translated by E.A.W. Badge), covering the life of Alexander, reveals a picture of defeated Alexander.

Legacy of Manu and Arya in Other Cultures

Manu finds common usage in cultures, as in the Vedic Manu, the Teutonic Manus, the first Egyptian king Menes, the Polynesian Menehune, etc. Danu is a Vedic progenitor goddess and in Celtic tradition Danu is also a progenitor goddess, as in 'Tuata te Dannan', or 'Children of Danu'. The word Arya is found in many cultures, as in the Ayar founders of the Incas, or in the Polynesian word Ari'I, meaning 'chief' or 'noble.' We also have the 'Eire' of Ireland, and the word 'aristrocat' also has its roots in the word Arya. In Sumerian we have the word Ara meaning 'lofty', and some say the name Sumeria comes from the Sanskrit 'Soma-Arya'.

Indian Connections with Greeks and Egyptians

In a book called 'India in Greece', author Pococke suggests many clues connecting ancient Greece with ancient India. Although somewhat speculative, many of the author's points make much more sense than many of the presently accepted theories. For example, the first Greek king is said to have come from Gaia. If this is read as Greek, he would be thought of as coming from the earth. However, if read as Sanskrit, Gaia becomes Gaya, the famous holy city in India. Instead of coming out of the earth, it makes sense for him to have come from a historical place. Pococke also points out that the major mountain chain of Greece is called Othrys, and an ancient name of the Himalayas is the Adhri. In the Nordic tradition heaven is called Himmel, very close to the word Himalayas, the location of Kailash. In his book 'Art and Culture of India and Egypt' author S.M. El-Mansori proves the ancient connections between these cultures. This is a very important field of research that has not been given the attention it deserves.

Use of Swastika and Name Rama show Significant Indian Connections

The world-wide prevalence of Swastikas has also not been adequately explained, nor has the prevalence of the name Rama. Rama is found in the Vedic culture, in Egyptian history, Assyrian, Native Americans, notably amongst Incas, in Europe, Arabia, etc. We find the name and word Rama to have the same divine and auspicious connotations wherever it is used. Also there is some question as to the true location of 'Lanka'. Was it located in the present Sri Lanka or was it located at the equator in and around the Chagos Islael area? Some have also questioned the authenticity of Emperor Ashoka's Buddhism and see his 'Dharma-Vijaya' to be the 'righteous conquest' of Vedic emperors like Sri Rama, King Prithu, and Maharaja Yudhisthira (*Glimpses of the Vedic Nation* by Balshastri Hardas). If this is a fact, the implications are enormous. India's history has been so distorted that it appears every era of its history needs to be reviewed. Amongst all this, glaringly obvious is the Vedic civilization evidenced by the Sarasvati-Indus civilization.

Falsity of Notion of a Pre-Vedic Culture

Frawley's paradox has exposed the falsity of the supposed Pre-Vedic basis of this culture. The amazing thing about all this is that the evidences of common Vedic World heritage are so prevalent that it obviously took a calculated effort to distort the truth. A real historian or a sincere student can never be satisfied with distorted truths. In the investigative search for historical facts, we obviously cannot rely on biased and misguided views. This is especially true for Indian historical researches. To get to the truth, we must access the ancient truths as recorded in the ancient scriptures of ancient India. We must replace the biased and unscientific fallacies of current mainstream Indian studies with a scientific fact-finding approach, measured with a healthy dose of respect for the grand achievements of the ancients. The greatness of the ancients is self-evident from their monolithic structures to the amazing oral preservation of the Vedic literature. We can read in these achievements the character and noble quality of these people and their culture. The modern theories which make every grand structure a tomb or place of human sacrifice, that portray every divine doctrine as an experiment in social engineering or a form of tyranny, lack credibility and border on the fantastic. Like the idea that the presumed Vedic authors, while crediting Vyasadev for it all, ingeniously and accurately noted the astronomical, geographical and scientific realities of a bygone era, all in the name of perpetuating a hoax.

Objectivity Demands Revision of Indian History

The modern historians/theorists, being emotionally attached to their beliefs, reject revisionism, though revision is a necessary part of most endeavors. The truth is that an investigator of facts immediately forfeits his ability to gather facts, by rejecting evidences in an off-hand way. In the same way, a historian who is unwilling to weigh historical evidence on the scale of objective science and logic, forfeits the ability to be an accurate historian. History is a field of study that should rise above the emotions, prejudices, and agendas of a current era. History seeks to be a window into the past. To color or taint historical past events with present day ideologies is unscientific, to say the least. A real historian must have the facts, in order to offer a true account of the past. The wonderful thing about truth is that it cannot be altered. The truth in history is solid and immutable, even in the face of many distortions. We are reminded here of the Vedic proverb '*satyameva jayate*'—'Truth alone prevails'.

The accuracy of the Vedic sciences, such as Sulbasutras, is evidenced in the book by Rajarama, '*The Politics of History*'. It is a self-evident truth relating to matters, both mundane and spiritual. Its continuity throughout the ages, points to an organic culture that synchronicizes with the natural laws of the universe. The Aryan/Indo-European race invasion/migration theories were invented to fulfill the colonial designs. But now with these theories proven false, we are left with a vacuum. Only the historical truths of the Vedic scriptures and traditions can justly and accurately fill the void. The implications of this demand a complete review of the current theories of not only the ancient Indian history, but also the ancient history of the entire world.

Community and Power in Kautilya's Arthasastra

JOYOTPAUL CHAUDHURI
Political Science Department
Arizona State University
Tempe, AZ 85257-2001

Kautilya's Arthasastra, after its rediscovery over 50 years ago, has become an integral part of the history of Indian ideas. Some early Western commentators did not regard it as impressive political theory, but useful as a window on ancient India. Another line of thought was anxious to show that Kautilya anticipated Machiavelli and is as impressive as Aristotle. Yet another section of literature primarily concentrates on Kautilya's balance of power model.

The current paper approaches the Arthasastra from the perspective of political theory. This involves some understanding of the epistemological and normative foundations of Kautilya's analysis. Then Kautilya's major positions are seen through some key, cross cultural and perennially important conceptual categories of how meaning is given to "community" and "power." This approach avoids, in large part, the rancours of colonialism and colonialism in scholarship and also bypasses the purely temporarily and spatially specific historical details of the Mauryan dynasty.

Introduction

Intellectual parochialism is ubiquitous and is not limited to any one part of the world. Western universities in the treatment of the development of political thought, for the most part, have continued with the standard sequence of Plato to Machiavelli, Machiavelli to Marx and contemporary political thought. Increased sensitivity to non-western traditions has resulted in an occasional course or a special topic treatment of non-western political ideas. We have evolved a bit away from Hegel's remark that "the Hindoo is incapable of . . . reflection"[1] and from the perspective of a well known twentieth century scholar in the history of political ideas, W.W. Willoughby, who had this to say about Asian political ideas:

> At times certain checks upon the exercise of autocratic power may have been attempted, but in almost universal practice the ruler's will know no hindrances.[2]

---

[1]Quoted from Hegel's Philosophy of History, in: P. Sil Narasingha, *Kautilya's Arthasastra,* Peter Hang, New York, 1981, p. 1.

[2]Westeral Woodbury Willoughby, *The Political Theories of the Ancient World,* Longman's Green and Company, New York, 1903, p. 19.

Reversing the misconception about Asian political thought is not an easy task and is not being attempted in this essay. Rather the task herein is to take Kautilya's *Arthasastra* and attempt to share a sense of its place in comparative political thought. This involves some understanding of the epistemological issues, the core concepts of political theory (such as community and authority) and some tactic knowledge of the development of Western and non-western traditions.

Kautilya's work represents an important tradition in Indian intellectual history. Kautilya's "saintly king" provides a model of Vedic political leadership and provides a sense of the statecraft of Hindu revivalists today. Kautilya's work also gives us a sense of early thought on realism in domestic policy and in international relations.

Authorship, Style and Epistemology

Kautilya's *Arthasastra* was apparently composed and written somewhere around 320 B.C. and most Indian scholars regard Kautilya to be the master teacher Chanaka—the strategist responsible for the rise from relatively humble origins of Chandragupta the founder of the Maurya dynasty, who laid the first cornerstones of the Indian state. Kautilya may well have been a denotative derivative of his clan or "gotra," namely "kutila gotra"[1] . Indians can have several names.

Kautilya's work is referred to by other writers in the historical literature[2]. Kautilya's work had its ups and downs in reputation in Indian history and was eventually "lost" till this century. Then "dramatically" a full length palm leaf manuscript came into the hands of Dr. R. Shamasastry of Mysore in 1904 who, subsequently, published the text, an English translation of the text and other reference material. Later, another manuscript of the same *Arthasastra* and additional fragments were also found. The enormously detailed text is mainly in prose form but intermingled with aphorisms and rhythmic verses. Since the pioneering Shamasastry edition, there have been several other translations in different languages. The text is spotted with condensed Sanskritic abstract nouns, powerful denotative statements, intuitive insights and esoteric terms, but is it also often very hyperfactual in its details on public administration. But then many contemporary administrative classics are not written in flights of poetry either. The tendency to use esoteric rather than discursive terminology often hides the analytical content of Indian classical writers, particularly for Western readers. If one looks at the classic coordinates for cross-cultural analysis of self, space and time, Kautilya's premises on all three are inter-related and clear cut. He

[1]See introductory discussion on text and authorship in L.N. Rangarajan (ed.), *Kautilya, The Arthasastra*. Penguin Books, New Delhi, 1992. pp. 13–14.

[2]For a brief but clear discussion of the historical references to Kautilya, see Sil, pp. 140–144.

understands the idea of an ultimate universe but his immediate concerns are with "Bharat":

> "The area extending from the Himalayas in the north to the sea [in the south] and a thousand *yojanas* wide from east to west is the area of the King-Emperor (Chakravartikshetram)."[1]

After the end of the Alexandrian incursion in northwest India, Bharat became the playing field for the universal emperor. In matters of time, the current sensed time is important. Without a current temporal, material, political and economic base, the pursuit of timeless spiritual liberation is not possible.

In matters of selfhood, Kautilya is neither a western individualist nor is he a Buddhist with the latter's "sunyata" or "anatman" (no self). Kautilya's self is ultimately indifferentiated in eternity (santana dharma), but temporarily discrete yet interdependent providing the basis for a communitarian approach with a hierarchical division of labor. Epistemologicially and broadly, Kautilya is a "naive realist" in that entities have empirically perceptible properties and a combination of observation, analysis and extension can ferret out and capture their behavior. It is interesting that the three key foundational philosophical systems that he mentions as being worthy of study are all dualists, namely Samkhya, yoga and materialism[2].

The dualism refers to the intrinsic distinction between the selfhood of conscious being (purusas) and the external world (prakrti). For the later Upanishads, Shankara's "advaita vedanta" (non-dualism) and for Buddhism (*anatmam* = no self) the distinction is artificial, non-existent or unreal. Samkhya provided a broad umbrella in whose shade various dualisms were nurtured. The ancient yoga philosophy (not the yoga practices)[3] also logically emphasized the self controlled observer and materialism saw consciousness as a reflection or extension of the external world.

Kautilya shares with the Dharmasastras, including Manu, a general commitment to dualism. His particular brand emphasizes the importance of "artha"—material well being as the gateway to "dharma" or righteousness[4]. Kautilya's discussion of his "method" further emphasizes his philosophical dualism. He organizes his terms of discourse into numerous "classes" and definitions like early Aristotelian botanists. There is no "logos" or Platonic reason heare. "Reasoning" is a disciplined quality which the observer brings to bear in examining a subject. Thus,

---

[1]Rangarajan (Ed.), *Arthasastra*, p. 743.

[2]Rangarajan (Ed.), *Arthasastra*, p. 106.

[3]Yoga practices can be reconciled with other philosophies as well.

[4]For a brief but clear discussion of dualism in Samkhya and Yoga, see Phillips Stephen, *Classical Indian Metaphysics*. Chicago: Open Court, 1995, pp. 12, 26, 86.

> "Reasoning is used to prove an assertion. In asserting, that artha alone is supreme, the reason is given: 'because dharma and karma depend on artha'."[1]

In other words, "artha" is out there in the external world as substance or resource. Good intuitive "reasoning" should show that without controlling artha, the good life is not possible.

Comparative Analysis: Power and Community

Kautilya's *Arthasastra* is rooted in the development of the Indian philosophical tradition and can be examined accordingly. But given its theoretical content, it is also important to understand its place in comparative political theory. Since the study of political theory is dominated by the western political tradition, a brief examination of the similarities and differences may be in order.

Kautilya's work is typically and classically Indian with respect to the preference for referring to ideational frames of reference rather than linear chronological events or regimes. Except for the important but brief reference to the Nanda dynasty and, thereby to the Greek invasions of Alexander and later his designee Seleucos, Kautilya's temporal references are ideational: to Manu, to Samkhya philosophy, to the Vedas and to tribal and republican polities. Though Kautilya was generally acknowledged to be a specific individual rather than the more mythical Manu, there could be commentaries by Kautilya's followers that could have crept into later texts as gloss. Given the combination of the Indian oral tradition, translation into regional languages and perishable palm leaf manuscripts one has to tolerate chronological ambiguities to deal with the substance of Kautilya's work.

Community: Kautilya and Aristotle

Kautilya is closer politically to Aristotle than to Plato. For Aristotle, politics is the queen of the sciences. For Kautilya, also, without "arthasastra", i.e. the science of political economy, the opportunity to pursue other aspects of the good life is not possible. Kautilya has a conception of distributive justice under the umbrella of a political community. Unlike Aristotle's preoccupation with the city state, Kautilya pursues the ideal of a hegemonic, larger "universal" community.

Kautilya's "naive realism" also parallels Aristotle's qualitative physics where qualitative properties are attached to entities. Kautilya's entities also have teleological purposes. However, unlike Aristotle, Kautilya limits his discussion to the arthasastra leaving the discussion of biology, rhetoric and general metaphysics to other writers in the dharmasastra tradition.

---

[1]Rangarajan (editor), *Arthasastra*, p.103.

Power: Kautilya and Hobbes

Like Hobbes, Kautilya is concerned with the achievement of security through state activity and speaks of the importance of the state as a dominant institution in society. Like Hobbes, Kautilya has a conception of the state as a creator of order out of anarchy. However, unlike Hobbes' materialism, Kautilya also has moral goals, the progress of righteousness (dharma). Kautilya's social contract involves the creation of a myth that is part of political socialization. The concept of legitimacy in Kautilya is less materialistic than in Hobbes, because of Kautilya's conception of the self allows great leeway for moral judgment.

Power: Kautilya and Machiavelli

The literature on Kautilya is full of many, though often brief, comparisons with Machiavelli[1]. Both are representatives of political realism, the importance of state building and power. Both are interested in relating psychology, politics and leadership. Both are interested in maintaining a civil religion and both are skeptical of the reliability of mercenaries in war. But the differences between them are considerable.

Kautilya has a deeper commitment to political economy and public administration. Encouraging activity and productivity is more important to Kautilya than to many other classical Indian writers.

Of course, some Marxists may see in Kautilya's economy a defense of emerging feudalism. But if one looks past Kautilya's contemperaneous examples to the principles one can see advice that is less fixed by time and place. Political leadership is an important economic variable in the coordination of the public and private sector. The importance of production is primarily in agriculture but also in manufacture. Without productivity in agriculture other functions can begin to crumble. The work ethic inculcated in the Sudra caste is important for the expansion of agriculture.

The agricultural division of labor is complemented with manufacturing and the work of skilled artisans. Kautilya's conception of the work ethic includes quality control by the state and punishment of dishonesty and theft. Consumer protection measures are described in great detail. The importance of trading is clearly recognized but state enforced standards govern fraud in materials in labor and in transactions.

---

[1]See Joyotpaul Chaudhuri, "Ethics and Politics in the Golden Age of Indian Poltical Thought", M.A. thesis, University of Oklahoma, Norman, Oklahoma, 1961. The author, thirty-six years ago, overemphasized the similiarities between Machiavelli and Kautilya. Some of the comparisons are still valid, but the thesis has a bibliography of early comparisons.

Power and Diplomacy

Aristotle and Machiavelli were both aware of the importance of external security for the state. Kautilya, however, goes far beyond both in developing an extensive theory of international relations[1].

There are many parallels between Kautilya and the work of Hans Morgenthau and other foundation writers on twentieth century political realism in the study of international politics. Although some of the content is defined differently, Kautilya's "anga(s)" or limb parallels political realism's "element(s)" of natural power. In political realism "diplomacy" is the connecting thread and so it is in the case of Kautilya.

> The power of good counsel (good analysis and good judgement) is superior [to sheer military strength]. Intelligence and (knowledge of) the science of politics are the two eyes (of a king). Using these, a king can, with a little effort, arrive at the best judgment on the means (the four methods of conciliation, sowing, dissension, etc.) as well as the various tricks, stratagems, clandestine practices and occult means (described in this treatise) to overwhelm even kings who are mighty and energetic.
>
> Thus, the three components of power - enthusiasm, military might and the power of counsel are in ascending order of importance[2]

For Kautilya, domestic and foreign policy are intimately related in more ways than one. Most importantly, domestic stability enhances fluidity in international diplomacy in keeping with what Modelski has called the recurring paradox in Indian polictics[3].

Power and Administration

For domestic stability among other things, Kautilya discusses the need for an extensive administrative machinery which takes merely a quarter of the space of the book. National administration is divided into about thirty-four different departments, each with a chief (adhyaksha) and appropriate subordinates. Forestry, mining, mint, state trading, weights and measures, surveying, alcohol, shipping, passports, textiles, jails and other major functions are listed. The job descriptions and qualifications are specified for each administrator.

There are long lists of administrative procedures, codes of ethics and sanctions

---

[1]See George Modelski, "Kautilya: Foreign Policy and International System in the Ancient Hindu World", *The American Political Science Review,* Vol. LVIII, September 1964, pp. 549–560.

[2]L.N. Rangarajan (Ed.), *Kautilya, The Arthasastra*, Penguin Book, New Dehli, 1992, p. 628

[3]Modelski, p. 559.

for wrong doing. For stealing gems from the treasury, for instance, if found guilty, the sanction is death[1].

Power And Jurisprudence

In addition to the administrative system, Kautilya also outlines a system of jurisprudence including codification of offenses, roles of judges, a policy manual for prisons and rules of evidence and procedure. Essentially, the Kautilyan system is a system of arbitration rather than adjudication, therefore, the codes and sanctions are not only violation specific but caste and gender specific as well.

The harshness of codes[2] is softened by Kautilya's advice to take into account the "special circumstances of the person convicted and of the particular offense."[3] Compassion is also to be shown to "a pilgrim, an ascetic, anyone suffering from illness, hunger, thirst, poverty, fatigue from a journey, suffering from an earlier punishment, a foreigner, or one from the countryside.[4]

Special categories of persons who have withdrawn from society for spiritual reasons can substitute penances and rituals for fines. Kautilya is also more "liberal" than Manu on divorce, remarriage of widows and even occasional mixed caste marriages.

In jurisprudence, even though Kautilya is primarily interested in statecraft, he is not a strict legal positivist. The primary source of the law is the "dharma", i.e., spiritual principles and norms written in texts (shastras). The shastras are superior to customary law (sociological jurisprudence). The edicts of the king (positive law) become relevant when the relationship between the operational rules of the "shastras" and the utlimate "dharma" (natural law) is unavailable[5].

With the emasculation of the 4th amendment in the U.S. Constitution, the rights of suspects have become ambigous at times. Kautilya, on suspects, may not satisfy ACLU members but there are some protections. Thus, for instance in criminal investigations, Kautilya states:

"Because of the difficulties of (conducting a proper) investigation, no one shall be arrested for a crime committed more than three nights earlier, unless he is caught with the tools of the crime."[6]

---

[1]Rangarajan (Ed.), *Kautilya*, p. 299.

[2]A humorous example of the softening of codes with an element of consent appears in his listings of "choices" open to those convicted of capital punishment. A person could *choose* being gored to death by an elephant. This "meritorious" way of departing should be preceded by "oblatory gifts" of the following: a drona of rice, a jar of wine, garlands and a piece of cloth to clean the tusks. Rangarajan, *Arthasastra*. p. 497.

[2]Kautilya, p. 493.

[3]Kautilya, p. 493.

[4]Kautilya, p. 380.

[5]Kautilya, p. 458.

Community and Polity

Given the order of the dharmasastras, the natural law and recognition of a civil religion, Kautilya's polity is not a modern secular polity—but it is a quasi-secular polity parallelling the English conception of a religious (Church of England) establishment balanced with a secular administrative system and de facto, if not de jure, freedom of religion.

As G. Bhagat notes, the Kautilyan policy in the Mauryan dynasty prescribed tolerance for the beliefs of the many plural Hindu sects with differences in beliefs and for the Buddhists, the Jains and many other "protestant" groups such as the "Ajivikas"[1].

One of the aspects of the Kautilyan state that is sometimes misunderstood is the internal security system. Kautilya urged a system of covert security for investigative work in dealing with other political systems and also for law enforcement and keeping informed about administrative dishonesty and subversive activity. Bhagat quotes Will Durant speaking critically that the "one defect of this (Maurya) government was autocracy and, therefore, continued dependence upon force and spies".[2] However, if one reads the *Arthasastra* carefully, Kautilya's remarks, in context, parallel the informational role of a Federal Bureau of Investigation domestically and the USIA and Central Intelligence agency in diplomacy and their primary reporting lines to the executive branch.

We come now to Durant's remark on autocracy. Remembering Alexis de Tocqueville's theses in *Democracy in America* is important in understanding the structure of Kautilya's polity. Kautilya is clearly advocating the building of the state and of executive power. But Kautilya's king, while symbolically sovereign, has greater limitations on his actual power than Robert Filmer's king, Hobbes' sovereign or modern "democratic" executives and their cloak of national security.

After saluting Brihaspati and Sukra—the mythical founders of the study of politics—Kautilya points out his role in overthrowing the autocracy of the Nanda kings[3]. He, unlike Hobbes, proceeds to point out that even anarchy is better than misrule or autocracy:

> "*Varam na rajyam na kurajarajyam* .
> (It is better not have any government than to have one of a bad ruler.)"[4]

---

[1]G. Bhagat, "Kautilya Revisited and Revisioned", *The Indian Journal of Political Science*, **51**(2), April-June 1990, 191.

[2]G. Bhagat, p. 187.

[3]Kautilya, p. 100.

[4]Sil, p. 65.

This is not the statement of an autocrat who rules only by dependence on force and spies. People are the most active ingredients of the state:

> "*na hyajano janapado rajyamajanapadem va bhavatititi.*
> (there is no country without people and no kingdom without a country.)"[1]

Kautilya's emphasis on the role of the people comes from his concern about legitimacy and the need for creating a moral (dharma/dharmic) yet "secular" community through the "science" of statecraft.[2] Of course, Kautilya is no democrat though he is familiar with some early principles of democracy, including equality, extensive debate, elected rulers and representation that were the ingredients of some early Indian Buddhist and tribal republics[3]. He actually advocates political and military acquisition of republics because of their instability unless the republics were lined up in a strong league or confederacy. Elaborate confederacies must be treated with equality and respect because the formation of viable leagues and confederacies are possible only when internal dissension is not extensive.

While the Kautilyan polity clearly specifies the authority of the state, there are elaborate limits on that authority, from both qualitative and quantitative standpoints. Kautilya's state implies clear symbolic and coordinating authority of the king in the context of considerable decentralization of power among "guilds", "corporations", caste and family organizations. There are semiautonomous institutions under the umbrella of the state for tax purposes and consumer protection[4]

Kautilya's polity is one of the best examples of de Toequeville's characterization of traditional societies which combines principles of de jure state power with de facto decentralization. Further, everyone is integrated into community through the multiple but intimately familiar world of family, caste, village and guild. Kautilya's society is a very specialized society coordinated by a state which exercises power with accurate information, legitimacy and with the right amount of "danda" or power.

---

[1]Sil, p. 65. 25. 26. 27.

[2]The specialized study of politics distinct from theology occurred very early in Indian thought even before Kautilya. Note the following: "It is, however, a remarkable fact that the study of statecraft and cognate topics branched off at an early period in the history of the race from the general stream of Vedic culture and formed and independent branch of knowledge which might be called a secular science, were it not for the pronounced distinction of the Hindu mind to conceive the secular life as the antithesis of the religious." U. Ghoshal, *A History of Hindu Political Theories*, Oxford University Press, Calcutta, 1923. p. ix.

[3]See M.V. Krishna Rao, *Studies in Kautilya*, Munshiram Manoharlal Publishers Pvt. Ltd., 1958 (Revised 1979), New Dehli, p. 5. Rao proceeds to list a large number of democratic rulers who came to grief because of dissensions and disunity.

[4]Rao, p. 42.

Power is not only distributed in the base of the pyramid it is also shared in a de facto manner at the top. The council of ministers is not supposed to be a group of cronies—their advice and consultation is crucial to good government. There is no "oriental despotism" here. The king, preferably, should have some martial experience but should be a "saintly" king who understands "dharma" and whose goal is to create an environment where morality can be pursued.

An important part of "dharma" is role differentiation. Thus, the distinction between brahminic knowledge and khattriya governance is important. A king can dismiss his Brahmin advisers but he needs to still give them their dignity. Also, governance is not just limited to khattriyas—it is simply preferable that princes be of noble birth so that they would be more easily acceptable and sociologically ready for assumption of power. Kautilya's protege, the founder of the Maurya dynasty, was apparently Sudra in origin[1]. The Sudra were still considered "Arya" though they were generally more involved in agricultural labor than in Brahminic scholarship or Khattriya governance.

Kautilya's approach to caste is thus not primarily racial but functional though he does use the term "varna" for caste which sometimes is roughly, but not incompletely, translated as "color". Kautilya is, therefore, primarily interested in the communitarian aspects of caste, guild and family associations as linkages for the building of a larger community and the state is the architectonic instrument for strengthening and protecting the community and insuring justice. It would be a mistake then to regard Kautilya either as equivalent to Machiavelli, at least of the Prince, or Manu who is more fundamentally interested in the preservation of caste. Kautilya's interest is both more political than Manu and more communitarian that Machiavelli's Prince. Like de Tocqueville, he is wary of the alienation and instability that egalitarianism can create and is interested in a limited government which recognizes the importance of identity and communitarian links to a political system which respects legitimacy and recognizes evenhanded but distributive justice.

The state has both it administrative and economic infrastructure in its civil service system and state enterprises. But the state's direct ownership of the means of production in terms of land remains small[2] and the state created "positive law" remains within the boundaries of the dharma—the moral order. The Kautilyan state internally avoids the extremes of disorderly anarchy and political tyranny. Since domestic and international politics are interconnected the state also avoids the excesses of anarchy/"matsyanaya" (the logic of the fish—large fishes living on little fishes) and the tyranny in its approach to foreign policy and international

---

[1]Sil, pp. 16, 29.

[2]Bhagat, p. 193.

system. The active and energetic ruler (vijigishu) must strive for a moral hegemonic (chakravartin) role in the international system. The hegemony results in a loose knit[1] international community where diversity and local authority, role of mediatory states[2] and cooperative confederacies is acknowledged in the context of realism and the mutuality of interests between diverse states.

Temporarily, Kautilya was interested in a "chakravartin" power from the ocean to the mountains. Theoretically, it deals with the chakravarartin exercising a moral but hegemonic role in the center of a wheel of linked states expanding to the geopolitical circumference of world affairs[3].

Some Conclusions

Kautilya's *Arthasastra* is the capstone of the development of classical Indian political theory which acknowledges the importance of a moral tradition but which emphasizes the study of politics, to borrow Aristotle's phrase, as the queen of sciences. Like Machiavelli, Kautilya is not interested in pure philosophy but in political theory. Unlike Machiavelli, he operates within the boundaries of a moral framework (dharma). Thus, the intrinsic goals (dharma) and the extrinsic instrumental values (artha) are inter-related. Kautilya, therefore, cannot be dismissed as an aberration in the development of Indian philosophical traditions. His political realism simply is part of one line of thought. Like many Indian thinkers, Kautilya does not have a western atomistic or bracketed or monadic concept of self. However, unlike the universal non-dualistic conception of selfhood and the external world represented in the later Upanishads and the post-Kautilyan Shankara's non-dualism (advaita vendanta) Kautilya's interdependent self is contextually differentiated into the caste specific duties of the dharmasastras. Kautilya is concerned about building a community with the naturally connected, but role differentiated self in the context of the empirically current framework of time and space. Even though Kautilya's literary style is different from Hobbes he shares with Hobbes the tight linkage between the premises of an imperfect world of motion and the means of making it livable.

A critique of Kautilya is, therefore, more viable if directed at his Dharmasastra premises than their extension into political realism which Kautilya shares with Manu and the political realism of the Santiparvan in the epic Mahabharata. The critiques could arise from Indian or Western philosophy. In Indian philosophy, Kautilyan's premises are different from Advaita Vedanta (Atma = Brahman), i.e. the unity of the internal and external worlds. Kautilya's premises of righteous

[1]Modelski, p. 555..

[2]Modelski, p. 557.

[3]See again, George Modelski's APSR article on Kautilya and the International System.

conquest (dharma vijaya) are also different from the Buddhists who are more committed to a universe of conciliation and mediation rather than political expansion. Some early Buddhist regarded Kautilya as wicked.[1]

In this century, Dr. Bhim Rao Ambedkar led some untouchables out of Hinduism because of casteism into more egalitarianism and also reportedly burnt a copy of the Code of Manu. Ambedkar would have been critical of Kautilya's premises, since like Manu, Kautilya accepts the varna system

From the standpoint of western thought, Kautilya's premises about "dharma" are considerably different from the context of Christian theologies. Marxists will tend to regard Kautilya as a defender of feudal society. But the western perspectives have their own parochialisms. Kautilya's premises do not include a Jeffersonian theory of rights but Kautilya goes about limiting government in other ways. In turn, Jeffersonian theory has its own problems of hypocrisies and inconsistencies in application. Intrinsically, Jeffersonian perspectives ran roughshod over aboriginal land rights in America. The application of Jeffersonian rights has run into its own difficulties such as the emasculation of the fourth amendment rights.

Kautilya's premises are quite clear and deeply rooted in the development of Indian political thought. Some of his discussion on political realism, of the nature of community, and political leadership are important landmarks in the development of Indian thought and should be integrated into the study of the development of human thought about politics. The study of Kautilya can add to cross cultural intellectual history, to the understanding of Hindu political revivalism and early political realism in diplomacy.

---

[1]Sil, p. 137. Reference to the Buddhist trait Manjusrimulakalpa which calls him wicked (durmati) irrascible (krodhana) and profane (papaka).

The Evolution of Sanskrit Language and Literature and Its Impact on Modern Languages.

RASIK VIHARI JOSHI
El Coleglo de Mexico A.C.
Camino Al Jusco. No. 20, Codigo Postal 0100, Mexico, D.F.

The title of this paper covers a wide range of the History of Sanskrit Literature. It is hardly possible to make full justice with the topic. Even an attempt to register the names of authors and titles of works will make a number of volumes. However, I am making a humble attempt to give a glimpse of this vast and enormous literature the importance of which is beyond doubt. Sanskrit literature is divided into two major parts, viz., (i) Vedic and (ii) Classical. The word Veda means knowledge—science of knowledge. Vedic literature consists of the Samhitas, Brahmanas, Aranyakas, Upanishads and Sutras. The Samhitas are four in number—Rig Veda, Yajur Veda, Sama Veda and Atharva Veda. Each of these Vedic Samhitas has an interrelation and development of thoughts in the remaining four parts of Vedic literature. Rig Veda consists of 1028 hymns or suktas, covering about 10,000 stanzas, and is the oldest literary document available to humanity. Its lucidity of language, depth of thought, rythmic meters, musical resonance and treatment of a variety of subjects are a matter of wonder for indologists. Thanks to the accents in the Vedas and eight types of recitation that the text of the Samhitas is preserved in its original form without interpolations. A traditional Vedic scholar can correct even an error of an accent in the printed text. A change in accent either in the last or the first sylable thus totally changes the meaning of the word. The accents of the Rig Veda and of the Sama Veda are different. A scholar expert in the Rig Veda would not be able to recite correctly even one stanza of the Sama Veda. It is well known that the text of the Rig Veda is repeated in the Sama Veda with the exception of 75 hymns, but the apparently similar text thus denotes a different meaning as per the accent.

To elucidate I may be permitted to refer to an incident of Vedic mythology. Indra the king of gods used to welcome his preceptor Brihaspati every day in his court. He used to get up from his throne along with all other gods, come up to the gate of the hall to receive him. He bowed down to Brihaspati and requested him to take seat on his right side. When Brihaspati was seated, Indra and all gods sat also. One day some gods advised Indra that he was the king of gods and Brihaspati was only a Brahmin priest, therefore what was the necessity to demonstrate so much honour? In case Brihaspati had transcendental perception he certainly would know the respect you deserve. Next morning on the arrival of Brihaspati, Indra and all gods remained seated on their respective thrones. Indra saluted Brihaspati "Good mornig, Sir! You are welcome. Please take your seat." Hearing this Brihaspati was annoyed and felt insulted. He returned from the gate of the Assembly Hall and dissappeared. The news reached the demons. The Vedic cult, as we know, was centred around the sacrificial fire. The Vedic yajña consisted of the offering of oblations of clarified butter, rice boiled in milk, etc. into the sacrificial fire along with the chanting of Vedic hymns. Every wish could be fulfilled with the performance of yajñas par excellence—to get a son or a beautiful wife, to defeat an enemy or to acquire prosperity or kingdom, or to get knowledge, wisdom and fame. The demons attackedthe gods, knowing well that the wise men had abandoned the gods. In the absence of the advice of the wise Guru Brihaspati the gods began to lose the war. Indra approached a rishi named Tvasta with a request to become his Guru in the absence of Brihaspati. Tvasta declined but he advised that his son Visvarupa could be approached for the same purpose. Visvarupa had three heads, symbolically representing three Vedic lores. Visvarupa accepted to be his Guru and organized a yajña in order to augment the spiritual force of gods so that the demons could be defeated in war. According to Vedic mythology Vishvarupa was related both to the Devas and the Daityas. As such, he was offering oblations into the sacrificial fire silently even for the spiritual strength of the Daityas. When this fact came to the notice of Indra he became furious, took out his thunderbolt and killed Vishvarupa. The news of the murder of Vishvarupa reached his father Tvasta who was terribly annoyed and then invited Vedic priests to organize a yajña in order to get a son who could kill Indra. On the last day of this yajña the priest asked Tvasta to offer half a coconut filled with clarified butter in the yajña kunda reciting the following mantra: "*Indrasha-tro pravardhasva.*" The accent in this mantra is on the last syllable of the word *Indrashatro.* But Tvasta in his anger and pride put the accent on the first syllable. According to Vedic grammar when we put the accent on the last syllable there is a tatpurusha compound, meaning the enemy or killer of Indra may appear. When we put the accent on the last syllable it becomes a bahuvrihi compound meaning "may a person appear whose enemy is Indra." So Vrtrasura appeared. There was a big fight between Indra and Vrtrasura and Indra killed him. Since then Indra had one more epithet that is Vrtraghna which corresponds to Varathragna of Avezta.

There are two approaches to decide the date of the Rig Veda. One is the Indian traditional approach and the other is the modern scientific approach along the principles of history and comparative philology. The orthodox Indian point of view is that the Vedas are apaurusheya, that is to say that the Vedas were never written by a man and were received by ancient rishis in the state of abstract meditation through transcendental perception. The Vedas represent universal cosmic laws. This aspect was highly elaborated in the Mimansa system of Indian philosophy, stating that sound was eternal and was a quality of space. As such sound is manifested by friction of two objects in space and to space it returns and assumes the unmanifest form. The modern scholars ascribed the date of the Rig Veda along historical principles. Bal Gangadhara Tilak in his *Orion* and Winternitz in his *History of Indian Literature* placed the Rig Veda in 6000 BC and 4500 BC respectively on the basis of astronomical calculations. We read in the Rig Veda of vernal equinox on Krttika nakshatra (Tauri alcyone constellation) and this according to B.G. Tilak occurred in 6000 BC. Winternitz calculated that the equinox on Mrgashira nakshatra (Orionis constellation) occurred in 4500 BC. However now the indologists hold that the Rig Veda cannot go before 2500 BC. This supposition is based on the theory of Aryan migration from Central Asia.

The Sanskrit language and the Upanishadic literature first became known to the Western scholars by the Latin translation of fifty Upanishads by a French scholar Anquetil Duperron. This Latin translation was based on the Persian translation ordered by the Mughal prince Dara Shikoh. This drew the attention of the German philosopher Schopenhauer. Thanks to the indefatigable efforts of Sir William Jones, Colebrooke and others that Sanskrit was made known to the western world. By and by the Sanskrit language was recognized, in its oldest and latest forms, as representing the Indo-Germanic Aryan stock.

Eugene Burnouf the great French guru of all Western gurus was the first scholar to point out the similarity of language and mythology between the Vedic Aryans and the people of Iran. In his monumental work *A Commentary on Yasna*, Burnouf pointed out that the yajña of the Rig Veda and yasna of Avezta were equivalent terms. Immediately after this Paris became a centre of Indo-Iranian studies. Scholars like Max Muller from Germany, Salisbury from the USA and Gorressio from Italy all flocked to Paris to study Sanskrit with Burnouf. It was the beginning of comparative philology when European scholars became accurately acquainted with the Sanskrit language. By and by developed the French, German, Dutch and American schools of Indo-Iranian studies and Sanskrit unanimously became recognized as the oldest language of the Aryan people. Let us recall that none of the other six principal members of the Aryan family has left any literary monument; and so is the case with Iranic, Hellenic, Itallic, Celtic and Letto-slavic languages.

As we know there is no image worship in the Rig Veda. The applications of Rigvedic mantras and rituals were later introduced in the Brahmana texts and image worship was brought in with the contact of Dravidians. Some of the Vedic Aryans soon became free from rituals and in the Aranyakas and Upanishads we come across seeds of the philosophical tree. The ideas of Brahman and Atm an (macrocosmos and microcosmos) that is the universal and the individual reality became rooted. In the Sutra literature, Sutras such as Grihya Sutras (domestic rituals), Srauta Sutras (Vedic rituals), Dharma Sutras (rules of society) and Sulva Sutras (rules of geometry) developed.

The word Sanskrit means "purified and well ordered." The sutrakara Panini, the great Sanskrit grammarian, in 500 BC, in his Astadhyayi, consisting of about 4000 sutras, remarkably gave a permanent form to Sanskrit language. The varttikakara Katyayana and the bhasyakara Patanjali by 150 BC gave to the Sanskrit langage a stereotyped but standard form which remained the same throughout the centuries even up to date. I may mention that Sanskrit is not an artificial version of grammarians, as often held, because the development from the Vedas through the Brahmanas and Upanishads can be clearly traced. Panini designates Sanskrit as Bhasa or language, which is akin to the language of the Brahmana and Upanisad.

It may be observed that Sanskrit was not only a language of religion, poetry, literature or philosophy, but of all Indian sciences such as Ayurveda, Jyotish, mathemathics, Shilpashastra, Mantrashastra and Tantric literature. Only the Hinayana Buddhists and the Jainas adopted the Pali and Prakrit languages in their early writings; otherwise the whole of India expressed her best thoughts for 7000 years in Sanskrit, which united Indian culture, giving it a synchronous form in spite of obvious differences of speech, racial, geographical, social and economic nature. However, it is noteworthy that even the Buddhists and Jainas switched over to writing in Sanskrit about the 1st century AD.

The twelve North Indian languages, namely Hindi, Marathi, Gujarati, Bengali, Oriya, Assamese, Rajasthani, Panjabi, Kashmiri, Nepali, Bihari and Haryanvi, are directly derived from Sanskrit. The grammatical structure and the basic vocabulary of all these languages is the same as that of Sanskrit. If these languages are made free from the barriers of script, it is very easy to understand all of them with the background of Sanskrit language. The impact of Sanskrit was so great that even the South Indian languages accepted a great amount of Sanskrit vocabulary. Tamil, Telugu, Malayalam and Kannada languages have 75% , 80%, 90%, and 70% of Sanskrit words. If Malayalam poetry is transcribed in Devanagari script, a good Sanskrit scholar can understand 90% of it.

Coming down to the epics, namely Ramayana and Mahabharata, we come across many variants from standard Sanskrit as laid down by Panini. The *Mahabharata*, a huge epic, is considered as an encyclopaedia of Indian culture. It is 30 times larger than *Paradise Lost* and seven times larger than *Iliad* and *Odyssey*. It is said that whatever is available in the *Mahabharata* can be found everywhere, and whatever is not found in it is not available anywhere else.

There were eight grammatical systems in ancient India: Aindra, Chandra,

Kashakrtsna, Hema, Kapala, Katantra and Paninian. Panini was the foremost. Even in the line of Panini there are several texts, commentaries and subcommentaries, expounding the philosophy and word formation. The two approaches to the study of Paninian grammar namely Astadhyayi and Siddhanta Kaumudi with numerous Sanskrit commentaries and expositions give ample proof to the continued interest in the structure of Sanskrit language.

The epic literature was followed by Puranic literature. The 18 Mahapuranas and 18 Upapuranas consist of hundreds of thousands of elegant Sanskrit verses. Only the *Bhagavata Purana* is composed of 18,000 verses. It is said that the test of a warrior's skill is made in the battlefield, the test of the purity of gold is made on the flame of fire, the test of a chaste wife is made during calamity and the test of scholarship is made in the *Bhagavata Purana.* The great French savant Eugene Burnouf, having heard this saying, put himself to the study of the *Bhagavatam* during a period of thirty years and published his French translation of the first nine books in eight huge folio volumes. The Puranic literature represents the development of the popular Hindu thought and religion.

We also come across in the epics variants from Paninian forms. Even the poets of Sanskrit inscriptions in India and in Southeast Asia often depart from them due to their inability to comply with the strict grammatical rules of Panini. But I may point out that apart from this, Sanskrit language has not suffered any change in the course of centuries. Likewise in the technical and non-Brahminical works we find laxity of grammatical forms. In early Buddhist writings there was an intentional disregard to the Paninian rules.

A striking example of the deviations from Paninian rules can be easily traced in the Gatha literature and Samadhiraja Sutra. Even in later Brahmanical works, there was a tendency to deviate from Paninian rules in order to impress upon people the archaic nature and the antiquity of their works, especially in the Tantric literature. There is ample evidence of Prakritism and careless Sanskrit in Bower manuscripts, and also frequently in the context of popular mantras.

As a vast vocabulary of Sanskrit entered into Dravidian languages, so a large number of Dravidian words also entered into Sanskrit through Sanskritization. The classical Sanskrit literature is enormous. It is kept in published and unpublished form. The published form can be divided into the following:

1. Poetry (Mahakavya, historical kavyas, shastra kavya, stotra kavya and giti kavya and khandakavya)
2. Prose
3. Campu (prose and poetry combined)
4. Tales and fables
5. Dramas

References are scattered to suggest that a large field of kavya literature existed during first century BC to fifth century AD. Even Panini in fifth century BC is supposed to have written a mahakavya called *Jambavati Vijayam* and Patañjali in second century BC refers to a kavya written by Vararuci. Patañjali also refers to three akhyayikas (historical tales) named *Vasavadatta*, *Sumanottaka* and *Bhaimarathi*, two Sanskrit dramas named *Kamsavadha* and *Balibandha* quoting a few verses from them.

There is continuity of kavya style in Sanskrit literature. Sanskrit is a living language. Unlike old Greek and Latin, Sanskrit has a remarkable continuity in all branches of literature, right from the dramas of Asvaghosa, Kalidasa and Sudraka, through Visakhadatta, Harsa and Bhavabhuti, to the modern Sanskrit dramas of Yatindra Vimala Choudhuri and Vanamala.

Poetry and versification dominate Sanskrit literature. The tradition of mahakavyas, kandhakavyas, erotic poetry, devotional poetry, didactic poetry and shastric poetry has continued up to modern Sanskrit literature—hundreds of Mahakavyas such as those of Jiva Nyaya Tirtha (*Kuru Pandaviyam*), Sridhara Sastri Varnekar (*Sivaji Vijayam*), Rasik Vihari Joshi (*Mohabhangam*) and Hri Narayana Diksit (*Bhisma Caritam*). The Sahitya Akademi Award was instituted about 30 years ago for creative Sanskrit writing or translation into Sanskrit of standard works from Indian or European languages. Equally the State Academies in India such as Delhi Sanskrit Academy, Uttar Pradesh Sanskrit Academy and the Academies of Rajasthan and Madhya Pradesh etc. give awards for creative Sanskrit writing every year. Hundreds and thousands of new Sanskrit plays and kavyas, short stories and prose kavyas are published in India every year. There are periodical research journals such as *Sagarika*, *Vimarsa* and *Sanskrit Susuma*, daily newspapers such as *Sanskritam* and weekly papers such as *Pañcajanyam* and *Gandhiva*. Also, there are Sanskrit films such as *Shankaracharya* and Sanskrit radio programs and staging of Sanskrit plays.

The principles of literary criticism have their own line of continuity. The Alamkara school, its origin and development into five schools, namely Alamkara, Riti, Vakrokti, Dhvani and Rasa, have played a very significant role in the development of Sanskrit poetry and poetical thought. One can easily find out the gradual and steady development of Sanskrit poetry upto date. Ananda Vardhana (8th century AD) the founder of Dhvani school, Abhinavagupta (11th century AD), Rajasekhara, Kuntaka, Ruyyaka, Dhanañjaya, Mahima Bhatta, Bhojadeva, Ksemendra, Mammata, Vishvanath, Appaya Diksita and Pandit Raj Jagannath, all were great Sanskritists and founders of new theories of literary criticism up to 17th century AD.

It will not be fair if I do not say a few words about the religio-philosophical Sanskrit literature. On the strength of Vedic religion there developed several religious schools in India. Primary mention may be made of Shaivism, Vaishnavism and Shaktism, and within these subreligious sects by and by several subsects flourished, such as the branches of Kashmir Shaivism, Pashupata, Mahesvara, and Virasaivism. Equally mention may be made in Vaisnava tradition to Nimbarka, Ramanuja, Vallabha, Madhva and Caitanya. Each of these sects has produced a large number of Sanskrit treatises. As we know, in ancient India it was a precondition for an acarya to write Sanskrit commentaries on the Upanishads, Brahma Sutra and Bhagavad Gita if he wanted to establish a school of thought. Later Bhagavata Purana acquired a similar importance. Besides, a number of original Sanskrit works and subcommentaries came forward from the following acaryas of the sects.

The six orthodox schools of Indian philosophy, namely Purvamimamsa, and Uttaramimansa, Sankhya and Yoga, Vaishesika and Nyaya, have an enormous body of Sanskrit literature. The Nyaya has two branches: (a) Pracinna Nyaya, and (2) Navya Nyaya. Navya Nyaya began from *Tattva Cintamani* of Gangesa Upadhyaya (11th century AD). When Sanskrit became known to Western scholars there grew a lot of curiosity and interest in the study of Navya Nyaya. But due to the terse style and technical terminology of Navya Nyaya they could not understand the texts, only smelt them and put them aside. By and by when Sanskrit manuscripts were taken abroad, there developed great centres for the study of Navya Nyaya such as Harvard and Vienna Universities.

I would like to conclude this paper by refering to some of the most important centres of Indology that keep collections of Sanskrit manuscripts, namely, Puna, Madras, Varanasi, Calcutta, Jodhpur, Kathmandu, Paris, New York, Harvard, Berlin, Heidelberg, Oxford, Cambridge and London. In all these centres more than a million Sanskrit manuscripts are kept, many of which have not been brought to light. Descriptive catalogues of Sanskrit manuscripts published from Puna, Madras, Calcutta and Paris, etc. are available and they are waiting for Sanskrit scholars to work in this direction. Today manuscriptology is well developed and there are ample opportunities for scholars to work in this field.

This brief note concludes that Sanskrit language and literature have been flourishing through the ages upto date with ever increasing force and vigour. In old Greek and Latin there is nobody today who writes poetry or philosophy, while in Sanskrit we have every year hundreds of new books. Thanks to our ancient Acaryas who maintained this life force of Sanskrit which is living even today.

Jñāna: Hindu India's Greatest Gift to the World

KLAUS K KLOSTERMAIER
Department of Religion
University of Manitoba

The widespread discontent of Western intellectuals both with the scientific and the religious establishments can be understood as dissatisfaction with the Western Rational Tradition that has shaped the modern world for the past three-hundred years. It is suggested here that *jñāna* as understood by the Hindu tradition would provide the basis for a more adequate rationality and a truer religiosity with major implications on all levels.

Erwin Schrödinger, winner of the Nobel prize for Physics in 1933, introduced a lecture on the "Spirit of Science" in 1946 with a quote from Śankara's *Brahmasūtrabhāṣya* (Schrödinger 1946: 491). Schrödinger stated that the search for the Self and its relationship to the Absolute had so much occupied the attention of Indian thinkers, "who were the equal of Plato, Spinoza and Kant as far as depth and grandeur of perception are concerned," that they neglected the investigation of objective nature "which surrounded them for centuries the same way as it surrounds us." Rather than criticizing the Indian sages for what they did, or had neglected to do, Schrödinger thought that they had an important contribution to make to our scientific world: "The subject of every science is always the spirit and there is only that much true science in every endeavour, as it contains spirit." He wished to see "some blood transfusion from the East to the West" so as to save Western science from spiritual anemia. In another lecture series he explicitly affirmed his conviction that Vedantic *jñāna* represented the (only) true view of reality—a view for which he was prepared to even offer empirical proof (Schrödinger 1964).

Aldous Huxley, a 20th century giant in the realm of Humanities, whose *Perennial Philosophy* is not only an unsurpassed anthology of world religions but also an outline for a universal religion, similarly suggests that Vedāntic *jñāna* is the key to unlock the gate to the meaning of human existence. In the first chapter Huxley parallels the famous dialogue between Śvetaketu and his father Uddālaka Aruṇi from the Chāndogya Upaniṣad with statements from a variety of mystics and philosophers. These he comments: "Based upon the direct experience of those who have fulfilled the necessary conditions of such knowledge this teaching is expressed most succinctly in the Sanskrit formula *tat tvam asi* . . . and the last end of every human being is to discover the fact for himself, to find out Who he really is" (Huxley 1973: 2).

Statements like these, which could be multiplied easily, suggest a fundamental dissatisfaction by prominent Western intellectuals with both Western science and religion and express the conviction that Vedantic *jñāna* could show the way out from the present dilemma.

I. Jñāna for a More Adequate Rationality and a Truer Religiosity

While in the popular mind science still proceeds triumphantly and the notion of "truth" is virtually synonymous with "scientific finding", uneasiness with present-day science is growing among the avant-garde of thoughtful scientists themselves. Not only have scientists signed petitions that would limit the application of some of their discoveries for ethical reasons, some also warn against replacing traditional pre-scientific and non-scientific insights by science as is often done today. Erwin Chargaff, one of the most prominent bio-chemists of our time, speaks of the "metaphysical nausea" that gripped him, the "existential terror" that struck him when hearing about the detonation of atom bombs over Hiroshima and Nagasaki. He castigates the mindlessness of a science that has degenerated into a sort of stock-market speculation and he warns of a scientific totalitarianism. "The great pendulum of birth and death, the darkness and mystery of human destinies; the great concepts that for many thousands of years spoke to the mind, and even more to the heart of humanity—reconciliation and charity, redemption and salvation—have they all been pushed aside and annihilated by science? I do not believe so. But if it really were the case, then science would carry a guilt even greater than its most embittered detractors have asserted" (Chargaff 1977: 53) Science, he had said somewhere else, is not a substitute for religion and philosophy. It has to understand its limits and not attempt to define reality, but be content with investigating it.

Physicist Roger Jones would go even further and contend that modern science failed to do even that. Instead of investigating reality, modern science has built up a system of mutually interlocking concepts, none of which really have any reality content, and none of which explain what science talks about. "Starting with Copernicus and Bacon, we began to take as synonymous with truth itself, any collection of hypotheses that explain all the appearances. We began modern idolatry . . . we have not only dehumanized science but also lost sight øf our integral connection with the continuing body of scientific and philosophical thought that goes back 2500 years . . . and beyond that to the mythic origins of religion and philosophy" (Jones 1982: X). The shortcoming of the rationality of modern science is not its lack of consistency, but its deficient connection with reality in more than a pragmatic and a commercial sense.

Many have pointed out that science, far from solving the questions it initially set out to answer, has moved away from these very questions. Physics, which emerged as science with the claim to rationally investigate the qualities of things perceived by the senses, eventually denied the existence of qualities altogether. Instead of explaining the nature of colour, it reduced colours to a set of differing wavelengths in the electro-magnetic spectrum. The very nature of the sensible world thus ceased to exist in a meaningful manner. Similarly biology, initially meant to explore the nature of life, turned into a science that eliminated the concept of life altogether, setting its goal to reducing every expression of life to the laws of physics and chemistry, looking at nature "with a dead man's eye" (Roszak 1973: 143). The same happened in psychology. Instead of illuminating the idea of soul, as the great classical philosophers had attempted to do, much of modern psychology denies its reality and restricts itself to quantifiable observations of physiological reactions, again largely in terms of physics and chemistry.

In spite of all the efforts of modern science, the real world of things is still around us. Colours and sounds are undeniable common experiences, giving rise to the arts without which life would be so much the poorer. Life is as surprising, exhilarating, tragic and mystifying as ever. The soul refuses to quit. A recent article in *The Scientific American* suggested that "the mathematical models now used in many scientific fields may be fundamentally unable to answer certain questions about the real world." (Casti 1996) What we need, obviously, is not a reality that conforms to modern scientific rationality, but a rationality that is more adequate to comprehend reality as it is.

Post-moderns have targeted the "logo-centrism" of (modern) Western thought as source of much that is wrong with it. It appears, however, that what post-modernists oppose is not so much the *lógos* as understood by the Platonic tradition, but the *logic* of Bacon and Descartes and their followers who initiated the "modern western rational tradition." The Platonic Socrates took his clues from the Delphic oracle's *gnôthi sautón*, and the *lógos* whom he followed faithfully unto his death was not a scientific theory but an all-embracing reality-principle. Finding the *lógos* of everything meant relating everything to the in-depth self-understanding which preceded it. The *lógos* was not sought in order to control natural processes but to find guidance in public and private life. The fact that questions of measurement, problems relating to quantitative aspects of external reality are easier to solve and can be answered with greater precision than questions of ethics and metaphysics does not permit the conclusion that these are the only meaningful questions to ask.

Our entire scientific enterprise—and with it a large part of our public educational effort—is largely dedicated to avoiding the great human questions rather than addressing them. The reduction of rationality to the mathematical manipulation of data, which finds its epitome in the computer, not only restricts the scope of science and makes it ignore questions of meaning, it also convinces the average scientist and the masses who believe in science that questions of meaning, questions relating to the Self, are "unscientific" and thus not worth pursuing. Research into such questions apparently "does not pay." Modern science leaves out, on principle, questions which include the entire range of ethics, of aesthetics, of spirituality. Nobody in one's right mind would contend that these are not vital areas for the well-being of individuals and societies.

The "Western Rational Tradition" which has guided modernity since the 16th century has come under attack. While it had helped the West to emancipate itself from an oppressive mediaeval religious, cultural, intellectual and political authoritarianism, it proved impotent in the face of 20th century cultural and political developments. The Western Rational Tradition was essentially individualistic, humanistic, bookish, academic. It did not comprehend what was happening when the Industrial Revolution changed the lives of many millions of ordinary people. It did not understand the implications of the colonial expansion that was associated with it. It was content with formalizing and universalizing education in the mode of the Western Rational Tradition and attempting to turn Asians into Europeans. The Western Rational Tradition was unable to prevent the World Wars, which effectively underminded its authority at home as well as in the colonies. It was unable to prevent the rise of dictatorships in the heartlands of Europe where it was supposed to have established itself most securely. Ironically, it was through the willing co-operation of representatives of that Western Rational Tradition that these dictatorships could not only succeed but even receive support from the institution most typically its creation, the modern universities. The list goes on. The disintegration of societies, the large-scale break-up of human relationships, the destruction of the natural environment—the Western Rational Tradition has not been able to prevent any of these, or to offer solutions to humankind how to overcome them.

Proponents of the Western Rational Tradition like to give it credit for the development of parliamentary democracy and "value-free" science. The only alternative to this tradition, which they seem to know of, are authoritarian government and theocratic "faith"; the condition from which the Western Rational Tradition liberated Western Europeans in early modern times. Asian alternatives are rarely considered, and more often than not rejected as unworkable in the West which is not willing to sacrifice its rational and liberal traditions. Simplistically the "other" is conceived as the total negation of one's own. The only "other" to the specific scientific Western notion of rationality is thought to be irrationality; the "other" to parliamentary, party-based democracy must be "autocracy." That type of thinking neither recognizes the limits of these specific historic forms of "rationality" and "freedom," nor the vast range of alternative "rationalities" and forms of good government found elsewhere and in other historic periods. While it is becoming increasingly clear that the Western Rational Tradition is no longer viable, and that liberal democracy based on the political party system has often become a travesty of itself, there is, of course, little willingness to return to the status quo ante. One does not have to.

Those of us Westerners, who decided to go into Asian Studies did so (in most cases) not because of some romantic attraction to ancient Asian poetry and art, but because of a felt need for a widening of the intellectual (and practical) horizon of Western culture. From information picked up before making Asian Studies our specialty we recognized that here was an intellectual tradition and a way of life that deserved respect and attention and that could possibly teach us something about our own institutions and about humankind in general. The proven long-term stability of many Eastern societies, the ideal of harmony of human relationships, the intuitive depths of understanding expressed in its literatures and its arts are not just "facts" to be registered, or "exotica" to be marvelled at, but human achievements that must be studied for the sake of the survival of humankind. While often enough failing to live up to these ideals, traditional Asian societies nevertheless possessed parameters for the "good life" that had validity, and a sure sense for enduring values.

To sharpen the focus for the purpose of this paper to the specific rationality that characterized the Western Rational Tradition and that clearly has proven inadequate, the Indian notion of *jñāna* provides an alternative that is neither "irrational," nor simply another variety of instrumental reason. It is a depth-dimension of "reason" in which the theoretical and the practical join, free from many of the shortcomings of Western Enlightenment rationality, such as its antireligious animus, which can be explained only by the singleminded Western identification of "religion" with an authoritarian and clericalized Christian Church.

Jñāna allows us to expand the range of rationality, which has been narrowed down time and again during the last few centuries, till it became completely identified with formalized logic and mathematics. To be sure, also in Indian traditions attempts were made to narrow down the meaning of *jñāna* to sect-specific understandings of it. However, Indian mainstream tradition was always able to keep *jñāna* open. *Jñāna* allows us to re-connect rationality with reality, overcoming the truncated rationality of the modern West, which bracketed out the source and end of all human thought. There is no need for the pathetic dichotomy between philosophy and theology, whose representatives are more concerned with building walls between each other than addressing real issues of substance. An appeal to *jñāna* is an appeal to the humane in thought and deed, to the integrity of thought and life, the continuity of consciousness and reality. While it contains elements of both "faith" and "science" as commonly understood in the Western tradition, it is different from both and overarches them.

For the average person *jñāna* will appear in the form of *jijñāsā*—a reaching out to understand rather than the possession of definite "wisdom." The existential nature of *jñāna* forbids it to have it expressed in dogmas and formulae. Although such formulae have been attempted—e.g. the Advaitic *brahma satyam jagat mithyā*—the Advaitic understanding of *jñāna* is not necessarily the only one and the formula can be interpreted in many different ways. *Jijñāsā* as constantly renewed attempt to reach *jñāna*—a search informed by some inkling, a spark of illumination, some kind of spiritual gravity—is the response to new challenges and questions from the level of *jñāna.* Whatever flaws his attempt may have had (and all *jijñāsā* is flawed) Sarvepalli Radhakrishnan may serve as an example of a *jijñāsi* of our time—someone who qualified as traditional Vedāntācārya by virtue of commenting upon the *Bhagavadgītā,* the *Upaniṣads* and the *Brahmasūtra* and who, in addition (and partly in his commentaries) engaged the important questions of his age and day and gave advice to high and low on how to deal with them. Less conspicuously many contemporary Vedāntins have done and are doing this as well. Vedāntic *jñāna* will remain alive only in the ongoing *jijñāsās* of those who look into themselves as well as into the world around them and try to match the two visions.

The exemplary character of *jnāna* consists in its synthesis of object and subject knowledge, its refusal to divide the world into fact and value, its insistence on rationality as reality, which does not exclude anything. It combines an insight into nature with reflection, objective knowledge with self-cognition. It implies and demands an ethic, a discipline as antecedent to its application. By seeing *ātma-jñāna* as irreducibly linked to *brahma-jñāna*, and both as the depth-level of any type of knowledge, it infuses into the human drive towards knowing the dimension of the *unum necessarium*, the one thing needed to save ourselves and the world in which we live.

II. Historicity and "Life-Historicity"

For every modern educated humanist "historicity" is central to any kind of hermeneutics (Campbell 1992). For those subscribing to it there are no "eternal truths" to be investigated, but only historical expressions, historical contexts and historical roots to everything, especially to the religious traditions. The very use of the word "traditions" instead of "religions" may be indicative of this historicity-consciousness. While agreeing with much of what historical consciousness has taught us, we may add the perspective of "life-historicity," especially when dealing with literary expressions of Indian religions. People are either baffled or otherwise react negatively against the otherwordliness found in many Vedāntic writings that seem to express disregard for nature, life, youth—all the things that are highest "values" for us (post-)moderns. Critics seem to forget that these texts were never meant to be read by the uninitiated and not intended for them. As part of the hermeneutical pre-suppositions of interpreting such texts, one will have to accept the *adhikāris* demanded by the writers. That may militate against the "modern" prejudice which assumes that everyone is/or ought to be in a position of reading/understanding any text whose grammar and vocabulary he or she knows. It also goes against the "post-modern" prejudice that disregards any and all intentionalities of authors as inhibiting the limitless freedom of the reader to read out of, or into, the text whatever one likes.

Underlying these assumptions is egalitarianism gone too far. While one requires training and a license to be permitted to clean rooms or to sell newspapers, when it is a matter of interpreting the most difficult matters concerning nature, humankind and God, every person is considered equally (un-) qualified. Again, it seems appropriate to expect a young person to do elementary and high school mathematics before enrolling in university courses. However, when it is a question of reading Vedāntic texts any or no qualification seems sufficient. Behind such attitudes lies, of course, profound disrespect for this kind of knowledge, disregard for the unknown, lack of appreciation for anything that does not translate into cents and dollars.

Jñāna, as understood by the Hindu tradition, is "life-historical," i.e. it does not reflect "everyman's idea of the world" and it is assumed to arise only at the end of a long process of mental and spiritual maturation. It is "privileged" knowledge, even "hierarchical" knowledge, but not in the sense of a "Herrschaftswissen," i.e. knowledge used to control and exploit for one's own purposes either humans or nature. Admission to this kind of training requires ethical as well as intellectual qualifications. The very interest in *jñāna* presupposes a certain nobility of mentality and it gives an upward direction to a person's intellectual search.

The *Aparokṣānubhūti,* a standard treatise on Advaita Vedānta, ascribed to Śankara, details the presuppositions for *jñāna*-seeking in the following manner:As pre-preparation it requires "worship of God" (*Hari toṣana*), austerities *(tapas)* and fulfilment of obligations appropriate to one's *varṇa* and one's stage in life (*āśrama*). Preparation properly speaking requires detachment (*vairāgya*), discrimination (*viveka*), ethical virtues (*samādiṣatsampatti)* and interest in emancipation (*mumukṣa*). Only then can one embark on the quest for *jñāna* in the hope of gaining insight into reality.

The way in which these pre-conditions are formulated require already life-historicity as "hermeneutics": Otherwise they sound offensive or "impossible." A Western author in a recent article dealing with Hindu attitudes to ward nature took offence at the way the *Aparokṣānubhūti* defined *vairāgya*: "It is not difficult to imagine what attitudes toward nature our taxi-driver might learn if he chanced to read, or hear a sermon based on verse four of this text: 'Pure non-attachment is disregard for all objects—from the god Brahmā down to plants and minerals—like the indifference one has towards the excrement of a crow.' Would this inspire him to revere nature as spiritual life, or would it rather teach him the irrelevance of nature to spiritual life?" (Nelson 1991: 300).

In the light of the foregoing it should be clear that a text like the *Aparokṣānubhūti* was not aimed at taxi-drivers, to begin with. It was meant for novices in an Ashram, people intent on making the search for ultimate truth their sole occupation. It was clearly not meant to teach environmentalism, however noble that may be. Surely some Śāṅkara texts could be found that would be more suitable for that purpose. If a present-day Śaṅkarācārya were asked to address a gathering of environmentalists, he probably would not quote *Aparokṣānubhūti* verse 4 but would say something along the lines of Śaṅkara's commentary to *Brahmasūtrabhāṣya* I,1,2. To get to the core of the matter: Our Western critic seems to have misunderstood the very intention of the text quoted. Far from denigrating nature and instilling indifference towards nature in the sense in which the Western outsider understands it, the text tries to promote *vairāgya* (as it explicitly says), i.e. an attitude that refrains from physical and emotional appropriation of nature for selfish purposes. It discourages all graspingness and does so by employing an effective metaphor. One is not likely to induce a spirit of renunciation in someone by describing that which one is told to renounce as the most valuable thing in the world. That would be perverse.

Someone whose major concern is still with the world—and this is not only a legitimate, but a necessary concern for the *gṛhastya*—will not be able to appreciate *vairāgya* and should not practice it. However, not only in Śāṅkara's but in every age many people become progressively disillusioned, disappointed, disaffected with "normal life" as they grow older and wiser. A person normally earns little gratitude for the good deeds done throughout a long life. The daily grind involved in making a living even in good times wears people thoroughly out. Most people have to fight even for minimal recognition of their worth. Wars, famines and bad times in general that so many have to live through in addition are not helping to create an impression that ordinary life is just one great feast. The kind of pseudo-heaven which Disney-worlds try to create has to be paid for with hard dollars and the sort of eat-your-cake-and-have-it religion of American televangelists will turn off each and every thinking person.

Śankarācārya was convinced that the liberation achieved through the cultivation of *jñāna* was a universal human goal and that sooner or later every living creature would attain it. Not satisfied with teaching disciples who had already renounced the world, he also composed stotras summarising *jñāna* for the general population. Some of these hymns, in which the insufficiency of wealth, power and sense gratification is contrasted with the peace, bliss and everlastingness of *ātman-brahman*, are extremely popular today among Hindus and recited at many religious gatherings by all those present. (Mahadevan, 1970) Vedānta is a thinking person's religion. *Vicāra*, reflection, thought, deliberation is the means to *jñāna*. The "interest" that informs this kind of search is circumscribed by the questions to which *jñāna* is helping to find answers: "Who am I? How did this world arise? And who is its creator? Of what is the world made?" These kinds of questions are neither answered by religions, as normally understood, nor by science. But they are crucial questions. They require a kind of rationality that is different from both "faith" and "instrumental reason."

Jñāna is "life-historical" also insofar as it considers the "ethic" of a person as indispensable condition for "knowledge." The claim to be on the way to truth—*brahmajijñāsā*—can only be made after certain qualities of character have been established—freedom from passion, from egotism, from ambition—otherwise it is sheer hypocrisy. *Jñāna* would also expose the fallacy of a "value-free" science: Knowledge is a value by and in itself and truth-search is a definite value-orientation. If it is not, it is a perversion. *Jñāna* could not be used to support the machinations of a criminal government, which science can and does very well, as we all know. Mahatma Gandhi could serve as a contemporary example for *jñāna*: His life, which he described as "Experiments with Truth" was a contemporary *brahma-jijñāsā*. Gandhi was dedicated to serving his people in a very concrete and practical way. But he also knew that this service was contingent on his ability to "live the truth," on his inner connection with the ultimate, on the purity of his motives, and on the ethical character of his actions. The proof for the truth of a thought of any depth is not its logical coherence, but the day-to-day life of the author who stands behind it. The "value-freedom" of science is the secular equivalent to the mediaeval Church's notion of the efficacy of sacraments *ex opere operato*. It absolves the authors from any ethical responsibility of their actions—and does not convince anybody. In matters of spirit the spirit matters!

The "triple knowledge of the Vedas," and the constant harmonisation of inner and outer reality, of sidereal and terrestrial truth, the effort to interiorize experience and to project it from within, gives a peculiar flavour to Indian *jñāna*. It can never be as dogmatic as Christian faith or as singleminded as Western science. It must leave much open—the balance is always precarious, the equilibrium dynamic. On principle *jñāna* is open to progress. Classical Indian writings are always warning not to take logical arguments too far—the underlying "revealed truth" is a greater truth than the small truths argued about with logic.

Conclusion

Brahmajijñāsā as an effort towards "meaningful knowledge," as reality-search and as ethical orientation can be real only in living persons, not in formulae or institutions. *Brahma-jijñāsā* is not an excuse to withdraw from the real life-concerns of one's time. Quite the contrary. It implies an engagement at a much deeper level and with a much greater stake in the outcome. There was practical wisdom in the traditional Hindu provision that only a person who had fulfilled all the usual obligations towards family and society was entitled to enter upon *brahmajijñāsā*. While the inner and outer independence of the *vānaprasthī* and the *saṁnyāsī* was essential, the search itself was seen as of utmost importance for family and society. Such mature seekers based their search on concrete knowledge and experience of "real life." They did not become "other-worldly" in the wrong sense, i.e. they did not imagine a parallel world without the problems of this world, but they plumbed the ultimate dimension of the world we all know or believe to know.

Brahmajijñāsā is not so much the preserve of professional philosophers as the intellectual, spiritual, moral quest of mature people with all kinds of backgrounds. In our age it would be especially the scientists who, in their search for truth about nature have reached limits of objective knoweldge and who have become aware of the ethical dimensions of their undertaking. They would be eminently qualified to embark on *Brahmajijñāsā* and to throw light from this search onto the ordinary world in which we live. Among the traditional reflections which were considered leading to *jñāna* were topics that have occupied all scientists for their life time. However, the crucial question, a question usually considered with the appropriate seriousness only at a somewhat advanced age, is "Who am I"? Indian tradition provides a variety of answers to this question, differentiated according to the level of consciousness a person has reached. However, at the ultimate level, the *turīya*, the answer to this question coincides with the question of what is reality. Not in a megalomaniac egotism but in a complete abandonment of the small 'I'-consciousness for the sake of the universal consciousness: the *tat* and the *tvam*, the *ātman* and the *brahman* become one and the same, because there *is* only one reality.

Jñāna is Hinduism's greatest gift to the world and Hindus will earn the respect and gratitude of the world for keeping *brahma-jijñāsā* alive. The world needs it and seeks it. In the context of the most recent ecological theory *atma-jñāna* (Self-Realization) is emerging as prime motive for ecologically responsible action (Zimmermann 1994). Hindu-India has given many gifts to the rest of the world in the areas of mathematics, linguistics, logic, religion, etc. Nobody today doubts that India has been one of the great original centres of civilisation which has had a global impact for thousands of years. In my presentation I restricted myself to just one such gift which India gave and continues to give to the world: *jñāna*. I restricted myself to *jñāna* not only because it belongs to my own area of work and competence, but because I believe it to be the root and crown of all the other gifts. It is an intangible, but it transforms all of reality by the ultimate perspective it generates. It is the humanly appropriate way of understanding not only the world around us but ourselves as well. It is, I venture to say, the thing we most need today everywhere.

REFERENCES

Richard Campbell, *Truth and Historicity,* Clarendon, Oxford, 1992.

John L.Casti, "Confronting Science's Logical Limits", *Scientific American*, October 1996, 102–105.

Erwin Chargaff, *Voices in the Labyrinth*, Seabury, New York, 1977.

Swami Gambhirananda (Trans.), *Brahmasūtrabhāṣya of Śrī Śaṅkarācārya,* Advaita Ashrama, Calcutta, 1965. .

Aldous Huxley, *The Perennial Philosophy*, Harper, New York, 1973.

Roger S. Jones, *Physics as Metaphor*, University of Minnesota, Minneapolis, 1982.

T.M.P. Mahadevan, *Hymns of Śaṅkara*, Madras, 1970.

Lance Nelson, "Reverence for Nature or the Irrelevance of Nature? Advaita Vedanta and Ecological Concern," *Journal of Dharma*, **16**(3), 1991, 282–301.

Sarvepalli Radhakrishnan (Ed. and Trans.), *The Principal Upaniṣads*, Allen & Unwin, London, 1953.

Theodore Roszak, *Where the Wasteland Ends*, Doubleday, Garden City, 1973.

Erwin Schrödinger, "Der Geist der Naturwissenschaften," *Eranos Jahrbuch*, 1946, 491–520.

______, *My View of the World*, Cambridge University Press, London, 1964.

Swami Vimuktananda (Trans.), *Aparokṣānubhūti or Self-Realization of Śrī Śaṅkarācārya*, Advaita Ashrama, Calcutta: 1955.

Michael E. Zimmermann, *Contesting Earth's Future: Radical Ecology and Postmodernity*, University of California, Berkeley, 1994.

The Scientific Aspects of Vedic Dharma

KAMLESH KAPUR
146-29, 33rd Ave., Flushing, NY-11354, USA

This paper overviews scientific aspects of Vedic Dharma and the vast literature related to it. As is well known, a distinctive feature of Vedic Dharma is that it gives a total view of the individual in this vast cosmic reality—its relation to the natural phenomena, root world, living organism, cosmic world and the intelligence/energy permeating through all these. It further analyzes the individual—his goals, his evolution through life and his self-fulfilment. Since his consciousness is superior to all else in the material world, his responsibility towards the continuation, preservation and progress is also greater. His actions assume a new significance. Vedic Dharma analyzes the fundamentals of actions—the modes of action, the motivators of actions which ultimately end up shaping and reshaping social dialectics.

In the various fields of western sciences—Physics, Chemistry, Biology, Psychology, Bio-chemistry and now Quantum Physics—some of these subjects are dealt with rather exhaustively. The most wonderful (awesome it might be added) part of the Vedic Dharma is that all of this is described exhaustively and in an integrated way. It was done by the sages and the thinkers millenniums ago when people of the colder climates were still dealing with problems of survival. Vedic Dharma has been and still is the citadel of vast knowledge guiding the confused bewildered humanity torn by their inner enemies (five doshas—lust, anger, greed, ego and attachment) and oppressed by hypocritical systems of violence and power struggles.

With the help of appropriate and direct references to the excerpts from Vedic literature, these scientific facts are analyzed, important beliefs are linked with modern thinking and the basics of Vedic Dharma are explained in the language, terminology and logic of modern sciences. The purpose of this unique approach is that people who are the products of Western educational system should acquire a proper understanding of Vedic Dharma, enabling them to continue it, preserve it, and hopefully improve their own life styles !!

Introduction

In the past four decades or so the world has been moving towards a closely knit entity—both in the economic sense and on the level of inter-communication and networking. It has become imperative that we broaden the knowledge of diverse cultures, create lasting bridges of cooperation and unbiased understanding so that we can foster a truly global partnership of purpose. To that end an attempt is being made to analyze the scientific and psychological aspects of Vedic Dharma—more commonly known as Hinduism. Vedic Dharma—the creator and moulder of complex Indian culture—is scantily described, a little understood and widely misunderstood. It is not surprising that our own second generation of Indians refer to themselves as A, B, C, D's[1]. Undoubtedly they are bereft of the knowledge of Vedic Dharma and its scientific aspects or its psychological underpinnings. To dispel this ignorance and to correct their distorted view, an attempt is being made to describe and analyze the scientific aspects of Vedic Dharma. Although many of the basic beliefs are discussed yet most could not be, because of the constraints on the length of the paper. For example, scientific explanation of important rituals is not discussed, nor is the theory discriminating perception, perceiver, and the perceived. Most of the points discussed in this paper are well established by modern science and are taught to young students. These may seem elementary to the reader. Many may even exclaim, "off course we know all this." But the point being made in this paper is that these were not only known to the sages in the Vedic age but are the very basis of Vedic Dharma. Why has this not been explained scientifically? In the past couple of centuries, history has been interpreted by people belonging to colder climates—many of them killing animals, eating animals, and living like animals. The nations, like individuals, create myths, illusions, and fallacies to perpetuate the established socio-economic structure.

Some basic premises of Hindu view

The basic premise of Hindu Dharma differs from those of other religions. According to Hindu view:

(a) Life is not random.

(b) Nothing in nature or in the universe is a coincidence. The universe is not a summation of random actions, events or a totality of coincidences.

(c) Hindus think of the well being of entire humanity and the universe as a part of their Dharma. Dharma, it may be pointed out, in Sanskrit, is defined as '*Dharayati iti dharma*' or that which sustains creation is Dharma.

Here creation includes all life—fauna and flora. Man is superior to all other life forms because he has intelligence and consciousness of his purpose in life. The day he loses sight of his responsibility of sustaining creation or the righteous actions, he loses Dharma. Dharma thus transcends any narrow organizational definition given by a religious group.

Dharma is the code of righteous conduct. The righteous conduct in line with

---

[1]A, B, C, D's mean American born confused desies. Desies are from their native country.

the preservation of all life and nature is eternal, hence, Vedic Dharma is called Sanatan Dharma. Applicable in all times and at all places, this code of conduct sustains and helps the progressive evolution of man—his mind, body, emotions and consciousness, family, society, and the environment. It recognizes unity in nature and promotes oneness between vegetation, living entities, the world, and the energy that reverberates through all this. This type of dharma creates a truly peaceful environment for universal family—the one that is described as *Vasudhaiva Kutumbakam.* Hinduism has been shaping the thought processes and the lifestyles of the countless people through the past millennia, not only because it is universal and objective but because it is the most scientific.

The Reality Of Nature

The nature and all living things are composed of five elements, *akasha* (space), *vayu* (air), *agni* (fire), *jala* (water) and *prithvi* (solid). The same ratio of the solid and water that composes the earth, composes the human body. Thus, one can conclude and extrapolate that the elements in living things on other planets would be probably in exactly the same composition as the material nature on that planet.

Tattva Bodha[1] describes the evolution of these elements thus: at first there was *akasha*, from that *vayu* is born, from air *agni* is born, from these *jala* comes, and then from liquid comes the *prithivi.* This is the principle of nature. It may be noted that the Vedic Dharma does not place a time frame on the creation. The creation is infinite, its evolution is on a continuum, hence, this too is in the infinity loop and timeless. The matter composed of these five elements is indestructible and the sum total is always the same. All it does is evolve, change and mutate. Is not this what modern science believes in and teaches us? The material nature and living entities in it are beginningless and endless; they only go through different changes because of their innate nature. In the *Bhagwad Gita,* Lord Krishna says "I, you and all those present today were born before, are here today, and will be there in the future."[2] The only thing is that the form changes and evolves higher or lower. The intelligence, energy and consciousness that permeates is indestructible, so is the matter. The only difference between the body and the consciousness is that the former is subject to change—it is small, it grows, it decays to be born again perhaps in different ways and in different forms. Lord Krishna makes the point more lucid thus, "What is born must die and what dies must be born since no one can stop this cycle of creation. Why brood over it?"[3] He further states, "This world is like a Banyan tree with its roots upward and

---

[1]*Tattva Bodhah—Akasadvayuh, vayostejah, tejasa apah, adbhyah prithivi.*

[1]*Srimad Bhagawad Gita,* Chapter 2, shloka 11, 12.

[2]*Srimad Bhagawad Gita,* Chapter 2, shloka 26..

branches downward. . . . Extending downwards and upwards, the branches of this tree are fed by the three modes of nature. The sense objects are its twigs, fruititive action—the upward and downward roots, which are omnipresent—bind us all to human society."[1] Later this matter was presented by Aristotle and his followers who laid down the basics of Formal Logic for the West. Aristotle maintains that whenever there is a change, the form changes but the essence of material nature and the aggregate of elements remain the same. He describes three types of change—locomotive (place), property (alteration), or quantitative (size). The change from one simple body to another is material change—the essence of natural phenomena. The questions of who created the universe and when or why are meaningless intellectual exercises in logic. These are also futile from the point of view of self-fulfillment, self-realization or setting up one's goals. Human body has the same composition. From *akasha,* the organ of hearing is evolved, from *vayu* the sense of touch, from fire or *agni* the sight, from liquid or *jala* the taste and from prithvi the smell. After describing this in detail, the Vedas conclude *Evam pindabrahmayor ekam sambhutam*—meaning, in this manner, the identity between the living being and the universe (microcosm and the macrocosm) is established.[2]

The next question is: how is this identity established and why do we all interact with other life forces and living organisms differently? The Vedic Dharma broadly describes three modes of interaction

(a) In the mode of goodness and awareness—which is called *sattva.*

(b) In the mode of passion—which is called *rajas.*

(c) In the mode of ignorance—which is called *tamas.*

His thinking either makes him identify with the nature, the natural phenomenon (which manifests threefold attributes too) and the energy/intelligence that pervades it. Alternately, it can alienate him from these forces. The *sattva* mode establishes complete identity, the *rajas* makes him enjoy it but not in the mode of total consciousness of consequences and in the *tamas* mode, man tends to master, pollute, deface and destroy nature. This brings us to the next point. What is the reality of mind? Why some people act in the *sattva* mode and some in the other two?

The Reality of Mind

Each person is born with his own innate *samskaras* (imprints of *a priori* experiences and their consequences) and genetic make up. These are further influenced by the station of his parents, his education, other socio-economic and

---

[3]Ibid., Chapter 15, shloka 2.

[4]*Tattva Bodha.*

political forces. Those with noble *samskaras* would tend to act in the mode of *sattva*, while others with less noble *samskaras* may act in the other two modes. The three genetic formats, broadly speaking, are heat (*pitta*), air (*vata*) and lymph (*kapha*). Each type tends to have a different temperament, which then determines his or her interaction with the material nature and its complex organizations. It is significant that we understand the psychological aspects of Vedic Dharma, because on the proper understanding of this depends the social dialectics and man's own evolution. What, then, is the mind?

(a) Is it intelligence?
(b) Is it judgment?
(c) Is it discernment?
(d) Is it consciousness?

The mind is recipient of sensory perceptions. Hence, Lord Krishna considered it as a sense, *indriya*. He tells Arjuna, "Among the senses, I am *Manah*."[1] It may be noted that Vedic Dharma differentiates between different folds of consciousness—intellect, discernment, judgment, ego, etc. The mind acts through impulses and reflexes with the five organs of perception. The master of mind is the Manah.[2] Decision and doubt are the nature of the mind. Therefore, it is constantly in agitation. Lord Krishna says, "*Mano durnigraham chalam.*"[3] No doubt it is out of control but through austere discipline (*Vairagya*) and constant practice (*Abhyasya*), it can be controlled. The nature of intellect is to decide the course of action. Education, experiential knowledge, discernment and sensory perceptions help. Ego and sense of achievement interfere and provide the necessary motivating force and impetus. The ruling force of '*chetana*' is the divine intelligence. It is summed up thus: "*Etesam panchatattvan samashti satvikamshad manas, buddhi ahankaar chitta antahkarnaani sambhutani.*"[4] Meaning, from the *sattva* aspects of these five elements are born—the mind, the intellect, ego, memory and consciousness. These are the inner instruments as differentiated from the outer instruments—eyes, ears, nose, tongue and skin. *Chetana*, the watchdog, is referred to as *Atma*. In the *Bhagwad Gita*, it is described thus: "It is an element, a very dense element. It is seen as amazing, described as amazing and heard as amazing. Many are absolutely unable to understand its real form."[5]

The mind has five main traits called *doshas*—lust, anger, ego, greed and attachment. These are the motivators to reach goals. Again, these goals may be *sattva*, *rajas* or *tamas*. These motivators generate ambitions and desires. Out of

---

[1] *Srimad Bhagawad Gita*, Chapter 10, shloka 22
[2] *Tattva Bodha.*
[3] *Srimad Bhagawad Gita*, Chapter 6, shaloka 35
[4] *Tattva Bodha*
[1] *Srimad Bhagawad Gita*, Chapter 2, shloka 29.

control, these can cause imbalance in nature and the society. The Vedic Dharma emphasizes total control of the senses. This is conquest of the self. The difficult journey to this end is through self-awareness and self-control. The two terms used in this context are *maryada* (rectitude) and *samyam* (self-control). These are perimeters of action and behavior. Acts done outside their bounds and motivated by the five *doshas* generate desire for certain outcomes. Hence, these are fruitful actions, followed by an unending trail of hopes, fears and misery. This, in turn, destroys one's perspective and one's psyche. In the *Bhagwad Gita*, it is lucidly discussed thus: "One may contemplate on sense objects, such a person develops attachment for them, such attachment leads to lust and from unconsummated lust anger arises. Anger clouds judgment and bewilders memory. When memory is bewildered, intelligence is lost which causes total moral collapse."[1]

Escapism /Yielding to desires vs. equanimity

The modern psychology developed by Western thinkers questions self-control. They consider it as suppression. Their therapy includes letting the patient give vent to anger and yield to desires. Even by Western logic, this can present a contradiction. Since the wants and desires are unlimited, how can the trail of misery end? Chasing transient desires, instead of leading to bliss, can put a person in a bewildering loop of a cat chasing its tail. At its best, it can cause anguish. At its worst, it can lead to personality disorders by putting individual identity at cross social purposes. Some of the recent thinkers are now moving towards acceptance and equanimity as a part of the therapy. Candid recognition of desires and one's limits is a prelude to awareness and acceptance. This is a step towards the conquest of the Self. Lord Krishna says, "The wise neither mourn for the dead nor for the living."[2] Equanimity not only creates bliss and detachment from outcomes but it also helps us to deal with grief and loss. It can, verily, lead to liberation of the mind from the shackles of illusion, duality of purpose, confusion and conflict states which mutate one's mind and distort one's perspective. The Vedic Dharma emphasizes that the natural state of mind is bliss and not anguish. The yogis strive to attain the state of '*sat-chit-anand*'. It may be noted that control of the senses is not tantamount to renunciation or inaction. It is action performed through self-realization. The next logical question is: What is the Self? Who am I?

Who Am I?

In the *Tattva Bodha*, *Atma* is defined thus, "Distinct from the material, subtle, and causal bodies, being beyond the five sheaths, as a witness to threefold

---

[2]Ibid., Chapter 2, shloka 63.

[3]Ibid., Chapter 2, shloka 11.

experience, of the form of existence, awareness and bliss, is 'I'—the *Atma*, the Self."[1] The five elements, five *jñanendriyas* (senses of perception), and eight senses (*indriyas*) are very much parts of the Self. They establish links with the outer reality—with or without the guidance of the consciousness and influenced or uninfluenced by the five traits of character.

Evolution of the Self

According to one's *Samskaras* and the genetic format, an individual starts his evolution, laying down the bounds of his actions—his *karmakshetra*. Through an integrated educational process, he becomes the knower. He acquires self-control and learns the basic tenets of Vedic Dharma. During the same process, he sets his goals and finds his role in society. Through his *Karmas* and self-realization, he has the opportunity to lay down the foundations of a blissful life of success and self-fulfillment. Lord Krishna says, "In my opinion, until the mind is controlled, self-realization is difficult, but when a person is able to steady his mind through right means, he is sure of success."[2] The right means are meditation, *yoga,* practicing self-discipline and determination. A person is, then, free from false ego, false pride of strength, lust, anger, desire for accumulating material possessions; thus reaching the stage of self-realization.

One of the most scientific parts of the Vedic Dharma is the division of life in four phases, called *Ashramas*. Why is it considered scientific? It is considered so, because it is in accordance with the biological clock of the individual, especially the women. The first *Ashrama* is *Brahmacharya*, when one acquires knowledge, skills and self-control to define and fulfill his quest, his duties and his responsibilities. He builds his character and morals. He learns about his Dharma. The second phase is *Grihastha Ashrama*—the onset of married life. He creates and raises a family. Once the process of procreation ceases, the next phase begins—the *Vanaprastha Ashrama*. A person gradually detaches himself from the material world and its *Maya* (illusion). At this juncture, it is the correct sociological attitude. Attachment causes unnecessary interference in the life of the children, leading to avoidable anguish. This is also the onset of spiritual evolution and the time to get involved in the larger social purpose. A few then reach the ripe old age to be in the *Samnyasa Ashrama* which is the next phase. His personal evolution is thus described in the *Bhagwad Gita*:

> "All living beings are constantly struggling with the material modes of nature,thus sustaining and continuing the universe."[3]

---

[1] *Tattva Bodha.*

[2] *Srimad Bhagawad Gita,* Chapter 6, shlokas 35, 36.

[1] Ibid., Chapter 7, shloka 5.

Man evolves, struggles, and achieves his goals, going through these four phases of life. This brings us to the next part of the Vedic Dharma.

The Fundamentals of Action (Karma) and Reincarnation

The theory of action and reaction is the basis of social and individual dialectics. Vedic Dharma views these actions and reactions on a continuum, transcending several life spans and encountering numerous hurdles in the path of evolution of consciousness. Briefly explained again, there are three types of *Karma.* Those performed in the mode of goodness and truth are *Sattva.* Those in the mode of passion and enjoyment are *Rajas* and those which are performed out of ignorance, the five *vikaras* or the impulses are *Tamas.* Individual *karmas* performed freely affect the social dialectics. A clear understanding of this point is crucial in these times. Many believe that the society has nothing to do with the individual *karmas* because it is not affected by these wrongs. Half of the miseries of the world are because of this myth. Let us take an example. A child is accidentally conceived by an unwed mother. The simple free act of perhaps one time of sense gratification has a triple social effect: (a) the child is raised without a natural father; (b) he has an impaired identity without a father, affecting his relations with other children, because he has a strong tendency to over-assert his masculinity; (c) once the act is performed, it places an avoidable economic burden on other members of the society. The laws of *Karma*, like the Hegelian social forces, are inexorable and unmitigating. Such accidents and contigencies may follow wars and other disasters when the male population dwindles down, but such broken families should not be the norm. When women lose morality and chastity, children thus born do not follow the tenets of religion. In the *Bhagwad Gita*, Arjuna points out the dire consequences in these words, "O Lord! annihilation of families causes the women to lose their morality and chastity and give birth to mixed children who lead both the enemies and the remainder of their families towards evil and destruction."[1]

The Theory of Action

The theory of action entailed in *Karma* is that the reactions do not leave one at the end of one's life. They follow one in several life spans, as we are trapped in the continuity loop of life and death. It may be emphasized again that death is the juncture when immortal consciousness leaves the body to find another abode and the five elements composing the body change and merge into the same five elements composing the entire nature. Being trapped in the cycle of death and birth is reincarnation. Self-interested *Karma* creates bondage in the form of reaction. Aristotle admits, " . . . action for an end is present in things which come to be and are by nature."[2] A reaction can be compensatory or punitive. To expect no individual

---

[2]*Srimad Bhagawad Gita,* Chapter 2, shloka 20.

consequence or social effect is pure delusion in the mode of darkness. Once initiated, whether spontaneously, impulsively or consciously, an action has to run its natural course to its ultimate conclusion. It has to generate reactions—immediate or long run, individual or social, desired or undesired. Causation is innate in the laws of material nature. *Karma* is at once the cause and its own effect. It is the cause of a new chain reaction; it, most certainly, is the outcome of previous *karmas.*

The Motivators of Action

The five motivators are lust, anger, greed, ego and attachment. They give rise to the desires and impulses . Many times, one is dragged in the reaction of *karmas* of one's near and dear ones.

What, then, is the Sattva Karma?

(a) Letting consciousness be the controller of sensory perceptions is *karma.*
(b) Letting determination guide the five sensory perceptions is also *karma.*
(c) Waiting for right opportunity for action is also *Karma.*

What then is the purpose of Sattva Karma?

(a) *Karma* performed out of duty.
(b) *Karma* performed for the general public welfare.
(c) *Karma* in accordance with the general laws of nature.

Such a *karma* is *yajña*[1] and such a detached *karma* is worship, and it is free of bondage. Lord Krishna says to Arjuna, "A worker free from material attachments and arrogance, who is determined but remains indifferent to success or failure is a worker in the mode of goodness." [2] The body acting on the material nature through voluntary and involuntary Karmas creates reactions and these reactions create ripple effects on the society (the family, the neighbours and the nations) and generate the fundamental forces of social dialectics. The reactions are of three types, depending on the initial *karma.* "Acts performed in goodness result in purification of mind, those done in passion result in agony and distress and those in ignorance result in foolishness. . . . From the mode of goodness arises knowledge, from that of passion greed, and from the mode of ignorance only madness and illusion are born."[3] These outcomes lead to social growth, decadence or annihilation. Natural history of mankind suggests that nothing ever stays the same. The rise and decline of civilizations prove this, that which reaches the peak comes down to reach another peak later. However, unlike the Hegelian social

[1]Aristotle, *On Generation and Corruption..*
[2]*Yajña*—it means sacrificial ceremony..
[3]*Srimad Bhagawad Gita,* Chapter 18, shloka 26.
[1]*Bhagawad Gita,* Chapter 14, shlokas 16, 17.

dialectics, where man is the victim of the collective forces and social currents, or is swayed and led by these, the Vedic Dharma says that the individual has immense power. It is his *karmas* which create those social currents and that collective force, the same way that his mind creates his own hell and heaven. Through his *karmas*, he makes his destiny and largely affects those of others.

Ralph W. Emerson, who was an erudite scholar of the Vedas and books on the Vedic tradition wrote about the role of *karma*, "Fate is nothing but deeds committed in a prior state of existence." He was referring to outcomes and reactions as fate. If *karma* is in the hands of the individual, then the outcome also is in his power. So, what are the fundemental governing forces of action? Ideally, it is the awareness of his duty to fulfill the social purpose. Most of the time, however, they are ignorance, illusion, sense gratification, and transient desires. The selfless detached action brings positiveness in human evolution and promotes peace and harmony and the Yogis dwell on that. Henry D. Thoreau describes it in these words, "One may discover the root of a Hindu religion in his own private history, when, in the silent intervals of the day and night, he does, sometimes, inflict on himself like austerities with stern satisfaction." Such Yogis attain serenity and they work for peace. Inner strength and inner peace according to Vedic Dharma are not contradictory to each other; they go together hand in hand. One who attains equanimity, whose mind is without duality, confusion and conflict, is the one who is in true bliss. No wonder, millions of people all over the world chant the *Shanti Mantra* every day and several times in a day.[1] Steadfast in all circumstances, viewing the world as his family, the self-realized person reaches the pinnacle of *Shanti*. Such a one is a *Yogi*. In the *Mahabharata*, Lord Krishna says that such a person is like a galaxy; even if he wants to change his destined course, he cannot!

An enduring culture has a hold on its people which does not end with the passage of miliennia in spite of catastrophic changes in all else around them. Why doesn't it? And how is it still the guiding light for millions of people? Vedic Dharma gives inner strength. It is equally applicable to current realities as to the life styles of ancient times. It corresponds to intellect, logic and the current set of experiential knowledge of physical sciences. It helps us:

(a) cope with change,

(b) find ways to forge fresh paths to truth,

(c) readjust approach to newly defined quests.

Rarely does Dharma have greatness, durability and a strong scientific base. Through this reading, it is hoped that the younger generation, especially of

---

[2]*Shanti Mantra:* "Let there be peace in the space, peace on the earth, peace in water, peace in the world of medicines, peace in vegetation, peace in the world, peace in the universes, peace everywhere, peace in my senses, and peace in my intellect.

Indians, would feel that Vedic Dharma is not just to be preserved as sets of scriptures amidst the annals of history of religions, but it is to be continued as a vibrant force, inspiring rethinking, rekindling intellectual strength and strengthening intellectual roots. Its proper understanding can force a reappraisal of values and provide stronger perimeters of behavior and righteous conduct, especially today, when most people find themselves at intellectual dead ends !! To the extent the individual is in conflict, the society is in conflict, the nation is in conflict, and the whole world is in conflict—United Nations or no United Nations—for the seeds of conflict, confusion, delusion, uprootedness from one's environment, and alienation from one's Dharma are in the mind of the individual. Therefore, only the individual has to make up his mind to strive for the state of serenity (*Shanti*) and bliss (*Ananda*). Only then can the ideal of world peace be conceivable as well as achievable.

Ancient Indian Culture and the Concept of Ashram

GOBARDHAN BAHADUR KARKI,
Brahmcharya Ashram, Dang, Nepal

The paper presents two ancient Vedic systems. First, the scientific system for the universe and the division of time on earth in terms of kalpas, manus, yugas etc. and, second, the ashram system for guidance of people for living a fruitful life as human beings on the earth. Also examined are roots of certain words, names, customs and findings around the world that show that at one time in history the Vedic discipline and science prevailed widely.

Introduction

Vedic literature talks of a universe composed of innumerable heavenly bodies, and the events in the universe on the scale of space and time. Talking of space, according to the Vedic scriptures, this planet which is known in Sanskrit as *Prithvi,* was divided in seven regions, called *dwips.* One of them was known as *Jambudwip.* This *Jambudwip* comprised the whole of modern Asia. Jambudwip was divided in nine *versas*, one of them was *Ila-versa*. The *Ila-versa* was later named as *Bharatversa* after a great King Bharat of the land.

Vedic seers, who were scientists, studied the structure of the universe comprising of many heavenly bodies. They formulated that every heavenly body undergoes cycles of formation and dissolution. They called the time span from formation to dissolution of *Prithvi* a *'kalpa'*, and gave them names. The present kalpa is known as Sweta-baraha-kalpa. Kalpas are divided in periods of 14 *Manus*. Presently it is period of 7th *Manu*. A *Manu* lasts for approximately for seventy-four *chaukadi*. Each *chaukadi* is formed of four *yugas*—known as *Satya-yuga, Treta-yuga, Dwaper-yuga, and Kali-yuga*. The present *Manu* is called *Vaibatswat Manu*, in which 27 *Chaukadis* have expired. The *Kali-yuga* is the shortest with a span of 4,32,000 years. *Dwaper*'s period is understood to be 8,64,000 years, of *Treta* 12,96,000, and of *Satya* 17,28,000 years. Thus the total time of a *chaturkadi* is 43,20,000 years. The last *Dwaper-yuga* concluded when Lord Krishna cast his temporal body. It was after the great Mahabharat war ended. It is the 5,097 (in 1996) year of present *Kali-yuga*. The present *kalpa* that has completed 1,95,58,85,097 years is calculated to last a total of 4 billion years.

There are several proofs given in support of this calendar. At one time this whole planet was populated by what may be called Vedic people, who practiced Vedic disciplines and science. The evidence is found in many names and customs found in different parts of the world that have Vedic roots.

Interpretations of Several Terms used in the World

Let us examine the roots of word 'Atlantic'. As is well known, the English letter 'T' replaces two sounds त (dental) and ट (palatal) of Sanskrit. A Sanskrit equivalent of 'Atlantic' therefore with dental sound is अतलान्तिक - अतल + अन्तिक, which means 'the lowest or end of the floor level'. This obviously makes sense for use of the word 'Atlantic' for a great ocean. Then there are words like 'Sumali', 'Mali', 'Maya' currently used for places and people of different parts of the world. These are Vedic words, proving their Vedic connection. Similarly, the word Aztecs is a corruption of Sanskrit आस्तिक- (*astika*) (believers in God). Also 'Incas' used for ancient residents of Peru and other parts of South America is made from 'Ina' which in Sanskrit means 'Sunworshipers'. In Madagaskar Island on the eastern coast of East Africa, several names are linked to Rama.

In terms of remnants of Vedic customs, these are also seen quite widely. A native tribe in north Australia performs a kind of dance after painting a third eye on their forehead, this is obviously Shiva-dance. In Mexico, a festival falls during Dasshara / Navratri time and is called 'Ram-Sita'.

There are some strange connections of Vedic episodes to North America. The word California is the corruption of Sanskrit 'Kapil-Aranya', place of the famous story of Kapil Muni who turned to ashes sixty thousand sons of King Sagara, who had found the sacrificial horse in his *ashrama*. The Ash Mountain Park of California and the Horse-Island of Alaska corroborate the facts of this story. Also, Mula Burma of Koeti and Bornio present the evidence of Yagas and Yagyans.

The evidence is not limited to names and customs alone. In North and British Honduras several idols of Ganesha were found by excavations. In Egypt, during excavations, an inscription was found which describes a treaty between Rameses and Hittites where Mitra and Varuna, the Vedic deities, are mentioned as witnesses.

It may be mentioned that ancient Vedic science has other dimensions of spiritualism and mysticism. Their search was not limited to the outside universe, but also studied and organized psychological aspects. They found practices that can enhance a person's abilities and capabilities. They talked of various siddhis, powers of accomplishing various feats. Sankhya and Yoga are accounts of in-depth psychic discoveries of ancient Indians. These theories and practices are aspects of what is called Nigama, but there were other seekers whose search, called Agamas, unfolded the mysterious side of mantras. They mastered the sound waves mechanism through composition and the chanting of mantras. The action was much more effective than the electric or magnetic waves which they understood well.

Division of Ashram

Vedic seers realized that man is a social being and has great potential for a useful and fruitful living. This is accepted in every society. However, there is perhaps no society where, on a large scale and in very extensive scale, guidance is made available for leading a life of fulfillment and where peace is formulated in the concept of 'Ashram system'.

Normally, the life span of a human being is taken to be of hundred years—this is reflected in the oft-repeated Vedic chant '*jibem sarada satam*'. The preceptors prescribed four ashrams each of 25 years in the life of a human being.

In the first ashram of 25 years, called brahmacharya-ashram, an individual is to be carefully raised, educated and trained so that in the remaining three periods he could be productive and could lead an enjoyable life. This is the period of instilling good behavior and habits in an individual. This norm is reflected in the Sanskrit shloka '*Janmad jayate sudra sanskarad dwija uchchate, Veda-abhyasi bhavet vipra brahma janati brahmana*'—'at birth one is *sudra*, by *sanskars* one becomes *dwij* (cultured, twice-born), then by practicing the Vedas become *vipra* (wise or knowledgeable), and by acquiring knowledge of absolute God (Brahma) one gains brahmanhood (enlightenment)'. Here it is necessary to understand the meaning of the word '*sudra*'. It means a person living at the sense level, very close to what can be called animal behavior. From early childhood, parents and society, by constant efforts, take care of the physical and mental growth of the individual, guiding him in all matters and giving him the discipline of not lying and also of not harming others, etc., even such small matters as what to eat and what not to eat. The practice of Yama and Niyama makes a child develop control and adopt good principles in life. The individual grows as a disciplined and enlightened person equipped with essential norms, ethics, effective skills to earn livelihood.

Having completed twenty-five years, a person enters the second stage called *grihasta* or the stage of domestic responsibilities. In this stage, an individual gets married and leads a conjugal life, rears children and serves the society in all different ways.

By reaching 50 years, in the next stage of 25 years called *vanprasth*, an individual should develop a change in outlook and inculcate an attitude of detachment. The person should relish solitude in life and should mostly concentrate on spiritual growth. He, helping others, pursuing spiritual advancement, gradually reaches the age of seventy five.

Beyond 75 years of age is the time of complete renunciation called sanyas. An individual should now withdraw completely from the worldly affairs and should dedicate fully to spiritual advancement. The individual now contributes to the society by presenting the example of a living embodiment of peace and serenity to those who come in touch with him or her. Thus is lived a human life of full accomplishments and fulfillment.

Impact of Ashram System

The Ashram system organized the individual and the society. It paved the way to develop clear codes of conduct for individuals in the society. It was linked to another important social division called *varna* system, wherein at any given stage, different tendencies determined his or her vocation in life in a coordinated fashion. It developed on a scale of human aspiration a sense of becoming an integrated personality and the values of responsibility, service and detachment. Finally it makes an individual realize the highest philosophical truth of '*Atma mokshaya, jagad hitaya cha*', i.e., 'the world's greatest service by an individual is to live a life that leads to liberation of the self.'

REFERENCES

1. Shrimad Bhagwat Gita, *Gita Press, Gorakhpur, India.*
2. *Goswami Tulsidas:* Ramcharit Manas, *Gita Press, Gorakhpur, India.*
3. Durga Saptasati, *Gita Press, Gorakhpur, India.*
4. Devi Bhagwat, *Gita Press, Gorakhpur, India.*
5. *H.H. Sri Chandra Shekharendra Saraswati:* Aspects of our Religion, *Bhawan's Book University, Kulpati Munshi Centenary Edition.*

At the Source of Indo-Georgian Historical Ties
(A Short Review)

NIKOLOZ KENCHOSHVILI
Tibilisi, Georgia, (Europe)

In accordance with traditional historiography the first historical ties (mostly economical) between ancient Georgia (Kolha-Kolheti) and India are fixed in antique period: for example Plavius Ariene notes that on the left bank of the river Phazisi (the present river Rioni in the west of Georgia) is located the town of Phazisi (the name of the present seaport Poti, at the West Georgian Black Sea shore) where could be heard the speeches in sixty different languages, among them Indian languages too.

The French Georgianologist Mari Brosse in his work "The Life of Kartli (Georgia)" (Tbilisi, 1849, p. 129) outlines that the direct or indirect commercial, political and cultural type ties between Georgia and India might have been taking place from times immemorial. Later this idea was accepted and developed in different ways by many other Georgian scholars dedicating several significant works, but the problem fundamentally never had been explored. So in this direction the present article (published in Georgian language, in the journal *Tsiskari*, in December 1993) may be considered as the first attempt of fundamental research of the Indian phenomenon's reflection in different Georgian sources, describing the historical and cultural intercommunications between ancient Georgia and the Indian subcontinent.

Taking into consideration and comparing the publications of the last decades in linguistics, archaeology, ethnography, anthropology etc. we can logically conclude that hypothetically the historical and cultural elements of communication between ancient Georgia (Caucasus) and Sindhu Valley civilization are observed even from 4–1 millenium B.C., that is while intensive migration periods in the Near East (including Caucasus), towards Iran and the Indian sub-continent until the invasion of Greeks (Alexander the Great) on India.

Naturally, the statement of the question in this way again is reminding that none of the civilizations of the world was formed in complete isolation without intercommunication with other civilizations of nearer or remote regions. In this respect neither Georgia nor India are exceptions, namely, the Near East should be considered as a "connecting bridge" between the Caucasian (including ancient Georgian) and the Indian sub-continent settlements in the period of formation of the cultures of the Proto-Georgian and Mesopotamian Sindhu-Valley civilizations (Dravidian), Sumers, Akhadians, which in historiography commonly is considered as an integral part of the history of the spiritual and cultural life of ancient Georgia. (See works of Kipert, Homel, S. Kramer, F. Bop, Fogt, M. Brosse, A. Snanidze, M. Tsereteli, N. Berdzenishvili, I. Javakhishvili, J. Sharashenidze, Z. Kiknadze, Z. Gamsakhurdia, etc.)

T. Gamkrelidze and Ivanov (see *Indo-European Languages and Indo-Europeans*, Tbilisi, 1984, p. 890) suppose that namely South of Georgia up to Mesopotamia are those regions (territories) where the linguistic and cultural intercommunications were accomplished in the 4th millenium B.C. (that is the most intensive tribe migration period towards India).

So Proto-Dravidians, those of Mediterranean origin, moving towards North-East on the way to neighbouring India, could not avoid communications with the relative civilization of ancient Georgia (Caucasus) resulting in mutual linguistic, cultural or any other type of ties, borrowing and dispersing of common words, mythology, symbols, etc. Namely this was the reason that made T. Emanow and Burrow make an attempt to compare Georgian and Sanskrit languages, or some other scholars to compare the ancient Persian alphabet (Zaden) with the Georgian. However, there are certain linguistic resemblances between Indo-Iranian and Georgian. For example, the Sanskrit *wist* (= mosti) in Georgian is *mustu*; the Sanskrit *kudi* (= brush) in Georgian is *kudi* (= tale); the Sanskrit *mala* (= garland) in Georgian is *mala* (= spinal, like garland); the Sanskrit noun *bandha* (= tie) in Georgian is used as a verb *bandva* (=to tie); but the Sanskrit verb *mil*(*na*) (= to meet, to connect) in Georgian is used as a noun *mili* (= connecting pipe). The Sanskrit root *mar* (= to kill, to hit) in Georgian is carrying the same sense, to kill, grave or the sense of eternity in the words sa-*mar*-e (= grave), dasa-*mar*-eba (= to kill), *mar*-adi (= eternal).

The Indo-Aryan words *tanu* (=body), *ena* (=tongue), *nav* (=boat) in Georgian are the same: *navi* (=boat), *tani* (=body), *ena* (=tongue, language). According to R. Mukherji *Tantra* (in Tantrism) means the extension (like growing body) of process of inner consciouness of self. These three words *tan*, *en*, *nav* are met in Dravidian and Sumerian languages too (I. Javakhishvili and A.Lipin). The German Georgianologist Heinz Fanrich considers the resemblance of Iber-Caucasian (Proto-Georgian) and Dravidian languages to have a system character (*Ibero-Caucasian and Dravidian Languages*, Tbilisi, 1972 (in Georgian) and *Kartwelisch und Dravidianische spachparallelen*, Berlin, 1991 (in German)). It is interesting to note the following proto-Georgian and proto-Dravidian lexical parallels: *tsitel* (=red) in Georgian and *tsitai* (=red) in Tamil; *tsuri* (=udders) in Georgian and *tsuro* (=udder) in Tamil; *karri* (=wind) in Georgian and *karri* (=wind) in Tamil; etc.

The Georgian anthropologist M. Abdushelishvili (working several years in

India) supposes that the Dravidians (origin North-West or Near East) were in communication with ancient Mesopotamians (Sumerians) and Iranians too.

So the builders of Sindhu Valley civilization, being bearers of a semitic culture at the first stage of migration to the valley of river (nadi) Sindhu could lay the base of "Brahmi language" (Brahmi Lipi) which is considered to be of Phoenician origin. Perhaps R. Pataridze is also right in proving that the ancient Georgian alphabet "Asomtavruli" is also of Phoenician origin. While comparing "Sohgaura's" copy plate scripts with the ancient Georgian alphabet "asomtavruli" (see drawing N4) the resemblance between them can be easily noticed.

D. Struve in the preface of D. Makey's book *Ancient Culture of Sindhu Valley* (Moscow, 1951) notes that the Dravidian slave-keeping society was very close to that of Sumerian one and indicates to the similarity of iconography and mythology, proving the religious closeness to Sumerian (that is, proto-Georgian) and Sindhu Nadi. A. Kondratev in his research *Proto-Indian Script* (Moscow, 1976, p. 484) outlines that I.A. Uodel made the first attempt (experiment) to read proto-Indian script—Brahmi Lipi—through the Sumerian language.

The Sumero-Akhadian king's name "Naramsin" in Indian mythology is known as "Narasimha" and the Khatian king's name "Ganish" in India is known as "Ganesh."

Perhaps it is not by chance that S.C. Chatterjee considers that the significant portion of Indian civilization is of non-Aryan origin. But the historian R.C. Majumdar considers that Dravidians of Mediterranean origin were more civilized than those proto-Australoids that came to the Indian subcontinent much earlier.

All the above mentioned enables us to presume that the word "Sumer" can be interpreted in the following way in the ancient Indian language Sanskrit: *su* (Surya) = sun, *mer* (Meru) = mountain full of sunshine that is the place of Sumerians, that is, *sumera* (golden coloured mountain or lotus filled up with sunshine). So we may think hypothetically that by the inhabitants of Sindhu Valley *sumera* had been called Mesopotamians (Sumerians, Arkhadians, etc.).

As another source of proto-Indo-Georgian ties may be considered the period of invasion of Aryans in ancient Iran and India through the Caucasus—namely through Georgia (see L. Klein's map of migration of Aryans), resulting not only in linguistic inter-borrowing, but in inter-influencing and interchanging of cultural phenomena too. In Khetian texts a lot of horse-breeding Aryan terminologies are met (see T. Klizarenkova, *Rigveda: Selected Hymns*, Moscow, 1072, p. 7, Preface).

The Georgian ethnologist S. Makalatia considers that the Indo-Iranian deity "Mitra" in the ancient Georgian paganic calendar is known as the month of Mirsoba (March). With the name of "Mitra" (god of Sun) are connected also the ancient Georgian theoporistic names as "Mitridatte," "Mihraan," later transformed in the modern Georgian name "Mirian."

The existence of eurotic dancers (like "devadasies") in the North mountain regions of ancient Georgia, S. Makalatia prescribes to the worshipping of the cult of the phallus (Shiva-Lingam) in Caucasus in the paganic epoch. M. Vodbolski outlines that on the "Phiala" excavated in Armazi (ancient Georgian monument in the center of Georgia) the horse is expressed, which is the animal used to be sacrificed by idol-worshippers. In the first chapter of *Brihadaranyakopanisad with Commentaries of Sankaracharya* (1965, sixth edition), we read: "On the head of the sacrificial horse is the dawn, its eye the sun, ..." (p. 6).

Some of these common cultural phenomena penetrated into ancient Georgia, not only during the migration of Aryans through Georgia (Caucasus), but later too, suppose through ancient Greece or Anatolia, or through any other way of the Near East, in some way towards India too.

While exploring the sources of Indo-Georgian historical or cultural ties, we meet with certain other aspects to which no attention has been paid by modern scholars, e.g., the French ethnographist of the last century, Abbe J.A. Dubois, who spent nearly twenty years in South India and was greatly appreciated by Max Muller, presumes: "At the time when the Hindus began to regard the waters of the Ganges, Indus and Godavari as peculiarly sacred, and to attribute to them those cleansing properties which could purify both soul and body, the inhabitants of Colchis (that is, ancient West Georgians, N.K.) and other peoples living near the Phasisi (the author means river Phasisi—the present river Rioni, N.K.) credited the waters of that river with the same efficacy amongst the Egyptians." Accordingly, the habit of cremation in ancient India amongst the Hindus was widely spread in ancient Georgia too (in the second millenium B.C.). At that time—considers the well-known Georgian historian I. Javakhishvili—the chiefs of ancient Georgian tribes, after their death, were burnt and the ashes, together with their chariots, rifles and other belongings, were put in a large, deep burial mound. It is of great interest that Abbe J.A. Dubois had the following opinion on the origin of Brahmanism (Brahmins):

> "I don't trace the origin of the Brahmins either to Egypt or to Arabia, and I believe them to be descendents not of Shem, as many argue, but Japheth. According to my theory they reached India from the north, and I should place the first abode of their ancestors in the neighbourhood of the. Caucasus."
>
> "Mago's name and Gaudama's, commonly called Gotama, Ma or Mahu, signifies "great," so that Gotama must mean the Great God or Magog."
>
> "Furthermore, pagan history adds weight to these conjectures of mine on the origin and antiquity of Brahmanism. Learned men allude to more

than one Prometheus. According to the Greeks the most celebrated of them all is a son of Japeth."

"Why should not Brahma and Prometheus be one and the same person? The Hindu divinity is known also under the names of Brama and Prume in some of their tongues. All these names bear resemblance to Prometheus (chained in Georgia on the Caucasus mountains, N.K.) or the god Preme of the Greeks."

"But admitting that Tartary or neighbourhood of the Caucasus was the birthplace of the Brahmins, it is not easy to decide the precise date of their arrival in India. It appears certain, however, that they were already established there in a flourishing condition more than nine centuries before the Christian era (see Dr., 1, 2)."

These considerations of Abbe J.A. Dubois seem rather truthful as in the history of Georgia of this time and later, Brahman-type saints were called "Shishvelmartalni" (half-dressed true men) or later as "Gimnosophist" (Brahmans) which probably should have looked like contemporaries of Jain Digambhars (dressed with heaven).

Abbe J.A. Dubois' hypothesis, in a particular sense, at least from the point of chronology of formation of Vedic ideas or creation of Vedas itself, proves the 129th Sukta of the fourth book concerning the creation of the world by Brahma. In this portion of the Vedas we easily can note a certain resemblance of connotation with the creation of the world in the Old Testament.

> 1.2. The earth was without form and void, and darkness was upon the face of deep, and the Spirit of God was moving over the face of the waters . . ."

In Veda (in the above mentioned portion) we read:

"उनके अतिरिक्त सब शून्य था ॥२॥

सृष्टि-रचना से पूर्व अन्धकार ने अन्धकार को आवृत किया हुआ था । सब कुछ अज्ञात था । सब ओर जल ही जल था ।"

Of course these judgements, in particular sense, are the subject of a separate discussion, and are going outside the frame of the main problems raised in the present article, but it is beyond doubt also that all the above given arguments cannot solve the problem of the sources of historical, cultural or any other type of ties between ancient Georgia (Caucasus) and India. But, anyway, it is out of question that all these problems are tightly bound with the historical processes that had taken place in the Near East and the Indian subcontinent, being an integral part of the history of ancient Georgia and Sindhu-Valley civilization too.

The Relevance of Ramayana to Mankind as it Enters the 21st Century

VIDYA SAGAR ANAND
Chairman
European Council of Hindu Organizations

> Outward attributes alone do not lead to spiritual consciousness, nor do they bring one nearer to God. For one's sense must at all times be subservient to God's name. The eye that looketh not towards God had better be blind. The tongue that uttereth not His Name had better be dumb. The ear that heareth not His Praise had better be deaf; and the body that performs not His Service had better be dead. —*Sheikh Farid*

A spiritual void in the present world

The world has, thanks to the jet engine, become a global village. We need not necessarily travel to be familiar with each other over remote distances, there's the all-pervasive computer, the wonderfully democratic Internet, the intrusive fax machine and the increasingly prevalent satellite TV. But the question is: Have we been brought together spiritually, morally and ethically?

The fact is that all over the world there is an appalling poverty of the spirit, despite immense wealth and unprecedented technological and scientific change. Alcoholism, sexual abuse, addiction to chemically synthesized hard drugs, and other forms of moral degradation are the order of the day. Especially in the materially developed West, there is immense dissatisfaction, a desperate search for the philosopher's stone that will finally reveal the secrets of mental peace, calm and tranquillity, which, in turn, will lead to a higher state of spiritual and cultural development.

As a citizen of the world, now finally and firmly anchored in London, after many voyages across the globe, I have seen and continue to see the ravages wrought by excessive, untamed and meretricious materialism. I, of course, am privileged to come from a country, which thousands of years ago came face to face with the challenges posed by a surfeit of materialism. Fortunately this was preceded by the age of saints, philosophers and sages who had long predicted the problems inherent in material development itself.

Those wise men saw the contradictions very early and warned of the evil, pain and grotesque distortion of the mind and personality that are the direct consequence of the idolatry of wealth.

Ramayana, a book to show the way

There are many fine books on these subjects by ancient scholars. But I do not think I am alone when I say that the great epic of Ramayana provides very cogently, very lucidly and very elegantly, and yet very practically, the eternal truths which are indispensable for the rescue of man now teetering on the brink of self-destruction.

The Ramayana points troubled, tortured and spiritually disembodied Man, not just in the West, but also in the East, in the direction of the redemption of Man. Here in the pages of the Ramayana are played out the great dramas that still haunt us when man made history by organizing government, administration, a taxation system and a body of laws, and the rule of law itself. A community came into being with a new morality. Men were compelled to be good by law. But laws in themselves cannot produce a responsible society.

The natures of men, their complex characters, their economic and social circumstance, the level of their learning, wisdom and ignorance, their vices and virtues, their ambitions, their vanity and their altruism, are all portrayed with incomparable thoroughness and honesty in the Ramayana. The heroes are here and so are the villains. The weak and the strong, the courageous and the cowardly, the dilettante and the scholar, the mercenary and the patriot, the caring and the callous, and the conscientious and the frivolous. We are repelled by the ugly, we are moved and inspired by beauty.

Ramayana presents role models for humanity

Can there, for instance, be a gentler, more virtuous woman than Sita? Can there be a gentler and nobler man than Rama? Self-effacing Lakshmana is the personification of humility, loyalty and decency, utterly selfless and resolute.

Today, it is fashionable to speak of role models, heroes and heroines who can inspire the young. India, indeed Asia, has produced many great and noble sons and daughters. A famous scholar once said that the Public Hero is the embodiment of his people's love of freedom, of fairness, of pride, of independence and valor. This is not a recent development. The Ramayana chronicled such pure and unalloyed virtues thousands of years ago.

The qualities of selflessness, love of one's nation and love of justice, so movingly recorded by Ramayana, have filtered through the ages orally. In villages where people cannot read, they gather to listen to the local story-teller vividly recapture the spirit and the atmosphere of those stirring times.

The great leaders who have shaped the destiny of India, and continue to shape it, have all been consciously or unconsciously influenced by the Ramayana and its eternal verities.

How much has the time changed!

People say rather cynically today that the old certainties are no more and that we live in entirely changed circumstances, implying that the law of the jungle, the survival of the fittest, have superseded love for one's fellow men, loyalty to one's country, community responsibility and consideration for the underprivileged and the disadvantaged.

This is a superficial view. It is, of course, the monopoly of laissez-faire market economies. But while the countries of Asia are marching in the direction of market economies, our legislators are making sure that the market is not a god unto itself, and that it is answerable not just to a handful of the rich, but also to the entire community.

Story of robber Valmiki questioning ill-gotten gains

You cannot run away from centuries of the most humane philosophy, particularly as enshrined in the glorious pages of the Ramayana. But how did the great epic, the incomparable Ramayana, so admired and respected, not just by Asians, but also by learned scholars from the West, come to be written? How did this monumental, Titanic work of literature, philosophy, social conduct and even economics, survive the turbulence and vicissitudes of centuries? To whom are we, the inheritors of this grandest of all master-pieces, indebted?

In a lecture to the Shakespeare Club, Pasadena, California on January 31, 1900, Swami Vivekananda took up the story.

> There was a young man who could not support his family. he was intelligent and athletic but in the absence of suitable employment, he turned to robbery. He preyed on people going about their business in a peaceful way; he robbed them and with these ill-gotten gains he supported his aged parents, his wife and children.
>
> One day, a great sage called Rishi Agastya chanced to pass his way, and the robber set upon him. The sage asked him: "Why do you wound and kill people in this way? What is the purpose of this sinful action?"
>
> "With the proceeds I support my family," the robber replied.
>
> The sage: "Are members of your family party to your crimes?"
>
> The robber: "They most certainly are."
>
> The sage: "Tie me up, and please go home and ask your family whether they approve of what you do."
>
> The robber did just that. He first asked his father: "Father, do you know how I support you?"
>
> Father: "My son, I don't."

Robber, "I kill and steal from people."

Father: "I am astounded, get away you outcast."

Next, the robber asked the same question of his mother, who also said she was unaware of his activities. When he told her the truth she was uncompromising: "How horrible!" And when the son asked if she shared his sin, she coldly retorted: "I never committed robbery."

He questioned his wife along these lines after confessing to his criminal way of life. Asked if she were a party to his sins, she replied: "By no means. You are my husband and it is your duty to support me."

The robber's eyes were thus opened to the enormity of his foul deeds. He said to himself: "This is the way of the world—even my nearest and dearest relatives have disowned me." He returned to the sage, released him and pleaded, "Save me! What must I do to redeem myself?"

The sage told him: "End your criminal career now. None of your family loves you now that they know how you earn your money. They will share your prosperity, but the moment you have nothing they will desert you and disown you. Therefore worship Him who alone stands by us whether we are doing good or evil. He never leaves us, for love never drags us down, knows no barriers, no selfishness." The sage then taught him how to pray.

Ramayana teaches how wicked can be transformed.

The former robber gave up everything and went into the forest to pray. There he went on praying and meditating, and he forgot himself so completely that the ants came and built their mounds around him.

After many years, a voice commanded, "Arise, O sage!"

Thus aroused he replied, "Sage? I am no sage, I am a robber."

"Robber no more," said the voice, "a sage you are. Your old name is gone. But now, since the meditation was so intense that you did not even observe the anthills around you, your name henceforth shall be Valmiki, he that was reborn in the anthills."

Valmiki—the power of his erudition and the skill of his pen are so awe-inspiring that we hesitate to link him with mortal men—was the author of this enduring tome.

Long before the first Pyramid was built, long before the Olympic flame was lit in ancient Greece, and long before Remus and Romulus had laid the first brick of Rome, Valmiki, who loved and respected life in all its splendid and poetic diversity, whether it be the magnificently plumed bird in the sky, the fleet-footed and gentle deer of the forests, or unpredictable Man himself, once witnessed an act of such mindless cruelty as to haunt him for a long time. A female deer was playfully teasing her male partner, when suddenly an arrow pierced its tender heart. Valmiki, hurt, shocked and outraged, condemned this vile deed with all the eloquence at his command. It is said that at this precise moment of poetic lament, a voice from heaven commanded Valmiki to create in the same poetic meter the life and deeds of Rama.

Valmiki Ramayana—A great work of world literature

Instantly, Valmiki took up his pen and wrote in seven sections, twentyfour thousand couplets full of the most compelling imagery, idiom and metaphor, and wisdom and nobility. Thus was born a unique literary and philosophical masterpiece, one of the greatest works in world literature. Many centuries later, the illustrious Milton wrote: "A good book is the lifeblood of a Master Spirit." He could well have had the Ramayana in mind; indeed if this man of such vast learning had had the privilege of reading the Ramayana, it is almost certain that he, too, would have been humbled by its wisdom.

The Ramayana, so deliciously sweet, so compellingly eloquent, lent itself beautifully to the declamations of the great Thespians of the time. Scenes from the Ramayana were enacted in the earliest theatres of India, often clearings in forests, with nature's splendors for the backdrop. It is said that even the fiercest animals sat down and listened, enthralled by the actors reliving some of the most memorable moments of the Ramayana. This touching reverence by members of the animal kingdom was to be expected, for was not the Ramayana inspired by a tragedy involving one its members, brutally slain by the arrow of an inhuman butcher?

Ramayana—its appeal to intellectual and unlettered alike

Bards in India, such as feature in the pages of Middle Ages lore, also carried the Ramayana with them to recite on their travels in a more leisurely and civilized age when people had the time and intelligence to appreciate stirring works of literature. Vivekananda wrote: "The writers of all the epics wrote in symbols of all they saw, felt and experienced. With inspired skills they painted glowing pictures. Do not get submerged in the quagmire of interpretations. Take them as they are and judge them only by the effect they have on you."

It has to be noted that the Ramayana was not only read at religious festivals, it was also celebrated at literary gatherings. And it is hardly surprising that the economic, yet graceful, style of the Ramayana provided a model for scores of poets, writers, dramatists and composers from early times to the present

Earlier giants of Indian literature, men like Kalidasa, Bhatti and Bhavbhuti, to name but a few, generously acknowledged their inspiration and style to the Ramayana. The Ramayana is still as revered today as when it was first published several thousands of years ago, because it is not abstract or wholly remote from the lives of people, nor does it set impossible targets for human perfection. It operates within the parameters of life's reality, recognizes the limitations and weaknesses of men, though it does not condone them, and sets achievable targets for good conduct. It stresses humility, reminding us of an observation by another great sage, Aurobindo. The latter, who also fell under the spell of Valmiki's magnum opus, wrote: "A tree laden with fruit bows its branches."

Ramayana and human virtues

The Ramayana refused to have any truck with irrational and absurd views, which are still being propagated today. The false prophets stridently assert that there must be a distinction between justice and morality, the inference being that justice cannot always be just for technical, economic or class reasons, that morality and truth are relative, that the debate about means and ends is unreal and futile. These Jeremiahs put forward the fatalistic view that human behavior cannot be changed because we are all predestined for a certain trend and end.

The Ramayana believes in the essential nobility and purity of Man. Although I have used the word "Man" throughout this text, let me stress that this is not due to a sexist attitude. The Ramayana, ahead of its time, witness its emancipated analysis of the character of Sita, rejected the idea of women's inferiority, though recognizing the biological differences between men and women. To use an old phrase, let me reiterate that in this text man embraces woman.

The Ramayana is also an optimistic document, and has no time for cynicism or skepticism, recognizing very early that such cynicism under the guise of intellectualism, distorts human values, exalting evil and pouring scorn on virtue. This does not mean that the Ramayana, like certain creeds that followed, believed in its own divine invincibility. On the contrary, the idea was not to produce a set of dogmas, stone tablets with indelible truths, but to challenge men and women to look anew at life, look at it more critically, and always strive for moral and ethical improvement.

It is this undogmatic approach that has led to the production of innumerable commentaries by so many scholars determined to show there are many ways of interpreting the great truths of the Ramayana.

That's what Valmiki intended. He did not want to regiment the minds of men, nor did he seek a blind devotion to its teachings. Mental slavery is totally alien to the very tolerant Hindu faith that gave birth to the Ramayana. Think for yourselves, but also understand that there are some truths which are unassailable. It is in this spirit of reason that one should approach the Ramayana.

Huge progress has been made in the struggle to rid ourselves of the pernicious caste system. But there are still powerful enclaves of reaction, the so-called fundamentalists, who in order to justify the perverse religious, cultural and spiritual enslavement of their fellow men, have even mendaciously attempted to seek justification in the Ramayana for criminality of the system.

Look in its humane and rational pages and you will never find a single line in favor of the monstrous system of human bondage. The Ramayana, on the contrary, positively affirms the brotherhood and equality of men. The Ramayana says clearly and unequivocally that a man can only justifiably adorn the mantle of a specific caste so long as the qualities of that particular caste are manifested in his character.

A man of ungovernable temper and wild and reckless passions, selfish, ruthless, greedy, boorish and bereft of refinement, cannot be called a Brahmin, nor high born.

Caste, the Ramayana reiterates, is the inner man, not the outward form. Wherever there is conflict between the two, the accident of birth is irrelevant. It is the sullied and discredited inner self of the sinner that cheats him of the rights to the caste one inherits from birth. What is noticeable here is that while caste in the negative and oppressive sense is rejected, merit and morality-based class is used to reward men of intellect, of virtue, of nobility and purity of thought.

These people, who had ample and abundant opportunities to justify their status with morally uplifting conduct, have forfeited whatever claims they may have had to be treated in a manner worthy of their original station in life. One must not only respect others, one must also be able to respect oneself, which is much harder unless one is a victim of self-delusion. Shakespeare got it right when he said, with the conviction and sharpness of a man familiar with the Ramayana, "This above all, to thine own self be true." Therefore, it behoves all who claim to be the true followers of Rama, but who are presently engaged in campaigns of hatred and intolerance, violence and harassment, which go against all that Rama stood for, to pause for a while, if they are capable of so doing, and reflect on the absurdity and meanness of their actions.

If they can, however, see the folly of their ways, they help to usher in Ramrajya, a divine mix of spiritual and moral bliss. They can indeed drink deeply from the well-springs of the nectar of rectitude and morality. But the killings and crimes of desecration are nothing but aasuric actions from people masquerading as the custodians of the true spirit of the Ramayana. Indeed, these people are nothing more than the devotees of the enemies of Lord Rama.

Ramayana—Women and family

I have already referred to the anti-sexist content of the Ramayana. Permit me to return to this very topical subject. Currently it is strongly engaging the minds of the great thinkers of the feminist movement, not just in Europe and America, but also in Asia. The Ramayana has decreed a very special and revered place for women in our society.

Kabir recited the following story from Mahabharat:

> "Kausik was a great sage. Once he was resting under a tree when a female crane, perched on a bough, defecated. The droppings fell on the sage's head.. The sage was furious and cursed the bird, which fell down dead. The sage proceeded to the nearby village to beg for alms. The housewife was racing against time to prepare her husband's meal and neglected the sage. The hotheaded sage uttered a mighty curse. This had no effect on the woman. She told him that she was no female crane, but a *pativrata*, over whom no one had power except the husband."

Yet there is widespread physical abuse, humiliation and exploitation of women in our society. In the name of Lord Rama all our actions should be devoted to the ending of domestic violence and degradation of our women.

Sita embodies all those virtues which we associate with Indian womanhood. She did so precisely because of the love and respect her husband showered on her. She, in turn, with her fine intelligence, her virtuous conduct in the most dangerous circumstances, and her courage in the face of death was most worthy of that love. For Rama, Sita was a companion, friend and wife, never a servant, never an object of lust. Let us never forget this, and let us remember too that until a certain invasion, our women were never in purdah, a system totally alien to the Indian way of life. Unfortunately, the people behind the purdah were also supported by reactionary fundamentalists in our midst. Some of the violence against women starts right from their conception, when efforts are made to abort them. If it is a male child, there is none of the fear, anxiety and self hate that greets the birth of a female child. Yet many do not realize the dangers of interfering so mindlessly with Nature. Nature knows what it is doing, it knows the need for a correct sex balance. If you start killing off the female of the species. apart from the criminality of such an act, you are also endangering society itself.

Can you think of the terrible social, economic, emotional and even sexual consequences where the ratio of young men to young women is preponderantly in favour of young men? Why are the followers of Lord Rama not taking up the cudgels against the oppressors of the Ahalyas, Anusyuas or Shabris of our age?

The fundamental teaching of the Ramayana is the sanctity of the institution of the family. The family is society in miniature, with the same code of behavior, though not formalized, holding them together. There is a unifying bond, sharing, caring, discipline and responsibility. Nowhere has the family been so strong as in India. Even in the many unjust societies of the Indian diaspora, the unity of the family has been a protective barrier against racism, poverty and the ever-present threat of cultural deformity.

Sadly, however, even in our societies, family unity is being weakened by alien concepts like aggressive assertiveness and selfish individuality in which every man is expected to plough his own furrow. Respect for elders, respect for our moral code, respect for our culture are all being eroded and undermined in the name of modernity. The role of father, brother, neighbour and citizen, in short the very dignity of human beings, is being cynically devalued. Those who, like myself, have spent a great many years in the diaspora, are deeply conscious of the significance of the family unit and its indispensability in an insecure, generally hostile and culturally alien climate. The family has been our mainstay, and in Britain where our thrift, energy and professional, business and academic success have aroused envy and respect in equal measure, there is a grudging admiration for our family structure, the comfort, security, love and discipline that enable individuals to be strong, confident and secure. Fortunately, despite all the destabilising tendencies of modernity, the family unit is not gravely threatened either in India itself, or in the diaspora. It is the Ramayana which sharply brought home to us the blessings of family and community unity, especially when dark and destructive forces threatened us. It is because Rama in his darkest hour was so majestically supported by family and community that he was able to triumph over a deadly enemy.

Ramayana and social justice

The Ramayana is a constant in our lives. It never changes. Its pages are there for us to consult and enjoy, they are also there for our spiritual enlightenment and our moral betterment. The Ramayana urges men and women to be vigilant, both in the defense of freedom, and also in defense of community and society. No man, it is said, long before John Donne wrote those famous lines, is an island. We are all interconnected, interrelated and responsible for the common weal. Even the hermit in his cave, unless he has a death wish and seeks to cut himself completely from humanity, has to come out from time to time for the nutritional and social sustenance provided by his fellow men. And it especially behoves the individual endowed with intellectual powers to show moral integrity, always protecting the weak against the strong. It is not often that people will behave with the same fairness as did Rama in a celebrated case of misconduct by Bali. Sugriva was the aggrieved victim of injustice at the hands of his brother, Bali. Rama intervened promptly and justly, restoring the rights of Sugriva. That is the essence of the rule of moral law, that no man is above it, regardless of his power. position, wealth or responsibility.

Like Lord Rama, one should be objective and detached, but committed to the truth. Here from the Ramayana is a firm declaration of these principles, "A man should try to be a guest in his own house and guest in his own thought. He is there to speak the truth, but who is he? Some clod the truth has snatched from the ground and with fire has fashioned him into a momentary man? Without the truth he is a clod again. Let him find his superiority in not wanting superiority, find the riches of love which possesses that which it does, the riches of poverty, the height of lowliness, the immensity of today and, in the passing hour, age of ages." Tukaram [4] says: "It is true, it is true—three times I say it is true."

In India, too, the land which gave us such luminous treatises on right conduct and respect for basic human rights, we see the dignity of our fellow men still being churlishly trampled on. The awareness of such shameful deeds is sharpened in our consciousness by Vishvamitras of the Ramayana, that the Dasrathas in our inner selves are not prepared to let our Raghunandans go with the Rishis to do battle with the forces of evil. The result is that the aasuric forces are rampant, creating havoc in our world. According to the Ramayana, when the Kshatriyas failed to stand up for the good and the righteous, an incarnation in the person of Parashurama appeared to weed out those so-called protectors. It is said that after this powerful purge of evil forces by Parashurama, Lord Rama came into the world to teach by example, how Kshatriyas should behave, and how they should serve the society.

But are we prepared to go in the direction to force the divine to destroy and create? A true devotee of Lord Rama used to live in a small hut. One night, thieves came to steal from him, and found two young men, looking like Lord Rama and Lakshmana, guarding his abode, bows and arrows at the ready. When in the morning, the repentant thieves fell at the feet of the saintly Rama's devotee and told him of the vision of his protectors, tears trickled down the eyes of the devotee who immediately threw out his meager belongings from his home. He was filled with remorse that Lord Rama had to go to so much trouble to protect his 'unworthy' property.

For all the straying from the path of virtue, truth and justice, one must not be pessimistic about our world, bearing in mind that in all societies the eternal struggle is between the forces of good and the forces of evil. No sooner do we slay one evil dragon than another rears its unpleasant head. What we must strenuously and conscientiously deny the forces of evil is the final victory they so desperately crave.

This is where the teachings of the Ramayana can help those who desire a better and juster world. We must take its real message, its truths and moral challenges into every home, and ensure that it becomes the cherished possession of every single man, woman and child.

The world was also in crisis, threatened by the forces of darkness, when Tulsidas appeared in the 16th century with a divine mission. In the 15th and 16th centuries a number of individuals and groups cynically exploited the divine to further their squalid political and ideological ambitions. Ill-digested ideas, the stagnant state of Buddhism and the indifference of the rulers to matters temporal had resulted in inertia and spiritual and moral degradation.

Akbar, the Mughal, had a subtle style—sensuous, seductive, with social and political corruption inimical to the country's moral infrastructure, its Dharma. Akbar strove to destabilise the Indian way of life. His methods lulled the people into complacency, and sought to subvert the national consciousness through the back door. In India, people succumbed en masse both to Akbar's iconoclastic sword and his corrupt material advances without much resistance. The Kavya of Valmiki was written in classical Sanskrit.

This language had, however, long lost its vernacular credibility. It was no longer the lingua franca of the masses. It was but natural, therefore, that new faiths and new philosophies in the language that people understood were rapidly attaining credibility.

These are the concluding lines of Tulsidas' Ramacharitamanasa:

> "This glorious, holy, purifying, blessed and most limpid Manasa lake of Shri Ram ever begets happiness, nay it bestows both wisdom and devotion and wipes out delusion, infatuation and immunity. It overflows with the waters of love. Men who devoutly plunge into it are never scorched by the heat of the world." [5]

This was a particularly difficult time for non-Muslims, who were cruelly oppressed in their own land by an alien power and alien faith. This was the century that inspired the immortal works of the mighty Tulsidas, Guru Das, Guru Nanak, Nabha Das, Malik Mohammed Jayasi, Rahim, Raskhan, Keshav Das and, above all Kabir Das.

Despite the oppression, it has to be noted that some of the most famous names in the renaissance of Indian literature and philosophy are those of several Muslims. Naturally the works of Tulsidas and Kabir had a profound effect. Both believed in the masses and not the elite, and their message, couched in simple yet startling prose and poetry, aroused in the masses strong feelings against their oppression and the decline of moral, cultural and spiritual values. Tulsidas' fame spread all over India with the publication of his masterpiece, the Ramacharitamanasa. Perhaps the most eloquent tribute to Tulsidas came from the genial and unselfish Nabha Das, who wrote that Valmiki has been born again as Tulsidas. In his famous poem, Bhaktamala, Nabha Das says:

For the salvation of beings in this perverse Dark Age Valmiki has become Tulsi
In the former Treta age, he made the thousand million verses of the Ramayana,

Of which but one letter can redeem even a man who has slain a Brahman.
Now he has again published abroad God's many wonders as a comfort for all devotees,
And intoxicated with the love of Rama's feet he repeats his Name both night and day according to his vow.
Thus he has secured an easily accessible boat for crossing the boundless ocean of existence;
For the salvation of beings in this perverse Dark Age Valmiki has become Tulsi." [6]

The age of Tulsidas was no different to our own, characterised by brigandage and honesty, cowardice and heroism, selfishness and altruism and cruelty and kindness. As in the modern age, however, in the age of Tulsidas the forces of darkness as opposed to the forces of light were on the ascendant, threatening to prise power from the hands of the virtuous. Those who were supposed to be guards had become robbers, and 'look-outs' beckoned the hordes to pillage. There was not the slightest shred of respect for human dignity and basic human rights.

The people were corrupted by pie-in-the-sky promises. Tulsidas warned the populace:

"These men of evil deeds declare
Tomorrow shall I gain a youthful body
Tomorrow, earth and wealth,
Tomorrow, shall I join the kingly throng
Being mere gnats they cry,
Even Mount Meru sinks beneath our weight.
Tulsi, many houses have fallen on account of these wrong ways,
Many houses are now falling
And many houses yet will fall;
But seeing it and hearing it and having it explained to them,
But even yet it is not clear those men,
And not one of them has ever added that
Tomorrow is the time of death." [7]

Unfortunately, the false prophets are as powerful today as they were in the era of Sant Tulsidas and Valmiki. Today, with advanced satellite technology, radio, television and Internet can take any message into communities millions of miles away. While negative messages, sometimes highly immoral and offensive, are also being conveyed under the guise of freedom of speech, it is possible to use the same media intelligently and responsibly to put over the wise teaching of the Ramayana.

For instance, Kabir says:

"This world has given millions of names to the Lord
But repeating them gives not the salvation
Few indeed are to know the Original Name
Which is the Lord in active form—creating and sustaining the universes
Few, indeed, are those who worship the Name."

But we must rise above our immediate mental quagmire to benefit from the spiritual bliss at hand. For according to Ramacharitamanasa of Tulsidas, Lord Rama says in an address to his subjects:

"Neither I say which is not right, nor I say with the authority of a king, therefore you do whatever you think right after listening to me."

But today, those in power and those seeking power, are intolerant of any opposition or dissent, filling the jails with those who seek to frustrate their greedy materialistic ambitions. However, as history continually teaches us, brave men with a moral conscience have always stood up to tyranny—in our own age to powerful parasitical imperial powers and for the destruction of apartheid. Men like Bonhoeffer and Gandhi did not care about the torture and death that faced them when they took on the forces of evil. They showed with a grandeur that will forever be writ large in the pages of the history of mankind, that human souls can soar high over the walls of prisons and concentration camps of the tyrants and the oppressors. No chains are strong enough, no torture is so painful that they can delay permanently the rebirth of freedom.

"The light of the epic of Ramayana shines on all alike
So speed the essence of the Ramayana from soul to soul
And waft its fragrance from pole to pole." [10]

Sometimes the pain of oppression is so intolerable that people long for that great rescuer, death. The Ramayana, however, counsels against despair and pessimism. Tyranny and darkness engulf our world only when the good cease to be vigilant and when they cease to resist. [11]

Hitler thought that his tawdry and blood-drenched Third Reich would last a thousand years, and many modern tyrants also suffer from similar delusions of grandeur. The latter, wherever they may be, in Asia, Europe, America, Africa or Australia, should familiarise themselves with these instructive words from the Ramayana:

"Where the land is kingless,
The cloud lightening-wreathed and loud-voiced,
gives no rain to the earth.

Where the land is kingless,
Men do not meet in assemblies,
nor make lovely gardens and temples.

Where the land is kingless,
The rich are unprotected, and shepherds and
peasants sleep with bolted doors.

A river without water, a forest without grass,
A herd of cattle without a herdsman,
Is the land without a king." [12]

The Ramayana does not offer an easy way out from the destruction of tyranny. In the great conflicts recorded by the Ramayana in which the forces of good and evil are arraigned against each other, the battlefields are covered with corpses not just of men of evil but also men of virtue. When they entered the good fight, the heroes, driven by an indestructible love of liberty and justice, knew the risks and fought conscious of the fact that they may never again return to the arms of their beloved families.

The Ramayana shows vividly through such examples that the fight against evil can only be the work of men of honour, purity and integrity.

The Ramayana rejected the widely held theory of Original Sin [7]. In ancient Indian scriptures, the best political system had been defined when there was no law of punishment as no one was expected to do anything wrong to merit punishment. Dand is the word for 'stick' which is kept by a Sanyasi who renounces the world. Goswami Tulsidas again refers to this in Ramacharita-manasa: "In Ram Rajya, 'Dand' was only known for the holy stick taken by Sanyasis and there was no other meaning of the word. It is quite clear that there was no conception of punishment at that time." [13]

We have referred before to society, and its resemblance to an over-extended family. In the concept based on Vasudhaiva Kutumbakam—the world is a family: "In this context, Ramayana conveys the message that if any system or order which is governed by a right person or persons who take into consideration the spiritual or the human values and translate them into practice then not only the whole environment becomes congenial but nature also showers grace. Human relations obviously take a turn for the better, and society resembles a vast family of Man." [14]

But no work, however great or wise, deserves respect if it is stuck in a time warp. The matchless genius, the tremendous vision, the timeless wisdom and the poetic compassion and humanity of the Ramayana make it a uniquely remarkable body of philosophy in the sense that though it was written many thousands of years ago, it is as relevant as ever to the vastly changed but equally turbulent conditions of the closing stages of this century, and the centuries to follow. [15]

We constantly talk of a higher stage in the evolution of Man. There is another stage, accessible albeit with some difficulty; this is the highest stage of Man's development. True, it looks as forbidding and as intimidating as Everest. But let us not forget that Everest too was conquered by that Great Sherpa, Tensing.

In the same spirit, provided we are humble, provided we accept that we are not pre-destined to sin, and provided we learn and practise the teachings of the Ramayana, the greatest book ever written, we will never scale the Everests of human perfection, but we can certainly help to create a better world—a world where:

"They shall beat their swords into ploughshares
And their spears into pruning hooks.
Nations shall not lift up swords against other nations,
Nor shall they learn war any more;
They shall sit—each one under his vine and under his own fig tree
And none shall make them afraid: to do justly, to love mercy
and to walk humbly with God." [16]

The Ramayana, as a modern sage, Bhagavan Sri Sathya Sai Baba, has so eloquently said, transcends the milestones of history and the boundaries of geography. It has shaped the attitudes and habits of many generations and has struck root in the consciousness of peoples, propelling them in the direction of Truth, Righteousness, Peace and Love. [17]

In July 1996, in a memorable debate on the moral decline of Britain, Dr. George Carey, the Archbishop of Canterbury, said: "You cannot take moral behavior for granted. It need to be redefined, re-examined, and nurtured again and again. It is my hope that we will find ways of strengthening the moral fibre of the nation in the days ahead." [18]

It is my own humble belief that thousands of years ago, the Ramayana foresaw with almost scientific accuracy, the moral and spiritual decline of nations, and took a concrete, positive view, forcefully reminding Man of the dangers of selfishness and the irresponsibility of rejecting the concept of society. What we need now is not only a global economy but a rational global philosophy based on the teachings of Ramayana, to act as a rudder for mankind as it enters the 21st century.

References

[1] *The Complete Works of Swami Vivekananda*, Volume IV, Advaita Ashramam, Calcutta, 1962, pp. 63–65.

[2] Ibid.

[3] Isaac A. Ezekiel, *Kabir, the Great Mystic*, Radha Soami Satsang, Beas, 1992, p. 88.

[4] C. Rajwade, *Tukaram, Saint of Maharashtra* as quoted in Isaac A. Ezekiel, op.cit., pp. 160–184.

[5] Nabha Das: *Sri Bhaktamala* (Edited by Bhagvan Prasad Tupkala), Lucknow, 1936, pp. 304–305.

[6] Tulsi Das, *Sri Ramacharitamanasa*, Gita Press, Gorakhpur, India, p. 782

[7] Raymond Allchin, Tulsi Das's *Kavitavali*, translated with introduction, George Allen & Unwin, London, 1964, p. 177.

[8] Isaac A. Ezekiel, op. cit., p. 96.

[9] Lallan Prasad Vyas, *Role of Ramayana and the Future World Order*, Vishwa Ram Darshan (Souvenir), New Delhi, 1993, pp. 28–33.

[10] V.S. Anand, *Savarkar, The Evolution of Indian Nationalism*, Woolf, London, 1967, pp. 77–78.

[11] Lallan Prasad Vyas, op.cit., pp. 28-33.

[12] A.L. Basham, *The Wonder that was India*, London, 1954, pp. 265–266.

[13] Lallan Prasad Vyas, op. cit., pp. 28–33.

[14] Ibid.

[15] Ibid.

[16] V.S. Anand, *Hindus of Europe have come of Age*, Paris, 1984, p. 6.

[17] Sri Sathya Sai Baba, *Ramakatha Rasavahini* (The Sweet Story of Rama's Glory), Volume 2, Sri Sathya Sai Books, Prasanti Nilayam, India, p. 1.

[18] *The Times*, London, July 3, 1996.

BIBLIOGRAPHY

Anand, V.S., *Hindus of Europe Have Come of Age*, Paris, 1984.

Anand, V.S., *Savarkar, A Study in the Evolution of Indian Nationalism*, C. & A. Woole, London, 1967.

Bagchi, P.C., *Studies on the Adhyatma Ramayana*, Calcutta, 1935

Basham, A.L., *The Wonder that was India*, London, 1954.

Basham, A.L., *History and Culture of the Indian People*, Bombay, 1957.

Bhagavan Sri Sathya Sai Baba, *Ramakatha Rasavahini* (The Sweet Story of Rama's Glory), 2 volumes, Prasanthi Nilayam, India, 1981.

Brockington, J.L., *Righteous Rama*, Oxford University Press, 1984.

Ezekeil, Isaac A., *Kabir, the Great Mystic*, Radha Soami Satsang, Beas, India, 1966.

Grierson, Sir George, "Notes on Tulsi Das", *Indian Antiquary,* **XXII,** 1893, 264–274.

Growse, F. S., *The Ramayana of Tulsi Das*, Allahabad, 1877–1881.

Hawley, John Stratton, *Sur Das, Poet, Singer, Saint*, Oxford University Press, 1984.

Hill, W.D.P., *The Holy Lake of the Acts of Ram*, Oxford.

Vyas, Lallan Prasad, *Role of the Ramayana and the Future World Order*, Vishwa Ram Darshan (Souvenir), New Delhi, 1993.

Nabha Das, *Sri Bhakta Mala* (edited with commentary by Bhagavan Prasad), Rupkala, Lucknow, 1936 (in Hindi).

Rajwade, C., *Tukaram, Saint of Maharashtra*, Bombay.

Sukla, R.C., *Jayasi Granthavali*, Benaras, 1949

Vaudeville, C., *Etude sur les sources et la composition du Ramayana de Tulsi Das*, Paris, 1955.

The Caste Consciousness in Ancient India and the Distortion of Hindu History

JEROME TEELUCKSINGH
522 Riverside Drive
Lange Park, Chaguanas, Trinidad, West Indies

This paper examines the existence of social ranking in ancient India which eventually led to the development of a society divided according to the Varnasrama social system. This system involved the four divisions of social and occupational castes. Evidence of caste restrictions in ancient religious literature such as the Mahabharata also added to the caste consciousness which was practised in ancient India.

Fallacies such as the Aryan-Dravidian clash in 1500 BC, the origin of the Aryans and the use of warped models of Hindu chronology and its negative impact on the study of ancient caste relations are also analyzed.

The possible existence of an earlier simple ranking in society before the Varnashrama social system is also considered. Other possible factors leading to the entrenchment and justification of caste groupings are also included.

New evidence by revisionist historians and scholars is also incorporated to confirm their correction of ancient Hindu history and show its positive impact on revolutionising the existing knowledge of the caste system.

> They are to keep the society in a state of peace and prosperity. The qualities mentioned herein (for each caste) are explained as transcendental qualities meant for making a person progress in spiritual understanding so that he can be liberated from the material world[1]

This quote from the religious literature—the Bhagavad-Gita—explains the purpose for the social institution known as "Varnasrama" which is the institution dividing society into four divisions of social and occupational castes. The Varnasrama social system described in the Vedic literature was a natural system of social organization essential for the creation of an ideal society. The underlying purpose of the Varnasrama social system was to provide a structure which allowed

[1]*Bhagavad-Gita,* translated by A.C. Swami Prabhupada, Bhaktivedanta Book Trust, Los Angeles, 1994, p. 522.

the ancient Hindus to work according to their natural tendencies for spiritual advancement.

The four major castes based on their work and their qualities consisted of the Brahmanas (intellectuals and priestly class), the Ksatriyas (government and military class) the Vaishyas (farmers and businessmen) and the Sudras (workers). The spiritual divisions were Brahmacharya (student life), Grihastha (married life), Vanaprastha (retired life) and Samnyasa. These meticulous divisions offer a glimpse into the merits of the social divisions of a society. One modern scholar, Banerjee, echoes the belief of the caste system as being beneficial and harbouring cordial relations:

> No professional class was self-sufficient, yet each class was indispensable. Each class had the initiative to contribute its best to the society as a whole.[1]

The distorted view of the origins and development of the caste system in ancient India has been due mainly to the work of European and American historians. The imperialism and colonization tactics of the Britishers to rewrite and thus discredit the history of Vedic civilization have infiltrated into the educational system throughout the world.

The false, superficial and unscientific epistemology that the Aryans were a superior race of foreigners who invaded India in 1500 BC continues to be propagated in colleges and universities. There is no geographical, cultural or anthropological evidence to indicate the supposed Aryan-Dravidian interaction of 1500 BC. Revisionist historians such as Bhagwan Gidwani and Dr. Deen Chandora are at the forefront of the school of thought which deems the Aryans as the original inhabitants of ancient India in 5000 BC where they lived as practising Hindus. This historical fact is further supported by Dr. David Frawley of New Mexico who, by using satellite technology, cultural anthropology and Indological studies agreed that the Aryans were the original inhabitants of India and later moved westward to Europe through Gandhar when the Sarasvati river dried up thousands of years ago.[2]

This revolutionary work is in contrast to the description by the British of the Aryans in India. The gravitation of the Aryans to the top of the caste system and their pivotal role in ancient India is no surprise because the Aryans were to be used as comparable ancestors of the later British rulers.

Obviously this genre of thinking led to preposterous theories which served as the justification for the social and cultural holocaust of India's history. Men such as Max Müller, the 19th century Oxford Sanskrit professor, used philological

---

[1]B.N. Banerjee, *Hindu Culture, Customs and Ceremony*, Delhi Print, India, 1979, p. 128.

[2]David Frawley, *Gods, Sages and Kings: Ancient Secrets of Ancient and World Civilizations*, Passage Press, Utah, 1990.

evidence and showed that the Aryans came from the Steppes of Central Asia. Similarly, Gordon Childe in "The Aryans" based his conclusion on cultural and archaeological evidence that the original home of the Aryans was South Asia.

The descriptions of the Aryans in the Rigveda have led many Western scholars to imaginatively construct not only the "Aryan invasion" of 1500 BC, but to determine the impact of the Aryans on the Harappan and Mohenjo-Daro civilizations—a devious scheme to portray the Aryans as a more advanced culture and a more complex society than the Dravidians, which automatically elevated the status of Aryans in the social ranking.

The Ramayana and the Mahabharata have evidence of a rich civilization and a highly evolved society; thus there was no need to depend on any foreigners for an advanced life. Neither is there any evidence to prove that the Dravidians were a dark-skinned people, inferior in religion, culture, customs or habits.

The research by Frawley, Chandora and Gidwani is important in understanding the past theories of the caste system. Because it is believed by some historians that the source of this social division and class distinction which constituted the basis of the caste system was pivotal in the Aryan-Dravidian clash of 1500 BC. One such misinformed historian, Herman Kulke, in "A History of India" believed that "colour (varna) served as a badge of distinction between the free Aryans and the subjugated indigenous people."[1]

Another Western scholar, with a racial theory, Louis Dumont, believed that the origin of the caste system was due to the encounter between two postulations—the invaders (Aryans) who were seeking to preserve the purity of their blood by the creation of closed groups and the conquered people (Dravidians)[2]. Other historians on ancient India's past have described the Aryans as a race—tall, fair and blue-eyed. There has been the eager acceptance of the theory in Western circles, that since the "invaded" Aryans had to fight enemies for a long time, they divided themselves into three classes; so normal work would not suffer.

These theories and historians could not have been further from the truth. In an unsceptical and unhistorical manner, Western civilization has accepted distorted ancient Indian history. On further analysis, it is revealed that the word "Dravid" describes people who are rich, dealing with money, precious metals and business transactions. The Dravidians have been unfairly and wrongly described as a lowly, subjugated people under the "superior" Aryans. In reality, the Dravidians were the backbone of their society as moneylenders and accountants in charge of the Treasury.

---

[1]Herman Kulke and Rothermund Dietmar, *A History of India,* McKay Chatam Ltd., 1986, p. 40.

[2]Louis Dumont, *Homo Hierarchus: An Essay on the Caste System*, University of Chicago Press, 1970, p. 27.

Similarly the definition and use of the word "Arya" (or Aryans) has been abused and corrupted and linked to the caste system signifying power, purity of blood and ability to rule. In contrast, Yogi Aurobindo gives a completely different definition which now questions the high position given to Aryans:

> The word Arya expresses a particular ethical and social order of well-governed life, courage, gentleness, purity and humanity, compassion, protection of the weak, liberty, observance of social duties, eagerness for knowledge, respect for the wise and the learned and the social accomplishment. There is no word in human speech that has a nobler history.[1]

It is believed that the hierarchy of the caste system owes its origins to the ancient "varna" system of the Vedic period which was more an occupational division of the underdeveloped Aryan society in the four occupational groups. Evidence of an already existing tension and bias among ancient groups is found in the later Vedic text:

> It (the sthali, an earthen milkpot) is made by an Arya, with perpendicular sides for the communion with the gods. In this way it is united with the gods. Demonical (Asurya) indeed is the vessel which is made by a potter on the potter's wheel.[2]

Indeed, the notion that the social caste systems became rigid much later when the Arabians, Persians and Moghuls attacked and destroyed the Vedic civilization is an acceptable historical fact. However, it cannot be assumed that only these foreign invasions were instrumental in shaping caste lines. Just as the Rigveda was composed as a text in 4600 BC, yet its songs of oral tradition were sung for thousands of years by Hindus, similarly the caste system was in existence for thousands of years in the Indus-Sarasvati period but in a less rigid manner.

In Vedic times, the caste system depended entirely upon occupation and not birth. People in this ancient period could have changed castes with professions and even intermarriage among groups was common. This lends itself to the theory that there might have been in existence before the Varnasrama social system, a simple social ranking with fewer rigid rules which would have gradually ungergone changes and adaptations in the society's social, political and economic structure.

In ancient India, the growth of occupational specialization meant the strengthening of caste restrictions and less social mobility. There is the argument, whether caste was mainly a social or religious distinction. It appears to be a

---

[1]Yogi Aurobindo, *Arya*, Vol. 1, 1963.

[2]*Satapatha Brahmana*, I.4.1, pp. 14–16.

mixture of not only social and religious factors but economic as well. Possibly different tribes had different criteria for distinguishing different classes from each other.

Indian scholars are often neither immune nor aware of the distorted Hindu chronology being propagated worldwide. One such scholar, Gokhale Balkrishna, adopts the Westernized stereotypical view of the prejudices of Aryans. He believed:

> Aryans frowned upon interracial marriages, racial fusion proceeded apace both through the institutions of marriage and concubinage and the adoption of non-Aryan priests by various Aryan tribes.[1]

There cannot be the belief that certain restrictions among tribes and races were weak or ineffective in ancient India. The Mahabharata relates an incident in which caste consciousness was apparent. Devayani, daughter of Sukracharya, was rescued from a well by Emperor Yayati of the Bharata race and she wanted to marry him but was prevented from doing so because interestingly:

> A Kshatriya maiden could marry a Brahmana according to the ancient tradition but it was considered wrong for a Brahmana maiden to marry a Kshatriya.[2]

This illustration of "anuloma" or the practice of marrying men of higher castes was legitimate but the reverse practice "pratiloma" which was marriage with men of lower castes was forbidden by the Sastras. Thus the flexibility of this aspect of the caste system was no longer apparent.

The Mahabharata provides another development in the caste system which involved the concept of dharma (duty), reinforcing consciousness during the Mahabharata period. It is a story by sage Markandeya about Kausika, a proud Brahmana who learnt the true meaning of dharma from Dharmavyadha, a lowly despised butcher.

In the domain of the origins and development of the caste system there is little or no consensus among historians and religious thinkers. One view holds that during the Vedic period the Sudras were allowed to read from the Upanishads, Mahabharata and the Puranas but not the Vedic Samhitas. This denial of the Sudras was yet another development contributing to their relegation to the base of the social order.

However, it was not only the exclusion of the Sudras from the Vedic rites and prayers but also the tales of the origin of the groupings were against their favour! According to the "Purusha-Sukta" hymn of the Rigveda, Purusha is identified

---

[1]Gokhale Govind Balkrishna, *Bharatavarha: A Political and Cultural History of India,* Sterling Publishers of India, 1982, p. 16.

[2]*Mahabharata,* translation by C. Rajagopalachari, Bharatiya Vidya Bhavan, Bombay, 1976, p. 129.

with the universe and the source of the Sun who produced the Brahmanas from his mouth, the Kshatriyas from his breast, the Vaisyas from his thighs and the Sudras from his feet (hymn 10, 90).

One scholar, Romesh Chunder Dutt, in "A History of Civilization in Ancient India" believed that the ancient Sutrakaras had written to show that the different castes sprang from the union of men and women of different original castes.[1]

Inaccurate, prejudiced viewpoints devoid of anthropological and scientific data have made the role of the Brahmana confusing. On learning of the role and function of the Brahmana as researched by certain scholars, one wonders "whether the ideology of the caste system and its divisions were maintained to serve the self-interests of the Brahmanas?"

Not only was the Brahmana's life one of sacraments, religious rites, sacrifices and divine grace, an ideal Brahmana was supposed to renounce all worldliness and interact with the world without losing purity. A well known Indian scholar, Bhattacharya, believed that the Mahabharata takes the stance indicating that it was neither birth, purification rites nor learning but upright conduct as the only criterion by which to judge a Brahmana.[2]

Understanding the origins of the caste system has been made more difficult by the distortion of historical events by North Atlantic historians of the 19th and 20th centuries. This was a blatant attempt to protect the tenets of Christianity from being undermined. The Christian view of the world being created around 4004 BC[3] strongly contradicted the Hindu chronology that the total period elapsed since the dawn of Vedic civilization is 1,960,853,096 years[4] and that the glorious Indus-Sarasvati age had begun from 9000 BC.

Thus it was necessary for the British and European historians to hatch the devious plot that the Rigveda was written in 1000 BC, that the Mahabharata period was 400 BC to 400 AD and the Ramayana period was 200 BC to 200 AD. Attempts to rectify this historical deception is difficult despite archaeological and literary evidence which proved that the Mahabharata War took place in 3137/3138 BC.[5]

The important event which changed ancient Indian history occurred on April 10th, 1866. This secret, politically motivated meeting was held in the Royal

---

[1]Romesh Chunder Dutt, *A History of Civilization in Ancient India,* Vol. 2, BC 320 to AD 1000, Vishal Publishers, India, 1972, p. 84.

[2]J.N. Bhattacharya, Hindu Castes and Sects, Ghatack, Delhi, 1973, p. 16.

[3]See margins in Genesis of the King James Version of the Bible.

[4]Karam Narain Kapur, "Age of Mahabharata War," *Vedic Light,* April 1981, p. 21. See also: Karam Narain Kapur, "Vyas and Zoroaster," *Vedic Light,* February 14, 1982, p. 17.

[5]Deen B. Chandora, "Hindu Dharma," *Vedic Light,* Sarvadeshik Arya Pratinidhi Sabha, New Delhi, India, November 1991.

Asiatic Society of London to craft the theory of the Aryan invasion of India. Thus it appeared that:

> India was ruled all along by outsiders and so the country must remain a slave under the benign Christian rule.[1]

This cunningly crafted theory to justify the rule over India was a tactic designed to lead to the continued exploitation and domination of Indians.

The effects of this "engineering" of ancient history has affected the caste system. A corrupted version of the caste system gradually prevailed and the original Varnasrama social system is no longer in existence. The destruction of the social structure in India and the resulting "caste" system is now used by the rich to exploit and oppress the poor. By tampering with their ancient history the British have left a legacy of confusion and destruction amongst one of the greatest and oldest civilizations in the world. Two articles in the journal *The Wilson's Quarterly*, "Hinduism by any other name" and "Naming Hinduism"[2] provide solid evidence that the European impact was only a short-term, negative one but the repercussions will continue to haunt India for many years.

---

[1]Swami Jyotirmayanand, *Vivekanand—His Gospel of Man-Making with a Garland of Tribune and a Chronicle of His Life and Time with Pictures,* M.V. Naidu St. Panchavati Cheetput, Madras, India, October 1986.

[2]John Stratton Hawley, "Naming Hinduism," *The Wisdom Quarterly*, Summer 1991, pp. 20–34 and Wendy Doniger, "Hinduism by any other name," *The Wisdom Quarterly*, Summer 1991, pp. 35–41.

Limitations of Modern Thought with the Ancient Light of India: Freeing the Modern Mind to See the Truth in a New Dimension

JOSEPH A. WARREN
1012 W, Washington, Lansing, MI 48906-4839, USA

DEBORAH DAVIS
89 Moultine Creek Circle, St. Augustine, FL 32086, USA

The focus of this paper is to explore how modern scholars can use the traditions of ancient India to illuminate the framework of modern thought to reveal its content and conceptual limitations. Its purpose is to explore how ancient India can be an illuminating guide to critics to analyze modern scholarship, especially in the fields of psychology and medicine.

Introduction

The gift of ancient India is the path of liberation for those who seek the infinite freedom of absolute consciousness. By showing humans how to see and experience life beyond the confines of conditioned social limitations, the traditions of India have provided the light of awareness to illuminate the limitations of the modern mind in all expressions of its constricted consciousness.

The focus of this paper is to explore how modern scholars can use the traditions of ancient India to illuminate the framework of modern thought to reveal its content and conceptual limitations. Its purpose to explore how the light of ancient India can be an illuminating guide to critique modern academic scholarship, especially in the fields of psychology and medicine.

The ability of modern travel and communications technology to reduce and open the barriers between the various parts of the global community has facilitated our ability to access the insights of other cultural traditions. To those who see this interaction as a threat to their own cultural hegemony, it is interpreted as the clash of cultures. To those who see this as a window of opportunity to explore new dimensions of life, it is seen as the dawning of the golden age of expanded awareness.

The ability of participant-scholars and others to access esoteric and hitherto isolated traditions has opened a door to the rich diversity of the human experience. Each new cultural tradition that becomes available to scholars is, in essence, a new tool to understand and explore the treasury of life. Arising from this process are a myriad of new approaches and disciplines one can use to explore the insights offered by other cultural traditions.

In the western world, one discipline, known as anthropology, has attempted to provide scholars with academic tools to traverse the diversity of cultural traditions. Born of the western intellectual tradition, it has recently been compelled to confront its own intellectual and conceptual limitations in an effort to grasp the illusive nature of what is considered to be "reality" in the western metaphysical framework. It is, in essence, the search for a concept to embrace all concepts so that one might have a firm foundation upon which one can build an intellectual framework of reality. The assumption behind this search is that one will then have a framework to evaluate mutually contradictory cultural views of reality. By seeking a commonly accepted conceptual framework, one can minimize or eliminate individual and cultural perceptual biases and provide a basis for evaluating cultural expressions of common human problems.[1]

To better understand the problem this approach presents, what if one were to apply this process to understanding the individual experience of being in love? Could one ever grasp intellectually this most precious and profound human experience? Can a person undergoing the transformational experiences of love ever reduce and express those experiences in symbolic, conceptual, and transmittable forms that can be used by another to convert these forms back into the experiences of the first person? Obviously not, as love is one of the most subjective and private, inner transformative experiences one can undergo. Likewise, when one undergoes a love experience, the intellectual and conceptual need to understand it shrinks in comparison to the experience of it.

We would briefly and generally summarize the western intellectual approach to understanding life, and then illustrate how the methodologies and approaches

---

[1] For an excellent discussion of the history and dynamics of this tradition, see Richard A. Shweder's *Thinking Through Cultures: Expeditions in Cultural Psychology* (Cambridge, Mass: Harvard University Press, 1991). See especially the chapters entitled "Post-Nietzschean Anthropology: The Idea of Multiple Objective Worlds," and "Culture Psychology: What Is It."

used by Indian traditions reveal the limitations of the western conceptual framework. We will also use yoga to critique modern Western thought patterns.

A Review of Ancient Indian Tradition

The traditions of ancient India provide one with a powerful experiential practice and analytical tool to explore, experience, and understand reality beyond the limitations of the western intellectual and scientific traditions. These ancient Indian traditions provide not only a metaphysical framework of reality, but the tools to access its depths, and then go beyond the constricted conceptual frameworks inherent in the intellectual expressions of reality. These ancient traditions open the door for modern scholars to explore and experience a reality far beyond the western intellectual heritage's ability to understand and grasp the nature, experience, and meaning of life.

This thesis rests upon the perception that Truth, by definition, can never be distorted. It is only our human perception of the Truth and our world that is distorted. Once the perceptual barriers, basically the tyranny of the senses, are removed, one is able to experience and intuitively know the Truth that gives rise to everyday reality. The Indian traditions discussed in this paper are, in effect, a powerful source of illumination and grace that reveal the limitations of modern thought like a light behind a cloth reveals not only its warp and weave but the holes, cracks, and tears in it as well.

My Buddhist friends playfully chide Western scholars with the observation that they are extremely happy that the West has finally reached a level of intellectual sophistication that it can now begin to understand what the ancient traditions of India are trying to teach. As the West enters the technical cyber world of "virtual reality" (the maya of maya), ancient insights from the wisdom teachings will be needed even more.

Six Modes of Western Scholarship

If one were to summarize the operational mode of the dominant Western scholarly approach to life it might be condensed as follows:

First, reality is experienced through the senses and conceptualized primarily through the truncated symbolic language of thought and the abstract language of mathematics. One may draw inferences about what may exist beyond one's sensory awareness, but it cannot be said to exist until it is scientifically proven using the senses to verify it. Thus, the West is locked into a small world bounded by sensory perception and ghostly inference. The dominant culture of the West has forgotten about direct experience and *jnana*, that is, spiritual knowledge.

Second, the West arranges its conceptual framework as an expression of the ego structure, and then anchors itself in it, thinking the ego structures are the true and only expression of reality. Each new advance in Western knowledge is merely an extension of the conceptual framework of the ego model. For example, in Western psychology, each new therapy is a permutation of the ego model, which extends the language of existence further and further, but fails to cross over and go beyond the confines of thought. It fails to cross over from the head to the heart, from the secular to the sacred.

Third, the Western conceptual framework of the ego model is designed to confine and control, rather than to liberate, one's awareness. As a result one's awareness is conditioned into beliefs so that the culture can control and manage everything. Western culture places very little value on freeing oneself from collective social "support" systems to explore the reality beyond it. Instead, Western culture focuses on reinforcing one's attachment to the so-called political and economic freedoms, instead of a true psychological and spiritual liberation from the confinement of one's conditioned awareness.

Fourth, Western cultures tend not to honor processes that might lead one to free oneself from the collective view of reality. The educational process, for example, is designed to focus and narrow one's awareness to smaller and smaller areas as one matriculates through the system. In the absence of any cultural support for an individual to seek liberation, few individuals in Western cultures do so. Those few who manage to escape the confines of the cultural control mechanisms tend to be ridiculed and rejected by "those in control" as non-conforming misfits, or are seen as saints to be idolized, but not followed.

Fifth, the West does not seek to honor one's inner life as being as important as one's outer life. Consequently, Western societies have been structuring their cultures for the last 400 years or so to keep the population anchored in the so-called "rewards" of materialism, rather than to seek the sacred life of a *jivanmukti*. Unlike traditional Indian society, which encourages and nurtures one to seek spiritual liberation, Western societies seem to fear the presence of individuals that they cannot control through the conventional social and political means.

Sixth, Western cultures do not have methods or processes that enable one to go deep within oneself. Even modern Western depth psychology cannot match the power of meditation and the yogic tradition to explore one's inner world and liberate one's consciousness. Although, a new practice, HeartMath,[2] may be the first flowering of this continent's nascent yoga. HeartMath consists of practices

[2] HeartMath was created and developed by Doc Lew Childre as an inner fitness system. For further information write: Institute of HeartMath, 14700 West Park Avenue, Boulder Creek, California 95006, (408) 338-8700, fax (408) 338-9861, Internet: hrtmath@netcom.com.

that bring thinking, emotions, and intuition in line with the intelligence of the heart. These are done individually or with others—colleagues, co-workers, family members. HeartMath is not a therapy; most therapies, in asking people to "process" their emotions, have resulted in a decline in active citizenship. In the short run, HeartMath prevents stress/distress in the moment, then creativity increases, and eventually there is a gain in human development.

West has opportunity to India's comprehensive model

Over the last century the Western tradition has opened the door to re-orienting its focus of awareness, with the emergence of quantum physics. As the Western intellectual tradition moves from the "material atom" to the "energetic atom," India offers the West a comprehensive model and method to dis-identify from the sensory world, go beyond the ego and the forces of duality, to the deep inner core of Being—to the universe of pure consciousness to experience the liberation of constricted awareness through the ultimate freedom of Absolute Consciousness.

When one can detach from the confines of the sensory perceptions and intuitively experience the Self, the core of timeless Being, and how consciousness manifests the reality that occupies our surface awareness, then the pieces begin to fall into place.[3] To enter this state of awareness requires a shift in the direction of the questions that are asked about what is "out there" to an understanding of the dynamic relationship between researcher and researched, self and other, seer and scenery.

Since Western scholars tend to live and find meaning more in the mental and sensory world, Buddhist Inner Science is an excellent point of departure to sharpen the mind and to cut away much of the mental baggage Westerners bring to the search for liberation. It is a tradition that helps one to refocus one's attention and awareness to the subtle realms of one's inner universe.

Similarly, other wisdom traditions such as that of Native Americans and the re-emergence of the goddess in women's spirituality offer ways to the recovery of meaning in the post-modern West. They offer ways to cross over from the secular to the sacred.

---

[3] See one author who helps westerners, who are not conversant with the Indian Traditions, bridge this gap of understanding. Amit Goswami, Ph.D., with Richard Reed and Maggie Goswami, *The Self-Aware Universe: How Consciousness Creates the Material World* (Jeremy P. Tarcher, G.P. Putnam's Sons, New York, 1995). Also see, Heinrich Zimmer "On the Significance of the Indian Tantric Yoga [1931]," in *Spiritual Disciplines: Papers from the Eranos Yearbooks*, Bollingen Series XXX, Volume 4, edited by Joseph Campbell (Princeton University Press, Princeton, 1960).

As the twentieth century draws to a close, hopefully the next century will bring a new appreciation of what the ancient traditions of India can offer the modern world to create a new awareness of what human consciousness is capable of becoming with the appropriate attention and nurturing. Hopefully this will lead to a new and dynamic synthesis of conscious awareness that will help free humanity from its current constricted awareness to fully explore the gifts of human life and consciousness.

The Lord Buddha and His Great Thoughts

K.N. Shrestha
Chairman of W.C.B., Nepal

First of all, we should know that the Lord Buddha was the son of a king who ruled a state on the Himalayan slopes in Nepal. He was married at nineteen to the beautiful Yashodhara. He hunted and played in his sunny world, and it was amidst this rosy life that a profound discontent descended upon his spirit. It was the unhappiness of a refined mind that seeks. He reasoned that the existence he was leading was not the reality of life. It was the unhappiness of a sublime soul, who realised that his life was not real in fact. The sense of sickness and death, the insecurity of life for the common man and the cruelty to which our fellow men are subjected all engulfed the sublime mind of Gautama.

While he was meditating upon this, he was given the happy news that his wife had given birth to his son. Then he realized that this was an added bond to the material world. He was convinced that it is the duty of all men and women to strive to leave the world a better place than they had found it.

He determined to leave in quest of truth and enlightenment. He entered the bed chamber of his queen and cast one last loving look at his beautiful slumbering wife and his bonny baby boy. Then he walked out into the dark night in quest of enlightenment. He made his way to a resort of hermits. Gautam became versed in all the metaphysics of the time. But his acute mind was dissatisfied with the solutions offered him. He was in quest of a more lofty, more sublime edification of the spirit and conduct of the human race.

One day despite his enfeebled state he was passing the jungle floor pondering upon his pursuit. All of a sudden he collapsed unconscious, due to long fasting and his troubles.

He disconcerted his disciple companions by requesting for ordinary food and discontinued his mortifications. His disciples abandoned him in absolute disillusion. Gautama wandered away alone.

So it happened to the great Gautama. He had seated himself under a great tree by the side of a river where he got a clear vision; the divine illumination dawned upon him. He is said to have sat all day and all night and then he rose to impart his precious vision to the world.

Gautama's teachings revolutionized the religious thoughts and impressions throughout the Asian region. The Buddha did not forget Self as was the common practice among all Asian ascetics. He concentrated upon Self and strived to destroy it.

This was the gist of his teaching the canons of life which resulted in curing the woeful and tragic conditions of human existence.

If the profound wisdom of the Lord Gautama Buddha had been adhered to by the leaders and people of this world, the nations of the world would be ruled in wisdom and by virtue, and then wars and all other evils of our civilization would vanish from the face of the earth for ever.

Lord Buddha had attained the supreme enlightenment in Bodha Gaya in his 35th year. He spent 45 years in preaching his teachings to make this world a better place to live in.

Buddha's contributions

(a) Buddha was the first man to proclaim the sovereignty of man.

(b) Buddha was the first person to conduct research into the human psyche and its functions.

(c) Buddha was the first thinker to declare that man needs:

(1) the freedom of thinking,

(2) the freedom of conscience,

(3) the freedom from ignorance,

(4) the freedom from casteism.

(d) He declared:

(1) A man does not attain the status of Brahmin (a learned man) by birth nor does he become a Chandala (a person of low status) by birth.

(2) A man turns into a Brahmin or a Chandala by his accomplishment or shallowness.

(e) Buddha's discovery:

(1) The Four Noble Truths,

(2) The Noble Eightfold Path

(3) The Theory of Independent Origination.

The Four Noble Truths

(a) There is suffering (a dissatisfied state of mind resulting from a man's failure to get what he wants).

(b) There is the cause of suffering.

(c) The cause of suffering can be ended by a thorough understanding of the Theory of Dependent Origination, the Theory of Cause and Effect.

(d) The way to end suffering is the Noble Eightfold Path.

The Noble Eightfold Path

Sheela (Moral Conception)

(a) To speak the truth,
(b) To do good to others,
(c) To conduct right-living but not causing any pain to others for one's own benefit.

Samadhi: Right concentration (passing away for ever)

(a) To have wide thinking about the basic realities of life in terms of the awareness of the world's state of flux.
(b) To be aware of activities of the mind which is very wayward and inconsistent.
(c) To be aware of the wholesome or the unwholesome state of mind. If your thinking is unwholesome for you and others, it is to be discarded. If it is wholesome for you and others, it is to be accepted.

Right View

(a) The world is ever changing,
(b) The world is in a state of flux,
(c) The world is burning, and
(d) The world is vibrating.

Right Determination

(a) To make every active effort in the attainment of the status of the Buddha.
(b) To be always thinking in terms of doing good to others, the feeling of friendship, compassion, joy and equanimity.

The Theory of Dependent Origination

Once we accept that the world is impermanent, one has to realize that craving is the root cause of all suffering. Until man has conquered his personal interest, his life is troubled and tragic.

A Definition of V. Buddhasa

Buddhasa Bhikku sincerely believed that world peace is possible if humanity would only conquer selfishness which is the cause of all conflict and troubles. We will find it useful in our own spiritual lives for a lasting peace. All religions may be different, separate and incompatible. But people think and speak according to their personal feelings, then come to each other. The highest understanding of Dhamma will bring the realization that the things called "religion" do not exist after all. There is no Buddhism, there is no Christianity, there is no Islam. A person with some knowledge, however, knows that pure water can be found in every kind of water. If we take rain water, canal water, sewer water or toilet water, and if we distill it, we will get pure water. As for those elements which make it impure or look different, they will all be pure. When we look at things from this viewpoint, if they appear different, it is because we are making judgements on the basis of external forms. There is only a certain nature which can be named whatever we fancy. We can call it Dhamma, we can call it truth, we can call it "God" or whatever. They just go about teaching us to live unselfishly. Please try to understand this correctly. There is only one nature, only Dhamma. This reality cannot be considered to be any particular thing; it cannot be anything other than Dhamma. It cannot be Thai, Chinese, Indian, Arab or European. It cannot be black, brown, yellow, red or white. It cannot be Eastern or Western, Southern or Northern. Nor can it be Buddhist, Christian, Islamic or anything else. So please try to reach this Dhamma, for then you will have reached the heart of all religions. We think that our religion is different from the other religions, because we have failed to understand and have not realised our own truth; we look down upon other religions and praise only our own. We think of ourselves as a special group; we think of ourselves as God's Chosen. We have many of these blind beliefs. Such ideas and beliefs show that we are still ignorant, very foolish indeed. Real Buddhism is to know how to get without getting and take without taking, so that there is no frustration and no suffering at all. We are afraid to think that there is no religion, that there is no Buddha, Dhamma or Sangha. For this reason, after the passing away of the Buddha, there appeared many new systems of religious practice. If we speak in Dhammal language, however, there is nothing to say, nothing to get, nothing to have, nothing to be happy about, no suffering, nothing at all. We call this voidness.

Craving classified into three parts

(a) *Karma Tanha* (craving for worldly pleasures, trans. as the origin of thirst and passion which results in the painful state of emotional conflict which ensues from failure).

(b) *Bhava Tanha* (craving or the lure of eternal living which is impossible).

(c) *Bi-bhava Tanha* (the imaginative conception of non-existence of the other world).

"Understand these three to be filth and obstacles to the gates of the city of liberation: adhering solely to morality and ascetism, mistaken view of self-individuality and doubt." (Nagarjuna's Letter)

These three types of cravings are called Avidya (ignorance). Out of ignorance comes out Sankhara (habit) and out of Sankhara comes out Vijnana i.e. awareness of consciousness, which produces the six sensory organs: eyes, ears, nose, tongue, body and mind. These six sensory organs produce touch which further produces sensations—happy, unhappy, gross, mild or neutral sensations. They all lead to unhappiness. But if ignorance is ceased, everything ceases.

The adventure of Buddha heralded the dawn of new revolutions—social, philosophical, economic, ethnic and cast-based, because Buddha openly declared that he was against the division of human beings into:

1. Brahmins (the educated class who feel themselves superior to others).
2. Kshatriyas (the warrior class without education).
3. Vaishyas (the business class also without education).
4. Sudras (the most lowly class destined to serve the above three classes and in rendering their services to do the most menial jobs).

Buddha openly declared that everyone can become a Buddha. Man shapes his own destiny by himself, not by any gods and goddesses as preached by the Vedic people in ancient Bharatavarsha.

Buddha's declaration of equality between man and woman also brought about a new epoch of:

(a) Democracy,
(b) Democratic socialism based on friendship, compassion, joy and equality,
(c) No necessity of any kind of unseen God and a Super One,
(d) Initiation of taking up scientific researches, approaches and conclusions.

Once the existence of God, the Almighty, is accepted, the thinking capacity of a man becomes dead and he becomes a slave to his thought created by man himself due to his inability and lethargy to search deep into Nature and Life. The advent of Buddha before 6th century B.C. generated a new world of scientific and logical thinking, thus coming in conflict with the so called Brahmins working as priests and exploiting the ignorant masses by introducing false systems of philosophy at that time. Theisms, both mono- and poly-, got a setback because of Buddha's revolutionary thinking. During the time Lord Buddha was preaching, there were sixteen republics in the northern part of ancient India—what is now called "Bharatavarsha." There was no political division between Nepal and India. The actual term used was "Jambudwip." Nepal was situated in the Himalayan slopes, the northern part. India fell south of Nepal and in the subcontinent. Recently, the exact spot where the Buddha was born was located at Lumbini and it has been highlighted by CNN, BBC, NIPPON and world's various TV stations and international organizations. The holy Lumbini is a proper place in Nepal.

Buddha's advent is the beginning of modern science, pragmatic philosophy and logical thinking ending the culture of blind belief, blind regard, blind faith. Buddhism is not a religion. It is a way of life. In fact, Dr. Rhys Davids, Dr. Albert Einstein, Prof. Dani, H.G. Wells, Bertrand Russell—all declare that the Buddha's approach to life is the only path to obviate war and the erroneous wastage of human intellect in futile pursuits. Buddha was the first man to proclaim the sovereignty of man in the whole life of history. His teaching on meditation also shows that our ego has been swindling us all, and that man can achieve goodness only when his ego lessens. When in the equanimity of meditation, we see that all our plans and schemes reveal themselves—an extremely precise "*inner expansiveness.*" The sovereign man can be through the attainment of Nirvana. Buddha was the first man to undertake research into human psyche and its functions. Gautam Buddha, through the immaculate purity of his mind and meditation, achieved the sublime enlightenment, never before accomplished, and laid the path for all humanity to culminate likewise.

The Great Nagarjuna

After the time of Gautam Buddha came a great philosopher to carry out and extend the work which he had started. He holds an almost unequalled place among the ranks of the Buddhist saints. Nagarjuna expounded the work of the Shakya Muni Buddha for the benefit of humanity and lent it a validity and dynamism which has continued to sustain it even to this day. One should be justified in asserting that his interpretation represents the true importance of the doctrine of Buddha and the essence of Buddhism. Nagarjuna's life will always be some sort of an enigma due to the numerous legends that have crowded it. Nevertheless, the fact that such a man, who was responsible for the great achievements in the elucidation and propagation of the Buddhist doctrine, did exist is borne out by the presence of his legacy in the form of the works that are attributed to him. Despite the elusiveness of the chronology, character and other aspects of this great luminary of the Buddhist philosophy, numerous historical, archaeological and theological records declare the existence of this unequalled expounder of the Buddhist philosophy. Nagarjuna's explanation of the real Buddhism is revolutionary.

Nagarjuna is said to have been born into a Brahmin family at Konda in South India. He was inspired by Buddha's teaching that human desires are the root of all suffering and tribulations. He was a master of Buddhist scriptures and precepts and was the author of numerous books on Buddhist philosophy and metaphysics. Nagarjuna possessed many tantric powers which he reportedly derived from the Naga sages during of his sojourn with them. We learn from historical accounts that Nagarjuna consented to his own death by decapitation at the hands of the son of his dearest friend, King Gautamiputra. In his book *Suhrillekha* he provides the aspirants to Buddhism with the essential knowledge of the Buddhist path to liberation and a comprehensive summary of the principles of the religion. Conclusively, few teachers of Buddhism have contributed as much to the propagation and elucidation of the teachings of Lord Buddha, the *Enlightened One,* as Nagarjuna.

The Great Emperor Ashoka

When he ascended the throne, Ashoka followed the example of his father and grandfather in striving for the conquest of the Indian peninsula. In 255 B.C. he invaded Kalinga, a small country on the east coast of India. He was a great success in this military adventure but was alone among conquerors who was so overcome by the cruelty and horrors of this war that he renounced it in totality. He would have no part in wars or conquests forthwith; he would never in future be responsible for human suffering and misery. He adopted the peaceful doctrines of Buddhism and promulgated a royal declaration that henceforth his conquests would be conquests of men's souls and spirit, through the sublime precepts of Buddhism. He contributed vast benefactions to Buddhist teaching and to a better and more energetic criticism of their own accumulated literature for corruptions and superstitious accretions that had accumulated very rapidly in the pure, profound and simple teachings of this great Asian Light. Missionaries were sent by Ashoka to Kashmir, to Persia, to Thailand, to Ceylon (Srilanka), to Alexandria and to the entire Indochina region, and the profundity and the absolute intellectual depth of Buddhist teaching spread into a vast area of Greater Asia, eventually finding its way and blowing like a gentle, refreshing wind into China, Korea and the islands of Japan. It was as if the races of Asia were reaching a stage of adolescence after a childhood of some 20,000 years.

Ashoka the Great was far in advance of his age but left no prince and no organization to continue the work he had so eagerly and energetically commenced. Within a century of his demise the great days of his reign were only a glorious memory in a shattered and decaying country. The priestly caste of Brahmins, the highest and most privileged caste in the Indian social structure, has always been opposed to the frank and open teachings of Buddhism.

Conclusions of Buddhist Philosophy

The holy ones means "those who understand deeply and have no attachments." You will have died to yourself from the very start. Everything has died at the moment of its birth. There never was an "I" and "mine." This is just a mental concept and a product of thoughts. There is nothing substantial or permanent upon which it is based. There is only cause and conditions. So do not let attached thoughts and feelings based on "I" and "mine" arise. Suffering can only happen to an "I" and it's "mine." With attachment to something, happiness is turned into pain, goodness into a form of suffering.

We may say "I" and "my" according to social conventions, but do not let them exist in the mind or heart. Leave such words outside, do not let them into the mind; do not believe them. We ought always to train ourselves this way, that is, "Mouth is one and mind another." The mouth says one thing, but the heart should know. There is no good, no evil, no virtue, no sin, no happiness, no suffering, and finally, not even any religion. This is the highest level of religion. Now let us consider the fact that non-attachment is the highest Dhamma. It is the heart of every religion. It is the essence of Dhamma. If there is God, it can only be found right there, in non-attachment.

Each conception of "I am," "I was" or "I will" is a birth as well as a death. This is the meaning of "birth" and "death" in Dhamma language, although physical birth has happened so long ago. To destroy this kind of birth is "Nibbana." The fact that this "I" will never be born again may be called "non-birth." You may call it "death" if you prefer. Now let us consider a word from the Christian scriptures, such as "life." Jesus Christ surrendered his life for human beings (Matt. 20:28). Jesus allowed them to kill the life of his body, which is the only meaning of "life." It now refers to a life that can never be killed. It is a life which will never know death. "To die" means that the bodily functions have stopped, which is the kind of death we can see with our eyes. The end of happiness, the end of peace, the end of everything. This is the meaning of "death" in Dhamma language. Most of us die this way many times in a day. There is no gain, no loss, no happiness, no suffering, no good, no evil, no merit, no sin, no male, no female. There is absolutely nothing at all that can be separated and polarized into opposites. So get free of all such attachments and the mind will be void. Whatever and whenever we practise non-attachment, there and then is Dhamma practice. And to the voidness surrender all of the fruits. We shouldn't think that the teaching of non-attachment is found only in Buddhism. But I feel that many religious people don't yet understand their own religion. Nothing can be obtained without an investment. The Buddha said that Nibbana is given free of charge. Nibbana, the coolness and peace experienced when there is no attachment doesn't cost a penny. This means that we can practise for the sake of Nibbana without spending any money. Christ invited us to drink the water of life for which there is no charge. Further he called us to enter Eternal Life, which means to reach the state where we won't die again. "Let him take the water of life without price." This call, which is taught in Buddhism: Give your everything and take nothing back. Don't receive any payment, we won't have to pay anything. We spend a lot of money trying to buy Nibbana. Nibbana is our first concern and requires no money. Jesus added further that "what you received without pay give without pay." If something is obtained for free, we ought to pass it on for free too. When we get something for free, we must give it away for free. The Dhamma of each religion is something to be obtained for free. Once we have got it, we are obligated to pass it to our fellow human beings for free. Also don't try to get any benefits out of it in return. That which we get for free is called "Nibbana." But we are born again at once. Because we need to be reborn, when we are born anew, we are born into Eternal Life, which is true life. The Buddha spoke in the same vein: There will be no more suffering by understanding this fundamental principle. Always living under the burn of ego and egoism is death. The word "reborn" means a life without ego, free of "I" and "mine." This is the true life which can never die. That continuous "I" and "mine" was death in Dhamma language. Any ego is a fire that should be cooled down. To make things easier, we should remember that the word "Nibbana" means "to cool down." Thus we discover that the way to apply Dhamma to cool ourselves is in Nibbana—absolute coolness—called Buddhism.

In this day the doctrine of wisdom expounded by the noble and sublime Buddha is propagating into most of the countries of the world—East, West, North and South. More and more people are getting aquainted with this valuable doctrine and we can anticipate that the people of the world will cultivate a superior love and respect for each other culminating in peace and freedom from strife.

Freedom to think

When a large number of people know the nature of their minds, as thought in Buddhism, of the word "the insider," someone who seeks the truth within the nature of himself.

Freedom of conscience:

To quote the Dalai Lama

> "The basis on which Buddhists accept the concept of rebirth is principally the continuity of consciousness. In other doctrines consciousness may be termed as soul or spirit etc. The fact remains that human existence in life depends entirely on our constantly transforming self."

Freedom from ignorance

Gautam Buddha was the first person to preach against casteism. The priestly class has ever been opposed to this frank and open teaching. This doctrine was certainly the most revolutionary teaching and has only in this century been taken with a certain degree of seriousness.

Buddhism and Lamaism in Tibet

There are four traditions in Tibetan Buddhism or Lamaism:

1. Nyingma Tradition

In the seventh century Buddhism came to Tibet during the reign of King Srongtsen Gampo (650) who married the Nepalese Princess Bhrikuti. She was a devout Buddhist disciple. There were three remarkable personalities who popularized the great teachings of the Lord Buddha in this Himalayan state. These were: (1) King Trisong Datsen of Tibet, (2) the Abbot (Abbess) Shantarakshita of Nalanda, and (3) King Trishong Sambhava from a Himalayan state of India who is known as Guru Rinpoche and as a second Buddha in Tibet. These three personalities established the tradition which is called "Ngagyur Nyngma" in the oldest Buddhist institute in Tibet. There are three main sectors in the Ngagyur Nyngma tradition:

(a) The distant economical lineage,
(b) The close lineage of spiritual treasure,
(c) The profound pure vision.

Guru Rinpoche's teaching is called Lamaism. Guru Padma Sambhava appears on Terton and speaks through a man. Many luminaries had appeared in this tradition since 1304 to 1900 in Tibet.

2. Kagyu Tradition

Kagyu tradition was founded by the Guru Ticope, who is known as Praina-bhadra. He was a great Tantric who was influenced by Malangi Guru, Nagarjuna and Indrabhuti as well as Sukha Siddhi of India. There are four Kagyu lineages of disciples. In fact the Kagyu lineage is a teacher who had a master mind and was most intellectual in various realisations and well experienced.

3. Shakya Tradition

The Shakya tradition was founded in the eleventh century by Khon Pui Wangpo Sungwa and his thirteen generations, who built the Shakya Monastery in 1073 and then the Shakya tradition was active in two sectors, one in the political and the other in the religious, in Tibet. Indian philosophers like Guru Rinpoche and Nagarjuna, the great Tantric, were also assimilated into the Shakya tradition in Tibet. The fame of his knowledge and scholasticism spread as far as Mongolia and China, from where he received invitations from the royal court. His nephew, Chogyal Phakpa (1235–1280) succeeded him as the fifth Gongma and the seventh patriarch of the Shakya school. During his time the Shakya tradition reached its political zenith, with the introduction of Mahayana Buddhism into China and Mongolia. The Mongolian ruler Kublai Khan, in devotion, offered the thirteen myrianarchies of Tibet to Chogyal Phakpa and thus Tibet was united under a joint spiritual and political authority. The five masters known to the Tibetans as Jetun Gongma Nga are regarded as the real founders of the Shakya tradition.

The Shakya tradition has the distinction of having a close connection with the other three major schools of Tibetan Buddhism. The Vajrakila lineage, which the Shakyas follow, originates from Guru Padma Sambhava, the founding master of the Nyngma school. The Shakyas have preserved, studied, expounded and disseminated their unique tradition for the past 800 years.

4. Gelumgpa Tradition

Gelumgpa or Mahayana principle (tradition) as a spiritual orientation and way of life was founded by Lama Tsongkhapa (je Rep) in the 14th century. It was propounded by Nagarjuna and Chandikirti, a great Buddhist philosopher and follower of Lord Buddha from Southern India. In fact there are three elements in the path for a whole-hearted wish for liberation—renunciation, Bodhicita and view of emptiness. In fact the Gelumgpa tradition is called the principle of Sutra and Tantra of Mahayana Buddhists, which was propounded by Lord Buddha through Nagarjuna, Manjushree and Maitreya.

The highest category meditation master, based on mystical experience, Lama Tsongkhapa, established the Gandon monastery in Lhasa in 1409, which was the greatest centre for all the Buddhists of Tibet at that time. Later Gandon became Gended and at last the Gelumgpa tradition became the new famous tradition. The Dalai Lamas also belong to the Gelumgpa tradition who have got a monastery in the Tsang province of Tibet. In fact Lama Tsongkhapa established the Genden monastery or the Genden school which became the Gelumgpa tradition (later) of today. Now there are many schools and colleges of this tradition.

So, now, these four traditions of Tibet spread all over the world after the Chinese attack on Tibet in 1959, otherwise the Tibetan Lamaism and the present Buddhist movement and the great thoughts would have been a folk lore today. It came out of Tibet at the correct time for mankind and their future lives as well as for the peace and non-violence in the world.

Why should we practise Buddhism?

Though every teacher says that his thoughts are the only truth and the others are wrong, there are so many centres for study. Buddha is kind and he says: Everyone should believe in anything after examining, thinking, trying and finding it correct. Buddhism is a holy religion of freedom. There are so many intellectual slaves who have lost their freedom falling into selfishness in the past. The power of propaganda and advertisement is so high that human beings have become slaves of it now. It is very very harmful for the past, present and future.

If we can't understand Lord Buddha and Buddhism, we would be very far from truth and peace.

It has nothing to do with individual and personal; it is impersonal. It is the law of nature, meaning Dhamma. So Dhamma means the God in Buddhism, which refers to the celestial being with creative and unseen powers.

Vinaya Dhamma

A historical Enlightened being was Gautam Buddha, who was born in Nepal

2600 years ago. At first many people abused Lord Buddha and did him physical trouble. Lord Buddha told the men: "Buddha means truth, truth means Buddha." The "Dhamma Vinaya" is your real teacher, which made Buddha, in fact, and after his passing away, Lord Buddha and his holy "Dhamma Vinaya" will be active as Lord the Buddha.

Remember some Buddist beliefs:

Enemy in Buddhism	It comes from our mind, is born in the mind and we can make friend instead of enemy in the mind.
World in Buddhism	In Dhamma language, the meaning of world is pain, an impermanent, changing and unsatisfactory condition of our mind.
Birth in Buddhism	Birth in Dhamma refers to the idea of the "I" and "me" ego which arises in the mind; so birth and death can take place so many times in one day of a man.
Death in Buddhism	Death means in Buddhism the same words "I," "my" and "myself". It can be many times in one day after saying it.
Life in Buddhism	Life in Dhamma refers to the deathless state, with the limitation, called Nibbana, where there is neither birth nor death. It should never come to an end.

We should try to live accordingly. Before long we will progress to a higher level on the path to voidness and freedom from suffering. Then we can do work of all kinds with a void mind and we can give all of the fruits to voidness. We will be able to eat the fruit of voidness. And so we will be able to die completely from the very beginning, that's the end of being a Buddhist—is the end of all religions. Don't waste the opportunity of being born a human and of having encountered Buddha-Dhamma. If we speak in Dhamma language, however, we would have to say this is the end of everything. There is nothing likely to be a problem ever again. Such a life can be called life for there is no more birth against illness or death.

ABSTRACTS OF PAPERS NOT INCLUDED IN THE PROCEEDINGS

Language, Chronology and Cultural Continuity in South Asian Archaeology

JIM G. SHAFFER, PH.D.

Dept. of Anthropology, Case Western Reserve Uni., Cleveland, Ohio 44106 USA

KEYNOTE ADDRESS

South Asian archaeology remains significantly influenced by ideas and interpretations proposed by the early prominent scholars (e.g., Marshall and Wheeler) that developed this area's archaeological record into one of international importance. However, seldom is it recognized these same ideas and interpretations significantly reflect eighteenth and nineteenth century European perceptions of history, language and ethnicity. At the same time these theoretical approaches continue to influence our understanding of even the most recent archaeological discoveries.

This paper will first discuss the historical background of South Asian archaeology as well as its theoretical limitations that continue to dramatically influence recent interpretations. Finally, the focus shifts to recent developments in the archeological and chronological data and they argue for a basic restructuring, rather than just new designations, of South Asian archaeology.

The Dilemma of the Aryan Ecumene: Sapta-Sindhu and the Sarasvati in Ancient India

SHIVA G. BAJPAI, PH.D.

Professor of History & Director of Asian Studies

California State University at North Ridge, North Ridge, CA 91330-8250

The problem of identification of the earliest region of the Aryan ecumene or homeland, and its frontiers, in Bharat (India) has been virtually an intractable one despite the endeavors of the international scholarship for over a century. The main reasons of this intractability have to do with the global albeit Eurasian dimensions of the Aryan question, and its corollary: the theory of Aryan invasion of India on the one hand, and, on the other hand, the presumptive non-Aryan characterization of the "Harappan Culture" or the Indus-Sarasvati civilization, first discovered by the archaeologists in the 1920s. The resultant mythic reconstruction of historical processes accorded an amazing role to the exploits of alien Aryan people, thus accounting for the demise of the splendid urban Harappan culture as well as the beginning of a new rural Vedic culture in c.1500 BCE in northwestern India. Although recent archaeological discoveries have chipped away the very foundations of such a reconstruction of the historical processes by the establishment indologists both in South Asia and abroad, they nevertheless cling to their quixotic theories by drawing on puzzling features out of the pandora's box of Eurasian Aryan archaeology, thereby preventing a meaningful and correct reconstruction of India's proto-history.

The dilemma of the Aryan ecumene in India stems from the larger Aryan phenomenon but centers on the identification of the Sapta-Sindhu or Saindhava region, the Rigvedic homeland and in it the place of the Sarasvati Plain, the epicenter of the Rigvedic culture. According to the Vedic testimony confirmed by the cumulative archaeological evidence both the Indus (Sindhu) and the Sarasvati were independent rivers that separately flowed into the western ocean. Thus, the interpretation of the term Sapta-Sindhavah by most scholars as the Indus and its seven tributaries is definitely wrong when it excludes the Sarasvati as there is no basis for treating it as the eastern affluent of the Indus. Further, gratuitous statements as to the Sarasvati forming the eastern frontier of the Sapta-Sindhu Region are misleading because these avoid confronting the fact that the Sindha or Sindhu of Sapta-Sindhu does not stand for the Indus river, rather denotes "river" in a generic sense. Thus a proper identification and correct interpretation of the term Sapta-Sindhavah ought to be "the Land of Seven Rivers", extending from the Sindhu (Indus) in the west to the Ganga in the east with the Sarasvati, the epicenter of the Rigvedic culture, in the middle. There could be a difference of views as to the names of the other four rivers of the Sapta-Sindha region and probably such was the case in ancient times as it certainly will be the case in modern scholarship.

My interpretation eliminates the rampant confusion in the extant scholarship, accords the proper and accurate place to the Sarasvati in the Sapta-Sindha region, and defines the western and eastern frontiers of the Aryan ecumene. Additionally, it is consistent with the post-Vedic definitions of Aryavarta (the Aryan country), the western frontier of which was never extended beyond the Indus regions despite the fact that the Atharva Veda mentions the Valhika, the area of northwestern Afghanistan. We have now defined clearly for the first time the frontiers of the Vedic Aryan homeland with its epicenter in the Sarasvati valley in India, which incidentally coincides with the mainland of the Indus-Sarasvati culture as well.

Long Ago and Far Away: Issues and Debates Regarding the Nature of Ancient Indian Music

GUY BECK, PH. D.
Department of Religion, Loyola University, New Orleans, LA

Ancient Indian music has been studied by Western scholars for over two hundred years, going back to Sir William Jones of the Asiatic Society. Debates have centered around the character of Vedic scales, the earliest ragas, which kind of instruments were used in the Vedic yagnas, the use of elementary notation, gender roles in performance, the dating of the earliest musical treatises, the music of the so-called Gandharvas whether human or celestial, and the possibility of borrowing from the ancient Greeks and other civilizations.

This paper will attempt to reconstruct parameters, based on the most reliable evidence, for a description of what the original music may have been like. Though many scholars agree that the present classical music of India does not resemble the ancient music, the author's work in the area of sacred sound in the Vedic literature, along with his recent research into North Indian temple music and dhrupad, will shape the discussion and hopefully shed some light on what are normally dark corners of historical studies and ethnographic studies.

The Origin of the Aryans: Some Linguistic Considerations

EDWIN F. BRYANT, PH.D.
Columbia University, New York
(Now: Department of Sanskrit, Harvard University, Boston, MA, USA)

There has been considerable and increasing controversy, of late, about the origins of the Indo-Aryan speakers. A significant body of scholarship has developed, in India, which can be termed 'Indigenous Aryan' school, which claims that the Indo-Aryans were autochthonous to the subcontinent and not invaders or immigrants as is generally held. This group, which consists predominantly of philologists, historians and archaeologists, draws particular attention to the impossibility of definitively identifying Aryan speakers with any intrusive element in the archaeological record.

The external origin of the Aryans, however, was a theory predicated on linguistic evidence. Irrespective of the status of the archaeological debate surrounding the Aryan presence on the subcontinent, most detractors of the Indigenous Aryan school ultimately refer to the linguistic evidence as conclusive in this regard. The Indigenous Aryan school has not critiqued the linguistic dimension of this problem with the same gusto as it reconsidered the archaeological and philological evidence.

This paper, which is a section of a dissertation examining the whole 'Aryan-Invasion' debate, examines the most compelling feature of the linguistic evidence, namely, the evidence of a linguistic substratum in Sanskrit texts. The bulk of the paper consists of an overview of most of the research published in the area that I am aware of. As a historian, I felt compelled to undertake this overview in order to examine the linguistic evidence commonly used to support the theory of Indo-Aryan migrations into the subcontinent. In the paper, however, I conclude that the opinions of the principal linguists in this area have differed quite considerably with regard to this linguistic substratum, thereby problematizing the value of this method as a significant determinant in this debate. I suggest, therefore, that the evidence of a linguistic substratum cannot be used as definitive evidence to support the theory of Aryan migration.

Women in Ancient Indian Civilization

MAYA A. CHAINANI, PH.D.
6185 Hidden Canyon Rd., Centreville, VA 22020

A critical study of Vedic literature reveals that women of all strata of society were held in high esteem in the Vedic Age. They were variously designated and addressed as mother, owner of the house, and wife, etc.. The woman in her role as wife enjoyed the position as owner of the house. She even wielded her authority over her father-in-law and her mother-in-law, like a queen in the house. They were entitled to wear the sacred thread and to study the Veda.

This paper, based upon citations from ancient Indian literature, will highlight the rights of women, the duties of women, and the status of women in the Brahmanas, smrtis, Ramayana, and the Mahabharata to show that woman had a very special place in ancient India, and that her position has become lessened due to the onslaughts of history.

Vaishnava Thought-System (Vaishnavism) since Antiquity

A.N. CHATTERJEE, PH.D.
Reader in History, University of Delhi, Delhi 110007, India
(E-4/21A, Model Town, Delhi 110009)

Vaishvanism represents an ancient Hindu religion. The word 'Vaishnavism' is derived from *'vaishnava'* meaning worshipper of Vishnu or His numerous manifestations. Early beginnings may be traced in the Rig Veda where we see the reference of Vishnu. Thereafter, Vishnu occupies a more prominent place. Some of the Upanishads have developed this theme. In the Puranas, Vishnu has a leading place. The subsequent development can also be traced in the Bhagvat Gita and Srimad Bhagavata.

This paper will trace how Vaishnavism blossomed under the *Alvaras* and the *Acharyas*. The process under which it reached its climax during the period of *Sri Chaitanya*, the founder of Gaudiya School will be highlighted. The entire Vaishnava thought-system, when taken as a whole, is complex, extensive and unlimited.

The paper also goes into some of the universally accepted and fundamentally important Vaishnava ideas. These ideals and concepts will be enumerated. In this regard, there shall also be elaboration of the path of devotion or 'bhakti'; the doctrine of Incarnation, Vaishnava ethical outlook.

Adhyatmic (Spiritual-Psychological) View of the Vedas

DAVID FRAWLEY

American Institute of Vedic Studies, P.O. Box 8357, Santa Fe, NM 8357

Modern Western scholars have seen the Vedas only as a kind of primitive nature worship. Most traditional Indian scholarship, particularly of the Sayana line, regards the Vedic Samhitas as a kind of ritual worship or Karma-kanda. However the idea that there is a spiritual or psychological, *adhyatmic,* meaning in the Vedic mantras is also very old, being mentioned in the *Brahmanas* and *Upanishads*, and in traditional Vedic exegis like the *Nighantu* and *Nirukta*. Medieval commentators like Madhvacharya also took it up. Important modern Hindu teachers like Swami Dayanand Saraswati of Arya Samaj and Sri Aurobindo have championed it in modern times and used it as the basis of their Yogas.

In this presentation, we will explore the adhyatmic interpretation of Vedic mantras and deities and see how the mantras apply on many inner levels. Relevance of Vedic mantras to Yoga and Vedanta will be examined, along with their relationship with *Vedangas* and *Upvedas*, like *Ayurveda*. The contention is that all the later developments of Hindu thought and culture can be found, at least in their essential form, in the original mantras of the Rig Veda itself. The Vedic Samhitas contain both *jnana* (spiritual knowledge) and *karma* (ritual), depending upon how they are viewed. Spiritual knowledge is not limited to the Upanishads only but is the very essence of the Veda which is crucial for any real understanding of ancient India or the spiritual legacy of humanity.

Elective Affinities: The Influence of "Ramayan" on Mizo Religion and Culture

SUJIT K. GHOSH, PH.D.
2 Sonali Complex, Ambicapatty, Silchar, Assam 788004, INDIA

The Mizos (previously known as Lushais), are believed to have migrated from the Chin-hill area of Burma. The story of Ramayan is not an influence on their religion and culture after their migration to India. The Mizo story of Rama—this major folktale is called '*Khena Leh Manate Unau Thawnthu*'—does not seem to have Valmiki origin. However, its impact is not marginal, Rama and Lakshman (Rama and Khena) are accorded divine status, and before planting rice, their blessings are invoked, for good crop.

Indo-Iranian Civilizatioan

DR. PALLAN R. ICHAPORIA
253 Adams Dr., Wonelsdorf, PA 19567

The Ancient Proto-Iranian culture is very similar to Proto-Indo-Aryan culture and this should be because both are derived from the same common Indo-Iranian stock. The undivided Indo-Iranians have passed a considerable time in their central Asia common home, growing up with common religious thoughts and customs, that need to be reconstructed by comparing the Veda and Avesta.

The Indo-Iranians worshipped many gods and abstract deities. This lasted till their migration to South moving separately from each other, one group occupied the Iranian plateau (later on called Iranians) while other continuing towards the Indus plains (later on known as Indo-Aryans). It is possible that they turned their backs upon each other and developed their distinctive civilizations.

This paper will examine this split and separation and how different religious thoughts came into vogue, together with similarities so profound in the post-Zarathushtra development in Zoroastrian Iran with reference to so many common words found in the Avesta and the Vedas.

In the field of religion, prophet Zarathustra of Iran was more successful in his reformation, but the similarities in the Later Avestan religion and Vedas are so prominent to prove the same previous identity vis-a-vis the civilization of the Gathas which in a way, became the reformed civilization of Iran

The Space-time and Quantum Physics with respect to the Ancient Hindu Wisdom of Maya

ASHOK JAIN, PH.D.

Professor of Physics, Pennsylvania State Uni., Lahmen, PA

The Indian *Rishis* called this universe as an illusion or *maya*. It was their real experience, not just a philosophical statement. The fact is that what we know about this world through our senses is not the *reality* or the *truth*. The new physics of the atom, space-time, quantum, non-locality, universe supports this ancient Hindu wisdom of *maya*.

In this paper we first formulate these ideas of new physics in a simple language. Then these are employed to explain the experience of yoga, meditation, samadhi, and other Hindu topics such as reincarnation, *karma*, and enlightenment.

Women in Ancient India

H.H. BRAHMAVADINI KRISHAN KANTA, M.A., B.T.

Parivrajika, Brahmarishi Mission, 1246 North Mantine St., Kent, OH 44240

Vedas, Upanishads and the epics give numerous examples showing the great position of women in ancient India. They were respected for being great philosophers, politicians, psychologists, teachers, administrators, law makers and successful householders, etc. Many hymns were composed by them. Vaak Abharni composed 'Devi Sukta', Shraddha Kamayani the 'Shraddha Sukta', Yami Vaivasvati mandal tenth in the Hymn 154, etc.

This paper will present, from Rigveda, the contributions of the women of the Vedic age.

Glimpses of Vedic Civilization:

AVANINDRA KUMAR, PH.D.

Professor of Sanskrit, University of Delhi, Delhi-110007, India

There is an enormous divergence of opinion among historians, anthropologists, archaeologists, geomorphologists, geologists, literateurs, linguists and the like in regard to the origin and evolution of a civilization in any part of the world let alone India. The crux of the problem is whether or not India is, in verity, the cradle of the most primeval civilization in the world. There is no gainsaying the fact that Western scholars have, by and large, given a biased view of the early beginnings of Indian civilization. If one wants to trace the origin of Indian civilization then the Vedas are the best and only authentic documentary evidence. It has been established beyond doubt that Vedic civilization flourished in the land of seven rivers—Sapta-Sindhu. A majority of Vedic hymns were composed on the banks of Sarasvati, the Drishadvati, the Apaya, the Sindhu and other rivers of Punjab.

In this paper a candid attempt has been made to remove the cobweb of confusion, ambiguity and distortion that has shrouded the true spirit of the history of Indian civilization. For quite some time the views and interpretations of Western scholars have been in focus. However, profound studies have been made by Indian scholars as well as by some Western scholars, which go to show that Indian civilization is the oldest civilization in the world. Several issues have been handled in this paper based on Rig Vedic writings.

Kapila and the Samkhya Philosophy

BIJOY MISRA, PH.D.

Department of Astronomy, Harvard University, Boston, MA 02138

Apart from the Vedas, the Samkhya theory of cosmology has had the most profound influence on Indian culture and civilization. The date of Samkhya development is around the date of Gautama Buddha and possibly both Samkhya and Buddhistic cosmologies were developed as rational inquiries as opposed to mystical speculations of the Vedic literature. Very little is known about the life and works of Kapila, who is recognized as the originator of the Samkhya line of thought. On closer examination, the material appears to be the product of a school of inquires rather than that of a single individual.

Kapila has been considered as a "teacher" in Hindu scriptures and possibly he headed an organized place of learning during the time. The identification of space (Akasa) as the first element in nature and the subsequent evolution of air, fire, water and earth presents the theory as a systematic development rather than the ad hoc assumption in Aristotelian cosmology. The paper compares the Samkhya view with the Aristotelian view and provides indications on the completeness of the ancient cosmological models.

India-Hindu History: Examining Time-Line in a Broad Setting

MADAN MATHRANI

17714 Arvida Dr., Granada Hills, CA 91344

There is a general talk that the ancient Hindus had poor sense of history and that they have left no historical records and written history. This is however not true. The Hindu *itihas* (history) is found in Ramayan, Mahabharata and other Puranas. For constructing a right modern account of ancient Hindu history there is need to intelligently and diligently use these accounts. The willful misrepresentation of Hindu history by Christian missionaries and the British who conquered India and wrote Indian History, introduced 'Aryan Race' and 'Aryan Invasion' theory with clear designs to malign Hindus and reduce their self-esteem to convert them to Christianity and secure British colonial rule. Macaulay, Max Mueller, Monier Williams were some of the European "scholars" involved in this. Their personal letters that recently surfaced from the British Archives, clearly expose their bias. Though the modern scholars have denounced the imperialists and their designs, they have not succeeded in removing the harm the imperialists and religious chauvinists have done to oppressed nations, such as India.

In this paper, we present an account of Indian-Hindu history time-line based on Hindu books of history. This has a very wide canvas, starting with creation of the earth, accounts of the eras, manvantaras, etc., as is presented in these books. We present evidence from Vedas, Purans, Ramayan, and Mahabharata and work of some of the modern scholars in establishing the age of crucial matters—Vedas, Rama, Krishna, and others—without whose history the Hindu history is of limited value, and largely irrelevant.

The Concept of Cosmology in Vedas

VIDYA NIWAS MISRA, PH.D.

M-3 Badshah Bagh, Varanasi, U.P. 221002, INDIA

The concept of cosmology is very basic for philosophy and science. It has been dealt in Vedas and other ancient literature of India. Surprisingly, it has come for a very comprehensive study there.

The paper presents this very fundamental concept the way it has been presented in Hindu scriptures. This highlights the scientific search of the ancient Vedic people, that parallels the modern searches in science. Here is man's search in a perspective for deeper further analysis.

Hindu Dharma and Human Rights

S.S. RAMA RAO PAPPU, PH.D.

Department of Philosophy, Miami University, Oxford, OH 45056

Human rights are an important matter for any human society . They are a part of *dharma* in Hindu line of thoughts. We seem to have moved away from a *dharmic* society to a *Right-bases* society. A document 'Hindu Declaration of Human Rights' has recently been drafted by G.C. Pande and Arvind Sharma. I propose to discuss things in this document. My presentation is divided in three parts.

In Part I, In order to put this document in perspective, I shall discuss

(a) the nature of human rights,
(b) the reasons why Hinduism is criticized for not recognizing human rights;
(c) ©the status of human rights in Hinduism before India accepted the Universal Declaration of Human Rights, 1948.

In Part II, I shall discuss the 'Hindu Declaration of Human Rights'. In Part III, I shall discuss the justification for the above document. Specifically I shall discuss here:

(a) The need for a *Hindu* Declaration of Human Rights when we have accepted the *Universal* Declaration of the Human Rights;
(b) Why the *Hindu* Declaration is grounded in the Hindu tradition not in some abstract conceptions of human rights, and therefore is more "realistic" and acceptable to the Hindu society;
(c) Why this document avoids the pitfalls of the *Universal* declaration of human rights.

Also, there is need to draft, at a future time, a secondary declaration of *non-human rights,* i.e., the rights of animals, environment, etc., that were included in the Hindu *dharmic* tradition but seem to have been forgotten in contemporary India.

Astrology: An Eye of the Society

DHARMA RAJ REGMI
President, National Astro-Science Committee
Prabhu Nivas, Dilli Bazar, Kathmandu, Nepal

Astrology presents evidence of advanced scientific achievements and its use for the welfare of man. We have found a lot of evidences, proofs, as well as records on ancient astrology of India. This developed from the works and observations of sages, who existed in all different eras and times. The ideas are presented in terms of heavenly bodies and forces as living entities. There is need to properly understand the notions and descriptions. Goddess Saraswati is considered the source of this knowledge. The Mercury, son of the Moon, is called the prognosticator. He is the store of Vedic knowledge. During *Treta yuga,* the supreme power holder, king Ravana, was an expert in the science of astrology. His father-in-law, Maya Danava, instructed by Surya Dev, was a great authority on astro-science.

The great names of ancient India, who could read and predict past, present and future are Bhrigu, Vashishta, Parasara, Garga, and Shiva etc.

In this paper, after outlining the place and tradition of astro-science, we propose to discuss the division of time given in terms of 18 yugas and 14 Manus, explaining the following:

(a) Ananta Yuga 51,960,000
(b) Avarta Yuga 4,086,000
(c) Tamangha Yuga 3,250,000

We would explain the position of Astro-science, as a shastra in the scheme of Vedas, Up-Vedas, and Shastras.

Ancient Hindu Theory of 'Creation': A Modern Scientific Comparison

BHU DEV SHARMA, PH.D.
Professor and Chairman, Department of Mathematics
Xavier University of Louisiana, New Orleans, LA 70125, U.S.A.

Man's earliest search must have started by trying to comprehend the nature of his universe. It came for intensive study. Several sutras of the Vedas, sections and portions of Upanishads, Smrities, Purans and other Hindu literature address to *sristi*, the emergence of universe.

In this presentation, first a review of the current scientific theories of creation of the earth will be outlined. Then material from various ancient Vedic sources, starting from Rig-Veda will be presented. Some modern scientific missing links will be pointed out and it will be argued, with deeper analysis, that the present scientific findings, on creation of the universe, support and seem to be leading to the Hindu understanding of *srishti.*

Mathematical and Scientific Contributions of Hindus from the Ancient

RAJENDRA SINGH, PH.D.
D. Houser Banks Professor, Dept. of Electrical & Computer Engineering
Clemson University, Clemson, SC 29634-0915

The contributions of Hindus in the field of philosophy and spirituality are rather well known. However, few people (including many Hindus) recognize that the modern science and technology also rests on the foundation laid by Hindus, way back. The numbers 1, 2, 3,... were invented by Hindus in India (refer the book, '*How Did We Find Out About Numbers*' by Issac Asimov) and the place-value system of representing any number using 10 (das—the decimal system) symbols 1, 2, ... , 9, and 0 were developed by Hindus. Since the

Europeans learned about the number system from Arab traders, the numerals are wrongly called Arab or Arab-Hindu numerals.

In this paper, we will mention the work and contributions of ancient Hindu mathematicians and scientists. Some key work of Hindus in the modern times will also be presented.

Status of Women in Ancient India

SAVITA VARMA, PH.D.
Department of Pre-School & Elementary Education, NCERT
Sri Aurobindo Marg, New Delhi-110 016, India

In this paper, in evaluating women's status in ancient India, two points have been taken into consideration:

I. Not to apply the modern norms, concepts and values to judge women of the past, though willy-nilly the modern values do come in as the reference point for any objective evaluation. Instead a holistic approach is considered more appropriate.

India is too large a country to lend itself for any one interpretation or one evaluatory statement on the status of women. It is not possible to make one definite comment on India which has about 60 socio-cultural regions. At times, it seems that variety and diversity are more predominant than the common features. In such a situation, both 'yes' and 'no' are correct in answer to a general question—Was the status of women in ancient India high?

If we dwelt upon point (ii), we were led into a whole range of interpretations, often contradictory into each other, for example: Woman as Goddess—an object of worship, and woman as an animal to be tamed through force and violence, woman as mother to be respected, loved and honored (Mother India—a popular concept throughout the country) and woman as wife whose duty is only to serve and sacrifice, woman as a scholar and a great warrior/crusader, and woman as an illiterate fool to be ignored.

Further, we examine women's position also from angles:

(i) Fair and equal treatment, and

(ii) Empowerment of women.

For this, it should be remembered that the concept of a welfare state/society is relatively modern. Ancient states/societies performed largely law and order and defense functions. When we talk about ancient societies, we talk about the way women were treated by individuals, not by the state/society.

In Indian philosophy and in conceptual terms, Indian women occupied a high position. All good values like woman as a symbol of divine affection and love, as a symbol of power (Shakti), faithfulness, devotion and sacrifice. In reality, whether she was treated that way is anybody's guess—or difficult to believe.

Ramayan: A Great Ancient Indian Ideal

LALLAN PRASAD VYAS
International Chairman, Int'l Ramayan Conference,
C-13 Press Enclave, Saket, New Delhi-110 017, India

Ramayan is truly the heart and soul of the age-old culture of India. Besides, it has been acknowledged as an important world classic, and has been translated into many languages of the world. The total human idealism supported by the great philosophy and culture of India translated into practice is the personality of Ram.

In this presentation, the great ideals of Ramayan, that have guided persons, the societies, and the governments to right conduct have been expounded. How this great work has influenced great men of our times is also elaborated. Its journey through the world is briefly outlined.

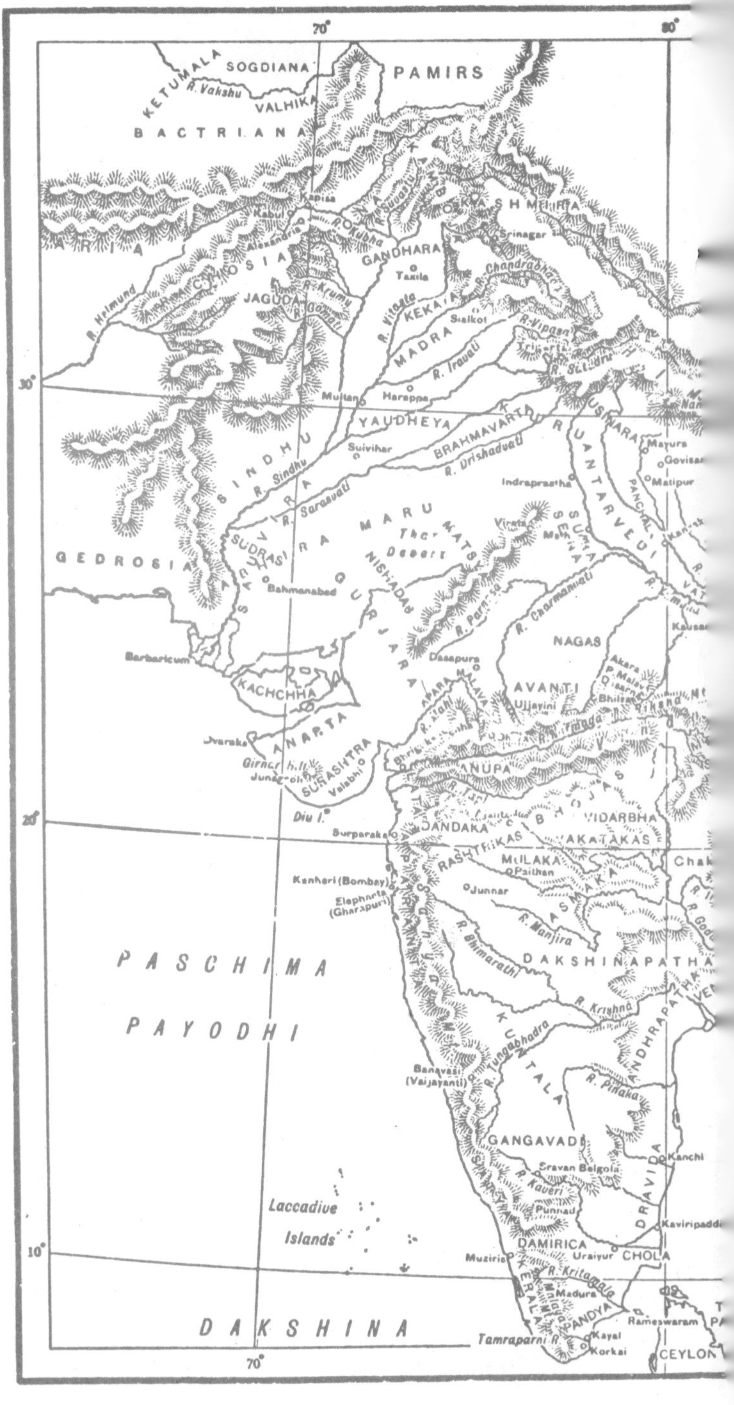

SOGDIANA
PAMIRS
KETUMALA
R. Vakshu
VALHIKA
BACTRIANA
KASHMIRA
Kapisa
Kabul
Alexandria
R. Kubha
Srinagar
ARIA
GANDHARA
Taxila
R. Helmund
JAGUDA
R. Krumu
R. Gomati
R. Chandrabhaga
KEKAYA
R. Vitasta
Sialkot
R. Vipasa
MADRA
R. Iravati
Multan
Harappa
YAUDHEYA
BRAHMAVARTA
Suivihar
R. Drishadvati
SINDHU
R. Sindhu
R. Sarasvati
Indraprastha
ANTARVEDI
PANCHALA
Mayura
Govisan
Matipur
MARU
Thar Desert
MATSYA
Virata
SUDRAS
GEDROSIA
NISHADAS
Bahmanabad
GURJARA
NAGAS
Barbaricum
Dasapura
KACHCHHA
AVANTI
Ujjayini
Bhilsa
ANARTA
Dvaraka
SURASHTRA
Girnar hill
Valabhi
ANUPA
Diu I.
VIDARBHA
Surparaka
DANDAKA
VAKATAKAS
RASHTRIKAS
MULAKA
Paithan
Kanheri (Bombay)
Junnar
Elephanta (Gharapuri)
R. Manjira
R. Bhimarathi
PASCHIMA
PAYODHI
DAKSHINAPATHA
R. Krishna
KUNTALA
R. Tungabhadra
ANDHRAPATHA
Banavasi (Vaijayanti)
R. Pinaka
GANGAVADI
Kanchi
Sravan Belgola
DRAVIDA
R. Kaveri
Punnad
Laccadive Islands
DAMIRICA
Uraiyur
CHOLA
Muziris
R. Kritamala
KERALA
Madura
PANDYA
Rameswaram
DAKSHINA
Tamraparni R.
Kayal
Korkai
CEYLON
70°
80°
30°
20°
10°